HANDBOOK OF FAMILY
DEVELOPMENT
AND INTERVENTION

Wiley Series in Couples and Family Dynamics and Treatment
Florence W. Kaslow, Series Editor

HANDBOOK OF FAMILY DEVELOPMENT AND INTERVENTION

EDITED BY
WILLIAM C. NICHOLS
MARY ANNE PACE-NICHOLS
DOROTHY S. BECVAR
AUGUSTUS Y. NAPIER

John Wiley & Sons, Inc.
New York • Chichester • Weinheim • Brisbane • Singapore • Toronto

Copyright © 2000 by John Wiley & Sons, Inc. All rights reserved.

Published simultaneously in Canada.

Library of Congress Cataloging-in-Publication Data:

Handbook of family development and intervention / William C. Nichols
. . . [et al.].
    p.   cm. – (Wiley series in couples and family dynamics and treatment)
Includes bibliographical references and index.
ISBN 0-471-29967-7 (cloth)
1. Family psychotherapy Handbooks, manuals, etc.   2. Family – Psychological aspects Handbooks, manuals, etc.   3. Family counseling Handbooks, manuals, etc.   I. Nichols, William C.
II. Series.
RC489.F33.H36   2000
616.898′158 – dc21
                                                                          99-37989
                                                                          CIP

Printed in the United States of America.

10   9   8   7   6   5   4   3   2   1

CONTRIBUTORS

Sylvia Acre de Esnaola, MA, clinical psychology, is a graduate student at the Department of Family Social Science, the University of Minnesota, St. Paul, Minnesota.

Joan Barth, PhD, is in private practice in suburban Philadelphia, in Doylestown, Pennsylvania. She is the author of *It Runs in My Family: Demystifying the Legacy of Family Illness* as well as many articles and book chapters, and is working on a book on unique mothers.

Dorothy S. Becvar, PhD, private practice in St. Louis, Missouri, is Founding Partner, The Haelan Centers™, a not-for-profit corporation dedicated to supporting growth and wholeness in body, mind, and spirit through therapy, education, and training.

Roni Berger, PhD, CSW, is Associate Professor, Adelphi University School of Social Work, Garden City, New York, and a consultant with the Jewish Board of Families and Children's Services, New York. Her clinical and research interests include stepfamilies, immigrants, and groups.

Ellen Berman, MD, is Clinical Professor of Psychology, Department of Psychology, University of Pennsylvania School of Medicine, Philadelphia, Pennsylvania.

Jerry J. Bigner, PhD, Department of Human Development and Family Studies, Colorado State University, Fort Collins, Colorado, is an internationally recognized scholar on parent-child relations who has performed specialized research in gay and lesbian parenting. He is also a therapist who has specialized in working with gay and lesbian families.

Pauline G. Boss, PhD, is Professor, Department of Family Social Science, University of Minnesota and a supervisor in its AAMFT doctoral program in marriage and family therapy, an AAMFT Approved Supervisor, and a family therapist in private practice. She is author of many research and clinical articles and several books, including *Ambiguous Loss* (1999, Harvard University Press).

Lee Combrinck-Graham, MD, is a child and adolescent psychiatrist who was trained to believe that people develop in family contexts. She is author of *Giant Steps,* and editor of *Children in Family Contexts,* and *Children in Families at Risk.* She practices at Family Services Woodfield in Bridgeport, Connecticut, and consults to mental health systems.

Darci Cramer-Benjamin, MA, is a doctoral student in family studies at the University of Connecticut, Storrs, Connecticut, and provides multisystemic therapy to families who have adolescents with severe behavioral disturbances for Catholic Charities in Niagara Falls, New York.

Shannon S. Croft, MD, is an Assistant Professor and child psychiatrist at Emory University School of Medicine, Department of Psychiatry and Behavioral Sciences at Grady Hospital, Atlanta, Georgia.

Adam Davey, PhD, Department of Child and Family Development and Faculty of Gerontology, the University of Georgia, is a family gerontologist studying intergenerational relationships, family caregiving, and research methods of studying development and family systems.

W. Todd DeKay, PhD, is Assistant Professor of Psychology, Whitely Psychology Laboratories, Franklin and Marshall College, Lancaster, Pennsylvania.

Manfred van Dulmen, MA (clinical child and adolescent psychology, Vrije Universiteit of Amsterdam), is a doctoral student, Department of Family Social Science, the University of Minnesota, St. Paul, Minnesota, and is interested in issues of risk and resiliency surrounding adolescent development in nontraditional families.

Jay S. Efran, PhD, is Professor of Psychology and Director of the Psychological Services Center at Temple University, Philadelphia, Pennsylvania. A Fellow of the American Psychological Association and the American Group Psychotherapy Association, he has written extensively on family and constructivist approaches to therapy, including coauthoring *Language, Structure, and Change: Frameworks of Meaning in Psychotherapy* (1990) with Michael D. Lukens and Robert J. Lukens.

Craig A. Everett, PhD, is Director, Arizona Institute for Family Therapy and is in private practice in Tucson, Arizona. He is Editor of the *Journal of Divorce and Remarriage* and serves on many editorial boards. He was formerly on the faculties and Director of AAMFT accredited graduate programs in Marital and Family Therapy at Florida State and Auburn Universities and is a Past-President of the American Association for Marriage and Family Therapy.

Raksha Dave Gates, MSc, clinical psychology, is a graduate student in the Department of Family Social Science, the University of Minnesota, St. Paul, Minnesota.

Mitchell A. Greene, PhD, is a psychologist at the Center for Psychological Services, in Ardmore, Pennsylvania, and an Adjunct Professor of Psychology at Temple University in Philadelphia. He works predominantly with children, adolescents, and their families.

Kenneth V. Hardy, PhD, is Professor, Marriage and Family Therapy Program, Syracuse University, Syracuse, New York.

Michele Harway, PhD, is Core Faculty and Director of Research at the Phillips Graduate Institute in Encino, California, is on the consulting faculty of the Fielding Institute, and has a private psychotherapy practice. She is the editor and/or author of many publications on domestic violence, including *Battering and Family Therapy: A Feminist Perspective* (with Marsali Hansen), and is President of Division 43 (Family Psychology) of the American Psychological Association.

Florence W. Kaslow, PhD, is Director of the Florida Couples and Family Institute; President, Kaslow Associates, PA; Visiting Professor at Florida Institute of Technology (Psychology Graduate Program); Visiting Professor at Duke University Medical School (Medical Psychology); board certified as a Clinical, Family and Forensic Psychologist by the American Board of Professional Psychology; President of the International Academy of Family Psychology; and President, American Board of Professional Psychology. She is Past-President of the International Family Therapy Association, and Division 43 (Family Psychology) and Division 46 (Media Psychology) of the American Psychological Association.

Nadine J. Kaslow, PhD, ABPP, is a Professor and Chief Psychologist at Emory University School of Medicine, Department of Psychiatry and Behavioral Sciences at Grady Health System, Atlanta. She is Chair of the Association of Psychology Postdoctoral and Internship Centers (APPIC).

Georgi Kroupin, MA, is a psychologist at the Center for International Health, Regions Hospital, St. Paul, Minnesota, where he provides individual and family therapy with refugees and immigrants with families from the former Soviet Union, Southeast Asia, Africa, Latin America, and other parts of the world, and is a doctoral student in family therapy at the Department of Social Science, University of Minnesota.

Tracey A. Laszloffy, PhD, is Assistant Professor, Marriage and Family Therapy Program, University of Connecticut, Storrs, Connecticut.

Megan J. Murphy, MS, is a doctoral student in Child and Family Development at the University of Georgia. She holds a master's degree in Human Development and Family Studies with a specialization in Marriage and Family Therapy from Colorado State University.

Augustus Y. Napier, PhD, is a writer, consultant, and lecturer in family therapy who lives in Brevard, North Carolina. His most recent book is *The Fragile Bond,* published in 1988 by HarperCollins. He is at work on a memoir called *Learning By Heart: Reflections on Marriage and the Family.*

William C. Nichols, EdD, ABPP, a Diplomate in Clinical Psychology and a marital and family therapist, is Adjunct Professor of Child and Family Development, the University of Georgia, and formerly was a professor at the Florida State University and other institutions, as well as in private practice for several decades. Currently President of the International Family Therapy Association, he formerly was President of the American Association for Marriage and Family Therapy and of the National Council on Family Relations. His latest book is *Treating People in Families: An Integrative Approach* (1996).

Mary Anne Pace-Nichols, PhD, President of The Nichols Group, Inc., Watkinsville, Georgia, is retired from the University of Georgia and formerly was on the faculty of Georgia Southern University. A family therapist, her specialty is human development.

Carol L. Philpot, PsyD, is Dean and Professor of Psychology, Florida Institute of Technology, Fellow of the American Psychological Association (APA), a Past-President of APA's Divison of Family Psychology, a member of the American Family Therapy Academy, and an American Association for Marriage and Family Therapy Approved Supervisor. Her book *Bridging Separate Gender Worlds: Why Men and Women Clash and How Therapists Can Bring Them Together* was published by the American Psychological Association in 1997.

Sharon J. Price, PhD, is with the Department of Child and Family Development and Faculty of Gerontology, the University of Georgia. Her current program of scholarship includes developing a textbook on families through the life span and conducting a qualitative study of widows who live on family farms.

Mark R. Rank, PhD, is with the George Warren Brown School of Social Work, Washington University, St. Louis, Missouri.

Sandra Rigazio-DiGilio, PhD, is an Associate Professor in the Marriage and Family Therapy Program at the University of Connecticut. Her writings have introduced and advanced an integrative approach to systemic treatment (systemic cognitive-developmental theory and practice).

Lita Linzer Schwartz, PhD, is Distinguished Professor, Department of Educational Psychology, Pennsylvania State University, Abington, Pennsylvania.

Greta Griffith Smith, PhD, Cherokee Health Systems, Talbott, Tennessee. Dr. Smith is completing her postdoctoral year as a full-time clinician in a community mental health center.

Ciloue Cheng Stewart, MSE (counseling), is in the Department of Family Social Science, University of Minnesota, St. Paul, Minnesota.

Sandra Volgy Everett, PhD, is Director of Clinical Training of the Arizona Institute for Family Therapy and in private practice as a clinical psychologist specializing in child and family therapy. She was formerly Director and Coordinator of Child Advocacy Services for the Pima County Conciliation Court, Chief Psychologist for the Tucson Child Guidance Clinic, and an adjunct faculty member at Florida State University.

Blong Xiong, MA, graduate student, the University of Minnesota, St. Paul, Minnesota, is on the board of directors of the Minnesota Council on Family Relations and of the Minnesota Parenting Association.

SERIES PREFACE

Our ability to form strong interpersonal bonds with romantic partners, children, parents, siblings, and other relations is one of the key qualities that defines our humanity. These relationships shape who we are and what we become—they can be a source of great gratification, or tremendous pain. Yet, only in the mid-20th century did behavioral and social scientists really begin focusing on couples and family dynamics, and only in the past several decades have the theory and findings that emerged from those students been used to develop effective therapeutic interventions for troubled couples and families.

We have made great progress in understanding the structure, function, and interactional patterns of couples and families—and have made tremendous strides in treatment. However, as we stand poised on the beginning of a new millennium, it seems quite clear that both intimate partnerships and family relationships are in a period of tremendous flux. Economic factors are changing work patterns, parenting responsibilities, and relational dynamics. Modern medicine has helped lengthen the life span, giving rise to the need for transgenerational caretaking. Cohabitation, divorce, and remarriage are quite commonplace, and these social changes make it necessary for us to rethink and broaden our definition of what constitutes a family.

Thus, it is no longer enough simply to embrace the concept of the family as a system. In order to understand and effectively treat the evolving family, our theoretical formulations and clinical interventions must be informed by an understanding of ethnicity, culture, religion, gender, sexual preference, family life cycle, socioeconomic status, education, physical and mental health, values, and belief systems.

The purpose of the *Wiley Series in Couples and Family Dynamics and Treatment* is to provide a forum for cutting-edge relational and family theory, practice, and research. Its scope is intended to be broad, diverse, and international, but all books published in this series share a common mission: to reflect on the past, offer state-of-the-art information on the present, and speculate on, as well as attempt to shape, the future of the field.

Florence W. Kaslow
Florida Couples and Family Institute

PREFACE

THE TERM *family development* is a deceptively simple one, seeming to denote a straightforward, perhaps unitary, concept. So obvious does the progression of the family through time seem to be, and despite a pervasive sense of crisis about this institution since time immemorial, the family as a focus of serious and methodical study is a relatively recent phenomenon in terms of both sociological and historical inquiry. Having undertaken to create a body of organized theoretical knowledge, however, social scientists have come face to face with the complexities characterizing the field of family studies. Similarly, as we have attempted in this book to address only that aspect known as family development, we have encountered challenges in several areas.

First, we were faced with the issue of defining what is meant by family. The inability to reach consensus regarding how the family is to be defined has proven to be an insurmountable stumbling block in many well-intentioned efforts by scholars and other professionals. An ever elusive concept, we have chosen in this book to use the term *family* loosely and to interpret it liberally, recognizing that variety and diversity are hallmarks of today's families. Chapter authors have been asked, therefore, only that they be as clear and precise as possible in choosing a definition, whether they are referring to a nuclear family of two parents and their children, an extended family, a single-parent family, a remarried family, or various other forms, either kin or nonkin networks and including gay and lesbian partners. By referring to the latter category of relationships as family, we are stretching the term well beyond a more restricted definition that demands that family must include an intergenerational or a biological relationship component. Our references to family are employed descriptively and not in any evaluative or normative sense. They have in common the facts that all consist of interacting personalities, all have a structure, and all undergo continuous processes of growth and change, as do their members.

The concurrent growth and change both of families and of the individuals who comprise them brings us to the second aspect of the challenge involved with a comprehensive survey of family development. That is, a search of the literature reveals little work in the area of integrating models of individual development with those of family development. Consistent with this trend, in the majority of the chapters in this book we present a variety of ways by which we may understand developmental dynamics from the perspectives of either the system as a whole or of the members of the system. A major exception is Chapter 11, in which the consideration of families in midlife explicitly includes discussions of the impact of adolescence as well as middle age on the family task of launching young adults. The ultimate responsibility for all of us thus remains that of recognizing that no one perspective, and certainly no one theory, can fully capture the phenomenon referred to as family development.

Indeed, the third aspect of our challenge relates to the myriad ways in which the processes of evolution and change may be understood. In recognition of the validity and utility in many different perspectives, rather than espousing a particular approach, we have opted to provide a sampling of perspectives that focus on the development of both families and family members. We have divided the book into five parts: Theories of Family Development; The Larger Social Context; Family Stages, Patterns, Processes, and Dynamics; Variations in Family Structure; and Families with Special Needs and Problems. Within each part the reader will find some of the ways each of these five perspectives has been translated into specific models or points of reference. For example, Chapters 1 through 4 (Part I) provide an overview of family development and then address evolutionary psychology, biological and genetic considerations, and constructionist conceptions. In Chapters 5 through 7 (Part II) the topics of discussion are socialization of gender roles, socialization of culture and racial/ethnic identity, and socialization of socioeconomic status. The family life cycle stages considered in Chapters 8 through 12 (Part III) are mate selection and marriage, childless couples, families with young children, families in midlife, and aging and the family. Included in our survey of variations in family structure Chapters 13 through 17 (Part IV) are discussions of adoptive and foster families, families with chronic physical illness, gay and lesbian families, immigrant families, single-parent families, and blended families. Families with special needs and problems in Chapters 18 through 22 (Part V) include families experiencing divorce; families experiencing violence; families with learning disabilities, physical disabilities, and other childhood challenges; families with chronic physical illness, and families experiencing death, dying, and bereavement. Despite our attempt to provide a broad survey, however, we are aware that there are probably as many approaches left without discussion as there are included. This, of course, speaks to the dilemma inherent in any effort to pin down or fully comprehend human behavior in all of its infinite variations.

Articulating the knowledge and understanding of human behavior relative to family development that we do have and translating it into practice represents the fourth aspect of our challenge. Our goal is to provide information that is both meaningful and useful to clinicians. Thus, wherever appropriate, the authors have been asked to consider not only developmental dynamics from a theoretical perspective but also their application in the therapy setting. In this regard we once again have opted for a broad focus, one which may hopefully prove useful and informative for representatives of all of the mental health professions. Whether working with individuals or with whole families, and regardless of therapeutic modality, we believe it is important to have an awareness of the larger contexts within which clients live and to be sensitive to the variety of developmental issues, tasks, and challenges that may have an impact on both clients and their families and on the potential for the therapy process to be effective.

William C. Nichols
Mary Anne Pace-Nichols
Dorothy S. Becvar
Augustus Y. Napier

CONTENTS

FOREWORD

Development is the timely theme of this new handbook appearing at the beginning of a new millennium. Development appears in this book in several different forms:

- In individuals and families
- As a framework to shape clinical thinking
- Describing the evolution of theories
- Tracing the history of recognition and attention to particular clinical problems

The model of family development formulated and popularized by Evelyn Duvall in the fifties (Duvall, 1957) still stands as an excellent example of how to adapt concepts that were developed for another purpose to a family framework. In this case, Duvall's model has endured as a straightforward sketch of changing family issues as individuals mature and age. This model and its developmental descendents rule the chapters that describe clinical issues in families through the life cycle.

Duvall's and others' standard developmental models need to be scrutinized in light of developing awareness of sociocultural forces, including ethnicity and economic status, among others, that lead to differences in expectations and outcomes. Leaving home, for example, is a significant marker of the end of adolescence for the individuals and a major adjustment for the families. But grown children may not leave home when their families have cultural rules about remaining in the home or when they are too poor to live independently. These social developments have required adjustments in our understanding and work with these families.

Developmental frameworks also appear in tracing the evolution of thinking about families in particular situations, such as divorce. In this instance, Florence Kaslow provides an historical account of how approaches to working with divorcing families evolved. The focus of attention to divorcing families has developed through the last 30 years. At the beginning we recognized that divorce was clinically important and developed means to evaluate and advise divorcing families. Then, divorce mediation was developed and has become a distinct profession. Even more recently, it has become a common practice in many states to require divorcing parents to participate in education about the effects of divorce on their children.

I would like to take some time in the Foreword of this book on development to look back on the development of the family field and to examine how developing forces have affected how we family clinicians define ourselves in the year 2000.

In the past 60 years, the evolution of family focus has evolved from two major forces. Force A has emanated largely from clinical concerns whereas force B has a more academic thrust. Force A has developed theory from practice, borrowing liberally not only from family sociologists, but also from anthropology, physics, mathematics, and ethology to explicate what has been found to be effective in clinical practice. Force B has come from more academically, research-oriented disciplines. Force B has contributed more of the solid, data-based understanding of family forms, organizations, and changes in response to the myriad of challenges facing the family, not the least among them the demands for change and accommodation to the developments of individual family members.

These two forces in the development of family therapy have usually run parallel courses. Clinicians developed ways to describe or even "map" family functioning, while researchers have developed carefully researched and validated assessment tools. The mapping device found in *Families and Family Therapy* (Minuchin, 1974) are very rudimentary. Family members are given identifying initials, M, F, S, or D. Boundaries (abstractions denoting distinctions between individuals, generations, or other functions) are represented by solid or dotted lines; distance is represented by distance, and hierarchy is represented by depicting members above or below the others. Force or movement can be represented by arrows. This is a simple sketch, clinically useful as a description of the moment, likely to change according to the tasks or demands the family faces at the time of mapping. Contrast this sketch with Olsen's FACES, a tool that identifies adaptability and cohesion in families through a self-report scale, where the report is often given by one or two family members. This tool has validity that allows for comparison of different families and for measuring different family styles against clinical presentations and outcomes. Clinicians benefit from the findings of the research, but usually do not employ these tools in their daily work.

Family thinking and clinical practice has developed in this bifurcated fashion throughout the last 50 or 60 years. On the clinical front (force A) the family field confronted, first, the simple challenge of assembling family members in the same room at the same time. This required logistics of persuasion, timing, and space allocation to be solved. Most important of these was persuading family members, particularly fathers, to participate in family therapy sessions. This was such a basic change in the way family members expected to receive treatment that dedicated family therapists often had to take the position that they would not see anyone unless the entire family came in. A second fundamental challenge, coordination of treatment in the life of a family, led to the important realization that therapy is not the center of people's lives. Particularly with families struggling with daily challenges, such as poverty or physical illness or employment instability, there are many distractions on the way to therapy and following the therapist's suggestions. Family clinicians realized that something had to happen in the therapy session; it had to make a difference; and it had to happen quickly, because the family might not have time to continue treatment. Focusing on the family's therapy in the context of other demands in their lives also led clinicians to view families as partners in the therapeutic enterprise. For example, instead of automatically giving a family an appointment for the next session, Carl Whitaker would ask them whether they would like to "do this again," and if so, when?

Another clinical development came from the observation that families didn't come in or stay in treatment if they felt blamed, criticized, or threatened by the therapist or the therapist's language and intentions. Family therapists learned to speak so that families could understand them, and to adjust their language accordingly. They learned to respect that people are usually doing the best they can, and that the families' limitations are usually based on constraints that are external, due to sociocultural forces, or internal, due to tradition, history, or constitution. This led to a virtual disintegration of categories of human emotional and psychological behavior, as each family's efforts to perform family functions became a study in itself; each family taught its eager therapist new things about how families can work. This, in turn, informed the currently popular narrative approach.

Force A practitioners visited many fields in an effort to formulate and communicate their experiences. They visited general systems theory to borrow equipotentiality, equifinality, and centripetal and centrifugal forces. From Norbert Wiener, cybernetics was adapted to understand recursive patterns and feedback loops. These observations were subsequently employed as deliberate clinical devices when the Milan group introduced circular questioning. The field visited Ilya Prigogene to apply entropy and negentropy to understanding family momentum, equating negentropy with love. The biologist Umberto Maturana provided other concepts to fuel these developments. Gregory Bateson was tapped for concepts of schizmogenesis and shapes of development (spiral, as in the whelk, where the history of the organism is visible in its emerging structure; and segmental, describing the maturation of bilateral symmetry). From ethology came the concepts of social attitudes and postures and how social context and status affect these. Claude Levi-Strauss was cited as a mentor on how to be an anthropologist with a family. From Kenneth Gergen and the post-modernists came notions of personal constructions (narratives) along with the optimism that narratives can change in the dialogic process, and changing narratives can change experience and behavior. Force A borrowed from other master therapists, such as Milton Erickson, Fritz Perls, Carl Rogers, and many others, including, of course, its own members, pioneers in family therapy.

The impetus behind force B has been academic and research oriented and better supported by data. Sociopolitical movements and their effect on the family have been the stimuli for developments in this line. Poverty; domestic violence; trends in marriage, divorce, and remarriage; and cultural diversity have been major influences on developments in family sociology as a contribution to clinical approaches to families. Additionally, there are sociopolitical issues, the most important being those relating to race, gender, and again, economics.

Force A is a driving clinical force; force B is a thoughtful force constantly challenging force A to have more support for its assertions, to be more sensitive and to include a wider awareness of sociopolitical context not only in work with individual families, but its theory making. For example, Structural Family Therapy flourished to assist families experiencing problems with their children. Structural Family Therapy emphasizes family hierarchy, maintaining generational boundaries, and differentiated roles and functions. Strategic family therapies work by disrupting recursive sequences in which symptom behavior is embedded; assessment of feedback loops (recursive sequences) assumes that all of the players in a sequence contribute to the process, outcome, and consequences. The feminist critique of family therapy challenged the unthinking maintenance of family hierarchy and distribution of power in families and in the strategic approach. Structural–strategic family therapists were criticized for failing to hold the powerful responsible for overpowering the weaker, or essentially blaming the victim, particularly in instances when less powerful family members, such as women and children, might be exploited and injured. To look at the interaction between a wife beater and his victim as circular or recursive, said the feminist critics (James & McIntyre, 1983), is to blame the victim and set her up for continued victimization. Feminists brought to light an observation buried in a study of "normal" adolescent families, that the mothers in these "normal" families often suffered from headaches and emotional distress (Leupnitz, 1988). Concepts of recursion and circularity in family interactions had been fundamental to leading clinical approaches to family treatment. Now, family systems thinkers have had to figure out how to hold concepts of hierarchy, power, and recurrent patterns in such a way that all can be accessed and used when they may be helpful and not disadvantage anyone. Some claim that violent men can not be seen in therapy with their abused mates, as, at best, this might condone the violence by examining the mate's behavior; at worst it might result in renewed and more intense violence. Yet when Virginia Goldener and Gillian Walker wondered why the violent couples they were treating stay together, they began to see these couples as clinging together, often in the face of outside forces to separate. They recommend that some of these couples can be treated by acknowledging and working with these strong attachments. On the other side of the argument, family violence researcher Neal Jacobson identified a group of violent men who are so unmoved by their violence (meaning that they show no physiological signs of arousal or stress during episodes of violence) that they cannot be safely engaged in treatment with the spouse. He doubted that they can be effectively treated at all. These observations led to the conclusion that there can be no singular approach to treating wife beating.

This handbook focuses primarily on the intersection of these forces A and B at the end of the century, where we find ourselves with many family forms, many cultures, and many transitional issues. The book reminds us that the family field continues to be fraught with tensions. Efran and Green present compelling evidence of biological destiny that challenges the premises of clinical psychotherapeutic interventions. They move back from radical environmentalism that has impelled the family therapy movement in its early years, to biological imperative. Since their chapter is followed with one on meaning-making through narrative, the contemporary, mature family clinician must continue to weigh conflicting ideas without discarding or choosing.

Perhaps it is too early to discuss the effects of biological approaches on the family field, and it is certainly too early to tell how the family field will incorporate wisdom from biological studies. Biological investigation into psychological expression (behavior, affect, and cognition) ranges from genetics (the human genome project) to neurobiology and location of behaviors at a synaptic and biochemical level. The finding that cognitive therapy and antidepressants have similar efficacy in the treatment of some forms of depression is encouraging to clinicians who work with the belief that change can occur in the dialogic process, the reshaping of patterned behaviors, or finding of options where families have been constrained. We become more encouraged by the observation that there appear to be changes in the neurochemistry of the brain in response to changes in behavior similar to those in response to pharmacological interventions.

The immediate effects of the fascination for biology, especially on the field of family, however, is the relegation of family treatment to adjunctive status while the principal activity for an individual experiencing emotional distress and misbehavior is to make a diagnosis and then treat the problem with medication. This is the principal and expected approach to managing all individuals who require intensive levels of care, such as psychiatric hospitalization or partial hospital care. In this instance, the biological approach and family/contextual treatment are either mutually exclusive, or, as noted above, the family treatment is considered to be adjunctive, and, therefore, optional. This emphasis on diagnosis and medication is also found in outpatient treatment where "medical necessity" is the catch phrase for providing insurance reimbursement for therapy. Treatment of many of the conditions described in this book, such as adjusting to a divorce, remarried family, or accommodating to foster care or adoption, will not be covered by insurance unless at least one family member is symptomatic, has a diagnosis, and is possibly even placed on medication.

This is particularly problematic when it comes to school-aged children where problems in learning, behavior, and adjustment are more often being diagnosed as due to a biologically based disorder, such as ADHD or an affective disorder. Families may be involved in the treatment of such children only for the purpose of assessing whether the child can be safely managed at home. Rarely is it considered that developmental or family interactional issues are significantly related to the problems and their potential solutions. Representatives of the health care "industry" and its providers may not consider that even if a child has a "biologically based" disorder that may respond to medication, there are also bound to be significant family interactional patterns that, when addressed in treatment, can reduce stress, reduce the child's dysfunctional behavior, and increase the sense of competence and control that families have over their lives. To give medication, when appropriate, *and* involve families in family therapy requires subscribing to what some may consider to be conflicting beliefs, recognizing the validity and limitations of each.

It is this commitment to entertaining, identifying, encompassing, and holding dear diversity—whether it be diverse theories, diverse cultural groups, or diverse versions of events—that seems to be the lasting legacy of the family systems movement. It is what Ivan Boszormenyi-Nagy referred to as multilaterality: someone can hold a position for him or herself while also acknowledging the validity of other family members' positions from their points of view. It is what Steve DeShazer spoke of as a multiocular viewpoint, suggesting that the clinician's mind might be like the eye of a fly, integrating multiple images into orienting information. At all levels of engagement with families, whether it be family therapy sessions, understanding sociopolitical influences on the family, or dealing with theories about dysfunction and change, family systems thinkers have learned to live with the plurality of ideas that are often contradictory or mutually exclusive, somehow accepting them all into the work that is family therapy.

Although this book features development as its unifying theme, it offers a diversity of ideas, theories, description of family types, and even of the notion of development itself.

The diversity of ideas and family forms described in this book impels those who believe in families as essential contexts for development and change to avoid closure on ideas or methods, and to be continuously open to learn from families, not only problems but solutions.

Lee Combrinck-Graham

REFERENCES

Duvall, E. M. (1957). *Family development.* Philadelphia: J.B. Lippincott.

James, K., & McIntyre, D. (1983). The reproduction of families: The social role of family therapy? *JAAMFT, 9,* 119–129.

Leupnitz, D. (1986). *The family interpreted.* New York: Basic Books.

Minuchin, S. (1974). *Families and family therapy.* Cambridge, MA: Harvard University Press.

PART I

THEORIES OF FAMILY DEVELOPMENT

CHAPTER 1

Family Development and Family Therapy

William C. Nichols and Mary Anne Pace-Nichols

THIS CHAPTER PROVIDES an introduction to the family development approach to understanding families and to the implications it has for family therapy. Briefly, it describes the relatively recent origins of family development theory, subsequent elaboration of the original ideas, some current perspectives on family development, and some of the ways in which family development ideas have been adapted by family therapists.

FRAMEWORKS FOR UNDERSTANDING FAMILIES

Family scholars and scholars from other fields have developed a variety of frameworks for studying and understanding families. By 1960, more than a dozen approaches were being used. Hill and Hansen (1960) selected a half dozen as the main theoretical frameworks on the basis that (1) they covered major dimensions of the family and (2) they could be clearly differentiated from each other. Five frameworks—institutional, structural-functional, situational, symbolic-interactional, and developmental—were later used as the theoretical orientations in Harold T. Christensen's influential *Handbook of Marriage and the Family* (1964). The first three developed out of attempts to understand culture and society. The fourth orientation developed out of efforts to understand personality development, particularly socialization processes and processes in the growth of "self." The fifth, developmental, was concerned specifically with family, with "an organization and setting for facilitating growth and development of families" (Hill & Mattessich, 1979, p. 164). The five are described briefly below.

INSTITUTIONAL

In the institutional approach, the major focus is on the family as an institution, and the emphasis is on historical and cross-cultural design (i.e., on the origin and development of the family institution and on comparisons between family institutions in various cultures as well as in different time periods).

STRUCTURAL-FUNCTIONAL

Structural-functional theory focuses on the family as a social system and how it operates, being concerned with whether any particular elements in the family either add to or subtract from the system's operation (i.e., is functional or dysfunctional). Interaction and interdependence connect these constituent parts of the family. The structural-functional approach is concerned with relationships between the family and other social systems as well as with the family's internal operations.

SITUATIONAL

This approach focuses on the situational settings that affect the behavior of family members. Although the family is also viewed as a unity of interacting personalities, the emphasis in the situational approach is on the social situation, which provides external stimuli that act upon family members, rather than on the family's interaction as such.

SYMBOLIC-INTERACTIONAL

As the name implies, the symbolic-interactional approach focuses on interaction among family members. E. W. Burgess (1926), who provided an impetus for this approach in the 1920s, defined the family as "a unity of interacting personalities." Essentially ignoring the major emphases of the institutional and structural-functional approaches—the relationships of the family as a transacting unit in society—the interactional approach emphasizes internal processes in the family—communication, status relations, role playing, decision making, stress reactions, and related phenomena.

DEVELOPMENTAL

The developmental approach, which had its roots in the 1930s and emerged in the 1940s, is a more recent entry into the theoretical frameworks field than the other four. The unique contribution that the family development approach has made to understanding families has been its emphasis on "family time," that is, with "the orderly changes which occur in most families over the life cycle" (Hill & Mattessich, 1979, p. 163). In contrast to other approaches, family development "is defined in terms of the progressive structural differentiation and the related transformations which the family unit experiences as it moves through the life cycle" (Hill & Mattessich, 1979, p. 161).

The older frameworks have limited value in explaining family change. According to Rodgers (1973), family sociologists have tended to approach the family in two basic ways: the institutional approach, which views broad patterns of family structures and time in broad sweeps; and the interactional approach, which looks at the internal dynamics of families, and thus makes it possible to examine the behavior of individuals and sets of persons in the family and in relation to other social organizations. The interactional approach is limited to short spans of time and to comparisons between them. The developmental theoretical framework "approaches the exploration of family phenomena in a way which accounts for both chronological and family process time" (Rodgers, 1973, p. 14). Rodgers uses the concept of family process time to refer to the periods in the life space of family within a given process (e.g., "they are getting an education" does not refer to chronological time but to a processual period).

THE BACKGROUND OF FAMILY DEVELOPMENT

The background out of which family development emerged and its early growth have been previously described in some detail, most notably by Hill and Rodgers (1964), Hill and Mattessich (1979), and Mattessich and Hill (1987). Hence, the coverage here will be brief, consisting primarily of broad stroke depictions, based on those sources. The reader is referred to the original sources in sociology for more complete treatment.

EARLY ORIGINS OF THE FAMILY DEVELOPMENT PERSPECTIVE

The family development approach can be described as emerging in 1948. Evelyn Millis Duvall and Reuben Hill, who had been collaborating in family studies since 1943, prepared a background paper for the National Conference on Family Life convened by President Harry Truman at the White House. In the paper they set forth a two-dimensional outline for plotting the developmental tasks of children and of parents for each of eight stages of the family life cycle (Duvall, 1971). They originally drew on two sources: (1) on symbolic interactionism (George Herbert Mead, E.W. Burgess, and Willard Waller) for their perspective of the family as an arena of interacting personalities, and (2) on the human development perspectives of Robert Havighurst and Erik H. Erikson for their ideas of "human development as marked by the mastery over the entire life span of progressively more complex developmental tasks" (Hill & Mattessich, 1979, p. 164).

Family development conceptualization continued to draw freely from other approaches. The notion of stages of the life cycle was borrowed from rural sociology, the idea of developmental needs and tasks from human development research and child psychology, and other concepts by which we may understand the family as a system of interacting actors from structure-functional and symbolic-interactional theory (Hill & Rodgers, 1964). The concepts of position, role, and norms were taken from the structure-functional approach, especially as these related to age and sex roles. The notions of boundary maintenance and of equilibrium seeking of the family as a social system were also borrowed from structure-function. The symbolic-interactional framework specifically furnished the conception of a system of interacting personalities, which has been used to modify the idea of role in role taking, role playing, role differentiation, and reciprocity of roles. Sociology of the professions and sociology of work provided the concept of career and the perspective of the family as, first, a convergence of the intercontingent career of husband and wife and, later, of children and parents (Hill, 1971).

Assumptions underlying the developmental framework nearly four decades ago were described by Hill and Hansen as follows:

1. Human conduct is best seen as a function of the earlier as well as the current social milieu and individual conditions.
2. Human conduct cannot be adequately understood apart from human development.
3. The human is an actor as well as a reactor.
4. Individual and group development is best seen as dependent on stimulation by a social milieu as well as on inherent (developed) capacities.
5. The individual in a social setting is the basic autonomous unit (1960, p. 309).

The possibility family development has for connecting with psychology's life span development (Hill & Mattessich, 1979) is, according to Hill, another outstanding feature of the developmental approach. Despite Hill and Mattessich's (1979) efforts, however, it cannot be said today that family development and life span development approaches have been closely related.

Family development emerges primarily in response to internal pressures such as the changing age composition of the family, but the contexts in which individuals are born, develop, and die also significantly affect developmental dynamics. That is, the historical time in which the family exists defines appropriate role transitions at certain chronological ages (e.g., school entrance requirements) and thus affects reorganization of family roles and entry into a new stage of development, and establishes normative prescriptions for family behavior for particular stages of development (Hill & Mattessich, 1979, p. 192).

THE FAMILY AS A SOCIAL SYSTEM

Early conceptualizations viewed the family as a closed unit, a view that did not last. By 1971, Reuben Hill was calling for a reconceptualization, specifically questioning whether the views of the family as a simple, closed, equilibrium-seeking, and conformity-oriented system implied in the structure-function approaches were appropriate. Rather, he saw the family as a complex, adaptive system that was ever changing and growing, selectively opening to transactions with other systems. Hill made some specific suggestions as to how system theory enhanced the theoretical bases of the family development framework (Hill, 1971).

Viewing the family as a social system, family development theory emphasizes several familiar system theory concepts (Hill & Mattessich, 1979) including the following:

Interrelatedness of parts: System theory involves the notion that the parts of a system are connected such that change in one part of the system influences other parts of the system. Positions and roles in a family thus are interdependent. Family development is concerned primarily with two kinds of positions: (1) age positions, which are modified by gender, and by the norms of ordinal position; and (2) relatedness positions, which are connected in normatively specified ways as paired positions (e.g., husband-wife, father-son, mother-daughter, father-daughter, mother-son, and brother-sister).

Boundary-maintaining system: The family has semipermeable boundaries. That is, it is partially closed and may exclude the external world when dealing with internal family issues. At the same time, families build liaison roles into family positions (e.g., roles of husband and wife for linkage to community) and develop rules for conducting transactions with other social institutions and groups (e.g., employers, school). The family is therefore semi-open to societal demands and environmental changes that require adaptations in the family.

Change over time: Hill and Mattessich indicate that, in order to account for changes in the family system over its formation, expansion, contraction, and dissolution, "the developmental approach focuses primarily on the changing role content of positions which occurs chiefly due to changes in age norms for these positions" (1979, p. 167). These content changes result in alterations in expectations and behavior of the occupants. In turn, such changes, of course, affect roles that are reciprocally related to the changing position.

An excellent description of systems theory and its application to marriage is provided by Steinglass (1978).

Through the research, teaching, and writing of Duvall, Hill, Roy Rodgers (1962, 1973), and others, the family development perspective became widely known. Duvall's textbooks on family development, which first appeared in 1957, introduced the material to generations of students. Although family development has had its critics, there is evidence that even today this perspective is accepted as the framework for understanding families by a high percentage of family scholars and specialists. Recently, when more than 100 family scholars were queried about how favorable they were toward 11 different theories, family development and family systems were tied for second place, behind only symbolic interactionism theory (Klein, 1994).

FAMILY DEVELOPMENT AND THE FAMILY LIFE CYCLE

A distinction needs to be made between two concepts, family development and the family life cycle. These terms have often been used interchangeably, but refer in the main to different phenomena. Family development is the broader concept and refers to all "transactional coevolutionary processes connected with the growth of a family" (Falicov, 1988b, p. 13). These include processes of continuity and change associated with work, geographical location and migration, acculturation, serious illness, or other patterns that have a major impact on family life such as psychological processes. The family life cycle label is placed on those significant events related to the arrival and departure of family members such as the birth or adoption of children, child rearing, the departure of children from the home, occupational retirement, and loss by death (Duvall, 1957).

The Life Cycle Concept

Originally used in a study of family poverty in England (Rowntree, 1906) early in the nineteenth century, the life cycle concept—defined in terms of expanding and contracting family size or on the age of children—came to be widely employed by rural sociologists in a number of studies in the United States during the 1930s and 1940s. Paul Glick (1947, 1955, 1957) provided the bridge from the use of life cycles as demographic categories to their use as a guide for describing the content of stages of living across the family life span. He demonstrated historical changes in American life cycle patterns, including the appearance of a new stage in families of the 1940s and 1950s between the departure of the children and the death of one of the spouses, and illustrated some of the effects of these changes on families, including particularly differences emanating from the earlier marriages of the times and the longer life span of the spouses.

Duvall (1971) divided the family life cycle into stages, focusing on the oldest child, the parents (couple), and the work career of the husband-father. An adaptation of this is listed below.

Stage 1: Married couples (without children)
Stage 2: Childbearing families (first child birth to 30 months)
Stage 3: Families with preschool children (oldest child 30 months to 6 years)
Stage 4: Families with schoolchildren (oldest child 6 to 13 years)
Stage 5: Families with teenagers (oldest child 13 to 20 years)
Stage 6: Families as launching centers (oldest child leaves home to last child leaving home)
Stage 7: Middle-aged parents (empty nest to retirement)
Stage 8: Aging family members (retirement to death of both spouses)

Some problems were evident with the Duvall formulation from the beginning. Aside from gender biases, nuclear family assumptions, and a middle-class orientation, there were difficulties in viewing the family as proceeding step by step through the stages with the oldest child and then repeating the process with younger children. Rodgers (1962) restated the conception, using the idea of categories instead of stages and providing categories on the basis of several different children rather than simply the oldest. Instead of eight stages, he provided for 24 categories and related the concepts of norm, positions, and roles to one's "positional career" and the "family career." Rodgers suggested that the family life cycle notion be replaced with the family career concept, which had been set forth by Bernard Farber. Farber (1956, 1959, 1961) had dealt with the development of the family as a set of mutually contingent careers, which referred to events in the life course of individual family members that affect other family members, for example, leaving home (Aldous, 1996). The family career concept would become an exceedingly important part of family development literature, particularly in the work of Rodgers (1973) and Aldous (1978, 1996).

The Developmental Tasks Concept

In the early stages of the family development approach, the life cycle was conceptualized as involving a series of developmental tasks to be performed at appropriate stages throughout its course. The concept of developmental task was set forth by Robert Havighurst as follows:

> A developmental task is a task which arrives at or about a certain period in the life of an individual, successful achievement of which leads to his happiness and to success with later tasks, while failure leads to unhappiness in the individual, disapproval by the society, and difficulty with later tasks. (1953, p. 3)

Duvall declared that family developmental tasks run parallel to individual developmental tasks. She noted:

> Family developmental tasks are those growth responsibilities that must be accomplished by a family at a given stage of development in a way that will satisfy its (1) biological requirements, (2) cultural imperatives, and (3) personal aspirations and values, if the family is to continue to grow as a unit. (1971, pp. 149–150)

Duvall indicated that the family development perspective means that families "go through predictable stages of development that can be understood in terms of the development of the individual family members and of the family as a whole" (1971, p. v). Thus, both individuals and families have developmental tasks to perform in Duvall's schema. According to Klein and White (1996), use of the developmental tasks concept involved an attempt to integrate age-graded and stage-graded social norms with the ontogenetic maturation of individual members.

Originally based primarily on biological foundations, the concept of developmental tasks has undergone redefinition over the years. Rodgers (1962, 1973) drew the concept of developmental tasks closer to systems theory and role theory. Using fairly standard role theory concepts, Rodgers defined a role as a set of expectations for an actor in a group. These roles are based on norms. Role behavior is what an actor does in response to role expectations. Position is the location of an actor, the sum total of the roles occupied by an actor in a system. As one moves through the life cycle, he or she plays a series of roles sequentially (role sequence). The set of concurrent roles that provide the content of a position at any given time constitute a role cluster. Two or more sets of role clusters held concurrently by two or more occupants of positions in an interlocking system at a given time comprise a role complex. When all the role clusters that occur in a given position sequentially during its life in the group are linked together, the result is referred to as the *positional career.* The family career is composed of all the role complexes (i.e., all the role clusters that exist concurrently at one point in time) linked together sequentially over the life of the group.

Rodgers redefined developmental tasks as a set of role expectations or norms that arise at a particular point in the career of a position in a social system. If these norms are incorporated by the incumbent of a position as a role or part of a role cluster, integration and temporary equilibrium result with respect to a role complex or set of role complexes. If they are not incorporated, a lack of integration, the pressure of sanctions, and difficulty in incorporating later norms into the role cluster of the position result (Rodgers, 1973, p. 51).

Believing that the developmental tasks concept becomes redundant with the age-graded and stage-graded ideas of norm and role, Rodgers (Rodgers & White, 1993) ceased to include it among the central concepts of family development theory, and, as noted, along with Aldous (1978, 1996), replaced the family life cycle concept with the more sequential idea of the family career concept.

FAMILY STRESS

Research and theory on family stress (Hill, 1949, 1958; McCubbin et al., 1980) also modified the original family development framework. As Falicov (1988b) has noted, the integration of concepts from stress theory into family development theory was important in several ways:

- The idea that stages were discrete or discontinuous was changed when the notion of transitions between stages was added, primarily from Rapaport's (1963) concept of developmental crises, leading to the view that the periods between stages were discontinuous and those within stages were continuous because the family was relatively stable during stages.
- The clinical relevance of the family development approach was improved when the idea was accepted that stress was distributed throughout the family life cycle.
- The idea that stressors "pile up" on a family (Hill, 1949), forcing it to cope with multiple, unanticipated stresses at the same time, fits well with clinical observations.
- The dynamic processes of coping and adaptation lessened the possibility of viewing family development in a static fashion.
- The changes increased the potential for perceiving family symptoms as unsuccessful efforts at adaptation, a view that was already held by some family therapists.

FAMILY DEVELOPMENT TODAY

Family development perspectives today obviously are different from those of earlier decades. Some of the changes have been described in the preceding pages. Rather than attempting to sketch the complex interweaving of changes that have occurred, at this juncture we are going to set forth several current perspectives on family development. Our emphasis is on the portions of the family development perspectives that have implications for therapeutic work rather than on implications for research and theory development.

ONTOGENETIC AND SOCIOLOGICAL VIEWS OF DEVELOPMENT

The concepts of change and development within the family were not clearly differentiated by the early family development adherents, the two concepts sometimes being used interchangeably. In recent decades, two distinctly different conceptions of development have appeared. Ontogenetic development—which is based on the genetic capacity of a species to progressively acquire language and thought—has been emphasized by child development specialists (cf. Piaget, 1952, 1971). A sociological conception of development typically followed by family development scholars concentrates on moving across normatively expected family events (White, 1991). In contrast to the rigid sequencing of an ontogenetic approach such as that espoused by Piaget, family development stages can follow a number of ways of sequencing. Thus a sociological perspective on development appears to conform more closely to observations that considerable variety is witnessed in families and that cultural factors often appear to affect what occurs.

FAMILY DEVELOPMENT AND INDIVIDUAL LIFE COURSE ANALYSIS

Over the last three decades or so, apart from family development theory, a kind of analysis of individual event histories has emerged that is focused to a significant degree on family events (Klein & White, 1996). Some would include individual life course analysis within the arena of family development (e.g., White, 1991), whereas others (e.g., Aldous, 1990) view it as different from family development.

THE FAMILY CAREERS DEVELOPMENTAL PERSPECTIVE: JOAN ALDOUS

Aldous (1996) has stated that family development concentrates on how families change over their lifetimes, how they live out their months and years, and on the alterations they are likely to experience. She refers to family careers as another term for family development—and says that she uses family development, family career, and family life cycle interchangeably—noting that this approach "provides markers for dividing families' social clocks into segments" (Aldous, 1996, p.3).

Family development focuses on "somewhat expectable changes over time in families. These include the coming together of couples and, for most, the birth of their children and their eventual departure from home" (Aldous, 1996, p. 7). Not all families follow the same sequence of events (e.g., some families are created through births to unwed mothers, and others through remarriage by one or both parents following divorce, and thus have different courses than a first-time married couple who have children). Aldous (1978) perceives stages as qualitatively distinct periods in a family's life course, which are marked off by transitional events. Family development does not include nonfamily aspects of the life course of individuals or occurrences to individuals that do not affect the lives of other family members.

Assumptions of the family development framework today include the following:

1. Since family behavior is the sum of the previous experiences of family members that are incorporated in the present and in their expectations for the future, what occurred in the past constrains a family in the present; there are linkages with the past, but such linkages are limited (Magrabi & Marshall, 1965). As Aldous (1996) notes, the family's level of task performance depends partly on limits set by past achievements or failures, for example, how the family maintains itself in terms of physical maintenance, preserving social order, or socializing members and maintaining morale limits to some degree its task performance at the next stage.

2. Families develop and change over time in similar and consistent ways. Although not all families follow the same sequence and there are some ethnic, social class, and other differences, families sharing the same stage sequences can be assumed to show certain behavioral features in common.

3. Family members and others in the society set time-specific tasks that the family members perform (e.g., based on family, school, and work careers, and on social meanings attached to the family member's age). Members seek changes due to events outside the family as well as from expectations held within the family. These factors constitute explicit sources of alterations in family life and account for the timing and sequence assumptions of the family development approach.

Table 1.1 illustrates the point that the importance of various tasks waxes and wanes over the family life cycle.

Family, as the term is conceptualized by Aldous, shares with other groups the following common elements: (1) membership based on mutual consent, blood, or adoption; (2) a relatively long duration or the expectation of relatively long duration, typically including a common residence; and (3) the performance for its members and for society of important functions (e.g., social control, physical maintenance, socialization, reproduction, and morale maintenance). Using this definition, a variety of groups—including a married couple and their children; a man and a woman living together in consensual union for several years; two women sharing a residence they jointly own; a parent, his or her child, and the child's child; or a remarried couple with his, her, and their children—can be referred to as families. In contrast to some other perspectives, Aldous' definition does not require the presence of two generations, but recognizes that the intimate relations involved in living together today can include a single generation, such as "empty nest" couples whose children have left home, couples who have never had children, and homosexual partners.

The three criteria that Duvall and Hill (1948) originally used for establishing stages—change in family composition, developmental stages of the oldest child, and the retirement status of the husband-father—obviously do not suffice for many recently emerging nontraditional family forms (Aldous, 1996). As compared to the traditional sequence, families today can be out of sequence (do not pass through stages in the traditional order, e.g.,

TABLE 1.1.   Major Tasks by Stage Across Family Life Cycle

Stage	Tasks
Formation	Morale maintenance Social control
Childbearing/ child rearing years	Reproduction Physical maintenance Socialization
Children leaving home	Social control Morale maintenance
The middle years	Morale maintenance
Final years	Physical maintenance Morale maintenance

Source: Adapted from Aldous, J. (1996) Family careers: Rethinking the developmental perspective. Thousand Oaks, CA: Sage Publications, 67.

begun by childbirth instead of marriage), truncated (skip stages, go through divorce), or recycled (repeat stages, e.g., remarried partners relive stages by having another child).

A DYNAMIC PERSPECTIVE: JAMES M. WHITE

White describes the parent-child bond, the consanguineal bond, as the principal character-istic of the family group. His definition is: "A family is an intergenerational, social group organized and governed by social norms regarding descent and affinity, reproduction, and the nurturant socialization of the young" (1991, pp. 6–7). Family development is expected to explain the transition between stages.

White (1991) asserts that a theory of family development is concerned with delineating patterned changes in families across time and therefore emphasizes dynamics (Klein & White, 1996; White, 1991). The family development approach acknowledges the impor-tance of individual development, but its main focus stays on "the development of the fam-ily as a group of interacting individuals and [as] organized by social norms" (Klein & White, 1996, p. 120). White views the notion of the family career as the core construct for a dynamic approach to understanding family development, since the concept of a career involves a sequence of events (or stages) over time: "A family career is composed of all the events and periods of time (stages) between events traversed by a family" (Klein & White, 1996, p. 131). White (1991) says that a family stage implies that there has been at least one family transition event, and that an event indicates both the end of one stage and beginning of the succeeding stage (e.g., a child's birth signals the end of the marital dyad stage and the beginning of the early family stage).

Family stages are defined by institutional norms, which construct relatively unique peri-ods (stages) that are bounded by family transition events. Family and individual behavior thus are seen as being guided by social norms rather than ontogenetic causes (Klein & White, 1996). Sequencing and timing norms for families (and individuals) come not only from within the family but also from other social institutions and from the norms syn-chronizing the timing of events between institutions. Hence, the path that a family may fol-low on the basis of family institutional norms is only a probable path, not one that is explicitly determined. Development therefore is stochastic in nature, and some of the fac-tors that affect the transition from one stage to another are not known and cannot neces-sarily be specified, according to White (1991). He defines family development as "the process whereby stages of family life are sequenced so that the probability of any stage is determined by the duration of time in a specific previous state" (White, 1991, p. 42).

White therefore argues against the assumption that the order of stages in family devel-opment is invariant and that it is necessary to meet developmental tasks for a stage before a family can move to the next stage. Rather, he holds that a family's probability of making a transition to another stage depends on the stage the family presently occupies and the length of time it has been in that stage. For example, a family consisting of a couple and a young child is not likely to enter the launching stage for more than a decade, whereas a couple with a late teenager probably will be entering the launching stage within a few years. Thus, he sees development as a process in which the probabilities of a transition are related to the family's current stage and the duration of its time in that stage.

Are transitions between stages to be viewed as discrete leaps or as gradual and contin-uous changes? The answer appears to be "either" or "both." As Hill and Mattessich (1979) noted, at its beginning the family development approach emphasized discontinuous change brought on by the transformational sequences of the behavior of children that demanded a major reorganization of family role scripts. More experience and observation disclosed that both discontinuity and continuity can be found in family stages. There are parts of the family life cycle where the stage breaks are sharp and discontinuous because of such complexities as a "pileup of changes in plurality patterns, in employment and residential statuses, and in sheer number of role renegotiations required" (Hill & Mattessich, 1979, p. 181). At the same time there are stage breaks that involve only age changes in children (e.g., entrance of the oldest child into adolescence). Klein and White (1966) present the argument that transitions are generally tied to a discrete event, such as a child being born or attaining a given age, and that these events change things for families. Controversy likely will continue to prevail regarding whether change is continuous or discontinuous. Whether in reference to family development or with regard to individual development, no simple answer is adequate (Gormly & Brodzinsky, 1993).

CULTURE-SPECIFIC CONTENT IN STAGES

The emergence of a multiplicity of family forms has long since elicited the criticism that the stage concept cannot be used to cover multiple family forms. It originally appeared as a notation that there was no single-parent families stage. Klein and White (1996) indicate that the criticism was appropriate when stages were given culture-specific content but does not fit with recent versions of family development theory in which stages are based on patterns of family life or possible membership structure.

A caveat may be entered against eliminating the culture-specific content approach entirely. Hill (1986) constructed life span careers by stages for several forms of single-parent families—divorced, widowed, and remarried women—offering one way of dealing with the complaint that the family life cycle approach did not include such families. The argument can be made that constructing models of tasks for families and especially marital couples can be helpful for therapeutic work, as long as the content is consistent with the norms of the culture and population with which one is working. Clinical experience indicates that such models (Nichols, 1988, 1996; Nichols & Everett, 1986) not only are useful on their own but also when employed in conjunction with such constructs as Sager's "marital contracts" ideas, which deal with individual expectations (Sager, 1976).

FAMILY DEVELOPMENT AND INDIVIDUAL LIFE SPAN DEVELOPMENT

Family development, as noted earlier, is concerned not only with families but also with individuals. One of the major challenges to professionals concerned with human development would appear to be that of bringing together a family development perspective and a life span development perspective and learning from both, as Hill and Mattesich (1979) essentially recommended two decades ago.

Life span developmental psychology emerged after family development, coming on the scene in the 1960s and 1970s (Baltes, 1979). Life span development theory was a welcome addition in that it concentrated on the individual throughout the life span, rather than focusing on childhood and assuming that behavior became fixed during one's early years. This perspective implies, of course, that behavior can be modified or remedied during one's adulthood. Erikson (1950) had said that personality could be changed later, but that it was easier for things to be done right the first time. Development is perceived as occurring throughout life as a consequence of the changing interaction of biological, physical, psychological, cultural, historical, and social influences (Gormly & Brodzinsky, 1993). Both the lifelong emphasis and the view that development and behavior must be comprehended in contextual terms render the life span development perspective significant for family development. The increasing differentiation of personality structure (e.g., alterations in mental abilities, physical skills, and social competencies) stimulate changes in family behavior and organization, just as changes in family organization and behavior influence the development of child and adult personalities (Hill & Mattessich, 1979).

The continuous interaction of the individual (and the family) and the environment, including other reciprocating systems, is part of the understanding of human behavior. The contextual emphasis of Russian psychologist Lev Vygotsky (1978) sounds remarkably close to the stance of family developmentalists and family therapists. He held that the study of human behavior cannot be conducted in a cultural vacuum because human behavior is guided by cultural norms, expectation, and values.

CHANGE PERSPECTIVES IN INDIVIDUAL DEVELOPMENT

The life span development approach involves the study of constancy and change in behavior throughout an individual's life. Two major views have prevailed among developmental psychologists with regard to individual growth. One holds that growth occurs gradually and is stable, proceeding in a continuous manner. When the behavior that began in childhood culminates in complex and mature behavior in adulthood, it does not change. The views of behaviorist B.F. Skinner, who perceived that the same mechanisms regulated development throughout the life cycle and emphasized quantitative rather than qualitative change, are an example of this perspective.

The second view perceives growth as discontinuous. It is seen as occurring in stages that are qualitatively different from one another. That is, differences between children and adults are regarded as qualitative rather than quantitative. Periods of quite limited change may be followed by times of rapid, dramatic alteration in growth in a stagelike manner. The order in which development occurs from one stage to another is viewed as the same for all persons, although the rate or speed at which they develop may vary among individuals. The views of Jean Piaget fit into this second perspective.

Development has been described in a dialectical fashion by Riegel (1975) in an analysis of adult life crises. A double interaction between individuals and sociocultural conditions produces crises or conflicts between individuals, between groups, and between groups and individuals. Individuals, according to Riegel, through their constructive development create historical changes and sociocultural conditions, in turn, change the individuals. Crises and conflicts should be regarded constructively and as the basis for development.

Like family development, life span development is marked by transitional periods, the primary task of which

> is to terminate the existing life structure and initiate a new one. This involves a reappraisal of the current structure, exploration of new possibilities for change, and a movement toward crucial choices that will provide the basis for a new life structure. (Baltes & Brim, 1979, p. 6)

Some significant life events are based to a notable degree on both personal choice and changes in the human being's body. Certain standards of physical maturity (and chronological age), as well as choice, are required in order to be married, for example.

FAMILY DEVELOPMENT AND FAMILY THERAPY

One of the earliest appearances of a family development perspective in family therapy literature occurred with the posthumous publication of an article by social worker Frances Scherz (1971). Drawing heavily on the work of Theodore Lidz (1963), particularly the notion of the interactional nature of development in which each family member's development affects others' development, Sherz's perspective was compatible with the developing family system theory. She regarded family tasks "as universal in the sense that, despite differences in social and family cultures and rapid changes in family lifestyles, every family apparently needs to live through the same tasks" (1971, p. 363).

FAMILY DEVELOPMENT CONCEPTS IN SELECTED FAMILY THERAPY ORIENTATIONS

Falicov (1988b) has presented an analysis of how certain developmental concepts are used in six major family therapy approaches—the structural, strategic (Jay Haley), brief (Mental Research Institute), systemic (Milan group), psychodynamic/intergenerational, and symbolic-experiential therapies. Each approach is described in terms of what changes during development, how it changes, the family dysfunction(s) involved, and the theory of change utilized in the therapy approach (i.e., whether change is viewed as continuous or discontinuous or both and the directionality of the change).

The views therapists hold regarding developmental change have some rather obvious implications for the therapeutic techniques and goals chosen. For example, those who think that developmental change can occur only through discontinuous change are likely to favor paradoxical techniques for use with impasses. Intergenerationally focused family therapists can be expected to explore the therapist's family of origin in order to increase a therapist's objectivity as well as for didactic purposes (Falicov, 1988b).

It should be noted that some family therapists in the approaches listed above have reservations about the value of the family life cycle in particular. Richard Fisch (1983) has indicated that the family life cycle is no longer a central concept in the thinking of the Mental Research Institute's brief therapy model, for example.

CLINICAL ADAPTATIONS OF THE FAMILY LIFE CYCLE

The family development perspective, especially the life cycle concept, soon was being adopted by family therapists (e.g., Haley, 1973; Glick & Kessler, 1974; Solomon, 1973). Subsequently, it has become a mainstay of family therapy literature (e.g., Carter & McGoldrick, 1980a, 1980b, 1988, 1999; Nichols, 1996; Nichols & Everett, 1986).

The 1970s and 1980s witnessed the emergence of a variety of modifications of the family life cycle concept for use by clinicians. Some of those, listed chronologically, follow.

Haley (1973). In describing the therapeutic work of Milton H. Erickson, Jay Haley presented a family life cycle framework. Implicit in Erickson's therapy was the view that symptoms appear when there is a disruption or dislocation in the life cycle of a family. Haley noted that while Erickson focused sharply on symptoms, his larger goal was to resolve the problems so that the family can get the life cycle moving again. The stages included the following:

The courtship period: Changing the young adult
Marriage and its consequences

Childbirth and dealing with the young
Middle marriage difficulties
Weaning parents from children
Retirement and old age (the pain of old age)

Solomon (1973). A five-stage clinically oriented framework that included developmental tasks was proposed by M.A. Solomon. Each stage posed a life crisis situation that had to be resolved if the family were to continue adaptive growth. These included:

Stage 1: The marriage. Two tasks are involved: ending the primary ties with one's parents and redirecting those family of origin energies into the marriage.

Stage 2: The birth of the first child and subsequent childbearing. Here the tasks involve consolidating the marriage and establishing parental roles.

Stage 3: Individuation of family members. Continued modification of roles and dealing with the evolving individuation of each family member across time are the tasks for this stage.

Stage 4: Departure of the children. The couple has the primary task of revamping their parental roles in order to become established as parents of adult children.

Stage 5: Integration of loss. Major tasks here involve dealing with social, physical, and economic changes that accompany old age.

Howells (1975). Seven stages or phases were delineated by Howells (1975, pp. 93–104): phase of courtship (informal partnership), phase of early marriage (legal partnership), phase of expansion, phase of consolidation, phase of contraction, phase of final partnership, and phase of disappearance. Each phase was concerned with changing structures and functions.

Barnhill and Longo (1978). Barnhill and Longo retained Duvall's stages, but split stage 5 into 5 and 6, as follows:

Stage 5: Family with early adolescent (oldest age 12 to 16, possible younger siblings)
Stage 6: Family with young adult (oldest age 16 to 20 until first child leaves home).

Their major emphasis was on the transitions from one stage to the next; they set forth nine key issues in the transitions:

Transition to Stage 1: Commitment. During the late courtship, wedding, honeymoon, and parenthood transition, the partners deal with breaking away from their respective families of origin and forming attachment to their new partner and family.

Transition to Stages 1–2: Developing new parent roles. This comes during the transition from spousal to parental roles and includes new roles with extended families.

Transition to Stages 2–3: Accepting the new personality. The family needs to accept the development of a new personality in the family and the normal dependency of the infant.

Transition to Stages 3–4: Introducing the child to institutions outside the family. The family needs to accept the child's independent relationships with and adjustment to school and other outside institutions and to deal with feedback from outside the family.

Transition to Stages 4–5: Accepting adolescence. Critical issues here include developing a sexual identity for the teenager, integrating the individual into peer group culture, and the effects on family relationships.

Transition to Stages 5–6: Experimenting with independence. The family needs to accept the oldest child's movement into late adolescence and young adulthood, gradually lessening his or her primary ties with the family of origin and permitting independent, counterdependent, and adult strivings to emerge.

Transition to Stages 6–7: Preparation to launch. Several role transitions are required—for both the parents and the child—in order for the oldest child to depart and move toward developing his or her own family of procreation.

Transitions 7–8: Letting go—facing each other again. Generally, this involves a new three-generation arrangement in which the parents are able to let go of their offspring and face each other as husband and wife alone again; for the children to leave the parents to themselves; and for new roles of grandparent (for the parent) and parent (for the children) to develop.

Transitions 8–9: Accepting retirement, old age, or both. This requires the transition of the first generation couple to a new lifestyle without occupational career concerns and the transition of the second generation couple to concerns for the care of the older couple as well as for their own children.

Carter and McGoldrick (1980a, 1980b, 1988, 1999). The six-stage family life cycle proposed by Carter and McGoldrick (McGoldrick, 1980) stresses the centrality of transitions and the disturbance of the family system as members enter and leave the family. They perceive that life cycle transitions require second-order change (i.e., change of the system itself) in order for the family to proceed developmentally (Carter & McGoldrick, 1988). Their schema differs from most others in that coverage of the stages starts with strong emphasis on young adults who are between families, whereas marriage rather than the immediate postlaunching period has tended to be taken as the starting point for family life cycle description. Stages include leaving home (single young adults), joining of families through marriage (the new couple), families with young children, families with adolescents, launching children and moving on, and families in later life. Major variations in the family life cycle are covered in divorce, postdivorce, and remarried family frameworks.

The latest version of the Carter and McGoldrick work (1999) expands their approach to the family life cycle to emphasize more strongly than ever the combination of individual, family, and social perspectives. Multiculturalism and multicontextualism (the individual, immediate household, extended family, community and social connections, and larger society) are described and the use of these constructs illustrated for clinical work in intensely practical ways.

Nichols and Everett (1986; Nichols, 1996). For use with intact families, Nichols and Everett proposed a four-stage developmental-clinical framework. The broad categories are formation (mating and marriage), expansion (parental beginnings and subsequent years), contraction (individuation and eventual separation of youth), and postparental. Departing from one's family of origin is regarded as less a stage in its own right than as a process in which altering relationships within the family typically begins with the increasing differentiation of self in late adolescence and is further advanced by entering into a marital relationship. Where there is marital breakup and family reorganization, a fifth stage is proposed with divorce, single-parent living, and remarried families as the foci. Another explicit emphasis in this approach is the argument that particular attention needs to be paid to effective completion of developmental tasks and expectations within stages, as well as to dealing successfully with tasks associated with transitions from one stage to another.

FAMILY TRANSITIONS

The notion of transitions between stages has been particularly attractive to family therapists as a guide to occasions for potential conflict and as an index to the need for professional intervention. Aldous has succinctly stated the issues:

> Family career, with its temporal perspective, looks at conflicts that occur at expectable periods. Transitions between qualitatively different stages in family lives are likely to create stress and produce conflicts. Demands of family members for change or pressure from external events at these times cause disruptions of family routines. (1996, pp. 18–19)

These occasions for stress and conflict change throughout the family career.

The stage formulation described by Rodgers and White (1993) has been used by family therapists during genogram analysis, according to Russell (1993). She also notes that replacing the developmental task conception with the more probabilistic approach of Rodgers and White permits a realistic anticipation and acceptance of unpredictability in family life and provides assistance in problem solving (Klein & White, 1996).

Family therapists often distinguish between stages and transitions and assume that the changes that occur within stages are first order in nature and that change during transitions between stages is second order change (Falicov, 1988b). Exceptions include Carter and McGoldrick (1980), who write about transitions within stages and Breunlin (1988; Breunlin, Schwartz, & Kune-Karrer, 1992), who favors the concept of microtransitions and gradual change and movement instead of stages and transitions.

Carter and McGoldrick. Carter and McGoldrick (1980b) early recognized the stages and transitions of alternative or nontraditional family forms (the divorce family, postdivorce family, and remarried family), providing a description of the developmental issues and of the prerequisite attitude for dealing with the steps and transitions. For all families, they explicitly went beyond Haley's (1973) approach, which emphasized current life cycle stress. They divided anxiety in the family system into horizontal stressors, which were characterized as Developmental (life cycle transitions), and External (chronic illness, death, and others), and vertical stressors (family issues, myths, patterns), as these have been transmitted through the generations. With the vertical stressors, they thus added an emphasis on anxiety and stress handed down across the generations.

The family life cycle and oscillation theory: Douglas Breunlin. Breunlin (1988; Breunlin, Schwartz, & Kune-Karrer, 1992) offers a new framework with which to pull together information on development. Criticizing family therapists' narrow focus on the family life cycle, they provide a developmental metaframework and emphasize that individual development and the context as well as the family itself must be considered in the life cycle. They refer to increments in individual development that secure significant and related changes in the family as *microtransitions*. This approach holds that families negotiate microtransitions through oscillation. Briefly, new sequences of behavior and old sequences exist together for a period of time, and there is oscillation or a movement back and forth between the old and the new. Thus, distinctions between a stage and a transition lose their meaning and only transitions exist.

Breunlin and associates (1992) summarize the clinical implications of the development metaframework they propose under four headings: Level (Family, Individual, Biological, and Relational), Developmental Issue, Constraint, and Clinical Implication. They note that, although the levels are listed separately, a recursive relationship exists among them and caution that therapists should avoid focusing on a single developmental constraint. Also, they summarize developmental problems faced by a family under the two headings of Developmental Problem and Assessment. Under the rubric of Developmental Problem, they list Family Life Cycle Nodal Transitions (e.g., transition to adolescence; transition to old age); Individual Developmental Microtransitions (e.g., daughter oscillating, mother oscillating, father oscillating), Biological Development, and Relational Development.

The major contributions of the Breunlin group's approach may be its emphasis on paying attention to individual development and the context in which the family and individual are functioning and its attention to the gradual and recursive nature of transitions.

Family life cycle as spiral: Lee Combrinck-Graham. Examining the family life cycle as the context of individual development, Combrinck-Graham (1985, 1988) points out that the life of the family is not linear. Rather, she says that it does not begin at any particular point or end with an event such as the departure of children or with a death, but is better described as a spiral because things do not repeat themselves exactly. By looking at the relationships between individual life issues of different generations, it is possible to construct a relational picture of the family life spiral. When diagrammed, the family life spiral will be distorted because, says Combrinck-Graham, at some stages the family is held closely together and the major forces in the family are centripetal. At others, the members are more differentiated and oriented outside the family and the forces are thus centrifugal. The person whose life covers three generations will have three periods of centripetal family life and three periods of centrifugal family life.

A careful examination of the more recent family therapy adaptations of family development perspectives would seem to indicate that more attention is being given to the notion of transitions and that they may be either continuous or discontinuous, to the idea that understanding life cycle tasks can be useful in both reparative and preventive work with families, and that individual life cycles and development and the cultural contexts in which families function and change deserve more attention than they have received in the past.

CONCLUSION

Family development perspectives have been exceedingly important in the development and practice of family therapy. The value can be increased in the future, particularly if family therapists strive to integrate family development research and theory with individual development conceptualizations and cultural-contextual research findings. Rather than seizing on conceptualizations from decades past, such as the idea that stages in the family life cycle are totally predictable and rigid and that family problems stem primarily or totally from transitions between stages, for example, it is critical to the development of family therapy to continue to struggle to understand more completely the nature of family change that therapists can observe as they work with individuals, couples, and families. An essential part of this endeavor is maintaining contact with the research and theory development of family specialists who focus on increasing the understanding of family development. Provocative findings and speculations continue to come forth; the spring did not run dry in the 1960s, nor did the ideas adopted by family therapists in the 1970s mark the totality of what can be learned from family sociologists and psychologists concerned with individual development, as well as from their own clinical observations and research.

REFERENCES

Aldous, J. (1978). *Family careers: Developmental changes in family.* New York: John Wiley & Sons, Inc.

Aldous, J. (1990). Family development and the life course: Two perspectives on family change. *Journal of Marriage and the Family, 52,* 571–583.

Aldous, J. (1996). *Family careers: Rethinking the developmental perspective.* Thousand Oaks, CA: Sage Publications.

Baltes, P. B. (1979). Life-span developmental psychology: Some converging observations on history and theory. In P. B. Baltes & O. G. Brim (Eds.), *Life-span development and behavior (Vol. 2)* (pp. 255–279). New York: Academic Press.

Baltes, P. B., & Brim, O. G. (Eds.). (1979). *Life-span development and behavior (Vol. 2).* New York: Academic Press.

Barnhill, L., & Longo, D. (1978). Fixation and regression in the family life cycle. *Family Process, 17,* 469–478.

Breunlin, D. C. (1988). Oscillation theory and family development. In C. J. Falicov (Ed.), *Family transitions: Continuity and change over the life cycle* (pp. 133–155). New York: Guilford Press.

Breunlin, D. C., Schwartz, R. C., & Kune-Karrer, B. M. (Eds.). (1992). *Metaframeworks: Transcending the models of family therapy.* San Francisco: Jossey-Bass.

Burgess, E. W. (1926). The family as a unity of interacting personalities. *The Family, 7,* 3–9.

Carter, B., & McGoldrick, M. (Eds.). (1988). *The changing family life cycle: A framework for family therapy* (2nd ed.). New York: Gardner Press.

Carter, B., & McGoldrick, M. (Eds.). (1999). *The expanded family life cycle: A framework for family therapy* (3rd ed.). Boston: Allyn & Bacon.

Carter, E. A., & McGoldrick, M. (Eds.). (1980a). *The family life cycle: A framework for family therapy.* New York: Gardner Press.

Carter, E. A., & McGoldrick, M. (1980b). The family life cycle and family therapy: An overview. In E. A. Carter & M. McGoldrick (Eds.), *The family life cycle: A framework for family therapy* (pp. 3–20). New York: Gardner Press.

Christensen, H. T. (1964). Development of the family field of study. In H. T. Christensen (Ed.), *Handbook of marriage and the family* (pp. 3–32). Chicago: Rand McNally.

Combrinck-Graham, L. (1985). A model for family development. *Family Process, 24,* 139–150.

Combrinck-Graham, L. (1988). Adolescent sexuality in the family life spiral. In C. J. Falicov (Ed.), *Family transitions: Continuity and change over the life cycle* (pp. 107–131) New York: Guilford Press.

Duvall, E. M. (1957). *Family development.* Philadelphia: J. B. Lippincott.

Duvall, E. M. (1971). *Family development* (4th ed.). Philadelphia: J.B. Lippincott.

Duvall, E. M., & Hill, R. (1948). *Report of the committee on dynamics of family interaction.* Washington, DC: National Conference on Family Life.

Erikson, E. H. (1950). *Childhood and society.* New York: Norton.

Falicov, C. J. (1988b). Family sociology and family therapy contributions to the family development framework: A comparative analysis and thoughts on future trends. In C. J. Falicov (Ed.), *Family transitions: Continuity and change over the life cycle cycle* (pp. 3–51). New York: Guilford Press.

Farber, B. (1956). *A model for the study of the family as mutually contingent careers.* Unpublished Manuscript, University of Illinois, Urbana.

Farber, B. (1959). Effects of a severely mentally retarded child on family integration. *Monographs of the Society for Research in Child Development, 24.*

Farber, B. (1961). The family as a set of mutually contingent careers. In N. Foote (Ed.), *Consumer behavior: Models of household decision-making* (pp. 276–297). New York: New York University Press.

Fisch, R., Weakland, J. H., & Segal, L. (1983). *The tactics of change.* San Francisco, CA: Jossey-Bass.

Glick, I. D., & Kessler, D. R. (1974). *Marriage and family therapy.* New York: Grune & Stratton.

Glick, P. C. (1947). The family cycle. *American Sociological Review, 14,* 164–174.

Glick, P. C. (1955). The life cycle of the family. *Marriage and Family Living, 17,* 3–9.

Glick, P. C. (1957). *American families.* New York: Wiley.

Gormly, A. V., & Brodzinsky, D. M. (1993). *Lifespan human development* (5th ed.). Fort Worth, TX: Harcourt Brace College Publishers.

Haley, J. (1973). *Uncommon therapy: The psychiatric techniques of Milton H. Erickson, M.D.* New York: Norton.

Havighurst, R. J. (1953). *Human development and education.* New York: Longsman Green.

Hill, R. (1949). *Families under stress: Adjustment to the crisis of war, separation and reunion.* New York: Harper & Row.

Hill, R. (1958). Generic features of families under stress. *Social Casework, 49,* 139–150.

Hill, R. (1971). Modern systems theory and the family: A confrontation. *Social Science Information, 10,* 7–26.

Hill, R. (1986). Life cycle stages for types of single parent families: Of family development theory. *Family Relations, 35,* 19–29.

Hill, R., & Hansen, D. A. (1960). The identification of conceptual frameworks utilized in family study. *Marriage and Family Living, 22,* 299–311.

Hill, R., & Mattessich, P. (1979). Family development theory and life-span development. In P. B. Baltes & O. G. Baltes (Eds.), *Life-span development and behavior (Vol. 2)* (pp. 161–204). New York: Academic Press.

Hill, R., & Rodgers, R. H. (1964). The developmental approach. In H. T. Christensen (Ed.), *Handbook of marriage and the family* (pp. 171–211). Chicago: Rand-McNally.

Howells, J. G. (1975). *Principles of family psychiatry.* New York: Brunner/Mazel.

Klein, D. M. (1994, November). *Theory as data: An investigation of ourselves.* Paper presented at the National Council on Family Relations, Theory Construction and Research Methodology Workshop, Minneapolis, MN.

Klein, D. M., & White, J. M. (1996). *Family theories: An introduction.* Thousand Oaks, CA: Sage Publications.

Lidz, T. (1963). *The family and human adaptation.* New York: International Universities Press.

Magrabi, F. M., & Marshall, W. H. (1965). Family developmental tasks: A research model. *Journal of Marriage and the Family, 27,* 454–461.

Mattessich, P., & Hill, R. (1987). Life cycle and family development. In M. B. Sussman & S. Steinmetz (Eds.), *Handbook of marriage and the family* (pp. 437–469). New York: Plenum Press.

McCubbin, H., Joy, C., Cauble, B., Comeau, J., Patterson, J., & Needle, R. (1980). Stress and coping; A decade review. *Journal of Marriage and the Family, 42,* 855–871.

McGoldrick, M. (1980). The joining of family through marriage: The new couple. In E. A. Carter & M. McGoldrick (Eds.), *The family life cycle: A framework for family therapy* (pp. 93–119). New York: Gardner Press.

Nichols, W. C. (1988). *Marital therapy: An integrative approach.* New York: Guilford Press.

Nichols, W. C. (1996). *Treating people in families: An integrative framework.* New York: Guilford Press.

Nichols, W. C., & Everett, C. A. (1986). *Systemic family therapy: An integrative approach.* New York: Guilford Press.

Piaget, J. (1952). *The origins of intelligence in children.* New York: International Universities Press.

Piaget, J. (1971). *Biology and knowledge: An essay on the relations between organic regulations and cognitive processes.* Chicago: University of Chicago Press.

Rapoport, R. (1963). Normal crises, family structure and mental health. *Family Process, 2,* 68–80.

Riegel, K. F. (1975). Adult life crises: A dialectical interpretation of development. In N. Datan & L. Ginsberg (Eds.), *Life span developmental psychology* (pp. 99–127). New York: Academic Press.

Rodgers, R. H. (1962). *Improvements in the construction and analysis of family life cycle categories.* Unpublished doctoral dissertation, University of Minnesota, Minneapolis, MN.

Rodgers, R. H. (1973). *Family interaction and transaction: A transactional approach.* Englewood Cliffs, NJ: Prentice-Hall.

Rodgers, R. H., & White, J. M. (1993). Family development theory. In P. Boss, W. Doherty, R.W. Schumm, & S. Steinmetz (Eds.), *Sourcebook of family theories and methods: A conceptual approach* (pp. 225–254). New York: Plenum.

Rowntree, B. S. (1906). *Poverty: A study of town life.* London: Macmillan.

Russell, C. (1993). Family development theory as revised by Rodgers and White: Implications for practice. In P. Boss, W. Doherty, R.W. Schumm, & S. Steinmetz (Eds.), *Sourcebook of family theories and methods: A conceptual approach* (pp. 385–411). New York: Plenum.

Sager, C. J. (1976). *Marriage contracts and couples therapy.* New York: Brunner/Mazel.

Scherz, F. H. (1971). Maturational crises and parent-child interaction. *Social Casework, 52,* 362–369.

Solomon, M. A. (1973). A developmental, conceptual framework for family therapy. *Family Process, 12,* 179–188.

Steinglass, P. (1978). The conceptualization of marriage from a systems theory perspective. In T. J. Paolino & B. S. McCrady (Eds.), *Marriage and marital therapy: Psychoanalytic, behavioral and systems perspectives* (pp. 298–394). New York: Brunner/Mazel.

Vygotsky, L. V. (1978). *Mind in society: The development of higher psychological processes.* Cambridge: Harvard University Press.

White, J. M. (1991). *Dynamics of family development: A theoretical perspective.* New York: Guilford Press.

CHAPTER 2

Evolutionary Psychology

W. Todd DeKay

E VOLUTIONARY PSYCHOLOGY has emerged over the last decade as an important theoretical perspective within many branches of psychology, including cognition (Cosmides, 1989; Cummins, 1998; Silverman & Phillips, 1998), perception (Shepard,
1992), psycholinguistics (Pinker & Bloom, 1990), social psychology (Buss, 1990; Nisbett,
1990; Simpson & Kenrick, 1997), developmental psychology (Belsky, Steinberg, &
Draper, 1991; McDonald, 1992), psychopathology (Mealy, 1995; Nesse & Williams, 1994;
Wakefield, 1992), and personality psychology (Buss, 1991; Gangestad & Simpson, 1990).
Its promise lies not in entirely supplanting other psychological perspectives or research
programs but rather in adding additional layers of analysis and understanding to human
psychological phenomena and in providing a framework for integrating findings across
subdisciplines in psychology and across the social and life sciences.

Evolutionary psychology starts by posing three fundamental questions that have been
relatively neglected over the past century within the social sciences: (1) What are the origins of human psychological mechanisms? (2) What adaptive problems are selected for
their existence? (3) What functions were they designed to serve? Answers to these basic
questions can help psychologists to organize extant observations, place them within an
integrated theoretical framework that is unified with the other life sciences (Tooby & Cosmides, 1992), and help generate new theories about specific psychological domains.

Although an adaptationist approach, using modern evolutionary theory, has contributed substantially to many disciplines within psychology and the other social and life
sciences, applications to psychopathology, dysfunction, and psychotherapeutic
processes are relatively uncommon and underdeveloped (but see Glantz & Pearce,
1989). In that sense, this chapter can only attempt to anticipate the potential practical
applications that current theory and research might offer to the clinical, counseling, and
therapy communities. However, a developed understanding of the evolved psychological

The author thanks Martie Haselton for helpful comments on an earlier version of this chapter.

mechanisms underlying mating, parenting, and kinship, as well as how these mechanisms might be involved in various forms of dysfunction, can only strengthen therapeutic interventions.

Evolutionary psychology is a relatively young endeavor, although it has firm historical roots. The basic principles of the approach and the major research findings yielded to date have been reviewed extensively elsewhere (see Buss, 1995, 1999; Cosmides & Tooby, 1989; DeKay & Buss, 1992; Tooby & Cosmides, 1989, 1992; Wright, 1994), as have the historical foundations upon which evolutionary psychology rests (see Buss, 1999; Cronin, 1991; Wright, 1994). My goals here are more modest. They are to (1) provide a brief sketch of the historical and conceptual roots of modern evolutionary psychology, (2) provide an introduction to the fundamental principles and conceptual tools of modern evolutionary psychology, and (3) acquaint the reader with key theories, derived from general evolutionary theory, that relate in important ways to family dynamics and processes.

HISTORICAL ROOTS OF EVOLUTIONARY PSYCHOLOGY

DARWIN, EVOLUTIONARY THEORY, AND THE "MODERN SYNTHESIS"

Long before Charles Darwin sailed on the *Beagle* or wrote a word of text, there were "evolutionists" among the ranks of natural historians (including Darwin's grandfather). Evolution, defined simply as change over time, had been observed in the organic world for some time before Darwin. In addition, pre-Darwinian evolutionists frequently observed that species' characteristics often seemed to have specific purposes, or functions, and were characterized by a nonarbitrary correspondence with features of the environment. They solved a particular problem for the organism possessing them. Explanations for these observations included divine intervention, or creationism; catastrophism, or the idea that geological or meteorological events result in the sudden extinction of some species and the emergence of others to replace them; and the inheritance of acquired characteristics, proposing that organisms pass characteristics to offspring after developing them ontogenetically. However, none of these could adequately account for the entire range of observations while providing a scientifically useful framework for studying organic design (see Cronin, 1991, for a detailed historical review).

Darwin's contribution was to provide an elegant, parsimonious theory of species change that could account for the prevailing characteristics of organisms and provide a plausible, mechanistic account of how these characteristics come about and come to be apparently purposeful (Darwin, 1859). Darwin's theory was simple in its essence (see Figure 2.1). He proposed that, given limited carrying capacity (natural resources for sustaining life), there will result a natural competition for scarce resources. Organisms with characteristics that enhance their ability to compete in this struggle will reproduce at a higher rate than will those with characteristics that hinder their ability to compete, relative to other organisms. This process is iterated across generations, resulting in the accumulation of the most successful designs over time. These successful designs ultimately come to characterize the entire population. Speciation occurs when populations become reproductively isolated in some way (e.g., due to shifts in the geographical landscape) and the characteristics of the two population, now subjected to separate selection pressures, diverge. Darwin's theory involves three key components. First, *variation* must exist within a given population in the features, or characteristics, of individuals within that

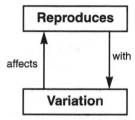

FIGURE 2.1   A simplified representation of the iterative process of selection proposed by Darwin. Any entity that (1) reproduces itself, with (2) a degree of variation, and where (3) the variations have potential effects on subsequent reproduction can be subject to evolution by selection. Organic evolution is perhaps just one example of the process (others have applied it to cultural evolution, Boyd & Richardson, 1985; Lumsden & Wilson, 1981; Dawkins, 1989).

population. Second, the existing variations must be, to some extent, *inherited,* or passed from parents to offspring. Finally, there must be some mechanism of *selection* among the existing variations. According to Darwin, there are two primary mechanisms of selection—natural selection and sexual selection.

Natural Selection

Many of the obstacles an organism encounters represent survival problems. An individual organism must live to reproductive age, and success relative to other individuals is partly a function of the length of its breeding life. Characteristics that aid in survival or in longevity can result in increased reproduction relative to alternatives. If the survival advantage persists across generations, the successful design will accumulate in the population, relative to alternatives, and will eventually come to characterize that population. This mechanism involves the selection of a design due to its effects on the survival, and hence reproduction, of the individual.

Sexual Selection

Ultimately, even survival problems are only problems in an evolutionary sense when they have an impact on the relative reproductive success of an organism. Darwin (1871) also argued that selection could operate through a slightly different mechanism—sexual selection. In sexual selection, one design is selected over alternatives because of the reproductive advantages accrued to the individual possessing it. This reproductive advantage occurs when a design results in some mating advantage, or when it leads to its bearer being preferentially selected as a mate by members of the opposite sex. Darwin argued that male peacocks' feathers and other species characteristics that appear costly to survival could evolve simply because of intersexual mating preferences.

Natural selection and sexual selection are really part of the same general mechanism. Designs succeed based on their effects on their own reproduction, relative to alternatives. Still, it is heuristically useful to distinguish those characteristics that were sexually selected and those that were naturally selected. The two mechanisms address two relatively distinct classes of adaptive problems. Natural selection results in adaptations that aid in survival (and, hence, reproduction) and that correspond to features of the physical environment. Sexual selection results in adaptations that solve reproductive, or mating, problems and that often seem counterproductive to the organisms' survival.

The Modern Synthesis

Although inheritance is an essential component of his theory, Darwin knew little about the actual mechanism by which characteristics are passed from generation to generation. We now know that the inheritance component of Darwin's theory is met by the operation of genes, or units of DNA. Genes provide a means for passing characteristics from parents to offspring in a way that tends to maintain the general integrity of the design. Changes in the structure of genes are relatively slow, allowing successful designs to be passed across generations with relatively few changes. In addition, genes provide for the variation component of Darwin's theory. Mutations, or random changes in the molecular structure of DNA, introduce random variations into the design of organisms. These random changes then become subject to the mechanisms of selection.

PREVIOUS APPLICATIONS TO SOCIAL BEHAVIOR

Ethology

A movement within biology emerged in the mid-1900s that emphasized the study of animals and animal populations within their natural habitat. This movement, called *ethology,* focused to a large extent on the social interactions of animals and on the functional properties of these interaction patterns (Alcock, 1989; Tinbergen, 1951). Ethology was guided by the premise that the behavior of organisms, like the bodies of organisms, is the product of a history of selection. As a result, animal behavior, if viewed within the appropriate natural context, should evidence functional properties. Behavior patterns emerge through selection because of their effects on the relative reproductive success of the animal exhibiting them. While ethology focused heavily on nonhuman species, ethological principles and methods have also been applied to humans, especially in the study of infant behavior systems (Ainsworth, 1973).

Sociobiology

In 1975, E.O. Wilson published a remarkable and equally controversial treatise on the functional properties of social behavior in animals, including humans. Wilson was taking ethology to the next logical application by adding a forceful theoretical framework to the sophisticated observational methods of ethology. Wilson argued that evolutionary theory would ultimately provide the means for a grand synthesis of the various life sciences (including human psychology) into one unified theory, called *sociobiology* (Wilson, 1975). Although Wilson included very little discussion of humans, the message was clear: Human behavior, like the behaviors of other animals, could only be fully understood from an evolutionary perspective.

Both ethology and sociobiology, however, proved limited in their usefulness to psychologists because of their emphasis on behavior and de-emphasis on the psychological structures that produce that behavior. The focus was on the current *adaptiveness* of the behaviors of individual animals and not on cognitive or neurological processes. As a result, they focused on a class of *outputs* of adaptations (behavior) rather than on the true functional design (psychological adaptations) of organisms.

MODERN EVOLUTIONARY PSYCHOLOGY

Evolutionary psychology is based on many of the same principles as ethology and sociobiology, but focuses on the psychological features of organisms, rather than on behavioral patterns per se. Evolutionary psychology rests on a few key concepts, including adaptation and adaptationism, the environment of evolutionary adaptedness, and psychological mechanism.

KEY CONCEPTS IN EVOLUTIONARY PSYCHOLOGY

The Three Products of Evolution

The central concept in evolutionary psychology is the concept of adaptation. Adaptations are not the only product of evolution, however. Evolution by selection generally produces three products—adaptations, incidental by-products of adaptations, and random effects (Buss, Haselton, Shackelford, Bleske, & Wakefield, 1998; see Table 2.1).

First, adaptations are reliably developing structures that exist in their current form because they helped solve a problem associated with reproduction (including survival problems) during the period of their evolution (Buss, 1990; Buss et al., 1998; Cosmides & Tooby, 1992). Adaptations are identified by evidence of special design for the solution of a reproductive problem, and by the reliability, efficiency, and economy of that design (Williams, 1966). For example, the mammalian umbilical cord is clearly an adaptation. It shows evidence of special design for the intrauterine provisioning of a fetus. In addition, the components of the umbilical cord, including its macrostructure and chemical properties, make it clearly suited to its proposed function.

The same standards that are applied to physiological characteristics in determining that they are adaptations must also be applied to proposed psychological adaptations. For example, sexual jealousy shows clear functional design (Daly, Wilson, & Weghorst, 1982), and the specific features of jealousy, including the typical activating contexts (Buss, Larsen, Westen, & Semmelroth, 1992), and the typical behavioral and affective outputs (Buss, 1988), show evidence of special design for solving an adaptive problem associated with preventing cuckoldry.

TABLE 2.1   Products of Evolution by Selection

	Candidate Examples	
Products of Evolution	*Physiological*	*Psychological*
Adaptations		
Inherited and reliably developing characteristics that came into existence through natural selection because they helped to solve problems of survival or reproduction during the period of their evolution.	Umbilical cord Hemoglobin Female mammary system	Parental love Jealousy Mate preferences
By-products		
Characteristics that do not solve adaptive problems and do not have functional design; they are "carried along" with characteristics that do have functional design because they happen to be coupled with those adaptations.	Belly button "Redness" of blood Male nipples	?
Random effects		
Characteristics produced by random forces such as mutations, sudden and unprecedented changes in the environment, or chance effects during development.	Shape of belly button Hemophilia Shape of nipples	?

Note: Partially adapted from Buss (1999). These examples are tentative and are dependent on future research addressing functional questions. To date, little is known about the psychological characteristics that are by-products or random effects because the analysis of psychological, as opposed to physiological, characteristics using this scheme is relatively new.

Second, evolution by selection produces by-products, or characteristics that do not have a proper function (they did not help solve an adaptive problem), but are carried through selection because they are linked in some way to adaptations. By-products are often characteristics of adaptations that have no functional properties themselves, but are present because of the functional properties of the adaptation. For example, bones certainly show evidence of special design, but the "whiteness" of bones, a product of the chemical components of bones, is a by-product. The whiteness of bones, per se, is irrelevant to their function.

By-products can also result when adaptations in one sex are carried over in some form (often inert) in the opposite sex. This can happen because of developmental necessity. For example, mammalian females (including humans) have functional mammary systems that show clear evidence of functional design for provisioning offspring. Mammalian males also have nipples, but these male nipples are seemingly functionless and are carried through selection because of the specifics of the developmental process of sex differentiation.

Third, the evolutionary process also produces random effects. Random mutations can cause idiosyncratic variations in the design of an organism. Most mutations are deleterious and are subject to strong selection that eliminates them from the population. Rarely, random mutations are beneficial to the organism and, if the benefits persist across generations, can proliferate throughout a population through selection. Some random mutations are effectively neutral. They do not appreciably help or hurt the organism and are not subject to elimination or proliferation through selection. These neutral effects can produce functionally neutral variations on the general design of organisms.

Adaptationism

Evolutionary psychologists typically assume by default that a given complex psychological feature is an adaptation, and proceed to formulate hypotheses about the design and function of that feature. This default assumption, or adaptationism, is appropriate for two reasons. The first reason is that evolution by selection is the only known natural process capable of producing complex, functionally organized, organic design. Simply stated, complex, organized features of the human mind, like those of the human body, are likely to be adaptations. Evolution by selection also produces functionless by-products of adaptations and random effects; however, adaptations are the only complex evolutionary product, and adaptations are the only product to evidence special design (see Buss et al., 1998; Williams, 1966). In addition, by-products and random effects are not immune to the selective process. Most by-products of adaptations, and most random effects due to mutations or developmental perturbations, will have nonneutral effects on organisms, and the process of selection will act upon variations in these by-products and random effects. Genes that reduce the harmful effects or build on potentially useful effects of the by-product will increase in frequency in subsequent generations. Thus, even by-products may eventually come to be functionally designed features of organisms (Buss et al., 1998; Gould, 1991).

The second reason that adaptationism is appropriate as a default position is a pragmatic one. The assumption that a given feature is an adaptation leads to useful and usually testable hypotheses about that feature. If a psychological feature is an adaptation, it will have properties that correspond in a nonarbitrary way to features of the environment. In addition, it will respond in predictable ways within appropriate contexts and will produce behavior, affect, or other psychological output that helped solve an adaptive problem over the course of human evolutionary history. Hypotheses about these properties, if well formulated, are usually testable and falsifiable. The alternative assumptions, that a feature is a by-product of an adaptation or is a random effect, lead to no hypotheses about the feature's structure or functional properties. These alternative assumptions are scientific dead ends and so they should be scientific alternatives of last resort. Of course, many features of human psychology will prove to be by-products of adaptations, random effects, or both. As a scientific matter, however, our understanding of human psychological mechanisms is more likely to accelerate by first applying adaptationist assumptions than by assuming the alternatives (for a contrary perspective, see Gould, 1991; Gould & Lewontin, 1979).

Evolved Psychological Mechanisms

Since the cognitive revolution, psychologists have become increasingly aware of the need to understand the internal cognitive and affective mechanisms that lead to behavior. Most psychologists have rejected behaviorism, but many have retained the behavioristic assumptions that the human mind begins as a relatively content-free, equipotential learning machine. Evolutionary psychology, by contrast, argues that evolved psychological mechanisms cannot be solely general-purpose, are likely to be saturated with content, and operate differently in response to external input about different adaptive problems. Just as the body is characterized by relatively specific mechanisms designed to solve particular problems (the heart, lung, and larynx), the mind is also likely composed of relatively specific psychological mechanisms, each designed to solve a particular adaptive problem.

Often, psychologists do not realize that all behaviors depend on psychological mechanisms plus input into those mechanisms. Environmental inputs alone cannot produce behavior in the absence of psychological processes designed to process the input. Even the most "simple" learning processes require complex psychological adaptations (Gallistel, 1990). These psychological adaptations represent the designs that are subject to selection and are, therefore, the appropriate focus of an evolutionary analysis of behavioral systems.

The Environment of Evolutionary Adaptedness

Every adaptation has its own period of evolution, called its *environment of evolutionary adaptedness* (EEA; Bowlby, 1969). The EEA is not really a particular historical time or place; it corresponds to the statistical regularities in the world that existed during the process of selection that led to a species typical characteristic (Tooby & Cosmides, 1992). Different adaptations have different EEAs because each adaptation resulted from unique selection pressures within a unique time frame. The EEA of a particular adaptation is a crucial element of an evolutionary psychological explanation because it helps to specify the conditions under which the adaptation was designed to operate. Under different conditions, the adaptation might lead to maladaptive outcomes, or might not function at all, absent relevant activating conditions. The functional design of an adaptation can only be understood in conjunction with the EEA of the adaptation. Adaptations solve problems of survival and reproduction within an ecological context. If you change the context, you often change the effects of an adaptation.

AN EVOLUTIONARY PSYCHOLOGICAL PERSPECTIVE ON MAJOR DOMAINS OF INQUIRY

Human Nature

According to evolutionary psychology, human nature is composed of many domain-specific, species-typical psychological mechanisms (Buss, 1991, 1995; Tooby & Cosmides,

1992). Psychological mechanisms are information processing devices designed to take in certain classes of information, operate on that information with a set of cognitive procedures or decision rules, and produce output in the form of behavior, physiological activity, affective responses, or information that serves as input to other psychological mechanisms (Buss, 1991, 1995; Tooby & Cosmides, 1992). Psychological mechanisms have design features that, during the appropriate EEA, helped solve a specific adaptive problem associated with reproduction. An evolved propensity to fear snakes, for example, has design features (e.g., sensitivity to stimuli that resemble snakes, activation of a "flight" response) that solved an adaptive problem of survival (and hence reproduction) over the course of human evolutionary history. An evolved preference for fertile mates, as another example, has design features (e.g., sensitivity to cues to health, sexual arousal upon detection of such cues) that solved an adaptive problem of reproduction over the course of human evolutionary history.

Just as the mechanisms of the body form an integrated system, evolved psychological mechanisms are linked with one another in various ways. The heart and lungs are separate, functional organs, and they are linked via the circulatory system. The mechanisms of the mind can also be studied separately, even though they are part of a larger integrated system. Analyses of each mechanism, along with studies of their integration, are central to an evolutionary psychological analysis of human nature.

Sex Differences

Evolutionary psychology offers a framework for predicting and understanding when we should and should not expect sex differences. Men and women are expected to differ only within domains where they have faced different adaptive problems over the course of human evolutionary history. Where the sexes have faced the same adaptive problems, we should see general similarity between men and women.

Most adaptive problems were not likely sex-differentiated problems. Ancestral men and women both faced the problem of maintaining body temperature, finding a suitable habitat, and preventing their mates from defecting from their relationship. We should, therefore, expect that the mechanisms that help solve these adaptive problems, such as shivering mechanisms, landscape preferences (Orians & Heerwagen, 1992), and jealousy (DeKay & Buss, 1992), are present in both men and women.

In those domains where men and women faced different adaptive problems we should expect corresponding sex differences. For example, sex differences in reproductive physiology create sex-linked adaptive problems. Fertilization and gestation are internal to women but not to men. Given that both sexes provide investment in children, this reproductive asymmetry creates an adaptive problem for men, called *paternity certainty*. For a man, there was always some risk of investing in another man's child due to the chance of cuckoldry. Investment in another man's child is an evolutionary dead end, and selection will favor adaptations in men that act to effectively reduce the chances of cuckoldry. Sexual jealousy (Buss et al., 1992) and tactics of mate guarding (Buss, 1988) are possible psychological adaptations in men designed to help solve this problem.

Individual Differences

Evolutionary psychology approaches individual differences within sex in a number of ways (Buss, 1991; Buss & Greiling, 1999). First, developmental contexts can shunt individuals into one of a set number of developmental trajectories. Such an approach views development as the activation of one developmental sequence from a limited "menu" of possibilities. This activation occurs because of some early ontogenetic environmental trigger, or cue, that provides information relevant to anticipating the future environment.

For example, Belsky, Steinberg, and Draper (1991) argue that the absence of an investing father during childhood shunts individuals (especially girls) into a relatively unrestricted and promiscuous mating strategy and the presence of an investing father shunts individuals into a relatively restricted and monogamous mating strategy. The cue (father presence vs. father absence) acts as a developmental trigger because it is correlated with the child's future mating environment. In father absent situations, the child is more likely to encounter a mating system characterized by unstable relationships and opportunistic mating. In father present situations, the child is likely to encounter a mating context characterized by stable relationships and monogamous mating. Belsky and associates (1991) argue that selection has fashioned this facultative developmental process because ancestral mating systems varied and individuals who had the ability to develop an appropriate mating strategy given the local context had a reproductive advantage over others.

Second, individual differences can result from different individuals inhabiting different environments. These different environments result in different inputs to species-typical adaptations and, hence, lead to different behavioral outcomes. For example, people married to highly desirable partners might be relatively prone to jealousy because they continually encounter jealousy-activating contexts such as others talking with, touching, or making eye contact with their mates.

Third, psychological individual differences can be "reactive" to physiological differences (Tooby & Cosmides, 1990). Individuals who are mesomorphic (muscular) are able to carry out a relatively aggressive social strategy whereas individuals who are ectomorphic (thin) might be forced to adopt a more diplomatic social strategy. These behavioral strategies are a product of psychological adaptations that take physiological information as input and often appear heritable because the physiological differences to which they respond are often heritable.

Finally, individual differences can result from "frequency-dependent" selection that produces adaptive genetic differences between individuals. Frequency-dependent selection occurs when two or more variants are maintained by selection in equilibrium, or in some stable proportion. Biological sex is an obvious example. As one sex increases in frequency, selection favors the other sex because mating opportunities will be more abundant. Therefore, in sexually reproducing species, the relative proportion of the sexes in a population usually remains stable. Psychological differences might also be the product of frequency-dependent selection. Gangestad and Simpson (1990), for example, argue that female sociosexuality, or the tendency to engage in promiscuous versus monogamous mating, is bimodal and this bimodal distribution is maintained by frequency-dependent selection. Note that this frequency-dependence hypothesis is in competition with the developmental hypothesis of Belsky and colleagues (1991). Both hypotheses are derived from evolutionary consideration, but which is correct (if either) will ultimately be determined by normal empirical research.

Cultural Variability

The analysis of cultural differences occupies a central place within evolutionary psychology for four reasons. First, an examination of various cultures allows researchers to test hypotheses about features of human nature that are presumably expressed across a wide range of environments. For example, some mate preferences are assumed to be universal and cross-cultural data can help evaluate that claim (see Buss, 1989a).

Second, an examination of cultural differences allows us to test hypotheses about evolved facultative strategies that take environmental and cultural input. For example, the relative importance placed on various characteristics in a potential mate might vary in a functional way with particular ecological conditions. Gangestad and Buss (1993), for example, found that the cross-cultural variation in the importance placed on physical beauty by men and women is a function of the prevalence of pathogens. Physical beauty provides a cue to good health and in geographical regions where parasites abound, physical beauty becomes a relatively important criterion.

Third, cross-cultural comparisons can be a source of hypotheses about the types of decision rules that comprise the human cognitive arsenal. Cultural research provides a sort of "natural experiment" in which people are exposed to a range of ecological and social circumstances. The behavioral and larger cultural outcomes across this range of experiences can provide information about psychological adaptations that might be rarely activated under particular cultural conditions. For example, Smuts (1992) has examined women's strategies for resisting male aggression across cultures. Strategies that are activated in some cultural contexts (e.g., forming female coalitions) are often relatively absent in others because ecological and social circumstances vary across cultures. By looking across cultures, evolutionary psychologists can better understand the range of evolved strategies within the human psychological arsenal.

Finally, cross-cultural comparisons provide one way to examine the effects of novel environments on the behaviors produced by evolved psychological mechanisms. Humans evolved in a very different environment from the one inhabited today. This means that the human cognitive architecture is likely tuned to a very different set of ecological and social circumstances. Data from a range of current cultures allow an examination of the ways our evolved psychology is expressed in a range of conditions. For example, humans evolved under conditions where sugar, salt, and protein were rare but essential resources. As a result, humans evolved strong taste preferences designed to motivate the sustained search for these resources. These mechanisms become especially apparent when we see them operate in a modern context—one with an abundance of sugar, salt, and fat. They lead to potentially maladaptive but highly informative dietary patterns.

Pathology and Dysfunction

An evolutionary psychological analysis of the mind, including human nature, sex differences, and individual difference, has implications for understanding psychopathology and dysfunction (see Buss et al., 1997; Glanz & Pearce, 1989). From an evolutionary perspective, there are a number of possible ways that psychological adaptations can produce dysfunctional or subjectively distressful outcomes.

First, a mechanism can break down and fail to function due to physical insults, genetic defects, developmental perturbations, or other external effects. This mechanism failure is certainly possible with physiological mechanisms and is also possible with psychological mechanisms. One class of dysfunction involves this type of mechanism failure.

Another way that an evolved mechanism might produce dysfunction is if it becomes operative within a novel environment, or an evolutionarily unprecedented context. In this case, the mechanism might operate in its usual fashion but it might produce maladaptive or undesirable outcomes. For example, strong taste preferences for sugar, salt, and fat are adaptations to an environment characterized by a scarcity of these important resources. Given the unprecedented availability of these substances in the modern environment, these adaptations produce dysfunctional diets. These dysfunctions are not produced by mechanism failures. They are products of a normally operating mechanism within an unusual or novel context.

Finally, it is possible that an evolved mechanism that is operating in its proper fashion, within a context to which it is suited, produces subjectively negative effects. Subjective discomfort, psychological pain, or negative affect might result from normal and functional psychological processes. In medicine, asking functional questions helps sort out the subjectively negative symptoms of a functional physiological response from truly pathological processes. For example, physicians once treated the fevers associated with illnesses partly because of the discomfort fevers produce. However, fever is one of the functional responses of the body's immune system, and interfering with this process results in a prolonged, rather than shortened, illness (Nesse & Williams, 1994). Some forms of psychological discomfort or pain (e.g., some depressions and anxieties) might also represent functional responses to trauma or other important circumstances (see Nesse, 1990, 1991).

EVOLUTIONARY PROCESS VERSUS EVOLUTIONARY PRODUCTS

It is critically important within evolutionary psychology to clearly maintain the distinction between the process of evolution by selection and the resultant structural features of organisms. The evolutionary process, in conjunction with chance events such as mutations and environmental contingencies, involves differential reproductive success by virtue of differences in design. Organic designs increase in a population because of their effects on the reproductive success (inclusive fitness) of the organism(s) bearing them. A design's reproductive effects can be quite indirect. For example, kin-directed help might increase a kin member's social status, leading to increased mating opportunities for his or her children.

While the process of evolution involves reproductive effects, the principal results of this process, adaptations, are not necessarily directed at reproduction per se. The products of evolution include structural features (e.g., eyes, opposable thumbs), information processing mechanisms (e.g., perceptual systems, social cognition), and affective systems (e.g., sexual jealousy, romantic love). There is no reason to expect a general motivation to pass on genes, or a generalized ability to track one's relative reproductive success. In fact, that type of general reproductive strategy is rather unlikely for one important reason: That type of design is not evolvable.

For an organism to pursue a general motive for "reproductive success," or to adjust its behavior to maximize its own inclusive fitness, it must have psychological processes designed to evaluate its current fitness trajectory, decide if that trajectory could be improved, associate behaviors with increases or decreases in fitness, and predict the fitness outcomes associated with changes in behavior. Fitness consequences, however, are temporally distal to the organism. Fitness is not observable by the organism because it is determined in hindsight, based on the reproductive outcomes of an individual's ancestors. It is also not clear how the individual might decide what to do, assuming it could determine that its current fitness trajectory was not maximally positive. The problem is not sufficiently narrow to restrict potential solutions much beyond random trial and error, not a generally effective method for living things.

Rather than general motives or behavior strategies geared toward the general problem of maximizing reproductive fitness, evolution produces relatively specific solutions to relatively specific adaptive problems. These specific mechanisms were favored by selection because they led to a successful solution to a proximate problem that was possibly only distally related to the ultimate reproductive success of its bearer.

LEVELS OF ANALYSIS IN EVOLUTIONARY PSYCHOLOGY

General Evolutionary Theory

General evolutionary theory, in its modern synthesis with molecular genetics and incorporating the insights of "inclusive fitness theory" (see below), provides metatheoretical guidance to psychologists. Its focus on selection as the key creative force in evolution has some heuristic value but by itself does not get us very far. Evolutionary theory at this level of abstraction offers only a few general predictions (e.g., that adaptations cannot exist exclusively for the benefit of another species or conspecific competitors) and only the crudest heuristic value (e.g., events surrounding survival and reproduction take on special importance). This level of evolutionary theory is typically assumed true in its general outlines and is used to guide theory-building efforts within more circumscribed content domains.

Middle-Level Evolutionary Theories

The primary focus of scientific efforts within evolutionary psychology is theory and research targeted at a particular domain. Using general evolutionary theory, we can derive more specific theories about a class of phenomena. These middle-level theories must be consistent with the principles of the general metatheory but the general theory underdetermines theories at this middle level. The result is that these middle-level theories are often in competition with one another, or exist within a system of normal paradigm science (see below for four examples).

Specific Evolutionary Hypotheses and Predictions

From a well-specified middle-level theory, evolutionary psychology proceeds according to normal science. These middle-level theories suggest relatively specific hypotheses because they ideally specify (1) a psychological adaptation (information-processing mechanism), (2) the contextual features relevant to its operation, and (3) the result, or output of the adaptation when operating in a given context. These hypotheses can then be subjected to empirical verification or falsification, and middle-level theories can be re-evaluated based on the results. Typically, it is the middle-level theory or the more specific hypotheses that are actually being tested in empirical research within evolutionary psychology and not general evolutionary theory. The general theory is assumed true, as a guiding metatheory, and empirical results from testing specific hypotheses, derived from middle-level theories, do not alter the assumed truth-value of the general theory.

EVOLUTIONARY THEORIES ESSENTIAL FOR UNDERSTANDING FAMILY PROCESSES

Four theories, derived from general evolutionary theory, have proven especially useful for understanding the adaptive problems and evolved psychological mechanisms associated with kinship (see Table 2.2 for research examples using these theories). These theories provide a useful starting point for a functional analysis of family systems. Each theory has generated a great deal of research, and the following is meant only as a brief introduction.

THEORY OF INCLUSIVE FITNESS

Hamilton's theory of inclusive fitness (1963, 1964) revolutionized the ways biologists understood kinship systems in the animal kingdom. His proposition was quite simple.

TABLE 2.2   Examples of Adaptive Problems Associated with Family Dynamics

Adaptive Problems	*Research Examples*
Mating	
Selection and attraction of appropriate mate	Buss (1989a)
	Buss & Schmitt (1993)
	Kenrick & Keefe (1992)
Retention of mate following selection and attraction	Buss (1988)
	Buss & Shackelford (1997)
Preventing infidelity	Buss et al. (1992)
	Buss et al. (1999)
Kinship	
Recognition of putative kin	Christenfeld & Hill (1995)
Evaluating uncertainty of relatedness	DeKay & Shackelford (1999)
	Euler & Weitzel (1996)
	Gaulin et al. (1997)
Providing help preferentially to kin	Burnstein et al. (1990)
	Essock-Vitale & McGuire (1985)
	Smith et al. (1987)
	Judge (1995)
Parenting	
Establishing paternity certainty	Daly & Wilson (1982)
Allocating effort between parenting and mating	Buss & Schmitt (1993)
Allocating resources and attention between children	Daly & Wilson (1995)
Socializing children	Low (1989)

Hamilton suggested that the contribution of an individual organism's behavior to its own reproductive success (termed *classical fitness*) was only one component of the true reproductive fitness of an organism. In addition, selection favors designs that help their own reproduction through the bodies of other individuals (i.e., genetic relatives). A design's "inclusive fitness" is a function of the effects of that design on its own reproduction and the effects of that design on the reproduction of genetically related others, times the degree of relatedness between the individuals.

Selection can favor organic designs that include seemingly altruistic behaviors, as long as the reproductive costs to the helper are less than the reproductive benefits to the helpee, times the degree of relatedness between the helper and helpee. This theory helped explain the presence of intense parental investment in some species (including our own), preferential helping toward other kin members, the presence of sterile workers in some species (e.g., bees, ants, termites), and hundreds of other phenomena (see Trivers, 1985, for a review of many of these applications). Inclusive fitness theory represented a major addition to general evolutionary theory and is considered by most biologists and evolutionary psychologists to be so well supported that it is now included as part of the general theory.

THEORY OF PARENT-OFFSPRING CONFLICT

Although inclusive fitness theory emphasizes that closely related individuals, such as parents and offspring, have some confluence of genetic interests, and hence often help one another, their genetic interests do not perfectly coincide. Trivers (1974) pointed out that often what is in the "adaptive interest" of a parent is not the best option for offspring and often the best reproductive option for offspring conflicts with the best option for parents. This often results in conflicts between parents and offspring, for example, over the distribution of parental resources. From the parents' perspective, a relatively even allocation of resources among offspring is optimal because each offspring represents a roughly equal reproductive investment (assuming they are of roughly the same age and health status). For each offspring, however, the optimal parental allocation is quite different. A child is more closely related to himself or herself than to siblings (excepting identical twins), and so each child will prefer that parental resources be skewed in his or her favor (see Daly & Wilson, 1988, for a more detailed discussion). In addition, parent-offspring conflict often emerges over the timing of weaning. Parents typically favor an earlier separation because they will then be able to shift from parenting to mating. Offspring favor a later weaning because, from the child's perspective, parental investment in them is more reproductively valuable than parental investment in future siblings.

THEORY OF PARENTAL INVESTMENT AND SEXUAL SELECTION

Trivers (1972) proposed that the process of sexual selection, or the selective effects of the mating choices of one sex on the reproductive success of members of the opposite sex, is driven by fundamental asymmetries between the sexes. According to Trivers (1972), the sex with the higher obligatory parental investment (often the female) will be relatively more choosy in selecting a mate. This is because the high investing sex will often bear the brunt of investment in each offspring (investment that cannot be directed elsewhere), and so each mating decision is an important decision. On the other hand, the sex with the lower obligatory parental investment (often the male) will be less choosy and will engage in heightened intrasexual competition for sexual access to the higher investing sex. This is because each mating decision is relatively less costly and the limiting factor on their reproduction is not investment, but access to the investing sex. This theory has been used to help predict and understand sex differences in mate preferences (Buss, 1989a; Kenrick & Keefe, 1992), mating strategies (Buss & Schmitt, 1993), sexual fantasies (Ellis & Symons, 1990), and many other phenomena.

The theories of inclusive fitness, parent-offspring conflict, and parental investment were formulated with reference primarily to nonhuman species. They have also proven useful for understanding human mating and family processes. In fact, these three theories help place our understanding of human behavior and psychology within a larger comparative context. Another theory, the theory of strategic interference, is more recent and was developed primarily with reference to humans.

THEORY OF STRATEGIC INTERFERENCE

Strategic interference theory (Buss, 1994) is an attempt to place human conflicts within an evolutionary framework as well as to recognize that many human conflicts do not arise simply because two individuals are in competition for the same resource. Rather, conflict often occurs because one person's goal, and the strategy he or she employs to attain it, interferes with the goals and strategies of another person. Although it was formulated with reference to humans, its principles apply with equal force to nonhuman species. Strategic interference occurs whenever the enactment of a goal-directed strategy by one individual blocks, inhibits, or impedes the goal-directed strategy of another person.

Buss (1994) argues that many of the conflicts that exist between the sexes, including conflicts within marriages, can be understood as strategic conflicts. That is, aspects of the evolved reproductive strategies of men and women often conflict. For example, the theory of parental investment and sexual selection (above) leads to the prediction that women, compared with men, will be relatively choosy in their mating decision. One implication is that women will prefer to delay sexual intercourse longer than men in a relationship. In this case, the preferred mating strategies of men and women are in conflict because they differ in the preferred timing of intercourse. This often leads to conflicts within couples over this issue (Buss, 1989b).

CONCLUSION

Darwin's theory of evolution by selection is deceptively simple, yet its application to human psychology is fraught with difficulties and produces many common misunderstandings (for a more extensive discussion of common misunderstandings, see Buss, 1995, 1999; Dawkins, 1979, 1982). The moral and practical implications of evolutionary explanations within psychology are often a subject of debate and so it is important to make two common misunderstandings explicit.

MISUNDERSTANDING 1: THE "DETERMINISTIC FALLACY"

There is no reason to expect that evolved psychological mechanisms are any more resistant to deliberate interventions than any other proposed psychological structure. Adaptations owe their existence to a long history of selection but that fact is orthogonal to the issue of behavioral or psychological change. In fact, a deeper understanding of the functional design of psychological mechanisms can lead directly to more effective strategies for changing behavior. For example, the source of behavioral variations in a particular domain (e.g., developmental triggers, immediate contexts, frequency-dependent selection, reactive individual differences, or some other source) will largely determine intervention strategies. If extreme sexual jealousy is largely a function of the activation of psychological adaptations within a recurring environment, intervention will perforce focus on that activating context. If it is a function of developmental triggers, intervention will focus on adjusting rearing environments. All mechanisms, evolved or not, are alterable given the appropriate environmental intervention. Evolutionary analyses can help determine what those interventions must be.

MISUNDERSTANDING 2: THE "NATURALISTIC FALLACY"

The claim that something is an adaptation is not a moral claim about its value. Rather, it is a description of the process that led to some structural property of an organism. The decision about the moral or social value of an adaptation ought to be independent of its status as an adaptation. There is no bridge from "is" to "ought." In fact, we decide regularly that we do not value various products of evolution. Viruses, such as the human immunodeficiency virus (HIV), are clearly products of evolution by selection, yet their evolutionary status does not cause anyone to argue that we should value HIV or that we should not try to change or eliminate HIV. The same applies to our own evolved psychology. If people become sexually jealous, and if that often leads to violence and conflict, we can decide to fight those outcomes. If we do, an evolutionary analysis of jealousy will be essential because it will reveal the intervention strategies that are most likely to work.

Evolutionary theory has been effectively organizing and guiding empirical discoveries within biology for over a century but has only recently been reintroduced into psychology. When properly applied, an evolutionary approach to psychological phenomena can provide two important benefits. First, evolutionary theory offers the chance to organize the social and psychological sciences and integrate them with the other life sciences. Second, by asking fundamental questions about the causal origins of psychological mechanisms, an evolutionary approach promises to lead us to new discoveries about human nature and the differences between us.

REFERENCES

Ainsworth, M. D. S. (1973). The development of infant-mother attachment. In B. M. Caldwell & H. N. Ricciuti (Eds.), *Review of child development research (Vol. 3)* (pp. 1–94). Chicago: University of Chicago Press.

Alcock, J. (1989). *Animal behavior: An evolutionary approach* (4th ed.). Sunderland, MA: Sinauer.

Belsky, J., Steinberg, L., & Draper, P. (1991). Childhood experience, interpersonal development, and reproductive strategy: An evolutionary theory of socialization. *Child Development, 62,* 647–670.

Bowlby, J. (1969). *Attachment.* NY: Basic Books.

Boyd, R., & Richardson, P. J. (1985). *Culture and the evolutionary process.* Chicago: University of Chicago Press.

Burnstein, E., Crandall, C., & Kitayama, S. (1994). Some neo-Darwinian decision rules for altruism: Weighing cues for inclusive fitness as a function of the biological importance of the decision. *Journal of Personality and Social Psychology, 67*(5), 773–789.

Buss, D. M. (1988). From vigilance to violence: Tactics of mate retention. *Ethology and Sociobiology, 9,* 291–317.

Buss, D. M. (1989a). Sex differences in human mate preferences: Evolutionary hypotheses tested in 37 cultures. *Behavioral and Brain Sciences, 12,* 1–49.

Buss, D. M. (1989b). Conflict between the sexes: Strategic interference and the evocation of anger and upset. *Journal of Personality and Social Psychology, 56,* 735–747.

Buss, D. M. (1990). Evolutionary social psychology: Prospects and pitfalls. *Motivation and Emotion, 14*(4), 265–286.

Buss, D. M. (1991). Evolutionary personality psychology. *Annual Review of Psychology, 45,* 459–491.

Buss, D. M. (1994). *The evolution of desire.* New York: Basic Books.

Buss, D. M. (1995). Evolutionary psychology: A new paradigm for social science. *Psychological Inquiry, 6,* 1–49.

Buss, D. M. (1999). *Evolutionary psychology: The new science of the mind.* Boston: Allyn & Bacon.

Buss, D. M. & Greiling, H. (1999). Adaptive individual differences. *Journal of Personality, 67*(2), 209–243.

Buss, D. M., Haselton, M. G., Shackelford, T. K., Bleske, A., & Wakefield, G. (1998). Adaptations, exaptations, and spandrels. *American Psychologist, 53,* 533–548.

Buss, D. M., Larsen, R., Westen, D., & Semmelroth, J. (1992). Sex differences in jealousy: Evolution, physiology, and psychology. *Psychological Science, 3,* 251–255.

Buss, D. M., & Schmitt, D. S. (1993). Sexual strategies theory: An evolutionary perspective on human mating. *Psychological Review, 100,* 204–232.

Buss, D. M. & Shackelford, T. K. (1997). Form vigilance to violence: Mate retention tactics in married couples. *Journal of Personality and Social Psychology, 72*(2), 346–361.

Buss, D. M., Shackelford, T. K., Haselton, M. G., & Bleske, A. (1997). *The evolutionary psychology of mental disorder. The proper function model.* Unpublished manuscript, Department of Psychology, University of Texas at Austin.

Christenfeld, N. & Hill, E. (1995). Whose baby are you? *Nature, 378,* 699.

Cosmides, L. (1989). The logic of social exchange: Has natural selection shaped how humans reason? Studies with the Wason selection task. *Cognition, 31,* 187–276.

Cosmides, L. & Tooby, J. (1989). Evolutionary psychology and the generation of culture, part II: A computational theory of social exchange. *Ethology and Sociobiology, 10,* 51–97.

Cummins, D. D. (1998). Social norms and other minds: The evolutionary roots of higher cognition. In D. D. Cummins & C. Allen (Eds.), *The evolution of mind* (pp. 30–50). New York: Oxford University Press.

Daly, M., & Wilson, M. (1982). Whom are newborn babies said to resemble? *Ethology and Sociobiology, 3,* 69–78.

Daly, M., & Wilson, M. (1988). *Homicide.* Hawthorne, NY: Aldine.

Daly, M. & Wilson, M. (1995). Discriminative parental solicitude and the relevance of evolutionary models to the analysis of mativational systems. In M. Gazzaniga (Ed.), *The Cognitive Neurosciences* (pp. 1269–1286). Cambridge, MA: MIT Press.

Daly, M., Wilson, M., & Weghorst, S. J. (1982). Male sexual jealousy. *Ethology and Sociobiology, 3,* 11–27.

Darwin, C. (1859). *On the origin of species.* London: Murray.

Darwin, C. (1871). *The descent of man and selection in relation to sex.* London: Murray.

Dawkins, R. A. (1979). Twelve misunderstanding of kin selection. *Zeitschrifft fur Tierpsychologie, 51,* 184–200.

Dawkins, R. A. (1982). *The extended phenotype.* Oxford: Oxford University Press.

Dawkins, R. A. (1989). *The selfish gene* (Rev. ed.). New York: Oxford University Press.

DeKay, W. T. (1999). *An evolutionary-computational approach to cooperation and altruism: Grandparental investment as a test case.* Unpublished dissertation thesis, Department of Psychology, University of Michigan, Ann Arbor.

DeKay, W. T. & Buss, D. M. (1992). Human nature, individual differences, and the importance of context: Perspectives from evolutionary psychology. *Current Directions in Psychological Science, 1*(6), 184–189.

DeKay, W. T., & Shackelford, T. K. (1999). *Toward an evolutionary approach to social cognition.* Manuscript under editorial review.

Ellis, B. J., & Symons, D. (1990). Sex differences in sexual fantasy: An evolutionary psychological approach. *Journal of Sex Research, 27,* 527–556.

Essock-Vitale, S. M., & McGuire, M. T. (1985). Women's lives viewed from an evolutionary perspective. II: Patterns of helping. *Ethology and Sociobiology, 6,* 155–173.

Euler, H. A., & Weitzel, B. (1996). Discriminative grandparental solicitude as reproductive strategy. *Human Nature, 7,* 39–59.

Gallistel, C. R. (1990). *The organization of learning.* Cambridge, MA: MIT Press.

Gangestad, S. W., & Buss, D. M. (1993). Pathogen prevalence and human mate preferences. *Ethology and Sociobiology, 14,* 89–96.

Gangestad, S. W., & Simpson, J. A. (1990). Toward an evolutionary history of female sociosexual variation. *Journal of Personality, 58,* 69–96.

Gaulin, S. J. C., McBumey, D. H., & Brakeman-Wartell, S. L. (1997). Matrilineal bias in the investment of aunts and uncles. *Human Nature, 8,* 139–151.

Glantz, K., & Pearce, J. (1989). *Exiles from Eden: Psychotherapy from an evolutionary perspective.* New York: Norton.

Gould, S. J. (1991). Exaptation: A crucial tool for evolutionary psychology. *Journal of Social Issues, 47,* 43–58.

Gould, S. J., & Lewontin, R. C. (1979). The spandrels of San Marco and the Panglossian program: A critique of the adaptationist programme. *Proceedings of the Royal Society of London, 250,* 281–288.

Hamilton, W. D. (1963). The evolution of altruistic behavior. *The American Naturalist, 97,* 354–356.

Hamilton, W. D. (1964). The genetical evolution of social behavior. *Journal of Theoretical Biology, 7,* 1–52.

Judge, D. S. (1995). American legacies and the variable life histories of women and men. *Human Nature, 6,* 291–323.

Kenrick, D. T., & Keefe, R. C. (1992). Age preferences in mates reflect sex differences in reproductive strategies. *Behavioral and Brain Sciences, 15,* 75–133.

Low, B. S. (1989). Cross-cultural patterns in the training of children: An evolutionary perspective. *Journal of Comparative Psychology, 103,* 313–319.

Lumsden, C., & Wilson, E. O. (1981). *Genes, mind, and culture*. Cambridge, MA: Harvard University Press.

McDonald, K. (1992). Warmth as a developmental construct: An evolutionary analysis. *Child Development, 63*, 753–773.

Mealy, L. (1995). The sociobiology of sociopathy: An integrated evolutionary model. *Behavioral and Brain Sciences, 18*, 523–599.

Nesse, R. M. (1990). Evolutionary explanations of emotions. *Human Nature, 1*, 261–289.

Nesse, R. M. (1991, November/December). What good is feeling bad? The evolutionary benefits of psychological pain. *The Sciences*, 30–37.

Nesse, R. M., & Williams, G. C. (1994). *Why we get sick*. New York: Times Books Random House.

Nisbett, R. E. (1990). Evolutionary psychology, biology, and cultural evolution. *Motivation and Emotion, 14*, 255–263.

Orians, G. H. & Heerwagen, J. H. (1992). Evolved responses to landscapes. In J. Barkow, L. Cosmides, & J. Tooby (eds.), *The Adapted Mind* (pp. 555–579). NY: Oxfort University Press.

Pinker, S., & Bloom, P. (1990). Natural language and natural selection. *Behavioral and Brain Sciences, 13*, 707–784.

Shepard, R. N. (1992). The perceptual organization of colors: An adaptation to regularities of the terrestrial world? In J. Barkow, L. Cosmides, & J. Tooby (Eds.), *The adapted mind* (pp. 19–136). New York: Oxford University Press.

Silverman, I., & Phillips, K. (1998). The evolutionary psychology of spatial sex differences. In C. Crawford & D. L. Krebs (Eds.), *Handbook of evolutionary psychology* (pp. 595–612). Mahwah, NJ: Erlbaum.

Simpson, J. A., & Kenrick, D. T. (1997). *Evolutionary social psychology*. Mahwah, NJ: Erlbaum.

Smith, M. S., Kish, B. J., & Crawford C. B. (1987). Inheritance of wealth as human kin investment. *Ethology and Sociobiology, 8*, 171–182.

Smuts, B. B. (1992). Male aggression against women. *Human Nature, 3*, 1–44.

Tinbergen, N. (1951). *The study of instinct*. New York: Oxford University Press.

Tooby, J., & Cosmides, L. (1989). Evolutionary psychology and the generation of culture, part I: Theoretical considerations. *Ethology and Sociobiology, 10*, 29–49.

Tooby, J., & Cosmides, L. (1990). On the universality of human nature and the uniqueness of the individual: The role of genetics and adaptation. *Journal of Personality, 58*, 17–67.

Tooby, J., & Cosmides, L. (1992). Psychological foundations of culture. In J. Barkow, L. Cosmides, & J. Tooby (Eds.), *The adapted mind* (pp. 19–136). New York: Oxford University Press.

Trivers, R. (1972). Parental investment and sexual selection. In B. Campbell (Ed.), *Sexual selection and the descent of man: 1871–1971* (pp. 136–179). Chicago: Aldine.

Trivers, R. (1974). Parent-offspring conflict. *American Zoologist, 14*, 249–264.

Trivers, R. (1985). *Social evolution*. Menlo Park, CA: Benjamin/Cummings.

Wakefield, J. C. (1992). The concept of mental disorder: On the boundary between biological facts and social values. *American Psychologist, 47*, 373–388.

Williams, G. C. (1966). *Adaptation and natural selection*. Princeton, NJ: Princeton University Press.

Wilson, E. O. (1975). *Sociobiology. The new synthesis*. Cambridge, MA: Harvard University Press.

Wright, R. (1994). *The moral animal*. New York: Pantheon.

CHAPTER 3

The Limits of Change: Heredity, Temperament, and Family Influence

Jay S. Efran and Mitchell A. Greene

F AMILY WORKERS are accustomed to explaining behavior on the basis of child-rearing experiences, family system variables, and socioeconomic circumstances. Although some have a growing awareness of the potential importance of biological and genetic determinants, most clinical practitioners remain firmly tied to the analysis of parenting patterns and family environmental variables. This "radical environmentalist" (Lykken, 1995, p. 67) perspective has become so ingrained in the consciousness of the field that its validity is rarely challenged. Moreover, our dominant research tradition—what behavior geneticist David Rowe labels *socialization science* (1994, p. 24)—routinely endorses this view and excludes any serious consideration of hereditary variables (Tellegen et al., 1988).

The current focus on nurture (over nature) had its origins in the 1950s. The kinds of hypotheses that were popular in that era included the notion that childhood autism and schizophrenia were caused by "ice-box mothering," that aggression and delinquency were the unfortunate sequelae of inner-city poverty, and that male homosexuality was attributable to having a domineering mother and a passive father. Although each of those particular suppositions has since been questioned, the underlying "nurture assumption" (Harris, 1998) continues to dominate both developmental research and clinical practice.

However, the profession now finds itself at a crossroad. The research findings of the so-called new genetics (Efran, Greene, & Gordon, 1998) are prompting a sweeping reevaluation of the role of genes and other biological factors in shaping people's lives. Mental health professionals and developmentalists wishing to remain current will need to educate themselves about emerging findings in fields such as behavior genetics and molecular biology. This chapter is a survey of the major trends developing in those domains and their implications for family theorists and practitioners.

THE SHIFTING ZEITGEIST

This is not the first time that workers in the family field have had to face a potentially radical change in their preferred explanatory model. In the past, changes in the sociopolitical zeitgeist as well as the emergence of new research findings have occasioned distinct shifts in how patterns of psychopathology and family development were construed. In the 1920s, for instance, when refugees were pouring across U.S. borders, there was great interest in the principles of eugenics (Gould, 1998). Segments of the citizenry—already feeling threatened by the influx of immigrants—were receptive to the notion that people should protect the gene pool from "contamination" by foreigners. They considered it self-evident that a person's heritage was responsible for his or her moral defects and characterological flaws. Therefore, they believed that the only way they could ensure the survival of the culture was to encourage the genetically fit to procreate (positive eugenics) and to persuade or compel the less genetically fit to abstain from procreating (negative eugenics).

Geneticist Charles Davenport was one of the key American promoters of this philosophy. He had been inspired by an earlier visit to the United States by Sir Francis Galton, the British scientist and statistician credited with founding the eugenics movement. Under Davenport's leadership, eugenics groups organized large-scale public relations campaigns. They set up displays at state fairs and local carnivals across the country, preaching the hazards of indiscriminate reproduction. Such exhibits warned that "tainted families threatened the germplasm of civilization" (Hasian, 1996, p. 43). At special tents, fairgoers were given the opportunity to be examined and declared "eugenically fit." People could take a special genetically oriented physical exam, including a Wassermann test, IQ test, and psychiatric screening. Farmers visiting these exhibits were told that traits such as "feeblemindedness, epilepsy, criminality, insanity, alcoholism, [and] pauperism . . . run in families . . . the same way as color in guinea pigs" (cited in Hasian, 1996, p. 44). The message, obviously, was that those who made their living evaluating the pedigree of livestock ought to be at least as attentive to the heritage of their own offspring. This sort of eugenic call to arms motivated thousands to send information about their family background to central eugenic clearinghouses for analysis and "authentication."

It was not just a lunatic fringe of racists and fanatics who boarded the eugenics bandwagon. Prominent thinkers and social reformers—social workers, judges, and civic leaders from both ends of the political spectrum—championed eugenic policies and practices. The passage of the immigration restriction bill of 1924 was partly an outgrowth of these efforts. It was also in that period that Supreme Court Justice Oliver Wendell Holmes uttered his famous dictum—"Three generations of imbeciles are enough"—in defense of forced sterilization programs (Buck v. Bell, 1927).

In their heyday, eugenicists were able to marshal considerable scientific support for their position. However, as news of the Nazi atrocities spread, their evidentiary base was rendered moot. Not only were Hitler's genocidal programs justified on the basis of eugenic principles, but ironically, German scientists prided themselves on mimicking aspects of early eugenic initiatives of the United States.

By the late 1930s and early 1940s, scientists and social thinkers who had previously seen promise in Social Darwinist solutions to societal problems had beaten a hasty retreat. In fact, the backlash caused by the abhorrent Nazi ethnic cleansing policies was so extreme that it brought a halt to virtually all research that even smacked of genetic determinism. Over the succeeding decades, funding for such work dried up, and investigators who wished to pursue the possible links between constitution and behavior found their motives and methods constantly questioned.

Even today, there is considerable resistance to studying the genetic roots of behavioral patterns. Just a few years ago, Frederick Goodwin, the former head of the Alcohol, Drug

Abuse and Mental Health Administration, was forced out of office two days after merely suggesting that the biological precursors of aggression warranted further investigation (Adler, 1992; Wolfe, 1996). Goodwin did not help his cause by comparing urban gang violence to the behavior of adolescent male rhesus monkeys. His point may have been scientifically defensible, but it was a red flag for those already suspicious of the political agendas of genetic investigators.

In 1993, the announcement of a federally funded University of Maryland conference on genetics and criminal behavior drew such political heat that the meetings had to be called off (Angier, 1995a). A scaled-down version of the conference was eventually held, but not without incident. A group of about 30 protesters burst onto the premises, accusing conference participants of "pushing genocide" and "promoting Nazi propaganda" (Angier, 1995b, p. C8). By contrast, the conference itself was quite tame. Speakers actually argued in favor of increased funding for social rehabilitation projects, and no one came even close to proposing selective breeding as the "final solution" to inner city strife.

Although E.O. Wilson's 1975 book *Sociobiology: The New Synthesis* was more about ant colonies than human communities, the term "sociobiology" that he introduced has caused such a furor that many scientists have since found it politically prudent to avoid the term and instead call themselves evolutionary psychologists, behavioral ecologists, Darwinian anthropologists, and evolutionary psychiatrists—in other words, anything but sociobiologists (Wright, 1994).

More recently, psychologist J. Philippe Rushton (1995) was attacked for publishing a scholarly but politically incorrect book titled *Race, Evolution, and Behavior: A Life History Perspective*. His "gene-based evolutionary theory" posits multiple comparisons—some flattering, some less complimentary—between people of East Asian, European, and African descent. Most critics were uninterested in evaluating the evidence and pronounced his work "off limits" as a subject of legitimate inquiry. Similarly, the explosive reactions to the 1994 publication of *The Bell Curve* (Herrnstein & Murray)—an admittedly controversial treatise on intelligence, genetics, and race—have only sometimes focused on the data the authors report or the adequacy of their interpretations. The necessary scholarly debate has been frequently sidetracked by ad hominem attacks on the authors' personal credentials, motives, and politics (Redding, 1998).

THE RISE OF RADICAL ENVIRONMENTALISM

As World War I ended, American psychiatry retreated further from an emphasis on biological factors, choosing instead to focus almost exclusively on cultural and relationship variables. The mood of the mental health community was well captured by Harry Stack Sullivan's interpersonal approach. Beginning in the 1930s, Sullivan (1953) emphasized the primacy of early parenting transactions and the importance of the social context, replacing Freud's genetically fixed psychosexual stages with his own conceptions of relationship-relevant developmental epochs (Cushman, 1995). Freud's theory was further debiologized in 1950 by John Dollard and Neal Miller, who attempted to translate psychodynamic concepts into learning theory terms. Their translation minimizes Freud's instinctual emphasis, focusing instead on descriptions of the role parents play in shaping their children's behavior. Dollard and Miller saw psychopathology as a form of cultural discontinuity—for instance, habits reinforced by parents at home might not work well in other contexts. A pampered child, for example, might have trouble relating to other authority figures later in life.

This learning theory approach was expanded upon by psychologists Albert Bandura and Richard Walters (1963), who argued that even bizarre or unusual traits might have their genesis in very basic parent-child interactions and modeling processes. A cross-dresser, for instance, might have started out innocently imitating his mother's behavior. However, the cross-dressing might later be stamped in as a learned component of the person's sexual arousal patterns. The Bandura and Walters approach fit well with the emphasis of American psychology on operationalism and empirical science. Unfortunately, it also perpetuated the basic neglect of hereditary factors.

In the mid-1950s, psychiatrists Stella Chess and Alexander Thomas found themselves increasingly skeptical of the received view and dubious that the striking temperamental variations they observed in children "could be attributed to the parents' child care practices and attitudes" (Chess & Thomas, 1996, p. 181). They soon concluded that traditional case formulations omitted crucial elements. Tentatively at first, and more boldly thereafter, they began arguing that "individual differences in the *children themselves* [italics added] played an important role in their healthy or deviant development—and not merely the mother's influence" (p. 13). On the basis of their disaffection with traditional thinking, they launched an extensive longitudinal project that continues to this day. Their goal was to examine more carefully the interaction of temperament and parenting practices. However, not until the 1970s did their efforts begin to receive widespread recognition. Until then, most researchers and practitioners remained largely disinterested in the possibility of biologically rooted differences.

At about the same time that Chess and Thomas began investigating temperament variables, Gregory Bateson proposed a double-bind theory of schizophrenia (Bateson, Jackson, Haley, & Weakland, 1956). In short, Bateson and his colleagues attributed etiological significance to the strained communication patterns observed in schizophrenogenic families. They believed, for instance, that mothers were issuing contradictory messages, overtly inviting closeness while simultaneously expressing disgust in the nonverbal channels. Unfortunately, the ultimate payoffs of focusing on individual parenting styles, family constellations, and boundaries have been disappointing. The double-bind thesis itself has failed to receive empirical support and has largely been abandoned (Liem, 1980; Sluzki & Ransom, 1976). Indeed, it is likely that the strained communication Bateson believed he observed was the result of dealing with a schizophrenic individual rather than the cause of that person's symptoms.

Moreover, as psychotropic medications were introduced, clinicians had to acknowledge that Thorazine quieted a person's hallucinatory voices more quickly and reliably than any of the therapies derived from family analysis, and the introduction of the lithium salts quickly revolutionized the treatment of bipolar disorder. Thus, the kinds of patients who originally interested Bateson and others such as Murray Bowen were increasingly being medicated rather than therapized. (Some therapists have now adopted an educational role, teaching families with psychotic individuals how to reduce stress. This is based on research suggesting that high levels of emotional reactivity in families can exacerbate psychotic symptomatology, e.g., Hooley, 1998; Lenior, Linszen, & Dingemans, 1998.)

Although clinicians have gradually ceded the primary care of the psychoses to biological psychiatry, they continue to see themselves as playing a central role in the treatment of other—nonpsychotic—conditions. Yet, this assumption is increasingly threatened by the growing list of disorders for which medications are being seen as appropriate and for which genetic mechanisms are being implicated. The list of problems and traits now presumed to have genetic "connections" includes irritability, murderous rage, hyperactivity, anxiety, circadian rhythms, risk taking, alcoholism, attention deficit/hyperactivity disorder, nicotine addiction, delinquency, homosexuality, ego strength, resilience, social phobia, depression, the eating disorders, nail-biting, dyslexia, shyness, panic disorder, and post-traumatic stress disorder. According to behavior geneticists, even something as apparently malleable and environmentally responsive as human happiness is more dependent on genetic "set points" than on the flow of everyday events (Goleman, 1996).

THE HUMAN GENOME PROJECT

The expanded list of "likely suspects"—conditions thought to have genetic underpinnings—is partly attributable to the creation of the government's $3 billion Human Genome Project. Headed by physician and geneticist Francis Collins, the project's goal has been to map, by the year 2005, the three billion chemical units that make up our DNA (Wade, 1998a). The genome contains all the chromosomes of a particular organism—in other words, the genetic instructions to make and operate the organism. Because of competition from the private sector, the Human Genome Project has now gone into high gear, moving up its completion date by 2 years (Wade, 1998b). Scientists affiliated with the project optimistically estimate that one third of the genome—roughly half of the genetic material—will be sequenced by 2001 (Wade, 1998c).

Even though only a small proportion of the estimated 100,000 genes have been fully investigated, the resulting findings in medicine and psychology have already justified the enthusiasm of the project's founders. The past few years have witnessed the discovery of many new disease genes, including the pinpointing of the genetic bases of more than 15 types of cancer. Progress has also been made in establishing the etiology of various forms of vascular disease and mental retardation. In 1993, the gene associated with Huntington's disease was located, and researchers continue to make headway deciphering the riddle of Alzheimer's. The Human Genome Project is expected to unravel the underlying causes of thousands of additional conditions, including sickle-cell anemia, Tay-Sachs disease, myotonic dystrophy, certain forms of deafness, and cystic fibrosis. Genetic culprits for any number of esoteric disorders, such as von Recklinghausen neurofibromatosis (benign tumors of nerves, muscles, and other tissues), osteogenesis imperfecta (brittle bones), and Niemann-Pick disease (fat metabolism defects) have also been identified (Weiss, 1995).

The success of all this genetic detective work has been enhanced by a dizzying array of technological breakthroughs. For instance, the arsenal of imaging techniques that started with the CT (computed tomography) scan has grown to include positron-emission tomography (PET), functional magnetic resonance imaging (fMRI), magnetoencephalography (MEG), and magnetic resonance spectroscopy (MRS). One of the latest entries in this alphabet soup is the PET reporter gene/PET reporter probe. It enables researchers to track single gene actions in a living human brain (McIntosh, 1998; Nasrallah & Pettegrew, 1995; Wolfe, 1996). Of course, DNA testing, a dinner-table topic ever since the O.J. Simpson trial, is another example of a technology that has rapidly increased in sophistication and ease of use over a remarkably short time span.

As marvelous as these hardware achievements are, the findings that intrigue—and potentially threaten—family workers owe as much to innovations in statistical tools and research designs as to the invention of sophisticated diagnostic equipment. Twin and adoption studies, in particular, have profited from advanced data analytic procedures as well as the increased availability of large-scale data banks (Bouchard & Propping, 1993; Rowe, 1994). Liberalized social policies have also made it easier to access information about adoptions and foster placements. Few agencies, for instance, remain committed to selective placement policies (i.e., the practice of matching the characteristics of adoptive and biological parents). Thus, even transracial adoptions are no longer a rarity. This new diversity of adoptive circumstances allows researchers to construct clearer and more detailed maps of how biological and environmental forces interact. Furthermore, by applying state-of-the-art model fitting designs, researchers can maximize the usefulness of a data set by combining information from different relatives into a single coherent genetic road map.

LEARNING FROM REUNITED TWINS

One of the best ways to disentangle the effects of hereditary and environmental factors is to observe what happens when identical twins—genetic carbon copies—are reared in different environments and by different parents. That methodology was used to advantage by psychologist Thomas Bouchard in the well-known Minnesota study of identical twins reared apart (Bouchard et al., 1990; L. Wright, 1997; W. Wright, 1998). In 1979, Bouchard was captivated—along with the rest of the country—by press reports about the so-called Jim twins (Watson, 1981). These gentlemen, both named James by their biological parents, had been separated at birth but were reunited at the age of 39. Although they had no contact with one another, their lives eerily followed similar pathways. Not only did they work similar jobs, but they had similar hobbies and habits. Both owned a dog named Toy, drank the same brand of beer, chain-smoked the same brand of cigarettes, and married a woman named Linda. When each of them divorced and remarried, it was to a woman named Betty. Perhaps equally remarkable, both Jims independently built circular wooden benches around backyard trees and painted them white.

Following an appearance on the Johnny Carson show, the Jim twins told their story countless times to newspaper reporters and magazine editors. In the midst of this publicity, Bouchard, who had already been involved in twin research, saw the potential of inviting such individuals to his Center for Twin and Adoption Research for intensive investigation. Separated twin pairs—particularly those like "the Jims" who grow up having little or no awareness of each other—do not struggle to "differentiate" from one another, nor do their parents have opportunities to accentuate their differences or similarities. Thus, they simply grow up "being who they are," providing a natural experiment on the effects of having a particular genetic complexion. As Bouchard was to learn, such twins often come astonishingly close to being human clones.

Following Bouchard's study of the Jim twins, many other pairs of separated twins were located and invited to the University of Minnesota for interviews and tests (Lykken, 1997). By this point, the number of pairs studied exceeds 120 (Wright, 1998). Those who came from distant locales often met each other for the first time at the airport or when they showed up at the laboratory. Uncanny coincidences occurred. For example, two sisters, without having had any prior contact, both arrived in beige dresses and brown velvet jackets. Another two realized that they had both "chosen" to wear seven rings, two bracelets on one arm, and one bracelet on the other. In addition to these striking similarities in dress and appearance, Bouchard's team documented impressive concordances in temperament, habits, sense of humor, intellectual ability, and psychiatric history.

Initially, Bouchard—who was originally trained as a social psychologist—did not include any attitude scales in his battery. Along with most of us, he assumed that attitudes were strictly social and environmental affairs. Subsequently, he learned otherwise. Apparently, even attitudes and values can have hereditary components. For example, researchers have determined that about 60% of the variance in authoritarianism scores is attributable to genetics (Bouchard, 1997). In some research, small but distinct genetic components seem to be connected with very specific beliefs, such as whether or not one advocates the death penalty, supports the use of censorship, or favors divorce as a solution to marital difficulties (Eaves, Eysenck, & Martin, 1989). Of course, it is anybody's guess as to exactly how such obviously culture-bound decisions might be tied to elements of genetic and biological structure. In speculating about the possible links, it is useful to bear in mind that although the discovered correlations in this domain are significant, they account for only a small proportion of the variance—in other words, they are tendencies, not inevitabilities.

The Minnesota sample included twins with quite diverse backgrounds who lived in different countries and under different economic circumstances. Although they were sent to different school systems, they often had remarkably similar academic achievement levels. One pair of twins had been brought up in different religious traditions. Oskar was raised in a fatherless family in Germany. He considered himself to be Catholic and a member of the Hitler Youth. His brother Jack, on the other hand, lived with his father and was raised as a Jew in Trinidad. He had spent some time in Israel, working on two kibbutzim. Despite these differences, they both arrived at Minnesota wearing virtually identical wire-rimmed spectacles. They wore matching blue shirts (with epaulettes) and trimmed their mustaches in the same style. Both men had the habit of reading magazines from back to front, storing rubber bands on their wrists, and dipping buttered toast in their coffee. Such similarities are typical of the many coincidences Bouchard and his colleagues discovered that seem quite characteristic of identical twins but almost unheard of with fraternal twins.

GENETICS AND FAMILY INFLUENCE

Although anecdotes abound, they do not prove anything. However, they are backed up by a considerable and growing body of more formal research evidence that underscores the contribution of genetics to personality. According to behavior geneticist David Lykken (1995), the average heritability of psychological traits seems to be about 50% when based on single measurements, and perhaps 70% when based on estimates of the stable component of the traits (e.g., on the means of repeated measurements). A highly consistent and stable trait like IQ has a heritability on the order of 75% for single measurements, rising to perhaps 85% when corrected for instability (Lykken, 1995, p. 108).

Martin Seligman, a past president of the American Psychological Association, recently reexamined the "large and well-executed" body of research on childhood determinants. He concluded that there are "huge effects of genetics," "large effects of recent life events," and "small or no effects of childhood events" (1995, p. 1). In his book *What You Can Change and What You Can't* (1993), Seligman summarizes this state of affairs bluntly: "The shared childhood environment . . . has virtually no effect on adult personality" (p. 299). In other words, "The whole kit and caboodle that American developmental psychology bet on came up with a bust."

Following heredity, the so-called nonshared environmental events seem to matter the most, accounting for 15 percent to 50 percent of the variance in most twin and adoption studies (Seligman, 1993). Unfortunately, nonshared environment is a hodgepodge category that does not tell us very much. Along with measurement error, it includes events as diverse as prenatal accidents, educational experiences, peer relationships, and chance encounters—in short, everything and anything that cannot easily be classified as either hereditary or shared family influence. In that sense, the "nonshared" category is a necessary artifact of these research designs, a pigeonhole into which to plunk, at least temporarily, all the factors not specifically being investigated. Ironically, some family experiences end up being lumped in this catchall category. These include parent behaviors or family circumstances that affect one child but not another. Most sibling interactions, too, are classified as "nonshared" because each child experiences them differently. Later, in discussing gene-environment correlations, we will return to a consideration of these sorts of particularistic and idiosyncratic influences.

However, for the moment, we want to emphasize that shared family environment factors—those elements of family structure and parenting style to which all siblings are presumably exposed—keep showing up at the bottom of the influence barrel (e.g., Bouchard, 1994; Hetherington, Reiss, & Plomin, 1994; Pinker, 1997; Rowe, 1994). In other words, except for severe abuse or neglect, the variables on which many family therapists and researchers have bet the professional farm seem to have virtually no predictable impact on a child's developmental trajectory.

A parent's behavior may certainly contribute to making a child's daily existence pleasant or stressful. However, surprisingly, such parental actions do not automatically or inevitably affect the child's later adjustment (Rowe, 1994). Thus, the traditional view of child development seems to have granted parents both too much credit and too much blame for how their children turn out. As author Judith Harris (1998) argues, the impact of parents on children—beyond genetic heritage—is more indirect than direct. For instance, the neighborhood in which parents live matters because it helps determine who their children will have opportunities to befriend (or not befriend). In fact, Harris views peer-group dynamics—a nonshared influence—as ultimately more important to a child's development than the particulars of parent-child interaction on which therapists and researchers typically concentrate.

Like Harris, developmentalist Sandra Scarr—a past president of the American Psychological Society—contends that developmental researchers have overemphasized parenting patterns and neglected peer influences (1996). For instance, she notes that research has never established a link between middle-class parenting practices and favorable child outcomes. In other words, a mobile over an infant's crib, the latest educational toys, and trips to zoos or museums do not appear to have any lasting effect on a child's academic performance or overall life success. We have been misled into thinking these things are important largely because of a series of spurious correlations: Because middle-class children usually do well academically, we simply assume that their parents must be doing something right (Scarr & Weinberg, 1978). Consider, however, a series of cross-cultural comparisons between Guatemalan village children and youths raised in the Boston suburbs (Kagan & Klein, 1973; Kagan, Kearsley, & Zelazo, 1978). The Guatemalan youngsters were rarely played with as infants and were given far fewer opportunities than children in the United States for physical or social exploration—they had no middle-class "pampering." Yet, by age 10 they were roughly identical to the Boston children in both intellectual and maturational development.

In Seligman's view, the bottom line is that "how we were raised—by martinets [or permissive parents]; how we were fed—on demand or on schedule, on breast or on bottle; even mother's death, parents' divorcing, and being second-born exert, at most, small influences on what we are like as adults" (1993, p. 237). Based on this conclusion, he recommends that professionals reexamine their fundamental beliefs:

> All of us who think that traumatic experience is important in human growth—and I have devoted most of my research life to this issue—must read this literature and discuss it. If you think you can dismiss this literature out of hand because you somehow know that childhood events cause adult psychopathology, you are simply wrong. (1995, p. 1)

THE HAZARDS OF SOCIALIZATION SCIENCE

Is it possible that both clinicians and researchers have been so misled about the relative causal significance of hereditary and shared family environmental factors? The simple answer is "yes." The clinical window through which socialization science investigators and therapists observe people's behavior favors noticing environmental similarities and overlooking constitutional concordances. Behavioral resemblances are outwardly visible and thus usually dominate people's perceptions and stories. Moreover, under ordinary circumstances, the influences of nature and nurture are complexly intertwined and people have no easy vehicle for teasing them apart. The effects of genetic overlap can only be "seen" under specialized research conditions. A woman (and her therapist) may firmly believe that her compulsive tidiness derives from observing her mother clean house all those years. However, it is just as likely—actually it is much more likely—that their near-identical cleaning styles are due to their shared genes rather than their shared experiences.

Among developmentalists, the view that family patterning is critical to child development persists as an article of faith. Similarly, family workers remain wedded to the belief that early childhood experience has particular significance (e.g., Harris, 1998; Rowe, 1994; Scarr, 1996). These notions basically lack research support. To quote psychologist Robyn Dawes (1994), they are components of a contemporary folk tale as pseudoscientific as a "belief in a mountain god" (p. 223). The evidence suggests that beyond reasonable standards of nurturance and environmental stimulation—what Scarr (1992) refers to as "good-enough parenting"—little else has much long-term impact.

Socialization researchers have repeatedly been unsuccessful in documenting strong effects of parenting. However, they rationalize such failures by continually attributing them to methodological shortcomings such as small sample size or insensitive measuring instruments (Harris, 1998). Moreover, in *The Limits of Family Influence* (1994), Rowe contends that more or less the entire "collection of socialization studies . . . do not provide a shred of evidence about rearing experiences, because they have failed to eliminate the influence of genes" (p. 19). Scarr (1996), also, bemoans the continued willingness of journals to "publish studies that make environmental inferences from confounded designs" (p. 150).

To make matters worse, authors of such studies frequently violate a cardinal research canon by drawing causal conclusions from strictly correlational data. Consider the large, growing, and influential literature based on John Bowlby's (1969) "attachment theory." Using an object relations perspective, Bowlby (1988) posited that "insecurely attached" children will have more trouble negotiating life tasks than youngsters who have formed stronger and more stable mother-child bonds. In the literature, bonding difficulties are frequently attributed to incompetent or inconsistent parenting. However, the exact causes of bonding weakness remain a mystery. In fact, some argue that weak bonds are as likely to be due to inherent temperamental characteristics of the child as the practices of the parent (Fox, Kimmerly, & Schafer, 1991). In other words, some children are apt to have trouble connecting emotionally with their parents no matter how they happen to be treated (e.g., Finkel, Wille, & Matheny, 1998). Furthermore, particular parents and children may very well share genetic attributes that make bonding a problematic process for both of them.

At present, there is simply no sound evidence causally linking insecure attachment to inadequate parenting (Lamb, 1987). In fact, some data suggest that bonding can occur quite successfully in normal children under a wide range of environmental conditions. Even less than sterling day care, for instance, does not seem to result in long-term effects (Scarr, 1997). Moreover, day-care placement does nothing to impede mother-child bonding except, perhaps, in cases where developmental difficulties are already present (NICHD Early Child Care Research Network, 1997). Thus, all we can legitimately say at present is that secure attachment is an indication of healthy maturation and that the precise causes of bonding weakness—both genetic and environmental—await further investigation.

THE GENETICS OF DIVORCE

Divorce researchers are another group who often mistake correlation for causation (e.g., Wallerstein & Blakeslee, 1989). Furthermore, they regularly overlook genetic factors. Yet, divorcing couples (and their children) are hardly a genetically random sample of the general population (Rowe, 1994). Divorcing adults may have distinctive genetic profiles and atypical mental health histories. Twin studies, for example, show a heritability of divorce of about 52%. In other words, if one identical twin divorces, the odds that the other will follow suit is about six times greater than average (McGue & Lykken, 1992). Furthermore, the effects do not seem to be merely due to social precedents, such as having witnessed other family members separate. In short, investigators who want to pinpoint the deleterious effects of divorce are now obliged to take into account both the predivorce psychiatric status of the family members involved and the genetic legacy that children of divorce share with their parents. Few doubt that children from broken homes experience higher than average rates of mental illness and marital distress, but that does not mean—as many have too glibly assumed—that their difficulties stem from the divorce process itself or from any associated child-rearing lapses.

WHY IS THERE A CYCLE OF VIOLENCE?

Another hazard of family life—the so-called cycle of violence—has recently been capturing headlines. This is the notion that because abused children have witnessed violence, been subjected to violence, or both, they will be prone to perpetuate the cycle by abusing their own spouses or offspring. Actually, the vast majority of such children—fully 70%—never engage in any violent or abusive behavior (Feldman, 1997; Widom, 1989). Another 30% do go on to be violent or abusive. However, it is not necessarily their early environmental experiences that causes them to act out. Again, it is important to remember that abusive parents pass on their genes as well as their behaviors (Harris, 1998; Wright, 1998).

We already know, from many behavior genetic studies, that antisocial and destructive tendencies have inherited components (e.g., Bohman, 1996; Mednick, Gabrielli, & Hutchings, 1984; Slutske et al., 1997; see also Stoff, Breiling, & Maser, 1997). Lykken (1995) estimates that the stable component of aggressiveness (measured across time) may be as much as 80% genetically determined. In adoption studies, the sons of criminal individuals who have been "transplanted" into law-abiding families shortly after birth remain at substantial risk for unlawful and aggressive activity. Improved parenting seems to do virtually nothing to quell their antisocial leanings. On the other hand, there is no noticeable rise in criminality associated with being raised in an antisocial household except for those individuals who are already genetically at risk (Hamer & Copeland, 1998). For example, in a study of over 1,000 Iowa families, children raised in problematic homes had a 500 percent greater likelihood of engaging in aggressive and delinquent behavior—but only if their biological fathers also had histories of antisocial behavior (Cadoret, Yates, Troughton, Woodworth, & Stewart, 1995). Similarly, Bohman (1996), reporting on rates of petty crime in Sweden, found elevated rates for children whose adoptive and biological parents had criminal backgrounds. Again, children without a predisposing genetic liability seemed relatively impervious to the degree of criminal activity surrounding them.

It follows from this sort of research that a good many of the 30% of youngsters who perpetuate "cycles of violence" might very well do so no matter how or where they were raised. Again, correlation does not equal causation, and the relevance of the genetic connection cannot be discounted.

In the highly publicized trial of Jesse Timmendequas—the man convicted of sexually assaulting and murdering 7-year-old Megan Kanka in New Jersey—lawyers argued that he should be spared the death penalty because of the horrendous childhood he endured (Lounsberry, 1997a, 1997b, 1997c, 1997d). The implication was that his upbringing was somehow responsible for his sexual proclivities. In an early report, his brother Paul was quoted as saying that Jesse had been sexually molested by his father and had been forced to watch the rape of a young girl. This is, of course, the cycle of violence scenario in a nutshell—a troubled childhood propelling someone toward later sexual and aggressive transgressions. However, Jesse's brother then recanted much of his testimony, raising doubts about the degree of childhood abuse Jesse actually suffered or witnessed.

The evidence, as reported, does not permit any firm conclusions about the origins of Jesse's antisocial behavior. Jesse is reputed to have had mild brain dysfunction and, according to the published reports, both he and his parents share a history of impulsive behavior—exactly the kinds of characteristics that make genetically linked criminal and psychopathic behavior more likely. Similarly, his father reportedly drank heavily and had a history of incarcerations and run-ins with the authorities. Regrettably, the focus of the case was lopsided—every aspect of Jesse's rearing environment was explored, but his genetic background and the hereditary background of his parents was barely considered. Thus, the publicity surrounding the case gives more credence to the cycle of violence hypothesis than it deserves.

In assessing the contribution of genetics to antisocial tendencies, several points warrant emphasis. First, adoptive studies of criminality and related behaviors speak only to relative degrees of risk. Even among high-risk youngsters, only a small proportion actually run afoul of the law. In that sense, heredity is never destiny. Second, children who are, let's say, unusually destructive do not inherit some mysterious criminal gene that impels them to act badly. What they inherit is a confluence of physical and psychological characteristics that make delinquency and criminal activity more probable (and profitable). For boys, this usually includes a muscular build, fearlessness, aggressivity, impulsivity, thrill-seeking, and, not infrequently, mental dullness (Lykken, 1995). However, as with other assemblages of characteristics, just a small variation in the genetic formula or exposure to just the right combination of life experiences can move the person onto a completely different pathway. That is why Lykken, writing about the antisocial personality, recommends that such youngsters be channeled, whenever possible, into challenging, self-esteem–building activities such as football and mountain climbing. "The potential psychopath," he writes, "is not 'born bad' but he is born difficult" (p. 84). One can, after all, emerge a hero or a villain with much the same (genetic) stuff (Gallagher, 1994).

GENE-ENVIRONMENT CORRELATIONS

In discussing genetics, it is almost impossible to avoid the trap of relying too exclusively on percentages and quotients, as if these told the whole story. Such mathematical recipes always convey an artificial and overly simplistic picture of how nature and nurture actually combine to shape a person's life trajectory. As Lykken (1995) notes, "The traditional argument over nature versus nurture is plainly fatuous, like asking whether the area of a rectangle is more dependent on its length or on its width" (p. 85). In Lykken's view, we must always be thinking in terms of nature via nurture rather than nature versus nurture.

The facts of people's existence depend on how their biological structure selects, shapes, and responds to particular environmental triggers (Rutter, 1997). Environmental responsivity is a biologically contextualized phenomenon. In other words, biochemistry always plays a role in determining what a child will notice and absorb. Sending children to ballet school, Little League, or art class does not ensure that they will emerge skilled dancers, ballplayers, or artists or that they will even develop an interest in such pursuits. A writing assignment that constitutes a turning point in the life of one child may simply bore or frustrate his or her classmates.

By the same token, experiences that strike observers as horrendous and universally devastating, such as being separated from one's parents in wartime, may have no lasting effects on some children. We have to recognize that organisms do not really respond to "objective events." They live in and respond to unique "effective environments," constructed on the basis of their changing needs and basic biological rhythms (Bouchard, 1994). That is why, as theoreticians and clinicians, we would do better to think of genetic endowment and environmental exigencies as simply being two sides of the same experiential coin (Efran, Lukens, & Lukens, 1990).

In dealing with such matters, behavior geneticists like to distinguish three different types of "gene-environment correlation"—active, evocative, and passive (Rutter, 1997). The first category refers to how people's biology induces them to shape their own environments. For example, children with natural athletic abilities can be expected to gravitate toward sports, while parents of budding musicians may find their children spontaneously tapping out tunes on the family piano. Often, such genetically primed urges seem to materialize out of thin air, requiring little in the way of external prompting or encouragement. As the father of a 6-year-old put it, "My daughter just suddenly began to breathe art. Now she wakes up and goes to bed with a pencil in her hand."

The concept of "evocative" gene-environment correlations refers to the unique responses people elicit from others. People continuously respond more or less automatically to the details of our physiognomy, temperament, body build, intelligence, and so on. Parents and teachers may set out to treat children equally, but it is an impossible task. Each child wittingly and unwittingly seduces and extracts particular reactions from others. As we implied earlier, even two youngsters brought up under one roof are actually living in two different households. The parental rebuke that deeply wounds one child may simply roll off the back of another. Of course, this is one reason that shared factors regularly fail to account for much of the variance in family studies.

The third category—passive gene-environment correlation—refers to how a child's experience is molded by being around genetically similar individuals. For instance, a musically gifted child with musical parents will automatically have access to opportunities and experiences—for instance, the piano we mentioned earlier—that other children miss. This type of gene-environment nexus is labeled "passive" because it evolves independently of a child's initiatives or a parent's conscious goals or plans. Of course, more often than not, passive, active, and evocative influences merge, creating a distinctive "fit" between a person's genetic makeup and the surrounding social ecology.

THE AVERAGE EXPECTABLE ENVIRONMENT

Geneticists use heritability ratios in their attempt to predict behavior under typical circumstances, where everything else can be assumed to be equal. When conditions diverge too much from this "average expectable environment," all bets are off (Scarr, 1992). Consider the case of phenylketonuria, the inherited metabolic disease that once doomed children to irreversible brain damage. Nowadays, through the use of a simple urine test and a special diet, such youngsters can be expected to develop more or less normally. In other words, a small environmental adjustment has completely changed the developmental odds, even though these children's genetic structure remains the same.

Similarly, although height is the quintessential example of a stable, inherited trait, height charts have to be revised every time nutritional habits improve. The larger point is this: Just because something has a high heritability quotient does not mean that environmental circumstances are irrelevant. As behavior geneticist Rutter (1997) notes:

> Heritability estimates describe only what is the case now and have no implications for what could, or would, happen if circumstances changed. Even very high heritability estimates do not imply that changes in the environment cannot bring about big effects. (p. 391)

For example, virtually all of us are born with a biologically "prepared" fear of snakes and spiders—an attribute that had considerable survival value in the wild (Seligman, 1971). However, this does not prevent us from overcoming our "natural" squeamishness toward such creatures and even adopting them as household pets.

Because heritability quotients are essentially ratios, changing either the numerator or the denominator changes the resulting estimate. Lykken (1995) explains it this way: "Heritability must increase when environmental variance decreases; when environmental differences are reduced, the total trait variance gets smaller, so the *same* [italics added] genetic effect becomes a larger fraction of the total" (p. 73). For example, the high figures usually cited for the heritability of intelligence are not just an indication of the power of genes. They also reflect the homogeneity of educational experiences for the students typically tested. Most, for instance, have daily access to the spoken and written word, to hours of television programming, and so on. If educational environments in our culture were more variable, heritability estimates for intelligence would decline. Thus, such figures are never absolutes. They are just estimates of the relative weight of genetic and environmental influences in specifiable contexts.

THE MOLECULAR PERSPECTIVE

Although twin and adoption studies enable behavior geneticists such as Bouchard and Lykken to quantify the effects of heredity, they are not designed to pinpoint the location of particular genes. Molecular genetic studies serve that purpose. Usually, there is a synergy between the two approaches: Behavior geneticists survey the general landscape, proposing domains in which genetic pay dirt might be found. Molecular geneticists then move in to excavate more deeply, exposing the details of the neurobiological substructure (Plomin, 1997).

Lately, molecular geneticists have made considerable progress by following leads suggested by behavior geneticists. This has been particularly true in tracking the genetic bases of temperament. For instance, two recent studies—one in the United States and one in Jerusalem—have illuminated individual differences in risk taking. These investigators found that people with the long form of a particular gene (D4DR on chromosome 11) are more likely than others to engage in hazardous or sensation-seeking behavior (Benjamin et al., 1996; Ebstein et al., 1996). Although the specific neurological mechanisms still need to be spelled out, dopamine chemistry in the brain is clearly implicated.

Dopamine is the neurotransmitter in the brain that some call the "pleasure chemical," partly because it has been associated with the "high" that results from drug use. In fact, as far as the nervous system is concerned, a cocaine high is a dopamine high (e.g., Volkow et al., 1997). By inhibiting the operation of a particular "transporter" molecule, cocaine allows dopamine levels to soar to dizzying heights. The long form of D4DR associated with increased risk taking does something similar but at much more modest levels. One working hypothesis concerning the sequence of events is that elevated dopamine levels raise a person's pain threshold, thereby tempting him or her to take more chances.

The related behavior genetics work shows strong linkages between risk taking and gene structure (Zuckerman, 1994). For instance, in a study of 442 pairs of twins, novelty-seeking scores correlated .59 for identical twins but only .21 for fraternal twins. Additional analyses suggested that about 58% of the overall variability in sensation seeking is due to genetics (Hamer & Copeland, 1998). Moreover, because the Minnesota group reports essentially the same figures for twins reared apart, it follows that sensation seeking is little affected by rearing practices.

Molecular researchers have also determined that short and long gene forms play a role in modulating levels of anxiety and neuroticism (Lesch et al., 1996). For instance, having the short form of certain transporter genes is associated with higher than average levels of fretfulness. In this case the affected neurotransmitter is serotonin, which—not surprisingly—happens to be the primary target for Prozac and a variety of the other popular antidepressants. The transporter gene in question helps regulate serotonin levels in the brain by governing the process of reuptake. Under conditions of inefficient reuptake, more serotonin is left free to roam around the system.

We should note that for both risk taking and neuroticism, the influence of any specific gene is relatively small (e.g., 10 percent for the gene linked to risk taking and 4 percent in the case of neuroticism). However, molecular geneticists expect to soon locate additional genes that contribute to each of these behavioral proclivities (4 or 5 in the case of risk-taking, and as many as 15 for neuroticism). When pooled, the total variance attributable to identified constitutional factors is thus expected to climb into the 40 percent to 60 percent range (Hamer & Copeland, 1998).

Interestingly, a set of twin studies at the Medical College of Virginia (Kendler, 1996; Kendler, Neale, Kessler, Heath, & Eaves, 1992) suggests strong similarities in the genetic structures of people who are anxious and those who are depressed. After studying about 4,000 twins, the Virginia team reported that both anxiety and depression are 33 percent to 46 percent heritable. This accords well with previous findings. However, they also found an almost 100 percent overlap in the heritability of these conditions—that is, people with either symptom have essentially the same gene pattern. At least at the genetic level, the conditions appear to be "kissing cousins" (Roy et al., 1995). This agrees with the growing evidence for the comorbidity of anxiety and depression (e.g., Regier, Rae, Narrow, Kaelber, & Schatzberg, 1998; Sartorius, Uestuen, Lecrubier, & Wittchen, 1996) and helps account for the vexation clinicians often experience in attempting to disentangle these syndromes (Barbee, 1998).

HAPPY CAMPERS AND GRUMPY OLD MEN

Happiness was the subject of a John Stossel television special on the ABC network. In his documentary, Stossel dramatically demonstrated the difference between children who seemed continuously bubbly, interested, and responsive, and those—videotaped in the same play environment—who appeared sullen and disengaged. Such contrasts are quite familiar to anyone who has taught nursery school or who has spent any time interacting with groups of children. Stossel's broadcast correctly emphasized that such basic temperamental differences are due more to genetic endowment than to particular life circumstances—they tend to be lifelong dispositions. A child's play behavior at 4 years of age is predictable from measurements made as early as when the child is 4 months old (Fox, Schmidt, Calkins, Rubin, & Coplan, 1996). Resilience, too, is a trait that generally makes an early appearance and remains relatively fixed throughout life (Butler, 1997). Children classified as resilient by researchers—and followed into adulthood—were typically described by their mothers as having been "active, cuddly, and good-natured" (p. 26) babies.

Moods in adulthood and old age have also been shown to be predictable on the basis of earlier, stable personality dispositions (e.g., Costa & McCrae, 1990). Researcher Charles Emery and his colleagues (Emery, Huppert, & Schein, 1996) studied a sample of 3,000 British citizens and found that people's neuroticism scores were good indications of whether they would be content or distressed in their twilight years. Even gerontologists are now urging that we rid ourselves of the stereotypic notion that grouchiness is a symptom of aging. They maintain that grumps are born, not made. In other words, grumpy old men are likely to be grumpy young men who have gotten older (Goleman, 1987; Rybash, Roodin, & Hoyer, 1995).

The implications of the temperament literature are that genetic factors make up at least 50 percent of a person's characteristic mood level. However, when moods such as contentment are sampled on a number of different occasions (thereby improving the reliability of the measurement), the heritability figure goes still higher, jumping to a whopping 80 percent (Lykken & Tellegen, 1996). This has led molecular biologist Dean Hamer of the National Cancer Institute to conclude that only 2 percent to 3 percent of our general demeanor can be attributed to specific environmental triggers (Hamer & Copeland, 1998). Even major life perturbations seem to affect a person's emotional outlook only briefly, typically for 3 months or less, and rarely for more than a year. Researchers Edward and Carol Diener report that following a serious illness or the loss of a relationship, people generally rebound relatively quickly to their characteristic emotional set points (Goleman, 1996). In other words, even winning the lottery will not ensure a satisfying life. The worriers among the contest winners will soon find new—perhaps more expensive—problems to fret about.

Evidence about the stability of mood has been quite consistent across laboratories, research methods, and study populations. For example, David Lykken and Auke Tellegen of the Center for Twin and Adoption Research at the University of Minnesota report that identical twins reared apart have very similar satisfaction levels on any given occasion, the correlation between their scores being about .53 (Lykken, 1997). When measured over longer time periods, their mood synchronies are reported to be even more striking. For instance, a twin's current level of well-being can be successfully predicted using information that had been collected a decade earlier from his or her twin. This cross-twin, cross-time correlation (.54) is the maximum that can be expected given the reliability of the measuring instruments. Furthermore, such predictions are more accurate than any based on the person's contemporary social, educational, economic, intellectual, or marital circumstances. In contrast, fraternal twins—even if reared together—show virtually no such correspondence in mood.

THE ROOTS OF INTROVERSION

Thanks to 30 years of careful and persistent research by Harvard developmentalist Jerome Kagan (1994), shyness or social reticence is a temperamental trait that has been well studied. Kagan writes that about 15 percent of children display a long-term pattern of inhibition that not only includes unusual fears, phobias, and risk avoidance but also strong heart-rate reactivity to any form of psychological intrusion. Many such individuals turn out to have light blue eyes, an ectomorphic body type, and atopic allergies—that is, allergic reactions related to hereditary hypersensitivities. At the other extreme are the 15 percent of youngsters who tend to be unflappable and outgoing. Sixty percent of those youngsters have dark eyes and the kinds of broad faces and mesomorphic body builds that fit some of our stereotypes. These are the children who are likely to run up and greet a stranger or to daringly speed down the hill on their new bicycle. Like most of us who were reared as radical environmentalists, Kagan was initially reluctant to accept the evidence that biological determinants held so much sway over these central behavioral patterns. However, as he told *Atlantic*

Monthly, "I was dragged kicking and screaming by my data to acknowledge that temperament is more powerful than I thought and wish to believe. . . . That's where I am, not out of prejudice but out of realism" (Gallagher, 1994, p. 42). Kagan's pioneering investigations of social caution have now been replicated and extended by others. For example, Hamer and Copeland (1998) report on a large-scale twin study at the Institute for Behavior Genetics at Boulder, Colorado, that attributes fully 60 percent of inhibited behavior in infants to heredity. Moreover, the figure rises to between 70 percent and 90 percent if one solely considers children who are at the extremes of the introversion-extraversion dimension.

DIRTY PHENOTYPES

Compared to their successes in the temperament domain, molecular researchers have generally struck out in their attempts to track down the particular genetic determinants of major psychiatric syndromes such as schizophrenia and bipolar disorder. At this writing, scores of promising hunches have gone exactly nowhere. One recent hypothesis is that there is a link between schizophrenia and a gene on the upper arm of chromosome 6 (Angier, 1995c). However, few are optimistic that this claim will hold up any better than any previous leads.

It is not that anyone doubts that schizophrenia and other such disorders have genetic components. Concordance rates for schizophrenia are estimated to be about 48 percent for identical twins and 17 percent for fraternals (Matthysse, Levy, Kagan, & Benes, 1996). Put another way, the risk to a monozygotic co-twin is roughly 50 times greater than for an average citizen (Rose, 1997). Moreover, children of schizophrenic parents are just as likely to develop the disorder even if raised in other homes. By the same token, there is no increased risk of psychosis for children raised by a psychotic individual unless the child's biological parents were psychotic (Wender, Rosenthal, Kety, Schulsinger, & Welner, 1974). Bipolar disorder also has notable concordance rates. An identical twin's chances of developing the disorder increase 40-fold if he or she has an afflicted twin (Hamer & Copeland, 1998). In a study of mood disorder concordance, the identical twin of a person with bipolar disorder was similarly diagnosed 63 percent of the time. Of the remaining group, 17 percent showed evidence of major depression (but without mania) and an additional 17 percent appeared to have at least some indicators of mood abnormality. That leaves only 3 percent who could be said to be symptom free (Bertelsen, Harvald, & Hauge, 1977).

Establishing heritability in such disorders is a snap compared to isolating the culpable genes or mechanisms. In fact, some argue that the search for specific genetic underpinnings for these kinds of complex syndromes is a fool's errand. First, there are vexing diagnostic issues. For instance, should researchers consider schizophrenia a single entity (with a specific etiology), or is it really a family of conditions with multiple causes? Even if one adopts the single-entity approach, what diagnostic tool is precise enough to enable researchers to assemble a reliable sample? Unfortunately, fuzzy diagnostic criteria jinx a molecular search from the outset, virtually guaranteeing inconclusive results.

Geneticists consider disorders like schizophrenia "dirty phenotypes"; that is, because it can take so many different forms, it is difficult to unearth an underlying genetic commonality (Herbert, 1997). Alcoholism is another example of a dirty phenotype, and it too has proven difficult to research. Generally, the biological children of alcoholics have a four times higher than average risk of becoming addicted, even if they are separated at birth from their biological parents (Goodwin, Schulsinger, Hermansen, Guze, & Winokur, 1973;

Goodwin et al., 1974). Furthermore, children lacking a genetic predisposition for alcoholism seem able to escape addiction even when reared among alcoholics.

Research on alcoholism has been complicated by the fact that people misuse liquor in all sorts of ways and for all sorts of reasons. Therefore, findings discovered in one study and with one population often fail to be replicated in another. In an attempt to lift the haze, Cloninger (1987) has proposed distinguishing between Type I and Type II alcoholism. Type II drinking begins early, is predominantly a male phenomenon, and generally fits the public stereotype of the mean-spirited drunkard out on a binge or staggering back after a barroom brawl. On the other hand, the Type I pattern cuts across gender lines. Type I drinkers usually begin drinking in middle age and progress gradually, without manifesting the heavy drama of the Type II pattern. The Type II pattern tends to have a more certain genetic etiology. The heritability of an alcoholic predisposition in Type II drinkers is said to be as high as 90 percent, at least for men (Nathan, 1986).

Many researchers now take it for granted that mental illnesses involve many genes, all acting in concert. This makes the genetic sleuthing complicated enough. However, the complexity of the task is multiplied because certain genes have the power to affect how other genes operate. Some genes are even capable of being turned on or off by environmental triggers—events ranging from viral infections to sensory deprivation. In short, the nervous system has so much built-in plasticity that tracing even rudimentary causal chains can be a perilous undertaking. No wonder that deciphering aspects of the human genome has been "assigned," with high priority, to a new U.S. Defense Department supercomputer capable of handling 1,000 trillion operations per second. Again, remember that it is details about specific genes and mechanisms that are still foggy—the importance of the genetic connection is unquestionable. Both personality patterns and the majority of psychiatric illnesses have been shown to have distinct genetic roots.

WHERE DO WE GO FROM HERE?

Lykken observes that "the long night of radical environmentalism . . . is coming to an end" (p. 71). However, few of us have seriously begun incorporating a hereditary perspective into our theories of family development and psychotherapeutic practice. Both in the clinic and the laboratory, we continue to implicitly or explicitly blame parents for how their offspring turn out. We continue to base suppositions about child development on flawed socialization research. We continue to pathologize and search for fancy explanations for individual differences that are natural and legitimate, although not always convenient. We continue to concentrate on minor parenting differences while overlooking other potentially more significant sources of influence such as peer associations, sibling relationships, and community demographics.

Especially in the clinic, we continue to promise clients unrealistic temperament transformations. Let's face it: Bob Dole's dour disposition is simply not going to metamorphose into Bill Clinton's crowd-pleasing affability any time soon, no matter how many therapeutic experts he decides to consult. Actually, to the extent that people's basic dispositions change after childhood, it is virtually always in the direction of their becoming more and more like their blood relatives (Bouchard et al., 1990). Researcher John Gunderson notes that "temperamental heredity is most fully expressed in maturity" (cited in Gallagher, 1996, p. 196). The phenomenon is perhaps best captured in that familiar but woeful refrain, "My god, I'm turning into my parents." For better or worse, as people age, the influence of their individualistic experiences tends to pale in comparison to what science writer Winifred Gallagher has called "the whisperings of neurotransmitters" (1994, p. 43).

Nevertheless, granting basic biology its due does not require jettisoning our interest in environmental analysis or abandoning our confidence in the value of therapeutic conversation. Although "personality can't be totally transformed," admits science writer Winifred Gallagher (1996), "it can be renovated" (p. 177). In fact, the findings of the new genetics open additional possibilities for therapists willing to explore the intriguing complexities of gene-environment interactions and correlations (Efran et al., 1998). After all, genes do not produce effects in an environmental vacuum any more than viruses cause illnesses in the absence of a suitable host. As psychologist Howard Gardner (1995) reminds us, although "genes regulate all human behavior . . . no form of behavior will emerge without the appropriate environmental triggers or supports" (p. 73). Thus, the job of both family researchers and clinicians is to understand more about the limits of biology and help people design lives that take full advantage of their internal and external worlds. In this regard, we have begun thinking of ourselves as preaching a modified, biogenetic version of the traditional AA serenity prayer, urging family members to accept their fundamental character structures while maximizing their individuality and their opportunities.

We recall a sage high school football coach who counseled parents to "ride the horse in the direction it is going." Instead of trying to push each child to become the star quarterback, he suggested that parents work along with the parameters set by each youngster's distinct temperament and body build. He argued that some children were simply better suited to run track than to go out for football or wrestling. Similarly, clinicians and researchers would do well to avoid a one-size-fits-all mentality. We submit, along with Chess and Thomas (1996), that some children are born to be rambunctious hellions while others are innately hesitant and reserved. However, every style has advantages that can be cultivated and channeled.

Lykken (1995) contends that "it is no longer intellectually respectable or scientifically acceptable to offer interpretations of important human psychological phenomena that leave genetic influences out of account" (p. 86). Moreover, as paleontologist Stephen J. Gould (1998) warns, "We will never get very far, either in our moral deliberations or our scientific inquiries, if we disregard genuine facts because we dislike their implications" (p. 72). As the millennium approaches, the family field needs to revisit the role of genetics in everyday life and family pathology. Under the aegis of radical environmentalism, genetic components were shunned the way families sometimes exile an unwanted child. It is time to arrange a reconciliation.

REFERENCES

Adler, T. (1992, December). Violence research comes under attack. *APA Monitor, 23*(12), 18.

Angier, N. (1995a, September 19). Disputed meeting to ask if crime has genetic roots. *The New York Times,* pp. B5, B9.

Angier, N. (1995b, September 26). At conference on links of violence to heredity, a calm after the storm. *The New York Times,* p. C8.

Angier, N. (1995c, October 31). Gene hunters pursue elusive and complex traits of mind. *The New York Times,* pp. B5, B7.

Angier, N. (1996, November 29). People haunted by anxiety appear to be short on a gene. *The New York Times,* pp. A1, B17.

Bandura, A., & Walters, R. A. (1963). *Social learning and personality development.* New York: Holt, Rinehart & Winston.

Barbee, J. G. (1998). Mixed symptoms and syndromes of anxiety and depression: Diagnostic, prognostic, and etiologic issues. *Annals of Clinical Psychiatry, 10,* 15–29.

Bateson, G., Jackson, D. D., Haley, J., & Weakland, J. H. (1956). Toward a theory of schizophrenia. *Behavioral Science, 1,* 251–264.

Benjamin, J., Li, L., Patterson, C., Greenberg, B. D., Murphy, D. L., & Hamer, D. H. (1996). Population and familial association between the D4 dopamine receptor gene and measures of novelty seeking. *Nature Genetics, 12,* 81–84.

Bertelsen, A., Harvald, B., & Hauge, M. (1977). A Danish twin study of manic-depressive disorders. *British Journal of Psychiatry, 130,* 330–351.

Bohman, M. (1996). Predisposition to criminality: Swedish adoption studies in retrospect. In G. R. Bock & J. A. Goode (Eds.), *Genetics of criminal and antisocial behavior* (pp. 99–114). Chichester, England: Wiley.

Bouchard, T. J., Jr. (1994, June). Genes, environment, and personality. *Science, 264*(5166), 1700–1701.

Bouchard, T. J., Jr. (1997, May). Inheritance of authoritarianism and other social attitudes. In S. Scarr (Chair), *Genetics and personality: The search for why we think, act, and feel the way we do.* Presidential symposium conducted at the 9th Annual Convention of the American Psychological Society, Washington, DC.

Bouchard, T. J., Jr., Lykken, D. T., McGue, M., Segal, N. L., & Tellegen, A. (1990, October). Sources of human psychological differences: The Minnesota study of twins reared apart. *Science, 250*(4978), 223–228.

Bouchard, T. J., Jr., & Propping, P. (1993). *Twins as a tool of behavioral genetics: Report of the Dahlem workshop on what are the mechanisms mediating the genetic and environmental determinants of behavior?* Chichester, England: Wiley.

Bowlby, J. (1969). *Attachment and loss: Vol. 1. Attachment.* New York: Basic Books.

Bowlby, J. (1988). *A secure base: Parent-child attachment and healthy human development.* New York: Basic Books.

Buck v. Bell, 274 U.S. 200, 207, 47 S.Ct. 584, 585 (1927) (Oliver Wendell Holmes).

Butler, K. (1997, March-April). The anatomy of resilience. *The Family Therapy Networker, 21*(2), 22–31.

Cadoret, R. J., Yates, W. R., Troughton, E., Woodworth, G., & Stewart, M. A. (1995). Gene-environment interaction in the genesis of aggressivity and conduct disorders. *Archives of General Psychiatry, 52,* 916–924.

Chess, S., & Thomas, A. (1996). *Temperament: Theory and practice.* New York: Brunner/Mazel.

Cloninger, C. R. (1987, April 24). Neurogenetic adaptive mechanisms in alcoholism. *Science, 236*(4800), 410–416.

Costa, P. T., & McCrae, R. R. (1990). *Personality in adulthood.* New York: Guilford Press.

Cushman, P. (1995). *Constructing the self, constructing America.* Reading, MA: Addison-Wesley.

Dawes, R. M. (1994). *House of cards: Psychology and psychotherapy built on myth.* New York: The Free Press.

Dollard, J., & Miller, N. E. (1950). *Personality and psychotherapy: An analysis in terms of learning, thinking, culture.* New York: McGraw-Hill.

Eaves, L. J., Eysenck, H. J., & Martin, N. G. (1989). *Genes, culture and personality.* London: Academic Press.

Ebstein, R. P., Novick, O., Umansky, R., Priel, B., Osher, Y., Blaine, D., Bennett, E. R., Nemanov, L., Katz, M., & Belmaker, R. H. (1996). Dopamine D4 receptor (DRD4) exon III polymorphism associated with the human trait of novely seeking. *Nature Genetics, 12,* 78–80.

Efran, J. S., Greene, M. A., & Gordon, D. E. (1998). Lessons of the new genetics. *The Family Therapy Networker, 22*(2), 26–32, 35–41.

Efran, J. S., Lukens, M. D., & Lukens, R. J. (1990). *Language, structure, and change: Frameworks of meaning in psychotherapy.* New York: W. W. Norton.

Emery, C. F., Huppert, F. A., & Schein, R. L. (1996). Health and personality predictors of psychological functioning in a 7-year longitudinal study. *Personality & Individual Differences, 20*(5), 567–573.

Feldman, C. M. (1997). Childhood precursors of adult interpartner violence. *Clinical Psychology: Science and Practice, 4,* 307–334.

Finkel, D., Wille, D. E., & Matheny, A. P., Jr. (1998). Preliminary results from a twin study of infant-caregiver attachment. *Behavior Genetics, 28,* 1–8.

Fox, N. A., Kimmerly, N. L., & Schafer, W. D. (1991). Attachment to mother/attachment to father: A meta-analysis. *Child Development, 62,* 210–225.

Fox, N. A., Schmidt, L. A., Calkins, S. D., Rubin, K. H., & Coplan, R. J. (1996) The role of frontal activation in the regulation and dysregulation of social behavior during the preschool years. *Development and Psychopathology, 8,* 89–102.

Gallagher, W. (1994, September). How we become what we are. *The Atlantic Monthly,* pp. 39–55.

Gallagher, W. (1996). *I.D.: How heredity and experience make you who you are.* New York: Random House.

Gardner, H. (1995, Winter). Cracking open the IQ box. *The American Prospect, 20,* 71–80.

Goleman, D. (1987, March 24). Personality: Major traits found stable through life. *The New York Times,* pp. C1, C14.

Goleman, D. (1996, July 16). Forget money; nothing can buy happiness, some researchers say. *The New York Times,* p. C1.

Goodwin, D. W., Schulsinger, F., Hermansen, L., Guze, S. B., & Winokur, G. (1973). Alcohol problems in adoptees raised apart from alcoholic biological parents. *Archives of General Psychiatry, 28,* 238–243.

Goodwin, D. W., Schulsinger, F., Miller, N., Hermansen, L., Winokur, G., & Guze, S. B. (1974). Drinking problems in adopted and nonadopted sons of alcoholics. *Archives of General Psychiatry, 31,* 164–169.

Gould, S. J. (1998, March). The internal brand of the scarlet. *Natural History,* 22–25, 70–78.

Hamer, D., & Copeland, P. (1998). *Living with our genes: Why they matter more than you think.* New York: Doubleday.

Harris, J. R. (1998). *The nurture assumption: Why children turn out the way they do.* New York: Free Press.

Hasian, M. A., Jr. (1996). *The rhetoric of eugenics in Anglo-American thought.* Athens, GA: University of Georgia Press.

Herbert, W. (1997, April 21). Politics of biology: How the nature vs. nurture debate shapes public policy—and our view of ourselves. *U.S. News & World Report,* pp. 72–74, 77–80.

Herrnstein, R. J., & Murray, C. (1994). *The Bell Curve: Intelligence and class structure in American life.* New York: Free Press.

Hetherington, E. M., Reiss, D., & Plomin, R. (Eds.). (1994). *Separate social worlds of siblings: The impact of nonshared environment on development.* Hillsdale, NJ: Erlbaum.

Hooley, J. (1998). Expressed emotion and psychiatric illness: From empirical data to clinical practice. *Behavior Therapy, 29,* 631–646.

Kagan, J. (1994). *Galen's prophecy: Temperament in human nature.* New York: Basic Books.

Kagan, J., Kearsley, R. B., & Zelazo, P. R. (1978). *Infancy: Its place in human development.* Cambridge, MA: Harvard University Press.

Kagan, J., & Klein, R. E. (1973). Cross-cultural perspectives on early development. *American Psychologist, 28,* 947–961.

Kendler, K. S. (1996). Major depression and generalised anxiety disorder: Same genes, (partly) different environments—revisited. *British Journal of Psychiatry, 168*(Suppl. 30), 68–75.

Kendler, K. S., Neale, M. C., Kessler, R. C., Heath, A. C., & Eaves, L. J. (1992). Major depression and generalized anxiety disorder: Same genes (partly) different environments? *Archives of General Psychiatry, 49,* 716–722.

Lamb, M. E. (1987). Predictive implications of individual differences in attachment. *Journal of Consulting and Clinical Psychology, 55,* 817–824.

Lenior, M. E., Linszen, D. H., & Dingemans, P. M. A. J. (1998, January). The association between parental expressed emotion and psychotic relapse: Applying a quantitative measure for expressed emotion. *International Clinical Psychopharmacology, 13*(Suppl. 1), S81–S87.

Lesch, K., Bengel, D., Heils, A., Sabol, S. Z., Greenberg, B. D., Petri, S., Benjamin, J., Muller, C. R., Hamer, D. H., & Murphy, D. L. (1996, November). Association of anxiety-related traits with a polymorphism in the serotonin transporter gene regulatory region. *Science, 274*(5292), 1527–1531.

Liem, J. H. (1980). Family studies of schizophrenia: An update and commentary. *Schizophrenia Bulletin, 6,* 429–455.

Lounsberry, E. (1997a, May 18). In Kanka case, jury says guilty. *Philadelphia Inquirer,* pp. A1, A5.

Lounsberry, E. (1997b, June 18). Brother's testimony called into question. *Philadelphia Inquirer,* p. B2.

Lounsberry, E. (1997c, June 1). In the Kanka case, next test is on killer. *Philadelphia Inquirer,* p. A15.

Lounsberry, E. (1997d, June 22). No simple answers in treating pedophilia. *Philadelphia Inquirer,* pp. B1, B5.

Lykken, D. T. (1995). *The antisocial personality.* Hillsdale, NJ: Erlbaum.

Lykken, D. T. (1997, May). Happy is as happy does. In S. Scarr (Chair), *Genetics and personality: The search for why we think, act, and feel the way we do.* Presidential symposium conducted at the 9th Annual Convention of the American Psychological Society, Washington, DC.

Lykken, D. T., & Tellegen, A. (1996). Happiness is a stochastic phenomenon. *Psychological Science, 7*(3), 186–189.

Matthysse, S., Levy, D. L., Kagan, J., & Benes, F. M. (Eds.) (1996). *Psychopathology: The evolving science of mental disorder.* New York: Cambridge University Press.

McGue, M., & Lykken, D. T. (1992). Genetic influence on risk of divorce. *Psychological Science, 3,* 368–373.

McIntosh, H. (1998, November). Neuroimaging tools offer new ways to study autism. *APA Monitor, 29*(11), 15.

Mednick, S. A., & Gabrielli, W. F., Jr., & Hutchings, B. (1984, May). Genetic influences in criminal convictions: Evidence from an adoption cohort. *Science, 224*(4651), 891–893.

Nasrallah, H. A., & Pettegrew, J. W. (1995). *NMR spectroscopy in psychiatric brain disorders.* Washington, DC: American Psychiatric Press.

Nathan, P. E. (1986). Some implications of recent biological findings for the behavioral treatment of alcoholism. *The Behavior Therapist, 8,* 159–161.

NICHD Early Child Care Research Network. (1997). The effects of infant child care on infant-mother attachment security: Results of the NICHD study of early child care. *Child Development, 68,* 860–879.

Pinker, S. (1997). *How the mind works.* New York: W.W. Norton.

Plomin, R. (1997, May). Search for specific genes in personality. In S. Scarr (Chair), *Genetics and personality: The search for why we think, act, and feel the way we do.* Presidential symposium conducted at the 9th Annual Convention of the American Psychological Society, Washington, DC.

Redding, R. E. (1998). Bias without measure on The Bell Curve [Review of the book *Measured lies: The Bell Curve examined*]. *Contemporary Psychology, 43,* 748–750.

Regier, D. A., Rae, D. S., Narrow, W. E., Kaelber, C. T., & Schatzberg, A. F. (1998). Prevalence of anxiety disorders and their comorbidity with mood and addictive disorders. *British Journal of Psychiatry, 173*(Suppl. 34), 24–28.

Rose, R. J. (1997). Psychiatric genetics, science, and society. [Review of the book *Genetics and mental illness: Evolving issues for research and society*]. *Contemporary Psychology, 42,* 978–981.

Rowe, D. C. (1994). *The limits of family influence: Genes, experience, and behavior.* New York: Guilford Press.

Roy, M., Neale, M. C., Pedersen, N. L., Mathe, A. A., & Kendzer, K. S. (1995). A twin study of generalized anxiety disorder and major depression. *Psychological Medicine, 25,* 1037–1049.

Rushton, J. P. (1995). *Race, evolution, and behavior: A Life History Perspective.* New Brunswick, NJ: Transaction.

Rutter, M. L. (1997). Nature-nurture integration: The example of antisocial behavior. *American Psychologist, 52,* 390–398.

Rybash, J. M., Roodin, P. A., & Hoyer, W. A. (1995). *Adult development and aging* (3rd ed.). Chicago: Brown & Benchmark.

Sartorius, N., Uestuen, T. B., Lecrubier, Y., & Wittchen, H. (1996). Depression comorbid with anxiety: Results from the WHO study on "psychological disorders in primary health care." *British Journal of Psychiatry, 168* (Suppl. 30), 38–43.

Scarr, S. (1992). Developmental theories for the 1990s: Development and individual differences. *Child Development, 63,* 1–19.

Scarr, S. (1996). Best of human behavior genetics [Review of the book *Twins as a tool of behavioral genetics*]. *Contemporary Psychology, 41,* 149–150.

Scarr, S. (1997). Why child care has so little impact on most children's development. *Current Directions in Psychological Science, 6,* 143–148.

Scarr, S., & Weinberg, R. A. (1978). The influence of "family background" on intellectual attainment. *American Sociological Review, 43,* 674–692.

Seligman, M. E. P. (1971). Preparedness and phobias. *Behavior Therapy, 2,* 307–320.

Seligman, M. E. P. (1993). *What you can change and what you can't: The complete guide to successful self-improvement.* New York: Fawcett Columbine.

Seligman, M. E. P. (1995, August 19). Child-adult links. *Network of the Society for the Science of Clinical Practice* [sscpnet@bailey.psych.nwu.edu], pp. 1–3.

Slutske, W. S., Heath, A. C., Dinwiddie, S. H., Madden, P. A. F., Bucholz, K. K., Dunne, M. P., Statham, D. J., & Martin, N. G. (1997). Modeling genetic and environmental influences in the etiology of conduct disorder: A study of 2,682 adult twin pairs. *Journal of Abnormal Psychology, 106,* 266–279.

Sluzki, C. E., & Ransom, D. C. (Eds.). (1976). *Double Bind: The foundation of the communication approach to the family.* New York: Grune & Stratton.

Stoff, D. M., Breiling, J., & Maser, J. D. (Eds.). (1997). *Handbook of antisocial behavior.* New York: Wiley.

Sullivan, H. S. (1953). *The interpersonal theory of psychiatry* (Eds. H. S. Perry & M. L. Gawel). New York: W.W. Norton.

Tellegen, A., Lykken, D. T., Bouchard, T. J., Wilcox, K. J., Segal, N. L., & Rich, S. (1988). Personality similarity in twins reared apart and together. *Journal of Personality & Social Psychology, 54,* 1031–1039.

Volkow, N. D., Wang, G.-J., Fischman, M. W., Foltin, R. W., Fowler, I. S., Abumrad, N. N., Vitkum, S., Logan, J., Gatley, S. J., Pappas, N., Hitzemann, R., & Shea, C. E. (1997, April). Relationship between subjective effects of cocaine and dopamine transporter occupancy. *Nature, 386*(6627), 827–830.

Wade, N. (1998a, March 10). The struggle to decipher human genes. *The New York Times,* pp. F1, F5.

Wade, N. (1998b, May 17). International gene project gets life. *The New York Times,* p. 20.

Wade, N. (1998c, September 15). In genome race, government vows to move up finish. *The New York Times,* p. F3.

Wallerstein, J. S., & Blakeslee, S. (1989). *Second chances: Men, women, and children a decade after divorce.* New York: Ticknor & Fields.

Watson, P. (1981). *Twins: An uncanny relationship?* New York: The Viking Press.

Weiss, R. (1995, October 3). Are we more than the sum of our genes? *Washington Post Health,* pp. 10–12.

Wender, P. H., Rosenthal, D., Kety, S. S., Schulsinger, F., & Welner, J. (1974). Crossfostering: A research strategy for clarifying the role of genetic and experiential factors in the etiology of schizophrenia. *Archives of General Psychiatry, 30,* 121–128.

Widom, C. S. (1989, April). The cycle of violence. *Science, 244*(4901), 160–166.

Wilson, E. O. (1975). *Sociobiology: The new synthesis.* Cambridge, MA: Harvard University Press.

Wolfe, T. (1996, December 2). Sorry, but your soul just died. *Forbes ASAP,* pp. 211–223.

Wright, L. (1997). *Twins: And what they tell us about who we are.* New York: John Wiley & Sons.

Wright, R. (1994). *The moral animal: The new science of evolutionary psychology.* New York: Pantheon Books.

Wright, W. (1998). *Born that way: Genes, behavior, personality.* New York: Alfred A. Knopf.

Zuckerman, M. (1994). *Behavioral expressions and biosocial bases of sensation seeking.* New York: Cambridge University Press.

CHAPTER 4

Human Development as a Process of Meaning Making and Reality Construction

Dorothy S. Becvar

THIS CHAPTER CONSIDERS several streams of thought within the field of human development that are part of a shift away from a belief in a knowable world that exists separate from an observer and its corollary that there are universal human properties and laws that may be discovered and categorized. Described as a postmodern perspective, this shift in beliefs permeates not only the sciences but the fields of art, literature, and philosophy, among others. Within the behavioral sciences, a focus on the social and linguistic construction of a perspectival reality has spawned a variety of approaches to human development that emphasize subjectivity, reflexivity, and individual interpretation. Consistent with such an emphasis, therapists are encouraged to move into the conversational domain and to be sensitive to the individual differences and uniqueness of their clients. There is also a heightened awareness of the shared expertise of everyone involved. The influence of the larger social context is acknowledged, and an effort is made to understand the relational creation of identities. Therapy, like human development, is understood to be a process of human construction and intersubjective meaning-making.

BACKGROUND AND HISTORICAL CONTEXT

The kinds of approaches considered in this chapter are an outgrowth of a critique of psychology in general, and of developmental psychology in particular, which emerged during the second half of the twentieth century. According to Ingleby (1986), three main themes characterized this critique, including the propagation of "spurious norms of development" (p. 299), the "individualism of psychology" (p. 299), and "the reification of meaningful, purposive activity in a deterministic framework" (p. 300). In other words, psychologists were challenged to reconsider the notions that there were universal laws of human development that could be discovered through use of the scientific method; that the appropriate targets of study were individual characteristics rather than the person in context; and that the utilization of a deterministic framework that denied agency was appropriate given "the fact that growing up was not simply a matter of acquiring skills, but the site of complex political tensions between children, parents and the state" (p. 300).

Although such challenges were part of a more generalized critique of the modernist focus on "universal meta-narratives" (Kvale, 1992, p. 34), or on what has been called the "transcendent criterion of the correct" (Gergen, 1991, p. 111), it was only gradually that what is now known as a postmodern perspective evolved. However, building on the work of environmentalists in the field, psychologists began to pay more attention to social factors, acknowledging that human development can take many forms and that our ideas about childhood, maturity, and their various characteristics are culturally bound. Thus, behaviorism initially was succeeded by humanism and a resurgence of cognitive approaches such as those of Chomsky, who focused on the innate language acquisition devices of infants (Bruner, 1990a) and of Piaget, whose concern was cognitive development through a series of invariant stages (Bruner, 1992). However, such approaches continued to neglect the social dimensions of language and cognition:

> For Chomsky, the "deep structures" underlying cognition were not social artifacts, but inbuilt mechanisms. Piaget rejected such a rationalistic approach, seeing the structures as constructed but by the individual and in a uniform way, which had to do with the physical, not the social order. . . . The initial thrust of cognitive developmental psychology, therefore, was away from rather than towards, the study of mind-in-context. (Ingleby, 1986, p. 303)

Ecologically concerned researchers thus focused continuing criticism on the lack of contextual awareness in the experimental process out of which theories were created. For example, according to Bronfenbrenner (1979, p. 19), "much of developmental psychology as it now exists, is the science of the strange behavior of children in strange situations with strange adults for the briefest possible periods of time." Along the same lines but in a more scathing critique, Newman and Holzman (1996) describe the emphasis on scientific study as follows:

> The laboratory experiment is a *form of life* or, more accurately, a *form of alienation*. People "behaving like organisms" is a form or life/form of alienation, albeit usually a nondevelopmental one. From this perspective, the emptiness of psychology's knowledge claims is apparent; they violate psychology's own rules of investigation. (p. 81)

Challenges also were forthcoming from those who, like Bruner (1976), were investigating the social foundations of language. Others raised questions about the limits of theories (e.g., those of Erikson, Piaget, and Kohlberg), which describe development as proceeding through a series of invariant stages. Steenbarger (1991) notes three limitations of such stage theories that have been identified in the literature, including the inability of a linear approach to capture human development in all of its complexity; the inadequacy of invariant sequences to accommodate the influence of unique situations; and, by virtue of a belief in such invariant sequences, the inclusion of problematic value premises.

The dilemma, according to Kvale (1992), was the continuation of "the cognivist tyranny of the rule" (p. 50) and the need to know "why." The shift to a postmodern perspective, on the other hand, brought with it a view of individuals as historically and culturally rooted, with an emphasis on the local context as well as on the social construction of reality. Knowledge, from this perspective, is understood to be ambiguous and perspectival and there is acknowledgment of the validity of many ways of knowing. The object of study becomes conversation, with an emphasis on relationship. Further, an attempt is made to understand human activity through knowledge of the cultural, social, and historical situation in which the activity occurs. The ramifications of such a view for clinicians is that, "Rather than uncovering and adjusting an essential self (which is the modernist project), postmodern therapy entertains and privileges the construction of multiple selves as emergent by-products of situated action—for both clients *and* therapists" (McNamee, 1996, p. 151). Within the field of psychology, Gergen (1992) summarizes many of the forces out of which a postmodern perspective continues to evolve:

> There is increasing talk about the problematic values inherent in psychological research. Critical psychologists question the individualistic and exploitative ideology underlying such inquiry; feminists question the androcentric biases inherent in theory and method. There is increasing talk of epistemology. Constructivists raise questions concerning the possibility of a world independent of the observer. Constructionists turn their attention to the social basis of what we take to be knowledge. There is increasing talk of alternative methodologies. Phenomenologists undertake new forms of qualitative research. Hermeneuticist (or interpretive) psychologists explore the possibilities of dialogic methodology. There is increasing concern with forms of human interdependence. Ecological psychologists search for concepts relating person and environment. Ethogenecists turn their attention from events within the head to the social rituals in which we are enmeshed. Discourse analysts move from the relationship of mind and language to language as a system of social interdependence. There is increasing concern with theoretical as opposed to empirical issues. (p. 17)

In the following section we provide an overview of the main categories by which researchers and clinicians who embrace a more postmodern perspective currently are attempting to understand and describe human development. Also included are some of the representative theorists taking each of these positions. However, it is important to be aware that there is much overlap between categories, which can only be so neatly divided for purposes of discussion.

PERSPECTIVES AND DEFINITIONS

CONSTRUCTIVISM

According to Aldridge (1993, p. 1242), "Constructivism is based on the idea that individuals create their own knowledge through interactions with others and the environment." This active, rather than reactive (Mascolo, Pollack, & Fischer, 1997), process of knowledge creation has been described as including the three basic features of proactive cognition, morphogenic nuclear structure, and self-organizing development (Mahoney, 1988), that is, participation by the knower in what is known is a fundamental assumption of constructivism. Further, how one construes reality is understood to be a function of one's basic structure, or mental and symbolic processes. And most importantly, "individual human systems organize themselves so as to protect and perpetuate their integrity and they develop via structural differentiations selected out of their trial-and-error variations" (Mahoney, 1988, p. 9).

While the existence of a "real" world "out there" is acknowledged, constructivists emphasize that it can be known only indirectly, through the basic categories, concepts, and other organizational processes of our minds (Mascolo et al., 1997). As a consequence, the search for the truth or validity of knowledge is replaced by an emphasis on the viability or utility of a particular perspective or set of beliefs. What is more, the focus of attention is on the individual and his or her private reality. Building on the work of Kant and Vaihinger, Jean Piaget created a constructivist foundation in the realm of human development with his studies of individual processes of knowing, or "the construction of mental schemata in response to challenging experience, and the eventual assimilation of experience to these newly constructed schemata" (Shultz & Mareschal, 1997, p. 565). And it was George Kelly (1955) who was one of the first to utilize a constructivist perspective in the area of personality theory and psychotherapy, noting that "individuals attend to recurring aspects of their experience and abstract salient perceived similarities and differences from among these events, fashioning categories or forging distinctions that he called personal constructs" (Neimeyer & Neimeyer, 1993a, p. 6). However, current theorists have extended the work of both these pioneers. For example, Mascolo and colleagues (1997) summarize their "epigenetic systems approach" as follows:

> Like Piaget's notion of equilibration, constructive epigenesis suggests that the individual is active in coordinating subsystems of activity into larger wholes. However, unlike Piaget, we argue for the inseparability and mutual interpenetration of the biogenetic, cognitive-behavioral, and sociocultural systems. The concept of constructive epigenesis is far more open-ended than the notion of equilibration, which places the major burden of development on processes that are universal, intrinsic, and autonomous to the individual. Because constructive epigenesis stresses the inseparability of the systems that create cognitive activity, this notion provides a framework for understanding alternative trajectories in development as a function of individual differences [in] biogenetic and sociocultural systems. This concept stands in opposition to views that predict universal sequences of stages that are incited by processes endogenous to the child. (pp. 45–46)

In the realm of psychotherapy, Polkinghorne (1995) has become one of the primary spokespersons for a constructivist perspective. However, in addition to paying attention to the development of the meaning-making structures of clients, he believes it is essential that therapists also focus on their own internal processes in order to avoid the "sedimentation and rigidification of concepts" that previously was considered only relative to the subjects under study. Also essential is the need to engage actively with clients in an effort to understand as well as create new meanings as a function of a shared languaging process. He writes, "Piaget's work alerts practitioners to being open to new meaning and to resisting the comfort that comes from believing that they have finally come to understand psychotherapy" (p. 277). Similarly, Valsiner (1996, p. 300) notes, "The mind is the constructor of our notions of development."

DEVELOPMENTAL CONSTRUCTIVISM

Those whose work comes under the heading of developmental constructivism view meaning-making in a life span developmental perspective, as a process of maturation that includes alternating periods of change and stability. Accordingly, this process involves a continual unfolding "whereby old forms of knowing give way to more comprehensive forms as the knower constructs more epistemologically powerful (inclusive, viable, integrated) ways of making sense of the world" (Lyddon & Alford, 1993, p. 32). Thus theorists expand their focus to include, for example, the complex dialectic between development and learning:

> Qualitative stages of development result from certain dynamic nonlinear interactions between the task's demand characteristics, the developmental state (state of maturation plus the products of prior learning), and the modes of problem solving (executive-driven dynamic syntheses) and/or learning that the subject can afford—modes that vary with the time available, the subject's motivation, and the presence or absence of human mediators. (Pascual-Leone, 1995, p. 346)

In a related view, Kegan (1982, 1994) describes development as a process focused on both knowing and being as the individual continually redefines his or her relationship to the world in increasingly more integrated and coherent ways. Of crucial importance to this process are holding environments, which act as a major influence on the developing person's self identity. Such holding environments, or "cultures of embeddedness" composed of family, peers, teachers, or other close personal relationships, act to confirm, contradict, or provide continuity as the person's beliefs about such issues as trust, power, and intimacy evolve and mature. Mental development occurs as subjective experience is transformed into objectively observable information. The challenges encountered along the way are a crucial factor relative to the individual's perception of his or her self–world relationship. According to Strand (1997, p. 327), the clinical ramifications of such a perspective include the fact that the way in which clients engage in the process of reality construction, "namely, the distinction between what is subject and what is object," will be an important factor in determining both the cultural issues perceived as problematic as well as the "nature of the solutions they are capable of generating."

RADICAL CONSTRUCTIVISM

According to Ernst von Glasersfeld (1984, p. 24) radical constructivism refers to "a theory of knowledge in which knowledge does not reflect an 'objective' ontological reality, but exclusively an ordering and organization of a world constituted by our experience." While an objective reality may exist, we have no way of knowing the degree to which our representations of it are more or less accurate. The possibility of arriving at a point at which reality, or truth, can be known in an absolute sense, therefore, is denied by this perspective. Consistent with the views of Maturana and Varela (1987), we can no longer think in terms of progress. Rather, we recognize that all that is possible are new coordinations as we interact together, or structurally couple, in the various consensual domains that we create with others in language.

As such views are translated into thinking about human development and clinical practice, the main issues are (1) acknowledging that each of us invents our particular reality, and (2) recognizing that we always have the option of creating it differently (Watzlawick, 1984). The crucial area of focus is thus the individual's personal epistemology, or belief system, and the recognition that the most problematic epistemologies are those that do not have a conscious awareness of themselves (Bateson, 1972). As part of this awareness, there is also acceptance of the idea that "psychiatric diagnoses are in the minds of the observers and are not valid summaries of characteristics displayed by the observed" (Rosenhan, 1984, p. 118).

We are all constructors of knowledge as well as of reality, both clients and clinicians. The issue is not so much what we know but how we know. Indeed,

> radical constructivism views the construction of new concepts, principles, and theories as a continuous process, leading to new questions or new ways to make and transform records, and hence new knowledge and value claims. . . . New concepts, principles, and/or theories can lead to more parsimonious explanations and perhaps better prediction or control of events. The key point is that there is no end point in time when truth will be known. (Novak, 1993, pp. 185–186)

NARRATIVE THEORY

Proponents of narrative theory assume the storied nature of all thought and the related idea that meaning construction occurs as a process of storytelling (Howard, 1991). Included in such notions is the belief that scientific theories, or stories, are no more valid than those of, for example, philosophy, literature, clinical wisdom, or religion. That is, we all create our reality as a function of our stories. As described by Mair (1988):

> Stories are habitations. We live in and through stories. They conjure worlds. We do not know the world other than as story world. Stories inform life. They hold us together and keep us apart. We inhabit the great stories of our culture. We live through stories. We are lived by the stories of our race and place. It is this enveloping and constituting function of stories that is especially important to sense more fully. We are, each of us, locations where the stories of our place and time become partially tellable. (p. 127)

Thus, "Developmental understanding of life issues can be gleaned from a personal life story" (Hoshmand, 1993, p. 180). However, critical to an understanding of narrative theory is acknowledgment of the importance of relationship, or the recognition that storytelling requires a listener as well as a narrator, both of whom participate, or share in the co-construction of the narrative (Tappan, 1992). Further, rather than seeing development as a prescriptive, normative concept, a narrative focus considers the process of reflecting upon and giving meaning to the events in one's life and, in that process, the rewriting of oneself. According to Bruner (1990b):

> The major activity of all human beings everywhere is to extract meaning from their encounters with the world. What is crucial about this process of creating meanings is that it affects what we do, what we believe, even how we feel. This is true both for our subjects and for us who study them. (p. 345)

Indeed, the ability of a narrative focus to include the affective dimension and "to bridge the gap between cognition, emotion, and action that has traditionally marked the study of human development" (Tappan, 1992, pp. 376–377) is considered to be one of its most important features.

In therapy, the use of a narrative perspective may be understood as "the development of useful meta-abstractions" (Vogel, 1994, p. 247), or stories about our stories. For Howard (1991), life is equated with "the stories we live by"; psychopathology is understood as "stories gone mad"; and psychotherapy consists of "exercises in story repair" (p. 194).

That is, through the creation of new understanding about the narratives and abstractions currently in use, stories are rewritten in such a way that new experiences become possible. The goal is the creation of a new sense of coherence on the part of the client as she or he reorganizes her or his sense of self.

SOCIAL CONSTRUCTIONISM

Examining the social basis of knowledge is the goal of those who espouse a social constructionist perspective. Various functions, such as memory, attitudes, thinking, and emotions, which were once considered to be found within the individual, or as intrapsychic processes, are viewed from this perspective as social processes, or as constituents of relationships (Gergen, 1996). According to a social constructionist perspective, "becoming a competent person, indeed becoming a person at all, is . . . the appropriation from a common public realm of whatever is needed to round out and inform the mind of the developing individual" (Harre, 1986, p. 290). That is, the sociocultural is the source from which the individual emerges (Martin & Sugarman, 1996).

Along with relationships, language is a crucial area of focus for the social constructionist. Rather than being a reporting device for our experience, or representationalism, language is understood as a defining framework. That is, we experience reality in and through language in terms of the prepackaged thoughts of our society, what McNamee and Gergen (1992, p. 1) have called "forestructures of understanding." In other words, each of us is born into and assimilates preexisting forms of language in a culturally created linguistic system. In the process of socialization we learn to speak in accepted ways and simultaneously to adopt the shared values and ideology of our language system. Thus, our words express the conventions, the symbols, the metaphors of our particular group, for we cannot speak in a language separate from that of our community (Becvar & Becvar, 2000). In other words, "perhaps all of the fine grain of human psychological functioning is a product of the language that a person has acquired" (Harre, 1986, p. 288).

From such a perspective we move to thinking about therapy as conversation (Anderson, 1997) consistent with the proposition that individual development is entirely constrained by the kinds of conversations and social relationships experienced in one's particular cultural context (Martin & Sugarman, 1996). Accordingly, "As merely a manifestation of conversations and social relations, especially as captured in language systems, individual agents dissolve into the dialogue and social roles in which they supposedly are created and compelled to participate" (p. 297). Thus the self gives way to an emphasis on the variety of relationships by means of which we understand ourselves, a phenomenon for which Gergen (1996, p. 139) has proposed the term *relational sublime.*

Many theorists espousing a social constructionist orientation, as well as each of the other variations on the postmodern theme discussed in this section, have articulated approaches to human development. As will be discussed in the following section, some of these newer approaches represent an explicit attempt to bridge some of the categories described above. Others are more concerned with specific aspects of development, including cognitive development, language development, moral development, and personality development, and thus may or may not include more than one category. While varying in the degree to which each is consistent with the assumptions of a postmodern perspective, all share a focus on human development as a process of meaning making and reality construction.

DEVELOPMENTAL APPROACHES

BRIDGING THEORIES

Martin and Sugarman (1996) attempt to bridge social constructionism and cognitive constructivism by considering the role of both biological and sociocultural factors in human development. In contrast to the traditional separation of what is individual and private from what is social and public, these theorists suggest that comprehending psychological phenomena, including mind, selfhood, intentionality, and agency, requires the inclusion of both domains. They write:

> Our theory offers a mildly dualistic, developmental view of the emergence and evolution of the psychological, one which is premised on the core ideas of (a) a *shifting psychological ontology* that relies on the gradual emergence of imaginal and memorial capabilities and mediational functions, and (b) the *underdetermination* of these mediational capabilities and functions (and the psychologies they enable) from their sociocultural and biological origins. (p. 293)

Although the individual thus emerges from the social, she or he is not determined by or reducible to it. Rather, the social may be transcended to some degree as a function of our basic biology and neurophysiology as well as our unique personal histories. Conversational and relationship experiences organize thought and enable the meaningful construction of events and self-identities, out of which we create personal theories. There is great variety in the ways such personal theories of self are used to understand and reflect on activities and expectations. Further, the unique way in which each individual imagines possibilities and remembers past events plays a major role in the ongoing emergence of his or her specific psychological processes.

Similarly, the previously mentioned epigenetic systems approach of Mascolo and colleagues (1997) views the process of developing new cognitive structures as

> the active coordination of systems of action, thought, and feeling into new superordinate wholes within specific physical, social, and cultural contexts. Even though coordination of action at the organismic (agentive) level proceeds as a self-organizing process, it is nevertheless fully interpenetrated by biogenetic and sociocultural systems. (p. 36)

From the perspective of these theorists, the development of any complex thought or action on the part of the child proceeds through a series of stages, each of which is limited by the child's ability to create organized wholes through the coordination of the multiple elements of experience and behavior. This coordination, in turn, occurs as a function of each child's particular genetic/biological context as well as of the sociocultural system of which she or he is a part. Thus, while the process of development is similar among different individuals, there is no inevitable sequence of developmental stages shared by all.

Therapists operating in a manner consistent with the former theory are encouraged to focus on collaborative conversation and mutual interaction with the goal of helping clients achieve their goals through the elaboration and alteration of their personal theories. When the personal theories of clients, as well as the actions consistent with these theories, are inadequate, emotional problems are perceived and change is sought. As the therapeutic conversation is internalized, clients are able to utilize their new perspectives within their larger network in ways that are experienced as more meaningful and useful, and thus problem resolution is achieved (Martin & Sugarman, 1996). Although not explicitly stated in the latter approach (Mascolo et al., 1997), one can infer a similar therapeutic role given the importance of self-directed interpretive activity in the creation, differentiation, and integration of knowledge into more comprehensive forms.

COGNITIVE DEVELOPMENT

Moshman (1994) first considers the objectivist conception of rationality that he believes underlies the preponderance of research and theory in the area of human reasoning. He then proposes, "an alternative subjectivist account and ultimately integrate[s] the two perspectives to produce a view of rationality as a form of objectivity constructed via metacognitive reflection on, and developmental reconstruction of, one's subjectivity" (p. 246). Objectivity and subjectivity, in this view, are understood as complementary aspects of the knowing process. That is, one's knowledge is inevitably subjective to some degree, given that it is always viewed through a personal perspective. At the same time, to the degree that knowledge is constrained by and thus a function of a reality separate from the observer, it also is objective. In the development of rationality, one creates a metasubjective perspective through reflection on and reconstruction of previously implicit subject-object relationships. There is no specific endpoint, or defining moment when an ideal of rationality is achieved, however. Rather,

> We are rational to the extent that our most fundamental conceptions and modes of reasoning enable greater objectivity than did their predecessors. Rationality resides in the developmental process whereby our subjectivity becomes an object of reflection, thereby allowing the construction of a more objective metasubjectivity. (Moshman, 1994, p. 251)

For Pascual-Leone (1995), cognitive growth occurs as a function of the dialectical interaction between learning and development. On the one hand, he recognizes the innate basis of learning and development in the "general-purpose functional organization" (p. 338) embedded in the brain's structure. On the other hand, he also assumes that both reality construction and the performance of novel behavior are "explained by means of the capacity of a human organism to tacitly represent, and rerepresent . . . to itself the patterns of coactivation of its own schematic processes, which are informed by reality resistances" (p. 341). The power to represent is perpetuated through intentional actions generated by cognitive schemes. Such actions, in turn, affect the individual in such a way that new patterns of coactivation of schemes emerge. From this perspective it is assumed that

> the content and kinds of learning, the patterns of co-activation and co-functionality among schemes that become higher-order structures, and the dynamic interactions among developmental determinants that condition these learned structures are processes that 'mirror' epistemologically the true constraints of praxis and experience, filtered through the organism's current knowing/learning capabilities. These capabilities in turn result from prior learning and development. (Pascual-Leone, 1995, p. 346)

Given Moshman's (1994) view of rationality, therapy focuses on assisting clients with self-reflection on their thought processes. The goal of this reflection is change in the thought processes considered to be consistent with good reasoning. While not speaking specifically of this approach, nor of the cognitive growth model of Pascual-Leone (1995), Novak's (1993) vision of the therapeutic task from a constructive perspective seems to fit both. This, he believes, is one of empowering individuals "to optimize their phenomenal capacity to make meaning, including their awareness of and confidence in processes that are involved" (p. 190).

LANGUAGE DEVELOPMENT

In the area of language development we will consider the theory of Jerome Bruner (1990a, 1990b, 1992). Bruner focuses on the importance of interaction to the process of language acquisition, which he believes occurs as one uses language to accomplish a particular goal. He writes, "The child is not learning simply what to say but how, where, to whom, and under what circumstances" (1990a, p. 71). That is, language is understood as a problem-solving process (Gopnik, 1990). In this process, and before being able to express himself or herself fully in formal language, the child masters such communicative functions as indicating, labeling, requesting, and misleading. What is more, the learning of a first language is enhanced to the extent that there is a prelinguistic understanding of the situation in which a particular conversation is occurring: "With an appreciation of context, the child seems better able to grasp not only the lexicon but the appropriate aspects of the grammar of the language" (Bruner, 1990a, p. 71).

For Bruner, human growth and development cannot be separated from the distinguishing features of a culture, "what its people take for granted about the nature, the causes, and the expectable results of human mental activity—the things that need no further explaining in order to be understood" (1990b, p. 346). A sense of oneself as separate, as having control over one's world, emerges through the process of interaction with others. At first, children act out narratives that they then internalize as "'scripts' or 'plans' or 'procedures'" (p. 352). The next step in the process is to provide verbal support for what they are doing through the use of reasons, excuses, and justification. Their knowledge becomes more generative as the adults in their world scold or reason with them, giving them additional ways in which to narratively organize their previously more pragmatic understanding. Language development evolves along with the effort to make greater sense of the world in which such transactions are occurring.

As the child continues to mature, knowledge and skills are acquired relative to the specific domains (Bruner, 1992). Each of these domains is characterized by a set of principles and procedures that enable the use of intelligence in ways that may or may not apply in other domains. Bruner refers to these domains as "a culture's treasury of tool kits" (p. 230). No person has access to all tool kits, becoming expert in the use of some while remaining ignorant in the use of others. The differential access to and use of domain-specific tool kits may offer an explanation of the many different ways in which each person constructs reality: "Cultural products, like language and other symbolic systems, mediate thought and place their stamp on our representations of reality" (p. 231).

Such representations of reality continue throughout our lives to emerge in the form of narratives. That is, we organize our experience and our memory of various events in terms of stories, rationales, and so on. Rather than providing "true" explanations, however, such stories provide "a version of reality whose acceptability is governed by convention and 'narrative necessity' rather than by empirical verification and logical requiredness" (Bruner, 1992, p. 232).

Gopnik (1990) provides a summary of three themes characterizing Bruner's theory. These include the assumptions that cognitive development involves the formation and testing of theories and that children's semantic structures reflect these theories, which may differ from those of the adults in their world. The second theme is that knowledge is functional, or that it is engaged, enabling the child to accomplish something, particularly in the social realm. The third theme involves the importance of the social context of knowledge, or the notion that "knowledge requires a community, as well as a mind and a world" (p. 336). In all of this, the mind as well as reality are constructed (Olson, 1990), and thus each individual must be understood in all of his or her uniqueness, and the importance of the therapeutic conversation takes on new meaning. Indeed, by inference, one could understand that through exposure to new narratives, with their associated domain-specific tool kits, the therapist may assist the client in expanding his or her personal theories and thus facilitate his or her growth and development.

MORAL DEVELOPMENT

Postmodern approaches to moral development have been created on both narrative and constructivist assumptions. In the former instance, the narrative process is the means by which many authors have begun to understand the way in which one achieves moral authority. However, in a paradox described by Lourenco (1996):

> Narrative approaches run the risk of not being true narratives whenever they intend to be (normative) theories of moral development, and of not being true theories of moral development whenever they intend to provide narrative (and nonnormative) understanding of human experience. The effort to apply the idea of narrative to moral development runs the risk of distorting the very nature of both narrative and morality. Narrative reflects description and characterization rather than prescription and obligation . . . whereas morality addresses obligation and prescription rather than characterization and description. (p. 85)

Nevertheless, while embracing value neutrality and relativism, narrative approaches emphasize context, embeddedness, and the role of personal stories. Such stories are not to be judged but rather are to be heard. A focus on interdependence, relationship, and connectedness replaces the emphasis on "boundaries, separatedness, individualism" (Lourenco, 1996, p. 93) characteristic of overarching theories of moral development, such as that of Kohlberg (1981). The ethic becomes one of care and responsibility rather than of justice and rights (Gilligan, 1987).

Noam's (1993) theory builds on both developmental and constructivist ideas, considering the biographical path in which meanings about the self and other relationships are constructed and transformed. Defining the self as a process in which one structures thoughts, feelings, and actions about self, others, and the world, he believes "that morally evil or inactive people also lack a strong self and that establishing strengths in the self is often related to moments of moral conflict" (p. 211). Further, it is his position that "moral maturity needs to be judged by the relationship between the complexity of judgments and the capacity to transform judgments into positive adaptations" (p. 213).

For Noam, development is an interactive process in which all experiences influence the evolution and formation of the individual and his or her construction of reality. Recognition must therefore be given to "the internalized weaknesses created through participation in. the various social systems and networks that mark the contexts of development" (p.

216). In the process of developing meanings, new abilities and vulnerabilities are created that relate not only to moral development but also to the basic development of the self: "The abilities to be reflective and decisive, to weigh and judge, to delay and care, to keep narcissism in check and believe that one can make a difference—all these capacities contribute to moral judgment and moral action" (p. 219).

Noam sees therapy as the ideal context within which to explore vulnerabilities and their transformation. Therapists participate in strengthening the self of clients through the creation of trustworthy and respectful relationships. That is, "the self always learns about itself through the eyes of others, through how significant others view the self" (p. 234). Self-reflection and the creation of new understanding about past experiences are also important aspects of the therapy process. Indeed, a specific focus on instances in which an individual took a morally courageous position and acted on his or her beliefs facilitates the transformation of vulnerabilities into strengths. Thus, "what begins as a rigid application of moral rules can lead to explorations with more flexible evaluations of internal reality and to new relation capacities" (p. 236).

PERSONALITY DEVELOPMENT

Kegan (1982), as previously noted, takes a life span developmental approach to the development of relationships between subject and object in which he describes "a sequence of emotional, motivational, and psychodynamic organizations, as well as the now familiar [those of Piaget and Kohlberg] cognitive and sociomoral ones" (p. 72). The theory is based on the concept of the "motion of evolution," or "evolution as a meaning-constitutive activity" (p. 77), which is understood to be the context that generates as well as unifies both (1) thought and feeling and (2) self and other. The evolutionary activity of which Kegan speaks involves, on the one hand, the creation of objects through a process of differentiation and, on the other hand, the ways in which such objects are related to through a process of integration:

> Subject-object relationships emerge out of a lifelong process of development: a succession of qualitative differentiations of the self from the world, with a qualitatively more extensive object with which to be in relation created each time; a natural history of qualitatively better guarantees to the world of its distinctness; successive triumphs of 'relationship to' rather than 'embeddedness in.' (p. 77)

The theory describes the developmental process through a series of six stages, or types of balance, in subject-object relationships. For example, at birth the child is at the incorporative stage, operating as subject on the basis of reflexes with no sense of the other, or of objects. The succeeding stages include the impulsive, imperial, interpersonal, institutional, and interindividual. This progression of stages may be seen as a metatheoretical perspective in that it is understood to constitute a common ground for understanding various other developmental theories.

Kegan (1982) depicts his model by means of a helix, or spiral, in order to describe an ongoing process in which the individual seeks to resolve the tension between a desire to be both differentiated from (distinctness) and embedded in (inclusion) his or her context:

> The life-history I have traced involves a continual moving back and forth between resolving the tension slightly in the favor of autonomy, at one stage, in the favor of

inclusion, at the next. We move from the overincluded, fantasy-embedded impulsive balance to the sealed-up self-sufficiency of the imperial balance; from the overdifferentiated imperial balance to overincluded interpersonalism; from interpersonalism to the autonomous, self-regulating, institutional balance; from the institutional to a new form of openness in the interindividual. (p. 108)

As one operates from this perspective, what is important is a recognition that understanding another requires knowing where he or she is in the evolutionary process, thus having a sense of the way in which he or she makes meaning. An important aspect of this understanding includes both the degree to which the essential functions of confirmation, contradiction, and continuity are being provided to the individual within his or her culture of embeddedness and the absence or presence of support for the individual over time through his or her processes of growth, change, and transition. More recently, Kegan (1994) has added to this list the need to be aware of the kinds of consciousness that are demanded of individuals in a given society. That is, we must consider "the relationship between the principles we may possess and the complexity of mind that contemporary culture unrecognizedly asks us to possess through its many claims and expectations" (p. 34).

Based on his constructive-developmental framework, Kegan (1982) believes that what is suggested is "a kind of metatheory of therapy which, simply stated, amounts to viewing the therapeutic context as a culture of embeddedness in the facilitation of a troubled person's evolution" (p. 262). In the course of their interactions, the therapist understands that both he or she and the client are engaged in an ongoing evolutionary process. When pain is experienced it denotes resistance to the "motion of life" (p. 265) as the individual refuses to accept life experiences that are different from those planned for or anticipated: "We may hear grief, mourning, and loss, but it is the dying of a way to know the world which no longer works, a loss of an old coherence with no new coherence immediately present to take its place" (p. 266). The desired outcome is thus the creation of a new balance, of a new life, as each crisis is used as a springboard for the evolution of a construction of the world that is more articulated and does a better job of differentiating and reintegrating one's understanding of his or her prior balance.

In his consideration of the goal of therapy, Kegan (1982) avoids the polar opposites of either valuing some externally decided good or assuming that each person's way of making meaning is as good as any other way. Rather, the goal is to help the client move from a less-evolved to a more-evolved stage of meaning making in which one is better able to achieve a sense of truth. That is,

Each new evolutionary truce further differentiates the self from its embeddedness in the world, guaranteeing, in a qualitatively new way, the world's distinct integrity, and thereby creating a more integrated relationship to the world. Each new truce accomplishes this by the evolution of a reduced subject and a greater object for the subject to take, an evolution of lesser subjectivity and greater objectivity, an evolution that is more "truthful." (p. 294)

As we engage in such a process, however, therapists must be aware that the requirements of the order of consciousness implicit in what we say is consistent with the level of consciousness at which the client is operating and is thus able to understand (Kegan, 1994).

This awareness of the unique ways in which each individual participates in the process of meaning making and reality construction may be seen as a unifying thread in all of the approaches described in the previous two sections. And although therapeutic considerations have been addressed relative to each approach, it also is appropriate to be aware of some other ramifications for therapists of perspectives such as these. Thus, in the following section we conclude with a discussion of the more general issues of assessment and practice.

GENERAL CONSIDERATIONS AND FURTHER THOUGHTS

ASSESSMENT

As Efran and Clarfield (1992) note, there are some who would take the position that expression on the part of the therapist of what is right or wrong is inconsistent with the constructionist idea that all perspectives are to be viewed as equally legitimate. By contrast, consistent with their interpretation of constructionism, each person is understood to have personal preferences that she or he is entitled to express. What is important is the avoidance of the suggestion that such preferences represent objective truth or the "real" reality. That is,

> Constructionists are obliged to take responsibility for being advocates of particular positions. They are not enjoined from having them. Constructionists are even allowed to test their hypotheses using the canons of science, provided they keep in mind that science itself is a tradition involving a dialectic between the observer and the observed. It never yields value-free observations. (p. 201)

Similarly, conversation becomes the medium through which the activities of therapy occur rather than a tool to be adopted. Thus, the process of assessment remains valid as long as it is adapted to account for the inevitability of such factors as subjectivity, reflexivity, and individual interpretation as well as the importance of relationship and the larger context. In other words,

> Emphasis is placed, for example, on the primacy of personal meaning, the active role of the person as a co-creator of meaning, and the self-organized and developmental progressive nature of our knowledge structures. . . . Constructivist traditions emphasize processes of knowing and orient toward assessing the viability (utility) as opposed to the validity (truth) of an individual's unique worldview. (Neimeyer & Neimeyer, 1993a, p. 2)

Keeping in mind that the focus is on the meaning-making activity of the client, Neimeyer and Neimeyer (1993b) suggest that in constructivist assessment, the therapist is concerned with one or both of two avenues of exploration considered to be complementary to one another: "*process* (the examination of the flow of the client's moment-to-moment experience) and *structure* (the identification of enduring values, core beliefs, and central dilemmas that constitute part of the structure of the client's personal knowledge)" (p. 222). However, the techniques of assessment vary in terms of their directiveness. On the one hand, for example, there is the process of "streaming," which allows the client to speak freely without being constrained by conventional communication rules and permits the therapist to observe themes and patterns that may then be considered in dialogue together. At the other hand of the continuum is the process of "zigzag" interviewing in which systematic inquiries are made about individual constructions and related behaviors in order to understand how each member of a family experiencing a problem participates in the creation of an impasse or escalation. Techniques that fall somewhere in the middle between these two poles include content analysis of narratives, either spoken or written; analysis of group discourse; the use of personal journals or diaries; self-characterization sketches; exploration of personal belief systems and/or problematic reactions; and circular questioning. Regardless of technique, however, assessment is understood as an intervention that facilitates the evaluation of problems in such a way that new realities are created.

PRACTICE

In his discussion of postmodernism and its ramifications for an epistemology of practice, Polkinghorne (1992) makes a distinction between relativist postmodernists and affirmative postmodernists. Both groups affirm the assumptions that (1) we cannot know the world in any real or absolute sense; (2) what is real is composed of a "fragmented accumulation of disparate elements and events" (p. 148); and (3) human knowing consists of cognitive constructions by means of which each person makes meaning of the world. However, affirmative postmodernists also assume a neopragmatic stance, or one that "shifts the focus of knowledge generation from attempts to describe the real as it is in itself (theoretical knowledge and 'knowing that') to programs to collect descriptions of actions that have effectively accomplished intended ends (practical knowledge and 'knowing how')" (p. 151). The search is thus for actions that have previously been effective in situations similar to that which one is currently facing.

Based on the notion that five different types of cognitive processes are used by practitioners at different stages of their professional development (Dreyfus & Dreyfus, 1986), Polkinghorne (1992) underlines the shift away from knowledge based on external sources to knowledge based on experience:

> This knowledge primarily takes the form of cognitive patterns or prototypical models derived from the practitioners' tacit understandings of human function, from theories and models learned in training and from exemplary clinical experiences. The models are organized as collections of configurations or patterns, rather than formal, logically linked knowledge statements. In practice, understanding progresses to fit the unique configuration of the situation. This development of a contextually informed, particularized knowledge occurs by adapting and revising previously held general models until all elements of the situation are related into a meaningful whole. (p. 157)

As this position is translated into considerations about the training of therapists, one recognizes the importance of modeling and demonstrating success as well as of describing how therapy is done. In addition, trainees must experience their own successes and failures in order to acquire practical skill. Thus, as one grows in expertise about the doing of therapy, one also acquires understanding of the position that knowledge, about the world and about human development, as well as about therapy, emerges in the context of a process of meaning making and reality construction.

REFERENCES

Aldridge, J. (1993). Constructivism, contextualism, and applied developmental psychology. *Perceptual and Motor Skills, 76,* 1242.

Anderson, H. (1997). *Conversation, language and possibilities: A postmodern approach to therapy.* New York: Basic Books.

Bateson, G. (1972). *Steps to an ecology of mind.* New York: Ballantine.

Becvar, D. S., & Becvar, R. J. (2000). *Family therapy: A systemic integration.* Boston, MA: Allyn & Bacon.

Bronfenbrenner, U. (1979). *The ecology of human development.* Cambridge, MA: Harvard University Press.

Bruner, J. (1976). The ontogenesis of speech acts. *Journal of Child Language, 2,* 1–19.

Bruner, J. (1990a). *Acts of meaning.* Cambridge, MA: Harvard University Press.

Bruner, J. (1990b). Culture and human development: A new look. *Human Development, 33,* 344–355.

Bruner, J. (1992). The narrative construction of reality. In H. Beilin & P. Pufall (Eds.), *Piaget's theory: Prospects and possibilities* (pp. 229–248). Hillsdale, NJ: Lawrence Erlbaum Associates.

Dreyfus, H. L., & Dreyfus, S. E. (1986). *Mind over machine.* New York: The Free Press.

Efran, J. S., Clarfield, L. E. (1992). Constructionist therapy: Sense and nonsense. In S. McNamee & K. J. Gergen, (Eds.), *Therapy as social construction* (pp. 200–217). London: Sage Publications.

Gergen, K. J. (1991). *The saturated self.* New York: Basic Books.

Gergen, K. J. (1992). Toward a postmodern psychology. In S. Kvale (Ed.), *Psychology and postmodernism* (pp. 17–29). London: Sage Publications.

Gergen, K. J. (1996). Technology and the self: From the essential to the sublime. In D. Grodin & T. R. Lindlof (Eds.), *Constructing the self in a mediated world* (pp. 127–139). Thousand Oaks, CA: Sage Publications.

Gilligan, C. (1987). Moral orientation and moral development. In E. Kittay & D. Meyers (Eds.), *Women and moral theory* (pp. 19–33). Totowa, NJ: Roman & Littlefield.

Gopnik, A. (1990). Knowing, doing, and talking: The Oxford years. *Human Development, 33,* 334–338.

Harre, R. (1986). The step to social construction. In M. Richards & P. Light (Eds.), *Children of social worlds: Development in a social context* (pp. 287–300). Cambridge, MA: Harvard University Press.

Hoshmand, L. T. (1993). The personal narrative in the communal construction of self and life issues. In G. J. Neimeyer (Ed.), *Constructivist assessment: A casebook* (pp. 179–205). Newbury Park, CA: Sage Publications.

Howard, G. S. (1991). Culture tales: A narrative approach to thinking, cross-cultural psychology, and psychotherapy. *American Psychologist, 46*(3), 187–197.

Ingleby, D. (1986). Development in social context. In M. Richards & P. Light (Eds.), *Children of social worlds: Development in social context* (pp. 297–317). Cambridge, MA: Harvard University Press.

Kegan, R. (1982). *The evolving self: Problem and process in human development.* Cambridge, MA: Harvard University Press.

Kegan, R. (1994). *In over our heads: The mental demands of modern life.* Cambridge, MA: Harvard University Press.

Kelly, G. (1955). *The psychology of personal constructs, Vols. I & II.* New York: Norton.

Kohlberg, L. (1981). *Essays on moral development Vol. I: The philosophy of moral development.* San Franciso, CA: Harper & Row.

Kvale, S. (1992). Postmodern psychology: A contradiction in terms? In S. Kvale (Ed.), *Psychology and postmodernism* (pp. 31–57). London: Sage Publications.

Lourenco, O. (1996). Reflections on narrative approaches to moral development. *Human Development, 39,* 83–99.

Lyddon, W. J., & Alford, D. J. (1993). Constructivist assessment: A developmental-epistemic perspective. In G. J. Neimeyer (Ed.), *Constructivist assessment: A casebook* (pp. 31–57). Newbury Park, CA: Sage Publications.

Mahoney, M. J. (1988). Constructive metatheory: I. Basic features and historical foundations. *International Journal of Personal Construct Psychology, 1,* 1–35.

Mair, M. (1988). Psychology as storytelling. *International Journal of Personal Construct Psychology, 1,* 125–138,

Martin, J., & Sugarman, J. (1996). Bridging social constructionism and cognitive constructivism: A psychology of human possibility and constraint. *The Journal of Mind and Behavior, 17*(4), 291–320.

Mascolo, M. F., Pollack, R. D., & Fischer, K. W. (1997). Keeping the constructor in development: An epigenetic systems approach. *Journal of Constructivist Psychology, 10,* 25–49.

Maturana, H., & Varela, F. (1987). *The tree of knowledge.* Boston: New Science Library.

McNamee, S. (1996). Therapy and identity construction in a postmodern world. In D. Grodin & T. R. Lindlof (Eds.), *Constructing the self in a mediated world* (pp. 141–155). Thousand Oaks, CA: Sage Publications.

McNamee, S., & Gergen, K. J. (1992). *Therapy as social construction.* London: Sage Publications.

Moshman, D. (1994). Reason, reasons and reasoning: A constructivist account of human rationality. *Theory and Psychology, 4*(2), 245–260.

Neimeyer, G. J., & Neimeyer, R. A. (1993a). Defining the boundaries of constructivist assessment. In G. J. Neimeyer (Ed.), *Constructivist assessment: A casebook* (pp. 1–30). Newbury Park, CA: Sage Publications.

Neimeyer, R. A., & Neimeyer, G. J. (1993b). Constructivist assessment: What and when. In G. J. Neimeyer (Ed.), *Constructivist assessment: A casebook* (pp. 207–223). Newbury Park, CA: Sage Publications.

Newman, F., & Holzman, L. (1996). *Unscientific psychology: A cultural performatory approach to understanding human life.* Westport, CT: Praeger.

Noam, G. G. (1993). "Normative vulnerabilities" of self and their transformations in moral action. In G. G. Noam & T. E. Wren (Eds.), *The moral self* (pp. 209–238). Cambridge, MA: The MIT Press.

Novak, J. D. (1993). Human constructivism: A unification of psychological and epistemological phenomena in meaning making. *International Journal of Cognitive Construct Psychology, 6,* 167–193.

Olson, D. R. (1990). Possible minds: Reflections on Bruner's recent writings on mind and self. *Human Development, 33,* 339–343.

Pascual-Leone, J. (1995). Learning and development as dialectical factors in cognitive growth. *Human Development, 38,* 338–348.

Polkinghorne, D. E. (1992). Postmodern epistemology of practice. In S. Kvale (Ed.), *Psychology and postmodernism* (pp. 146–165). London: Sage Publications.

Polkinghorne, D. E. (1995). Piaget's and Derrida's contributions to a constructivist psychotherapy. *Journal of Constructivist Psychology, 8,* 269–282.

Rosenhan, D. L. (1984). On being sane in insane places. In P. Watzlawick (Ed.), *The invented reality* (pp. 117–144). New York: Norton.

Shultz, T. R., & Mareschal, D. (1997). Rethinking innateness, earning and constructivism: Connectionist perspectives on development. *Cognitive Development, 12,* 563–586.

Steenbarger, B. N. (1991). All the world is not a stage: Emerging contextualist themes in counseling and development. *Journal of Counseling and Development, 70,* 288–296.

Strand, P. S. (1997). Toward a developmentally informed narrative therapy. *Family Process, 36*(4), 325–338.

Tappan, M. B. (1992). Commentary. *Human Development, 35,* 376–383.

Valsiner, J. (1996). Whose mind? *Human Development, 39,* 295–300.

Vogel, D. (1994). Narrative perspectives in theory and therapy. *Journal of Constructivist Psychology, 7,* 243–261.

von Glasersfeld, E. (1984). An introduction to radical costructivism. In P. Watzlawick (Ed.), *The invented reality* (pp. 17–40). New York: W. W. Norton.

Watzlawick, P. (1984). Components of ideological "realities." In P. Watzlawick (Ed.), *The invented reality* (pp. 206–247). New York: W. W. Norton.

PART II

THE LARGER SOCIAL CONTEXT

CHAPTER 5

Socialization of Gender Roles

Carol L. Philpot

"IS IT A BOY OR A GIRL?" This is among the first questions asked immediately after the birth of an infant. Once an individual knows the gender of a child, there follows a flood of assumptions regarding the direction that new life will take. Never mind that the assumptions may be inaccurate. The reality is that even today, at the end of the twentieth century, for most people the stereotypes predominate.

Gender is probably the most basic category into which we sort people, more basic even than age or race. Although the expectations that accompany gender may differ across cultures, there are some roles that seem to be common in all but the most isolated and esoteric civilizations. Throughout the world women are valued for their beauty (although the standards of beauty may differ), their ability to bear children, and their nurturance, whereas men are valued as providers and protectors. How is it that the roles of men and women came to be divided in this manner?

THEORIES OF GENDER ROLES

There are many theories that attempt to explain the pervasive differences between the genders that people perceive to be true. These include biological, evolutionary psychological, anthropological, historical, and religious explanations, as well as the theory of gender socialization.

BIOLOGY

No one would deny that there are biological differences between females and males. Much research has been done on the biological basis for differences in aggression, visual-spatial ability, verbal ability, quantitative ability, hormonal effects, depression, intelligence, and physical strength. Scientists (Archer, 1987; Hyde & Plant, 1995) have argued that most differences found are too small to be clinically significant or alternatively (Fausto-Sterling,

1985) that such research does not control for the effects of socialization and thus cannot claim to support biological differences alone. Recently, through the use of magnetic resonance imaging, researchers (Gur, 1995; Shaywitz & Shaywitz, 1995; Witelson, 1989) have discovered structural and functional differences in the brain based on gender. However, it is only speculation that these differences are responsible for perceived cognitive and behavioral differences. For example, Witelson has discovered that the corpus collosum in the female brain is thicker than that in the male brain. This could be the explanation for women's "intuition," their ability to use both sides of their brains at once, and their greater facility with language, and for men's tendency to compartmentalize, but there is no physical proof to that effect.

EVOLUTIONARY PSYCHOLOGY

Buss (1995) has suggested that many of the differences between the genders can be explained by the adaptive demands made of men and women in the quest to procreate. His theory states that males needed sexual access to many reproductively valuable women while females needed commitment from a male who could provide for and protect the young. Thus psychological differences between the genders were perpetuated by mate selection. Although interesting, this theory only accounts for a small portion of the observed gender differences, in particular stereotypical differences in sexual behavior.

ANTHROPOLOGY

Some scholars (Doyle, 1989; Harris, 1977; Kelly, 1981) believe that in an attempt to provide a division of labor, early humans assigned roles to those most biologically suited to accomplish the task (i.e., child care for women, protection for men). Thus women and men developed the skills and attributes that were needed for their assigned tasks. Although this theory accounts for some broad role differences, it does not explain the many other observed gender differences that are discussed below.

HISTORY

According to many historians, the development of the concepts of property and hierarchy (Ehrenberg, 1989), the beginnings of warfare (Harris, 1977), the discovery of the male role in reproduction (Buss, 1995), the ascent of patriarchy (Doyle, 1989), the advent of capitalism, and the industrial revolution (French, 1985; Harris, 1977) all had an influence on the development of gender roles over time. The hypothesis is that the biologically stronger male began to perceive women and children as property, which enhanced his status, but which he needed to protect from competing males. Furthermore, women and children could provide the labor necessary to build his estate in exchange for food and shelter. Although it could be argued that this was an interdependent relationship, in a patriarchal society, the male was on top of the hierarchy, the female beneath. Theoretically, then, gender attributes are a result of centuries of playing these assigned roles.

RELIGION

In Western society, religious beliefs were simultaneously affected by and strengthened the patriarchal value system. For example, Greek philosophy divided mind (associated with male) and body (associated with female) and encouraged the control of mind over body. Christianity emphasized control over sexual instincts, which it associated with the less spiritually developed, highly sexualized female (Doyle, 1989; French, 1985). Thus wives were urged to obey their husbands, who were more spiritually developed. The influence of such belief systems on the expectations held by many regarding males and females cannot be ignored.

GENDER SOCIALIZATION

In the last three decades, psychologists have proposed another theory for perceived gender differences, one that encompasses the above explanations and yet offers the possibility of divergence from the norm. This is the theory of gender socialization. This theory proposes that, although biology plays a part in gender, most of the differences observed between the genders are a result of learning passed down across generations and reinforced by society. Thus, gender socialization theory acknowledges biological differences and recognizes psychological, anthropological, historical, and religious influences, but sees these influences as a result of knowledge transferred through successive generations.

PREVAILING GENDER ROLE MODELS

There are two major theoretical models that have laid the foundation for psychological research on gender. These are the gender identity paradigm, most frequently associated with Sandra Bem (1974), and the gender role strain paradigm, proposed by Joseph Pleck (1981).

GENDER IDENTITY PARADIGM

The gender identity paradigm assumes that individuals have an inner psychological need to develop a gender identity and that development of this gender identity is a requirement of healthy functioning. According to this paradigm, a person's healthy development depends on how well he or she conforms to the stereotypical masculine and feminine roles set by society. Masculinity and femininity are not seen as polar opposites, but complex independent constructs that include attributes, roles, values, behaviors, preferences, and so on. Individuals are believed to possess masculine or feminine traits. Two of the most prominent researchers of the gender identity paradigm are Sandra Bem and Janet Spence.

Bem (1981) described individuals as either schematic or aschematic with regard to gender. A schematic individual will organize his or her thinking in such a way as to see distinct differences between males and females that are predictable. The aschematic individual, on the other hand, is open to the possibility that a person can have unique characteristics that do not have to fit the stereotypical female or male gender schema. Bem (1974) developed the Bem Sex Role Inventory (BSRI) to measure the extent to which persons identify themselves with socially endorsed roles and characteristics for their gender. In addition to masculinity and femininity scores, individuals can also obtain scores on androgyny and undifferentiation.

Spence and Helmreich (1978) developed the Personality Attributes Questionnaire (PAQ) to measure the extent of instrumentality and expressiveness endorsed by individuals, with the assumption that in general, expressive characteristics are socially desirable for women whereas instrumental attributes are socially desirable for men. Spence, who believes that effective individuals possess both instrumental and expressive traits, created the Masculinity-Femininity Scale on the PAQ to measure the extent to which an individual could combine both.

GENDER ROLE STRAIN PARADIGM

A great deal of research in the area of gender differences has been conducted using these two instruments, with the gender identity paradigm as a defining construct. In 1981, however, Joseph Pleck proposed the gender role strain paradigm as an alternative method for conceptualizing gender. Pleck views gender as a social construct. That is, he believes society sets the rules regarding what is considered masculine and feminine and then punishes people who do not comply with those rules. He states that many people violate gender roles and suffer the negative psychological consequences. Others overconform to gender roles because they fear the consequences, but overconforming can lead to dysfunction. He identified three kinds of strain experienced by individuals when they attempt to conform to society's prescription of gender: discrepancy strain, dysfunction strain, and trauma strain.

Discrepancy strain occurs when individuals perceive a discrepancy between what they believe society expects of them and what they truly are. For example, society demands that males perform athletically; however, not every adolescent male can be on the football team. Society also demands that women fit in a size eight or below, but not every woman is built like a Barbie doll. These people will suffer discrepancy strain because they do not fit the ideal that society has prescribed for their gender.

Some of the rules that society makes regarding women and men produce dysfunctional individuals. For example, a woman who believes she should be a size eight when genetically she is not, may develop a life-threatening eating disorder in order to accomplish the impossible. A male who thinks society demands that he show no emotion may develop high blood pressure or suffer a heart attack, because his suppressed emotions take a toll on his physical body. In other words, in order to meet society's demands, men and women become dysfunctional.

In the process of gender socialization, girls and boys experience trauma. Little boys are told that they cannot cry, are pushed away from their parents at a young age, and as adolescents are forced to perform various manhood initiation rights that are traumatic. Little girls learn quickly that they are not as important as boys, that they are valued for their bodies, and that they are vulnerable to rape and physical abuse. The experience of accepting society's gender prescription is traumatic in and of itself.

GENDER AND SOCIAL CONSTRUCTIONIST THEORY

In this chapter, we use the social constructionist explanation for gender roles. That is, gender is viewed as a construct that is created by society and differs for different age groups, socioeconomic groups, ethnic groups, and even geographical areas. According to this perspective, gender is taught and reinforced by society through the process of gender socialization and is not a biologically based inherent set of traits. Because gender is not a property of individuals, but a social construct, it can be deconstructed. Behavior that is learned can be unlearned. Therefore those aspects of gender roles that are seen as detrimental to men and women can be changed. They are not immutable.

PROCESS OF GENDER SOCIALIZATION

People learn what is expected of males and females through several processes, which can be broadly categorized as (1) modeling, (2) cognition, and (3) reward and punishment (Basow, 1986; Lott, 1994).

MODELING

Children learn by copying and as soon as they can tell the difference between boy and girl, they strive to be like their same sex models. Models can be parents, peers, siblings, teachers, television and movie stars, story characters, sports stars, musicians—anyone who is frequently encountered by the child. As mentioned previously, Bem (1974, 1981, 1982, 1983, 1984, 1987) proposed that there are sex-typed and non–sex-typed individuals. The former process information according to their gender schema and strive to meet the cultural stereotype of their gender, while the latter do not. So children who are sex-typed copy the behavior of same-sex role models and reject the behavior of the other gender, thus limiting their repertoire to that which they perceive to be socially acceptable. This unquestioning acceptance of the cultural norm and effort to meet its requirements perpetuates the stereotypes. Indeed the stereotypes become a self-fulfilling prophecy.

The roles that women and men typically occupy in society also serve as a model for children. Although much has changed in the last several decades, traditionally men held positions of authority and power and women were relegated to dead-end service jobs that paid poorly or were housewives, which paid nothing. Today more and more women are occupying positions of power in law, medicine, politics, and so on, which presents a more positive role model for girls than was once the case. Nevertheless, for many children, their closest role models (i.e., their parents) present a stereotypical power differential with regard to education, careers, and finances, reinforcing the idea that men have more opportunities to succeed than do women. Furthermore, women still handle most of the housework and child care even when they are employed full-time (Hochschild, 1989), which indicates to little girls that if they do go to work they will be working a double shift while their brothers will not. Although superwomen may have more financial and political power, the inequity of the workload remains a problem. On the other hand, society still does not tolerate the unemployed, financially dependent male. Little boys quickly learn that they will be financially responsible for women and children when they grow up and to shirk this responsibility damages their manhood.

COGNITION

Society, rather arbitrarily, labels some things as female (pink), some as male (blue). For example, until recently, hurricanes were given only female names, implying that females have similar characteristics as hurricanes. In the Bible, God is referred to as the Father, implying that God-like behavior is male. Furthermore certain behaviors such as showing emotion, providing nurturance, and acting giddy, are considered appropriate for females whereas others, participating in contact sports such as football, slapping each other on the back, or defending yourself by physical violence are acceptable for males. These behaviors are labeled male or female and people who deviate from the acceptable norms are labeled deviant, even though both genders are entirely capable of participating in all the behaviors mentioned. Dolls, doll houses, cook sets, and jewelry kits are labeled for little girls, while footballs, trucks, and army men are labeled for little boys (Bradbard & Endsley, 1983; Cobb, Stevens-Long, & Goldstein, 1982; Downs, 1983; Schwartz & Markham, 1985; Ungar, 1982). Children begin to divide the world into male and female cognitively and then act in a stereotypically gender appropriate manner. Again, the gender stereotype becomes a self-fulfilling prophecy.

Language also plays a part in gender role socialization. Feminist linguists (Lakoff, 1975, 1990; Tannen, 1990) have pointed out how the accepted placement of male and female designations reflects and perpetuates society's hierarchy. Phrases such as man and wife, men and women, his and hers, he and she place the woman secondary to the man. It is their contention that children cognitively absorb the unspoken message that perpetuates the notion that men are more important than women. The acceptance of this hierarchy by both genders then affects the way they relate to one another. Indeed, Tannen (1990) has demonstrated that men and women adopt different communication styles partially due to this power differential.

Geis (1993) found that people are so influenced by what they have been taught is male and female that they perceive what they expect to perceive despite evidence to the contrary. That is, they interpret the behavior of others based on their gender, thus misinterpreting or failing to perceive any behavior that deviates from the gender norm. This creates a self-fulfilling prophecy from which it is very difficult to escape. As can be understood from this discussion, cognition plays a large part in absorbing the social messages regarding gender and in perpetuating them.

REWARD AND PUNISHMENT

Gender training begins at birth. Parents reward behavior differentially based on the gender of the infant. Girl babies are treated more gently, cuddled, and serenaded (Lerner, 1968; Williams, 1987) while male babies are tossed in the air and tickled. Mothers tend to withhold touch from boy babies at an early age (Goldberg & Lewis, 1969). Boys are subjected to more physical punishment than girls and do not get comfort for minor injuries (Hartley, 1974; Lambert, Yackley, & Hein, 1971; Weitzman, Eifler, & Ross, 1972). Girls are kept closer to their mothers and receive more protection from their parents (Chodorow, 1978), while boys are more likely to be left alone (Fagot, 1978). Fathers exhort their sons to squelch emotions so that they do not appear vulnerable (Choti, Marston, & Holston, 1987).

At an early age, children absorb the messages from the media that make it clear that those who conform to the gender norms receive rewards while those who do not are derided, rejected, and devalued. In general, movies, books, television, music, magazines, and children's stories portray females who are valued for their beauty, who put relationships, particularly with men, above all else, who defer to males, who are emotional and illogical, and who expect males to protect, provide for, and rescue them (Courtney & Whipple, 1983; Dominick, 1979; Downs & Gowan, 1980; Downs & Harrison, 1985; Dworkin, 1981; Griffin, 1981; Reinartz, 1975; Weitz, 1977). Males are portrayed as aggressive, active, achievement-oriented, frequently violent, and sexually promiscuous (Mellen, 1978; Weitz, 1977). Children quickly learn to emulate those characteristics that will provide them with the reward of acceptance. Indeed, examples of males who have power and wealth due to their achievements and of women who have power and wealth because of their beauty or their relationship with a powerful male abound. Of course there are exceptions, but the stereotype predominates.

In school, girls are positively reinforced for compliance and neatness while boys are rewarded for correct answers (Sadker & Sadker, 1985). Boys are more often acknowledged than girls when they raise their hands to answer a question. Researchers (Harway, 1980; Harway & Astin, 1977) have found that males are encouraged to further their education beyond high school, while females, even bright females, are less likely to be supported in this endeavor. The clear implication is that males are valued for achievement and females for compliance.

Religion also plays a role in rewarding differential behavior for women and men. Fiorenza (1983) and Ruether (1983) found that children who receive formal religious education in any of the major religions of the world learn that women are to serve God, husband, and children and that men serve only God, but must provide for and protect women. These roles are rewarded by God and conform to gender stereotypes.

During adolescence peers have a major influence over gender roles. Girls are rewarded by their peers for their popularity with boys and not for academic achievement (Belenky, Clinchy, Goldberger, & Tarule, 1986; Chafetz, 1978; Weitz, 1977). Therefore they develop interests in make-up, clothes, dieting, and appearance, often endangering their lives with eating disorders. Adolescent boys achieve status with peers through fighting, sports, sexual activity, risk taking, and alcohol use (Fasteau, 1974; Gilmore, 1990). Male bonding during adolescence also includes the rejection or degradation of anything labeled female in order to achieve their identity as separate from and dominant over women (Hartley, 1959).

As adults men and women continue to be differentially reinforced. Women continue to judge themselves and other women by their beauty and their relationships with men (Kolbenschlag, 1981; Russianoff, 1981; Wolf, 1991). Women who do not have a husband and children feel incomplete despite excellent career success because they are judged by society as having missed the most important function in their lives. Furthermore, women who are single mothers face poverty (Weitzman, 1985), which provides even more incentive to value marriage above all. Men, on the other hand, live in a hierarchical world, judged by their career success (Bernard, 1981; Doyle, 1989). Respect, financial benefits, beautiful women, and prestige in society are all the spoils of having won in the competitive male world.

GENDER CO-EVOLUTION

A discussion of the process of gender socialization would not be complete without an explanation of the power of co-evolution. As discussed above, people learn how to be women and men through modeling, cognition, and reward and punishment. Women play a very large role in men's socialization by imposing expectations on them and rewarding or rejecting them based on their ability to meet these expectations. Likewise, men have certain expectations of women and mold women by a process of reward and punishment. This process occurs both at the larger societal level as well as one on one. An example or two may help to clarify. Cheerleaders encourage football players to be competitive, aggressive, and even physically violent in order to win the game. They reward the best players with their attention, praise, and sexuality. Thus they mold young males to be competitive, aggressive, and sometimes violent. They participate in his choice of values and behavior in this way. And then they complain that these same males are too macho, not in touch with their feelings, too focused on sports, and insensitive. At the same time, males find women who wear make-up, have Barbie-doll figures, and dress in sexy clothes very attractive. They reward these women by giving them attention, gifts, and even offering marriage. They thus mold young women to put a high value on appearance, to diet (perhaps to extreme), and to spend large amounts of money on make-up and clothes. This participation in molding the interests and choices of women occurs as they reward specific behavior. But then they complain about the shallowness of women who only think about their looks and the cost of their clothes and make-up.

Gender co-evolution is the process of influencing the development of the other gender through cognition, modeling, and reward and punishment. Each gender has the power to affect the values, characteristics, and conduct of the other by changing its expectations and rewarding nonstereotypical behavior. This is particularly effective in close relationships such as parent/child, wife/husband, or close friendships, but has the potential to work elsewhere as well. The concept of gender co-evolution is an important one because, once understood, each gender can recognize that it participates in the socialization process and can discover how to work together to deconstruct those aspects of gender socialization that they find detrimental.

OUTCOMES OF GENDER SOCIALIZATION

As a result of gender socialization, many men and women develop in what might be considered different cultures, and therefore adopt different value systems, personality characteristics, communication styles, problem-solving techniques, roles, attitudes toward sexuality, and expectations of marriage and family. These cultures overlap in many ways, but females and males place a higher priority on different aspects of each category, which leads to misunderstanding, conflict, and dissatisfaction between the genders. A brief summary of these differences is presented below.

VALUES

Most human beings have a need for both affiliation (connection with others) and autonomy (control over one's own destiny). A cornerstone of marital and family theories is finding a solution to the affiliation/autonomy conflict in human relationships. Finding a balance between these two needs can be tricky since most people feel the need to please others in order to be accepted and belong, but experience the attempt to please others as an encroachment on their autonomy. Many researchers and scholars (Brooks, 1992; Chodorow, 1978; David & Brannon, 1976; Dinnerstein, 1976; Gilligan, 1982; Majors & Billson, 1992; Miller, 1986; O'Neil, 1982; Pleck, 1981) have pointed out that men and women prioritize different values in this autonomy/affiliation dilemma, which then has an effect on every other aspect of their lives. In general men are reinforced for being autonomous, women for being connected to others. Adopting these values as priorities then affects the personality characteristics that each gender develops.

PERSONALITY CHARACTERISTICS

For males, a priority on autonomy means they want to avoid coming under someone else's control at all costs. They perceive the world in a hierarchical fashion and measure their success by where they fall in this hierarchy. They therefore become competitive, goal-oriented, and aggressive, and seek to exert power and control over themselves, nature, machines, and other people. Their focus is on winning the spoils, whether that be a game, an award, a high salary, a promotion, more land, or more electronic toys. Therefore they emphasize the actual accomplishment of a task, the doing, which is often referred to as *instrumentality*. Since reaching the top rungs of the hierarchy is a major goal, males find it necessary to suppress the softer emotions, such as fear or shame, which might indicate weakness before a competitor. This often results in their loss of the ability to identify or express their own emotions (alexithymia). The rules of manhood require that they use reason, abstract rules, logic, and principles to gain dominance. If all of that fails, they may resort to physical force, rather than submit to the will of someone else. Their primary interest is in the external world—work, politics, sports, science, law, medicine—not on the internal world of family and marriage. Consequently, men who are strongly influenced by their gender socialization are competitive, domineering, aggressive, logical, rational, emotionally repressed, controlled, and sometimes violent.

For women whose priority is affiliation, cooperation, compassion, and dependency, even submission is preferable to losing the connection with the "other." Women place a priority on nurturing others, empowering them to accomplish and succeed. They do not see the world as a hierarchy, but as an egalitarian organization where everyone helps everyone else. They are rewarded for expressing their emotions and for understanding the emotions of others. They are less task-focused and more relationship-focused, which means they will take time to tend to the needs of others while working toward a goal. Their concern for others leads them to concentrate more on the internal world of family and relationships, and diverts their attention from affairs in the external world. This, plus the fact that women who work outside the home make 75 cents on the dollar compared to men doing the same job (Decade of the Woman, 1992), frequently puts women in a dependent position. It should be mentioned that the women's movement has done a great deal to rectify this situation, but the pressure to nurture others and prioritize relationships still remains. Women who are strongly influenced by their gender socialization are nurturing, expressive, spontaneous, emotional, cooperative, compassionate, dependent, and sometimes irrational.

COMMUNICATION STYLES

Tannen (1990) has shown that men use communication to impart knowledge, to criticize, to demonstrate their superiority, to provide solutions, to offer advice—in other words, to place themselves favorably on top of the hierarchy. Women, on the other hand, use communication to provide understanding and support, give praise, validate others, and share intimate experiences (i.e., to affiliate or connect with others). These different communication styles create misunderstanding, and they create a disadvantage for each gender in a different arena. The male communication style dominates in the public arena, as men interrupt, speak loudly, critique others, and present their arguments in such a way as to win the debate, while women, using their stereotypical deferential, tentative, and polite communication style will be ignored or dismissed. On the other hand, the male communication style does not foster intimacy, which puts men at a disadvantage in the personal arena. Men find it very difficult to express themselves emotionally or to offer self-disclosure, the building blocks of an intimate relationship for women. They often do not understand what women want in the way of intimate conversation and feel inadequate to the task. Therefore, they frequently shut down verbally and the relationship suffers as a result.

PROBLEM-SOLVING TECHNIQUES

Scholars have long proposed that there is a gender preference for instrumental versus expressive behavior (Spence & Helmreich, 1978). Since as a rule males are more interested in producing results and attaining a position of authority and power in the hierarchy, they are more likely to use instrumental behavior to solve problems. That is, they are task-oriented and look for solutions to problems. In doing so, they often elevate themselves in relationship to the person owning the problem, because they are able to provide advice, use critical thinking to find answers, and produce actual solutions (Tannen, 1990). Additionally, men often prefer to think things through in solitude until they have come up with a solution, rather than verbalize their thought processes (David & Brannon, 1976; Doyle, 1989).

Women, on the other hand, are often more concerned about the relationship between themselves and the person owning the problem. They recognize the sharing of problems as an opportunity to connect on an emotional level (Tannen, 1990). They are sensitive to the feelings of the other individual and are more likely to commiserate, explore concerns, and empower the other to find his or her own solutions. Although men and women can use both problem-solving techniques, some researchers (Spence & Helmreich, 1978; Tannen, 1990) have found that they seem to have a preference for one over the other. This may lead to conflict between the genders. When women seek closeness through sharing problems and get solutions they feel put down. When men do not share problems because they prefer to be self-reliant and maintain their status on the hierarchy, women feel shut out.

SEXUALITY

Both biology and socialization play a part in differences between the genders when it comes to sexuality. Women are socialized to want a satisfying emotional relationship with a sex partner and to expect monogamy (Hite, 1987), while men are socialized to want recreational sex with multiple partners on a very frequent basis (Farrell, 1987; Zilbergeld, 1992). Men are focused on performance, are expected to be the initiators and always interested, are aroused by visual stimuli (often determined by the media), and often see orgasm as a goal to be attained (Brooks, 1995; Zilbergeld, 1992). Women are socialized to be the gate-keepers; that is, it is up to them to determine how far a sexual encounter will go. Meanwhile women are also socialized to use their beauty to obtain what they want in life (Wolf, 1991) and will often use their sexual powers for nonsexual ends (Williams, 1987).

It is easy to see how conflicts can develop in the area of sexuality. Men are not well trained to provide women with the intimacy they crave in a sexual relationship. Women are not well trained to provide men with the casual recreational sex they see in the media. Men who have been socialized to want multiple partners are expected to give up this fantasy for a monogamous relationship in order to have ready sex (Farrell, 1987). Men who are trained to be initiators may very well misread a woman's seductive behavior when she really has no intention of following through on a sexual encounter. The potential for conflict abounds.

ROLES AND EXPECTATIONS

Despite the advances in women's position in society in the United States in the last 30 years, societal pressure to fulfill century-old roles still remains. Men are expected to provide for and protect their families (Bernard, 1981; Deaux & Hanna, 1984; Doyle, 1989; Farrell, 1993; Gould, 1974). Women are expected to handle the child care and housework (Hochschild, 1989; Schwartz, 1994). Men are trained from birth to become warriors. That is, they are taught to deny fear and pain, embrace anger, be brave, stand up to other men, and come to the assistance of women and children in need (Doyle, 1989).

In the last decade, women have begun to take a more active part in protection roles, serving as firepersons, policewomen, active military, and so on. Yet even today, these roles are expected to be filled by men while the women who do so are considered special. Furthermore, although 71 percent of women in two-parent families are employed outside the home (Hoffman, 1989), the man who does not work to support his family is considered a failure. A man is defined by the work he does, while the woman is not (Bernard, 1981; David & Brannon, 1976).

At the same time, despite the fact that men are taking a more active role in parenting in the last decade (Jump & Haas, 1987; Kimmel, 1987; Levant, 1994; Levant & Kelley, 1989; Pleck, 1987), the vast majority of housework and child care still falls to the woman, whether or not she is employed full time (Hochschild, 1989; Levant, 1992). Hochschild found that even when men helped with the home care, women still retained executive responsibility for getting the job done. This situation has resulted in women putting in as much as 80-hour work weeks due to what Hochschild entitled the *second shift*. Furthermore, the woman who relegates child care to a baby-sitter while focusing on her career risks social condemnation (Public Eye, 1995) and possible loss of custody. Both men and women are criticized and punished by employers for taking time away from work for family concerns, although businesses are harsher on men than women, seeing males who put family first as slackers unworthy of promotion (Pleck, 1993). Most of corporate America has still not recognized that in 71 percent of families, both parents work. There is a need for child care and flex-time to be provided by business (Silverstein, 1991) that goes unfilled. In the meantime, when someone must miss work in order to handle childhood emergencies, it is most often the woman who is expected to do so. Likewise, the recent call for family values in politics emphasizes the importance of mother (not father) being at home for the children in order to improve the moral fiber of our country. Despite changes in the last several decades, public opinion still holds that women should be primarily responsible for rearing children, men for financially supporting them.

NEGATIVE RESULTS OF TRADITIONAL GENDER SOCIALIZATION

For decades, feminists have pointed out the negative results of gender socialization for women and have called for changes. More recently, since the development of the gender role strain paradigm by Pleck (1981), men have recognized that rigid gender socialization is detrimental to men as well. The negative results of gender socialization for both genders are summarized below.

WOMEN

McGrath, Keita, Strickland, and Russo (1990) found that the incidence of depression among women worldwide was twice that of men. These researchers attributed that depression to, among other things, the supportive and dependent role that women are expected to play with relationship to their spouses and children. That is, they are expected to give up their own needs, dreams, and wishes in order to ensure that their families are happy and fulfilled. This means, in practical terms, that they live where their spouse's career demands they live, they give up career opportunities of their own in order to follow their husbands, they defer to the wishes of their spouse and children, they serve the needs of spouse and children, and they have no time for themselves and very little autonomy over their lives. A life sacrificed for others seems unimportant; women who have given up themselves have no self-esteem. The result of this role is depression. Furthermore, the values that are labeled feminine by society are held in lower esteem in our culture than are male values. If a woman adopts male values, she is punished for being unfeminine. If she adopts feminine values she is dismissed as defective, less than a man. She cannot win. Her self-esteem suffers another blow.

Worldwide, women make 75 cents on the dollar compared to men working at the same job (Decade of the Woman, 1992; Ferraro, 1984; U. S. Department of Labor, 1985 [as cited in Lott, 1994]). This situation leads to poverty (Morgan, 1991; Weitzman, 1985) or economic dependence for many women. Thus women will endure an unhappy and perhaps abusive relationship in order to provide for themselves and their children. Furthermore, a woman's preoccupation with child care and housework does not allow her the time for or access to experts in the external world in the areas of politics, law, medicine, economics, and so on. Her lack of knowledge in these areas puts her at a disadvantage compared to her male counterpart whose work puts him in regular contact with professionals. The women's movement has made great strides in changing some of these problems for a handful of upper-middle-class Caucasian women. Unfortunately, however, a majority of women still experience these disadvantages. Such problems are a direct result of socialization messages that women should serve their spouses and children in the home rather than focus on their own education and career and that males' employment is more important and valuable than that of females.

Since woman are taught to define themselves through their relationships, they will often feel like failures if they do not have a male partner even when they are very successful in their careers (Russianoff, 1981). They will defer major decisions such as where to live and whether to purchase a house until they find their lifelong partner (Dowling, 1982). They may monitor their relationships closely, often creating unnecessary conflict with their partners because they believe it is their job to keep the relationship satisfying. They tend to defer to their partners, cooperate more than they would like, take blame for problems, and try to change themselves in order to preserve the relationship. In other words, they give up power and lose themselves because they have been socialized to believe women are nothing without a man. In addition, because women are taught to be nurturing, to empower others, to cooperate and encourage, they frequently lose the ability to express anger or assert themselves. Instead they turn anger inward and become depressed.

Women suffer role overload when they take on the second shift (Hochschild, 1989) and the third shift (keeping oneself beautiful through exercise, diet, surgery, cosmetics, clothing) (Wolf, 1991) and become totally exhausted. As if that were not bad enough, some women suffer eating disorders (Bloom, Glitter, Gutwill, Kogel, & Zaphiropoulos, 1994; Gutwill, 1994; Root, 1990) as a result of attempting to fulfill the socialization messages regarding their appearance. The socialization messages that tell a woman that she is only valued for her body can be very detrimental.

MEN

Because people tend to think of males, at least some males, as being privileged to occupy a position of influence and power in today's world, it is sometimes difficult to recognize that male gender role socialization is also detrimental. Nevertheless, traditional male socialization has many negative impacts.

Males die 10 years earlier than women. Researchers attribute the shortened life span in part to the psychosomatic illness of cardiovascular disease with its resultant heart attacks and strokes. It is believed that the pressure to achieve, to compete, to repress emotion, and to control oneself contributes to the higher incidence of cardiovascular disease in men (Waldron, 1976). Men are less likely than women to visit doctors for routine checkups because it is not manly to do so (Nathanson, 1977). Therefore, illnesses that might have been prevented are missed until it is too late. Males also die younger due to risk-taking behavior that is encouraged by the aggressive "macho" attitude that young men are expected to achieve in order to be accepted and respected by peers. Young men go through an initiation that requires that they do dangerous things like drive too fast, drink too much, or physically challenge one another in fights (Harrison, Chin, & Ficcarrotto, 1989; Herek, 1987; Verbrugge, 1985). As mentioned above, men also take over the majority of the protector role in society, which means they are more likely to die in war or in life-threatening occupations (Farrell, 1993). Despite the privileges that come with masculinity, malehood is a danger to one's health (Harrison, 1978).

Males are also restricted in their need to define themselves through their careers (David & Brannon, 1976; Doyle, 1989; O'Neil, 1982). The pressure to make money and provide for their families prevents them from being able to fully explore their creativity or to fulfill other dreams or pursue other adventures. The result is that many men become depressed at midlife and frequently shirk their responsibilities in order to live life more fully. Others become bitter and resentful. The focus on career also separates men from their children. Many men would prefer to have more time with their families but are prevented from doing so because of societal pressure to achieve at work.

As stated earlier, many men suffer from alexithymia, the inability to recognize or express their emotions. Because they have been taught to suppress emotions that are soft or weak during the warrior training, they experience such emotions as a "buzz" (Levant & Kopecky, 1995) and can neither identify their feelings nor discuss them with significant others. This dysfunction places them at great disadvantage in intimate relationships with women, children, and other men. Instead of communicating their needs with others, they seek to avoid the uncomfortable feelings by distracting themselves through activity or drugs. Thus, problems never get resolved. Also affecting the male's ability to develop intimate relationships with women is his tendency to divert all tender feelings into sexuality and to objectify women's bodies (Brooks, 1995).

Men suffer from defensive autonomy (Levant, 1996). As little boys become aware that they are different from Mommy, they feel the need to pull away and be separate from her in order to develop their own sexual identity (Chodorow, 1978). As they get older, they fear engulfment if they allow their emotional dependence on women to show. They come to see closeness with a woman as a loss of masculinity. They resist suggestions or requests made by women because responding to such requests or suggestions might imply they are controlled by women (O'Neil, 1982). Furthermore, they avoid intimacy based on the sharing of soft emotions. Such behaviors severely limit a man's ability to develop a long-term, satisfying relationship with a woman.

Men also avoid emotional intimacy with other males. In a hierarchical system where competitors are always looking for the weaknesses in each other in order to climb to the top, it is dangerous to be emotional, vulnerable, and open (Nardi, 1992). Many men also isolate themselves from other men because they are homophobic. They fear that the expression of emotional closeness with another male through conversation or a physical display of affection indicates that they are homosexual (O'Neil, 1982), which in our society is still viewed very negatively despite increased tolerance over the past decade. This fear of closeness means that many men live lives of isolation and loneliness, never experiencing the connection with others that is considered an important part of a fulfilling lifestyle. All of these dysfunctions are a direct result of the rigid gender messages men receive as they grow up.

EFFECTS OF THE WOMEN'S AND MEN'S MOVEMENTS ON GENDER ROLES

Until Betty Friedan wrote *The Feminine Mystique* in 1963, male and female gender roles in the United States were fairly clearly defined. Most women and men who were reared before 1963 had clear role models and specific directives that they either accepted or rejected. As can be seen from the above discussion, many of the old value systems have been successfully challenged by the women's movement in the last three decades. More recently, the men's movement has called for changes in men's gender socialization as well. However, century-old messages do not die easily. Instead, both men and women of today are faced with a difficult dilemma. The new rules are overlaid like transparencies on top of the old. So rather than following a new set of clearly defined rules about gender roles, younger generations are faced with confusing, contradictory, and conflictual messages.

For example, new women are expected to be competitive, career-oriented, assertive, self-sufficient, decisive, independent leaders who can hold their own with men in the businessplace. However, they are still expected to be nurturing, supportive, emotionally sensitive, cooperative, relationship-oriented, and willing to sacrifice themselves for their spouse and children. They are also expected to not only contribute half (or more) of the family income, but to do the housework, the child care, and to keep their Barbie-doll bodies in perfect condition for their sexually hungry spouses. There are two problems with this picture. The first is that there is not enough time in a lifetime to perform all of these functions well even if a woman did measure up to the Superwoman Syndrome, which is the model held up for women today. The Second and Third Shifts mentioned above take their toll both physically and emotionally. By the time the Superwoman has accomplished all of her daily tasks, there is no time left for herself or for simply enjoying life. Therefore, new women often find themselves in angry conflict with spouses who will not give up their time for themselves in order to do housework or take care of the children. Or, alternatively, they insist on ownership of the child care and housework so that it must be done their way (which is usually the way their professional-housekeeper mothers did it). This then creates altercations with husbands who are willing to help but want to do it in a different, usually short-cut manner. In other words, they would bring home fast food rather than cook a hot meal or use paper plates, rather than having to do the dishes.

Second, the various roles require different and often contradictory skills. Because women have had several decades now to practice their skills, one of the things they have learned to do is switch channels. That is, they have learned how to be nurturing and supportive at home with husband and children, but competitive and decisive at work. Nevertheless, there are times when the two roles simply clash and choices have to be made. For example, problems arise when she gets a promotion that requires moving and he does not wish to move. Or more frequently, when a child gets sick and both spouses have major presentations to give at work. The old ideas regarding the greater value of the man's career often surface at times like these. They can either be reinforced by the earning power of the man versus his wife, or less often contradicted by the financial considerations.

Likewise for men, the new rules say they should be emotionally sensitive, show the ability to cry, be willing to take care of their children, help with the housework, be verbally expressive, and focus more on their families. But at the same time they must still make more money than she does and if possible provide for her and the children while they are little so she does not have to work outside the home. He should make enough money to give her things (house, car, vacations, jewelry) even though he goes to the children's school play and Christmas party. He should help with the housework but he should do it her way. He can take care of the kids, but he must remember that she is the child-care expert. He should be emotionally vulnerable, but still be able to fight off an attacker, if that becomes necessary. He should be able to express his softer emotions, but he cannot be so much of a wimp as to scare her into thinking she must take care of him instead of vice versa. He should be sensitive to her sexual needs, but still should be the initiator. The problem for the man is that he does not know how much to modify the old and how far to go with the new. He treads a tightrope. At the same time, he dislikes many of the changes that have come with the new rules because they mean more work and less autonomy for him. The conflicts between the new woman and the new man are complicated by the fact that the new rules have not been totally accepted by either gender.

DANGERS OF GENDER-BLIND PSYCHOTHERAPY

In the 1970s, feminist psychologists began to critique the psychological theories and practices of the time through a feminist lens. Studies (Brodsky & Hare-Mustin, 1980; Chesler, 1972; Mowbray, Lanir, & Hulce, 1984) found that clinicians had a double standard of mental health with different expectations for female and male clients. Women who were more emotional, dependent, compliant, and submissive were considered typical, but neurotic, while women who were ambitious, assertive, and achievement-oriented were considered psychologically maladjusted. Marriage and children were considered necessary ingredients for women's happiness, but not for men. It was also found that women used psychotherapy more than men, were more often hospitalized, and were prescribed drugs more often for mental disorders (Anderson & Holder, 1989; Fidell, 1981; Mowbray et al., 1984). Furthermore, women were sometimes sexually abused by male therapists (Bates & Brodsky, 1989). Explanations for this discrepancy include (1) the compliant and dependent behavior encouraged in females at the time; (2) the tendency of women to solve problems through talking about them as opposed to male instrumentality or diversion tactics; and (3) the detrimental effects of women's roles in society. The feminist critique also extended to personality and developmental theories that held male autonomy in high esteem and failed to address the importance of affiliation and connectivity. Using measures of mental health based on a male value system and male experience caused disadvantage to females who were not respected for being different, but viewed as defective.

Much has changed since the 1970s. The blatant abuses mentioned above are less prevalent. Therapists no longer automatically assume a woman should be compliant or married with children in order to be healthy. On the other hand, gender training affects therapists in such subtle ways that they often perpetuate the detrimental effects of gender socialization by simply assuming things must be as they have always been. Today therapists must be aware of how the different socialization messages given to women and men will affect not only their perceptions and lives, but also how they participate in therapy. Only recently have writers (Brooks, 1992, 1996; Brooks & Silverstein, 1995; Cleary, 1987; Diamond, 1987; Levant, 1990; Long, 1987; Mintz & O'Neil, 1990) begun to point out the link between gender socialization and men's psychopathology, such as alcohol abuse and domestic violence, as well as their reluctance to participate in therapy. For example, the male emphasis on self-reliance, emotional suppression, instrumental versus expressive methods of problem solving, and competition makes psychotherapy a very threatening environment. Not only do they feel inadequate to the task, but they are also in danger of losing ground on the all-important hierarchy.

GENDER-SENSITIVE PSYCHOTHERAPY

Gender-sensitive psychotherapy can be systemically defined as therapy that is sensitive to the influence of men's and women's gender socialization and roles on the effectiveness and outcome of psychotherapy. Philpot, Brooks, Lusterman, and Nutt (1997) have proposed a model of gender-sensitive psychotherapy based on guidelines developed by the Division of Family Psychology of the American Psychological Association (Philpot & Brooks, 1988). These guidelines suggest that therapists should

1. Be knowledgeable about the differing perceptions of reality for men and women growing out of biological differences, male-female developmental theory, socialization in a capitalist-patriarchal society, value systems, levels of moral development, role definitions, and real power differentials in the political, economic, and legal arenas.
2. Understand the implications of the current literature in women's studies, men's studies, and gender-difference research.
3. Be familiar with the theoretical bases for understanding gender differences and be aware of the uses and limitations of the theories.
4. Impose no limits on the roles to be played by males or females and impose no limits on the potential for growth by either sex.
5. View the often predictable dichotomies of distancer-pursuer, expressive-instrumental, logic-emotion, and function-form as inevitable, but perhaps exaggerated, results of socialization rather than intrapsychic pathology.
6. Approach therapy from as androgynous a perspective as possible, given the limitations of their own gender, maintaining an awareness of the special needs of men and women and of the techniques that will most facilitate treatment for each.

MAJOR CONCEPTS OF GENDER-SENSITIVE PSYCHOTHERAPY

Both clients and therapist must understand and accept certain concepts that form the foundation of gender-sensitive psychotherapy. These include the gender ecosystem, gender socialization, androgyny, empathic knowing, gender co-evolution, gender strain, and the gender role journey. Although several of these concepts have been discussed at length, a brief description of each follows.

GENDER ECOSYSTEM

A system refers to a group of interrelated individuals that has a boundary around it, such as a family, a couple, or a sibling group. An ecosystem is a large system such as ethnic groups or religions that share beliefs, attitudes, expectations, and behavior. Male and female gender ecosystems often transcend even ethnic and national cultures in the amount of influence they have over an individual's expectations and attitudes.

GENDER SOCIALIZATION

As discussed in a previous section, this term refers to the process of learning what it is to be a man or a woman through modeling, cognition, and reward and punishment.

The gender-sensitive psychotherapist believes that women and men have the capacity to adopt all human values, whether those are labeled feminine or masculine by our society. A belief in the value of androgyny must be conveyed to the clients so that they can understand it is acceptable to be both rational and emotional, both instrumental and expressive, both connected to others and autonomous. Individuals must feel free to access attributes that have been traditionally assigned to the other gender whenever appropriate.

Empathic knowing refers to the kind of deep understanding that comes with having heard and shared the experience of the other with empathy. A goal of gender-sensitive psychotherapy is to help clients reach a point where they sense the pain of the other gender, give up defensive posturing, and work together to change the restrictive nature of rigid gender messages.

As previously explained, gender co-evolution is the process of evolving as a man or woman together. Males and females have a great deal of influence over the values, behaviors, and attitudes of the other gender by how they react and what they choose to reward and punish. Recognizing the role one plays in the shaping of the other is empowering because it gives both genders the ability to bring about desired change by refusing to endorse rigid gender expectations of the other.

The gender role strain paradigm delineated by Pleck (1981) has been described earlier in this chapter. Therapists may need to raise the consciousness of their clients in order that both genders understand the detriments of rigid gender socialization and become motivated to change.

O'Neil and Egan (1992) have coined the term *gender-role journey* to describe the process of moving from a place of total unconscious acceptance of traditional gender roles to empathic knowing accompanied by a commitment to break detrimental gender patterns together. The journey consists of five steps: (1) unconscious compliance, (2) vague dissatisfaction with gender messages, (3) consciousness-raising accompanied by anger and blame, (4) taking responsibility for self and making unilateral changes, and (5) empathic knowing and proactive change. Clients will predictably move through these stages during therapy.

THERAPEUTIC TECHNIQUES

The field of gender-sensitive psychotherapy, which is based on the research coming out of the men's and women's movements, is relatively new. Techniques have been developed by a handful of therapists (Levant, 1992; Levant & Silverstein, in press; Lusterman, 1989; Markman & Kraft, 1989; Philpot, 1991, in press; Philpot & Brooks, 1995; Philpot et al., 1997), but as yet none have been empirically validated (Levant & Philpot, in press). A few of the techniques common to most models are described below.

VALIDATION AND NORMALIZATION

A very important and delicate task that befalls the therapist is that of validating the experience of both male and female simultaneously. Often the couple is polarized around an issue, believing that only one of their perceptions could be right and trying desperately to elicit positive judgment from the therapist. The therapist must provide each partner an opportunity to present her or his side of the issue in a way that does not blame the other. When a problem is presented that has clear gender roots, it is the opportune time for the therapist to normalize the perception and to educate the client regarding traditional gender socialization. This can be done in such a way as to demonstrate that the process of gender socialization has victimized both partners and that neither is responsible for those rigid rules. It is helpful to avoid toxic issues at first, until the couple is well into the process of therapy and both partners feel heard by the therapist. Gaining distance from present issues by having the clients discuss early gender training learned from parents and teachers is also useful. The therapist must interrupt any exchanges that blame the other gender for the problem. This then reduces defensiveness and allows partners to hear each other—the first step to empathic knowing.

PSYCHOEDUCATION

A major portion of the therapist's job will be educating the clients regarding the process and stereotypical results of gender socialization. This can be done in the therapy session, through videotapes and movies, and through bibliotherapy. The goal is to facilitate the gender role journey of both partners through education.

GENDER BROKER

The therapist will serve as a gender broker (Pittman, 1985), reframing, explaining, and translating between the genders. Using the metaphor of different cultures or different worlds, the therapist can serve as mediator and diplomat, decoding the message from one gender into the frame of reference of the other. Likewise, the therapist can teach each gender how to understand the other and how to talk the other's language. This process goes beyond simply translating language. The therapist can also explain attitudes, behaviors, feelings, expectations, and values in the same manner. The goal here is to change the client's attitude from that of wanting the other to be exactly like oneself, to one of understanding, accepting, and appreciating differences, and working together to meet mutual goals.

UNIFICATION AGAINST THE SYSTEM

It has long been understood that a scapegoat helps to bring people together and create bonds. When the clients stop blaming each other for their predicaments and begin to blame the rigid gender roles they have absorbed, they are well on their gender role journey. Although there are many good things about gender socialization, the therapist can unite the couple against those detrimental aspects of gender roles, so the couple will form a team to bring about change. This is done through a process of validation, normalization, and psychoeducation.

EMPATHIC INTERVIEWING

At some point the therapist will want to use basic communication skills to get the clients to listen to each other's gender stories. Particularly important are open-ended questions, active listening skills, reflection, the avoidance of interruptions and defensive responses, and validation of the needs and concerns of the other. It sometimes helps to explain to the couple that you want them to interview the other as if for a newspaper article, with no preconceived notions and no sense that what the other says reflects on them in any way. They should basically just be curious about the other partner's experience.

GENDER INQUIRY

Philpot and associates (1997) have developed a model of questions organized in developmental order regarding gender messages received since birth. The goal of the gender inquiry is to bring insight regarding the fact that gender messages come from the larger culture and are passed down across generations. The questions do not have to be asked in a rigid sequential manner, but are offered as a guide for the therapist. The therapist conducts the gender inquiry with one spouse in the presence of the other, so that both can learn from this process. The purpose of the inquiry is to teach the clients that the gender ecosystem is at the core of many of the misunderstandings between the spouses, to depersonalize the conflict, to demonstrate how each gender molds and influences the other across generations, to expand cognitive maps, and to offer the possibility of change for this and future generations. The interested party is referred to Philpot and colleagues (1997) for an indepth discussion of these and other techniques illustrated by case examples.

CONCLUSION

Gender has a very large influence on the way people think, feel, and behave. It cannot be ignored by therapists without peril to the therapeutic endeavor. In this chapter I have attempted to sensitize the reader to the importance gender plays in the lives of our clients and in our methods of conducting therapy. Rigid gender roles can be detrimental to both genders and to our relationships. Men and women have the capacity to access all human traits and to play all human roles, when appropriate. Traditional gender socialization has the effect of training us to reject half of ourselves. The goal of gender-sensitive psychotherapy is to help our clients, and incidentally ourselves, become whole again.

REFERENCES

Anderson, C. M., & Holder, D. P. (1989). Women and serious mental disorders. In M. McGoldrick, C. M. Anderson, & F. Walsh (Eds.), *Women in families: A framework for family therapy* (pp. 381–405). New York: Norton.

Archer, J. (1987). Beyond sex differences: Comments on Borrill and Reid. *Bulletin of the British Psychological Society, 40,* 88–90.

Basow, S. (1986). *Gender stereotypes: Traditions and alternatives.* Monterey, CA: Brooks/Cole.

Bates, C., & Brodsky, A. (1989). *Sex in the therapy hour: A case of professional incest.* New York: Guilford Press.

Belenky, M., Clinchy B., Goldberger, N., & Tarule, J. (1986). *Women's ways of knowing: The development of self, voice, and mind.* New York: Basic Books.

Bem, S. L. (1974). The measurement of psychological androgyny. *Journal of Personality and Social Psychology, 42,* 155–162.

Bem, S. L. (1981). Gender schema theory: A cognitive account of sex typing. *Psychological Review, 88,* 354–364.

Bem, S. L. (1982). Gender schema theory and self-schema theory compared: A comment on Markus, Crane, Bernstein, and Siladi's "self-schemas and gender." *Journal of Personality and Social Psychology, 43,* 1192–1194.

Bem, S. L. (1983). Gender schema theory and its implications for child development: Raising gender-aschematic children in a gender schematic society. *Signs, 8,* 598–616.

Bem, S. L. (1984). Androgony and gender schema theory: A conceptual and empirical integration. In T. B. Sonderegger (Ed.), *Nebraska Symposium on Motivation: Psychology of gender.* Lincoln: University of Nebraska Press.

Bem, S. L. (1987). Gender schema theory and romantic tradition. In P. Shaver & C. Hendrick (Eds.), *Sex and gender* (Vol. 7, pp. 251–271). Newbury Park, CA: Sage Publications.

Bernard, J. (1981). The good provider role: Its rise and fall. *American Psychologist, 36,* 1–12.

Bloom, C., Glitter, A., Gutwill, S., Kogel, L., & Zaphiropoulous, L. (Eds.). (1994). *Eating problems: A feminist psychoanalytic treatment model.* New York: HarperCollins.

Bradbard, M. R., & Endsley, R. C. (1983). The effects of sex-typed labeling on preschool children's information-seeking and retention. *Sex Roles, 9,* 247–260.

Brodsky, A. M., & Hare-Mustin, R. T. (1980). *Women and psychotherapists: An assessment of research and practice.* New York: Guilford Press.

Brooks, G. R. (1992). Gender-sensitive family therapy in a violent culture. *Topics in Family Psychology and Counseling, 1,* 24–36.

Brooks, G. R. (1995). *The centerfold syndrome: How men can overcome objectification and achieve intimacy with women.* San Francisco, CA: Jossey-Bass.

Brooks, G. R. (1996). Treatment for therapy-resistant men. In M. Andronico (Ed.), *Men in groups: Insights, interventions, and psychoeducational work* (pp. 7–19). Washington, DC: American Psychological Association.

Brooks, G. R., & Silverstein, L. B. (1995). Understanding the dark side of masculinity: An integrative systems model. In R. F. Levant & W. S. Pollack (Eds.), *A new psychology of men* (pp. 280–336). New York: Basic Books.

Buss, D. (1995). Psychological sex differences: Origins through sexual selection. *American Psychologist, 50,* 164–168.

Chafetz, J. (1978). *Masculine/feminine or human?* (2nd ed). Itasca, IL: Peacock.

Chesler, P. (1972). *Women and madness.* Garden City, NY: Doubleday.

Chodorow, N. (1978). *The reproduction of mothering.* Berkeley, CA: University of California Press.

Choti, S., Marston, A., & Holston, S. (1987). Gender and personality variables in film-induced sadness and crying. *Journal of Social and Clinical Psychology, 5,* 535–544.

Cleary, P. D. (1987). Gender differences in stress-related disorders. In R. C. Barnett, L. Biener, & G. K. Baruch (Eds.), *Gender and stress* (pp. 39–72). New York: Free Press.

Cobb, N. J., Stevens-Long, J., & Goldstein, S. (1982). The influence of televised models on toy preference in children. *Sex Roles, 8,* 1075–1080.

Courtney, A. E., & Whipple, T. W. (1983). *Sex stereotyping in advertising.* Lexington, MA: Heath.

David, D., & Brannon, R. (Eds.). (1976). *The forty-nine percent majority: The male sex role.* Reading, MA: Addison-Wesley.

Deaux, K., & Hanna, R. (1984). Courtship in the personals column: The influence of gender and sexual orientation. *Sex Roles, 11,* 363–375.

Decade of the Woman. (1992, December 31). *Providence Journal Bulletin,* p. A8.

Diamond, J. (1987). Counseling male substance abusers. In M. Scher, M. Stevens, G. Good, & G. Eichenfield (Eds.), *Handbook of counseling and psychotherapy with men* (pp. 332–342). Newbury Park, CA: Sage.

Dinnerstein, D. (1976). *The mermaid and the minotour: Sexual arrangements and the human malaise.* New York: Harper & Row.

Dominick, J. R. (1979). The portrayal of women in prime time, *Sex Roles, 5,* 405–411.

Dowling, C. (1982). *The Cinderella complex.* New York: Pocketbooks.

Downs, A. C. (1983). Letters to Santa Claus: Elementary school-age children's sex-typed toy preferences in a natural setting. *Sex Roles, 9,* 159–163.

Downs, A. C., & Gowan, C. (1980). Sex differences in reinforcement and punishment on prime-time television. *Sex Roles, 6,* 683–694.

Downs, A. C., & Harrison, S. K. (1985). Embarrassing age spots or just plain ugly? Physical attractiveness stereotyping as an instrument of sexism on American television commercials. *Sex Roles, 13,* 9–19.

Doyle, J. A. (1989). *The male experience* (2nd ed.). Dubuque, IA: William C. Brown.

Dworkin, A. (1981). *Pornography: Men possessing women.* New York: Perigee/Putnam.

Ehrenberg, M. (1989). *Women in prehistory.* London: British Museum Press.

Fagot, B. I. (1978). The influence of sex on parental reactions to toddler children. *Child Development, 49,* 459–463.

Farrrell, W. (1987). *Why men are the way they are.* New York: McGraw-Hill.

Farrell, W. (1993). *The myth of male power.* New York: Simon & Schuster.

Fasteau, M. (1974). *The male machine.* New York: McGraw-Hill.

Fausto-Sterling, A. (1985). *Myths of gender: Biological theories about women and men.* New York: Basic Books.

Ferraro, G. A. (1984). Bridging the wage gap: Pay equity and job evaluations. *American Psychologist, 39,* 1166–1170.

Fidell, L. (1981). Sex differences in psychotropic drug use. *Professional Psychology, 12,* 156–162.

Fiorenza, E. S. (1983). *In memory of her: A feminist theological reconstruction of Christian origins.* New York: Crossroad.

French, M. (1985) *Beyond power: On women, men and morals.* New York: Ballantine Books.

Friedan, B. (1963). *The feminine mystique.* New York: Norton.

Geis, F. L. (1993). Self-fulfilling prophecies: A social psychological view of gender. In A. E. Beall & R. J. Sternberg (Eds.), *The psychology of gender* (pp. 9–54). New York: Guilford Press.

Gilligan, C. (1982). *In a different voice.* Cambridge: Harvard University Press.

Gilmore, D. (1990). *Manhood in the making: Cultural concepts of masculinity.* New Haven, CT: Yale University Press.

Goldberg, S., & Lewis, M. (1969). Play behavior in the year-old infant: Early sex differences. *Child Development, 40,* 21–31.

Gould, R. (1974). Measuring masculinity by the size of a paycheck. In J. Pleck & J. Sawyer (Eds.), *Men and masculinity* (pp. 96–100). Englewood Cliffs, NJ: Prentice Hall.

Griffin, S. (1981). *Pornography and silence: Culture's revenge against nature.* New York: Harper & Row.

Gur, R. (1995). Sex difference in regional cerebral glucose metabolism during a resting state. *Science, 267,* 528–531.

Gutwill, S. (1994). Women's eating problems: Social context and internalization of culture. In C. Bloom, A. Glitter, S. Gutwill, L. Kogel, & L. Zaphiropoulous (Eds.), *Eating problems: A feminist psychoanalytic treatment model* (pp. 1–27). New York: HarperCollins.

Harris, M. (1977). *Cannibals and kings.* New York: Random House.

Harrison, J. (1978). Warning: The male sex role may be hazardous to your health. *Journal of Social Issues, 34,* 65–86.

Harrison, J., Chin, J., & Ficcarrotto, T. (1989). Warning: Masculinity may be hazardous to your health. In M. S. Kimmel & M. A. Messner (Eds.), *Men's lives* (pp. 296–309). New York: Macmillan.

Hartley, R. E. (1959). Sex role pressures and the socialization of the male child. *Psychological Reports, 5,* 457–468.

Hartley, R. E. (1974). Sex role pressures and the socialization of the male child. In J. Pleck & J. Sawyer (Eds.), *Men and masculinity* (pp. 7–13), Englewood Cliffs, NJ: Prentice-Hall.

Harway, M. (1980). Sex bias in educational-vocational counseling. *Psychology of Women Quarterly, 4,* 412–423.

Harway, M., & Astin, H. S. (1977). *Sex discrimination in career counseling and education.* New York: Praeger.

Herek, G. M. (1987). Of heterosexual masculinity: Some psychical consequences of the social construction of gender and sexuality. In M. S. Kimmel (Ed.), *Changing men: New directions in research on men and masculinity* (pp. 68–82). Newbury Park, CA: Sage Publications.

Hite, S. (1987). *Women and love: A cultural revolution in progress.* New York: Knopf.

Hochschild, A. (1989). *The second shift: Working parents and the revolution at home.* New York: Viking Penguin.

Hoffman, L. (1989). Effects of maternal employment in the two parent family. *American Psychologist, 32,* 544–657.

Hyde, J., & Plant, E. A. (1995). Magnitude of psychological gender differences. *American Psychologist, 3,* 159–161.

Jump, T., & Haas, L. (1987). Fathers in transition: Dual-career fathers participating in child care. In M. Kimmel (Ed.), *Changing men: New directions in research on men and masculinity* (pp. 98–114). Newbury Park, CA: Sage Publications.

Kelly, M. (1981). Development and the sexual division of labor: An introduction. *Signs, 7,* 268–278.

Kimmel, M. S. (1987). Rethinking "masculinity": New directions for research. In M. S. Kimmel (Ed.), *Changing men: New directions in research on men and masculinity* (pp. 9–24). Newbury Park, CA: Sage.

Kolbenschlag, M. (1981). *Kiss Sleeping Beauty good-bye.* Toronto: Bantam.

Lakoff, R. T. (1975). *Language and women's place.* New York: Harper & Row.

Lakoff, R. T. (1990). *Talking power: The politics of language.* New York: Basic Books.

Lambert, W., Yackley, A., & Hein, R. (1971). Child training values of English Canadian and French Canadian parents. *Canadian Journal of Behavioral Sciences, 3,* 217–236.

Lerner, I. M. (1968). *Heredity, evolution, and society.* San Francisco: Freeman.

Levant, R. F. (1990). Psychological services designed for man: A psychoeducational approach. *Psychotherapy, 27,* 309–315.

Levant, R. F. (1992). Toward the reconstruction of masculinity. *Journal of Family Psychology, 5* (3&4), 379–402.

Levant, R. F. (1994). *Desperately seeking language: Methods for treating alexithymia.* Paper presented at the Annual Convention of the American Psychological Association, Los Angeles, CA.

Levant, R. F., & Kelley, J. (1989). *Between father and child.* New York: Viking.

Levant, R. F., & Kopecky, G. (1995). *Masculinity reconstructed.* New York: Dutton/Plume.

Levant, R. F. (1996). The new psychology of men. *Professional Psychology: Research and Practice* 27(3), 259–265.

Levant, R. F., & Philpot, C. L. (in press). Conceptualizing gender in marital and family therapy research: The gender role strain paradigm. In H. Liddle & D. Santisteban, (Eds.), *Family psychology intervention science.* Washington, DC: American Psychological Association.

Levant, R. F., & Silverstein, L. (in press). Integrating gender and family systems theories: the "both/and" approach to treating a postmodern couple. In S. H. McDaniel, D.-D. Lusterman, & C. L. Philpot (Eds.), *A casebook for integrating family therapy.* Washington, DC: APA Books.

Long, D. (1987). Working with men who batter. In M. Scher, M. Stevens, G. Good, & G. Eichenfield (Eds.), *Handbook of counseling and psychotherapy with men* (pp. 305–320). Newbury Park, CA: Sage Publications.

Lott, B. (1994). Women's lives: *Themes and variations in gender learning.* Pacific Grove, CA: Brooks/Cole.

Lusterman, D.-D. (1989). Empathic interviewing. In G. Brooks, D.-D. Lusterman, R. Nutt, & C. Philpot (Chair), *Men and women relating: The carrot or the stick?* Symposium presented at the Annual Conference of the American Association for Marriage and Family Therapy, San Francisco.

Majors, R., & Billson, J. M. (1992). *Cool pose: The dilemmas of black manhood in America.* Lexington, MA: Lexington Books.

Markman, H. J., & Kraft, S. A. (1989). Men and women in marriage: Dealing with gender differences in marital therapy. *The Behavior Therapist, 12,* 51–56.

McGrath, E., Keita, G., Strickland, B., & Russo, N. (1990). *Women and depression: Risk factors and treatment issues.* Washington, DC: American Psychological Association.

Mellen, J. (1978). *Women and their sexuality in the new film.* New York: Dell.

Miller, J. B. (1986). *Toward a new psychology of women* (2nd ed.). Boston: Beacon Press.

Mintz, L. B., & O'Neil, J. M. (1990). Gender roles, sex, and the process of psychotherapy: Many questions and few answers. *Journal of Counseling and Development, 68,* 381–387.

Morgan, L. (1991). *After marriage ends: Economic consequences for midlife women.* Newbury Park, CA: Sage Publications.

Mowbray, C., Lanir, S., & Hulce, M. (1984). *Women and mental health: New directions for change.* New York: Haworth Press.

Nardi, P. M. (Ed.). (1992). *Men's friendships.* Newbury Park, CA: Sage Publications.

Nathanson, C. A. (1977). Sex roles as variables in preventive health behavior. *Journal of Community Health, 3,* 142–155.

O'Neil, J. M. (1982). Gender-role conflict and strain in men's lives. In K. Solomon & N. Levy (Eds.), *Men in transition: Theory and therapy.* New York: Plenum Press.

O'Neil, J. M., & Egan, J. (1992). Men's and women's gender role journeys: A metaphor for healing, transition, and transformation. In B. R. Wainrib (Ed.), *Gender issues across the life cycle* (pp. 107–123). New York: Springer.

Pittman, F. (1985). Gender myths: When does gender become pathology? *Family Therapy Networker, 9,* 24–33.

Philpot, C. L. (1991). Gender-sensitive couples' therapy: A systemic definition. *Journal of Family Psychotherapy, 2*(3), 19–40.

Philpot, C. L., & Brooks, G. R. (1988). *Guidelines for gender-sensitive psychotherapy.* Unpublished manuscript.

Philpot, C. L. (in press). Someday my prince will come. In S. H. McDaniel, D.-D. Lusterman, & C. L. Philpot (Eds.), *A casebook for integrating family therapy.* Washington, DC: APA Books.

Philpot, C. L., & Brooks, G. R. (1995). Intergender communication and gender sensitive family therapy. In R. Mikesell, D.-D. Lusterman, & S. McDaniel (Eds.), *Integrating family therapy: Handbook of family psychology and systems theory* (pp. 303–325). Washington, DC: American Psychological Association.

Philpot, C. L., Brooks, G. R., Lusterman. D-D., & Nutt, R. (1997). *Bridging separate gender worlds: Why men and women clash and how therapists can bring them together.* Washington, DC: American Psychological Association.

Pleck, J. (1981). *The myth of masculinity.* Cambridge, MA: MIT Press.

Pleck, J. (1987). American fathering in historical perspective. In M. S. Kimmel (Ed.), *Changing men: New directions in research on men and masculinity* (pp. 83–97). Beverly Hills, CA: Sage Publications.

Pleck, J. (1993). Are "family-supportive" employer policies relevant to men? In J. D. Hood (Ed.), *Work, family, and masculinities.* Beverly Hills, CA: Sage Publications.

Public Eye: Does father know best? (1995, March 20) *Time,* pp. 40–45.

Reinartz, K. F. (1975). The paper doll: Images of American women in popular songs. In J. Freeman (Ed.), *Women: A feminist perspective* (pp. 293–308). Palo Alto, CA: Mayfield.

Root, M. P. (1990). Disorder eating in women of color. *Sex Roles, 22,* 525–536.

Ruether, R. R. (1983). *Sexism and God-talk: Toward a feminist theology.* Boston: Beacon Press.

Russianoff, P. (1981). *Why do I think I am nothing without a man?* Toronto: Bantam Books.

Sadker, M. P., & Sadker, D. M. (1985, March). Sexism in the schoolroom of the 80's. *Psychology Today,* pp. 54–57.

Schwartz, L. A., & Markham, W. T. (1985). Sex stereotyping in children's toy advertisements. *Sex Roles, 12,* 157–170.

Schwartz, P. (1994, September 7). How men act as parents can improve marriages. *St. Paul Pioneer Press,* AE.

Shaywitz, S., & Shaywitz, B. (1995). Sex differences in the functional organization of the brain for language. *Nature, 373,* 607–609.

Silverstein, L. (1991). Transforming the debate about child care and maternal employment. *American Psychologist, 46,* 1025–1032.

Spence, J. T., & Helmreich, R. L. (1978). *Masculinity & femininity: Their psychological dimensions, correlates, and antecedents.* Austin: University of Texas Press.

Tannen, D. (1990). *You just don't understand: Women and men in conversation.* New York: Ballantine Books.

U.S. Department of Labor, Bureau of Labor Statistics. (1985). *Employment and earnings, April 1985.* Washington, DC: U.S. Government Printing Office.

Ungar, S. B. (1982). The sex-typing of adult and child behavior in toy sales. *Sex Roles, 8,* 251–260.

Verbrugge, L. M. (1985). Gender and health: An update on hypothesis and evidence. *Journal of Health and Social Behavior, 26,* 156–182.

Waldron, I. (1976). Why do women live longer than men? *Journal of Human Stress, 2,* 1–13.

Weitz, S. (1977). *Sex roles: Biological, psychological and social foundations.* New York: Oxford University Press.

Weitzman, L. (1985). *The divorce revolution: The unexpected social and economic consequences for women and children in America.* New York: Free Press.

Weitzman, L., Eifler, E., & Ross, C. (1972). Sex-role socialization in picture books for preschool children. *American Journal of Sociology, 77,* 1125–1150.

Williams, J. (1987). *The psychology of women* (3rd ed.). New York: Norton.

Witelson, S. (1989). Hand and sex differences in the isthmus and genu of the human corpus collosum: A post-mortem morphological study. *Brain, 112,* 799–835.

Wolf, N. (1991). *The beauty myth.* New York: Morrow.

Zilbergeld, B. (1992). *The new male sexuality: The truth about men, sex, and pleasure.* New York: Bantam Books.

CHAPTER 6

The Development of Children and Families of Color: A Supplemental Framework

Kenneth V. Hardy and Tracey A. Laszloffy

INDIVIDUAL AND FAMILY developmental theories are valuable frameworks for understanding human experience. Many of the major developmental theories have made enormous contributions toward conceptualizing human growth. However, few individual or family developmental theories explicitly address issues of race and racial oppression. Given the substantial variations that exist between groups on the basis of race, the lack of attention to this variable seems like a rather large oversight. This is particularly true with respect to the experiences of children and families of color whose lives are deeply affected by racial devaluation.

This chapter briefly reviews and critiques from a racial perspective the theories of five major developmental theorists: Sigmund Freud, Erik Erikson, Jean Piaget, Lawrence Kohlberg, and Evelyn Millis Duvall. This is followed by a discussion of how the lives of children and families of color are affected by virtue of living in a society that devalues them racially. Because of the specific challenges created by living in such an oppressive context, children and families of color must negotiate several unique tasks in addition to those that are specified in traditional developmental theories. Hence, the developmental framework proposed in this chapter is intended as a supplement to existing theories.

OVERVIEW OF THE MAJOR THEORIES

FREUD

Freud was the architect of psychosexual theory, which conceived of development as occurring primarily from birth through the early years of childhood. He suggested that development involves five stages: oral, anal, phallic, latency, and genital. Each stage is closely tied to biological maturation and the gradual unfolding and development of the three major elements of personality, the id, the ego, and the superego. According to Freud's theory, personality development involves the struggle between the forces associated with these three parts of personality. The id represents the unconscious mind, which is motivated by instinctual drives, wishes, and impulses; the superego represents the superconscious mind, which is motivated by conscience and ensures conformity with internalized social norms; and the ego represents the conscious mind, which exists between the other two and is the central part of the personality (Freud, 1962, 1963).

ERIKSON

Erikson, considered a neo-Freudian, also conceived of individual development in terms of the ego. In Erikson's formulation, however, the ego is present from birth and it is essentially conflict free. As the individual begins to grow and develop, the ego gradually becomes embroiled in a series of developmentally based conflicts that involve negotiating oppositional tensions between the need to grow and the need to stay the same, and between the interests of the ego versus the interests of society. Erikson outlined eight age-based stages of psychosocial development through which he believed all people develop. Each new stage is characterized by the onset of a preordained developmental crisis that consists of conflicting forces that the individual must negotiate. The extent to which a crisis is successfully resolved affects the overall health and viability of one's ego and has significant implications for the degree to which future developmental crises are functionally resolved (Erikson, 1963).

PIAGET

Piaget conceptualized development in terms of cognitive processes that are reflected in four age-based, developmental stages, including sensorimotor, preoperational, concrete operational, and formal operational stages. Piaget believed these stages unfolded in accordance with a biological blueprint and that each successive stage builds on the former one(s). According to Piaget, as a child grows, she or he develops increasingly complex and sophisticated cognitive functions that are characterized by "transformations of earlier modes of understanding to qualitatively different organizations of knowledge" (Green, 1989, p. 189). Hence development occurs in a linear fashion, without the possibility of regressions or the loss of skills or abilities that have already been acquired. In each stage of cognitive development, children experience two opposing tendencies, assimilation (the absorption of new information) and accommodation (the appropriate application and utilization of this knowledge). Both of these tendencies are mediated by equilibration, which is the process of adaptation that balances the two (Piaget, 1963, 1966): "Equilibration can be viewed as the process of change in which individuals move from the equilibrium of one stage, through a transition of disequilibrium, to a hierarchically integrated new form of equilibration at the next stage" (Green, 1989, p. 167).

KOHLBERG

Kohlberg focused on how children grow and develop morally beginning during the preschool years and advancing through childhood into adulthood. He defined morality in terms of justice and fairness and argued that it is based on cognitive rather than emotional processes, and that behaviors are not necessarily indicative of one's stage of moral reasoning. Like Piaget, Kohlberg believed children develop through biological, age-based stages of moral development that are closely tied to cognitive development. Also like Piaget, Kohlberg posited that stages of moral development involve qualitative transformations from one level of reasoning to the next such that each new stage of development involves the hierarchical integration and reconstruction of former stages.

Moral judgments are specialized cognitive functions that require the ability to compare multiple perspectives. When an individual has two contradictory beliefs, this creates a conflict that invokes cognitively based moral principles that are used to resolve the conflict. As individuals continue to grapple with cognitively based moral conflicts, their thinking processes become increasingly organized and more adaptive. There are three levels of moral development, preconventional, conventional, and postconventional. Each levels consists of two stages that are extensions of underlying cognitive operations (Kohlberg, 1975, 1984).

DUVALL

Family development stands in contrast to theories of individual development. Beginning in the 1940s an interdisciplinary group of scholars considered the first models of family life cycle theory. By 1957, one of these scholars, Evelyn Duvall, utilized census data to propose the first complete family life cycle model. Although a variety of alternatives to this model have been advanced during the last 50 years, Duvall's model is widely used today. It remains one of the most popular and well-known models of family development.

According to Duvall, families progress through eight stages: getting married, childbearing, preschool years, school-age years, teenage years, launching, middle-aged parents, and aging family members. During each stage of development, she identified a variety of tasks families have to complete before progressing successfully to the next stage of development (Duvall, 1988; Duvall & Miller, 1985).

CRITIQUE

As issues of diversity have gained greater recognition within the human sciences, a growing body of scholars have endeavored to critique the ways in which developmental theories have failed to consider the unique life experiences of people of color. There is much debate regarding the extent to which racial and cultural variations necessitate changes in the underlying assumptions, concepts, and conclusions of major developmental theories (Mattessich & Hill, 1987; Norton, 1983; Phinney & Rotheram, 1987). There are those who have argued that these theories fail to address racial, ethnic, and cultural variations and that this undermines the credibility and overall applicability of these theories. Others have asserted that these theories are based on universal processes that transcend racial and cultural variations. A number of cross-cultural studies have in fact demonstrated that many of the concepts and processes that Freud, Erikson, Piaget, and Kohlberg identified apply to individuals irrespective of cultural variations. The cultural biases of Duvall's family life cycle theory are more obvious and the theory has been much criticized for its heavy reliance upon culture-specific assumptions about what constitutes a family, the experiences families will have, and when these will occur (Aldous, 1990; Mattessich & Hill, 1987; Rodgers & White, 1993).

As cited by Gibbs and Huang (1998):

> While maturational processes are undeniably universal and occur with only minor variations across racial and cultural groups, many social science researchers have shown that these processes are subject to wide ethnic variations in their behavioral manifestations, their symbolic meanings, and their societal responses. (Phinney & Rotheram, 1987, p. 5)

The value of the position Gibbs and Huang have advocated is that it recognizes the universal basis of many of the underlying processes associated with major developmental theories, while also acknowledging that there may be important variations based on race and ethnicity. For instance, all children may indeed advance through the four biologically based stages of cognitive development that Piaget identified, and yet there may be critical racially based variations between groups of children that affect how these advances occur.

Despite the fact that the developmental processes identified by the major individual theories have a genetically grounded dimension that is not culture specific, social contexts inevitably play a role in shaping how these processes occur. For this reason, when applying these theories to an individual or members of a group, it is important to have some understanding of their social context. Unfortunately, none of these theories addresses this issue in a meaningful way. Even in the case of Erikson's theory, where the social context is an integral concept, little attention is given, for example, to exploring the effects that the societal devaluation of people of color has on healthy ego identity development.

A more comprehensive understanding of the developmental experiences of children and families of color requires some appreciation of the racial context within which people of color live. As the following section explicates, this is a context that is overwhelmingly characterized by racial devaluation.

DEVALUATION

For children and families of color residing within the United States, theirs is an existence that has always been and continues to be confined to this nation's borderlands. Despite impressive political, economic, educational, and social gains over the past several years, people of color are still regarded as "other" by a society that built its wealth and secured its position of power in the world on the backs of generations of people of color.

To make room for the white colonial invaders, countless indigenous peoples were forcibly removed from their homes and more often than not, were simply murdered as a way of making the land "safe" for the white Christian settlers. To feed the ravenous appetite of a newly emerging market economy, millions of Africans were ripped away from the bosom of their homes only to have their blood, sweat, and tears fertilize the Southern crops that supplied the Northern factories upon which our modern American economy was founded.

While it may be tempting and consoling to reflect upon the history of this nation with pride and nostalgia regarding our many great accomplishments, we must also acknowledge that our beauty is tempered by our ugliness, our compassion by our cruelty, our pride by our shame. Just as we have freedom, liberty, and equality as venerable legacies that powerfully shape our modern American character, we must also recognize that racism, elitism, and xenophobia are a part of the legacy that has molded our national identity. As much as we believe that life, liberty, and the pursuit of happiness are inalienable individual rights, we also comfortably deny these rights to entire groups. The ease with which this occurs stems from a deeply held, often unconscious belief that people of color do not qualify for these rights because they somehow are a little less than human.

Within this society, to be anything less than human is tantamount to "not being." As a society, we are incapable of recognizing the beinghood of anyone who is not human, as evidenced by our indescribably cruel treatment of nonhuman animals. Our careless disregard for other life forms is routinely justified with a dismissive and flippant, "But they're not human," which translates into, "they do not exist as beings, only as thoughtless, feeling-less, unaware objects." An object cannot think or feel. Any object has not a soul, does not form relationships with other living beings, and has no sense of self-awareness. An object is just a thing (Spiegel, 1996).

In the dominant schema of Western ideology, anyone who is not fully human is no bet-ter than an object and is surely treated as such. Objects are treated with flagrant disregard because they are incapable of experiencing pain or hurt. In this society, to be deemed an object is to be automatically relegated to a status whereby issues of equal treatment are irrelevant. One of the notable achievements of the U.S. system of government is that we grant equality and justice to all, but the catch is that these "all" include only those who are recognized as fully human. As this nation's history reveals, long before we embraced the noble virtues of equality and justice, we were consumed by a virulent form of racism that categorically denied the humanity of people of color. What better evidence of this can be found than in our most sacred document, the Constitution, that guaranteed the virtues of freedom, liberty, and equality, but denied these to blacks on the grounds that they were three-fifths of a human being.

While our ignorance and cruelty have evolved over the past 200 years and no longer are as blunt and audacious as they once were, they remain within us nonetheless. This part of ourselves we must see. If we are ever to have any hope of becoming the just and noble soci-ety we claim ourselves to be, all of us, white, brown, black, and all the shades in between, must begin by seeing the ways in which an ideology of otherness, hatred, and dehuman-ization toward people of color continues to shape contemporary life in the United States.

A survey of contemporary U.S. society reveals numerous examples of how we objectify people and devalue people of color by assaulting and/or denying their humanity—their beinghood. One of the ways this occurs is through language. The power of language to con-struct reality is undeniable. Language gives meaning to our experience. According to Moore (1992), "Language not only expresses ideas and concepts, but it actually shapes thought. If one accepts that our dominant white culture is racist, then one would expect our language—an indispensable transmitter of culture—to be racist as well" (p. 331).

For children and families of color in the United States, the very act of hearing common everyday expressions of speech involves the systematic socialization that one is inherently inferior or bad. In fact, linguistic devices that devalue people of color are so commonplace that most of us never think about them consciously. When we are forced to focus on the underlying connotation of these words and phrases, it is typical for most people, including people of color, to respond with skepticism, "Oh, it's just an expression," "It doesn't mean anything," "It's a reference to a color not a racial group." These refrains speak to how deeply ingrained negative valuations of blackness and darkness are in the minds of most people, including people of color.

The devaluation of people of color also is manifest through one of our society's most powerful institutions, the media. The power of the media cannot be overemphasized. It both reflects and creates our culture. It is both a mirror and a chisel, simultaneously carv-ing the nuances of our social identity while projecting the image of who we are back to ourselves. Whether one is surveying films, television shows, magazines, print and elec-tronic advertisements, or any other form of media, the representation of people of color remains constant. Most images reflect whites, and when people of color are represented, more often than not these depictions are unidimensional and stereotypical. The messages that children of color receive are that they either do not exist in the world at large, or they exist only in negative ways.

At almost every turn, children and families of color are confronted with systematic devaluation. When children go to school, they generally learn history lessons that deny the contributions of their ancestors, they read textbooks that do not depict people who look like them, and the food they are served in the cafeteria is not like the food they eat at home. When they go shopping they have to contend with being followed and harassed for crimes they did not commit, buying products that do not have pictures on the covers that look like them, and shopping around to find stores that specially carry the types of foods, styles of clothes, and health and beauty supplies that are designed with them in mind. When they go to the movies, they will have to rush to see the few films that have racial relevance to them because these mysteriously disappear from theaters almost as soon as they are released. In other words, in addition to coping with any number of "normal developmental struggles," the realities of racial devaluation create unique developmental dilemmas for children and families of color. Consequently, a framework is needed that acknowledges these unique dilemmas and illuminates how they can be conceptualized and addressed within the context of existing developmental theories.

UNIQUE DEVELOPMENTAL TASKS FACING PEOPLE OF COLOR: A SUPPLEMENTAL FRAMEWORK

The following section presents a supplemental framework for conceptualizing the unique developmental tasks faced by children and families of color in a society that devalues them. This framework is not intended to replace more traditional models of individual and family development, but rather to augment them. In addition to considering how children of color, like white children, must negotiate the transition from one psychosexual or psychosocial stage to the next, or the advancement from one stage of cognitive or moral development to the next, or how a family evolves from one life cycle stage to another, we would encourage a consideration of how the unique developmental tasks outlined in the following section interact with these more traditionally recognized developmental processes. Hence, the framework proposed below is intended to supplement traditional developmental theories.

NEGOTIATING THE DILEMMAS OF SILENCE AND OF SPEAKING

Objectification and devaluation, as stated previously, are similar processes, if not the same. Both involve assaulting and/or stripping a person or group of their beinghood. When this occurs, silencing is inevitable. Silencing involves denying a person or group their "voice." The term *voice* is a metaphor for the ability to define one's experience for one's self and to speak on one's own behalf. Obviously, having a voice threatens the process of objectification. The presence of a voice challenges the reality that one is an object. After all, objects cannot speak. Objects have no self-awareness, they lack the capacity to think and feel, let alone to speak. The mere act of speaking, irrespective of what one speaks about, defies the notion that one is an object. Moreover, the act of speaking poses the threat that one may choose to speak directly against the notion that she or he is an object. For this reason, from the perspectives of oppressive systems, the process of silencing plays a crucial role in ensuring that transformation of beings into things.

There is a powerful historical precedent for the silencing of people of color in this country. From the first cross-racial encounter that occurred on these shores, whites have lashed out brutally against people of color who have dared to speak on their own behalf and who have challenged white dominance. It was common practice to mutilate and even kill those persons of color who dared to speak. Even nonverbal forms of speaking were prohibited, as in the case of a person of color daring to look a white person in the eyes. Such an act defied the notion that one lacked subjecthood. It was an act of resistance against the notion that people of color lacked a self and a soul.

The denial of the right to vote and access to educational opportunities are clear examples of how institutional barriers were created to silence people of color. After all, without the right to vote, the interests of groups of color were not represented politically, which effectively denied their voices. Similarly, preventing access to a meaningful education was tantamount to silencing since the knowledge and skills that come with an education often are necessary preconditions for "being heard."

Despite the gains of civil rights legislation during the second half of the twentieth century, the silencing of people of color remains a deeply entrenched artifact of racial oppression and devaluation. Today, as was true during earlier periods, "silence is golden." A person of color who is silent is in one sense safer than one who dares to speak, at least to the extent that safety is defined in pragmatic ways (i.e., physical, economic, political). Many parents of color realize this and therefore strive to protect their children by teaching them to conform to the rules that demand silence, rather than resist them. I (KVH) still recall my mother telling me as a child, "you'd better watch that mouth, one day it's going to get you in trouble." I now understand that what my mother was really saying was that she feared for me as a black man in this society because she knew all too well that my verbosity put me at risk. She rightfully feared that I would be punished if I did not learn how to modulate my voice appropriately.

At the same time that there are benefits associated with conforming to the rules around silence, there also are costs. Not having access to one's voice is the essence of feeling powerless and hopeless. When persons or groups are unable to speak for themselves, a small piece of their soul dies. They are forced to bear witness to the murder of their own beinghood, which is devastating. Herein resides the dilemma. Those who speak up and resist the silencing process risk losing their lives or opportunities that are critical to their physical survival. Yet for those who remain silent and do not speak up, each time a little more of their soul dies. It is the essence of a double bind.

The dilemmas of silence and of speaking pose complex developmental challenges. In addition to negotiating the developmental tasks specified in Freudian, Eriksonian, Piagetian, Kohlbergian, or family life cycle theories, children and families of color must negotiate the dilemmas of silence and of speaking. Parents of color are faced with the difficult job of trying to teach their children how to attain a healthy balance in the midst of an unhealthy situation. If they are successful, they will find ways to help their children learn when it is vital to remain silent and when they can dare to take a few carefully calculated steps toward speaking. This is a job that is daunting to many parents of color because they either have not worked this out successfully for themselves, or because their fear for the children is so great that it overrides their capacity to approach this issue in a meaningful way.

Annie, who is African American, remembers that she was seven years old when she was first confronted with the dilemmas of silence and of speaking. She lived in Little Rock, Arkansas, with her parents and two younger sisters. The city had just integrated the schools for the first time, and when Annie set out on her historic journey to school that first day, she did so with her father firmly by her side. She remembers that she felt safe with him by her side. She liked it. But as they approached the new school, Annie could see a mob of white people standing outside. They looked angry and hateful. She could feel the hate in their eyes as she and her father drew closer to the front doors of the school. "Nigger go home," a white man shouted from the crowd. And then suddenly Annie saw something come hurling from the crowd. It smashed into her father's clean yellow shirt that her mother had pressed that morning. It was a tomato and it made a horribly red, pulpy mess across her father's shirt. Then suddenly a second hit. This time a tomato smashed into the side of Annie's head. She could feel the cold pulp running into her ear. Annie's fear was immediately flushed over by rage. How dare these people treat her and her father so disrespectfully. They'd be sorry for this. Her father, the man she had revered since she was old enough to say "daddy" wouldn't take this. He was the strongest, most noble man she had ever known. But what was happening? Her father simply looked down at his shirt and then at Annie's hair. He wiped them both and then he pressed forward. He never said a word! Annie was horrified. He never said a word! Suddenly he looked smaller to her, weaker, sadder. Annie wanted to say something, to shout at her father, "Say something!" She wanted to shout at the people in the crowd. But she, like her father, never said a word.

Annie was a grown woman when she told this story for the first time. Telling the story was critical because it represented the key moment in her life when she was first faced with the dilemmas of silence and of speaking. Telling the story also was critical because it allowed her to speak for the first time about a painful experience that had remained buried for years. As that seven-year-old child, Annie witnessed her father's silence in the face of injustice and it both enraged and defeated her. For years she felt secretly angry with her father for not speaking up. While she understood the threat the crowd presented, as a child who needed to believe her father was strong and powerful, it destroyed a piece of her to see his silence, which she equated with weakness. Yet like her father, she learned that day to remain silent in the face of degradation and pain. It was a lesson she resented her entire life, but she had learned it nonetheless, and while it helped her survive more than 20 years with white teachers, professors, employers, and neighbors, at a deeper, much harder to see place within her, she had suffered terribly with the wounds associated with silence.

As a grown woman and as a mother of two children, Annie found herself struggling with the task that requires her to teach her children how to negotiate the dilemmas of silence and of speaking. When Annie first came to therapy with sons who were 8 and 11, it was clear she was struggling. She was frustrated with her older son, whom she described as "quiet and angry and always listening to that trashy rap music and fussin' about having to pull his pants up." She routinely reprimanded her youngest for what seemed to be "typical eight-year-old" antics (note the developmentally based description). For example, at one point he got up to try and look through the one-way mirror. Annie promptly told him that was none of his business and he'd better sit down immediately. This interaction is typical of many we see with African American families and other families of color. Because of the dilemmas of silence and of speaking, many parents of color greatly restrict their children's freedom and mobility out of their fear for their safety. They realize that their children do not have the same degrees of freedom that white children have, and from an early age, they begin to socialize their children to censor their freedom of expression. At stages and ages of development where the preponderance of theories suggest it is natural and healthy for children to engage in an exploration of their world, to be curious and experiment, many parents of color feel the need to greatly restrict their children's boundaries. While on one hand, the realities of living in a racially oppressive society necessitate this socialization, on the other hand, it can foster feelings of fear, rage, and insecurity in children.

The loud, obstreperous behavior sometimes observed in teenagers of color often can be linked back to highly restricted childhoods where many of them felt so confined and suffocated that they feel compelled to lash back as a form of protest when they enter adolescence. But, of course, assuming this defiant stance of speaking loudly has an associated price, the very thing their parents fearfully tried to protect them against. It is not uncommon for adolescents of color to be suspended or expelled from high school at two to three times the rate of their white counterparts. The arrest and conviction rates for criminal wrongdoing are disproportionately higher among teens of color compared with whites. Unless we believe that teens of color are just worse than white teens, these are but a few tangible examples of the price many teens of color pay for speaking up. And among those who do not speak, the price is still high, although in other ways. Consider, for example, that Annie's father died at age 39 of a massive heart attack, and that she, like too many African Americans, suffers from hypertension. The dilemmas of silence and of speaking create a double bind that children and families of color must struggle to negotiate at the same time that they must contend with the myriad of other "normal developmental tasks."

Therapists can play a pivotal role in helping parents of color to help their children negotiate the dilemmas of silence and of speaking. The first step often entails helping parents to "voice" their concerns about their children's use of their own voices. In other words, many parents of color greatly fear the repercussions their children encounter if they dare to have a voice in public. This fear leads them to begin early on to teach their children how to contain and suppress their voices in the private spaces of their homes and communities, with the hope that this early learning will translate into an appropriate level of restraint once their children enter the more public spaces of the broader society (e.g., schools, shopping malls, job sites). Therapists can create a "safe space" in therapy where parents can begin to challenge their own silence by speaking of the ways in which they worry about their children's safety. Helping parents begin to express their fears and worries is a critical initial step in helping them eventually help their children to negotiate successfully the dilemmas of silence and of speaking.

As parents give voice to their fears, they experience directly the healing power associated with being able to assert one's voice and to name one's experience. They have the opportunity to feel how vital it is for their children to have similar opportunities. By recognizing the value in being able to speak, parents can wrestle with the complexities associated with their need to have their children learn how to be silent, and their need to have their children learn how to speak on their own behalf. Ultimately, it is important for therapists to imagine and explore ways in which their children can master the art of balancing silence with speaking, which includes knowing when to hold back and knowing when to assert one's voice. This balancing requires the development of good assessment skills in terms of being able to determine when it is best to not speak versus when there are latitudes that may support taking a calculated risk.

Therapists can also help parents explore ways of teaching their children to become "cultural ventriloquists." This involves learning how to assert one's voice indirectly, through a channel that is not obviously linked to the projecting source. One technique that we often use in therapy with adolescents involves asking them to bring in a song that they feel represents them and their lived experience. For example, at our request, Annie's oldest son

Dwayne brought to therapy a song by the late rap artist 2 Pac entitled "Trapped." We asked him to play the song in therapy and then explain to his mother why he connected with it. Dwayne explained that through the song, 2 Pac was expressing the frustration many young black males experience by virtue of living in a racist society that does not value them as human beings. According to Dwayne: "2 Pac understands what it's like. It's like we're trapped with no room to breathe, no space to live. No one wants to hear what we have to say, or even wants us to be here in this world. Either we're not noticed at all, or when we are, it's just to get rid of us."

The song Dwayne played in therapy "gave voice" to his sense of voicelessness. Through the song, he was able to speak about the ways in which he felt silenced. Through the song, Dwayne asserted his voice and shared with his mother the struggles and frustrations he felt as a young black male. With some coaching, Annie was able to validate what Dwayne was feeling, and she talked with him about their shared struggles as African Americans. Most powerfully, Annie was able to articulate her worries as a black mother who feared for her son's safety, while at the same time recognizing how critical it was for Dwayne to find avenues for expressing himself and for exploring and asserting his identity in spite of the forces that threatened to suppress and limit this exploration process. Similar to what Dwayne was able to find through 2 Pac and his songs, therapists and parents can encourage children and adolescents of color to utilize socially acceptable avenues (e.g., sports, performing arts, music, writing) for "channeling their voices" and balancing the dilemmas of silence and of speaking.

NEGOTIATING THE DILEMMA OF RAGE

When a person or group is systematically silenced and their beinghood degraded and denied, rage is inevitable. Rage is a natural response to pain and injustice (Hardy & Laszloffy, 1995). For people of color, the dilemma that rage presents is that few socially sanctioned opportunities for its expression exist. In fact, the unspoken rule is that people of color do not have a right to feel rage that is related to the ways in which the voices of people of color are silenced: their rage is also subject to suppression and denial.

Rage is an intense and potentially threatening emotion. The threat that the rage of people of color presents for whites is threefold. First, expressions of rage challenge the notion that people of color are merely objects since objects cannot feel rage or any other emotion for that matter. Second, expressions of rage, either implicitly or explicitly, implicate whites in the perpetration of racially based wrongdoings. Finally, most people are not free to observe expressions of rage without automatically associating them with violence. Hence, when a person of color becomes enraged, white people, in recognition of their guilt (even if this recognition is unconscious), fear that rage will culminate in violence and they will be the targets of both. For these reasons, whites as a collective, endowed with institutional power, exert a great deal of energy toward curbing, containing, suppressing, and denying the rage of people of color.

One of the ways this occurs is by shaming people of color for their rage. Common expressions such as "he's just so angry" or "she's hypersensitive" all serve to punish people of color for their rage. The hidden message is that their rage is not justified and that there is something inherently wrong with them for having this feeling. People of color are punished for their rage in more active ways as well. The high numbers of children of color who are removed from classrooms for "behavioral problems" are but one example of this. While there may be any number of reasons for acting out behaviors among children of color, many times such incidents are related to racial struggles and race-related rage that teachers often misunderstand.

Because of the ways in which people of color are shamed or otherwise punished for their rage, many simply attempt to suppress and deny this emotion. However, rage is energy and energy cannot simply be erased. It must be channeled or transformed. When rage is buried within, this energy builds until one way or another it finds a release. There are two primary ways in which this tends to occur. First, rage may be released toward one's self. A person can turn the brunt of his or her rage upon himself or herself, which almost always causes grave harm. The high number of people of color who suffer with addictions involving eating (sugars and fats), alcohol, and other drugs, as well as the alarming numbers who commit suicide or are afflicted with heart disease, hypertension, strokes, and diabetes are indications of rage turned inward (Hooks, 1995).

The second way suppressed rage can be released is in the form of an explosion that erupts after rage cannot be contained a moment longer. These explosions generally are directed at others. When these occur, the energy that is released represents energy that has accumulated over an extended period of time, which contributes to its intensity. Such explosions can range from verbal screaming to acts of physical aggression. The point here is that when a person or group is subjected to experiences with devaluation, it is almost a forgone conclusion that they will experience rage. Because rage is energy, it cannot simply "go away." It must find an outlet for expression. The task facing children and families of color is not a matter of how to avoid feeling rage, or how to eliminate rage, but rather how to find ways to constructively channel rage. The operative word is constructively.

Jose and his family had moved to the United States from Puerto Rico when he was 10. Jose immediately realized that he was an outsider in this new land. Back on the Island he knew he was dark-skinned, and he realized there were negative connotations associated with this, but he had never experienced the type of blatant rejection and dismissal that were directed at him in the United States. Here he felt a sense of isolation and disregard that felt so totalizing it was as if nothing else about him were of importance.

On his second week in school, the gym teacher said to him, "Hey little Taco, you'd better get in out of the sun, you don't need any more color." The bluntness of the comment and its offensiveness stung like a slap in the face. There also were the children who made fun of his accent and the girls who wanted to know about the fancy palm-lined beach resorts of the Island, as if that was all his home represented to them. At last Jose thought he would find some solace when he heard there was another Puerto Rican boy in school, Luis. He was devastated, however, when Luis rejected him, saying to Jose "You're black, not Puerto Rican."

Overwhelmed by his sense of racial and cultural isolation and denigration, Jose quickly fell behind in his academic work. His teacher assumed he was a slow learner and an unmotivated student, that is, until the day he physically attacked a classmate. At that point he also became a "bad kid" in the eyes of his teacher and the school. Jose's experiences reveal several important issues related to rage and children of color. First, Jose's story demonstrates how children of color are subjected to racial devaluation. But more important, his story illustrates how these experiences are often overlooked, misunderstood, or both by the very adults who most need to understand. For instance, Jose's teacher and the school principal never once considered the ways in which his difficulties were rooted in conditions outside of himself. Hence, Jose, not his conditions, were labeled as the problem. Consequently, his learning opportunities were greatly stifled. He was placed in a class that failed to access his true academic potential, and he was burdened with demeaning labels that impaired his social competence. It should not require much effort to imagine the ways in which these factors affected Jose's cognitive and social development. Because of the dynamics of racism and devaluation, the positive, growth-enhancing challenges that would have maximized his development were replaced with shame, invalidation, and hopelessness.

While teachers and schools often misdiagnosis the academic and behavioral problems children of color manifest, interestingly many parents also struggle in this regard. Depending on their own growing-up experiences, some parents of color find it extremely difficult to help their children to cope constructively with their rage. For example, Jose's parents were mystified by their son. They questioned him at great length and were extremely concerned about him, but they were unable to assemble the pieces of Jose's experiences to assess what was actually happening for him. This was, in part, related to their experiences as children. Jose's father also suffered as a child because of his dark complexion; and because his feelings were never validated by the adults in his life he was left to deal with them all alone. The way he managed to survive was by burying his feelings and avoiding them altogether. As an adult who had never learned how to deal with his own feelings of rage, Jose's father could not allow himself to consider the ways in which his son was enduring experiences that were similar to his own childhood.

With respect to Jose's mother, who had a very light complexion, she did not understand her son's pain because it was not a part of her own lived experience. Hence, for different reasons, both his parents were unable to provide Jose with the support he needed to understand what he was experiencing and to find healthy ways of dealing with his feelings.

Some parents of color are actively aware of and sensitive to their children's struggles with rage. However, their fear that their children's rage will invite punishment from the world around them propels many of them to move quickly to suppress their children's rage. Unfortunately, suppressed rage becomes more of the problem and not the solution. For example, much of Jose's rage was suppressed. Most of the time he appeared quiet and withdrawn. He rarely spoke with other students or participated in class. He did not know how to articulate what he was experiencing inside, so most often he said nothing, even when he was asked directly to explain himself. As a result, his rage remained suppressed most of the time. But rage is energy, and at some point this energy must find a release. The day he attacked another student was an example of the explosive release of rage that had been suppressed for far too long. On the surface, the infraction that invited his attack seemed so minor (the other boy had taken his pencil), but in reality it reflected an accumulation of rage that he had been holding for months because he did not understand his feelings and did not know how to deal with what was happening to him.

Therapists can play a vital role in helping parents of color to recognize and ultimately help their children appreciate that rage is a natural, healthy response to pain and injustice, and when appropriately channeled, it can be a source of healing and transformation. They can also point out the dangers of suppressed rage, which can lead to aggression either directed at self (e.g., drug abuse) or others (e.g., violent explosions). Moreover, they can emphasize how certain "problem behaviors" are actually symptoms of mischanneled rage, which is closely linked to the failure to negotiate successfully the dilemmas of silence and of speaking. Clarifying this relationship is critical because it has important implications for how parents and other adults respond to children's "problem behaviors." More often than not, the response is punishment. However, the inappropriateness of punishment as a dominant response becomes evident once one realizes that what underlies "problem behaviors" is almost always (mischanneled) rage and pain. As therapists assist parents in understanding the roots of children's "problem behaviors," they are better posed to assist parents in exploring responses other than punishment. In other words, they can encourage parents of color to work with their children to develop more constructive ways of channeling rage and of dealing with the underlying pain. In a related manner, parents can assume an active role in challenging others who may rely too heavily on punishment as a tool for responding to their children's mischanneled rage. For example, with therapy, Jose's parents became more aware of the roots of their son's "problem behavior." Aided by this understanding, one step they took to help Jose involved meeting with his teacher to explain that his behavior was a symptom of his suffering, not his defiance. They challenged her to see Jose as more than a bad, unmotivated student and asked her to create opportunities in the classroom that would help him deal with his sense of alienation, pain, and rage.

It is not easy for adults to teach children how to channel rage constructively. As a society we have zero tolerance for rage. Consequently, many adults lack a clear sense of how to deal with rage constructively in their own lives, let alone in the lives of children. Based on their own childhood experiences with rage, as adults, many parents struggle with how to help their children negotiate this complex emotion. Yet, it is imperative that they help their children find methods of dealing with rage such that it is not turned inwardly upon themselves or suppressed until it explodes, putting both self and others at risk. Such a balancing is difficult to achieve.

It is critical to bear in mind that the task is not "to rage or not to rage," but rather "how to rage." This creates challenges for parents of color who must resist the messages from the dominant society that are aimed at denying and covering up rage. They must embrace in themselves a powerful and threatening emotion as a way of helping their children to do the same. Therapists can play a critical role in helping parents of color work through their own rage so that they eventually do the same for their own children. Therapists working with parents of color can begin by gently encouraging these parents to recognize and name their own rage and to connect it to experiences associated with being a person of color in a racist society. It is imperative for therapists to model validating rage, normalizing its existence and affirming the right to have rage.

Once rage has been uncovered, named, and validated, it becomes possible to explore how one has learned to handle this rage. What pathways did the person develop for channeling rage and in what ways have these pathways been a benefit and a liability? For example, one benefit to the person who tends to bury rage involves determining punitive and disengaging reactions from others who feel threatened by rage. On the other hand, by burying rage inside, this person endures the full burst of this intense emotion, which can result in depression and/or various self-destructive behaviors such as drug use or suicide. Eventually this exploration should lead to experimentation with developing alternative pathways for channeling rage, specifically, pathways that are constructive in nature. For instance, during therapy, Jose's father was encouraged to develop a positive channel for his rage that involved volunteering his time to establish a local group for Latino youth.

As part of his service, Jose's father helped teach Latino children about their history and culture and he encouraged them to be sociopolitical activists for the rights of Latinos living in the United States. He also organized a youth conference aimed at examining issues facing "Latino Youth in Contemporary U.S. Society." These activities enabled Jose's father to embrace the rage he felt regarding his oppression as a Latino and to channel it constructively. More important, as he was able to do this for himself, he was able to help Jose do the same. Jose was one of the most active members of his father's group. At the conference, he gave a moving speech about his experiences as a Puerto Rican male in the United States. Both their involvement in the group and the conference provided a vehicle for father and son to channel constructively the rage they felt in response to their devaluation as Latinos.

NEGOTIATING THE DILEMMA OF SELF-HATE

The dominant theme underlying the racial oppression of people of color is that they are inferior. We already have gone to great lengths to outline some of the major ways in which this belief is conveyed on a daily basis. What is important to appreciate is that when one encounters this message over and over, in almost every nook and cranny of one's existence, at some point it is inevitable that one will start to believe it. What we are referring to here is the phenomenon of internalized oppression. After being conditioned to believe that one is "less than," one finally begins to believe it, and the resulting emotional consequence is a profound sense of self-hate.

Expressions of self-hate can be directed at one's self in the literal sense, or they can be directed at one's self in the symbolic sense. For example, the alarmingly high black-on-black homicide in many urban areas can be interpreted as an example of self-hate directed at one's symbolic self. Consider the remarks of a young African American male, Kareem, who said:

> This society doesn't care about us as black people. All they do is build more prisons and fill them up with us. Every time we see them put up another prison it's like they're saying they don't care about us. Like they want us gone so they don't even have to look at us. Sometimes just for fun, we'll just go down a few 40s and go shoot a nigger. Hell, there's nothing else to do but get bombed and waste a nigger. That's what they want us to do anyway. It don't matter, it's just a nigger.

Kareem's words are chilling. For those who do not live in the borderlands where Kareem lives, it is almost impossible to relate to what he's saying. But make no mistake, while it may seem hard to understand how deeply this young man and his peers hate themselves, their hatred is only a glimmer of the hatred this society has for them. Because this hatred is not directed toward whites, most whites find it hard to see all the ways in which society conveys this ugliness as loudly and as crisply as Kareem's words indicate. But he is living proof of just how clearly, persistently, and stridently this message is sent to people of color living in this society.

One of the most poignant and disturbing manifestations of self-hate among people of color involves the color complex. This refers to a color caste system that exists among people of color whereby distinctions are made about the relative worth and value of an individual based on the lightness or darkness of her or his complexion. The color complex represents the internalization of the same proracist ideology that establishes whites as superior to all people of color. Hence, the very ideology that results in whites unjustly discriminating against all people of color on the basis of skin color is simultaneously reinforced by people of color who value and reward those among them who are light-skinned and devalue those who are dark-skinned.

The use of spanking as a form of physical discipline or punishment (depending on your perspective) can be seen as another indicator of self-hate. While this practice is defended with almost religious-like conviction by many parents of color, we believe it raises a number of complex and disturbing questions regarding the internalization of both the ideology and methods of the oppressor. Consider for a moment that during the days of slavery, the preferred method of disciplining or punishing (again, depending on your perspective) of slaves was physical beatings. Slavemasters believed they were justified in their use of force. This justification was rooted in their belief that they were mightier than their slaves and that their "might made right." Because they saw themselves as having authority over their slaves, they believed it was justified to use physical force as a way of bending slaves to their will. Many slavemasters strongly believed that if they failed to use physical force, their slaves who became unruly would start to think they had more power than they were entitled to have. They feared their slaves would not respect them and would begin to entertain ways of exerting greater degrees of freedom and autonomy. They feared their slaves would defy their will. Ironically, these are all the same arguments we hear when we talk with parents who believe in the use of physical force as a method of disciplining their children.

While there are people of all races who support the use of spanking, and while they will invoke similar arguments, this method of disciplining is especially prevalent among people of color, particularly African Americans. We think this is ironic and disheartening when we consider the historical record. There is something profoundly disturbing about how much those African Americans who defend their use of physical disciplining sound like the white slavemasters who defended their right to strike those whom they felt were their underlings. While this is undoubtedly a controversial point, we believe spanking of children is both an artifact of slavery and an expression of self-hate that is directed at the symbolic self (i.e., one's children).

As we have attempted to explicate, there are numerous ways in which people of color can manifest self-hate. The dilemma that self-hate creates is that for many people of color, the behaviors they engage in as an expression of this self-hate often appear on the surface to serve a more beneficial goal. Hence, in the case of parents who spank their children, the intended goal is to discipline children and socialize them to behave in responsible and appropriate ways. Individuals who fall prey to the color complex are often trying to find ways to elevate themselves and minimize their suffering. In the case of Kareem, who spoke of "shooting a nigger for fun," he was attempting to distance himself from his pain by shrugging his shoulders at it, as if to say, "Okay, so this is how it is, I won't let it get to me." Expressions of self-hate are complicated. Sometimes they seem like the only form of power an oppressed person can exercise. It is almost like saying, "Since I'm going to die no matter what, I'll kill myself before you kill me." Seen in this light, expressions of self-hate create the illusion of control and power.

At other times, expressions of self-hate involve playing along with the rules of the dominant society ("acting white") as a way of trying to reap the rewards of whiteness. From this perspective, self-hate is a strategy used to reduce suffering and increase rewards. The problem, however, is that self-hate, ultimately, is about destruction. Therefore, while it may seem more empowering to kill one's self rather than be killed, in the end, one is still dead. The same is true with respect to the phenomenon of "selling out" to whiteness by trying to pass. Despite the surface level gains an individual may obtain, again, one ultimately dies because one kills the part of self that is essential to the survival of one's soul.

Eddie was 18 and the son of a Lakota Sioux mother and a Mohawk father who were both killed in a car crash when Eddie was seven. His aunt became his legal guardian and because she believed it was in Eddie's best interest, he spent most of his growing up years in a government-operated boarding school. There he received a marvelous miseducation that taught him nothing of who he was. The most significant mention of Native American people was found in his history books that told the typical Christopher Columbus Creation Story. Beyond that, it was as if his ancestors had not lived. The majority of what Eddie knew of himself and his roots had been fed to him through B-grade Hollywood movies that had taught him Indians were either savage barbarians or nearly mute idiots. The closest he had come to interacting with the sacred symbol of the Sioux, the Thunderbird, was in the form of the Thunderbird car his best friend was driving. There were the few words of his ancestral Sioux language that he had learned from his grandmother when he was only a few years old, but those were buried away with the painful memories of the boys who laughed at him when he used those words during his first few days of school.

As far as Eddie was concerned, his parents may have been Indians, but he was not. He had been raised by whites and with whites. He spoke like whites, thought like them, and even dated them exclusively. He would never consider lowering himself to date an Indian girl. He considered his white girlfriends as affirmation of his whiteness and the status associated with it.

To those who observed Eddie from afar it was easy to see that he was strongly white identified, and there was even the illusion that perhaps it was all right. After all, for all practical purposes he had been reared as a white person. Moreover, he seemed proud of his whiteness. He seemed secure and focused. The only problem was that underneath, in a place within himself that few could see, the other side of Eddie's infatuation with whiteness was his revulsion with his Indianness. Eddie hated all that was Indian, and therefore he hated a significant part of who he was. It would have been one thing if his love of whiteness had been balanced with a love of Indianness. But this was not the world within which Eddie was living. Because Eddie's love of whiteness was a mask that hid his hatred of his Indianness, Eddie was at risk of destroying himself, either literally or symbolically. There already were signs of this occurring.

On one occasion Eddie and a group of his white friends verbally harassed a young Indian man who had been handing out leaflets educating the public about Indian rights. Eddie was the most vicious in his attack upon the young activist. On one level this may seem surprising because one might have expected Eddie, as a fellow Native American, to have greater sensitivity to the young man. But because of the power of his self-hate, Eddie was becoming as cruel in his treatment of other Native Americans as the most vicious white racist.

Years later in therapy, Eddie eventually came to appreciate the relationship between his cruelty toward the young man he had harassed and his sense of self-hate. In retrospect he eventually realized he needed to harass that young man in front of his white friends as a way of proving he was worthy of their friendship. Because he never felt like he truly belonged, he found himself repeatedly acting in ways that were designed to convince his friends, and himself, that he did belong. The way he tried to prove this was by attacking anything and everything that was a representation of Indianness. He attempted to destroy all traces of himself as a way of proving over and over again that he was not who he was—that he was not the person he had learned to hate so deeply.

Eddie's story is so vital because it illuminates the dangers associated with not seeing and confronting the self-hatred that people of color are oriented toward. In a society that had taught him to hate and deny his Indianness, he was faced with the task of recognizing his self-hate and challenging himself to resist it, in fact to transform it into self-love.

The task of seeing, resisting, and transforming self-hate into self-love is nothing short of a countercultural act. The love of self requires an active, purposeful effort. For people of color, it is an act of will that stands against the thrust of the dominant social order. It is oppositional and boldly defiant and while it offers the promise of spiritual liberation, it also poses risk. To love is to risk because where there is love, there is the risk of loss. Daring to love one's self means risking pain and loss. Had Kareem dared to love himself, he would have had to risk the pain he would have felt each and every time another brother was gunned down on the street or carted off to prison. If Eddie had dared to love himself, he would have had to risk the pain associated with each and every time his Indianness was denigrated, marginalized, or decimated by racial hatred. If he had dared to love himself, he would have had to speak when it may not have been safe, and hence he would have had to risk the loss of approval, of opportunities, and perhaps even of his life.

Before therapists can aid children of color in transforming self-hate into self-love, they must first support parents of color in undertaking this transformation within themselves. An integral part of this transformation involves accessing the courage within "to speak," and more important, to give voice to the numerous painful messages of devaluation that all people of color internalize to varying degrees. Therapy can serve as a space where clients of color can name experiences, feelings, and messages they carry within them that suggest to them they are "less than." For example, to assist Eddie in his therapy, his aunt Rosa was included in the therapy.

During the second session that Rosa attended, she told the therapist she was disturbed that Eddie only dated white women. The therapist pursued this point by asking Rosa what meaning she attached to Eddie's behavior. After much effort, Rosa finally articulated that she believed Eddie's behavior emanated from a belief he held that Indian girls were not good enough for him. The therapist asked Rosa how this made her, as a Native American woman, feel. Immediately tears came to Rosa's eyes. As a Native American woman herself, Eddie's rejection of women like herself felt personal. Moreover, it tapped into a deep sense of pain she carried around within herself that related to all the ways in which she felt devalued as a Native American woman.

Rosa flashed back to childhood and all the times she hated her dark hair and eyes that never seemed as pretty as the little white girls with their curly blonde locks, blue eyes, and powdery skin. She spoke of the times over the course of her life that she received the message that she was the lowest among the low, worthless as both a woman and as an Indian. She recalled the times she had been rejected romantically by both Native American males and white males as a young girl and as a young woman. She spoke of the pain she experienced when her husband of almost 10 years had an affair with a white woman. It was not simply that he had been sexually unfaithful, but that the woman he betrayed her with was white. It reinforced every agonizing belief she has ever had about herself as being "less than."

With the therapist's encouragement, Rosa shared the litany of stories within her about the ways she had learned to hate herself. While her telling of these stories did not change them, the mere act of saying them aloud and having them validated initiated a process of liberation and healing for Rosa. With the therapist's support, Rosa was also able to access the profound rage she felt with respect to her devaluation. During the fourth session she attended, Rosa cried and screamed uncontrollably, releasing for the first time the pain and rage she had been burying within for so long.

The therapist actively worked with Rosa to begin challenging her stories of self-hate. She reminded Rosa of her own words: "I got so many messages that taught me to see myself as worthless." The therapist used this to make the point that what Rosa felt toward herself was not innate or inevitable. It had been taught and learned. And in the same way, it could be unlearned.

Within the next few weeks, Rosa followed the therapist's advice and began reading books authored by Native American women. She was amazed how much she shared with these other women, but more important she found inspiration in the stories they told of how they had found unique ways of resisting self-hate. Rosa also reconnected with two cousins whom she had lost contact with years earlier. Through these reconnections, Rosa began to explore other ways of seeing herself as an Indian woman. She and her cousins began to recount stories of their childhood together that provided an alternative to the stories of self-hate that were strong within her. For example, Rosa felt joy when she rediscovered a forgotten memory of a time when she and her cousins, as young girls, had gone swimming together naked one hot summer day. They spent the entire afternoon swimming, laying in the sun on the grass, and brushing each other's hair. This was a long lost memory of a time when Rosa had felt her body and spirit were in harmony with each other and with the natural world. She remembered the feeling of peace and love she had felt for herself and her cousins. She remembered how on that day she felt beautiful and the touch of her cousins' long black hair in her hands was like silk. It was pure joy. This memory provided a powerful contrast to the other stories of inferiority, shame, and pain.

Gradually, Rosa began to develop a consciousness of resistance that was active and intentional. This consciousness closely scrutinized the messages of inferiority and worthlessness. This consciousness purposefully resisted the negative stories and guided Rosa in weaving together the stories of love and goodness about who she was as an Indian woman. Rosa began a journal in which she noted her daily acts of resistance and recorded her stories of love.

The initial session when Rosa had cried about the ways in which she felt devalued by Eddie's rejection of Indian women greatly affected Eddie. For the first time, he was challenged to think about his behavior in a new way, both in terms of how it might represent some piece of self-hate within him and also in terms of how it affected someone he cared for a great deal. It was the first time that Eddie saw his refusal to date Indian women as a symbolic rejection of his aunt, and, in some way, of himself. Eddie continued to struggle with what he had experienced during that therapy session, but his greatest challenges came when Rosa was able to engage with him directly about her struggles with self-hate as a Native American and about her concerns for him. As Rosa opened herself up, Eddie was given permission to access and explore similar parts of himself. This process was deeply emotional. It tapped into intense feelings of grief, rage, and shame, but with the therapist's initial support, Rosa was able to validate Eddie's feelings and stay connected with him as he worked through them.

Part of the healing process also involved Rosa apologizing to Eddie for the ways in which her own self-hate had led her to betray him, to not do a better job of protecting him and helping to teach him how to love himself in spite of the hate around him. She also asked him to join with her as she continued her journey to reclaim herself. One thing she asked Eddie to do was to attend a Mohawk ceremony as a way of reconnecting with the part of themselves that they each had lost. This also was a way to begin building a network with other Native Americans who could lend support in their journey to resist self-hate and nurture self-love.

As should be evident by this point, a critical relationship exists between achieving self-love and finding the courage to speak. One cannot live in silence and achieve self-love. Despite the risks that speaking engenders, it is an essential aspect of achieving self-love. To speak on one's behalf is a declaration of one's inherent value and worth. Self-love also requires the constructive channeling of rage. It is impossible to love self while being eaten alive by rage. Those who love themselves are able to use rage as a powerful force for positive transformation of their lives and the world around them. Hence, if it is not already clear, the tasks associated with transforming self-hate into self-love are inextricably tied to the task of negotiating the dilemmas of silence and of speaking, and the task of channeling rage constructively. The degree to which one is able to negotiate successfully the latter two tasks has powerful implications for how one is able to negotiate the former.

CONCLUSION

In addition to working through the developmental tasks associated with traditional theories, children and families of color are simultaneously faced with unique tasks associated with their racial devaluation. Further, the extent to which parents of color are able to help their children depends to a large extent on the degree to which they have been able to help themselves. It is difficult for parents to take their children someplace where they themselves have never gone. And yet, the health and viability of the lives of children of color requires no less than every effort from the adults in their lives to help them successfully negotiate the tasks they face as children of color that they must contend with in addition to all those other "normal developmental tasks."

Parents and other adults must act as cultural translators for children of color. Everything from watching television, listening to music, visiting the mall, going out to eat, attending school, participating in sports or other extracurricular activities, reading magazines or books, and simply walking down the street are all racialized experiences, and most of the racial messages embedded in these experiences devalue people of color. Hence, parents and other adults must become adept at helping children of color decode the underlying meaning embedded in this onslaught of messages, and they must provide them with strategies and tools to counteract this devaluation. They must act as a counter-cultural force that teaches children of color how to live within society while simultaneously developing oppositional resistance against the messages that society communicates about who they are and their appropriate place. They must help them learn how to achieve a balance between the dilemmas of silence and of speaking, of how to constructively channel rage, and how to transform self-hate into self-love. They must accomplish all of this as an integral aspect of promoting healthy ego identity development, the development of formal operational thinking, moral development, and the positive growth and transformation of family roles and relationships.

REFERENCES

Aldous, J. (1990). Family development and the life course: Two perspectives on family change. *Journal of Marriage and the Family, 52,* 571–583.

Duvall, E. M. (1988). Family development's first forty years. *Family Relations, 37,* 127–134.

Duvall, E. M., & Miller, B. C. (1985). *Marriage and family development* (6th ed.). New York: Harper & Row.

Erikson, E. (1963). *Childhood and society* (2nd ed.). New York: Norton.

Freud, S. (1962). *The ego and the id.* New York: Norton.

Freud, S. (1963). *A general introduction to psychoanalysis.* New York: Simon & Schuster.

Gibbs, J. T., & Huang, L. N. (1988). *Children of color: Psychological interventions with culturally diverse youth.* San Francisco: Jossey-Bass.

Green, M. (1989). *Theories of human development.* Englewood Cliffs, NJ: Prentice-Hall.

Hardy, K. V., & Laszloffy, T. A. (1995). "What we teach" by how we teach: The hidden dimension of multicultural education. *IMPACT on Instructional Improvement, 24*(2), 22–24.

Hooks, B. (1995). *Killing rage: Ending racism.* Boston: South End Press.

Kohlberg, L. (1975). The cognitive-developmental approach in moral education. *Phi Delta Kappan, 61,* 670–677.

Kohlberg, L. (1984). *Essays on moral development (Vol. II: The psychology of moral development).* San Francisco: Harper & Row.

Mattesich, P., & Hill, R. (1987). Life cycle and development. In M. B. Sussman & S. K. Steinmetz (Eds.), *Handbook of marriage and the family* (pp. 437–469). New York: Plenum Press.

Moore, R. B. (1992). Racism in the English language. In P. Rothenberg (Ed.), *Race, class and gender in the United States: An integrated study* (pp. 331–340). New York: St. Martin's Press.

Norton, A. J. (1983). Family life cycle, 1980. *Journal of Marriage and the Family. 45,* 267–277.

Phinney, J. S., & Rotheram, M. J. (1987). *Children's ethnic socialization: Pluralism and development.* Thousand Oaks, CA: Sage Publications.

Piaget, J. (1963). *The origins of intelligence in children* (2nd ed.). New York: Norton.

Piaget, J. (1966). *Psychology of intelligence.* Totowa, NJ: Littlefield, Adams.

Rodgers, R. H., & White, J. J. (1993). Family development theory. In P. G. Boss, W. J. Doherty, R. LaRossa, W. R. Schumm, & S. K. Steinmetz (Eds.), *Sourcebook of families theories and methods: A contextual approach* (pp. 225–254). New York: Plenum Press.

Spiegel, M. (1996). *The dreaded comparison.* New York: Mirror Books.

CHAPTER 7

Socialization of Socioeconomic Status

Mark R. Rank

IN THE 1940S, Billie Holiday began her classic song "God Bless the Child" by singing "Them that's got shall get; Them that's not shall lose; So the Bible said; And it still is news." Her words poignantly express the timeless but weighty importance that social class exerts on life outcomes. Just as gender, race, and ethnicity have been shown in prior chapters to impact and influence family process and outcomes across the life course, so too does socioeconomic status (SES). This chapter explores the relationship between SES and a variety of family dynamics.

SES has typically been measured through individual or household levels of income, education, and occupational status (Beeghley, 1996; Ganzeboom, Treiman, & Ultee, 1991; Smith & Graham, 1995; Sorensen, 1994). Researchers have utilized these variables in both a continuous and a discrete manner. Those relying on a continuous approach have either looked at the separate effects of these variables or have combined them into an overall socioeconomic index. Researchers using a discrete approach have generally divided the population into various classes, based on cutoff points for income, education, and occupational status. A common categorization has been to divide the population into an upper, middle, working, and poverty class. Both ways of conceptualizing SES will be used throughout this discussion of the research knowledge in the field.

The chapter is organized around many of the family topics addressed in the handbook. What is emphasized here, however, is the impact that SES has on these dimensions of the family. In addition, particular attention is paid to the effect that poverty has on various life outcomes and family processes. As we shall see, social class, and poverty in particular, often exert a profound influence on family dynamics. An understanding and appreciation of these influences would appear important in engaging in effective therapeutic interventions. The chapter is divided into two major sections. First, the impact of SES on family dynamics is examined. Second, the manner in which lower SES intensifies specific family problems is discussed.

IMPACT OF SOCIOECONOMIC STATUS ON FAMILY DYNAMICS

There has been a long and rich tradition in both the family and social stratification literatures that has examined the impact of SES on family dynamics. A number of studies have been produced during the twentieth century that have examined these issues, ranging from the Middletown books by Robert and Helen Lynd (1929, 1937), to the more recent work of William Julius Wilson (1987, 1996). In the sections that follow, the current state of knowledge regarding the relationship between SES and family dynamics is highlighted.

AGE AND LIKELIHOOD OF MARRIAGE

To begin, considerable research has indicated that individuals tend to marry others who are like themselves in terms of a range of demographic characteristics such as race, age, religion, residence, and so on (Kalmijn, 1998). This process is called *marital homogamy,* and applies to social class as well. Individuals with roughly similar levels of SES tend to marry one another. When individuals do marry outside their social class, women tend to marry up in terms of social class and men tend to marry down (Eshleman, 1997).

Research indicates that the higher one's social class (particularly in terms of education among women), the later the age at which individuals first marry (Cherlin, 1991). As women invest more in their education, there is a tendency to put off marriage until such training is completed and careers are launched. On the other hand, research suggests that for young blue-collar and working-class men and women (Rubin, 1976), getting married is often viewed as a means of defining oneself as an adult (in much the same way that having a child is often viewed among the underclass as a right of passage to becoming an adult). Consequently, an earlier age at marriage is found among the working class.

Ironically, a long line of ethnographic, sociological, and demographic studies have indicated that the likelihood of marriage is substantially reduced among the poverty stricken (Cheal, 1996; Lewis, 1966; Rank, 1994; Stack, 1974). The fundamental reason for this is that individuals contemplating marriage generally are seeking (or desire to be) an economically secure partner (Becker, 1981; Cherlin, 1996). Poverty undermines the availability of such partners. Hence individuals in these situations are more likely to forego marriage.

Most recent and well known within this vein of research has been the work of Wilson (1987, 1996). His analyses have focused on the increasing problems found within the inner city among African Americans and the reasons why such problems appear to have worsened over the last three decades. A critical factor in understanding the falling rate of marriage within the inner city population has been the recent economic restructuring that has resulted in the movement of capital and job opportunities out of central city areas. As Wilson writes:

> The black delay in marriage and the lower rate of remarriage, each associated with high percentages of out-of-wedlock births and female-headed households, can be directly tied to the employment status of black males. Indeed, black women, especially young black women, are confronting a shrinking pool of "marriageable" (that is economically stable) men. (1987, p. 145)

As a result, the rate of marriage within poverty stricken inner cities is considerably lower than that within the general population.

CHILDBEARING

Demographic data indicate that there is an association between lower levels of income and higher rates of fertility. For example, if we examine the total number of births per 1,000 women aged 15 to 44 in 1995, women residing in a family with incomes below $10,000 had a rate of 91.0; for those with a family income between $30,000 and $34,999 it was 60.6; and for those with a family income over $75,000 the number was 53.1 (U.S. Bureau of the Census, 1997). Looking at women aged 15 to 29 reveals an even more striking story—the figures are 132.7, 89.2, and 28.9. Increasing levels of women's education are also associated with lower levels of fertility.

Women at lower income and educational levels also tend to have children at earlier ages and are more likely to bear children out of wedlock. For example, the fertility rates per 1,000 unmarried women aged 18 to 24 reveal a rate of 300.9 for those with 0 to 8 years of education, 123.5 for women with 12 years of education, and 23.7 for those with 13 to 15 years of education (National Center for Health Statistics, 1997).

Three factors appear critical in understanding why lower income, and particularly poverty, are associated with these patterns. First, research indicates that the poor have less access to information regarding birth control (Luker, 1996). The poor are also least able to afford contraception (and specifically abortion). As a result, survey research indicates that poor women are more likely than nonpoor women to report that they have experienced an unwanted or unintended birth (Maynard, 1997).

A second reason for higher fertility rates, particularly among teenagers in dire poverty, is the perception of a lack of future opportunities (Dash, 1989). In a world of negatives, having a child may be seen as one of the few positive actions one can take. The Children's Defense Fund put this idea aptly by stating, "In many ways, the best contraceptive is a real future" (1985, p. 3).

Third, as noted above, having a child is often viewed in poverty stricken inner city communities as a right of passage to becoming an adult (Anderson, 1990, 1999; Stack, 1974; Wilson, 1996). This, in turn, increases the desirability and reduces the stigma attached to having a child at a younger age and out of wedlock.

SOCIALIZATION OF CHILDREN

In reviewing the research literature on the differences in patterns of socialization among children by social class, Adams (1998) notes that several broad generalizations can be made. Specifically, the higher the social class:

- The greater the parental demonstration of warmth.
- The greater the supportive role of the father in child rearing.
- The greater the emphasis on development and use of verbal skills.
- The greater the use of reasoning with the child.
- The less the use of physical punishment.
- The more discipline is based on intent rather than on the child's overt act.
- The greater the tolerance on parent's behalf for children's impulses.
- The greater the emphasis on independence, achievement, and creativity.

Much of the research from which Adams draws these generalizations is based on blue-collar versus white-collar parents' socialization styles.

Several arguments have been put forth to explain these social class differences. Perhaps most influential has been the work of Kohn (1963, 1979). Kohn has argued that these differences arise primarily because of the differences in the styles of work between white-collar and blue-collar occupations. White-collar jobs stress that individuals be able to deal with ideas, symbols, and interpersonal relations, resulting in much more freedom and creativity on the job. Blue-collar work tends to focus more on the manipulation of physical objects, resulting in the following of orders and the maintaining of discipline being valued work qualities. According to Kohn, these traits then carry over into how parents socialize their children. Middle-class parents tend to focus more on creativity, independence, and verbal skills when rearing their children, while working-class parents tend to focus more on conformity, discipline, and neatness (for empirical work examining this model, see Gerris, Dekovic, & Janssens, 1997; Luster, Hoades, & Haas, 1989; Spenner, 1998; Wright & Wright, 1976).

GENDER ROLES

Similar to the research dealing with socialization differences among children, much of the social class research on gender roles has been based on blue-collar versus white-collar marital comparisons (Halle, 1984; Howell, 1973; Komarovsky, 1962; LeMasters, 1975; Rubin 1976, 1994). This body of research has indicated that blue-collar families perceive their appropriate gender roles as more traditional (e.g., patriarchal authority, clearly defined spousal roles) whereas white-collar families have a greater tendency to espouse a more egalitarian view of gender roles (e.g., shared decision making; less well-defined spousal roles).

For example, blue-collar families are more likely to view a husband's role within the family as basically comprising that of the breadwinner, whereas the wife's role is viewed as the primary caregiver. As one of the working-class husbands in Rubin's book *Worlds of Pain* put it:

> That's just the way life is. It's her job to keep the house and children and my job to earn the money. My wife couldn't do my job, and I couldn't be as good a cook and housekeeper as she is. So we just ought to do what we do best. (1976, p. 100)

The irony of this is that blue-collar husbands often do not have the financial resources to support such a traditional division of labor and power structure. As Goode writes, "Lower-class husbands are more likely to claim authority simply because they are males, but actually concede more voice to their wives" (1982, p. 83).

With increasing SES, both husbands and wives are more likely to accept the legitimacy of egalitarian gender roles and to behave somewhat more in keeping with such a norm (Blumstein & Schwartz, 1983). For example, Rank (1982) found that increasing education, income, and occupational status for both wives and husbands leads to a more egalitarian power structure in terms of decision making. Likewise, studies focusing on the division of labor have found that increases in SES result in husbands contributing more to family housework and child care (Collins & Coltrane, 1995). However, it must be emphasized that although SES is associated with a greater acceptance of egalitarianism, research indicates that actual behavior often falls far short of this standard (Hochschild, 1989).

An exception to this pattern is found for extremely wealthy families. Those few studies that have focused on upper-class families (Daniels, 1988; Ostrander, 1984) have found a very traditional pattern and acceptance of gender roles. Ostrander argues that such behavior reflects a desire to maintain the privileges that those at the very top of the social class hierarchy enjoy:

A major consequence of upper-class wives' activities is to support the economic position of their husbands at the very top of society's hierarchy. As long as upper-class wives assume an accommodative and supportive function at home and in the community, their upper-class husbands are free to devote their full energies to managing the economic and political affairs for the society and to perpetuating the dominance of the upper class . . . To the extent that upper-class women are supportive of and subjugated by this traditional family structure—with its rigid division of labor between the sexes and its traditional subordination of women—the function of the upper-class family is reinforced. As the primary social form for the orderly transmission of power and privilege from generation to generation, the family confines the women who preserve it. (1984, pp. 68–69)

EXTENDED KINSHIP

Various anthropological studies have indicated that those in poverty are more likely to utilize a larger network of kinship (than the nonpoor) in order to exchange resources and services. This extended network serves as a coping mechanism for dealing with the uncertainties and hardships of poverty (e.g., Edin & Lein, 1997; Harvey, 1993; Lewis, 1966; Stack, 1974).

For example, in Stack's study of a poor, black community called The Flats, she found that it was virtually impossible for families to cover their various expenses and needs completely on their own. Consequently, a system of collective sharing arose within The Flats as an adaptive strategy to survive the daily uncertainties and deprivation of poverty. As Stack writes:

In the final months of my life in The Flats, I learned that poverty creates a necessity for this exchange of goods and services. The needs of families living at bare subsistence are so large compared to their average daily income that it is impossible for families to provide independently for fixed expenses and daily needs. Lacking any surplus of funds, they are forced to use most of their resources for major monthly bills: rent, utilities, and foods. After a family pays these bills they are penniless. (1974, p. 29)

This system of exchange encompassed a wide network of kin and friends within The Flats. Only through such a collective response were families able to get through the daily trials and tribulations of long-term poverty.

Likewise, in Harvey's (1993) ethnographic study of a white, displaced farming population that had located in a community called Potter Addition, a similar process of mutual sharing and obligation developed across a wide network of kin. Family and kin members could be counted on to help in various situations, just as they themselves would be counted on for mutual assistance by others.

AGING ACROSS THE LIFE COURSE

One of the significant impacts of SES on the process of aging across the life course is that social class tends to reproduce itself along the way. Various analyses have shown that while some amount of social mobility does occur (Blau & Duncan, 1967; Duncan, 1984; Featherman & Hauser, 1978) social class as a whole tends to perpetuate itself (Beeghley, 1996;

Wright, 1994). Those whose parents are from a working or lower class are likely to remain working or lower class themselves. Similarly, those whose parents fall into the upper class are likely to remain upper class.

The reason for this is that variations in economic and social class result in significant differences in resources and opportunities for children. Children from lower- or working-class backgrounds simply do not have the range and depth of opportunities as children from middle- or upper-class backgrounds. These differences in turn affect children's future life chances and outcomes (Berrick, 1995; Blank, 1997; Devine & Wright, 1993; Entwisle & Alexander, 1993; Lichter, 1997; Rank & Cheng, 1995).

Likewise, lower SES during the prime working years is associated with an elevated risk of poverty during the elderly years. Rank and Hirschl (1999) analyzed the elderly's likelihood of ever experiencing poverty between the ages of 60 and 85. For those who had graduated from high school, 20.4 percent would experience poverty at some point during their elderly years. However, for those who had less than 12 years of education, 48.4 percent would experience at least one year below the poverty line.

Rank (1994) uses the analogy of a modified game of Monopoly to illustrate this process. Rather than the players beginning with identical resources ($1,500) at the start of the game, the players begin with different sets of resources. Some begin with $5,000 and properties already acquired, some begin with the standard $1,500, and some begin with $250. Much as in real life, these advantages or disadvantages acquired before the dice have been rolled will have a strong impact on how well the individual players do in the actual game. Skill and luck are still involved, but are no longer as important given the prior advantages or disadvantages with which each player begins. It should come as no surprise that players with $5,000 will wind up winning most of the games, while players beginning with $250 will end up losing most of the games. As this game analogy illustrates, prior advantages or disadvantages due to social class carry over into life trajectories as individuals age. This is one of the most significant effects that social class has on the manner in which the life course unfolds for both individuals and their families.

FAMILY PROBLEMS AND DIFFICULTIES

In this section several areas where social class impacts and intensifies family problems are discussed. These include physical health, the stunting of children's development, marital stress, dissatisfaction and dissolution, and family violence. Research indicates that lower SES, and particularly poverty, is associated with greater difficulties in each of these areas. However, it must be noted that these family problems exist across the spectrum of social class (e.g., although family violence is more likely to occur in lower-class families, it is by no means the exclusive domain of such families).

PHYSICAL HEALTH

One of the most consistent findings in epidemiology is that the quality of an individual's and family's health is negatively affected by lower SES, particularly impoverishment. Poverty is associated with a host of health risks, including elevated rates of heart disease, diabetes, hypertension, cancer, infant mortality, mental illness, undernutrition, lead poisoning, asthma, dental problems, and a variety of other ailments and diseases (Klerman, 1991; Leidenfrost, 1993; Sherman, 1994; Williams & Collins, 1995). The result is a death rate for the poverty stricken approximately three times higher than that for the affluent (Pappas, Queen, Hadden, & Fisher, 1993). As Leidenfrost (1993) notes in her review of the literature, "Health disparities between the poor and those with higher incomes are almost universal for all dimensions of health" (p. 1).

The connection between poverty and ill health exists for several reasons, beginning with the lack of an adequate diet. Living in poverty often means having to do without a sufficiently balanced diet and adequate intake of calories (Clancy & Bowering, 1992; Poppendieck, 1997; Uvin, 1994). Several large-scale studies have indicated that those in poverty routinely have bouts of hunger, undernutrition, and/or a detrimental altering of the diet at some point during the month (Breglio, 1992; Cook & Brown, 1992; Physician Task Force on Hunger in America, 1985; U.S. Conference of Mayors, 1994; VanAmburg Group, 1994). This risk affects children, working age adults, and the elderly (Cohen, Burt, & Schulte, 1993; Food Research and Action Center, 1991).

For example, an elderly woman in Rank's *Living on the Edge* described how she could not afford a balanced diet, which then compounded her health problems:

> Toward the end of the month, we just live on toast and stuff. Toast and eggs or something like that. I'm supposed to eat green vegetables. I'm supposed to be on a special diet because I'm a diabetic. But there's a lotta things that I'm supposed to eat that I can't afford. Because the fruit and vegetables are terribly high in the store. It's ridiculous! I was out to Cedar's grocery, they're chargin fifty-nine cents for one grapefruit. I'm supposed to eat grapefruit, but who's gonna pay fifty-nine cents for one grapefruit when you don't have much money? But my doctor says that that's one thing that's important, is to eat the right foods when you're a diabetic. But I eat what I can afford. And if I can't afford it, I can't eat it. So that's why my blood sugar's high because lots of times I should have certain things to eat and I just can't pay. I can't afford it. (1994, p. 59)

Having enough food on the table is thus a constant battle among families in poverty. As Dan Glickman, the Secretary of Agriculture, aptly noted:

> One in three of our kids live in families that do constant battle with hunger—whether it's missed meals the last few days before a paycheck, or skipped medical appointments in favor of putting food on the table. These kids are at constant risk of malnutrition and the lifetime of chronic illness that can accompany it. (Glickman, 1997)

A second reason for the connection between lower SES (and specifically poverty) and ill health is less access to medical care. Although Medicaid and Medicare have helped to increase the access of the poor to health care, when use of health services is compared to need for services, low-income households still have the lowest rate (Wolfe, 1994). Furthermore, a number of the poor and near poor have no insurance whatsoever (approximately 40 percent), and when insurance is carried, it is often restrictive in terms of what is covered (Bok, 1996).

A third reason for the connection between lower SES and decreased physical health is that poor families are more likely to be residing in unhealthy and stressful physical and mental environments. Living in a safe and decent neighborhood becomes less likely as one approaches the lower end of the SES scale. Poverty significantly limits the ability of families to buy into a high quality of life neighborhood. For example, a poverty stricken mother of two teenagers described her neighborhood as follows:

The territory is horrible. Across the street is the place that's been hitting the news lately. And it's really bad, 'cause when we go away, on weekends, we go down to my older son sometimes. And you really don't know what you're gonna have left when you come back. Because the apartment next door has been broken into twice. And it's bad. You can never be comfortable at night 'cause ya can never leave your windows open. You have to lock everything up, because you never know. But I guess if you want reasonable, cheap rent, you have to. (Rank, in press)

In addition, racial discrimination in the housing market further restricts the options available to minorities, particularly African Americans (Jargowsky, 1997; Massey & Denton, 1993; Yinger, 1995).

Finally, less educational awareness regarding health issues helps to explain the relationship between SES and a family's physical health. Those with higher educational levels are more likely to be cognizant of potential health danger signs, as well as more likely to follow healthy life habits (Anderson & Armstead, 1995; U.S. Bureau of the Census, 1996).

STUNTED CHILDREN'S DEVELOPMENT

Related to the above discussion, low SES and particularly poverty have been shown to be associated with a stunting of physical and mental growth among children. Poor infants and young children in the United States are much more likely to have lower levels of physical and mental growth (as measured in a variety of ways) when compared to their nonpoor counterparts (Duncan & Brooks-Gunn, 1997; Korenman & Miller, 1997; Smith, Brooks-Gunn, & Klebanov, 1997). According to Schiller (1998),

[A] child born to a poverty-stricken mother is likely to be undernourished both before and after birth. Furthermore, the child is less likely to receive proper postnatal care, to be immunized against disease, or even to have his or her eyes and teeth examined. As a result, the child is likely to grow up prone to illness and poverty, and in the most insidious of cases, be impaired by organic brain damage. (p. 97)

Both the duration and depth of poverty intensify these negative outcomes. For example, in their research on poverty's effects on young children's cognitive and verbal ability and early school achievement, Smith and colleagues (1997) report:

Duration of poverty has very negative effects on children's IQ, verbal ability, and achievement scores. Children who lived in persistently poor families scored 6–9 points lower on the various assessments than children who were never poor. In addition, the negative effects of persistent poverty seem to get stronger as the child gets older . . . The effects of family poverty varied dramatically depending on whether a family was very poor (family income below 50 percent of the poverty level), poor, or near poor. Children in the very poor group had scores 7–12 points lower than did children in the near-poor group. (p. 164)

Likewise, in a study that examined the impact of the duration of poverty on children's mental health, McLeod and Shanahan (1993) found that the length of time spent in poverty was directly associated with children's feeling of unhappiness, anxiety, and dependence.

As children grow older, and if they continue to reside in poverty, the disadvantages of growing up poor multiply. These include attending inferior schools (Kozol, 1991), coping with the problems associated with disadvantaged neighborhoods (Brooks-Gunn, Duncan,

& Aber, 1997), residing in less educationally stimulating home environments (Mayer, 1997), having health needs left unattended to (Sherman, 1994), and a host of other disadvantages. By the time they reach their early twenties, poor children are often at a significant disadvantage in terms of their ability to compete effectively within the labor market, which in turn increases their risk of experiencing poverty as adults.

MARITAL STRESS, DISSATISFACTION, AND DISSOLUTION

Research has consistently found that poverty and lower income are associated with greater levels of marital stress, dissatisfaction, and dissolution (Voydanoff, 1990; White, 1990; U.S. Bureau of the Census, 1992). In essence, poverty and low income act to amplify the daily stress found in everyday life and its relationships. Married couples in poverty face significant economic stress that subsequently lowers their levels of marital happiness and well-being (Conger, Ge, & Lorenz, 1994). This, in turn, increases the likelihood that couples will attempt to resolve such dissatisfaction through separation and/or divorce.

As an illustration, when asked what brought about the separation of her second marriage, a mother of three young children replied, "Poverty (laugh). I mean really. Most of our fights were over money and time. Money and time" (Rank, in press). Similarly, a poverty stricken married woman discussed the problems in her relationship with her husband:

> We don't have the money. It makes us frustrated or mad with each other. We run out of things. We take that out on each other. 'Cause it makes you frustrated when you don't know where your next dollar's coming from. You just start in on money and it just brings on an argument. (Rank, 1994, p. 81)

Unemployment can often precipitate a fall into poverty (particularly for the working class since they are typically not that far above the poverty line), which results in a tremendous strain upon a marriage. Research has indeed shown that the impact of unemployment upon the marital relationship is quite deleterious (Vosler, 1996). Yet when blended with poverty, the combination can be particularly destructive (Voydanoff, 1990).

An example of this is revealed in an interview with a husband in his early thirties who had worked his entire life until suffering a back injury while on the job. He was asked about the types of day-to-day problems he and his wife were experiencing:

> Gettin' on each other's nerves all the time. For the previous 13 years I've been gone all day long every day. On the road sellin'. So all of a sudden that changes and you're stuck in one place. That's hard on me. It's hard on her. It's hard on the kids. You just can't get used to it. It's been very hard on the marriage and on the kids and on everything. 'Cause we weren't used to it. Connie had stayed home with the kids and everything. And that was her job, and she's very good at it. Raised the kids, and that's the way I wanted it and that's the way she wanted it. But since this has happened (the back injury) it's thrown everything into turmoil. Simply because if you're with someone 24 hours a day, seven days a week it gets pretty hard. (pause) So it's rough on the marriage. You know, more tension. (Rank, in press)

FAMILY VIOLENCE

Largely as a result of the kinds of stresses and economic strains just discussed, research has found that lower SES is associated with higher levels of domestic violence (Drake &

Pandey, 1996; Gelles, 1993a, 1993b; Moore, 1997; Sedlak & Broadhurst, 1996; Smith, 1990; Straus, Gelles, & Steinmetz, 1980). This is particularly true in understanding men's acts of domestic violence upon their wives (Anderson, 1997).

Take the above example of unemployment coupled with a drop into poverty. An out-of-work husband in Rubin's *Families on the Faultline* described his feelings as follows:

> It's hard enough being out of work, but then my wife gets on my case, yakking all the time about how we're going to be on the street if I don't get off my butt, like it's my fault or something that there's no work out there. When she starts up like that, I swear I want to hit her, anything just to shut her mouth. (1994, pp. 115–116)

As Rubin writes, "the stress and conflict in families where father loses his job can give rise to the kind of interaction described here, a dynamic that all too frequently ends in physical assaults against women and children" (1994, p. 116).

In addition, there is evidence to suggest that the greater acceptance of patriarchal authority among those with lower levels of SES (as discussed earlier under gender roles) also lends itself to a greater incidence of wife and child abuse. Physical violence is more likely to be seen by husbands and fathers as a legitimate tool in order to exert and maintain their authority (Collins & Coltrane, 1995).

CONCLUSION

This chapter has outlined several dimensions where SES exerts an important influence on the family. Just as gender, race, and ethnicity have been shown in prior chapters to impact on the family, so too does SES. These characteristics influence and shape the family in unique ways. As Rubin notes, the result is that:

> the family is a product of its time and place in the hierarchy of social institutions. American families are both similar and different—similar in that they share some common experiences, some elements of a common culture by virtue of being part of the same society; different in that class, race, and ethnic differences give a special cast to the shared experience as well as a unique and distinctly different set of experiences. (1976, p. 210)

Such an understanding would appear critical in dealing with families. In particular, economic distress and strain have been shown to be quite damaging to the family. Clinicians and family therapists see the daily fallout from these economic conditions in the forms of increased violence, stunted growth, rising numbers of single-parent families, and so on. The irony is that practitioners are generally unable to deal with the source of these problems (see Vosler, 1996, for a discussion of a multilevel social systems model that does attempt to deal with these issues on a much broader level).

Nevertheless, an awareness of the manner and process whereby SES impacts on the family provides an important background context for clinicians when confronting particular family processes and problems that have been discussed in this chapter. Just as family therapy often applies a systemic approach to understanding family dynamics, so too must we appreciate that the family is shaped by its hierarchical position in the system we call socioeconomic status.

REFERENCES

Adams, B. N. (1998). *The family: A sociological interpretation.* New York: Harcourt Brace.

Anderson, E. (1990). *StreetWise: Race, class, and change in an urban community.* Chicago: University of Chicago Press.

Anderson, E. (1999). *Code of the street: Decency, violent, and the moral life of the inner city.* New York: Norton.

Anderson, K. L. (1997). Gender, status, and domestic violence: An integration of feminist and family violence approaches. *Journal of Marriage and the Family, 59,* 655–669.

Anderson, N. B., & Armstead, C. A. (1995). Toward understanding the association of socioeconomic status and health: A new challenge for the biopsychosocial approach. *Psychosomatic Medicine, 57,* 213–225.

Becker, G. S. (1981). *A treatise on the family.* Cambridge, MA: Harvard University Press.

Beeghley, L. (1996). *The structure of social stratification in the United States.* Boston: Allyn & Bacon.

Berrick, J. D. (1995). *Faces of poverty: Portraits of women and children on welfare.* New York: Oxford University Press.

Blank, R. M. (1997). *It takes a nation: A new agenda for fighting poverty.* Princeton, NJ: Princeton University Press.

Blau, P., & Duncan, O. D. (1967). *The American occupational structure.* New York: John Wiley & Son, Inc.

Blumstein, P., & Schwartz, P. (1983). *American couples: Money, work, sex.* New York: William Morrow.

Bok, D. (1996). *The state of the nation: Government and the quest for a better society.* Cambridge, MA: Harvard University Press.

Breglio, V. J. (1992). *Hunger in America: The voter's perspective.* Lanham, MD: Research/Strategy/Management (RMS), Inc.

Brooks-Gunn, J., Duncan, G. J., & Aber, J. L. (1997). *Neighborhood poverty: Context and consequences for children.* New York: Russell Sage Foundation.

Cheal, D. (1996). *New poverty: Families in postmodern society.* Westport, CT: Greenwood Press.

Cherlin, A. J. (1991). *Marriage, divorce, remarriage.* Cambridge, MA: Harvard University Press.

Cherlin, A. J. (1996). *Public and private families: An introduction.* New York: McGraw Hill.

Children's Defense Fund. (1985). *Preventing children having children. A Special Conference Report, Clearinghouse Paper No. 1.* Washington, DC: Children's Defense Fund.

Clancy, K. L., & Bowering, J. (1992). The need for emergency food: Poverty problems and policy responses. *Journal of Nutrition Education, 24,* 12S–17S.

Cohen, B. E., Burt, M. R., & Schulte, M. M. (1993). *Hunger and food insecurity among the elderly. Project Report.* Washington, DC: The Urban Institute.

Collins, R., & Coltrane, S. (1995). *Sociology of marriage and the family: Gender, love and property.* Chicago, IL: Nelson-Hall.

Conger, R. D., Ge, X. J., & Lorenz, F. O. (1994). Economic stress and marital relations. In R. D. Conger & G. H. Elder, Jr. (Eds.), *Families in troubled times: Adapting to change in rural America* (pp. 187–203). New York: Aldine de Gruyter.

Cook, J. T., & Brown, J. L. (1992). *Estimating the number of hungry Americans.* Center for Hunger, Poverty and Nutrition Policy Working Paper No. HE01-090292. Medford, MA: Tufts University.

Daniels, A. K. (1988). *Invisible careers.* Chicago: University of Chicago Press.

Dash, L. (1989). *When children want children: The urban crisis of teenage childbearing.* New York: William Morrow.

Devine, J. A., & Wright, J. D. (1993). *The greatest of evils: Urban poverty and the American underclass.* New York: Aldine de Gruyter.

Drake, B., & Pandey, S. (1996). Understanding the relationship between neighborhood poverty and specific types of child maltreatment. *Child Abuse and Neglect, 20,* 1003–1018.

Duncan, G. J. (1984). *Years of poverty years of plenty.* Ann Arbor, MI: Institute of Social Research.

Duncan, G. J., & Brooks-Gunn, J. (1997). *Consequences of growing up poor.* New York: Russell Sage Foundation.

Edin, K., & Lein, L. (1997). *Making ends meet: How single mothers survive welfare and low-wage work.* New York: Russell Sage Foundation.

Entwisle, D. R., & Alexander, K. L. (1993). Entry into school: The beginning school transition and educational stratification in the United States. *Annual Review of Sociology, 19,* 401–423.

Eshleman, J. R. (1997). *The family.* Boston, MA: Allyn & Bacon.

Featherman, D., & Hauser, R. (1978). *Opportunity and change.* New York: Academic Press.

Food Research and Action Center. (1991). *Community childhood hunger identification project: A survey of childhood hunger in the United States.* Washington, DC: Food Research and Action Center.

Ganzeboom, H. B. G., Treiman, D. J., & Ultee W. C. (1991). Comparative intergenerational stratification research: Three generations and beyond. *Annual Review of Sociology, 17,* 277–302.

Gelles, R. J. (1993a). Poverty and violence towards children. *American Behavioral Scientist, 35,* 258–274.

Gelles, R. J. (1993b). Through a sociological lens: Social structure and family violence. In R. J. Gelles & D. R. Loseke (Eds.), *Current controversies on family violence* (pp. 31–46). Newbury Park, CA: Sage.

Gerris, J. R. M., Dekovic, M., & Janssens, J. M. A. M. (1997). The relationship between social class and childrearing behaviors: Parents' perspective taking and value orientations. *Journal of Marriage and the Family, 59,* 834–847.

Glickman, D. (1997). *Remarks of Secretary Dan Glickman at the FRAC annual dinner.* Food Research and Action Center, Washington, DC, June 17.

Goode, W. J. (1982). *The family.* Englewood Cliffs, NJ: Prentice-Hall.

Halle, D. (1984). *America's working man work, home, and politics among blue-collar property owners.* Chicago: University of Chicago Press.

Harvey, D. L. (1993). *Potter addition: Poverty, family, and kinship in a heartland community.* New York: Aldine de Gruyter.

Hochschild, A. (1989). *The second shift: Working parents and the revolution at home.* New York: Viking.

Howell, J. T. (1973). *Hard living on clay street: Portraits of blue collar families.* New York: Anchor Books.

Jargowsky, P. A. (1997). *Poverty and place: Ghettos, barrios, and the American city.* New York: Russell Sage Foundation.

Kalmijn, M. (1998). Intermarriage and homogamy: Causes, patterns, trends. *Annual Review of Sociology, 24,* 395–421.

Klerman, L. (1991). *Alive and well? A research and policy review of health programs for poor young children.* New York: National Center for Children in Poverty.

Kohn, M. (1963). Social class and parent-child relationships: An interpretation. *American Journal of Sociology, 68,* 471–480.

Kohn, M. (1979). The effects of social class on parental values and practices. In D. Reiss & H. A. Hoffman (Eds.), *The American family: Dying or developing?* (pp. 45–68). New York: Plenum Press.

Komarovsky, M. (1962). *Blue-collar marriage.* New York: Random House.

Korenman, S., & Miller, J. E. (1997). Effects of long-term poverty on physical health of children in the national longitudinal survey of youth. In G. J. Duncan, & J. Brooks-Gunn (Eds.), *Consequences of growing up poor* (pp. 70–99). New York: Russell Sage Foundation.

Kozol, J. (1991). *Savage inequalities: Children in America's schools.* New York: Crown Publishers.

Leidenfrost, N. B. (1993). *An examination of the impact of poverty on health.* Report prepared for the Extension Service, United States Department of Agriculture.

LeMasters, E. E. (1975). *Blue-collar aristocrats: Life-styles at a working-class tavern.* Madison, WI: University of Wisconsin Press.

Lewis, O. (1966). The culture of poverty. *Scientific American, 215,* 19–25.

Lichter, D. T. (1997). Poverty and inequality among children. *Annual Review of Sociology, 23,* 121–145.

Luker, K. (1996). *Dubious conceptions: The politics of teenage pregnancy.* Cambridge, MA: Harvard University Press.

Luster, T., Hoades, K., & Haas, B. (1989). The relation between parental values and parenting behavior: A test of Kohn hypothesis. *Journal of Marriage and the Family, 51,* 139–147.

Lynd, R. S., & Lynd, H. M. (1929). *Middletown: A study in modern American culture.* New York: Harcourt, Brace & World.

Lynd, R. S., & Lynd, H. M. (1937). *Middletown in transition: A study in cultural conflicts.* New York: Harcourt, Brace & World.

Massey, D. S., & Denton, N. A. (1993). *American apartheid: Segregation and the making of the underclass.* Cambridge, MA: Harvard University Press.

Mayer, S. E. (1997). *What money can't buy: Family income and children's life chances.* Cambridge, MA: Harvard University Press.

Maynard, R. A. (1997). *Kids having kids: Economic costs and social consequences of teen pregnancy.* Washington, DC: The Urban Institute Press.

McLeod, J. D., & Shanahan, M. J. (1993). Poverty, parenting, and children's mental health. *American Sociological Review, 58,* 351–366.

Moore, A. M. (1997). Intimate violence: Does socioeconomic status matter? In A. P. Cardarelli (Ed.), *Violence between intimate partners: Patterns, causes, and effects* (pp. 90–103). Boston: Allyn & Bacon.

National Center for Health Statistics. (1997). Birth and fertility rates by educational attainment: United States, 1994. *Monthly Vital Statistics Report Vol. 45, No. 10(S).* Washington, DC: U.S. Government Printing Office.

Ostrander, S. A. (1984). *Women of the upper class.* Philadelphia, PA: Temple University Press.

Pappas, G., Queen, S., Hadden, W., & Fisher, G. (1993). The increasing disparity in mortality between socioeconomic groups in the United States, 1960 and 1986. *New England Journal of Medicine, 329,* 103–115.

Physician Task Force on Hunger in America. (1985). *Hunger in America: The growing epidemic.* Middletown, CT: Wesleyan University Press.

Poppendieck J. (1997). The USA: Hunger in the land of plenty. In G. Riches (Ed.), *First world hunger: Food security and welfare politics* (pp. 134–164). New York: St. Martin's Press.

Rank, M. R. (1982). Determinants of conjugal influence in wives' employment decision making. *Journal of Marriage and the Family, 44,* 591–604.

Rank, M. R. (1994). *Living on the edge: The realities of welfare in America.* New York: Columbia University Press.

Rank, M. R. (in press). *In the shadows of plenty: Reexamining American poverty.* New York: Oxford University Press.

Rank, M. R., & Cheng, L. C. (1995). Welfare use across generations: How important are the ties that bind? *Journal of Marriage and the Family, 57,* 673–684.

Rank, M. R., & Hirschl, T. A. (1999). Estimating the proportion of Americans ever experiencing poverty during their elderly years. *Journal of Gerontology: Social Sciences, 54B,* 5184–5193.

Rubin, L. B. (1976). *Worlds of pain: Life in the working-class family.* New York: Basic Books.

Rubin, L. B. (1994). *Families on the faultline: America's working class speaks about the family, the economy, race and ethnicity.* New York: HarperCollins.

Schiller, B. R. (1998). *The economics of poverty and discrimination.* Englewood Cliffs, NJ: Prentice Hall.

Sedlak, A. J., & Broadhurst, D. D. (1996). *Third national incidence study of child abuse and neglect: Final report.* Washington, DC: U.S. Department of Health and Human Services.

Sherman, A. (1994). *Wasting America's future: The Children's Defense Fund report on the costs of child poverty.* Boston: Beacon Press.

Smith, M. D. (1990). Sociodemographic risk factors in wife abuse: Results from a survey of Toronto women. *Canadian Journal of Sociology, 15,* 39–58.

Smith, J. R., Brooks-Gunn, J., & Klebanov, P. K. (1997). Consequences of living in poverty for young children's cognitive and verbal ability and early school achievement. In G. J. Duncan & J. Brooks-Gunn (Eds.), *Consequences of Growing Up Poor* (pp. 132–189). New York: Russell Sage Foundation.

Smith, T. E., & Graham, P. B. (1995). Socioeconomic stratification in family research. *Journal of Marriage and the Family, 57,* 930–940.

Sorensen, A. (1994). Women, family and class. *Annual Review of Sociology, 20,* 27–47.

Spenner, K. I. (1998). Reflections on a 30-year career of research on work and personality by Melvin Kohn and colleagues. *Sociological Forum, 13,* 169–181.

Stack, C. B. (1974). *All our kin: Strategies for survival in a black community.* New York: Harper & Row.

Straus, M. A., Gelles, R. J., & Steinmetz, S. K. (1980). *Behind closed doors: Violence in the American family.* Garden City, NY: Anchor.

U.S. Bureau of the Census. (1992). *Studies in household and family formation. Current Population Reports, Series P23-179.* Washington, DC: U.S. Government Printing Office.

U.S. Bureau of the Census. (1996). *Statistical Abstract of the United States 1996.* Washington, DC: U.S. Government Printing Office.

U.S. Bureau of the Census. (1997). *Fertility of American women: June 1995 (update). Current Population Reports, Series P20-499.* Washington, DC: U.S. Government Printing Office.

U.S. Conference of Mayors. (1994). *A status report on hunger and homelessness in American cities.* Washington, DC: U.S. Conference of Mayors.

Uvin, P. (1994). The state of world hunger. *Nutrition Reviews, 52,* 1151–1161.

VanAmburg Group, Inc. (1994). *Second harvest. 1993 national research study.* Chicago, IL: Second Harvest.

Vosler, N. (1996). *New approaches to family practice: Confronting economic stress.* Thousand Oaks, CA: Sage Publications.

Voydanoff, P. (1990). Economic distress and family relations: A review of the eighties. *Journal of Marriage and the Family, 52,* 1099–1115.

White, L. K. (1990). Determinants of divorce: A review of research in the eighties. *Journal of Marriage and the Family, 52,* 904–912.

Williams, D. R., & Collins, C. (1995). U.S. socioeconomic and racial differences in health: Patterns and explanations. *Annual Review of Sociology, 21,* 349–386.

Wilson, W. J. (1987). *The truly disadvantaged: The inner city, the underclass, and public policy.* Chicago: University of Chicago Press.

Wilson, W. J. (1996). *When work disappears: The world of the new urban poor.* New York: Alfred A. Knopf.

Wolfe, B. L. (1994). Reform of health care for the nonelderly poor. In S. H. Danziger, G. D. Sandefur, & D. H. Weinberg (Eds.), *Confronting poverty: Prescriptions for change* (pp. 253–288). Cambridge, MA: Harvard University Press.

Wright, E. O. (1994). *Interrogating inequality: Essays on class analysis. socialism and Marxism.* London: Verso.

Wright, J. D., & Wright, S. R. (1976). Social class and parental values for children: A partial replication and extension of the Kohn thesis. *American Sociological Review, 41,* 527–537.

Yinger, J. (1995). *Closed doors, opportunities lost: The continuing costs of housing discrimination.* New York: Russell Sage Foundation.

PART III

FAMILY STAGES, PATTERNS, PROCESSES, AND DYNAMICS

CHAPTER 8

Making a Marriage

Augustus Y. Napier

W HILE MUCH OF LIFE proceeds by small, incremental choices, the decision to marry is truly a turning point; it is perhaps the most dramatic life-altering choice. Marriage attempts to link two lives across an immense range of experience: sharing intimate and mundane feeling, shaping sexual experience, creating the intricate organization of everyday time, pooling financial and emotional resources. Marriage is the entire coordination of two lives; it involves learning to be both separate and together, learning to allocate power, learning to play and work together, and perhaps the greatest challenge of all, learning to rear another generation. But marriage not only binds two individuals, it attempts to unify the separate "cultures" of their families: their customs, myths, rituals, prejudices, aspirations, beliefs, gender prescriptions, and memories.

Given the complexity of intimately juxtaposing two lives over many years, hopefully with a measure of pleasure and satisfaction, it is small wonder that so many marriages fail. Some current estimates are that upwards of two-thirds of first marriages will end in divorce (Martin & Bumpass, 1989). So our task here, looking at how we can help couples make better and more enduring marriages, is a very serious one.

WHAT IS A MARRIAGE?

At least one defining boundary that delineates marriage is a couple's public declaration—often before friends and family members, but sometimes before a single public official—to be loyal to each other and to love and support each other for a lifetime. While they are still denied the protection of law afforded to heterosexual pairs (Glaser, 1996), gay and lesbian couples are increasingly participating in marriage commitment ceremonies; for the purposes of this chapter, these couples will be assumed to be psychologically married, and to have the same problems and potentials as heterosexual relationships—with the added burden of living in a society that is often hostile to their partnerships.

In working supportively with gay and lesbian pairs, we can help them mitigate some of the effects of society's (and in many instances their families') disapproval (Laird & Green, 1996; Slater, 1995). We can also help them affirm the strengths in their relationships: Since they are not bound by the rigidity of traditional gender roles, gay and lesbian couples may develop more equality and deeper levels of intimacy than many heterosexual pairs (Green, Bettinger, & Jacks, 1996).

Although we may work with them in much the same way that we would with engaged or married couples, cohabiting couples are of course not married, and their dynamics are somewhat different from couples who have openly and publicly committed themselves to being married. Since marriage is such a dominant relationship in our society, the cohabiting couple often brings to therapy an implied (and sometimes unstated) agenda: Should we marry, should we break up, or should we continue to live together? If we address these implicit issues directly, our work with the couple can be more productive.

MARRIAGE TODAY

In 1960, the estimated median age of the marrying couple was 22.8 years for men and 20.3 years for women. In 1998, the typical man who married was 26.7 years old, the woman 25.0 years (U.S. Bureau of the Census, 1999a). At the same time that individuals are waiting longer to marry, they have begun having sex much earlier, often in their teens (Wolf, 1991). More than half of couples marrying today have lived together before marriage (Teachman & Polonko, 1990).

With greater mobility in our society, there is increasing heterogeneity in marital choice. While in the past a small community of relatively similar eligibles often dictated marital choice, individuals today are more likely to meet and choose partners from diverse backgrounds. For example, the number of interracial marriages alone more than doubled between 1980 and 1998 (U.S. Bureau of the Census, 1999b).

We need to be prepared to help couples adjust to the differences they bring to marriage: racial differences, differences in education and social class, ethnic and religious tradition, geographic origin, age, and prior marital experience. The therapist's best preparation for this task is a flexible attitude, an acceptance of cultural diversity, and a thorough grounding in multicultural perspectives (Hines, Preto, McGoldrick, Almeida, & Weltman, 1999). The accepting and knowledgeable therapist can help couples understand and cope with their differences, and can allow them to see the strengths that come with these differences.

THE SOCIAL AND EMOTIONAL CONTEXT OF MARRIAGE

As seen in our high rates of divorce, addiction, domestic violence, suicide, and abuse and neglect of children (Coontz, 1997), we live in a society with a great deal of personal distress. From the "cathartic" exposure of personal dilemmas on national talk-show radio and television, to the plethora of self-help books, to the burgeoning of self-help groups, to the factual and fictional "working through" of various social problems in movies and television, we also see a culture trying, sometimes desperately, to reveal, to understand, and to heal itself. It is as if the historical injunction to deny and conceal our personal vulnerability has been replaced by its polar opposite.

No ordinary human relationship is more vulnerable to these yearnings for emotional wholeness than marriage. This idealized relationship promises companionship, sexual satisfaction, economic collaboration, emotional support, and a depth of acceptance and love that will somehow compensate for the love we did not get as children. Marriage will give meaning and shape to our lives; it will fill some of the gaps in our own competencies and character (Aron & Aron, 1986, 1996). In short, contemporary marriage has implicit "therapeutic" import (Napier & Whitaker, 1978). When we look at the pressures on young adults during the decade of their twenties, when most first marriages are contracted, it becomes clear why they would be drawn to this "therapeutic" marriage.

COMPENSATION FOR THE FAMILY OF ORIGIN

Some young adults are fleeing chaotic or conflicted families; they may later realize that they married not out of a sense of the positive choice of a partner, but "to get away from home." Others may have separated from their families with a deep sense of incompleteness; they yearn for love or affection that they did not get from their parents. Some young adults are in conflict with their parents about their autonomy; they may choose a partner partly because their parents disapprove of this person. Still others may simply yearn for the safety and protection of the families from which they have "graduated."

LOSS OF THE TRANSITIONAL FAMILY

As they consider marriage, many young adults have lost, or are losing, the support of the "transitional family" of college, the military, or the temporary job in which many of their decisions were either made for them or could be deferred. Particularly in the urban setting, they face an increasingly pressured and competitive job world; they may be socially lonely.

DECISION PRESSURE

Individuals in their twenties have begun to feel the pressures of the aging process. At 25, they are halfway through the decade in which they expect to choose a career and to marry; as they near 30, this decade marker feels like a deadline. Men may feel anxious that they are not "established" in a promising job; women may be torn between the demands of their careers and their desires to have children. Worried about their fertility, women approaching 30 often feel an intense desire to marry.

A NEGATIVE RELATIONSHIP HISTORY

Individuals may be responding to a painful history in other relationships, including having been divorced. Rejection by a prior partner may create intense vulnerability and a need for confirmation. A history of an abusive past relationship may motivate the search for a protective partner. If the new relationship is the result of an affair that took place during a prior marriage, it is subject to some of the same risks as the "lifeboat" marriage that helps the young adult escape a painful family of origin. Relationships that are expected to "heal" prior relationships often bear a heavy burden of expectations, and they are vulnerable to disappointment.

PREMARITAL PREGNANCY

Premarital pregnancy is increasingly common, and is a serious risk factor for marriage (Teachman, 1983). Even if the couple is in love and may have planned to marry, the pregnancy may make them feel "forced" into marriage. In some instances the couple may have unconsciously "arranged" to become pregnant in order to help them break out of their ambivalence about or fear of marriage, but they may still feel cheated of the sense of choosing freely to marry.

COHABITATION

The couple may be influenced by the inertia of living together. Often one partner has wanted to marry for a while, and the other finally accedes. Since over half of marrying couples have lived together by the time they marry, the familiarity of habit may provide a powerful inducement to marry. Cohabitation may also reflect ambivalence in both partners about commitment to marriage.

Some marriages are overdetermined by intense needs and pressures, as when one seeks to find in the marriage a basic sense of self-worth, or when one is trying to escape a chaotic home or is fighting with parents for autonomy. Other marriages, such as in the acquiescence to the habit of living together, or to a sense that this is a reasonable and timely decision, are underdetermined (Napier, 1988). The two partners may feel very different degrees of "pressure" to marry: If the woman is pregnant, for example, she may feel very anxious to marry, and her partner may feel resistant or reluctant.

What constitutes a "healthy" marital choice? I look for what I have called an "integrated" choice of partner, or one that is a complex mixture of elements, where no single aspect of the choice seems to dominate (Napier, 1988). Yes, this seems to be a sensible decision (the partners have reasonably similar values, interests, and life goals, for example), and yes, there is a quality of passionate interest in the partner—and not simply sexual passion—that seems complex enough that both partners feel "confused" as to its exact nature. The sense of confusion may be positive because the partners represent to each other a mixture of qualities that are too intricate to define cognitively. Finally, the decision is strongly mutual; the marriage initiative is not "carried" by one person, with the other agreeing reluctantly or passively.

A PERSPECTIVE FOR THE THERAPIST OR COUNSELOR

This chapter is written for those who want more understanding of the world of marrying couples and who will be working with couples either in a clinical setting or in a marriage preparation program. While I will cite several structured tools for evaluating and teaching couples, my own experience has been largely in the clinical setting and has been interactive and personal.

The perspective of the therapist or counselor is an important aspect of this work. Do we attempt to be purely objective—administering questionnaires, teaching communications exercises, and avoiding advice—or do we become more personally involved, perhaps even advising a couple to go into therapy, or to delay or cancel a wedding? While both perspectives have validity, I believe that we are most helpful when we attempt to walk the difficult line between disciplined professionalism and a caring personal involvement.

I believe that crucial life decisions—among them whether and whom to marry, whether to divorce or not, whether to have a child and when—are indeed sacrosanct. They belong to the couple; we cannot know what is "right" for them, and we must finally defer to the interior and private wisdom of the two individuals. But I believe that we have certain obligations: to get to know our clients, inquiring as deeply as we dare; to speak honestly about our reactions to them and to their dilemmas; and to help them surface and reveal to each other their own interior thoughts, feelings, and reflections about the marriage they are about to undertake. The last is particularly important, since our clients are generally wiser about themselves than they know, and they are also highly likely to be defending against facing areas where they sense trouble exists for the relationship. How many times have we heard a divorcing client say, "I knew when I married that I was making a mistake." Yet no one was there to help that person bring that private knowledge to light.

I believe that we must sometimes confront couples, and individuals, forcefully, especially when we see something dangerous, destructive, or foolish taking place. This level of involvement is crucial when abuse or addiction issues surface in the relationship. As we work with couples who have very serious issues, we need good support (and referral) systems for dealing with these problems. We may need, for example, to push for a specialized treatment option for the violence-prone individual—before the marriage takes place.

A vital aspect of the couple's preparation for marriage is to help them examine whether there are major unresolved conflicts with their families of origin, conflicts that if addressed could make their marriage much less problematic. As therapists, we know how powerful loyalty conflicts can be, and how easily a new marriage can be invaded by the family of origin. Is the husband's family, for example, reluctant to let him separate from them, and are they working to undermine the couple's independence? Is she so hurt by her father's absence in her life that she hopes that her husband will be a substitute for her father? Does he anticipate that his wife will devote herself to taking emotional care of him in the way that his mother did, while she plans to have the high-profile career her mother did not have?

Helping couples develop perspective on the burdens of the scripts handed them by their families, particularly when these scripts put them on a collision course, can be vital to the couple's ability to anticipate and resolve these conflicts. I also believe that we need to be prepared—at least in the psychotherapy setting—to intervene in the extended family by convening that family. Often families are intuitively searching for a catalyst to force them to address old issues between them, and a couple's marriage can provide that opportunity.

We should be aware of the biases we bring to working with couples. Few of us can approach a client's decision to marry (or to divorce) without bringing strong feelings to the encounter. Rather than try to banish our own perspective, we can reveal it to our clients so that they can factor this information into what they take from us. Since my wife and I have been in a committed marriage for 35 years, when we work together as cotherapists, we are likely to approach the marrying couple with implicit enthusiasm about making a commitment and sticking with it. We tend to trust—sometimes naively—the intuitive wisdom of the partners' choice of each other. Therapists who have been divorced may have more freedom to suggest that a couple question the wisdom of their engagement, but they may also bring a certain skepticism about marriage itself. Whatever our marital experience, we bring strengths and liabilities to our clients. When we work didactically with couples, our personal biases are likely to be less intrusive, but even then we should be aware of them.

There are real advantages to working with couples in a male/female cotherapy team. So many couples' parents had highly conflictual or dysfunctional relationships that they often approach marriage with little first-hand knowledge of how a partnership works. The therapists need not be married to provide instructive modeling of warmth, consideration, and shared power; and the group format of many premarital programs may make coleading financially practical.

ATTRACTION: ISSUES OF SIMILARITY AND DIFFERENCE

While the large research literature on attraction and close relationships (for a recent review, see Berschied & Reis, 1998) is not always relevant to clinical concerns, this body of knowledge can cast helpful light on what attracts partners to each other, and it can indicate how different variables influence the outcome of these relationships.

Partners tend to meet through their personal networks. In one study, two-thirds of the respondents had met at least one member of their partner's network prior to meeting the partner (Parks & Eggert, 1991). Furthermore, the positive and negative opinions of the people in this network have a distinct influence on the relationship as it progresses (Surra, 1990).

What forces influence the attraction of mates? Several well-established principles seem to be at work, the most basic of which may be familiarity. Familiar people are usually considered safe and unlikely to cause harm (Hartley, 1946), leading us to want to interact with people whom we have seen or been physically near. Over time, however, familiarity may diminish our ability to capture our partner's sexual interest (Berscheid, 1985).

When someone expresses liking or esteem for us, we are likely to reciprocate that expression. As a relationship develops—and we learn more about our partner's sentiments—these reciprocity effects become stronger (Kenny, 1994). As clinicians who frequently focus on relationship problems, we might be reminded to help couples "uncover" and express to each other positive sentiments that they may be fearful of revealing.

We are powerfully drawn to someone who is similar to us. In fact, there is a great deal of evidence that attraction is a linear function of attitudinal similarity (Byrne, 1971). Since it was first asserted that, "On the average, similar individuals tend to marry" (Harris, 1912), research has repeatedly found that "like tends to marry like" on virtually every dimension studied, including personality dimensions (e.g., Caspi & Herbener, 1990). This affinity for the similar also seems true with regard to physical attractiveness, where individuals of similar levels of physical attractiveness seem to progress more rapidly in courtship and to marry (e.g., Price & Vandenberg, 1979). Once married, the more similar partners are in their sex-role performance expectations and in their leisure interests, the more satisfied they are (Houts, Robins, & Huston, 1996). Couples also tend to become more similar over time; for example, Gruber-Baldini, Schaie, and Willis (1995) found that couples became more similar in their verbal skills and attitudinal flexibility.

Based on clinical experience, I have suggested that we humans often feel very alone in the world, and that we have a deep yearning to marry someone who has the possibility of being a kind of "interior psychological twin" (Napier, 1988, 1999a). I find that even spouses who see themselves as distressingly different have striking underlying similarities. They may have had similar core experiences in their families of origin: Both are high-achieving "delegates," for example, or both have struggled with rejection by their parents; they may both have had learning disabled siblings, or absent mothers, or stern fathers. Both of their families of origin may have been preoccupied with their social image, or have been chaotic and messy, or frightened of sexuality. They may both have been "Oedipal" kids, with deep attachments to the opposite-sex parent. If we can help a couple identify these shared family patterns or themes, they can often deepen their sense of conscious identification with each other.

The couple's similarities can also create problems. If both, for example, are preoccupied with rejection, or with achievement, or with helping their families of origin, they can fail to see the extent to which their similarities lead them to overreact to their shared concerns.

Similarities between the partners may also lead them to make unwise decisions. For example, a couple can subtly collude in their both becoming gradually and seriously overweight, or in their making impulsive financial decisions. When both spouses are compulsive, they can overmanage their children. Scapegoating of a child also seems to be a shared marital process in which the couple "agrees" to focus their anger and frustration on a particular child (Napier & Whitaker, 1978).

Similarity between the individuals can be problematic if each sees in the other aspects of the self that he or she is frightened by or disapproves of (Napier, 1988). If the wife is overtly controlling, for example, and the husband more covertly controlling, he may blame her for a part of his own personality that he is not conscious of. Both partners may be uncomfortable about sex, but the husband may conceal his anxiety behind a constant pressure on his wife to have sex, while blaming her more obvious reticence. This projective identification, in which a negatively valued part of the self is projected on the other (for a discussion, see Scarf, 1987), can be difficult for couples to see; but if we can make them aware that these problems are shared, they can deepen their sense of common cause—although of course they need to stop the process of blaming the other.

Perhaps because we often see couples where the partners have contrasting personality traits, communication styles, or role positions, clinicians may be drawn to the theory that "differences attract," embodied by the complementary needs theory of Robert Winch (1958), which posits that differences between the spouses may "interlock" in ways that lend a positive tenor to the relationship. McGoldrick (1999), for example, citing Toman (1976) states:

> Couples who marry mates from complementary sibling positions tend to enjoy the greatest marital stability. In other words, the older brother of a younger sister will tend to get along best with a younger sister of an older brother. He will be comfortable with leading, she with following; and each will have grown up being familiar with a member of the opposite sex. (p. 246)

In reviewing the research on complementarity versus similarity in mate selection, Berscheid (1985) maintains that the weight of the research evidence is still on the side of similarity, and that evidence for complementarity is scarce. Based on clinical experience, I believe that we should be cautious in assuming that complementary role familiarity is necessarily healthy or provides long-term satisfaction in marriage:

> Tom and Shelly had been married for three years when they entered therapy. Tom was the youngest of three children and had twin older sisters. Shelly was the oldest of four children; all her younger siblings were brothers. While they initially felt comfortable with each other, Tom had grown to resent Shelly for what he saw as her attempts to direct and control him (something she clearly learned in dealing with her brothers), while Shelly was impatient with Tom's passivity and his difficulty taking initiative (a resistant stance he had taken with what he called his "twin controllers"). As Tom sensed Shelly's "disrespecting" him for not being her equal, he responded by having increasingly volatile temper outbursts. While the initial sessions focused on Tom's learning to control his outbursts, the deeper issue seemed to be his subordinate position in the marriage.

Since they tap familiar role experiences, complementary power arrangements (whether dictated by sibling position or other factors) may be comfortable for couples who are not highly oriented around marital equity, or "exchange orientation" (Murstein, Cerreto, & MacDonald, 1977). But for couples who value relationship equality, any habitual dominance pattern may become oppressive over time. As we examine dominance issues in marriage, we should be reminded that principles of equity are not of equal importance to everyone. Marital satisfaction is related to perceptions of equity between the partners only among spouses high in exchange orientation (Buunk & Van Yperen, 1991).

In a review of the relationship between power and marital satisfaction, Gray-Little and Burks (1983) found that egalitarian relationships (which are noncomplementary or "symmetrical") are the most satisfying for couples, but that traditional male-dominated marriages (complementary) run a close second in satisfaction. Wife-dominated pairs were far less satisfied than the other two types, a finding that has apparently been replicated across a number of societies. It would appear that complementary power arrangements are more satisfying for couples when they conform to historical norms than when they do not.

Theories of complementarity in mate selection tend to be accepted by our culture. Many people would assume, for example, that the masculine man and the feminine woman are a good match. Ickes and Barnes (1978) found that dyads composed of masculine men and feminine women typically get along less well and like each other less than do partners with similar sex-role orientations. Another study (Zammichieli, Gilroy, & Sherman, 1988) found that the traditional sex-typed couple is less satisfied than are other combinations. In fact, marital satisfaction seems to be strongly associated with the femininity of the partner, whether the partner is male or female (Antill, 1983; King, 1993). Lamke, Sollie, Durbin, and Fitzpatrick (1994) found that both men's and women's satisfaction with their relationships seem to be associated with the individual's own expressive competence, and with perceptions of the partner as feminine. Thus "symmetrical" orientations that lend themselves to the development of greater intimacy seem to lead to higher marital satisfaction.

A positive way to view distinct differences between partners is that while they may in some instances represent the partners' dependency on each other (he supplies the impulsive creativity, for example, she the element of planning and control), these differences also indicate the partners' attempts to "expand the self" by linking up with a partner with different traits, attributes, and abilities (Aron & Aron, 1986, 1996; Aron, Aron, & Smollan, 1992). In fact, Aron, Paris, and Aron (1995) found that after falling in love, people listed more words and phrases describing the self than they had used before, implying that they may have felt that they had acquired some of their partners' qualities. According to the Self-Expansion Model, plateaus in self-expansion may result in the reported decreases in romantic love over time, and this model posits that novel and exciting activities may offer possibilities for enhancing long-term relationships.

As we try to help couples understand the issues of similarity and difference that link and separate them, it is important that we evaluate these issues carefully, and that we not oversimplify them. A pattern that may produce dissatisfaction in one couple may be acceptable to another. Differences between the partners may divide them; they may also enrich the couple's experience.

While most partners represent a complex mixture of similarities and differences, their differences are likely to be more problematic. Are the spouses similar enough to be able to identify with each other's basic experience in life, or are they so different that they are having—or are likely to have—difficulty understanding each other? As more marriages are made between people from different geographic areas, races, ethnic groups, religious orientations, social classes, and even age groups, we need to help the couples be realistic about some of the challenges that these differences will present.

We should also not overlook the power of family loyalty (Boszormenyi-Nagy & Spark, 1973). Particularly if we were unhappy with aspects of our family of origin, we may be strongly attracted to a family with different dynamics and with new possibilities. But once we link up with a different family system, our loyalties to our own family may exert themselves in powerful and largely unconscious ways. It is much easier to make a conscious determination to break with our own family's patterns than it is to actually do so.

In my experience, the couple's families of origin are a fairly reliable indication of how successful the couple will be in overcoming their different backgrounds. If both families of origin support the marriage of—for example—partners from different religious backgrounds, the prognosis for the marriage is much better than if the couple has to battle their families as well as contending with their cultural differences. Marrying couples do not require the support of their families to have a successful relationship, but it helps tremendously if they have that support. If there is family opposition, it is very useful for the couple to know that this negative feeling can have a significant effect on them.

Hendrix (1988) maintains that we are drawn to marry someone who—if the marriage is to work—will require us to change in ways that we need to change, and that this incentive is present for both partners. This seems to me an attractive notion: that the differences between the partners are "strategically" chosen, and are part of both individuals' unconscious needs to change themselves. Are both partners willing to accept their differences and to try to learn from each other, or are they initially intrigued by these differences, only to later turn on the partner and say, "But I want you to be like me (and my family)?" It is important to help couples realize that there is an unconscious "strategy for growth" in their choice of each other, but that this growth rarely comes without pain and effort.

OF BIOLOGY AND ATTACHMENT

In recent years, there has been increasing interest in biologically based theories of human relationships. The evolutionary psychologists (see Buss, 1994; Kendrick & Trost, 1989) propose that while humans have been selected to maximize reproductive success (and thus maximize gene replication), there are gender differences in sexual strategies and mate preference. Buss and his colleagues found that men tend to prefer mates who are physically attractive, while women more than men prefer mates who have good earning potential and are college educated. Men are said to value beauty in women because it signifies youth and fertility, while women (who invest more in their offspring than do men) value men who can provide the safety and stability associated with good earning power, conditions that lend themselves to successful child rearing.

These theories have been hotly debated (for a lively, caustic rebuttal, see Angier, 1999). Recent research seems to suggest that women's mate preferences for men with good earnings potential are highly influenced by women's lower earning power in American society. Gangestad (1993) found that as women gain greater economic resources, they seem increasingly to prefer physically attractive men. However this theoretical argument sorts itself out, we need to be aware of the evolutionary psychologists' empirical findings, which have been confirmed across many cultures and across age and racial groups.

Of direct relevance for therapists who are working with couples are the attachment theories of John Bowlby (1973, 1980, 1982, 1988). In an attempt to explain the infant-caregiver bond, Bowlby assigns a central place to "relational schemata," which are concerned with security, dependability, and self-worth. Bowlby sees infants as developing an "attachment behavioral system" that keeps them in close proximity to adult caregivers, thus promoting their survival in evolutionary terms. This infant-caregiver "attachment" allows the infant to develop an "emotionally secure base" from which to explore the world, and it provides a safe haven when the infant feels threatened.

Out of the early experience with caregivers, the infant develops an "internal working model" that reflects the caregiver's availability and responsiveness. This internal model is believed to have two complementary components: one referring to the self ("Am I worthy or unworthy of love and attention?") and the other referring to the attachment figure ("Will my caregiver be available, sensitive, and responsive?"). This internal model organizes and summarizes historical experience, and it provides the individual with behavioral strategies that are useful in predicting and controlling social interaction.

Once formed in the infant, these internal working models are thought to structure that person's expectations, modes of information processing, and approach/avoidance motives in a way that is likely to elicit confirmatory feedback. Once an individual has learned to expect a secure or insecure attachment, he or she is likely to induce that response from others. In spite of the many differences between infant-caregiver relationships and adult romantic relationships (Hazen & Shaver, 1994), romantic relationships serve many of the same functions in adulthood that caregivers serve in childhood—providing a sense of security, for example—and feelings of romantic love may be considered manifestations of the attachment behavioral system (Hazen & Shaver, 1987).

In addition to the internalized schema of the self and the partner, other researchers have added a third schema, or the interpersonal "script" that specifies expected sequences of interaction in the relationship, as in, "If I act weak, my partner will take care of me." These interactional predictions are also generalized from past interactions (Baldwin, 1992, 1995).

Based on the types of infant-caregiver attachments observed by Ainsworth and associates (Ainsworth, Blehar, Waters, & Wall, 1978), Hazan and Shaver (1994) developed an attachment style classification system made up of (1) the secure style ("I find it relatively easy to get close to others and am comfortable depending on them"); (2) the anxious/ambivalent style ("I find that others are reluctant to get as close as I would like"); and (3) the avoidant style ("I am somewhat uncomfortable being close to others").

As researchers have explored these attachment themes, two patterns have emerged. First, attachment styles have been found to be persistent in individuals over time (Baldwin & Fehr, 1995; Kirkpatrick & Hazan, 1994). There is also evidence of the "transmission" of attachment style across the generations. Benoit and Parker (1994) found that maternal representations of attachment were associated with both their infants' and their own mothers' attachment classifications (cf. Fonagy, Steele, & Steele, 1991; Main, Kaplan, & Cassidy, 1985), evidence that fits my own clinical impression of the formative power of infant-caregiver relationships.

Second, attachment styles do not seem to be set in stone (Weinfield, 1996). In fact, healthy individuals seem to revise their attachment schemata in accordance with their ongoing experience. Kojetin (1993) and Kirkpatrick and Hazan (1994) found that changes in adults' attachment styles tend to reflect actual relationship experiences. While the degree to which attachment style is influenced by contemporary experiences is not well understood, both sets of findings (attachment experiences' persistence and malleability) can inform the clinician's experience.

While couples may be responding out of their separate historical experiences, it is crucial that we help them see that they can change their responses to each other, and that their marriage can become a powerful "corrective" experience that allows the partners to change their predictions of what they can receive emotionally from each other. This shift in anticipated (and realized) intimacy and security posits a "competing" experience of peer intimacy, which can at least partially ameliorate childhood injury or deficit (Johnson, 1996).

The tripartite typology of attachment styles is highly relevant to understanding couples' interactions, and attachment style is clearly related to marital quality. Individuals with secure attachment styles seem to pursue, and to anticipate achieving, intimate relationships with significant others (Collins & Read, 1994; Mikulincer, 1998). When they are stressed, they tend to acknowledge their dilemmas and seek out others for support. Their sense of security seems to allow them to develop cohesive and flexible relationships (Mikulincer, 1997; Mikulincer & Florian, 1999). They show more positive interactions with their partners (Cohn, Silver, Cowan, & Cowan, 1992), and are less likely to use destructive responses to marital conflict (Feeney, Noller, & Callan, 1994). In short, people with secure attachment styles know how to "connect" emotionally with people.

Individuals with insecure attachment styles have a history of painful and distressing attachment experiences (Bowlby, 1988; Shaver & Hazan, 1993). Those with anxious-ambivalent styles are worried about loss or rejection and respond with an overactivation of attachment behaviors. When stressed, they are likely to be clinging, rigid, and hypervigilant in attempts to remain close to others, behaviors that prevent them from attaining autonomy and self-confidence. These are the individuals we define clinically as "pursuers" (Guerin, Fay, Burden, & Kautto, 1987). They both seek and report fairly high cohesion in their marriages, but they are less flexible than individuals with secure attachment styles (Mikulincer & Florian, 1999). The partners of anxious-ambivalent individuals seem to want less closeness in the marriage, and we might infer that they are responding to the "possessiveness" of their mates (Mikulincer & Florian, 1999).

Individuals with avoidant attachment styles seem to deactivate the attachment system. Bartholomew and Horowitz (1991) split the "avoidant" style into two groups: those who are "fearful" of intimacy, and those who are "dismissive" of it. These individuals' painful interpersonal histories lend them to make negative predictions about their success in gaining support from others; when stressed, they tend to deny their feelings and to withdraw. Mikulincer and Florian (1999) conclude that avoidant attachment styles lend themselves to poor communication in marriage and are associated with misunderstandings and conflict. Clinically, we tend to associate the anxious-ambivalent (pursuer) styles with women, and avoidant (distancer) styles with men. Mikulincer and Florian (1999), however, found no significant gender differences in the distribution of attachment style.

The ways in which couples' attachment styles are "matched" will clearly make a difference in their relationship, and here we must rely on clinical prediction. If both partners have secure attachment styles, there would appear to be a good chance for their developing a marriage that is both intimate and flexible. Two anxious-ambivalent individuals would tend to have a very intense, perhaps enmeshed relationship characterized by vigilant, somewhat rigid maintenance of their connection. Avoidant partners are likely to settle into cool, distant relatedness; over time they might feel lonely and misunderstood. Mixtures of styles should produce more conflict, since the partners' interpersonal goals are different (Mikulincer & Florian, 1999). Of particular concern would be the anxious-ambivalent individual married to the avoidant person. This combination is likely to produce what I have termed the "rejection-intrusion pattern" (Napier, 1978), in which each person's style threatens the other's.

As we evaluate the emotional connectedness of couples, we should not only ask them about and observe their current interaction styles, but we should attempt to understand the childhood antecedents of those styles:

> When I met with them, Carl and Jennie were excited about getting married. Jenny was concerned, however, because at 42 she had not been married; Carl, 48, was worried because his first marriage had failed 10 years before. Carl had teenage and young adult children, and most of the premarital sessions concerned the couple's anxieties about how they would deal with Carl's ex-wife and his stormy daughter, who resented being "displaced" by Jennie.
>
> Both partners revealed that they had lost their mothers early—Carl when he was 6, and Jennie when she was 12. Carl had been reared by his father, and later by a stepmother as well; Jennie was "supervised" by her two older sisters. As teenagers, both had been sent to boarding schools. Understandably, neither wanted to deal with these early losses around the time that they were marrying, but both clearly had avoidant attachment styles. I commented that it might be fortunate that they had each found someone who could understand what it was like to lose a mother early, and that I hoped they would find each other supportive. "However," I added, "because of your early losses of your mothers, you may have an unconscious tendency to assume that if you love someone, you will lose them. In order to protect yourselves from this experience of loss in your marriage, you might have a tendency to keep somewhat distant from each other. If in a few years you find yourselves assuming that the other is unavailable emotionally, you might then consider psychotherapy as a couple."
>
> Several years later they did come for therapy, complaining that they had settled into a distant, if cordial, relationship, and that they both felt lonely. Therapy focused on helping them break through their habitual reserve, and on helping them risk the emotional closeness that they had found during their engagement.

EVALUATING RISK FACTORS IN MARRIAGE

Regardless of the stage of the couple's relationship—living together, engaged, or in early marriage—there are certain questions that we need to consider:

Are there background stresses (e.g., recent death of a parent) that make it difficult for one or both partners to evaluate the relationship separately from this stress?

How would the partners feel about the relationship if this stress could be dealt with effectively?

Are both partners psychologically "available" for marriage, or is at least one partner over-committed to another relationship (a former lover, parent, or sibling)? Separating from "prior entanglements" is often a prerequisite for developing a functional relationship.

Has one partner failed to achieve a developmental task, and does this circumstance make it difficult for the partners to be peers (the man, e.g., has never lived away from home and is engaged to an older woman who seems to promise to protect him from facing the world alone)?

Is there serious individual psychopathology in one partner (e.g., serious depression) that makes the relationship feel like "medication"?

Is there addiction, violence, or potential violence in the relationship? Has either individual suffered or witnessed addiction or violence in the family of origin?

Couples with these problems not only require more focused attention, but before the couple can do meaningful interpersonal work—on communication, for example—these difficulties may need to be addressed. Often couples with these dilemmas will require more than an educational process; they will need psychotherapy.

Evaluating the potential for violence is especially critical, since we should not "fuel" this acting-out process with interpersonal work until the threat of this behavior has been ruled out—often through structured treatment for the man. Even if there is only a single violent outburst on the part of the husband, this event can signal his wife that he intends to dominate the marriage—or else. Addiction is a similar issue for the therapist, in that meaningful interpersonal work may be futile if an active addiction process exists.

MOVING TOWARD AND INTO MARRIAGE

THE COHABITING COUPLE

Our client may be a couple who has lived together, sometimes for years. For this couple, the wedding day hovers somewhere in the indeterminate future. They may be in a profound impasse concerning at least one partner's ambivalence about marrying, or they may be struggling intensely and on the verge of breaking up. As one partner in an unmarried, highly conflicted pair complained, "This is worse than a marriage!" The high-conflict cohabiting couple needs psychotherapy, and they may need help in separating. When I work with such a couple, I also issue a disclaimer: Being in psychotherapy is a stressful process, and without the "protection" of a formal contract, therapy may destabilize, and perhaps hasten the end of, their relationship. (For an example of a brief intervention with a cohabiting couple, see Napier, 1999b.)

The cohabiting partners may, however, simply be anxious about committing to marriage. Their anxieties are grounded in their experiences: They may have grown up with parents who were unhappily married, or they may have had negative relationship histories themselves. They may be risk-averse individuals, or they may both have avoidant attachment styles.

In many instances, one of the partners is reluctant to marry, while the other is eager to do so. In my clinical experience, it is often the man who is more reluctant. This individual who is the "weak link" (with regard to commitment) has more influence in determining the fate of the couple's stability than does the "strong link" (Attridge, Berscheid, & Simpson, 1995). He or she may also be the individual with the most attractive alternatives outside the relationship (Waller & Hill, 1951), a corollary that is consonant with men's greater power in our culture, including in marriage (Falbo & Peplau, 1980; Krokoff, 1987).

Working with cohabiting couples who are polarized around commitment to marriage is a complex process. We do not wish to focus on the reluctant partner; the clinical adage, "Never pursue a distancer" (Guerin et al., 1987) is relevant here. Helping the "strong link" (committed) partner examine his or her script around rejection may be useful, as well as exploring other possible options if this relationship does not work out. Often, the committed partner has covert reservations about the relationship, but is more comfortable with being a "pursuer." Helping the committed individual become more empowered and autonomous often exposes the uncommitted partner's covert interest in maintaining the relationship. If the committed partner achieves more autonomy and the uncommitted partner does not respond, this relationship may not survive. Of course we also need to help the uncommitted partner examine his or her anxieties about a deeper level of involvement.

While this individual may on the surface be an emotional distancer, underlying anxieties may be about rejection (Napier, 1999a).

As the committed partner achieves more independence in the relationship, she or he may also be able to "call the question" about marriage:

Ellen and Sam, both in their late forties, had been dating (and occasionally living together) for five years. Sam had been chronically dissatisfied with his job; when he had an opportunity for promotion that involved a move to another city, Ellen, thinking that career success would help Sam's self-confidence, encouraged him to take the job. Sam's confidence in himself did increase dramatically, but even though Ellen agreed to move to his new city, he still held back from committing to marriage. At that point Ellen contacted me. After some work on her propensity for persisting in relationships with marriage-phobic men, Ellen realized that this pattern protected her from her own reservations about commitment. She decided to risk making an unambivalent move toward Sam: She would be in therapy with him, she would marry him if it worked out, but she would not wait another five years. For several months, Ellen flew to Sam's city for relationship therapy. Finally, Sam, who was profoundly attached to his mother, ended the relationship; after a period of intense grief, Ellen recovered and eventually entered a much more promising partnership.

One of the most complex dilemmas of the unmarried, living-together couple is an "unplanned" pregnancy. If the partners are deeply committed to each other, the pregnancy may be an unconscious way in which they have scripted taking the formal step toward marriage. If, however, the woman has unconsciously hoped that pregnancy would precipitate her partner into marrying her, he may feel manipulated; if he resists marriage, she will feel rejected. Whatever the couple's decision about their relationship and about the pregnancy, they are likely to feel bound to each other by the implied "necessity" of marriage; even if they want to be married, this sense of obligation may make them question their love for each other. In my experience, this doubt about being "really loved" by the partner is often related to the individual's feeling dutifully parented as a child—instead of being really loved. We need to help the couple explore and negotiate all their options. In this intimate decision-making territory, we should be wary of our own prejudices, lest we bias the couple (or one individual) toward an alternative with which we are more comfortable.

Long-term cohabiting couples often hesitate about committing to marriage for good reasons. Prolonged courtships are characterized by greater ambivalence and conflict, and by weaker feelings of love and attachment; couples with this pattern have a greater probability of separation or divorce after marriage (Huston, 1994; Huston, Surra, Fitzgerald, & Cate, 1981; Surra, 1987). Premarital conflict itself, while not apparently associated with the degree of love the partners feel for each other, predicts conflict after marriage and also predicts the level of marital satisfaction two years after marriage (Kelly, Huston, & Cate, 1985).

THE ENGAGED COUPLE

For the engaged couple, the wedding day is not a vague possibility; they have announced their intentions to marry, and often they have set the date. Once this announcement has been made, a complex and often ambivalent process begins. While engaged couples usually experience a period of euphoria—and the good feelings may spread among the "convinced" of their family and friends—the march to the wedding can be stressful for the couple and their families.

Our media-dominated society promotes a highly commercialized and intensely romanticized ideal of the matrimonial beginning. Even couples and families who want to create a relaxed and informal wedding find themselves getting caught up in "the wedding thing." The wedding day feels like an ultimate deadline; it is an announced public event, and seems unalterable. It also begins to feel like a performance: People will be watching and judging. Weddings today are also very expensive. One survey indicated that the average wedding costs $16,000; in the New York area, $25,000 is considered "inexpensive" (White, 1997). Even low-income families, who cannot afford expensive weddings, feel the performance pressures around this ritual.

Preparations for the wedding often precipitate intense involvement between the bride-to-be and her mother. Some mothers overinvest in the "wedding show," and begin to try to control the process; their betrothed daughters may feel displaced, ignored, and infantilized. Other mothers may not help enough, and their daughters may feel unsupported or rejected. Often mothers of brides-to-be are covertly grieving about the loss of their daughters and may conceal this sense of loss in busy promotion of the very process that they feel is cheating them. Husbands-to-be are likely to feel unimportant in the drama of the wedding, and they may be passive-aggressive in not following through on their obligations.

While both families of origin usually make efforts to collaborate in supporting the young couple's marriage, they often do not know each other, and they may not understand each other. The two families also have different histories and traditions, and they are to some degree different "cultures," sometimes literally. Social class differences between the two families can be painful for all, but especially for the "poorer" family. As the engaged couple attempts to design a wedding, they may continually collide with their families' cultural and class differences.

Familial structures in both families may be dislodged by the impending wedding. Old conflicts within the family of origin may come to the surface: For example, jealousy may flare between two sisters who have been competitive, and one has temporarily "won" by marrying first. Or a sister and brother have been especially close, and the brother became engaged as his sister is divorcing. Torn between his sister's needs and his bride-to-be, the brother develops intense headaches.

Old cross-generational triangles may also be aggravated by the planned marriage. The engaged daughter was always her father's favorite; he showered gifts on the couple but was hostile to his prospective son-in-law, while the mother felt left out of the wedding details. Extended family issues also surface around who is invited and how they are to be treated. "Politeness" may demand that people be invited to the wedding who will be very tense with each other. These tensions, which may escalate as the wedding approaches, are especially acute when postdivorce/remarried relationships converge on the young couple:

> When Eleanor and Jim announced their engagement, Eleanor was distressed to learn that her biological father, with whom she had a tenuous relationship, refused to attend the ceremony if Eleanor's stepfather, to whom she was much closer emotionally, was going to participate in the ceremony. Eleanor badly wanted both her "father figures" to at least come to the wedding, and she did not want to offend her father, whom she had worked to become closer to in recent years. With coaching, she began writing to her father, explaining her anxiety that she might need to choose between two men, both of whom she loved. She also wrote about how much she valued the growing closeness with her father, and how worried she was that he might not attend her wedding. After these letters, she had several long telephone conversations with her father,

followed by a visit to his home. She not only addressed her father's resistance, but since she believed that his wife was part of the refusal to attend, began to include her in the conversations as well. The result of these efforts was that both father and step-father participated in the ceremony; this event marked the beginning of much more cordial relationships between Eleanor and the households of each of her parents.

As we work with engaged couples who are caught up in these struggles, we can help them team with each other to de-escalate and "manage" these family tensions. The families of origin can also take steps to de-escalate conflicts; by working through the young couple, we may be able to make suggestions to the two families. The simplest intervention may be for the parents of the couple to meet without the engaged couple and to have some time to learn about each other. Since they are likely to be the most involved in the wedding process, it is especially important for the mothers of the couple to spend some time together.

If tensions within or between the families escalate seriously, we can assemble the family and help them talk out these issues, but this would be an unusual occurrence. Although there may be highly emotional encounters during the engagement, particularly between the bride and her mother, most of the time both the couple and their respective families remain on "good behavior."

Since there is often genuine and deep excitement in both families of origin and in the couple's friends about the advent of the marriage, and since the engaged partners want so badly to believe that all is well, misgivings about the marriage tend to remain submerged. Reluctant to interfere, and prey to the myth that love conquers all, friends and family of the couple may treat the couple's decision to marry—and the timing of the marriage—as inviolate. After one young woman divorced, her friends came forth, saying almost uniformly: "I didn't want to intrude, but I didn't think you were a good match; you seemed so different!" This tendency to deny problems is particularly unfortunate for the engaged couple, who may not be able to share—even with each other—their doubts about themselves, their partner, and the marriage they are about to enter.

Fortunately, the climate for seeking help is changing rapidly. Engaged couples may seek premarital counseling even if they are not experiencing serious difficulties—they may just want to be reassured that they have "done their homework." Cohabiting couples may also seek more intensive therapy rather than abandon a serious relationship. Society-wide concern about the high incidence of divorce has also led to a rapid increase in the number of outreach programs designed to prepare couples for marriage (see Appendix A and B). While these premarital programs sometimes have a difficult time competing with the ardor and denial of the engagement period, they represent an exciting development. Not only can we help these couples gain valuable skills, but if they later have difficulties, they are more likely to seek psychotherapy.

THE RECENTLY MARRIED COUPLE

Newly married couples experience the sharpest drop in marital satisfaction of any period in marriage, and the experience is similar for husbands and wives (Kurdek, 1998). While the downward slope of satisfaction seems to plateau by the fourth year of marriage, most couples are distressed and confused by this dramatic turnabout in their feelings for each other. The acute transition makes newly married couples likely candidates for divorce, but also good candidates for early intervention. How do we understand the forces operating in early marriage?

When two people cross the threshold into marriage, this symbolic passage changes the way they feel about each other and about the world. Suddenly, the tension rises; the stakes seem much higher than before they married. As marriage draws them closer, and as they bring more emotional needs to the cozy "settling-in" period—which can be very pleasant—they also begin to fear that they will trade autonomy for security. Each partner has a panicky fantasy: "This person is going to control me for life!" Small decisions that might have been made easily in the mutual-accommodation ethos of engagement suddenly become matters of intense debate. Having been freely sexual before marriage, they may complain that their sex lives have become tense and strained.

Power struggles are common in early marriage (and are responsible for much sexual dysfunction during this period), but deeper issues are the partners' mutual dependency and their lack of skill in communication and negotiation. Typically, each partner experiences the other as "like a parent"; to make matters worse, the partner who is perceived in this way may be induced into "role-playing" that parental figure (Napier, 1988). Both partners experience each other symbolically, as representing the same trade-off that they experienced in childhood: If I get support, I lose self-determination. If, at this stage, we ask the partners if they feel a bit as if they were back in their childhood families, they often answer, "Yes!"

In addition to symbolizing each other, newly married pairs also become aware that each has married a willful, self-interested individual from a strange tribe (family of origin) with strange customs. And each is married to someone with powerful loyalties to his or her "prior world" of friends, relatives, home city, ambitions and dreams, and daily habits. When couples realize how fragile their new marriage is in the face of these long-established relationships and patterns, they become easily threatened by the power of these old attachments. A new wife may become alarmed when her husband wants to hang out for long hours with his high school or college friends; he may be equally anxious about her fantasies about an old boyfriend.

Early marriage is perhaps the ideal time for serious intervention in the life of the couple. Their denial has been broken, and they are often quite uncomfortable; yet typically they have not yet developed deeply entrenched positions. In the psychotherapy setting, work with newly married couples is similar to work with any couple, with the proviso that newly married couples who are in a serious crisis may be more likely to divorce than are long-married couples. They have clear memories of being single, and often these crisis couples question the wisdom of their decision to marry.

STRATEGIES OF INTERVENTION

Three areas of focus seem particularly important with newly marrieds, but they are also relevant to cohabiting and engaged couples.

INTERRUPTING DESTRUCTIVE COMMUNICATION

There is ample research evidence that before they develop more satisfying ways of relating, many couples have dysfunctional communication patterns. Many outreach programs focus on teaching couples to interrupt destructive patterns and to substitute healthier ones. The work of John Gottman (1994a), who has studied couples intensively in the laboratory setting, has been particularly instructive in identifying couples' styles of relating. Gottman describes three basic types of couples: (1) validating pairs, who emphasize togetherness and friendship and who value the "we-ness" of their relationship over their individual goals and values; (2) volatile couples, who fight passionately and frequently but who know how to make up and have many positive connections as well; and (3) avoidant couples, who minimize their conflicts and make light of their differences rather than resolving them. All of these interaction types can have satisfying and stable marriages, if, according to Gottman, the ratio of positive to negative communications is 5:1 or greater. Negativity is not in itself detrimental if each negative comment is balanced by five or more positive communications.

Gottman finds that four types of communication are particularly destructive; he calls these "The Four Horsemen of the Apocalypse," in that if they dominate a relationship, they can lead to a cascade of negativity that often spells the doom of that marriage. Criticism involves attacking someone's personality or character, rather than a specific behavior, usually with blame. Contempt comes out of the intention to insult and psychologically abuse the partner, and it includes insults, name-calling, hostile humor, mockery, and various forms of nonverbal derision. Defensiveness comes out of an attempt to fend off criticism or contempt—without taking responsibility. It includes making excuses, cross-complaining (meeting complaint with another complaint), "yes-butting," repeating oneself, and taking anxious, rigid body postures. Stonewalling occurs when communication breaks down completely. The stonewalling spouse just turns off, ignores the other, withdraws, or minimizes communication. When stonewalling becomes habitual, the marriage is fragile. In a popular book for couples, *Why Marriages Succeed or Fail,* Gottman (1994a) offers advice tailored for specific interaction types.

We need to help partners interrupt cycles of attack and defense—first in our office, then at home. Before partners can make deeper shifts in their communications, however, we often need to "de-construct" their problematic communications. Can they be aware of and reveal what is "beneath" their postures of attack and defense? What feelings hide behind criticism, for example? Some possibilities include hurt, anger, sadness, sexual tension, anxiety, fatigue, disappointment, self-blame, and not feeling loved or desired. If the partner who feels criticized were not defensive, what would take the place of defense: acknowledgement of responsibility, apology, admission of hurt or sadness when feeling criticized, admission of covert self-blame, validation of the other's feelings?

As we help couples move away from harshness and blame to softer and more vulnerable self-exposure, we also need to help them respond positively to the risks each takes in self-revelation. If an individual is threatened by the partner's vulnerability, he or she may intuitively blame the partner to get him or her to return to a "tougher" stance, thereby reconvincing the risk-taker that it is not safe to expose such feelings.

Since interaction between the couple may initially be stressful and toxic, we may "triangulate" ourselves between the partners, working with each "individually" (in the presence of the other), broadening that individual's awareness of what lies beneath and within their stereotyped communications. When the partners become more aware of the nuances and richness within themselves, and when they begin to hear their partners more sympathetically (through the "translations" of the therapist/interpreter), they are then ready to find more palatable means of talking and listening to each other. While a number of systems for teaching healthy communication have been developed, one of the most useful has been presented by the Interpersonal Communications Programs (Miller, Miller, Nunnally, & Wackman, 1991). The principles in this program have been used by therapists in a wide variety of settings.

DEALING WITH FAMILY-OF-ORIGIN ISSUES

As we work with couples, we become aware that certain of their words, phrases, tones of voice, attitudes, or topics of conversation "trigger" responses in the other that seem to be out of proportion to the replies we would anticipate. These affect-laden responses stem from often-painful family-of-origin experiences that are reactivated by the spouse. The husband is indeed critical, but his wife seems devastated by his critique; as we inquire about her childhood, we find that her father's criticism was truly abusive. And what lies behind the husband's criticism? As his wife has sought protection from his criticism, she has withdrawn, reactivating the husband's sense that he is living with the cool, reserved mother of his childhood.

Since the reactivity of each partner increases the vulnerability of the other, these "interlocking" transferential issues are the most troublesome, and the likeliest to escalate. He grew up jealous of his younger sister, while she was "punished" by a jealous older brother; his jealousy of her easily sets them off on a course of attack and defense. Lest the partners become flooded with too much awareness, we must proceed carefully in raising awareness of childhood issues. We must also deal with each individual's guilt about being disappointed by or angry about perceived betrayal by the parents: "I expect you feel bad about talking about your parents in this way." It is also important that we establish bilateral focus on these issues; otherwise, one partner will feel singled out for "analysis."

The goal of this family-of-origin work is to give both partners cognitive tools for sidestepping these affective traps. Can each individual see the childhood issue that is being activated by the partner, and self-intervene, attempting to calm and reassure the interior self that is enraged or panicked by the spouse's behavior? It is also useful if the self-intervening individual can educate the partner about what is happening internally: "This is what I am experiencing, and here is what would help me deal with this situation." At the same time, can the mate who is contributing to this sense of alarm begin to understand the ways in which his or her behavior is provocative—and attempt to change the difficult "stimulus" for the partner's "response"? If both spouses can team to defeat these cycles of distortion and escalation, the sense of crisis and alarm in the relationship can decrease dramatically.

The couple's families of origin can intrude into the marriage through the bilateral reactivation of historical issues; but particularly if their families are reluctant to allow their adult children to individuate, they can also invade the marriage in the present. Bringing both families into the therapy process is a powerful and often effective intervention. While the reasons for working actively with the enmeshed family are palpably obvious, involving the disengaged family can also be productive. Individuals from disengaged families often bring too much emotional need to the marriage, and achieving deeper levels of connection with the family of origin can decrease some of this pressure.

Bringing the family of origin into the therapy process is a complex task, particularly for the younger therapist who may be intimidated by parents who too-closely resemble his or her own. Using a consultant/cotherapist for these sessions is often a reassuring and helpful adjunct to treatment.

NURTURING THE CONNECTION

Emotional connectedness is the soul of marriage, and helping young couples remain engaged and caring is the heart of our work with them. While spouses can "feed" their relationship in many ways—from sharing pleasurable experiences (dinners out, movies, long walks, little rituals like afternoon tea, and good sex) to cooperating through shared tasks and duties—the essence of connectedness is a communication process that works. This process helps the partners understand and move toward each other in ways that are nurturing, supportive, and affirming. While firmly rooted in the present and in a peer relationship, this kind of emotional link allows both individuals to feel "attached" in ways that reactivate early childhood bonds to parents or other caregivers. But even if those early experiences have been deficient, marriage can supply a vital sense of being cared about and "joined" by another that gives both lives increased meaning and value. It may be what helps married couples live longer than single individuals.

Helping couples develop secure ways of deepening their connectedness is complex work, but certain basic strategies are useful. In order to be more genuinely intimate (as distinguished from feeling "close," or in close proximity to each other), both partners need a sense of their own separateness. When partners are enmeshed (and these may be two anxious/ambivalent individuals), they often precipitate crises in order to establish boundaries in the relationship. Learning to be comfortably separate may lead to greater willingness to risk more genuine intimacy. Other couples remain quiet and distant, and we may need to coax them into taking even small steps toward each other. Still others cycle through the familiar sequence of criticism and defensiveness, which may proceed to contempt and stonewalling.

After we help couples interrupt destructive communication patterns, there is often a period of "silence" in the relationship; the spouses seem to be asking, "Now what?" If the partners can first expose their yearning for more caring and intimacy, we can then "coach" them on risking being vulnerable in reaching out for each other. As they attempt more intimacy, most couples become frightened and "spoil" the experience. But these couples can also learn to monitor their expressions of mutual anxiety, and they can catch themselves in the process of relationship sabotage. Often we find ourselves saying, "Don't give up; try again—did you see the tender look she gave you when you said that?"

It takes patience and hard work to build bridges of intimate connectedness between partners who, over the course of a lifetime, have learned to be wary of intimacy. As we become invested in and care about the couple who are bravely confronting their fears and anxieties, our own optimism and caring may be the chief instrument of therapy (Napier, 1998). For a more systematic treatment of building emotional connectedness in couples, see Johnson (1996).

This is an exciting time for working with couples (and their families). There is a society-wide concern about the high divorce rate, and a great deal of optimism among professionals and lay persons about preventing these family tragedies. The professional community is creating some excellent tools for evaluating and counseling couples; many organizations, from state legislatures to churches, are involved in outreach to couples. But more than crisis intervention is taking place. As we see from some of the marriage enrichment programs (Hunt, Hof, & DeMaria, 1998), and as we sense from the current ethos about marriage, there is a feeling abroad that marriage can be more than a good "working relationship," that it can be a rich, deeply rewarding link between people, one that sustains and nurtures human experience across the life course.

REFERENCES

Ainsworth, M. D. S., Blehar, M. C., Waters, E., & Wall, S. (1978). *Patterns of attachment: Assessed in the strange situation and at home.* Hillsdale, NJ: Erlbaum.

Angier, N. (1999). *Woman: An intimate geography.* New York: Houghton Mifflin.

Antill, J. K. (1983). Sex role complementarity versus similarity in married couples. *Journal of Personality and Social Psychology, 45,* 145–155.

Aron, A., & Aron, E. N. (1986). *Love as the expansion of "self": Understanding attraction and satisfaction.* New York: Hemisphere.

Aron, A., & Aron, E. N. (1996). Self and self expansion in relationships. In G. J. O. Fletcher & J. K. Fitness (Eds.), *Knowledge structures in close relationships: A social psychological approach* (pp. 325–344). Hillsdale, NJ: Erlbaum.

Aron, A., Aron, E. N., & Smollan, D. (1992). Inclusion of Other in the Self Scale and the structure of interpersonal closeness. *Journal of Personality and Social Psychology, 63,* 596–612.

Aron, A., Paris, M., & Aron, E. N. (1995). Falling in love: Prospective studies of self-concept change. *Journal of Personality and Social Psychology, 69,* 1102–1112.

Attridge, M., Berscheid, E., & Simpson, J. A. (1995). Predicting relationship stability from both partners versus one. *Journal of Personality and Social Psychology, 69,* 254–268.

Baldwin, M. W. (1992). Relational schemas and the processing of social information. *Psychological Bulletin, 112,* 461–484.

Baldwin, M. W. (1995). Relational schemas and cognition in close relationships. *Journal of Social and Personal Relationships, 12,* 547–552.

Baldwin, M. W., & Fehr, B. (1995). On the instability of attachment style ratings. *Personal Relationships, 2,* 247–261.

Bartholomew, K., & Horowitz, L. M. (1991). Attachment styles among young adults: A test of a four-category model. *Journal of Personality and Social Psychology, 61,* 226–244.

Benoit, D., & Parker, K. C. H. (1994). Stability and transmission of attachment across three generations. *Child Development, 65,* 1444–1456.

Berscheid, E. (1985). Interpersonal attraction. In G. Lindzey & E. Aronson (Eds.), *Handbook of social psychology* (3rd ed.) (pp. 413–484). New York: Random House.

Berscheid, E., & Reis, H. T. (1998). Attraction and close relationships. In D. T. Gilbert, S. T. Fiske, & G. Lindzey (Eds.), *The handbook of social psychology* (4th ed.) (pp. 193–281). New York: McGraw-Hill.

Bowlby, J. (1973). *Attachment and loss: Vol. 2. Separation, anxiety and anger.* New York: Basic Books.

Bowlby, J. (1980). *Attachment and loss: Vol. 3. Loss.* New York: Basic Books.

Bowlby, J. (1982). *Attachment and loss: Vol. 1. Attachment.* New York: Basic Books.

Bowlby, J. (1988). *A secure base.* New York: Basic Books.

Boszormenyi-Nagy, I., & Spark, G. M. (1973). *Invisible loyalties.* New York: Harper and Row.

Buss, D. M. (1994). Strategies of human mating. *American Scientist, 82,* 238–249.

Buunk, B. P., & Van Yperen, N. W. (1991). Referential comparisons, relational comparisons, and exchange orientation: Their relation to marital satisfaction. *Personality and Social Psychology Bulletin, 17,* 709–717.

Byrne, D. (1971). *The attraction paradigm.* New York: Academic Press.

Caspi, A., & Herbener, E. S. (1990). Continuity and change: Assortative marriage and the consistency of personality in adulthood. *Journal of Personality and Social Psychology, 58,* 250–258.

Cohn, D. A., Silver, D. H., Cowan, C. P., & Cowan, P. A. (1992). Working models of childhood attachment and couple relationships. *Journal of Family Issues 13,* 432–449.

Collins, N. L., & Read, N. J. (1994). Cognitive representations of attachment: The structure and function of working models. In K. Bartholomew & D. Perlman (Eds.), *Attachment processes in adulthood* (pp. 53–92). London: Jessica Kingsley.

Coontz, S. (1997). *The way we really are: Coming to terms with America's changing families.* New York: Basic Books.

Falbo, T., & Peplau, A. A. (1980). Power strategies in intimate relationships. *Journal of Personality and Social Psychology, 38,* 618–628.

Feeney, J. A., Noller, P., & Callan, V. J. (1994). Attachment style, communication and satisfaction in the early years of marriage. In K. Bartholomew & D. Perlman (Eds.), *Attachment processes in adulthood* (pp. 269–308). London: Jessica Kingsley.

Fonagy, P., Steele, H., & Steele, M. (1991). Maternal representations of attachment during pregnancy predict the organization of infant-mother attachment at one year. *Child Development, 62,* 891–905.

Gangestad, S. W. (1993). Sexual selection and physical attractiveness: Implications for mating dynamics. *Human Nature, 4,* 205–235.

Glaser, C. (1996, September 16). Marriage as we see it. *Newsweek,* 19.

Gottman, J. (1994a). *Why marriages succeed or fail.* New York: Fireside.

Gottman, J. (1994b). *What predicts divorce? The relationship between marital processes and marital outcomes.* Hillsdale, NJ: Erlbaum.

Gray-Little, B., & Burks, N. (1983). Power and satisfaction in marriage. *Psychological Bulletin, 933,* 513–538.

Green, R. J., Bettinger, M., & Zacks, E. (1996). Are lesbian couples "fused" and gay male couples "disengaged?": Questioning gender straightjackets. In J. Laird & R. J. Green (Eds.), *Lesbians and gays in couples and families* (pp. 185–230). San Francisco, CA: Jossey-Bass.

Grubner-Baldini, A. L., Schaie, K. W., & Willis, S. L. (1995). Similarity in married couples: A longitudinal study of mental abilities and rigidity-flexibility. *Journal of Personality and Social Psychology, 69,* 191–203.

Guerin, P. J., Fay, L. F., Burden, S. L. & Kautto, J. G. (1987). *The evaluation and treatment of marital conflict: A four-stage approach.* New York: Basic Books.

Harris, J. A. (1912). Assortative mating in man. *Popular Science Monthly, 80,* 476–492.

Hartley, E. L. (1946). *Problems in prejudice.* New York: King's Crown Press.

Hazan, C., & Shaver, P. (1987). Romantic love conceptualized as an attachment process. *Journal of Personality and Social Psychology, 52,* 511–524.

Hazan, C., & Shaver, P. (1994). Attachment as an organizational framework for research on close relationships. *Psychological Inquiry, 5,* 1–22.

Hendrix, H. (1988). *Getting the love you want.* New York: Harper and Row.

Hines, P. M., Preto, N. G., McGoldrick, M., Almeida, R., & Weltman, S. (1999). Culture and the family life cycle. In B. Carter & M. McGoldrick (Eds.), *The expanded family life cycle* (3rd ed.) (pp. 69–87). Boston: Allyn & Bacon.

Houts, R. M., Robins, E., & Huston, T. L. (1996). Compatibility and the development of premarital relationships. *Journal of Marriage and the Family, 58,* 7–20.

Hunt, R. A., Hof, L., & DeMaria, R. (1998). *Marriage enrichment: Preparation, mentoring and outreach.* Philadelphia, PA: Brunner/Mazel.

Huston, T. L. (1994). Courtship antecedents of marital satisfaction and love. In R. Erber & R. Gilmour (Eds.), *Theoretical frameworks for personal relationships* (pp. 43–66). Hillsdale, NJ: Erlbaum.

Huston, T. L., Surra, C., Firzgerald, N., & Cate, R. (1981). From courtship to marriage: Mate selection as an interpersonal process. In S. Duck & R. Gilmour (Eds.), *Personal relationships (Vol. 2)* (pp. 53–88). London: Academic Press.

Ickes, W., & Barnes, R. D. (1978). Boys and girls together and alienated: On enacting stereotyped sex roles in mixed sex dyads. *Journal of Personality and Social Psychology, 36,* 669–683.

Johnson, S. M. (1996). *The practice of emotionally focused marital therapy: Creating connection.* New York: Brunner/Mazel.

Kelly, C., Huston, T. L., & Cate, R. M. (1985). Premarital relationship correlates of the erosion of satisfaction in marriage. *Journal of Social and Personal Relationships, 2,* 167–178.

Kendrick, D. T., & Trost, M. R. (1989). A reproductive exchange model of heterosexual relationships: Putting proximate economics in ultimate perspective. In C. Hendrick (Ed.), *Close relationships: Review of personality and social psychology (Vol. 10)* (pp. 92–118). Newbury Park, CA: Sage.

Kenny, D. A. (1994). Using the social relations model to understand relationships. In R. Erber & R. Gilmour (Eds.), *Theoretical frameworks for personal relationships* (pp. 111–127). Hillsdale, NJ: Erlbaum.

King, L. A. (1993). Emotional expression, ambivalence over expression, and marital satisfaction. *Journal of Social and Personal Relationships, 10,* 601–607.

Kirkpatrick, L. A., & Hazan, C. (1994). Attachment styles and close relationships: A four-year prospective study. *Personal Relationships, 1,* 123–142.

Kojetin, B. A. (1993). *Adult attachment styles with romantic partners, friends and parents.* Unpublished doctoral dissertation. University of Minnesota, Minneapolis.

Krokoff, L. J. (1987). The correlates of negative affect in marriage. *Journal of Family Issues, 8,* 111–135.

Kurdek, L. A. (1998). Developmental changes in marital satisfaction: A 6-year prospective longitudinal study of newlywed couples. In T. N. Bradbury (Ed.), *The developmental course of marital dysfunction* (pp. 231–257). New York: Cambridge University Press.

Laird, J., & Green, R. J. (1996). *Lesbians and gays in couples and families.* San Francisco: Jossey-Bass.

Lamke, L. K., Sollie, D. L., Durbin, R. G., & Fitzpatrick, J. A. (1994). Masculinity, femininity, and relationship satisfaction: The mediating role of interpersonal competence. *Journal of Social and Personal Relationships, 11,* 535–554.

Main, M., Kaplan, N., & Cassidy, J. (1985). Security in infancy, childhood, and adulthood: A move to the level of representation. *Monographs of the Society for Research in Child Development, 50,* 66–104.

Martin T., & Bumpass, L. (1989). Recent trends in marital disruption. *Demography, 26,* 37–52.

McGoldrick, M. (1999). Becoming a couple. In B. Carter & M. McGoldrick (Eds.), *The expanded family life cycle* (3rd ed.) (pp. 231–247). New York: Allyn & Bacon.

Mikulincer, M. (1997). Adult attachment style and information processing: Individual differences in curiosity and cognitive closure. *Journal of Personality and Social Psychology, 72,* 1217–1230.

Mikulincer, M. (1998). Attachment working models and the sense of trust: An exploration of interaction goals and affect regulation. *Journal of Personality and Social Psychology, 30,* 273–291.

Mikulincer, M., & Florian, V. (1999). The association between spouses' self-reports of attachment styles and representations of family dynamics. *Family Process, 38,* 69–83.

Miller, S., Miller, P., Nunnally, E., & Wackman, D. (1991). *Talking and listening together.* Littleton, CO: Interpersonal Communication Programs.

Murstein, B. I., Cerreto, M., & MacDonald, M. G. (1977). A theory and investigation of the effect of exchange-orientation on marriage and friendships. *Journal of Marriage and the Family, 39,* 543–548.

Napier, A. Y. (1978). The rejection-intrusion pattern: A central family dynamic. *Journal of Marriage and Family Counseling, 4* (1), 5–12.

Napier, A. Y. (1988). *The fragile bond.* New York: HarperCollins.

Napier, A. Y. (1999a). Experiential approaches to creating the intimate marriage. In J. Carlson & L. Sperry (Eds.), *The intimate couple* (pp. 298–327). Philadelphia: Brunner/Mazel.

Napier, A. Y. (1999b). Experiential therapy with Dr. Gus Napier. In J. Carlson & D. Kjos, (Eds.), *Family therapy with the experts* (videotape series). Needham Heights, MA: Allyn & Bacon.

Napier, A. Y., & Whitaker, C. A. (1978). *The family crucible.* New York: HarperCollins.

Parks, M. R., & Eggert, L. L. (1991). The role of social context in the dynamics of personal relationships. In W. H. Jones & D. Perlman (Eds.), *Advances in personal relationships (Vol. 2)* (pp. 1–34). London: Jessica Kingsley.

Price, R. A., & Vandenberg, S. G. (1979). Matching for physical attractiveness in married couples. *Personality and Social Psychology Bulletin, 5,* 398–400.

Scarf, M. (1987). *Intimate partners: Patterns in love and marriage.* New York: Random House.

Shaver, P. R., & Hazan, C. (1993). Adult romantic attachment: Theory and evidence. In W. H. Jones & D. Perlman, (Eds.), *Advances in personal relationships (Vol. 4)* (pp. 29–70). London: Jessica Kingsley.

Slater, S. (1995). *The lesbian family life cycle.* New York: The Free Press.

Surra, C. A. (1987). Reasons for change in commitment: Variations by courtship type. *Journal of Social and Personal Relationships, 4,* 17–33.

Surra, C. A. (1990). Research and theory on mate selection and premarital relationships in the 1980s. *Journal of Marriage and the Family, 52,* 844–865.

Teachman, J. D. (1983). Early marriage, premarital fertility, and marital dissolution. *Journal of Family Issues, 4,* 105–126.

Teachman, J. D., & Polonko, K. A. (1990). Cohabitation and marital stability in the United States. *Social Forces, 69,* 207–220.

Toman, W. (1976). *Family constellation* (3rd ed.). New York: Springer.

U.S. Bureau of Census (1999a, January 7). *Estimated median age at first marriage, by sex: 1890 to the present.* Internet release.

U.S. Bureau of Census (1999b, January 7). *Interracial married couples: 1960 to present.* Internet release.

Waller, W. W., & Hill, R. (1951). *The family: A dynamic interpretation.* New York: Dryden.

Weinfield, N. S. (1996). *Attachment and the representation of relationships from infancy to adulthood: Continuity, discontinuity, and their correlates.* Unpublished doctoral dissertation, University of Minnesota, Minneapolis.

White, C. C. R. (1997, July 5). The price a woman pays to say "I do." *New York Times.*

Winch, R. F. (1958). *Mate selection: A study of complementary needs.* New York: Harper.

Wolf, A. E. (1991). *Get out of my life but first could you drive me and Cheryl to the mall?* New York: The Noonday Press.

Zammichieli, M. E., Gilroy, F. D., & Sherman, M. F. (1988). Relation between sex-role orientation and marital satisfaction. *Personality and Social Psychology Bulletin, 14,* 747–754.

APPENDIX A: PREPARE, FOCUS, AND RELATE

PREPARE (PREmarital Preparation and Relationship Enhancement) was developed by David Olson and his associates. A second version, PREPARE-MC is used with couples who intend to marry but have children from prior marriages. ENRICH, a very similar survey, is intended for married couples and longer-term cohabiting couples. MATE is designed for couples 50 or older who are marrying or making a major life transition such as retirement.

In PREPARE, the therapist receives a computer printout that assesses the couple's strengths and "growth areas" (or problems) in 12 categories: idealistic distortion, marriage expectations, personality issues, communication, conflict resolution, financial management, leisure activities, sexual relationship, children and parenting, family and friends, role relationship, and spiritual beliefs. Additional scales based on the Circumplex Model assess cohesion and adaptability in both the couple and their families of origin; a "family map" illustrates these patterns. Four personality traits are also evaluated: assertiveness, self-confidence, avoidance of problems, and partner dominance. There are slight variations on the other tests, but all are similar.

The therapist, who receives day-long training in use of the test and is guided by a Counselor's Manual, gives verbal feedback to the client but does not give the printed data to the couple. Couples use a 25-page workbook that assists them in communication and other relationship-enhancing exercises. [Life Innovations, Minneapolis. 800-331-1661]

FOCCUS (Facilitating Open Couple Communication, Understanding and Study), developed by B. Markey and M. Micheletto, is designed for use with groups or individual couples. It reflects the ideals of marriage as a sacred institution, including faith in God, with a commitment to permanency, fidelity, forgiveness, and openness to having children. There are four editions: Nondenominational, Christian Nondenominational, Catholic, and Alternate, the latter for the learning impaired. An additional 33 optional items are for interfaith, cohabiting, and remarrying couples.

FOCCUS assesses 19 premarital factors, including lifestyle expectations, personality match, personal issues, communication, sexuality concerns, family of origin issues, and religion and values. The computer printout lists all the statements of the 19 scales and indicates the items on which the spouses agree both with each other and with the preferred responses. Preferred responses are based on the authors' judgment as to the optimum response for the couple. By using "Patterns for Couple Study" and "Counselor Aids on Individual Items," the therapist and couple can discuss individual items of particular concern as well as item patterns. "FOCCUS for the Future," a 14-item form, can be used for consolidating information from the test and planning for the future. [Archdiocese of Omaha, 402-551-9003]

RELATE (RELATionship Evaluation), developed by T. B. Holman and associates, assesses four broad areas: personality characteristics, values, family background, and relationship experiences. The computer printout is self-interpretive and can be sent to the therapist or directly to the couple. Bar graphs illustrate how each partner rates the self and other in seven different personality areas including sociability, calmness, organization, flexibility, emotional maturity, happiness, and self-esteem. The second section compares partner agreement on values and attitudes in areas such as marriage roles, sexuality, children, and religion. In the third section a comparison is made of partner perceptions of family background experiences, including family processes, parental marital satisfaction, relationship with parents, family stressors, and parental and couple conflict resolution. The fourth section summarizes relationship experiences including couple communications styles, conflict styles based on John Gottman's research, and relationship satisfaction and stability. By skipping sections of the tests that refer only to dating or engaged couples, nondating or individuals such as friends or strangers can take the test, making it useful in classroom settings. [Provo, Utah, 801-378-4359]

APPENDIX B: ENRICHMENT PROGRAMS

American Association for Marital and Family Therapy (AAMFT)
1133 15th St. NW, Suite 300
Washington, DC
202/452-0109

Association for Couples for Marriage Enrichment (ACME)
ACME National Office
P.O. Box 10596
Winston Salem, NC 27108
800/634-8325

Coalition for Marriage, Family and Couples Education (CMFCE)
Diane Solee, Director
5310 Belt Rd., NW
Washington, DC 20015-1961
202/362-3332
(For directory of enrichment programs: www.smartmarriages.com)

Couple Communication Skills

Drs. Sherod & Phyllis Miller
Interpersonal Communication Programs, Inc.
7201 S. Broadway, Suite 11
Littleton, CO 80122
800/328-5099

Growing Together Program
Life Innovations, Inc.
PREPARE/ENRICH
P.O. Box 190
Minneapolis, MN 55440-0190
800/331-1661

Marriage Savers
Michael & Harriet McManus
9500 Michaels Court
Bethesda, MD 20817-2214
301/469-5870

National Marriage Encounter
4704 Jamerson Place
Orlando, FL 32807
800/828-3351
(Information about groups)

National Institute of Relationship Enhancement (NIRE)
Dr. Bernard Guerney
1191 Renwood Lane
North Bethesda, MD 20852
301/986-1479

PAIRS INTERNATIONAL
1152 N. University Drive
P.O. Box 840037
Pembrook Pines, FL 33084-0037
888/PAIRS-4U

Prevention and Relationship Enhancement Program (PREP)
Dr. Howard Markman
Center for Marriage and Family Studies
P.O. Box 102530
Denver, CO 80250-2530
303/759-9931

CHAPTER 9

Childless Married Couples

William C. Nichols and Mary Anne Pace-Nichols

T RADITIONALLY, THE SOCIAL EXPECTATIONS in the Western world were that adults would mate and produce children. Exceptions to this general rule of marriage and childbearing were rare and included primarily priests and others engaged in religious vocations, as well as individuals whose mental or physical handicaps would seem to preclude effective or normal parenthood. Otherwise, it was presumed that marriages would produce children. Eventually, love, marriage, and parenthood came to be construed as the normal order of things.

For many centuries, as an agrarian social order prevailed, children were valuable economic assets who could work with other family members to assist with both the production of agricultural products and animal husbandry. Children not only were expected to contribute to the family economy but also to support their parents in their old age (Schoen, Kim, Nathanson, Fields, & Astone, 1997). The biblical injunction to "be fruitful and multiply" thus appealed not only to religious values but also to the practical side of life. Although the religious ideology continued to be a part of the motive for many to produce offspring, following the advent of the industrial revolution and the rise of urbanism and the factory system children became an economic liability. As the complexity of society increased, extending children's economic dependency on the family and increasing the need for extensive education or training in order for them to enter the adult world of work, the costs of bringing them to adulthood continued to grow.

Long-term demographic, economic, technological, and social trends have drastically altered the traditional picture, making parenthood today much more of a voluntary, elective matter. Recently, as we have begun to transition into a service economy and an information society, children rather typically have come to be valued for social rather than economic reasons (Schoen et al., 1997). The "baby boom" in the decade-plus following World War II, which produced children at a remarkably high rate, peaked in approximately 1957 and declined until the early 1980s (Bianchi & Spain, 1986). The reasons for the decline in fertility rates in the United States are manifold, but in particular it is associated with the changing role of women in society. The increased and growing labor force participation of women and the characteristics and effects of the feminist movement are too well known to require discussion here.

Related to the broader trends in American and Western society in general in the 1960s and 1970s were a weakening of the imperative to marry, to have children, to remain married, to be monogamous, and to maintain distinctly different roles for the genders (Thornton, 1989). A major change that has evolved over time is the tendency of females to delay parenthood or to remain permanently child-free. By the 1990s, there was a definite increase in the proportion of women who did not bear their first child in their twenties but delayed the event until their thirties, as well as an increase in the proportion of females opting for nonparenthood (Bianchi & Spain, 1996). American women also are marrying later than even in the 1970s, when 6 percent of those aged 30 to 34 were single, as compared with 20 percent in 1994. The figures are 9 percent and 30 percent, respectively, for men (Bianchi & Spain, 1996). Many, including both females and males, seem to be making an explicit choice between the primacy of child rearing and career, although voluntarily childlessness remains uncommon (Schoen et al., 1997).

Schoen and associates (1997) point out that children create "social capital" (enduring social bonds among parents, siblings, grandparents, aunts, uncles, and friends) that the parents can use to fulfill their interests. They call this a significant and previously unappreciated reason why Americans want children and engage in the intentional behavior of producing children. This chapter is limited to a consideration of married couples and their attitudes and behaviors regarding the absence of children, whether the absence is voluntary or involuntary in nature.

DECIDING WHETHER TO HAVE CHILDREN

Many married couples do not make a conscious choice either to have a child or refrain from having a child. For them the determination occurs by default. The percentage of unintended pregnancies in the United States is estimated to be 57 percent (Institute of Medicine, 1995). The immediate concern here is not with those "nonstrugglers" but with those "strugglers" who do make a conscious decision regarding childbearing, those who make the "most fateful" (Whelan, 1975) or "most important" decision of their life (Bombardier, 1981). Their decisions often are made on the basis of a combination of deliberate and rational issues and emotional, sometimes irrational, and unconscious ideas, desires, and expectations.

Factors that seem to be significant when evaluating whether to have children include work, nonwork time, income, and type of job. Nock (1987) has argued that women remain child-free or limit their fertility based on the symbolic meaning that lifestyle and childbearing characteristics have for them, which is reflective of their view of the role of women in society. National survey data from the United States in 1987–1988 indicate that there are gender differences in several areas related to this decision: Child-free males were more pronatalistic than females; husbands rated the general importance of having children higher than did females; and husbands were more likely to want to have children (Seccombe, 1991).

However, gender, as well as age and ethnic background also may differentially affect the values associated with childbearing decisions. Southern Europeans tend to be more concerned with psychological and social identity than economic variables, as contrasted with Australians (Callan, 1980, 1982). Catholic women in the United States are less likely to be voluntarily childless and more apt to be involuntarily childless than non-Catholics (Poston, 1990). Among Hispanic American women, those choosing voluntary childlessness do so primarily because of dedication to career (Thomas, 1995). Persons under 30 have expressed a greater desire to have children and regarded parenthood as having more personal value than couples over 30, the older being more concerned with the costs of being parents than the benefits, and different costs being more important for males than for females. At the same time, younger persons (especially the males) tended to favor androgynous role identification more than the older (Gerson, Berman, & Morris, 1991).

Both couples who remain child-free and those who choose to be parents have been found by Cowan and Cowan (1992) to assume that having a baby will bring change, with portions of both groups expecting that a baby will produce more closeness, excitement, and joy and others in both categories assuming parenthood will lead to more distance between marital partners and to increased frustration and tension.

TYPES OF DECIDERS AND RESPONDERS TO INFERTILITY/PREGNANCY QUESTIONS

Cowan and Cowan (1992) identified several types of couples based on their responses to making a decision whether to have a child, to learning that they were not able to conceive, or to having the experience of a surprise pregnancy. These findings, which are consistent with our many years of clinical observations, have been adapted, as follows:

Decided Couples: Child-Free

With those who approached the question of parenthood in a deliberate way and definitely decided that they wished to remain child-free, the desire to avoid a repetition of what occurred in their family of origin was named as a major motivation (Cowan & Cowan, 1992). Single females wishing to have no children or only one child have been found to have strong career interests, to be financially and socially more independent in their future relationships, and to desire more role innovative practices (Callan, 1986).

Decided Couples: Parenthood

On the other side of the coin, those who deliberately and clearly decided to have children indicated that their desire to have a special and intimate relationship with their children and to experience the changes parenthood would make in their sense of themselves were at the top of their list of reasons for becoming parents (Cowan & Cowan, 1992).

Surprised and Frustrated Couples

Whether their plans to avoid pregnancy are disrupted by an unplanned pregnancy or they have decided to have children and find that they cannot conceive on their planned schedule or cannot conceive at all, couples may experience surprise, disappointment, and frustration (Cowan & Cowan, 1992).

Surprised but Accepting Couples

Of the expectant couples in their study, Cowan and Cowan (1992) found that one couple in seven were surprised when they learned of their pregnancy, but accepted the outcome.

Ambivalent Couples

Ambivalence (both positive and negative feelings on the part of both partners) was found in all the categories of couples (Cowan & Cowan, 1992). Although ambivalent, one feels more strongly in one direction and the other in the opposite direction in such marriages. The Cowans found in their sample that couples in this ambivalent category were likely to feel less positive about the marriage than couples in other categories. A clinical implication of this phenomenon is that such ambivalence may be a signal that there are serious problems with commitment to the marriage. The reluctance may signify a feeling that having a child would pull them farther into a marriage about which they feel uncertain.

Ambivalent-Conflicted Couples

This category contained couples whose strong conflict about having a child remained unresolved (Cowan & Cowan, 1992). This is, as encountered clinically, a matter of "one wants a child and the other doesn't" that has not been settled. Having to choose between two undesirable courses has been described metaphorically as a "Sophie's choice" situation, a continuing dilemma for many infertile couples: whether to accept infertility without treatment—as some do—and go against contextual norms or undergo treatment that may lead to postponing other life goals and experiencing other hardships, possibly without obtaining a remedy for their problem (Sandelowski, 1986).

Therapists who work with couples around childbearing issues thus need a variety of skills. They may be called on to help those torn between having a child or remaining childless. They also need to be able to assist those who encounter difficulties as a result of either being unable to have a child or of suffering sanctions because of the decision to remain child-free.

THE TIMING OF THE DECISION

Understanding how and when couples make the decision to have children or not is also important. Family background factors generally have seemed to be important in distinguishing between the early deciders and the postponers (Callan, 1986; Houseknecht, 1979). Early deciders, for example, were more likely to come from smaller families and to believe that concern with overpopulation influenced their decision (Callan, 1983). At the same time, Ramu (1984) found that such family background factors as family-of-origin size, birth order, and perceived parental happiness did not predispose a sample of Canadian couples to voluntary childlessness. Interestingly, couples from a random sample of the National Alliance for Optional Parenthood were found to be participating in a social movement for personal more than public welfare reasons and to be interested in securing support for their childless decision (Barnett & MacDonald, 1986). Reference group support and continuous related socialization during adulthood have been found to help shape the decisions of those who become voluntarily childless (Houseknecht, 1979).

The decisions and behaviors of one category of couples, the professionals who deliberately delay childbearing until after completion of advanced educational degrees and training as well as establishment of themselves in their careers, create new additions and variations to the family life cycle. Described as an elongated professional model (Fulmer, 1989), the typical pattern is either a few children or, in some cases, infertility following a decision sometime in their thirties or early forties to attempt to have children. This pattern may produce conflict with parents over the failure to follow expected patterns and norms, power conflicts within the marriage, and, in case of infertility, significant disappointment and unaccustomed feelings of helplessness. Paradoxically, during their twenties they may have experienced both an extended economic dependency and a troublesome separation from their family of origin as they obtained advanced education and training, followed a path different from that of their parents, and pulled apart without creating a new relationship of parents interacting with their own parents as grandparents.

It is interesting to note that the issue of wishing to have children and having children has been described as a catch-22 dilemma of marriage: Marital happiness is enhanced by the wish for a child but reduced by the implementation of the wish (Willén & Montgomery, 1996). At the same time, there is evidence to suggest that the presence of children has a positive impact on marital relationships (Wu, 1996).

EFFECTS OF CHILDLESSNESS

The effects of being voluntarily or involuntarily childless or child-free compared to having children have been investigated at different places throughout the family life cycle. Age 30 has been a widely used marker for such study. Summarizing empirical research, Menaghan (1989) found that it suggests that differences vary by gender and economic pressures and that childlessness past age 30 more negatively affected women than men.

No differences in affectional expression or consensus between partners from the two different categories was found by Somers (1993), although the involuntarily childless showed higher levels of dyadic cohesion and satisfaction. National survey data in the United States showed parents scoring higher than nonparents on measures of life meaning (Umberson & Gove, 1989). In an Australian study, parents scored higher on dyadic satisfaction (and had fewer quarrels and less talk of regrets about marriage and possible divorce), although voluntarily childless couples seemed to spend more time together talking and deciding about their lifestyle (Callan, 1984, 1987).

When compared with voluntarily childless women and mothers, infertile Australian women rated their life as less interesting and less rewarding but were more positive about the amount of love in their life and the amount of support they received from family and friends, and also indicated that they had more loving marital relationships than their parental and voluntarily child-free counterparts. Mothers and voluntarily childless ranked their life satisfaction higher in a similar fashion (Callan, 1987).

Perceptions and reports of experiences of being stigmatized because of childlessness, particularly voluntary childlessness, vary. The childless perceive themselves to be negatively stereotyped by family and friends (Somers, 1993). Husbands have been perceived as more psychologically healthy when they had children and wives have been viewed more negatively and liked less when described as voluntarily childless (Calhoun & Selby, 1980). Some research suggests that while there is a stigma attached to being voluntarily childless, such reactions are not universal and that being childless may lead to some positive social attributions (Lampman, 1995).

Studying couples across three stages of the family life cycle, Ishii-Kuntz and Seccombe (1989) found that parents whose children had left home were the most socially involved and "permanently" child-free couples were the most isolated. Their conclusion was that stronger marital support complements the isolation of childless couples. A study with a Canadian national sample of older adults revealed somewhat different results: Voluntarily childless couples went to social places and traveled as often as parental couples and went on outings and sought companionship with friends more frequently than parental couples (Connidis & McMullin, 1993).

PARENTHOOD AND CHILDLESSNESS IN THE LATER YEARS

Research findings on the effects of being childless or a parent during the senior years appear to be mixed and gender differences rather marked. Feelings of regret among older women over not having children vary somewhat with the context, changing over the life course and expanding in cultural systems that render childless women marginal (Alexander, Rubinstein, Goodman, & Luborsky, 1992). Significant differences in subjective well-being have been found between close and distant parents and between close parents and couples who are childless by circumstances but not with the voluntarily childless (Connidis & McMullin, 1993). Among older Canadian couples, the childless experienced levels of well-being similar to that of parents and reported undergoing less life stress (McMillan, 1996).

Childlessness has been found to have no significant effect on the well-being of married older women, but such factors as physical capacity, quality of social interaction, religiosity, and strength of social support are all positively associated with their well-being, and widowed mothers have been found to have better psychological well-being than widowed childless women (Beckman & Houser, 1982). Children have not been found to ensure greater acceptance of life, less loneliness, or life satisfaction of either women or men (Keith, 1983). Beckman (1985) declares that there is little direct research evidence in social gerontology that childless older men are less satisfied than others.

LOSS OF CHILD THROUGH SPONTANEOUS ABORTION

Miscarriage (spontaneous abortion) refers to the loss of pregnancy before 20 weeks of gestation. The experience of women who lose an embryo in this manner has been compared to that experienced following the loss of an infant or young child, although it tends to be shorter and often is less acknowledged (see Chapter 22 for further discussion). Leppert (1985) describes it as consisting of stages of shock, disorganization, volatile emotions, guilt, loss and loneliness, relief, and reestablishment. Couples and women typically need the most support and assistance in the guilt stage, where women in particular need to talk about their feelings, to cry, and to launch the grief process (Leppert, 1985). When the loss is through ectopic pregnancy, the couple encounters emergency surgery that leaves the woman with a scar, hospitalization and lengthy recovery, and grief over the loss of the fetus (Rosenfeld, 1985).

One in every 100 births is a stillborn. The couple typically must deal with a "wall of silence" from outsiders, who respond as if there never had been a birth or death, which prolongs and deepens the grief reaction. DeFrain and associates (DeFrain, Martens, Stork, & Stork, 1986), found that 28 percent of the mothers and 17 percent of the fathers in a study of stillborn experience in the United States had seriously considered suicide following the death.

PUBLIC ATTITUDES TOWARD THE CHILDLESS

There appears to be little room for doubting that those who remain childless—whether voluntarily or involuntarily—are often stigmatized and treated as if something were wrong with them. An Australian study, for example, found that the childless women were perceived as individualistic, nonconforming, intelligent, and self-fulfilled. The voluntarily childless were described as selfish, unusual persons, who were more likely to be pitied for their alternative view of social reality than to be applauded (Callan, 1983).

INFERTILITY

Approximately one in six married couples (Cooper-Hilbert, 1998; Sadler & Syrop, 1987; Speroff, Glass, & Kase, 1994) will experience infertility at some point in their lives. Infertility has two major aspects—the psychological and the medical. It is important to recognize with clients that it is a medical condition and not a sexual disorder; the couple's sexual relationship may be excellent, although not fertile. Infertility is defined medically as the inability to conceive a child after a year or more of regular sexual intercourse without contraception or as the inability to produce a live child if there have been a number of pregnancies (Bresnick, 1984; Shapiro, 1982). For women over 30 who have been unable to conceive, the time period is lowered to six months, after which time they are advised to seek appropriate medical help.

Psychologically, infertility is a life cycle crisis that results in a state of disequilibrium for couples who had expected to have a child and discover that they are not able to achieve their goal (Bresnick, 1984). Although it is possible that there may be some few instances in which psychological problems contribute to failure to have children, the psychological difficulties associated with infertility are essentially the result of reactions to failure to achieve pregnancy rather than a cause. In addition to its impact on physical health, infertility also affects the couple in several other significant areas: their psychological development, emotional well-being, and participation in the life cycles of their respective families (Menning, 1977). The couple may find that their parents are disappointed over their failure to produce grandchildren and that the parents may feel they have contributed to the failure (Burns, 1987). Emotional distance and estrangement may arise between the partners and their siblings who have children (McDaniel, Hepworth, & Doherty, 1992).

Within the marriage, one or both partners may feel that he or she has been betrayed. They may feel that the marriage "contract"—the spoken and unspoken expectations they brought into the relationship (Nichols, 1986, 1996; Sager, 1976)—has been violated and the "models of relationship" (Nichols, 1996) that each formed while growing up have gone unrealized.

Grief and its varied stages and manifestations (shock, denial, anger, guilt, self-blame, decreased self-esteem, and diminished control over their lives including feelings of helplessness) are common reactions of couples not only to the initial discovery or diagnosis of infertility but throughout the process of treatment and eventual resolution of the crisis (Sadler & Syrop, 1987; Shapiro, 1982). In some instances, the initial denial may mitigate against seeking definitive diagnosis and treatment. In others, it contributes to "physician hopping" as the couple continues to reject an infertility diagnosis and searches for a professional who will promise them a successful outcome. They may experience not only the common features of grief reactions but also such behavioral reactions as disorganization, fatigue, distractability, moodiness, obsessive behaviors and thoughts, and unpredictability (Valentine, 1986).

Social attitudes toward infertility and the couple's perceptions of such attitudes contribute to the stigmatizing and stereotyping of infertile couples. Canadian studies show relationships among perceptions, stigma, and social support. A sample of infertile women perceived that "normal" persons considered infertility to be caused by psychological or sexual malfunctioning or by the woman and that infertility overshadowed other characteristics in others' perceptions of them (Miall, 1985). When both men and women in infertile marriages were studied, it was found that couples thought that male infertility was more stigmatizing in the community than female, that infertility is caused by psychological factors or by male sexual dysfunction, and that it is a problem requiring diagnosis and treatment (Miall, 1994). Physically infertile women tend to feel more stigma, but women whose husbands are infertile control the information in order to protect their spouse (Miall, 1986).

EFFECTS ON WOMEN

Compared to voluntarily childless women and to mothers, infertile women have been found to manifest a strong need to be loved and an exaggerated sense of femininity. They also report better marriages than do mothers (Callan, 1989). At the same time, infertile women have reported less satisfaction with their lives as a whole and, compared with mothers, have rated their life as more lonely, less rewarding, less interesting, and as less content (Callan & Hennessey, 1988). Among women undergoing treatment for infertility, marital adjustment decreased with the length of the marriage (Chandra et al., 1991; Ulrich, Coyle, & Llabre, 1990) and with the course of treatment for infertility (Chandra et al., 1991). Link and Darling (1986) found that wives among couples undergoing treatment for infertility were significantly less satisfied with life than were their husbands.

EFFECTS ON MEN

Men in couples treatment for infertility who were able to accept a childless marriage were able to achieve better marital adjustment. In addition, better adjustment was more likely to occur especially when their wife was employed or had high earnings (Ulrich, Coyle, & Llabre, 1990).

EFFECTS ON THE MARRIAGE

Reports of the effects of infertility on marriages are somewhat mixed. Although infertility and the efforts of couples to cope with it can have deleterious effects on their marriage, mediating factors such as the relationship between self-esteem and commitment to the marriage can significantly affect their adjustment to being involuntarily childless (Abbey, Anderson, & Halman, 1992; Sabatelli, Meth, & Gavazzi, 1988). One-third of the women complaining of infertility in a clinical population in India also reported problems in marital functioning, with the greatest deterioration occurring for those from rural areas, those living in joint families, and those married longer than six years (Chandra et al., 1991). Greil, Leitko, and Porter (1988) found in a small sample of western New York infertile couples that interaction between husbands and wives and with medical professionals may lead the couple to ignore treatment options and to take wrong directions. The women perceived infertility as a major role failure, while the men viewed it as disconcerting but not tragic. Both saw it as a problem for wives.

Healthy couples gradually move toward resolution, learning to cope—to tolerate, overcome, or reduce the stress—and to gradually become able to confront the situation instead of denying it, according to Callan and Hennessey (1988). Cooper-Hilbert (1998) emphasizes that they must first face losing their dreams of becoming genetic parents or nurturing a child before they can effectively resolve their infertility.

SOURCES OF INFERTILITY

Physicians have noted that infertility may stem from a variety of sources, usually in some combination of factors. These include antisperm antibodies in either partner, retrograde ejaculation by the male, abnormal sperm motility, suboptimal sperm or lack of sperm, scar tissue from surgery or pelvic infections, blocked fallopian tubes, cervical mucus that prevents sperm from entering the uterus and fallopian tubes, endometriosis, hormonal abnormalities, failure to release an egg or irregular ovulation, repetitive miscarriage, inadequately prepared uterine lining, and advanced age of the female (above 35), as well as unexplained causes and stress (Metzger, 1998). Weinshal (1990) asserts that infertility is more common among women who came to adulthood in the 1960s, partly due to the fact that many of them delayed childbearing in order to launch their careers.

Physicians emphasize that infertility is a couple's problem. Current estimates of male factor infertility given by physicians from reproductive health centers on the Internet range from 25 percent to 45 percent, presumably from the respective physicians' clinical experience. RESOLVE, a national nonprofit organization in the United States that provides information, support, and advocacy for persons concerned with infertility, indicates that it is a male problem 35 percent of the time, a female problem 35 percent of the time, a combined couple matter 20 percent of the time, and unexplained 10 percent of the time.

STRATEGIES FOR COPING WITH INFERTILITY

Berk and Shapiro (1984) describe four major psychological factors that pertain to family therapy approaches to dealing with infertile couples: developmental crisis, emotional reactions to infertility, intrapsychic dynamics, and crisis resolution.

Referral of the couple experiencing difficulty conceiving to a physician who has a special interest and expertise in this problem area is an important step for the therapist, who may continue working with the couple in dealing with their emotional and relational issues. Metzger (1998) emphasizes that both partners should be evaluated by the physician simultaneously in order to formulate a complete understanding of why they are not conceiving. She notes that the assessment covers four areas associated with the reproductive process: the quality and number of sperm, maturation and release of an egg, barriers to fertilization, and barriers to the implanting and maintenance of pregnancy (Metzger, 1998, pp. 9–10).

Couples can seek pertinent information from the physician regarding the perceived causes of their difficulty, the rationale for the treatment approach to be taken, and an overview of the plan. They also can take an active part in educating themselves about infertility either through reading material furnished by the physician or obtained from other reputable health care sources. The couple also have the right to discuss with the physician or fertility specialist when a reevaluation and change of course will be planned if conception has not occurred. Metzger (1998) indicates that a change in treatment should be considered if three or four cycles of a particular treatment have not led to conception and suggests that both the infertility physician and the therapist can help the partners deal with such questions as whether to continue or stop infertility treatment and to discuss alternatives to parenthood. All professionals dealing with them should be aware that the couple experience a "chronic monthly hope-loss cycle" (Cooper-Hilbert, 1998), a kind of monthly emotional roller coaster (Atwood & Dobkin, 1992) that does not need to be sustained indefinitely.

Assisted Reproductive Technology (ART)

This term refers to a number of medical procedures in which human sperm and eggs are brought together in order to facilitate a pregnancy. They include:

IVF (in vitro fertilization). Sometimes called a "test tube" method, which is a misnomer, IVF consists of extracting eggs from a female's ovaries, fertilizing them in a laboratory, and then placing them into the woman's uterus through the cervix. The act of placing sperm and egg in direct contact minimizes the effects of antibodies in the reproductive tract. IVF was the first of the new reproductive technologies that provided women whose fallopian tubes are blocked the opportunity to become pregnant (Metzger, 1998). IVF was used in 70 percent of the ART procedures reported for 1995 (SART/CDCP—Society for Assisted Reproductive Technology and the Centers for Disease Control and Prevention, 1996).

GIFT (gamete intrafallopian transfer). In this procedure, eggs removed from the female's ovary are combined with sperm and the unfertilized eggs and sperm are placed with a laparoscope into her fallopian tubes through a small incision in the abdomen. This procedure was used in 6 percent of the ART procedures reported for 1995 (SART/CDCP, 1996).

ZIFT (zygote intrafallopian transfer). Used only 2 percent of the time for ART procedures reported in 1995 (SART/CDCP, 1996), this procedure involves taking eggs from the woman's ovary, fertilizing them in a laboratory, and placing the fertilized egg (zygote) in her fallopian tubes by means of a laparoscope through a small incision in her abdomen.

All three of these methods thus involve the use of the couple's own egg and sperm to develop fresh embryos.

Embryo cryopreservation. This method involves freezing tissues in order to preserve embryos that can be thawed and transferred into the female's uterus at some point in the future. This use of undonated eggs occurred in 14 percent of the ART procedures reported for the United States in 1995 (SART/CDCP, 1996).

Donor insemination. This procedure involves the use of an embryo from the egg of a female who donates it for transfer to a woman who is unable to conceive with her own eggs. Eight percent of the ARTS procedures reported for the United States for 1995 used donated eggs (SART/CDCP, 1996). Some evidence exists that suggests that couples are likely to have considered and rejected the adoption alternative before deciding to have a child by donor insemination. Such decisions are based on both practical and emotional reasons, including what they perceived as the positive aspects of donor insemination and the negative aspects of adoption (Daniel, 1994).

Surrogate pregnancy. Surrogacy occurs when a couple secures the services of another woman who conceives with the male's sperm and gives birth to the baby, using either her own eggs or eggs from the first woman, which are provided through the in vitro fertilization process. The baby is then transferred to the couple. This recently developed alternative is filled with both legal and psychological questions and hazards. Therapists may be engaged to work with the couple as they make a decision and/or to evaluate the female who will bear the child. Among the contingencies are the potential refusal of the surrogate mother to surrender the child to the couple and the possibility that the baby may not be normal at birth (Schwartz, 1987).

At this time there probably are too many unanswered questions for surrogacy to be *the* answer for infertile couples (Schwartz, 1991). A 1993 California court decision, for instance, upheld and enforced a surrogacy contract against the wishes of the woman who gave birth and wished to keep the baby (Morgan, 1994). Several states have enacted statutes to prohibit payment in connection with the adoption, and other areas remain murky (Katz, 1986). Debate continues over ethical and legal issues relating to the rights and welfare of the planned child, with donor anonymity seen as a significant problem in view of legislation aimed at reducing secrecy. The United Kingdom's 1990 Human Fertilisation and Embryology Act is but part of the picture for the British Isles (Snowden, 1993).

Some research indicates that infertility treatment has a definite impact on marital and sexual satisfaction for women both during treatment and afterward, suggesting that the long-term psychological effects of infertility treatment need to be considered by professionals who are working with women who have had such treatment unsuccessfully in the past (Pepe & Byrne, 1991). For infertile couples who become parents the change has been found to be associated with improved global life quality for the women and diminished life quality for all men except fertile men (Abbey, Andrews, & Halman, 1994).

The social and emotional development of children from the two most widely used reproductive technologies—donor insemination and in vitro fertilization—have been compared to naturally conceived children and adopted children quite favorably. No group differences were found for the children's emotions, behavior, or relationships with parents. Further, the quality of child rearing was found to be superior to that in families with a naturally conceived child (Golombok, Cook, Bish, & Murray, 1995).

At some point it should become apparent to the couple that biological parenthood is not going to occur for them. They can be helped to consider other options, such as adoption, alternative parenting, or childless living.

Adoption

Some couples may make application to adopt at the same time they are undergoing or beginning in vitro fertilization (Williams, 1992). Miall (1987) found that adoptive parents perceived that social beliefs hold that adoption is second best, adopted children second best, and adoptive parents not "real" parents. (See Chapter 13 for more information on adoption.)

SOME THERAPY ISSUES WITH CHILDLESS COUPLES

According to Mazor (1984) the first task of therapy with infertile couples involves helping them deal with the crisis that occurs when they recognize that a problem exists and start on the lengthy, expensive, and sometimes frustrating attempts at further investigation. The second task is to assist them in coping with the longer term issues of the meaning infertility has for them in the context of their life experience. The first task can be handled through short-term therapy or groups, whereas the second may require long-term and intensive therapy.

Couples may present with their difficulties in different ways. They may be direct, saying for example, "We have not been able to conceive and it's tearing us up." They also may be indirect, complaining about a poor sexual relationship and the partner's lack of interest, or one or both of the partners may engage in an extramarital affair in an effort to shore up damaged and slipping self-esteem.

APPROACHES TO THERAPY

The approach to treatment used with infertile couples depends in part on how they functioned prior to experiencing infertility. Some couples who had psychological problems and manifested behavioral dysfunction before encountering the infertility crisis continue to express their preexisting pathology and behavioral dysfunction, sometimes in even more overt forms. Other couples, who seemingly had functioned rather well as long as they did not encounter significant difficulty, fall to a less effective level when the fertility crisis opens the gate to the emergence of their underlying pathology. There are still other "normal" couples who had manifested an ability to cope adequately in the past in other crisis situations and who can return to normal functioning when the fertility crisis is resolved. Sufficient evidence exists to support the conclusion that psychotherapeutic help needs to be provided along with medical assessment and infertility treatment (Bresnick, 1984). Forms of therapy used with infertile couples range from cognitive-behavioral (Myers & Wark, 1996) to poetry therapy (Barney, 1992).

Assisting infertile couples involves several roles for the therapist, including working with their depression, strengthening and improving their relationship, helping them prepare for unsuccessful outcomes of infertility treatment, and consideration of alternative roles. Both Sadler and Syrop (1987) and McDaniel and colleagues (1992) stress the importance of the therapist being well educated in the medical aspects of infertility. Infertile couples are reacting both to the fact of their infertility (i.e., the impact of being unable to achieve their wish for a child on their own) and the effects of medical procedures and hormonal medications required for treatment. The reactions of women to hormonal medication while undergoing an IVF treatment cycle, for example, have been found to include fatigue, weight gain, headaches, moodiness, abdominal discomfort, irritability, and feeling "blue". Most of these reactions can also indicate that the person is experiencing depression. A considerable amount of therapy effort and time can be expended futilely if a therapist is not familiar with the medical aspects of fertility and does not recognize that reactions to medications are similar to depressive reactions or to the stress of being infertile.

Evaluating and treating couples struggling with infertility involves dealing with at least the following: determining why the couple decided to start a family; exploring the fears that the infertility treatment venture brings; ascertaining their coping styles, feelings of failure and guilt, feelings of loss of control, and their support systems; learning the effects of the treatment on their relationship; facilitating the grief process; and resolving the legal and ethical issues associated with the assisted reproductive processes (Sadler & Syrop, 1987).

STAGES AND EMPHASES OF THERAPY

Cooper-Hilbert (1998) delineates four stages of psychotherapy for couples who have a presenting or acknowledged problem of infertility and also includes a helpful list of suggestions for specific questions to be posed to the couple. Emphases 1 and 2, in particular, overlap and may invovled a back-and-forth movement in which therapy involves concentrating first on one factor, then on another, and back to the first in a circular fashion rather than in a strictly linear manner. These emphases may be described as follows:

Emphasis 1: When the couple enters in the midst of confusion and feelings of being overwhelmed, the therapist essentially normalizes their situation, helping both members to understand that their reactions are common to persons experiencing crisis and educating them about the medical treatment process, the side effects of infertility drugs, and their extended psychological stress. Coping strategies for the couple at this point include contacting RESOLVE (1310 Broadway, Somerville, Massachusetts 02144-1779) (Cooper-Hilbert, 1998; McDaniel et al., 1992), which enables them to secure support and information while learning that they are not alone, that others have similar difficulties and reactions, and that their feelings are normal; developing other interests; and constructing a new identity in light of the infertility information, which essentially means constructing a new world view (Atwood & Dobkin, 1992). RESOLVE also engages in advocacy and provides education regarding infertility to associated professionals.

After infertility treatment has begun, one of the more difficult times for the couple is the waiting period after they have gone through a series of tests and treatment. What will be the outcome? Typically, the waiting period is filled with mixtures of hope and fear, exacerbated by inevitable feelings of helplessness and lack of control. The marital partners must not only be supportive of one another but also must have some guidelines for how much they talk about infertility and with whom they talk. "Mini-max" rules are needed. That is, they need to talk about their feelings, to voice what they feel, but also to learn to recognize when they are reaching a point of diminishing returns, when talking about the problem is making things worse. It can be helpful, as in other forms of couple communication, to agree that either can call time-out if he or she is beginning to get too uncomfortable either about individual reactions or to get concerned about the effects on the relationship. The time-out includes the agreement that they will return to the subject at a later time after some respite, if both wish to take up the topic again. The three-week waiting period before a pregnancy test can be performed and the results of artificial insemination ascertained is one in which stress should be avoided as much as possible even while living with inevitable feelings of uncertainty. Chronic strain during lengthy infertility treatments may result not only in couple conflict but also individual symptoms and the need for other psychotherapeutic interventions.

Emphasis 2: The major issue here is on shifting away from the initial focus on the couples' crisis, loss, and negative aspects of their lives toward the revitalization of the marital relationship (Cooper-Hilbert, 1998). Following the establishment of a viable therapeutic relationship with the partners, acknowledgment of the pain they are suffering, and attention to exploring and working through at least part of their grief reactions, the therapist can move to dealing with the exploration of the old "contract" (Sager, 1976) and establishment of a new one between the partners. Before explicit attention is given to other matters, any serious couple or individual problems that have emerged need to be addressed.

Sadler and Syrop (1987) point out that the partners need to be helped to pull their sexuality, self-image, and self-esteem issues apart from the matter of childbearing. Cooper-Hilbert (1998) recommends that the marital relationship needs to be rebalanced so that infertility is demarcated as a couple's issue, rather than defined as a male or female matter. Examination of relationships with friends and extended family is a significant part of securing appropriate support, including determining who can be helpful and how to help them be helpful through what they say and do (Williams, Bischoff, & Ludes, 1992) as well as helping them construct a new and more appropriate relationship with their parents and siblings.

McDaniel and coworkers (1992) have suggested encouraging the couple to discuss the "secret" of infertility with trusted friends and relatives while setting limits on unhelpful inquiries. They might also review the extended family's reproductive history and explore the coping strategies used by other family members in dealing with infertility. They may suggest that the couple educate themselves regarding infertility treatment to increase their sense of control.

Emphasis 3: The couple needs to be helped to make decisions about their ongoing treatment (Cooper-Hilbert, 1998). The major foci are assisting the partners to discover tools that will help them to get past the crisis, to develop a plan, and to set goals. They may also need be assisted to assess the degree of control they have over their life, including control over setting goals and following desired options (within the limits of their physiology). They need to be helped, as noted above, to decide when and how to make an informed decision about ending medical treatment. This frequently involves having to make the painful decision to "give up the dream" and move on to search for and find meaning in other parts of their lives. Therapeutic tasks here typically include helping the couple to recognize how they make decisions and to understand the difficulties in establishing a new model for family living (Fulmer, 1989).

Emphasis 4: For couples who face the reality that they are not going to achieve a pregnancy, accepting infertility and achieving resolution become the major issues. At this point, the possibility develops for grieving the loss of the pregnancy possibility and having their own biological child. Resolving these painful issues brings them back to the juncture of deciding whether they will seek a child through adoption or continue living in a child-free state.

Following careful preparation on what the couple would like to accomplish in such sessions, family-of-origin sessions with each partner and his or her family of orientation (Framo, 1992) can be exceedingly useful in working out more appropriate relationships, whether or not a child is added to their marriage. However, it is important to note that a study of infertile women in Australia who underwent unsuccessful in vitro fertilization were, predictably, more depressed and had lower self-esteem than they did prior to treatment (Hynes, Callan, Terry, & Gallois, 1992). If they used problem-focused coping, they were likely to have higher levels of well-being, whereas if they used avoidance coping and sought social support, lower levels of well-being were found.

RELATIONSHIP WITH THE COUPLE

Can the therapist understand the pain and bewilderment of couples who are struggling with infertility? In addition to educating himself or herself regarding the psychological and physical-medical aspects of infertility and its treatment, the therapist needs to be genuinely concerned with understanding the marital partners as a pair and as individuals and sincerely committed to accepting their decisions and helping them to steer their own course. Does the therapist comprehend the gender differences, the differential reactions of husband and wife to the issues of having a child or not having a child?

Can the couple accept the therapist's ability and willingness to comprehend and accept their wishes and their pain and dilemma? What difference does it make whether the therapist has children? Whether the therapist is pregnant?

The questions of whether the therapist cares and understands and whether the couple accepts the fact that the therapist cares and understands need to be faced squarely any time that there is an inkling of a concern on either side. The clients can raise the issues. The therapist can raise the issues, "Can we work together?" "If you don't think I understand, help me understand. I'll do my best to understand how you feel and what you are going through, but be my teacher."

Knowledge and caring that can be conveyed to the partners and accepted by them appear to be much more important to helping them deal with what troubles them than any techniques of the therapist.

REFERENCES

Abbey, A., Andrews, F. M., & Halman, J. (1992). Infertility and subjective well-being: The mediating roles of self-esteem, internal control, and interpersonal conflict. *Journal of Marriage and the Family, 54,* 408–417.

Abbey, A., Andrews, F. M., & Halman, L. J. (1994). Psychosocial predictors of life quality: How are they affected by infertility, gender, and parenthood? *Journal of Family Issues, 15*(2), 253–271.

Alexander, B. B., Rubinstein, R. L., Goodman, M., & Luborsky, M. (1992). A path not taken: A cultural analysis of regrets and childlessness in older women. *Gerontologist, 32*(5), 18–26.

Atwood, J. D., & Dobkin, S. (1992). Storm clouds are coming: Ways to help couples reconstruct the crisis of infertility. *Contemporary Family Therapy, 14,* 385–403.

Barnett, L. D., & MacDonald, R. H. (1986). Value structure of social movement members: A new perspective on the voluntary childless. *Social Behavior and Personality, 14*(2), 149–159.

Barney, A. (1992). Infertility and crisis: Self-discovery and healing through poetry writing. *Journal of Poetry Therapy, 5*(4), 219–226.

Beckman, L. J. (1985, August). *Childlessness, family composition, and well-being of older men.* Paper presented at the annual conference of the American Psychological Association, Los Angles, CA.

Beckman, L. J., & Houser, B. B. (1982). The consequences of childlessness on the social-psychological well-being of older women. *Journal of Gerontology, 37*(2), 243–250.

Berk, A., & Shapiro, J. L. (1984). Some implications of infertility on marital therapy. *Family Therapy, 11*(1), 37–47.

Bianchi, S. M., & Spain, D. (1986). *American women in transition.* New York: Russell Sage Foundation.

Bianchi, S. M., & Spain, D. (1996). *Women, work, and family in America. Population Bulletin, 51*(3). Washington, DC: Population Reference Bureau.

Bombardieri, M. (1981). *The baby decision: How to make the most important choice of your life.* New York: Rawson Associates.

Bresnick, E. K. (1984). A holistic approach to the treatment of infertility. In M. D. Mazor & H. F. Simons (Eds.), *Infertility: Medical, emotional and social considerations* (pp. 36–52). New York: Human Sciences Press.

Burns, L. H. (1987). Infertility as boundary ambiguity: One theoretical perspective. *Family Process, 26,* 359–372.

Calhoun, L. G., & Selby, J. W. (1980). Voluntary childlessness, involuntary childlessness, and having children: A study of social perceptions. *Family Relations, 29,* 181–183.

Callahan, L. (1994). The crisis of fertility and its effect on the couple relationship. *Progress: Family Systems Research and Therapy, 3,* 19–35.

Callan, V. J. (1980). The value and cost of children: Australian, Greek, and Italian couples in Sydney, Australia. *Journal of Cross-Cultural Psychology, 11,* 482–497.

Callan, V. J. (1982). Australian, Greek, and Italian parents: Differentials in the value and cost of children. *Journal of Comparative Family Studies, 13*(1), 49–61.

Callan, V. J. (1983). Perceptions of parenthood vs childlessness: A comparison of mothers and voluntarily childless wives. *Population & Environment: Behavior & Social Issues, 6*(3), 179–189.

Callan, V. J. (1984). Childlessness and marital adjustment. *Australian Journal of Sex, Marriage, and Family, 5*(4), 210–214.

Callan, V. J. (1986). Single women, voluntary childlessness, and perceptions about life and marriage. *Journal of Biosocial Science, 18,* 479–487.

Callan, V. J. (1987). The personal and marital adjustment of mothers and of voluntarily and involuntarily childless wives. *Journal of Marriage and the Family, 49,* 847–856.

Callan, V. J. (1989). Psychological adjustment to infertility: A unique comparison of two groups of infertile women, mothers, and women childless by choice. *Journal of Reproductive and Infant Psychology, 7*(2), 105–112.

Callan, V. J., & Hennessey, J. F. (1988). The psychological adjustment of women experiencing infertility. *British Journal of Medical Psychology, 6*(2), 137–140.

Chandra, P. S., Chaturvedi, S. K., Isaac, M. K., Chetra, H., Sudarshan, C. Y., & Beena, M. B. (1991). Marital life among infertile spouses: The wife's perspective and its implications in therapy. *Family Therapy, 18*(2), 145–154.

Connidis, I. A., & McMullin, J. A. (1992). Getting out of the house: The effect of childlessness on social participation and companionship in later life. *Canadian Journal on Aging, 11*(4), 370–386.

Connidis, I. A., & McMullin, J. A. (1993). To have or have not: Parent status and the subjective well-being of older men and women. *Gerontologist, 33*(5), 630–636.

Connidis, I. A., & McMullin, J. A. (1996). Reasons for and perceptions of childlessness among older persons: Exploring the impact of marital status and gender. *Journal of Aging, 10*(3), 305–222.

Cooper-Hilbert, B. (1998). *Infertility and involuntary childlessness.* New York: Norton.

Cowan, C. P., & Cowan, P. A. (1992). *When partners become parents: The big life change for couples.* New York: Basic Books.

Daniel, K. R. (1994). Adoption and donor insemination factors influencing couples' choices. *Child Welfare, 73*(1), 5–14.

DeFrain, J., Martens, L., Stork, J., & Stork, W. (Compilers) (1986). *Stillborn: The invisible death.* Lexington, MA: D. C. Heath.

Framo, J. L. (1992). *Family-of-origin therapy: An intergenerational approach.* New York: Brunner/Mazel.

Fulmer, R. (1989). Lower-income and professional families: A comparison of structure and life cycle process. In B. Carter & M. McGoldrick (Eds.), *The changing family life cycle: A framework for family therapy* (2nd ed.) (pp. 545–578). New York: Gardner Press.

Gerson, M-J., Berman, L. S., & Morris, A. M. (1991). The value of having children as an aspect of adult development. *Journal of Genetic Psychology, 152,* 327–339.

Golombok, S., Cook, R., Bish, A., & Murray, C. (1995). Families created by the new reproductive technologies: Quality of parenting and emotional development of children. *Child Development, 66*(2), 285–296.

Griel, A., Leitko, T. A., & Porter, K. L. (1988). Infertility: His and hers. *Gender and Society, 2*(2), 172–199.

Houseknecht, S. K. (1979). Timing of the decision to remain voluntarily childless: Evidence for continuous socialization. *Psychology of Women Quarterly, 4*(1), 81–96.

Hynes, G. J., Callan, V. J., Terry, D. J., & Gallois, C. (1992). The psychological well-being of infertile women after a failed IVF attempt: The effects of coping. *British Journal of Medical Psychology, 65*(3), 269–278.

Institute of Medicine (1995). *The best intentions: Unintended pregnancy and the well-being of children and families.* Washington, DC: National Academy Press.

Ishii-Kuntz, M., & Seccombe, K. (1989). The impact of children upon social support networks throughout the life course. *Journal of Marriage and the Family, 51,* 777–790.

Katz, A. (1986). Surrogate motherhood and the baby-selling laws. *Columbia Journal of Law and Social Problems, 20*(1), 1–54.

Keith, P. M. (1983). A comparison of the resources of parents and childless men and women in very old age. *Family Relations, 32,* 403–409.

Lampman, C. (1995). Attitudes toward voluntary and involuntary childlessness. *Basic and Applied Social Psychology, 17*(1–2), 213–222.

Leppert, P. C. (1985). Women's grief reactions following spontaneous abortion. In W. F. Finn & L. G. Kutchner (Eds.), *Women and loss: Psychobiological perspectives. Foundation of Thanatology Series, Vol. 3* (pp. 63–65). New York: Praeger.

Link, P. W., & Darling, C. A. (1986). Couples undergoing treatment for infertility: Dimensions of life satisfaction. *Journal of Sex and Marital Therapy, 12*(1), 45–69.

Mazor, M. D. (1984). Emotional reactions to infertility. In M. D. Mazor & H. F. Simons (Eds.), *Infertility: Medical, emotional and social considerations* (pp. 23–35). New York: Human Sciences Press.

McDaniel, S., Hepworth, J., & Doherty, W. (1992). Medical family therapy with couples facing infertility. *American Journal of Family Therapy, 20*(2), 101–122.

McMillan, J. A. (1996). Family, friends, stress, and well-being: Does childlessness make a difference? *Canadian Journal on Aging, 15*(3), 355–373.

Menaghan, E. G. (1989). Psychological well-being among parents and nonparents: The importance of normative expectedness. *Journal of Family Issues, 10*, 547–565.

Menning, B. E. (1977). *Infertility: A guide for the childless couple.* Englewood Cliffs, NJ: Prentice-Hall.

Metzger, D. A. (1998). A physician's perspective. In B. Cooper-Hilbert *Infertility and involuntary childlessness: Helping couples cope* (pp. 1–21). New York: Norton.

Miall, C. E. (1985). Perceptions of informal sanctioning and the stigma of involuntary childlessness. *Deviant Behavior, 6*, 383–403.

Miall, C. E. (1986). The stigma of involuntary childlessness. *Social Problems, 33*(4), 268–282.

Miall, C. E. (1987). The stigma of adoptive parent status: Perceptions of community attitudes toward adoption and the experience of informal social sanctioning. *Family Relations, 36*(1), 34–39.

Miall, C. E. (1994). Community constructs of involuntary childlessness: Sympathy, stigma, and social support. *Canadian Review of Sociology & Anthropology, 31*(4), 392–421.

Morgan, D. (1994). A surrogacy issue: Who is the other mother? *International Journal of Law and the Family, 8*(3), 486–512.

Myers, L. B., & Wark, L. (1996). Psychotherapy for infertility: A cognitive-behavioral approach for couples. *American Journal of Family Therapy, 24*(1), 9–20.

Nichols, W. C. (1986). *Marital therapy: An integrative approach.* New York: Guilford Press.

Nichols, W. C. (1996). *Treating people in families: An integrative framework.* New York: Guilford Press.

Nock, S. L. (1987). The symbolic meaning of childbearing. *Journal of Family Issues, 8*, 373–393.

Pepe, M., & Byrne, T. J. (1991). Women's perceptions of immediate and long-term effects of failed infertility treatment on marital and sexual satisfaction. *Family Relations, 40*, 303–309.

Poston, D. L. (1990). Voluntary and involuntary childlessness among Catholic and non-Catholic women: Are the patterns converging? *Social Biology, 37* (3–4), 251–265.

Ramu, G. N. (1984). Family background and perceived marital happiness: A comparison of voluntary childless couples and parents. *Canadian Journal of Sociology, 9*(1), 47–67.

Rosenfeld, D. L. (1985). Personal loss in ectopic pregnancy. In W. F. Finn & L. G. Kutchek (Eds.), *Women and loss: Psychobiological perspectives. Foundation of Thanatology Series, Vol. 3.* (pp. 92–97). New York: Praeger.

Sabatelli, R. M., Meth, R. L., & Gavazzi, S. M. (1988). Factors mediating the adjustment to involuntary childlessness. *Family Relations, 37*, 338–343.

Sadler, A., & Syrop, C. (1987). The stress of infertility: Recommendations and interventions. *Family Therapy Collections, 22*, 1–17.

Sager, C. J. (1976). *Marriage contracts and couples therapy.* New York: Brunner/Mazel.

Sandelowski, M. (1986). Sophie's choice: A metaphor for infertility. *Health Care for Women International, 7*(6), 439–453.

Schoen, R., Kim, Y. J., Nathanson, C. A., Fields, J., & Astone, N. M. (1997). Why do Americans want children? *Population and Development Review, 23*(2), 333–358.

Schwartz, L. L. (1987). Surrogate motherhood I: Responses to infertility. *American Journal of Family Therapy, 15*(2), 158–162.

Schwartz, L. L. (1991). *Alternatives to infertility: Is surrogacy the answer?* New York: Brunner/Mazel.

Seccombe, K. (1991). Assessing the costs and benefits of children: Gender comparisons among husbands and wives. *Journal of Marriage and the Family, 53*, 191–202.

Shapiro, C. (1982). The impact of infertility in the marital relationship. *Social Casework, 63*, 387–393.

Snowden, R. (1993). Ethical and legal aspects of donor insemination. In C. L. R. Barratt & I. D. Cooke (Eds.). *Donor insemination* (pp. 193–203). New York: Cambridge University Press.

Society for Assisted Reproductive Technology and the Centers for Disease Control and Prevention (Compilers). (1996). *1995 Assisted reproductive technology success rates, national summary and fertility clinic reports.* Available on Internet.

Somers, M. D. (1993). A comparison of voluntarily childfree adults and parents. *Journal of Marriage and the Family, 55,* 643–650.

Speroff, L., Glass, R. H., & Kase, N. G. (1994). *Clinical gynecologic endocrinology and infertility* (5th ed.). Baltimore: Williams & Wilkins.

Thomas, I. M. (1995). Childless by choice: Why some Latinas are saying no to motherhood. *Hispanic, 8*(4), 50, 52, 54.

Thornton, A. (1989). Changing attitudes toward family issues in the United States. *Journal of Marriage and the Family, 51,* 873–893.

Ulrich, P. M., Coyle, A. T., & Llabre, M. (1990). Involuntary childlessness and marital adjustment: His and hers. *Journal of Sex and Marital Therapy, 16*(3), 147–158.

Umberson, D., & Gove, W. R. (1989). Parenthood and psychological well-being: Theory, measurement, and stage in the family life cycle. *Journal of Family Issues, 10,* 440–462.

Valentine, D. P. (1986). Psychological impact of infertility: Identifying issues and needs. *Social Work in Health Care, 11*(4), 61–69.

Weinshal, M. (1990). Practice sketch: Treating the infertile couple. *Family Systems Medicine, 8,* 303–312.

Whelan, W. M. (1975). *A baby? . . . maybe: A guide to making the most fateful decision of your life.* New York: Bobbs-Merrill.

Willén, H., & Montgomery, H. (1996). The impact of wish for children and having children on the attainment and importance of life values. *Journal of Comparative Family Studies, 27*(3), 499–518.

Williams, L. (1992). Adoption actions and attitudes of couples seeking in vitro fertilization: An exploratory study. *Journal of Family Issues, 13*(1), 99–113.

Williams, L., Bischoff, R., & Ludes, J. (1992). A biopsychosocial model for treating infertility. *Contemporary Family Therapy, 14,* 309–322.

Wu, Z. (1996). Childbearing in cohabitational relationships. *Journal of Marriage and the Family, 58*(2), 281–292.

CHAPTER 10

Families with Young Children: A Developmental-Family Systems Perspective

Nadine J. Kaslow, Greta Griffith Smith, and Shannon S. Croft

Children are intuitive guides to the shared unconscious of the family. When children are included in family therapy, boundaries of time, person, generation, and meaning become fluid. The parents, seeing themselves as children, slide back into associations from their childhood. As the image of potential transformation, the child prepares the way for future change. (Keith, 1986, p. 3)

IT IS CHILDREN'S playfulness, honesty, directness, guilelessness, and affective aliveness that makes their presence enhance the process of family therapy. In addition, family therapy is effective in treating a broad array of child problems (Diamond, Serrano, Dickey, & Sonis, 1995; Estrada & Pinsof, 1995; Shadish et al., 1993; Wells, 1988). Despite the case that has been building for the value of family therapy for children, remnants of the historical tensions between child therapists and family therapists (McDermott & Char, 1974; Montalvo & Haley, 1973) remain; many therapists are not comfortable conducting family assessments and interventions with infants and toddlers, preschoolers, and elementary school children. This is evidenced by the finding that many therapists include some but not all children in family sessions (Zilbach, 1986), and even when children are included in family therapy, developmentally appropriate adjustments to technique often are not made and the children's voices are not heard (Cederborg, 1997; Stith, Rosen, McCollum, Coleman, & Herman, 1996). The lack of appropriate inclusion of young children in family therapy may be attributed to the limited cross training in family therapy and child therapy (Korner & Brown, 1990) and the different interpersonal styles and techniques required to work simultaneously with adults and children in a complex system.

This chapter offers a developmental perspective on the family treatment of children from infancy through middle childhood. Family therapy with children requires that the therapist be knowledgeable about child and family development, developmental psychopathology, family systems theory, and techniques of culturally competent child and family assessment and intervention. Thus, to set the stage for a discussion of child-oriented family therapy, we provide demographic and descriptive statistics on families with young children, discuss child development and family development, and examine common presenting issues. Then, we discuss the why, when, and how of including young children in family therapy and families in the therapy of young children and explore models of family therapy with young children, including family play therapy, child-centered family therapy, parent training, and parent-infant therapy in an outpatient context.

DEMOGRAPHICS AND DESCRIPTIVE STATISTICS

The approximately 46.4 million children under age 12 residing in this country comprise nearly 18 percent of the population (U.S. Bureau of the Census, 1997). Of these children, 35.8 percent are children of color: 15.5 percent are African American, 15.1 percent are Latino, 4.1 percent are Asian American, and 1.1 percent are Native American (U.S. Bureau of the Census, 1997). These rates are on the increase. The number of children in poverty in the United States is alarmingly high, with 22 percent living in poverty (Ammerman & Hersen, 1997). Thus, therapists must have the skills to provide culturally competent family interventions for the large number of diverse young children who are likely to present to their offices and clinics.

Family therapists also must be attuned to the changing family composition of their young clients. Demographic data suggest that 68 percent of children live in two-parent families, roughly 23 percent of whom live in step or remarried families (U.S. Bureau of the Census, 1997). By the year 2000, approximately 40 percent of all children will live with a step-parent (Glick, 1989). Approximately one million children a year are affected by divorce. It is estimated that 28 percent of children live in single-parent families (Lugaila, 1998), with 85 percent living with their mothers, many of whom (40 percent) have never been married. Based on National Council on Adoption Statistics, in 1992 there were 51,157 unrelated domestic adoptions, of which half were infants, and in 1997 there were 13,620 foreign adoptions. Over a six-month period in 1996, approximately 114,000 children were living in foster care according to an estimate from the Adoption and Foster Care Analysis Reporting System. Further, more than 13 percent, 5 percent, and 3 percent of African American, Latino, and Caucasian youth, respectively, live in their grandparents' home (McGreal, 1994). These statistics underscore the need to assume an inclusive definition of family when working with young children and highlight the need for family therapists to develop expertise in working with multiple family constellations.

CHILD DEVELOPMENT

When working with families with young children, the family therapist must be knowledgeable about various aspects of child development. Here, we review salient aspects of the three stages of child development focal to this chapter.

INFANCY AND TODDLERHOOD

Infants are dependent on their primary caregiver(s). Given the enormity of their basic needs, infants place innumerable demands on their caregivers. Consistency and responsiveness in caregiving are required for the development of secure attachments and basic trust, which lay the foundation for healthy psychological development.

Toddlerhood is marked by the child's burgeoning independence, which comes with the increased mobility achieved with learning to walk. Toddlers experience a newfound mastery at being able to manipulate the environment and communicate their needs, wants, and preferences through words. Cognitive developments lead to object permanence by age two. The toddler's emerging sense of physical separateness often is accompanied by an awareness of the need for primary attachment figures leading to struggles around autonomy versus shame and doubt. During this developmental phase, children primarily engage in parallel play, and begin to enjoy symbolic imaginative play.

PRESCHOOLERS

The preschool years are marked by language acquisition and the use of words to communicate. Children become cognizant of their increasing capacity to master their environment, develop an awareness of complex familial relationships, negotiate their desires for special relationships with each caregiver, and engage in sibling rivalries. Preschoolers begin to use cognitive and interpersonal processes to modulate their own affects and control their behavior, develop the capacity for self-evaluation, and understand causality. Still, they view events in an egocentric manner and perceive the world in a magical and animistic light. Further, preschoolers begin to engage in mutual play, enjoy interacting with their peers, and their imaginative play becomes increasingly complex.

MIDDLE CHILDHOOD

Although we use the term *middle childhood* to refer to children ages 5 to 11, developmentalists appreciate differences between the early (5–7) and later (8–11) stages of this period. Middle childhood is marked by a shift from egocentrism to perspective taking. Children become more able to manage their distressing affects in a social context and understand connections between events and feelings. They manifest logical (cause–effect) thinking, exhibit increasing self-awareness and capacity to self-reflect, have more psychological and competency based self-assessments, realize the constancy of themselves and the immutability of their identity, make more comparative inferences about themselves, and develop the capacity for metacognition. Peer relationships become more prominent; children actively engage in mutual play, form clubs and groups, engage in competitive activities (e.g., game playing), and become invested in keeping secrets. Peer relationships are more often unisex than was the case in earlier stages. Children exhibit increased mastery of their bodies and channel self-expression through involvement in sports, the arts, and other hobbies that often entail trading and showing off collections.

FAMILY DEVELOPMENT

Just as developmental stages have been identified for individuals, family life cycle stages identify organizing transitions and adjustments encountered in families. Families with multiple children often face issues from multiple life cycle stages simultaneously, complicating a simple family life cycle conceptualization. Here, we deal only with the developmental tasks involved in being a family with young children and incorporate the work of Carter and McGoldrick (1989), L'Abate (1994), and Zilbach (1986).

COMMON TASKS FOR FAMILIES WITH YOUNG CHILDREN

With the arrival of the first child, the family begins to incorporate its first fully dependent member. This event leads to changes in role definition and responsibilities regarding child care, managing household responsibilities, earning a living, having adult relationships (e.g., partner, friends, extended family), and engaging in personally gratifying adult activities (e.g., sex, career, hobbies). Caregivers must learn to provide consistent nurturance without themselves becoming depleted, and find new forms of emotional gratification in the act of caregiving. As children mature, families must strive to be flexible enough to allow the child increasing independence, while consistently offering a holding environment marked by nurturance, support, and boundaries appropriate to the child's developmental level. The setting of appropriate boundaries requires that parents take responsibility by setting limits and exerting authority.

As children become parents and parents become grandparents, cross-generational family loyalties and roles shift. These shifts inform and are informed by the structure and boundary permeability of the newly formed family. When there are two or more caregivers, conflicts may emerge regarding cooperation versus competition with regard to parenting and parent-child relationships. The extent of these conflicts is likely to depend on the nature and quality of the caregivers' relationships with one another and the child, the roles and responsibilities of each caregiver, the personality characteristics and temperament of all involved, and parenting styles.

DYNAMICS FOR DIFFERENT FAMILY CONSTELLATIONS

A discussion of dynamics of different family constellations must take into account family's sociocultural context. Cultural group norms differ with regard to child rearing on such variables as gender roles in parenting; nature and extent of extended family involvement; and ideas and values regarding marriage, divorce, remarriage, foster care and adoption, and homosexuality. Thus, the dynamics discussed below will be influenced significantly by the cultural background of all family members involved in caring for the children.

Intact Families

In intact, two-parent families, the addition of a child shifts the family dynamics from dyadic to triadic. While this is also true for other family constellations (e.g., grandmother-mother caregiver dyad), the nature and complexities associated with this shift differ depending on the prior relationship of the caregivers. The birth of a first child requires previously childless couples to find new ways to maintain "couplehood" and to nurture their relationship, despite a significant decrease in time and energy for private time for the couple and a need to redefine the relationship.

In two-parent families with older children living in the home, the addition of an infant requires renegotiation of family role and responsibilities. Older siblings experience changes in the amount and nature of parental attention that they receive and may be expected to assume child-care responsibilities. Parents may find it challenging to meet the often simultaneous needs of children at different developmental stages.

Single-Parent Families

For single parents rearing children on their own, the demands of caring for a child or children by oneself can be overwhelming, both pragmatically and emotionally, due to the lack of having another adult with whom to share parenting responsibilities. For single parents, it is virtually impossible for them to find time for themselves. Because of these difficulties, extended family members often play vital roles in the care of young children.

Extended Family

While any extended family member may serve as a caregiver, most often it is a grandmother who live nears or with the family that serves in this capacity (McGreal, 1994). This is particularly true among certain ethnic groups (e.g., African Americans), for families in which the parents are adolescents, and for families in which a parent has a mental illness or a serious substance abuse problem. In three-generation families, the delineation of roles related to childcare often is complex and stressful, secondary to conflict regarding the balance of authority within the family and the appropriate ways to raise the child (e.g., amount or nature of discipline).

Divorced, Step, and Remarried Families

Divorced families struggle with the stresses of single parenthood, the complexities of maintaining a coparenting relationship with a person with whom one has severed an intimate partnership, the negotiation of custody and visitation arrangements, and the need for each parent to develop new support systems and intimate partnerships (Schwartz & Kaslow, 1997). In addition to these dilemmas, newly remarried families must contend with complex conflicting and ambiguous new roles and relationships, shifting boundaries, and reallocation of resources (Bray & Kelly, 1998; Visher & Visher, 1996).

Adoptive and Foster Families

In adoptive families, bonding depends on the interplay between the developmental stages of the child and the family at the time of the adoption, cultural similarities and differences between the adopted child and adoptive family, the child's personal history (e.g., maltreatment, foster care, history of prior attachments), and the caregivers' motivations for adoption (e.g., unable to have biological children, gay couple, humanitarian interests, caring for kin). Additional family tasks include forming a family story about the adoption, addressing divided loyalties, managing a child's curiosity about his or her biological parents and search for roots, and grappling with feelings about separation and loss (Combrinck-Graham, 1989). Foster families deal with similar issues, with additional difficulties related to the uncertainty of the length of the placement, the ongoing relationship with human service and legal agencies, and in some instances, with relationships with the child's birth family.

Gay and Lesbian Families

There is variability in the family structures of children with gay and lesbian parents that influence family dynamics: a blended family in which one partner has children from a previous relationship, a lesbian woman or couple whose child was conceived with sperm donation (via sexual intercourse or artificial insemination) from a known or anonymous donor who may or may not be included in the family structure, an individual or couple with a child conceived via the use of surrogacy, or an individual or couple with an adopted child (Cabaj & Purcell, 1997). While there slowly has developed an increased acceptance of gay male and lesbian couples, these couples experience intensified societal prejudices when they choose to add a child to their family. This also is the case for persons with children acknowledging publicly for the first time their sexual orientation as a gay man or lesbian.

COMMON PRESENTING ISSUES IN FAMILIES WITH YOUNG CHILDREN

Families with young children may present for therapy because the child manifests emotional, behavioral, or developmental difficulties and/or there are parental, sibling, or other family problems.

CHILD PROBLEMS

When a child begins to exhibit emotional or behavioral difficulties, or both, that interfere with his or her social and educational functioning, parents often first seek assistance from the pediatrician. This often occurs in response to day care or school personnel concerns about the child. Typically, youth who are referred to mental health services have complicated presentations and a high rate of comorbidity of childhood disorders.

Behavioral Problems

Children with disordered conduct are those most often referred for mental health services, comprising almost half of all referrals (Alexander & Pugh, 1996). These youth commonly manifest oppositional and defiant behavior toward authority, conflicts with peers, impulsivity, overactivity, tantrums, and destruction of property. The two most frequently reported disruptive behavior disorders are conduct disorder (prevalence of 1.5 percent to 16 percent) and attention deficit hyperactivity disorder (prevalence rate of 3 percent to 17 percent) (American Academy of Child and Adolescent Psychiatry, 1997a). Both disorders occur more often in boys than girls (American Academy of Child and Adolescent Psychiatry, 1997a). Disruptive behavior frequently reflects underlying emotional distress and a reaction to environmental stresses.

Emotional Problems

Children with depressive or anxiety disorders may be less disruptive in peer settings, but require mental health services for their social isolation and limited peer involvement, fears and inhibitions, withdrawal from pleasurable activities, low self-esteem, or appetite and sleep disturbance. Epidemiological data indicate that 2 percent to 5 percent of youth in community samples are depressed and 9 percent are anxious, with rates increasing with age (American Academy of Child and Adolescent Psychiatry, 1997b; Fleming & Offord, 1990).

School and Learning Problems

Many children are referred because of poor school performance that may be secondary to learning disorders (disorders of reading, written expression, mathematics). Estimates of learning disorders range from 2 percent to 10 percent (American Psychiatric Association, 1994). Behavioral and emotional problems may contribute to learning and academic performance problems. Conversely, learning disabilities often lead to low self-esteem and disruptive peer, teacher, and family relationships, contributing to the development of behavioral and emotional difficulties (Culbertson & Silovsky, 1996).

Developmental Disabilities

Many children are referred for mental health services for mental retardation and pervasive developmental disorders (e.g., autism, pervasive developmental disorder not otherwise specified). Epidemiological data indicate that mental retardation occurs in 1 percent of the population and autism is diagnosed in .02 percent to .05 percent of the population (American Psychiatric Association, 1994).

Physical Symptoms and Medical Problems

Children often are referred by their pediatricians for mental health treatment around physical complaints, symptoms, and disorders. Referrals run the gamut from physical symptoms with no known organic etiology (e.g., enuresis, encopresis, pseudoseizures) to somatic complaints (e.g., headaches, stomachaches) to problems coping with serious and/or chronic medical illness or physical disabilities (e.g., cancer, diabetes, sickle cell syndromes, visual or hearing impairment) (Roberts, 1995). Six percent to 12 percent of children have a serious chronic illness (Roberts, 1995). Children with physical symptoms and medical problems frequently manifest behavioral and emotional difficulties.

Links Between Child Problems and Family Dysfunction

Problems in a child are stressful to other family members and in some families may lead to dysfunctional interactions that maintain and/or exacerbate the child's difficulties. However, not all families with a psychologically disturbed or medically ill child become dysfunctional. On the other hand, consistent with a systemic perspective, many childhood emotional and behavioral problems reflect family system dysfunction. Thus, we now address those family factors that may precipitate, maintain, and/or exacerbate problems in the child.

FAMILY PROBLEMS

Parental Relationship Discord and Conflict

Studies reveal a high correlation between child maladjustment and marital discord, particularly for boys (Cummings, Davies, & Simpson, 1994). However, few studies examine whether marital problems cause child problems. Research does indicate that the following factors determine which children will have negative reactions to marital conflict: the child's perception of the destructiveness of the conflict, the child's perception of the threat to himself or herself, and the degree to which the child blames himself or herself for the conflict between the adults (Cummings et al., 1994).

Separation and Divorce

Cross-sectional and longitudinal research indicate that significant numbers of children manifest ongoing psychological and social difficulties associated with the stresses that accompany divorce (Wallerstein, 1991). Increased psychological difficulties in children postdivorce are predicted by levels of interparental conflict, and the interparental conflict-child adjustment link is mediated by the children's contact with both parents, the children's anger, and the children's capacity to seek support from their parents for help with emotion regulation (Lee, 1997). Conversely, children who adapt reasonably well to divorce come from families with low levels of parental hostility and parental rejection combined with consistent and appropriate disciplinary practices.

Remarriage

Stressful challenges associated with remarriage include the entry of a new member or members into the family (e.g., step-parent, step-siblings, half-siblings), the introduction of a step-parent into the coparenting team, and the complex alliances among all of the child's different caregivers (Whiteside, 1989). Children in remarried families adjust well when authoritative child-rearing styles are used by the caregivers (Hetherington & Clingempeel, 1992).

Parenting Problems

Problems in parenting associated with the development, maintenance, or exacerbation of child problems include difficulties establishing a secure attachment and bond, an inability to provide for the child's basic physical and emotional needs, trouble providing adequate stimulation to the child, problems playing with the child, a pattern of overprotection or underprotection or significant alternation between the two, problems handling the child's distressing affects, a lack of consistency in response to the child, a dearth of effective child management strategies for dealing with common child behaviors, communication difficulties (e.g., lack of clarity, criticalness, limited praise), a lack of agreement between caregivers, and limited skills in teaching the child. These difficulties may be attributable to relationship discord between caregivers, parental psychopathology, problems modulating anger, limited problem-solving and coping abilities, a lack of social and emotional support, and high levels of chronic or acute stress, or both, in the parent's life.

Family Violence

The physical and sexual abuse of children are major public health problems. Physically and sexually abused children often meet criteria for posttraumatic stress disorder (PTSD) and many manifest myriad difficulties including fears, depression, low self-esteem, physical aggression, hyperactivity, impulsivity, learning problems, oversexualized behavior, and peer problems (Kendall-Tackett, Williams, & Finkelhor, 1993). The functioning of families of physically and sexually abused children depends on the severity and duration of the maltreatment, the child's reactions to the maltreatment, the response of the nonoffending adults to the abuse, the perpetrator's relationship to the child, and the nature of the perpetrator's continued involvement in the child's life (Kendall-Tackett et al., 1993). Family variables associated with childhood maltreatment include poverty or limited financial resources, parental unemployment, single parenthood, young age of parents, four or more children in the home, parental substance abuse or mental illness, and limited social support (Kaplan, 1996; Wolfner & Gelles, 1993).

Children who witness domestic violence, another form of family violence described elsewhere in this book, often manifest a variety of somatic, psychological, and behavioral dysfunctions. Not surprisingly, young children have most serious difficulties when domestic violence results in the death of one or both of their parents.

Neglect

Many cases of child maltreatment also involve significant emotional, physical, educational, or medical neglect. Neglected children are more likely than nonneglected children to have insecure attachments, low frustration tolerance, low self-esteem, difficulties asserting themselves, impaired peer relationships, attentional problems, and symptoms of depression and anxiety (Kaplan, 1996). Child neglect often is associated with a number of parental problems: marital discord, immaturity, depression, substance abuse, unemployment and financial problems, lack of social support, and intellectual impairment (Kaplan, 1996).

Parental Psychopathology

Studies on the effects of schizophrenic adults suggest that these children were at risk for various forms of maladjustment (Watt, Anthony, Wynne, & Rolf, 1984). Similarly, children of depressed mothers evidence high rates of perinatal complications, a range of behavior and emotional difficulties, academic deficits, and impaired social competence (Kaslow, Deering, & Racusin, 1994). In addition, children of parents with anxiety, bipolar disorder, and substance abuse are at increased risk for myriad psychological difficulties (Lee & Gotlib, 1994). In all families in which one or more parents exhibit significant levels of psychopathology, it is the emotional availability of the parent that is crucial in determining the child's ability to adjust effectively (Lee & Gotlib, 1994).

Illness or Death of a Family Member

While many children whose parents have a medical condition fare relatively well, some of these youth have behavioral and emotional problems and low levels of social competence (Chun, Turner, & Romano, 1993). The nature and extent of the child's psychological difficulties is a function of the parents' level of psychological adjustment and the quality of the marital and the parent-child relationships (Armistead, Klein, & Forehand, 1995; Steele, Forehand, & Armistead, 1997). Similarly, youth who lose a parent to death suffer more psychological adversities than their nonbereaved peers, including depression, anxiety, disruptive behavior, impaired academic and social functioning, and low self-esteem (Silverman & Worden, 1992). The severity of children's psychological distress following the death of a parent depends on mode of death, child's age at the time of loss, subsequent caregiver behavior, and mourning behavior (Tremblay & Israel, 1998). Further, parental death leads to an increase in the number of stresses experienced by the child, which in turn lead to increased child distress (Thompson, Kaslow, Williams, Price, & Kingree, 1998).

Children also are quite affected by the illness, disability, and/or death of a sibling (Fanos, 1996). A child's adaptation to a sibling's illness is largely a function of the child's parents' coping and adjustment (Bettoli-Vaughan, Brown, Brown, & Baldwin, 1998; Brown, Doepke, & Kaslow, 1993). Bereaved siblings demonstrate increased levels of aggression, symptoms of PTSD, and impairments in social competence (Applebaum & Burns, 1991; McCown & Davies, 1995).

Sibling Problems

A number of sibling dynamics are associated with a young child's involvement in therapy. These include difficulties accepting the birth of a younger sibling, exaggerated sibling rivalry and competition, parental favoritism, physical aggression, and sibling incest and abuse (Bank & Kahn, 1982; Kahn & Lewis, 1988).

FAMILY INTERVENTIONS FOR YOUNG CHILDREN

Family Therapy: The Treatment of Choice?

When a young child is referred for evaluation and treatment, the clinician is confronted with questions of modality choice. This decision is complicated by the fact that historically there was an extreme polarization between individual child therapy and family therapy. Fortunately, in recent years, clinicians have espoused an integrative perspective that attends to family dynamics in individual child therapy, as well as the developmental and individual needs of all individuals. Some have discussed the conditions under which family therapy is the treatment of choice for young children. Specifically, Kaslow and Racusin (1990) argue that when there are adequate parental resources and the IP child has a reasonable degree of ego strength, family treatment—ranging from membership in formal family therapy to training parents in child behavior management techniques and guiding parents in vivo—is the treatment of choice. (p. 285)

In addition, guidelines have been developed for combining individual and family interventions (Racusin & Kaslow, 1994). For example, concurrent individual and family therapy is recommended when the child does not possess adequate ego strength and/or the parents' resources are compromised as evidenced by one or more of the following: (1) the child manifests significant symptoms and the parents exhibit considerable psychopathology or marital dysfunction contributing to impaired parenting; (2) the parents are able to help their children with some, but not all, aspects of their development; (3) the family engages in maladaptive interactions in response to the child's individual pathology; and (4) the family exhibits inadequate role function and poor communication patterns. Finally, couples therapy, in addition to family therapy that includes young children, may be indicated when marital problems are severe and require an intensity of focus and discussion of topics inappropriate for young children.

The remainder of this chapter focuses on clinical work with families with young children when family therapy alone or in conjunction with other modalities is the treatment of choice. Our discussion includes cases in which the child may or may not be the index person. Our review of family intervention approaches with young children focuses only on the major treatment approaches and is not meant to be exhaustive.

PLAY IN FAMILY THERAPY

The innovators of family play therapy were Satir (Satir, 1967, 1972) and Keith and Whitaker (Keith & Whitaker, 1981). Other significant contributors to the family play therapy movement include Ariel, Carel, and Tyano (1985), Combrinck-Graham (1989), Gil (1994), Griff (1983), Kobak and Waters (1984), and Zilbach (1986). These family play therapists integrate techniques from the play therapy field with interventions from the family therapy field in their work with children from birth to age 12 and their families.

By focusing family therapy around play, the therapist communicates that all members' thoughts and feelings are equally valued. Play is the medium through which adults and children can be engaged in a meaningful therapeutic process, find a common ground by which to communicate about themselves, grow in their understanding of one another, and resolve conflicts (Gil, 1994). Play lowers family members' resistances to sharing and change, which facilitates a deeper level of interaction characterized by fantasy, metaphor, and symbolism. Through play, a family's patterns of relating are highlighted and new meanings can be created (Schatz, 1998). Rather than the therapist interpreting the play, the therapist and family together cocreate a narrative understanding about the child and family's play (Larner, 1996). In addition, play facilitates alliances and attachments through engagement in a mutual and pleasurable activity (Gil, 1994; Zilbach, 1986).

Many family play therapists use board games, some of the most popular of which are *The Un Game; The Talking, Feeling, Doing Game; The Changing Family Game; The Family Contract Game;* and *Solutions.* These board games are designed to help families communicate more effectively, often about sensitive personal and family matters, and improve their problem-solving skills using a familiar game format.

In the Family Puppet Interview (Irwin & Malloy, 1994) families are instructed to create a story with an original plot using puppets. The puppets speak the dialogue, rather than narrate the story. Puppet play, which stimulates communication and demonstrates how a family organizes to engage in a mutual task and accomplish a goal, is recommended for highly intellectualized and analytical families.

Family art therapy (Kwiatkowska, 1978; Linesch, 1993) is a process through which family members engage in an expressive activity together. The informal and indirect nature of the communication in art therapy may alter maladaptive interactional patterns by facilitating emotional self-expression, lessening defenses and supporting the expression of unconscious thoughts and feelings, encouraging genuine communication between family members, and empowering family members to acknowledge and take responsibility for their behavior (Kwiatkowska, 1978; Linesch, 1993). The process of creation, the content of the art, and the family interaction stimulated by this production are essential elements. Commonly used family art techniques are the scribble technique, squiggle drawing game, free drawing technique, color your life technique, and kinetic family drawing technique.

The telling of stories is another strategy that supports spontaneous verbal interchanges and reduces resistance. The most frequently employed is a family adaptation of Gardner's Mutual Story Telling Technique (Gardner, 1971). Families are asked to cocreate a story with a beginning, middle, and end. The content of these stories and the process of creating them provides information about family dynamics. The family therapist may work with the family to create new and more effective story endings, a process that facilitates the resolution of family conflicts.

Family sculpting (Duhl, Kantor, & Duhl, 1973) involves the metaphoric use of space and movement for understanding one family member's perceptions of his or her family's relational dynamics. Each person is asked to physically arrange other family members, without words, according to his or her view of family relationships at a particular point in time (e.g., present, prior to or following a major family life event) or based on his or her desired family unit. The sculptor is encouraged to explain the creation and family members are invited to discuss the sculpture. Sculpting offers the individual the opportunity to express his or her perception of various aspects of the family structure and relationship patterns that often are difficult to communicate about in words. As a result, family members learn more about each other's views of the family.

CHILD-CENTERED FAMILY THERAPY

Child-centered family therapy (Andreozzi, 1996), a short-term, developmentally focused, structural dynamic treatment intervention, uses a family-initiated model of system change. This model includes practical exercises, structured activities, and interventions designed to normalize family processes, increase self-reflective capacities and an understanding of family processes in all family members, and build knowledge from within the family. This facilitates the family's development of more effective strategies for change. The approach emphasizes family strengths and competencies.

Five structured activities serve as the basis for this approach. Involvement in these activities is associated with increased understanding of family process, relationships within the family, and child development. The five activities are the family notebook, family photographs, family network drawing, living sculpture, and family role play. The family notebook activity consists of responses to a novel series of questions posed by the therapist meant to encourage families to think of themselves as a system and to increase their conscious awareness of the parenting style used within the family. In the family photograph activity, family members share three or four photographs; discussions of these photographs help participants explore past childhood experiences, current family system dynamics, and the parent-child relationship over time. In the family network drawing, the family illustrates its view of itself and its boundaries. This drawing includes information about the people, places, and relationships that currently shape, change, direct, and influence the adults and children within the family system. The living sculpture allows either a therapist or family member to physically move and position family members to represent family relationships. This technique allows family members to explore their feelings about their relative spatial-emotional positions in relation to one another. The family role play task asks family members to imagine what it feels like to be another family member, and to experience the world directly from another's perspective.

PARENT TRAINING

Parent training is a systemic and cognitively based intervention approach with the goal of providing information and imparting skills to parents in order to better equip them to address their child's problematic behaviors (Schaefer & Briesmeister, 1998). Therapists coach parents in new skills and ways of interacting with their child and supervise caregivers' implementation of these skills at home. In this treatment approach, caregivers are recognized as offering unique and intimate insights into the day-to-day routines, behaviors, and emotional reactions of their child. Parents and therapists work together and share their expertise to help the parents better help the child. This approach is accessible, understandable, maintainable, generalizable, ecologically valid, and time and cost efficient. As a result, adults are likely to seek out this treatment, to adhere to the protocol, and continue to apply skills learned over time. Parent training has been advocated for parent-child relationship disorders and for parents of children who manifest such psychiatric disturbances as attention-deficit, disruptive behavior, developmental, and habit disorders.

Parent training approaches for child emotional and behavioral problems can be classified under two broad categories: (1) behavior modification, and (2) relationship enhancement. Behavior modification interventions are based on operant conditioning and social learning theory and focus on altering antecedents and consequences of children's behavior. The most commonly used behavioral modification approaches for young children include the work of Barkley (1995), Eyberg (Eyberg, Boggs, & Algina, 1995; Eyberg & Boggs, 1998), Forehand (Forehand & Long, 1996), Patterson (1976), and Webster-Stratton (1996). These behavior modification interventions are the family-oriented child treatment approach with the most empirical support and validation (Eyberg, Edwards, Boggs, & Foote, 1998). Relationship enhancement approaches aim to strengthen caregiver-child relationships via improved communication, problem-solving skills, and corrective emotional experiences. For illustrative purposes, we briefly discuss one form of parent training namely Eyberg's parent-child interaction therapy for oppositional defiant preschoolers (Eyberg et al., 1995; Eyberg & Boggs, 1998), and one form of relationship enhancement, filial therapy as promulgated by Guerney and colleagues (Guerney, 1964), Ginsberg (Ginsberg, 1997), and Van Fleet (Van Fleet, 1994).

Parent-Child Interaction Therapy

Parent-child interaction therapy (Eyberg et al., 1995; Eyberg & Boggs, 1998) is designed for the parents of preschoolers with an array of psychological disturbances, most notably oppositional defiant disorder. This approach aims to teach children prosocial behavior, decrease inappropriate behavior, and teach parents to improve the quality of their relationship with their young child. This approach includes two basic phases: (1) child directed interaction (CDI), and (2) parent directed interaction (PDI). In the CDI component, parents are taught traditional nondirective play techniques and are encouraged to use warmth, attention, and praise as incentives for the child to develop appropriate play and improved self-control. In the PDI phase, the caregivers are taught to communicate clearly using age-appropriate instructions and commands, to provide positive and negative consequences following the child's obedience and disobedience, respectively, and to understand how the child's social environment shapes his or her behavior. These techniques can then be applied to novel situations as they arise, such that generalization of the child's enhanced self-control can occur. Empirical support for the efficacy of this model at posttreatment and follow-up has been found in a number of studies (Brestan & Eyberg, 1998; Eyberg et al., 1998).

Filial Therapy

Filial therapy is a relationship enhancement intervention approach that incorporates client-centered play therapy techniques. Developed by Guerney (1964) and popularized by Ginsberg (Ginsberg, 1997) and Van Fleet (1994), the goal of this approach is for the parents to learn how to function similar to a play therapist with their own children. This may be accomplished via some combination of the following: (1) The therapist explains to the parents the benefits to be derived for the child and for the parent-child relationship from the parent observing, encouraging, and participating in periods of self-directed play on the part of the child; (2) the parents watch the therapist play with the child and are taught to understand, but not interpret, the symbolism of their child's play; (3) the parents play with their child (or with another family's child if the work is conducted in a group context) and receive feedback from the therapist (and/or other group members) regarding their efforts to be nondirective, reflective of the child's play behavior, and empathic in their responses to their child and his or her play; and (4) after considerable in-session training, the parent and child engage in play sessions at home, take notes on these sessions, and return to the therapist for supervision on these play endeavors.

The philosophy underlying filial therapy is that play is the primary vehicle for relating with children. Empathically reflecting a child's feelings as expressed through the child's play communicates acceptance and encourages a sense of safety and security, which in turn supports the expression of deeper feelings and more genuine self-expression. A parent can be more effective than a professional therapist on the basis of the parent's emotional significance to the child and the fact that a child's anxieties that may have arisen within a family context may be best treated within the same venue. When a parent is the agent of therapeutic change for the child, the results may be more long lasting and fulfilling.

Filial therapy, typically recommended for children ages 3 to 12, has been used effectively for a wide range of child social, emotional, and behavioral problems, as well as for other families with various special needs. Specifically, filial therapy has been used for children who are depressed, anxious, perfectionistic, and those who have elimination disorders (enuresis, encopresis) and school problems (Van Fleet, 1994). It also has been found to be helpful with medically ill youth (Van Fleet, 1992). In addition, it is recommended for children of divorce, adopted and foster children, children with a history of abuse or neglect, and children whose parents have addictive disorders (Van Fleet, 1994). Further, filial therapy may be used preventively to improve family relationships, provide an enjoyable parent-child experience, and reduce a child's risk for future problems (Van Fleet, 1994). This treatment approach, however, is considered to be contraindicated when parents do not possess the intellectual capacity to learn this intervention, when the parents themselves are under such emotional stress that they are unable to focus in the requisite manner on their child's needs, and if the parent has been the perpetrator of a child's abuse (Van Fleet, 1994).

INFANT-PARENT PSYCHOTHERAPY

Infant-parent psychotherapy was developed by Fraiberg and colleagues (Fraiberg, 1980). Since its origination, a variety of models of infant-parent psychotherapy have emerged (Stern, 1995). Some of these approaches aim to change the parents' internal representations of their infants (Cramer & Palacio-Espasa, 1993; Fraiberg, 1980; Lieberman & Pawl, 1993), whereas other models are designed to alter the interactive parent-infant behaviors (Clark & Seifer, 1983; Field, 1982; McDonough, 1993; Trad, 1992, 1993). All of these approaches have been developed for, and used primarily with, high-risk infants.

Fraiberg's (1980) model serves as the basis for the infant-parent psychotherapy approaches that primarily target parents' internal representations of their young ones, and thus will be used as illustrative of these approaches. While myriad intervention techniques may be employed in this treatment model, the predominant feature is an emphasis on the "ghosts in the nursery" (i.e., parents' tendencies to reenact unresolved and/or repressed conflicts from their own childhood with their infants) (Seligman, 1994). Fraiberg's model includes three elements: (1) psychotherapy, (2) nondidactic developmental guidance, and (3) concrete support. The psychotherapy component involves helping parents increase their awareness of the ways in which they are reenacting their own unresolved traumatic childhood experiences with their own infants. This is accomplished via interpretation of the parent's behavior with the child and interpretation of transference dynamics vis-à-vis the therapist. Nondidactic developmental guidance refers to the practical side of this approach; the therapist offers advice regarding various aspects of the child's physical, cognitive, social, and emotional development. The therapist also provides direct support (e.g., referrals, practical assistance) and advocacy, which further serve to bolster the caregiving relationship.

Trad (1992, 1993) has delineated in the greatest detail a model for directly intervening in the parent-infant dyad, and thus his approach will be used to illustrate such models. In this approach, he uses a technique referred to as previewing, which is designed to help the caregiver anticipate the next developmental tasks of the infant and to encourage the infant's attainment of developmental milestones. This is accomplished via the parent functioning as an "auxiliary supporter" who facilitates the infant's experimentation with the relational consequences of attaining new aspects of development. The key components of previewing are (1) representation—the caregiver imagines the infant's next developmental tasks; (2) auxiliary partner—the caregiver devises behavioral exercises that help introduce the infant to developmentally appropriate new tasks in a manner that both offers a secure environment within which the infant can learn the tasks and that conveys that the parent will be available to help the infant make developmental gains; and (3) caregiver sensitivity to infant's cues—the caregiver communicates an awareness and acceptance of when the infant has become satiated with an exercise and wishes to return to a previous level of achievement. Intervention strategies that accompany this previewing work include perspective taking, representational exercises, contrasting the past and present, reconstruction, interpretation, counterprojection, and confrontation.

Stern (1995) underscores the fact that all of the infant-parent psychotherapy approaches appear to be effective in improving the parent-infant relationship and enhancing the child's development, which he attributes to commonalities between the various models. Common elements include the following: the interventions are brief (3 to 12 sessions) and most often weekly; a positive therapeutic alliance and positive transference are encouraged and not analyzed; and the clinical system includes the representations and actions of the therapist, the caregivers, and the infant.

CONCLUSION

Despite the fact that the family therapy literature is replete with assertions that it is extremely beneficial to include children in family therapy endeavors, many family therapists either fail to include children in an ongoing manner in the treatment or include them but do not conduct the treatment in a child-friendly manner (Rober, 1998). Effective inclusion of young children in family therapy requires that the family therapist stay current on the changing demographics of children and families in our culture, be informed about the complexities of child development and family life cycle issues as related to families with young children, remain abreast of common child and family problems that often precipitate referrals for mental health services, and be familiar with the range of nonverbal and action-oriented techniques and psychoeducational approaches for working with families with young children. To create a safe culture for children in family therapy, the therapy should be conducted in a child-friendly room. The therapist should include and form a positive alliance with all family members, help the caregivers explain the purpose of therapy, become acquainted with the child separate from the chief complaint, and adapt his or her verbal and nonverbal communication to the child's developmental level (Rober, 1998).

Perhaps most important, the therapist needs to be able to play with the child and the family and help the child and family play together. This enables the therapist and family to have a mutual and enjoyable experience, helps families "stay alive," and produces more rapid, effective, and long-lasting change (Keith & Whitaker, 1981). Play is universal and is associated with healthy psychological development, creativity, self-expression, and meaningful interactions (Winnicott, 1971). As such, family therapy with young children that incorporates play provides a vehicle for individuals of all ages to become more psychologically adjusted and to form more secure and positive attachments.

REFERENCES

Alexander, J. F., & Pugh, C. A. (1996). Oppositional behavior and conduct disorders of children and youth. In F. W. Kaslow (Ed.), *Handbook of relational diagnosis and dysfunctional family patterns* (pp. 210–224). New York: John Wiley & Sons, Inc.

American Academy of Child and Adolescent Psychiatry. (1997a). Practice parameters for assessment and treatment. *Journal of the American Academy of Child and Adolescent Psychiatry, 36,* 69S–193S.

American Academy of Child and Adolescent Psychiatry. (1997b). The practice parameters for the assessment and treatment of children and adolescents with anxiety disorders. *Journal of the American Academy of Child and Adolescent Psychiatry, 36,* 69S–84S.

American Psychiatric Association. (1994). *Diagnostic and statistical manual of mental disorders— Fourth edition (DSM-IV).* Washington DC: American Psychiatric Association.

Ammerman, R. T., & Hersen, M. (Eds.). (1997). *Handbook of prevention and treatment with children and adolescents.* New York: John Wiley & Sons, Inc.

Andreozzi, L. L. (1996). *Child-centered family therapy.* New York: John Wiley & Sons, Inc.

Applebaum, D. R., & Burns, G. L. (1991). Unexpected childhood death: Posttraumatic stress disorder in surviving siblings and parents. *Journal of Clinical Child Psychology, 20,* 114–120.

Ariel, S., Carel, C. A., & Tyano, S. (1985). Uses of children's make believe play in family therapy: Theory and clinical examples. *Journal of Marital and Family Therapy, 11,* 47–60.

Armistead, L., Klein, K., & Forehand, R. (1995). Parent physical illness and child functioning. *Clinical Psychology Review, 15,* 409–422.

Bank, S. P., & Kahn, M. D. (1982). *The sibling bond.* New York: Basic Books.

Barkley, R. A. (1995). *Taking charge of ADHD: The complete, authoritative guide for parents.* New York: Guilford Press.

Bettoli-Vaughan, E., Brown, R. T., Brown, J. V., & Baldwin, K. (1998). Psychological adjustment and adaptation of siblings and mothers of children with HIV/AIDS. *Families, Systems, and Health, 16,* 249–266.

Bray, J. H., & Kelly, J. (1998). *Stepfamilies: Love, marriage and parenting in the first decade.* New York: Broadway Books.

Brestan, E. V., & Eyberg, S. M. (1998). Effective psychosocial treatment of conduct disordered children and adolescents: 29 years, 82 studies, and 5272 kids. *Journal of Clinical Child Psychology, 27,* 180–189.

Brown, R. T., Doepke., K. J., & Kaslow, N. J. (1993). Risk-resistance-adaptation model for pediatric chronic illness: Sickle cell syndrome as an example. *Clinical Psychology Review, 13,* 119–132.

Cabaj, R. P., & Purcell, D. W. (1997). *On the road to same-sex marriage: A supportive guide to psychological, political, and legal issues.* San Francisco, CA: Jossey-Bass.

Carter, B., & McGoldrick, M. (Eds.). (1989). *The changing family life cycle: A framework for family therapy* (2nd ed.). Boston: Allyn & Bacon.

Cederborg, A. C. (1997). Young children's participation in family therapy talk. *American Journal of Family Therapy, 25,* 28–38.

Chun, D. Y., Turner, J. A., & Romano, J. M. (1993). Children of chronic pain patients: Risk factors for maladjustment. *Pain, 52,* 311–317.

Clark, G. N., & Seifer, R. (1983). Facilitating mother-infant communication: A treatment model for high risk and developmentally delayed infants. *Infant Mental Health Journal, 4,* 67–82.

Combrinck-Graham, L. (Ed.). (1989). *Children in family contexts: Perspectives on treatment.* New York: Guilford Press.

Cramer, B., & Palacio-Espasa, F. (1993). *The practice of mother-infant psychotherapies: Clinical and technical studies.* Paris: Universitaires des France.

Culbertson, J. L., & Silovsky, J. F. (1996). Learning disabilities and attention deficit hyperactivity disorders: Their impact on children's significant others. In F. W. Kaslow (Ed.), *Handbook of relational diagnosis and dysfunctional family patterns* (pp. 186–209). New York: John Wiley & Sons, Inc.

Cummings, E. M., Davies, P. T., & Simpson, K. S. (1994). Marital conflict, gender, and child's appraisals and coping efficacy as mediators of child adjustment. *Journal of Family Psychology, 8,* 141–149.

Diamond, G. S., Serrano, A. C., Dickey, M., & Sonis, W. A. (1995). Current status of family-based outcome and process research. *Journal of the American Academy of Child and Adolescent Psychiatry, 35,* 6–16.

Duhl, K., Kantor, D., & Duhl, B. (1973). Learning, space and action in family therapy: A primer of sculpture. In D. Bloch (Ed.), *Techniques of family psychotherapy* (pp. 47–63). New York: Grune & Stratton.

Estrada, A. U., & Pinsof, W. M. (1995). The effectiveness of family therapies for selected behavioral disorders in childhood. *Journal of Marital and Family Therapy, 21,* 403–440.

Eyberg, S., Boggs, S., & Algina, J. (1995). Parent-child interaction therapy: A psychosocial model for the treatment of young children with conduct problem behavior and their families. *Psychopharmacology Bulletin, 31,* 83–91.

Eyberg, S. M., & Boggs, S. R. (1998). Parent-child interaction therapy for opposition preschoolers. In C. E. Schaefer & J. M. Briesmeister (Eds.), *Handbook of parent training: Parents as co-therapists for children's behavior problems* (2nd ed., pp. 61–97). New York: John Wiley & Sons Inc.

Eyberg, S. M., Edwards, D., Boggs, S. R., & Foote, R. (1998). Maintaining the treatment effects of parent training: The role of booster sessions and maintenance strategies. *Clinical Psychology: Science and Practice, 5,* 544–554.

Fanos, J. H. (1996). *Sibling loss.* Mahwah, NJ: Lawrence Erlbaum Associates.

Field, T. (1982). Interaction coaching for high risk infants and their parents. In H. A. Moss, R. Hess, & C. Swift (Eds.), *Prevention in human services* (Vol. 1, pp. 5–24). New York: Haworth Press.

Fleming, J. E., & Offord, D. R. (1990). Epidemiology of childhood depressive disorders: A critical review. *Journal of the American Academy of Child and Adolescent Psychiatry, 29,* 571–581.

Forehand, R., & Long, N. (1996). *Parenting the strong-willed child.* Chicago: Contemporary Books.

Fraiberg, S. (Ed.). (1980). *Clinical studies in infant mental health.* New York: Basic Books.

Gardner, R. (1971). *Therapeutic communication with children: The mutual story telling technique.* New York: Science House.

Gil, E. (1994). *Play in family therapy.* New York: Guilford Press.

Ginsberg, B. (1997). *Relationship enhancement family therapy.* New York: John Wiley & Sons, Inc.

Glick, P. C. (1989). Remarried families, stepfamilies, and stepchildren: A brief demographic profile. *Family Relations, 38,* 24–27.

Griff, M. D. (1983). Family play therapy. In C. E. Schaefer & K. J. O'Connor (Eds.), *Handbook of play therapy* (pp. 65–75). New York: John Wiley & Sons, Inc.

Guerney, B. J. (1964). Filial therapy: Description and rationale. *Journal of Consulting Psychology, 28,* 304–310.

Hetherington, E. M., & Clingempeel, W. G. (1992). Coping with marital transitions: A family systems perspective. *Monographs of the Society for Research in Child Development, 57,* 1–242.

Irwin, E. C., & Malloy, E. S. (1994). Family puppet interview. In C. Schaefer & L. Carey (Eds.), *Family play therapy* (pp. 21–33). Northvale, NJ: Jason Aronson.

Kahn, M. D., & Lewis, K. G. (Eds.) (1988). *Siblings in therapy.* New York: Norton.

Kaplan, S. J. (Ed.). (1996). *Family violence: A clinical and legal guide.* Washington, DC: American Psychiatric Press.

Kaslow, N. J., Deering, C. G., & Racusin, G. D. (1994). Depressed children and their families. *Clinical Psychology Review, 14,* 39–59.

Kaslow, N. J., & Racusin, G. R. (1990). Family therapy or child therapy: An open or shut case. *Journal of Family Psychology, 3,* 273–289.

Keith, D. V. (1986). Are children necessary in family therapy. In L. Combrinck-Graham (Ed.), *Treating young children in family therapy* (pp. 1–10). Rockville, MD: Aspen.

Keith, D. V., & Whitaker, C. A. (1981). Play therapy: A paradigm for work with families. *Journal of Marital and Family Therapy, 7,* 243–254.

Kendall-Tackett, K. A., Williams, L. M., & Finkelhor, D. (1993). Impact of sexual abuse on children: A review and synthesis of recent empirical studies. *Psychological Bulletin, 113,* 164–180.

Kobak, R. R., & Waters, D. B. (1984). Family therapy as a rite of passage: Play is the thing. *Family Process, 23,* 89–100.

Korner, S., & Brown, G. (1990). Exclusion of children from family psychotherapy: Family therapists' beliefs and practices. *Journal of Family Psychology, 3,* 420–430.

Kwiatkowska, H. (1978). *Family therapy and evaluation for art.* Springfield, IL: Charles C Thomas.

L'Abate, L. (Ed.). (1994). *Handbook of developmental family psychology and psychopathology.* New York: John Wiley & Sons, Inc.

Larner, G. (1996). Narrative child family therapy. *Family Process, 35,* 423–440.

Lee, C. M., & Gotlib, I. H. (1994). Mental illness and the family. In L. L'Abate (Ed.), *Handbook of developmental family psychology and psychopathology* (pp. 243–264). New York: John Wiley & Sons, Inc.

Lee, M. (1997). Post-divorce interparental conflict, children's contact with both parents, children's emotional processes, and children's behavioral adjustment. *Journal of Divorce and Remarriage, 27,* 61–82.

Lieberman, A. F., & Pawl, J. H. (1993). Infant-parent psychotherapy. In C. Zeanah (Ed.), *Handbook of infant mental health* (pp. 427–442). New York: Guilford Press.

Linesch, D. (Ed.). (1993). *Art therapy with families in crises: Overcoming resistance through nonverbal expression.* New York: Brunner/Mazel.

Lugaila, T. A. (1998). *Marital status and living arrangements: March 1997.* Washington DC: U.S. Bureau of the Census.

McCown, D. E., & Davies, B. (1995). Patterns of grief in young children following the death of a sibling. *Death Studies, 19,* 41–53.

McDermott, J. F., & Char, W. F. (1974). The undeclared war between child and family therapy. *Journal of the American Academy of Child Psychiatry, 13,* 422–436.

McDonough, S. C. (1993). Interaction guidance: Understanding and treating early infant-caregiver relationship disorders. In C. Zeanah (Ed.), *Handbook of infant mental health* (pp. 41–26). New York: Guilford Press.

McGreal, C. E. (1994). The family across generations: Grandparenthood. In L. L'Abate (Ed.), *Handbook of developmental family psychology and psychopathology* (pp. 116–131). New York: John Wiley & Sons, Inc.

Montalvo, B., & Haley, J. In defense of child therapy. *Family Process, 12,* 227–244.

Patterson, G. R. (1976). *Living with children: New methods for parents and teachers* (Revised). Champaign, IL: Research Press.

Racusin, G. R., & Kaslow, N. J. (1994). Child and family therapy combined: Indications and implications. *American Journal of Family Therapy, 22,* 237–246.

Rober, P. (1998). Reflections on ways to create a safe therapeutic culture for children in family therapy. *Family Process, 37,* 201–213.

Roberts, M. C. (Ed.). (1995). *Handbook of pediatric psychology* (2nd ed.). New York: Guilford Press.

Schatz, I. M. (1998). Meeting noodle face Noah: Child oriented family therapy. *Journal of Family Psychotherapy, 9,* 1–13.

Satir, V. (1972). *Peoplemaking.* Palo Alto: Science and Behavior Books.

Satir, V. M. (1967). *Conjoint Family Terapy* (Revised ed.) Palo Alto, CA: Science and Behavior Books.

Schaefer, C. E., & Briesmeister, J. M. (Eds.). (1998). *Handbook of parent training: Parents as cotherapists for children's behavior problems* (Second ed.). New York: John Wiley and Sons.

Schwartz, L. L., & Kaslow, F. W. (1997). *Painful partings: Divorce and its aftermath.* New York: John Wiley & Sons, Inc.

Seligman, S. (1994). Applying psychoanalysis in an unconventional context: Adapting infant-parent psychotherapy to a changing population. *Psychoanalytic Study of the Child, 49,* 481–500.

Shadish, W. R., Montgomery, L. M., Wilson, P., Wilson, M. R., Bright, I., & Okwumabua, T. (1993). Effects of family and marital psychotherapies: A meta-analysis. *Journal of Consulting and Clinical Psychology, 61,* 992–1002.

Silverman, P., & Worden, W. (1992). Children's reactions in the early months after the death of a parent. *American Journal of Orthopsychiatry, 62,* 93–104.

Steele, R. G., Forehand, R., & Armistead, L. (1997). The role of family process and coping strategies in the relationship between parental chronic illness and childhood: Internalizing problems. *Journal of Abnormal Child Psychology, 25,* 83–94.

Stern, D. (1995). *The motherhood constellation: A unified view of parent-infant psychotherapy.* New York: Basic Books.

Stith, S. M., Rosen, K. H., McCollum, E. E., Coleman, J. U., & Herman, S. A. (1996). The voices of children: Preadolescent children's experiences in family therapy. *Journal of Marital and Family Therapy, 22,* 69–86.

Thompson, M. P., Kaslow, N. J., Williams, K., Price, A. W., & Kingree, J. B. (1998). The role of secondary stressors in the parental death-child distress relation. *Journal of Abnormal Child Psychology, 26,* 357–366.

Trad, P. (1992). *Interventions with infants and parents: The theory and practice of previewing.* New York: John Wiley and Sons.

Trad, P. V. (1993). *Short-term parent-infant psychotherapy.* New York: Basic Books.

Tremblay, G. C., & Israel, A. C. (1998). Children's adjustment to parental death. *Clinical Psychology: Science and Practice, 5,* 424–438.

U.S. Bureau of the Census. (1997). *Statistical abstract, 117th edition.* Washington, DC: Author.

Van Fleet, R. (1992). Using filial therapy to strengthen families with chronically ill children. In L. Vandecreek, S. Knapp, & T. L. Jackson (Eds.), *Innovations in clinical practice: A sourcebook (Vol. 11).* Sarasota, FL: Professional Resource Press.

Van Fleet, R. (1994). *Filial therapy: Strengthening parent-child relationships through play.* Sarasota, FL: Professional Resource Press.

Visher, E. B., & Visher, J. S. (1996). *Therapy with stepfamilies.* New York: Brunner/Mazel.

Wallerstein, J. S. (1991). The long-term effects of divorce on children: A review. *Journal of the American Academy of Child and Adolescent Psychiatry, 30,* 349–360.

Watt, N., Anthony, E. J., Wynne, L., & Rolf, J. (1984). *Children at risk for schizophrenia.* New York: Cambridge University Press.

Webster-Stratton, C. (1996). Early intervention with videotape modeling: Programs for families of children with oppositional defiant disorder or conduct disorder. In E. D. Hibbs & P. Jensen (Eds.), *Psychosocial treatment research of child and adolescent disorders: Empirically based strategies for clinical practice* (pp. 435–474). Washington, DC: American Psychological Association.

Wells, K. C. (1988). Family therapy. In J. Matson (Ed.), *Handbook of treatment approaches in childhood psychopathology* (pp. 45–61). New York: Plenum Press.

Whiteside, M. F. (1989). Remarried systems. In L. Combrinck-Graham (Ed.), *Children in family contexts: Perspectives on treatment* (pp. 135–160). New York: Guilford Press.

Winnicott, D. W. (1971). *Playing and reality.* London: Tavistock Publications.

Wolfner, G. D., & Gelles, R. J. (1993). A profile of violence toward children: A national study. *Child Abuse and Neglect, 17,* 197–212.

Zilbach, J. J. (1986). *Young children in family therapy.* Northvale, NJ: Jason Aronson.

CHAPTER 11

The Midlife Family:
Dealing with Adolescents, Young Adults,
and the Marriage in Transition

Ellen Berman and Augustus Y. Napier

THE MIDLIFE EXPERIENCE

Midlife—which is defined here as between the ages of 40 and 65 years—comprises a huge and rapidly changing span of human experience. Although the adult development literature is many decades old (Erikson, 1963; Jung, 1933; VonGennep, 1909/1960), it was only with the publication of Sheehy's (1974) *Passages* that the idea of life stages and the "midlife crisis" became part of the national vocabulary. Since then the portrait of midlife painted by the popular press is one of an intense and troubled time of life, one full of anguish and reorganization.

Midlife is doubtless a challenging time. During these years we must come to grips with the aging of the body; we have increasing difficulty denying the inevitability of death. The sometimes turbulent separation of adolescents from the family must be reckoned with, as well as the needs of our aging and often failing parents. Long-standing marriages may present their own hurdles: Patterns that have felt mildly unsatisfactory may suddenly feel intolerable; ambitions and yearnings squelched in the interest of family unity can come roaring to the surface. New marriages at midlife often begin laden with the complex histories and commitments of each partner, including their children and ex-spouses. Single parents may feel emotionally exhausted and financially stretched. For adults traversing midlife, it may feel that if they are ever going to achieve something or enjoy something, it must happen now, before the ravages of age claim them.

Nevertheless, an ongoing 10-year study of nearly 8,000 midlife Americans conducted by the MacArthur Foundation Research Network on Successful Mid-life paints a more sanguine picture. "On balance, the sense we all have is that midlife is the best place to be," summarized Orville Gilbert Brim, director of the study (Goode, 1999). Recent books in the MacArthur (MIDMAC) series include Lachman and James (1997), Rossi (1994), Ryff and Seltzer (1996), and Shweder (1998). (For a thorough bibliography of this impressive body of collaborative research, contact www.midmac.med.harvard.edu.)

The MacArthur team found that between the ages of 35 and 65 years, but particularly between 40 and 60 years, people reported increased feelings of well-being and a greater sense of control over many parts of their lives. A majority of participants in the study reported feeling better about their lives than they had 10 years before; many also estimated that they felt younger than their chronological ages. A minority of individuals (23 percent) reported undergoing a midlife crisis, and of that group only one-third described the crisis as being brought on by the realization that they were aging. The others attributed the sense of crisis to specific events in their lives unrelated to aging. Those who did experience a midlife crisis scored higher on a neuroticism scale and had higher levels of education.

Of those surveyed by the MacArthur research group, 70 percent described their health as excellent, and there was a strong sense of optimism among the midlife population about their health and the prospects for it in the future. Nor did menopause reveal itself to be the universal scourge portrayed by Sheehy (1991). A majority of women felt "only relief" when their periods stopped. Even during their fifties, the peak time for menopausal symptoms, half of those surveyed reported having few or no symptoms.

A striking finding was that on scores of psychological well-being, both men and women achieved gains in personal autonomy and in effective management of the surrounding world, but the women gained larger increments in these areas. This finding is consistent with the research of others that found increases in the sense of optimism and power in women as their children matured (Apter, 1995).

Despite the high rate of divorce in the United States, a majority of participants in this study described their marriages or relationships as stable and relatively happy. Certainly many had not had an easy life. The parents in the study had made substantial sacrifices to help care for their children. Women were more likely to have cut back on work or moved to flexible schedules, while men had worked extra hours to meet the costs associated with their children. Women felt that they shouldered the bulk of household chores and child care, and their husbands tended to overestimate their own contributions in this arena. However, 90 percent said that it was "not very likely" or "not likely at all" that their relationships would eventually break up. More than half reported that in the past year they had "never" thought their relationships were in trouble.

At the older end of the age continuum, both sexes reported a loss in "personal growth" and in the sense that their lives had a purpose. These older individuals were also less optimistic about the prospects for their health in the years ahead.

Although not the final word on midlife, this group of studies provides a valuable context for the clinician, whose clients are likely to be drawn from the 23 percent who have some kind of crisis during this time. Trouble may come from a number of quarters: from the problems of an adolescent or young adult child, from the couple's marriage, from the death or illness of a parent, from job loss, from an accident or non–age-related illness or trauma. Although midlife is complex, the perspective of the MacArthur study is that these are generally good decades for people, where most feel satisfied with their lives, and despite worries about the future make impressive personal gains.

Coincident with baby boomer researchers turning 40 and then 50, a remarkable number of books on midlife have surfaced in the last 10 years including (Anderson & Stewart, 1994; Apter, 1995; Berquist, Greenberg, & Klaum, 1993; Hunter & Sondel, 1989; Jones, 1989). Taken together, these books provide a comprehensive and generally positive look at the period.

Although this sense of well-being and of personal options may be true of middle and upper socioeconomic classes, the view of life for the less economically secure is not as rosy. As Blacker (1999) points out, with plant closings, corporate downsizing, and the increased reliance on technology in American industry, poor families face decreasing job opportunities. Working-class men whose work depends on their physical effort may feel old in their thirties, and without adequate health care, they may not live to enjoy retirement. Working-class women may expect to carry both full-time work and full-time homemaking throughout their lives, and they may be forced to work at unfulfilling jobs. This bleak picture seems particularly true for African American men who have high rates of heart disease and stroke.

THE MIDLIFE FAMILY

Vast changes in society have produced 12-year-olds with children, 45-year-old mothers with newborns, and 65-year-old men having babies with their new young wives while grandparenting their older children's offspring. Midlife parents may be dealing with children anywhere from age 1 to past 40. In addition, the modal couple is marrying later than at any previous time in the past 50 years, pushing the active childbearing period later in life for an increasing number of parents (US Bureau of the Census, 1999).

Because midlife is a span of 25 years, and active adolescence, even defined as 12–20, is only an eight-year period, much of midlife family life will be spent with either school age or young adult children. Adolescence, however, is such a complex and demanding time that the adolescent experience often dominates the research on the period, as well as consuming the attention of the parents. A predictable stress for the midlife family is the effort of rearing adolescents in a world that is more hazardous for teenagers, and more anxiety-provoking, than the one in which most of the parents grew up (Pipher, 1994).

Meanwhile, parents are dealing with midlife issues, which may impact their ability to deal with their rapidly changing children. Grandparents as well are experiencing change. While some become ill and need care, others may deal with aging by beginning new marriages or work projects. In many cases they are less available to provide emotional or practical support than they had been a few decades ago.

Given the rapid cultural changes and the lessened predictability of each stage of the life cycle for each generation, at any particular time the needs of different generations of the family may be in conflict or in synchrony.

The Adolescent Child

The child may need time, space, and security for the development of adolescent identity, and may need emotional and financial support in the process of leaving for work or college. The experience of adolescence has changed dramatically in this country in recent years, as teens are far more at risk than in years past. A 10-year study of adolescence by the Carnegie Council on Adolescent Development (1995) reported that nearly half of American adolescents are at high to moderate risk for alcohol and drug use, unprotected sexual activity, delinquency, eating disorders, victimization by violence, and depression (cf. Pipher, 1994). Today's child may be in particular need of a comforting familial holding environment. Near-adult children may wish for available and unchanging parents while learning how to connect with them as fellow "grown-ups."

The Parents

Parents, on the other hand, may need all of their own energy to deal with a midlife problem or a marital dilemma, and they may find the adolescent's need for attention and emotional expression a major trial. They may not be ready to see their children leave home, or they may be glad to have them out of the house so they can concentrate on a new marriage, travel, or a late-life baby. Although the major emphasis in the early family therapy literature has been on the parent who will not let go, parents are often ready to treat their child as independent long before the child is ready. Pipher (1994) found that the majority of parents seeking help for their adolescents were tried, overworked, overcommitted to a number of activities, and struggling with financial issues; often they had little emotional support. The troubled adolescent, then, is often underattended-to by beleaguered parents, and may demand parental limits and attention by acting out.

Marriages may improve or dissolve when the children leave home. One theme, as is evident in the MacArthur studies, reflects the increasing sense of happiness and well-being in some couples as their children are launched. The familiar "U-shaped" curve of marital satisfaction reflects a sharp downward drop in satisfaction after marriage, a trend that continues downward until the children leave, at which time the curve trends upward again (Glenn, 1990). We should note, however, that there is disagreement about the evidence of a U-shaped curve of marital satisfaction over time. As Bersheid and Reid (1999) report, in the absence of adequate longitudinal data, it is difficult to be confident about the estimates of the temporal progression of satisfaction in marriage. Some researchers (Vaillant & Vaillant, 1993) have found a continuous decline in satisfaction, particularly for wives.

Another theme is the rise in divorce around midlife. After the initial high rate of divorce in the first two years of marriage, the next peak occurs at around 15 to 18 years of marriage; there is a third spike after 25 to 28 years (Shapiro, 1996). These couples may be stressed by midlife changes and difficult adolescents, or may realize that, without their children to connect them and to give their lives meaning, there is little to hold them together.

The high incidence of divorce in midlife means that a high proportion of adolescents is exposed to at least some period of major stress; in acrimonious divorces, teenagers may endure several years of confusion and often a period of parental emotional unavailability as the divorced spouses rebuild their own lives. Single parents with several children may not have the emotional or financial reserves to focus on all of them, particularly if a child is at high risk (Sandmaier, 1996). Children with attention deficit disorder are especially vulnerable to family stress during adolescence (Everett, 1999). During and after divorce, parents may exhibit what Isaacs, Montalvo, and Abelson (1986) term *the abdication dynamic,* in which they are so demoralized by divorce that while they may go through the motions of parenting, they are essentially absent as effective parents in their children's lives.

The System of Parents and Adolescent or Launching Children
Key issues for the system of parents and adolescent or launching children include the process of retaining an emotional connection in the face of the rapid growth and change of the adolescent child. Gilbert (1997) found that teens who felt close to their parents engaged in fewer risky behaviors; high expectations for school performance also had a positive effect. The salient issue seems to be a level of parental involvement, of "paying attention," that leads teens to feel supported emotionally. Parents also face the difficult challenge of relaxing rules and giving adolescents appropriate control over their lives, while setting reasonable limits on a young person who may have poor judgment and limited experience in dealing with complex issues. It is also difficult to provide emotional support for adolescents who confide little about their dilemmas and who may seem much more independent

than they are. If the adults are in crisis or have leftover family-of-origin issues about adolescence or launching, these transitions will be particularly complex. In the larger family
system, illness in grandparents or other older family members may add still more stress.

The Adult Individual

Key issues for the adult individual in midlife include developmental and narrative change,
the search for greater meaning in life; work issues, including burnout, the entry into a second career, the threat of downsizing, and ageism in the workplace; and couple issues such
as the feeling of unfilled potential in each partner. If long-established patterns in the marriage seem to stand in the way of the individual's fulfilling his or her potential, the validity of the marriage may be called into question. As we examine these issues, we will draw
on concepts of human development within the family system, and on the concept of the
individual and family narrative.

As they complete age-related tasks, both individuals and systems change in consistent
ways. Struggles with developmental tasks introduce complexity and depth into the system,
increase the use of more mature defenses (Vaillant, 1977), and hopefully increase the wisdom and resilience of the individual and family.

THE CONCEPT OF NARRATIVE

The concept of narrative is one key to understanding the midlife family. In Chapter 4,
Becvar describes this process in some detail, and points out that "meaning construction
occurs as a process of storytelling" (p. 70). Many stories can be told about a particular
event, and the process of choosing a particular story is a complex one. Certain narratives
are situated in the culture and may change dramatically over time. For example, cultural
narratives around the abilities and needs of women have changed dramatically in the last
30 years.

At a private level, all events are "storied" by the person and family living them, and this
story constitutes their lived reality. For example, a family may see cancer in one of its
members as a sign of family weakness and helplessness, or as a proof of survival in the
face of terrible odds. The development of an adolescent identity is partly a development of
a consistent story of the self, mediated by peer and parental stories that reflect back to the
young person "mirrors" of themselves. Because midlife is changing so rapidly, there are
fewer cultural narratives about the "right" way to be. In adulthood there are also fewer biological imperatives than in childhood. Midlife in particular, therefore, is developed and storied according to the changing situation of the individual and of the family (Braverman &
Berman, 1997).

As a couple enters and begins to move through midlife, both partners are strongly influenced by the story of their parents' midlife experience. If a woman's stay-at-home mother
became depressed and demoralized when the children left home, she may panic at 40, dramatically increasing her workload, for example, or suddenly going back to college. Similarly, a man whose father fell apart emotionally and started drinking when he was fired at
50 may try to insulate himself from this possibility by deliberating leaving his job to
become an independent contractor.

As Becvar points out in Chapter 4, the individual's ideas about childhood, maturity, and
old age are profoundly related to cultural norms and belief systems. For example, the idea
of "launching" looks very different in cultures where young people remain in the parental
home until they marry and then move next door or into the family home or compound. The

definition of the proper role of elderly parents in this country ranges from independent good time occasional babysitters to family elders and advisors to primary child-care provider depending on the area of the country and ethnic group. Each role provides different satisfactions, fills different needs for independence versus connection, and affects the finances and moods of the participants. We should be knowledgeable about each family's cultural and ethnic traditions, and we should be wary of imposing our own values and prescriptions on them (Hines, 1998).

THE ADOLESCENT

TASKS OF THE ADOLESCENT

The adolescent individuates within an intense and ongoing relationship with parents whose presence is still central to his or her existence. Tasks that must be accomplished are developing a coherent sense of identity, developing some comfort with sexuality, connecting with peers, and learning competence in dealing with the adult world. In this process the adolescent begins the long journey of taking responsibility for the self, which culminates (hopefully) in mature functioning during the twenties. Adolescents must cope with rapid body change as they mature physically and sexually. The capacity to engage in moral and abstract reasoning develops as brain maturity progresses. As with any rapid change, this growth may be welcome or not, and may progress smoothly over time or in sudden spurts. Although adolescence can be a period of high volatility and risk for adolescents, it is seldom continuously turbulent and can be calmer and more comfortable than one would believe from reading the research (Gilbert, 1997).

Early adolescence is very different from later adolescence. Young teens may want more responsibility but most are clear that they do not yet want to be on their own. By midadolescence, there is an internal demand for self-determination—a wish to depend less on their parents and more on themselves or their peers for emotional support and guidance. In teens without a good sense of self-esteem or a comfortable peer group, this drive for autonomy can lead to intense loneliness and depression. Teens genetically vulnerable to depression may have their first episodes at this time; lonely children with a history of parental depression and high family stress are particularly vulnerable. Older teens are hopefully more secure in themselves and the world, better at controlling impulses and setting goals. A 16-year-old in this country can become an emancipated minor, hold a job, get married, or go to college early. In some areas it is still not unusual for 18-year-olds to get married and begin families. By this time values and personality patterns are somewhat set.

The sexual maturation of children and concurrent development of sex-typed cultural roles are central themes of the period. Sexual maturation in girls is seen as risky, not only in terms of potential pregnancy or rape but because of cultural confusion about women's sexuality. Our highly sexualized society still contains deeply ingrained ideas that "nice girls don't," while at the same time maintaining that sex is normal and healthy for teenagers (Brumberg, 1997).

Until recently, European-American culture encouraged a young woman to wait, without developing a sense of her own identity, to be claimed by a man. Girl's self esteem is still lower than boys throughout adolescence (Gilligan, 1982). On the other hand, male developmental norms compel bold and often risky behavior as a proof of manhood.

Because they can lose as well as gain a sense of "manhood," the imperative for boys to be strong and powerful has a dark side (Pittman, 1993). Fathers and mothers may deal very differently with their same and opposite sex adolescents (Steinberg, 1987). The boy's preference for his father, the discomfort of some fathers with their daughter's sexuality, and the mother's response to her daughter's individuation may all dramatically alter the family's patterns.

Teen behavior is highly culture bound. In most historical periods, adolescence as a separate period did not exist. Early teens were still regarded as children, and often looked like children; puberty did not occur until 14 or 15. By 15 or 16, children were full-fledged adult workers. Twentieth century Western culture, with its increasing demands for a technically educated population, encourages continued dependence on families and continued schooling into the twenties. The mainstream cultural narrative is that teens are rebellious, unmanageable, and part of a separate culture. For middle-class children, adolescence is a private community, a time of exploration and not much responsibility. However, poor and rural children may begin work along with school much sooner, or participate in caretaking in extended families; it is assumed that they will take their place in the community without much fuss. In some communities of urban poor where there are many struggling single mothers and the larger community of church and neighborhood has fragmented, teen males are often on the streets and out of parental control by age 13 or 14. They may replace parental control with that of a gang. In many Asian communities and in religious communities such as Orthodox Judaism and Amish sects where respect for parents is an integral part of the culture, overt teen rebellion is far less frequent, and obedience rather than experimentation is the norm. In these communities, teens and young adults continue to follow parental advice in most circumstances, at least until marriage and often beyond.

THE ADOLESCENT IN THE SYSTEM

The adolescent moves out into the world in fits and starts, periodically returning to a younger way of relating, and then demanding more rights or simply behaving in a more adult and distant way. In many families where basic values are shared and children and parents have had relatively comfortable and reasonable relationships, these are not all-out wars. The rebellions here are often around curfews, piercing, clothing, or specific religious practices rather than alcohol, drugs, or dangerous behaviors (Hill, 1987). Some adolescents individuate by quietly developing most of their "real" or emotional life outside the house, providing little information about this experience to parents. This distancing is somewhat more common among male children; females are more likely to demand recognition of their maturation and to struggle openly with their parents, particularly with their mothers (Apter, 1990).

Nancy Chodorow (1978) has written about the daughter's difficulty in separating from her mother, positing this individuation struggle as a long-standing and central aspect of the mother-daughter relationship, one in which the mother often projects her own needs onto her daughter. Chodorow, with others, sees the boy's development in terms of a much earlier separation from the mother, often earlier than the boy is ready for. Napier (1988) has commented on the difficulty for boys in pulling away emotionally from their mother without a secure and supportive link with the father. Noting that the culture has traditionally devalued the connection between mothers and sons, Silverstein (1994) has made a persuasive case that women can raise boys successfully in the absence of fathers.

Adolescents are part of patterns of division and coalition within the family, and their attempts at separation often threaten the parents. Adolescents also challenge the parents' authority, sometimes precipitating the parents into regression (as the adolescents remind the parents of their own parents or siblings). Some parents overreact, coming down much too hard on their adolescents, particularly if the adolescent threatens to repeat a traumatic experience in the parent's history. Some parents conveniently see their children as more mature and independent than they really are, and thus neglect these children's needs for support (Pipher, 1994).

Adolescents have a keen sense of justice and injustice. They sense fakery and hypocrisy and will often act up to force the family to face denied issues. They also see injustice in a parental relationship and are easily recruited into assisting the subordinate parent in defying the dominant parent. These teens are flattered to be invited into alliance within the parental generation and can quickly assume an omnipotent stance in challenging the dominant parent, almost always at their own peril. When adolescents challenge the dominant parent (with a covert wink from the one-down parent), they are often attacked by the dominant parent, and they may eventually be disavowed by the parent with whom they are in coalition. When this happens, the adolescent feels acutely betrayed and may disconnect from both parents. Occasionally, the subordinate parent will stand up for a child who is being treated unjustly, and marital issues in these families can escalate sharply.

Many adolescents are invisibly neglected (for a thoughtful discussion of this issue, see Stierlin, 1981). They may seem relatively responsible, but their underlying needs are not met by the parents, who may be preoccupied by their own problems: depression, addiction, marital issues, health concerns. Parents' willingness to ignore their adolescents' needs may have complex origins in the parents' own childhood neglect.

A common dynamic in the family with adolescents, particularly among older adolescents who are driving automobiles and are active in the outer world, involves a trading of anxiety about the adolescents' movement in this larger world. Parents are anxious about their children, but often are unable to articulate or describe this anxiety to their children without blaming them. Parents focus on dangers, with frequent warnings and scoldings. Adolescents are also anxious about their own vulnerability; by being provocative or by taking risks, they unconsciously signal their parents to worry about them. Parents then come down hard on their teens, who are relieved at not having to worry about facing the dangerous world—"My parents will do the worrying for me." So parents become the "bad guys" and the adolescent is preoccupied with getting around these anxious parents' limits and need not worry as much about becoming competent in the adult world. Parents may also be relieved to avoid their own relationship by focusing on their children's struggles. Adolescents who really need emotional support may opt instead for anxious surveillance; at least they are getting adult attention.

Adolescent radicalism is a powerful stimulus for parents. If the parents' own parents were authoritarian, they may allow their children to push limits in ways the parents never dared do. These parents may also be harsh with their teens when the parents' own internalized values are violated—"I couldn't talk to my parents that way, and even though I have allowed you to develop a wicked tongue, I must punish you for violating my parents' injunctions." Similarly, parents may be powerfully stimulated by their children's visible (and sometimes exhibitionistic) sexuality, and both encourage and punish sexual acting out. As a way of participating vicariously, a parent who is excessively involved with an adolescent may become deeply intrusive into the child's sexual adventures.

When adolescents sense that their parents are drifting apart emotionally, they may unconsciously seek a way of bringing the parents together. The adolescent may act out so dramatically that the parents are forced to team with each other. This is especially true when the father has been progressively distancing and the children worry that he will leave the family. Adolescent boys are particularly likely to mount such a challenge, because they feel that they urgently need a connection with their father in order to face the outside world. Often the boy's mother augments the crisis by becoming increasingly ineffective in dealing with the rebellious boy.

Adolescents may also challenge their parents' hypocrisy by embarrassing the family publicly. A minister's teenage son gets caught drinking on a school trip and is suspended from school, embarrassing both of his image-conscious parents. Underlying this challenge may be the adolescent's sense that if he or she is to get through adolescence and into adulthood successfully, the parents must be shocked into facing the family's hidden conflicts.

One of the things that can make this era so volatile is an "adolescent sensibility" in some parents. That is, if the midlife parents feel rebellious (often covertly) against the strictures of convention and obligation in their own lives, they may subtly encourage the boldness of their children, and they make take rebellious positions vis-à-vis each other vis-à-vis the adolescent. The outbreak of primitive emotion in the adolescent side of both generations may make rational thought and discourse problematic during these years. Parents in crisis (or workaholics or parents in the process of divorce) may also choose to ignore problematic behavior in their children until it blows up. To a large extent this is related to the age of the parents. Such issues may be far more likely with parents aged 45 than 55 years.

Stierlin (1981) has identified several patterns that develop between parents and adolescents as the separation process unfolds. Napier (1988) has made several modifications in Stierlin's typology that seem to make it applicable to a wide variety of clinical situations.

Bound Children

These children are tied in several ways to their parents: in an older-generational or parentified ("assistant parent") pattern; in a peer or Oedipal pattern, which can include the adolescent as buddy or friend to the parent; or the adolescent can be trapped in an infantilized or exaggerated child position. These teens are bound to parents because of parents' needs, and they are often thus prevented from individuating. These dynamics are common in the classic enmeshed family system.

Rejected Children

In spite of family therapy's early focus on enmeshment, rejected children constitute the largest group of symptomatic adolescents. Some adolescents are acutely rejected, as when a single mother remarries and her teenager, who has been her emotional support, feels suddenly displaced. Others have been rejected throughout life because of parental projections of badness. Another subset of children are invisibly neglected or ignored. Some of these may be the "good children" in a family that has a learning disabled or ill child, or that is struggling too much financially to have energy for quiet children. These children are sometimes high achievers who work very hard for small crumbs of parental approval. Some are the financially indulged children of well-to-do parents whose minds and hearts are elsewhere. These young people may be perceived as mature until they become dysfunctional.

Delegated Children

The "positive" delegate lives for the parents, who may be overly invested in this achieving child's school career or other exploits. These children are often not seen as troubled, yet they may live their lives in an effort to please their parents to such an extent that when they marry, they ignore the needs of their own children and spouse. Achievement-oriented fathers may have a favorite delegate child, but mothers without their own career interests may also overinvest in a child's star status.

The "negative" delegate gets covert reward for acting out. This is the teen who engages in multiple piercing and "dresses Goth" to challenge "square" dad, then is not supported by his mother who has covertly encouraged the rebellion. Negative delegates do get some reinforcement for their acting out, but it often comes at a high price. The classic rebellious family scapegoat is usually a negative delegate.

All of these dynamics are exacerbated by parental divorce. Every divorce constitutes a major family stress, and almost everyone in the family may be temporarily dysfunctional. Some teens recover rapidly and mature quickly, either speeding up their moves toward independence or developing a helping stance within the altered family. Teens caught in the crossfire between parents may be forced into one of the patterns described above. For example, the bound child may become one or both parents' emotional support through the divorce. One co-dependent adult client described her panic as a teenager when she realized that her mother was about to divorce her father. Afraid that her father would give up on life, she devoted her afternoons to watching television with him in an effort to cheer him up.

As we work with midlife families, it is important to remain aware that much adolescent misbehavior is unconsciously motivated by the adolescent's anxiety about the family's functioning. Although adolescents have their own interests at heart (they need adequate parenting), they are often willing to go to great lengths to expose the parents' marital problems, and to try to get the parents to change. In fact, we might think of the troubled adolescent as an amateur therapist in the midlife family (Napier & Whitaker, 1978).

LAUNCHING

The process of becoming an adult in a complex technological world is taking longer and longer. Becoming responsible for themselves financially and emotionally will often occupy adult children throughout their twenties. In the past, when young adults married and had children early, much of this maturation was done within the new family of procreation, which provided at least some boundaries and new rules within which to operate. However, the delayed age of marriage has left many late twenty-somethings with only their family of origin defined as family; therefore, the active engagement between parents and their young adult children may remain high. Although parents vary greatly in their ability to let go, young adults also vary greatly in their ability to take on responsibility for themselves. During this individuation period, the family may alternate between times of stability and times of turmoil, and adult children may orbit both close to and far from the nuclear family.

The parental process of remaining connected to a child who appears independent and out of the house is complex. It is hard for a parent who has not talked to a child in two or three weeks (or talked to them of anything of substance for months) to realize that the child is having constant conversations with them in his or her head. Particularly if the young person has been very close to the parents, there may be a period of distancing while the child learns to hear his or her own voice. Although this distancing is distressing to parents, it is seldom permanent. Many young adults take several years to choose a life's work and an intimate partner. Parents must learn to accept the child's choices, whether or not they coincide with the parents' dreams. When the parents accept their child's adult decisions, this child is often free to develop closer ties to the parents.

As the near-adults mature and begin to leave, both the parents and the children become anxious about this transition. How will the young adult fare in the adult world? How will the parents cope with the empty nest? The departure process is heavily influenced by social class, gender, and cultural issues. Girls of working-class parents may stay close by, while boys may be freer to separate from home. The more affluent family can afford for the children to go farther, as to a distant college; but many parents experience intense financial pressures as they help children with school or startup costs. Although these financial and emotional demands on the the midlife couple occur at a time when their earning power should be at its peak, any unplanned event—such as a job loss or the needs of failing older parents—can strain financial and emotional resources of the midlife couple. If their child is struggling psychologically or has a serious illness, the parents may be physically and emotionally exhausted by the demands placed on them.

The child who returns home after an attempt at individuation, or who remains at home much longer than in past decades, has become a familiar figure in the contemporary family (Aquilino, 1991). Although this near-adult may be at home largely for financial reasons—attending a nearby college or looking for a job—he or she may also be responding unconsciously to the family's emotional needs. This "adult" may have been poorly supported emotionally as a child and may return home in an unconscious effort to garner missed experience, sometimes with a particular parent:

> May and Terry, a lesbian couple, began a relationship in their forties. Each had been previously married. May's child, Amy, had been an adolescent during her mother's divorce and was very distressed by the divorce and May's change in orientation. She had ADD and had not done well in school. In addition, her relationship with May had always been conflictual. She began college but was unable to finish. She began to work in a nearby city, but spent most holidays and many weekends at May and Terry's house, arguing with her mother and sleeping a lot. May's guilt over the divorce and the problems of Amy's childhood led her to refuse to set limits on Amy's at-home behavior, infuriating Terry, who felt that the problem was Amy's irresponsibility. Therapy focused initially on helping May begin to set appropriate limits with Amy, then shifted to the deficits in Amy's relationship with her mother, and finally included work on Amy's relationship with her father. Amy also worked on issues regarding her learning disability. As Amy's relationship with her parents improved, the conflict between May and Terry abated.

It is difficult, however, for some parents to provide their adult children or even older and married children with emotional or financial support without attempting to control them, or without fostering an unhealthy dependence.

> Bob and Ginger, now in their early sixties, were very busy professionals when their four children were teenagers, and there was a good deal of conflict between them and their often undersupervised children. When their only daughter, Patricia, married a man from

Canada and had a child, Bob and Ginger began a campaign to persuade the couple to live near them. But because Bob was so controlling with the young couple, not only did Patricia's husband resist moving the family to Philadelphia, but he began to resent his in-laws coming to visit. Patricia was also angry about her parents' pressure, complaining that her parents were not available when she was a teenager and seemed eager to control her as an adult. Bob and Ginger sought therapy about their grief in feeling cut off not only from Patricia but also from another of their children; only with coaching did they begin to rebuild their relationships with their adult children.

When the empty-nest parents find that it is really their marriage that is empty, they may divorce, and their newly independent children may be drawn back to the family to help mediate between parents or to support them emotionally. Even when unhappily married parents do not divorce, the young adult may remain close to home because of concern about depression in one or both parents. In some instances, a parent may actively attempt to block the child's attempt to marry. In others, the adult child may marry but have difficulty developing loyalty to the new marriage. Because father absence is so common in our society (Pittman, 1993), sons—as substitutes for absent fathers—may have problematic ties to their families of origin, especially to their mothers. These bound sons may feel torn between their felt obligations to their mothers and the strong societal mandate to separate:

Tim, an only child, was his mother's closest companion after her divorce from Tim's father. As his father distanced from Tim as well as his mother, there was little support for Tim's efforts to leave home. When Tim began to date Sonya, she was the "girl with a bad reputation" in his high school, where Tim's mother was a teacher. Anxious about Tim's choice, his mother tried to break up the relationship; but the harder she tried to interfere, the more attractive Sonya seemed to Tim. Only when Sonya became pregnant did Tim's mother begin to accept the relationship, and then only grudgingly. Following their graduation from high school, Tim pushed for them to move in with his mother, where tensions between mother-in-law and daughter-in-law escalated sharply over issues of the care and control of the new baby. Sonya eventually took the baby and left, filing for divorce. Tim came into therapy several years later. He had remarried a woman with two children. Tim's mother remained a powerful force in his life; conflicts between Tim and his second wife also centered around his close ties to his mother.

In both of his marriages, Tim's wives had borne most of the burden of trying to set limits—and thus having conflict with—Tim's mother. Torn between his loyalty to his mother and his loyalty to his wife, Tim had retreated to a safer, neutral distance. In the therapy process, Tim's second wife learned to avoid fights with Tim's mother, and Tim for the first time began to stand up to her directly. As he did this, his marriage became less conflictual, but his mother's distress accelerated dramatically. With some assistance from her family doctor, she eventually joined a women's support group that helped her adjust to a life with less connection with her son.

In this as in many other interpersonal situations, the women in the system tend to be the main connectors. When problems occur, the apparent antagonists are likely to be the women as well, regardless of blood ties. Men who have not been socialized to take responsibility for intimate relationships may step aside and "let you and her fight." In mother-son conflicts, it is also common to blame controlling mothers, while the profound absence of fathers in the system may be the determining dynamic (Blankenhorn, 1995).

When it occurs, the turbulence of midlife may place marriages in both the parental and young adult generations at risk. If the marrying young adult responds to family turmoil by making a precipitous (and often early) marriage, this marriage is especially vulnerable to divorce (Glick, 1990). As we have noted, the midlife couple may be destabilized by the launching process, and may also be more likely to divorce. The fact that there are peaks of divorce in the first two years of marriage and around year 25 suggests that the transitions of midlife contribute to marital instability in both younger and older generations.

As we work with midlife families, we may have a good opportunity to intervene positively in the lives of young adults in the system. We may, for example, refer the marrying couple for premarital counseling where they can examine the choices they are making. If Tim's family had been in therapy when Tim was considering marriage for the first time, years of conflict and struggle might have been avoided.

The process of launching also demands that parents learn to add new members to the family: first, the partners of their young adult children, and then grandchildren. While the stereotypic mother-in-law believes that no one is good enough for her child, the truth is that parents are often happy to meet the partners of their children (and their families), and they often form close relationships with them. If the young adult has a series of long relationships that do not include marriage, the parents must also learn to accept and then lose not-quite-family members to whom they might be quite attached.

In some circumstances these parents may also find themselves as primary parents or backup caretakers of their grandchildren:

> At age 20, James and his girlfriend Pat had two children. Because the young couple worked weekends and were unable to find child care, James' mother Emma took over full care of the children during the weekend—in addition to her full-time job as a housekeeper. Although this arrangement created stress between Emma and her husband (and James' father) Tom, Emma felt better that the children were taken care of and that she had a good relationship with their mother. This arrangement continued even after James and Pat split up.

While the young adult who is struggling to separate from his or her family is often a good candidate for individual therapy, involvement of the family in treatment has many advantages. Not only can the therapist work with the young adult, but the deficits in the parents' relationship—or the stress of the single parent—can begin to be addressed. The successful transition for the adult child may necessitate the binding parent's learning to turn loose, but it may also involve becoming closer to a parent from whom the child has been cut off or distant. Becoming closer to a distancing parent may be just as important as gaining separateness from an over-close parent, as it frees the young adult from a persistent sense of rejection by this parent. Although family work may be initially focused on the young adult's difficulties, the emphasis may later shift to work on the midlife couple's relationship. Our clinical experience indicates that when the parents address their own relationship in therapy, the launching child is often freed to begin adulthood in earnest.

THE COUPLE AT MIDLIFE: LONG-TERM MARRIAGES

The midlife marriage is a core family subsystem under pressure. Although many of the stresses impinge from outside the marriage, there are also complex dynamics within the relationship that may have persisted over many years. During midlife, increasing external stress may intensify these dynamics or dislodge long-maintained patterns within the marriage. In fact, the couple may allow these stresses to impact them in ways that create a powerful incentive for change; indeed, both partners are likely to be unhappy about some of the long-term stasis in the relationship. Although the couple may on some level welcome change, they also fear it.

The following are some areas affected by the forces of midlife.

THE BALANCE OF POWER AND FULFILLMENT

Has this been an egalitarian marriage with equal but divided realms of power, or the more thoroughly egalitarian pattern of shared tasks—both, for example, participating in care of the home and the children? Has this been a traditional, male-dominated system? Or has the wife been the dominant person in the relationship? In their review of the relationship between marital satisfaction and marital power, Gray-Little and Burks (1983) found that egalitarian marriages are the most satisfying, that traditional marriages are not far below them in the approval of both partners, and that wife-dominated marriages are the least satisfying for both partners. Gray-Little and Burks state that the findings about unhappiness in wife-dominated marriages have been replicated worldwide, perhaps because in so many countries this arrangement runs counter to historical and cultural expectations.

Although marital power is determined by a wide range of attributes, from personality to IQ to gender, it is closely tied to success and earning power in the world of paid work. The partner with the highest income typically has the most power in the marriage (Blumstein & Schwartz, 1983). Although there are many types of power (including the power of helplessness) and many ways of dividing it (e.g., wife has more say in child-focused decisions and the husband final say in spending large sums of money), cultural norms still tilt toward the man's having final decision-making power over a wide range of areas.

A recurrent finding has been that women's power increases as the family's children mature; the MacArthur studies (Goode, 1999) confirm the general improvement in women's sense of control over their lives during this period. Particularly for the current midlife population, where the women often began their work involvement after the children were grown, wives may be deeply involved in new careers at the same time their husbands feel burned out by work and are ready to cut back. This discrepancy in work involvement may create conflict between the couple; it may also lead to a pleasant complementarity in the marriage in which the husband is freed to participate more actively in family life and home care while he supports his wife's career.

In families where the wife's career has been successful and her husband's more marginal, she may reach her peak work years while her husband continues to struggle or feels increasingly like an occupational failure. Husbands in this situation may become seriously depressed. The same kind of painful imbalance in functioning may also occur in the traditional family where the husband's career becomes increasingly demanding and financially rewarding just as the children are leaving home. Robbed of her sense of purpose and meaning in relation to her children, the mother of these individuating children may also become very depressed. Because current young-adult women with children are mostly in the work force already, men's and women's trajectories in midlife may become more similar in the decades to come.

Whatever the history of power sharing in the couple, midlife creates a sometimes intense push in both partners to live out their incomplete identities. The husband who has not been successful may urgently seek fulfillment. One man who had had a somewhat unsatisfying job and had done much of the child care while his wife was a busy physician, suddenly quit his job and started a software company. When a larger firm bought out his young company, he decided, without thorough negotiation with his wife, to accept a job at the company's regional headquarters, throwing the family into crisis. Although this marriage survived the husband's passive-aggressive coup, the wife left her thriving practice at great cost to herself, and the couple was in therapy for several years to work out this traumatic reorganization.

Clinically, one must look for the areas of overfunction and underfunction within the internal and external lives of the couple, and one needs to support the partners in balancing their experience in a way that is fulfilling to both. As couples work through the midlife years, it is important that each partner address his or her yearnings for different or more fulfilling experience, and that the couple thoroughly negotiate how they will live out these years.

INTIMACY AND SEXUALITY

As couples begin to confront the passage from youth to old age, their desire for greater intimacy and for deeper sexual fulfillment comes to the fore. Emotional distance, sexual problems, or both, that may have been frustrating when they were busy rearing children and building the family "establishment" may become intolerable. As each child leaves, the partners may feel increasing panic about what life will be like when the two of them are alone. These teenagers and young adults' emerging sexuality may increase the parents' awareness of their own sexuality, but the teenagers' late hours and their watchfulness of their parents may make privacy harder to find. The economic pressures on midlife parents may also leave them exhausted. They may yearn for more sexual satisfaction but find scant time or energy to pursue it. They may also fear facing the very issues that they intuitively know will emerge as they deal with their sexual relationship: early family-of-origin experiences around sexuality, and traumatic episodes within their marriage, such as a prior affair, which may need to be revisited.

Positive potentials for intimacy in the midlife family may come from several quarters: from the wife's increasing sense of control over her life, from the husband's greater interest in the life of feeling and inner experience, and from both partners' sense of general well-being. Often husbands have tired of the world of competition and hyper-rationality, and they sense what they have missed in the private world of relationships, not only with their children but also within their marriages. Of course the well-chronicled midlife crisis in which the man flees from his awareness of aging by having an affair with a younger woman is an option chosen by some. Although the affair can be a way in which either partner can leave a stale midlife marriage, the affair can also lead in some instances to a rejuvenated relationship, particularly if the couple seeks help (Napier, 1999).

In spite of the negatives of midlife couples' aging bodies, which may include the disturbances of menopause and men's slowing sexual response, most couples find their children's departure from the home a freeing and rejuvenating experience (Apter, 1995). Women may feel especially freed-up with the children out of the house, and men's greater willingness to be vulnerable and expressive may lead to increased tenderness and sexual pleasure between the couple. In following the data from the MacArthur study, Goode (1999) points out that midlife individuals often feel younger than they are, and that they are often not bothered by the signs of aging. Schnarch (1997) has been particularly emphatic in maintaining that the midlife couple's greater personal maturity produces increased sexual well-being in these marriages. The advent of Viagra has also altered the sexual dynamics of many marriages, bringing a sense of excitement to many aging men and their partners. In couples where the wife has been sex-avoidant, however, the husband's increased pressure for active sexuality may be a destabilizing force.

COMMITMENT

As children leave home, and as both partners achieve autonomy that may have been absent earlier in the marriage, the question of what holds them together becomes powerfully central. The couple must confront the meaning of their relationship on its own terms, without the practical justification of child rearing. If they have specialized in very different areas of life, can they find pleasure and companionship in joint activities? As they have more time together, can they have fun, or are they only "business partners"? Finding few activities that draw them together, couples may develop new and more shared interests, or they may remain in separate spheres. As couples approach the era when they are simply a couple again, they may reexperience some of the same conflicts and pleasures of early marriage: time to be alone together, but conflicts about how to organize that time. And where their specialized realms may have separated them over the years, they now need to build common activities and interests.

BOUNDARY ISSUES

As relationship patterns shift, the alignment of spouses with each other and significant others shifts. If the wife's most significant intimacy is with the youngest daughter, this daughter's departure may precipitate a depression in the wife, and the husband may be mystified by this development. A child who has left home and married may return following a divorce or economic setback, disrupting the couple's newfound intimacy. As they reenter the midlife couple's life, the parents' parents may ask for a level of emotional support that they did not give during the middle-aged adult's childhood. These sometimes-rapid fluctuations in the midlife family's boundaries demand flexibility on the part of the family, and rigidly organized families may have great difficulty with these shifts.

ACCUMULATED HISTORY

Years of living together have created a reservoir of accumulated need and feeling; the couple must find ways to deal with this backlog of affect and feeling. Where are the unprocessed traumas in the history of the relationship? What areas of affect have been difficult for the couple? What process areas need attention if the couple is to move past old injuries and grievances? Perhaps they have fought constantly and not allowed themselves tenderness or softer emotions. Perhaps there has been an underfunctioner and an overfunctioner—and both are tired of this sense of imbalance.

Midlife couples may overrespond to the patterns their own parents played out in midlife, attempting, as Boszormenyi-Nagy and Spark (1973) suggest, to "balance the books" on a perceived injustice in their own histories. In trying to rectify a historical inequity, they are likely to create a new imbalance in the present family. Misunderstanding and conflicts between the midlife partners may also grow out of the overdriven effort to avoid repeating the past. In one couple, for example, the husband saw his mother verbally abuse his father and witnessed the father's descent into depression and early death. The wife's father had treated her mother abusively, with the same tragic result. As these partners approached the age at which they had seen their same-sex parents deteriorate psychologically, each became extremely anxious about being treated disrespectfully and became hypervigilant about being controlled.

Although midlife adults may overcompensate in an effort to avoid replicating a parent's past, they are also strongly drawn to repeating a variation of that past. (See Napier, 1988, for several clinical examples.) For example, Chuck's father died of a heart attack at age 46, due in part to high levels of marital and job distress. Chuck believed he would die early as well. As he turned 40 he paid more attention to diet and exercise. He also quit his career as a chiropractor to go into home renovation, a way of reactivating his childhood dream of being an architect. Because he was new at the work and felt he had to make every moment count, he kept extremely late hours, exhausted himself, and alienated his wife. This precipitous job change created far more stress than he had before; at the point he entered therapy, he had developed high blood pressure.

The long walk through family-of-origin issues, past old hurts, and accumulated emotion is extraordinarily difficult for the couple to do alone. The therapist can provide a protected space where the couple can attempt to relive past hurts, where they can search for areas of forgiveness, and where they can seek support in developing a more positive narrative of their relationship. This work on their relationship narrative needs to include acknowledgment of the couple's prior successes, and it should take into account the intrinsic meaning of the narrative to both partners. If the couple seems to be considering divorce because the prospect of dealing with many years of accumulated anger seems too frightening, the therapist can try to offer a safe place—and emotional process—in dealing with these pressures.

NARRATIVE CHANGE

The powerful triggers of unfinished business in the couple interact with issues of aging to profoundly alter the couple's narrative. A quiet marriage that was previously identified with security may suddenly seem unbearably dull. One member of the couple may feel old and wish to retire as the other feels young again and wants adventure. The midlife process of life reassessment may cast a harsh glare on previous struggles. The therapist needs to help the couple examine the process of how and why their previous narrative no longer seems to fit, and to help them find new frames that allow for more creative thinking (Braverman & Berman, 1997).

COUPLE TYPOLOGY

Braverman and Berman (1995) have identified three general types of long-term marriages.

Generative Marriages
These marriages are basically alive and growing, but they may be at a temporary impasse. The emotional connection between the partners remains strong, and each person's change is relevant and involving to the other. In these marriages therapy usually takes off, and the couple uses the therapist to get past a temporary block or confusion.

Devitalized Marriages
In devitalized marriages the structure of the marriage and a basic sense of commitment remain, but the partners lead largely parallel lives, with most of their affect connected to their children, their friends, and their work. There may be submerged caring in these marriages, but there is also a lot of unexpressed anger and emotional distance. These couples are highly vulnerable to affairs and to a pervasive sense of boredom. The therapist's job

here is to explore any remaining affect and aliveness in the marriage, and to help the couple walk through the issues of continued commitment.

Toxic Marriages

In toxic marriages, projection and distortion create a sense of depression and dread that slow or halt the growth of each of the spouses. Depression, substance abuse, and emotional or physical abuse are common in such marriages. The therapeutic task is to decrease the damage; often a good deal of individual work is needed as well. For at least one of the partners, divorce may be a good solution. (For a thorough look at marriages in which one or both the partners have diagnosable disorders, see Carlson and Sperry, 1988).

NEW MARRIAGES AT MIDLIFE

New marriages at midlife are most often remarriages for one or both partners. Both their strengths and their weaknesses as remarried couples stem from the partners' previous lives. Twenty years of experience as adults usually provides the new spouses with more clarity on their own needs and wants, as well as more patience and wisdom. There may be more companionship and friendship in remarried relationships, and more intensity. On the other hand, the accumulations of a lifetime, from their separate histories of long-established habits and rituals, to the complexities of their finances, to their relationships with their ex-spouses and children, must somehow be managed. If both partners have matured as people, they may be able to handle some of the complexities of remarried midlife, but their chances of divorce remain higher than in first marriages.

If both partners have substantial conflicts with their ex-spouses, they may be tempted to focus their negativity on their former partners in order to avoid dealing with conflicts in their current marriage. The difficulties of their children from these former relationships may add to their temptation to avoid current relationship problems, and scapegoated children may become the targets for negativity among all the adults in these postdivorce and remarried couples. These complex step-families are described in Chapter 18.

THE COUPLE IN THE LARGER SYSTEM

At times during midlife, the couple is buffeted from all quarters by the winds of change; at other times there is relative quiet. Because of rapid change in children, younger midlife tends to be the most complex. The couple's opportunities for change are also dependent on larger system issues such as income and social class, career opportunity, and the differing positions of older men versus older women in society.

THE WORLD OF WORK

Although at one time the financial welfare of a family might have been tied to the continuity of the husband's job, often with one employer, the days of employment stability seem to be over, at least for the foreseeable future. Corporate reorganizations and downsizing have made employment uncertain even for the successful midlevel executive. Mergers and acquisitions make layoffs or major reassignments more likely for all employees, especially those without advanced skills or education. If both partners are employed—as they are in the majority of families—these dual incomes give the family greater options; they also make the family doubly vulnerable to employment instability.

Another force impinging on the midlife family is the atmosphere of intense pressure from the job. From the construction worker to the executive, the performance pressure in today's business environment is enormous: competition for contracts, inflexible deadlines, quotas, and loading of additional responsibilities bear heavily on the family (Jacobs & Gerson, 1998). Couples who badly want to make changes in their careers may continue to work at unsatisfying jobs solely for health care coverage.

Other families are disrupted by success. At a time when the needs of adolescent and young adult children for emotional and financial support are most intense, they may be overridden by a parent's promotion that necessitates a move to another city (or country). Not only are the adolescents taken out of the matrix of peer support that they need, but the other partner may be forced to leave a satisfying job. These decisions are often excruciating for couples, and they may be made without adequate processing by the couple: "Of course you can't pass up this opportunity." This kind of disruption is especially likely for the ambitious and successful employee who is approaching the height of his or her potential at work.

THE EXTENDED FAMILY

Several factors make providing support for the grandparent generation complex. The death or disability of one of the grandparents not only presents the midlife individual with his or her own grief, but the surviving grandparent may turn strongly to the younger family for support. Especially if a widow or widower moves near the midlife family, or must be moved nearby to ensure his or her care, the disruption in the lives of the sandwich couple can be severe. On the other hand, having grandparents nearby may be a helpful and supportive process:

> Joan, 41, and Peter, 42, a recently married couple, had a "difficult-to-raise" child. When the child was one, Joan decided not to return to work as a nurse, and her husband, a lawyer, became the sole breadwinner. Peter's long hours, and his exhaustion when he came home, made him less involved in family life. When Joan's parents retired, they decided to leave their home and move near Joan's new family. Within a year Joan's mother, with whom Joan had an intense and complex relationship, developed cancer. Although it was an enormously stressful time, Joan was able to support her parents through her mother's chemotherapy and finally her death. Joan felt good about her ability to remain strong, helpful, and involved with her mother, and this involvement did much to resolve the tensions in the mother-daughter relationship. After her mother's death, Joan's father took on a more active role with Joan's daughter. Joan began to know her father better, and she was also able to resume part-time work because of his availability for child care.

The needs and demands of the older parent can be especially difficult if the midlife adult was treated badly by that parent (or parents) as a child. It both feels and is terribly unfair for the older adult to turn in a needy and narcissistic way to the midlife adult who as a child received little support from this parent. These parental demands create both rage and guilt in the middle-aged individual, who often does not know how to manage these turbulent feelings and who—because of the parent's obvious vulnerability—may transfer anger to a spouse or adolescent child.

In many instances, relationships between the midlife siblings are disrupted by shifts in the needs of the grandparent generation. The individual who is singled out as the focus of the older parent's needs may have been the parentified caretaker in the original family; the reactivation of this role may seem especially unfair in the light of this individual's sibling's responses. In addition, this may be a time when older siblings become ill or incapacitated. Sibling relationships at this stage can be a source of great strength or great distress. Feuds between siblings in the midlife generation can involve their children as well, so that the adolescents lose potential sources of support from uncles, aunts, and cousins.

> Jessie, 48, took responsibility for moving her father—who suffered from dementia— near her home; with her husband's support she began to supervise the demanding father's care. Not only did these new responsibilities place strain on her marriage, but when her brother began to align with the father in resisting both the move and the attempts by the personal care home to care for the father, old resentments between brother and sister broke into open confrontation. Jessie's sister supported her efforts, but a coordinated plan to deal with the father evolved only when the three siblings met with a family therapist near the brother's home.

Although the physical and emotional decline of older parents can place acute demands on the midlife couple, these stresses, if dealt with openly and in a "teamed" way by the extended family, can also allow the resolution of long-buried historical events and feelings. Particularly as death draws near for older parents, they too may want to address these issues. This extended family work needs to proceed carefully, with consideration for the vulnerability of the older parent.

THE DIVORCED EXTENDED FAMILY

Just as the aging process may bring siblings and parents together in an effort to confront their difficult histories, the coming of age events of the individuating adolescents and young adults may also force a confrontation of long-standing angers and hurts in divorced (and often remarried) midlife parents. When the young adult, for example, graduates from high school or college, or marries, or has a baby, these ritual events often precipitate encounters between individuals who may have avoided each other for years but who may have conscious or unconscious needs to resolve old conflicts.

The marriage of the young adult is an especially potent event for postdivorce networks. If the young couple becomes our client, we may be able to help them negotiate this transition in a growthful way. Sometimes the challenge is for the young couple to manage a difficult situation with minimal conflict. At other times, one of the partners may want to do more than get through the public occasion; he or she may see the wedding (or other event) as an opportunity to resolve some old conflicts.

We may also be approached by midlife parents who are concerned about their relationship with their adult child. If the young bride-to-be, for example, wants to invite both of her divorced parents to the wedding, and her father and his new wife have a hostile relationship with the young woman's still-single mother, the parents may be able to initiate negotiations or conferences that can involve the entire network. The possibilities in this scenario are invariably complex, and intervention requires careful planning and a measure of diplomacy in assembling the extended family network. Preliminary meetings with subsets of this network and the evolution of certain rules for proceeding may be necessary. This kind of intervention may be more successful if a team of at least two therapists carries it out.

If it is done skillfully, work with the extended family, either the family of origin or the complex postdivorce network, can be satisfying for all concerned. The therapist's involvement in the complexities of these systems may allow the family to attempt—and succeed at—conversations that without the help of the therapist may seem too high-risk. The feelings held in abeyance by these family members provide a powerful "engine" that drives the therapy process; the therapist's job is to help the family manage these often turbulent feelings and to turn them toward a positive outcome. Although families may at first resist such meetings, it is our experience that they often want to resolve the old issues between them, and that the major work of the therapist is to keep the family focused on their stated agendas and to monitor the emotional safety of the conversations.

THE MIDLIFE INDIVIDUAL

In the past 25 years, the idea of a predictable life cycle for adults has undergone a series of changes. The dramatic alterations in adult life that we have described in this chapter have led some to question whether the concept of a predictable life cycle has any value at all. However, certain events that are biologically based are somewhat time-linked, and the idea of an individual life cycle as a way of organizing data still has usefulness, even if it cannot be seen as a definitive truth.

Ever since life expectancy increased past the 50-year mark, midlife has been a period of self-invention, more unpredictable than the textbooks would suggest. Because of this increased life span (expected age now 80 and rising), it is possible to have more marriages, second and even third careers, and time for more introspection or more regret and bitterness. The possibilities for reinventing the self and changing one's family, career, and lifestyle seem endless, and midlife can be a time of beginnings, endings, or both. In Sheehy's (1995) *New Passages,* she postulates a truly altered time line: provisional adulthood from 18 to 30, first adulthood from 30 to 45, and second adulthood from 45 to 85, with the fifties as the age of mastery.

BIOLOGY

The biological markers for early midlife include clear signs of aging—thickening waist (or more exercise to keep a slim one), and changes in hair, eyes, stamina, and short-term memory. Over the 20-year period, there is an increase in chronic and annoying illnesses, and some increase in life-threatening ones. Medical science has greatly improved both prevention and tertiary care, enhancing our ability to remain healthy. An unintended result is that not only health but also the appearance of youth are expected, at least in the affluent middle class. The obstetrical-gynecological community has made remarkable strides in allowing later and later pregnancies for women, which has altered the family life cycle and in some groups is now another way of being young. Sexual changes of midlife commonly involve some decrease in sexual interest for men and women, although sexual functioning is so connected to relational and self-esteem issues that it is hard to tell apart biology and life circumstances.

Menopause for women occurs in later midlife—age 50 to 55. Although the psychological changes attributed to menopause in the past are exaggerated, perimenopause (the period of hormonal irregularity preceding the end of menstruation) may set off difficult mood swings that have a negative impact on the family. (For a good review of menopausal issues, see Daniluk, 1998, pp. 241–270.)

Beginning in midlife, people who do not exercise are far more prone to heart disease and other illnesses. Men whose sense of self is dependent on serious athletic involvement will be increasingly troubled by decreased stamina and physical ability. Fewer women have their athletic prowess as such an integral part of their identity, but they may worry about changes in appearance or fitness. The biological changes of midlife often force a confrontation with the self, setting off the narrative changes described below.

IS THERE A MIDLIFE CRISIS?

The early midlife person today still faces the fact that young adulthood is over, even though old age may be far away. There is a sense of lost possibilities, for many options are closed, including the early adult belief in infinite possibility. One can have new and exciting sex and learn a great deal about oneself, but certain opportunities may be truly closed—ballet dancing as a career, for example—while others may appear closed. A man with a wife and small children and very little money probably imagines he cannot give up his job and go to medical school, although some people have done it. However, a person's life may still undergo enormous change. It is possible for a person who was alcoholic in early adulthood to get sober and get going, for an unskilled laborer to be retrained, for a woman to start a post–child-rearing career. It is possible for a man to go from CEO to carpenter, or as in the last election, from wrestler to governor. It is also possible for a man who ran the family business to find when the family business is sold that he has no skills outside the business, or conversely that he is more valued outside the family than in it.

Somewhere in the initial decade of midlife there is usually a transition period that is a critical period in the person's development. The midlife transition, or series of transitions, is essentially a narrative change. The midlife transition occurs when the narrative shifts to include the awareness of mortality, and the understanding that one is in the middle of life and not the beginning. Whether brought on by events or feelings, there is a period of life review in which the person reappraises his or her life, developing a coherent story about the past and present. On the basis of that review, the individual begins to plan for the future. Sometimes, minitransitions may occur. For example, a career woman may be surprised to discover at 39 that a life without children is empty and may downsize her career and have a baby. This may change her feelings about the past, and also her self-identity. This may allow her to feel young, since a person with a small child is still a young mother. When her child turns 14, she may abruptly experience herself as middle-aged. When she is 57 and that child leaves home, she may reevaluate her life again and make new life decisions based on that reevaluation.

Part of this evaluation process involves forgiving the self for sins of omission and commission. A person who feels that her mistakes are unforgivable or her future is hopeless will be unable to create a functional life. Depending on the story created, one may continue the previous life structure and enjoy it, spend the next several years creatively changing, or give up in despair.

Although the direction of change may not be predictable, the midlife transition causes each adult to rethink his or her place in the family. A 40-year-old may try to make peace with a parent or give up on them, may reconnect with an adolescent, or ignore him or her. It is the therapist's task to use the energy inherent in transition periods to promote growth and healthy connection.

Particularly in midlife, it is clear that the story one constructs is truly a construction rather than a truth, and that the definition of success or failure is about belief rather than reality. Because he compared himself to his great-grandfather who had been a senator (who ran for president) and to his father who had been a wealthy businessman, a reasonably well-known physician who ran a division of a department in an excellent medical school considered himself unsuccessful.

A midlife crisis occurs if the person cannot construct a narrative that makes sense, if one constructs a narrative of failure and becomes depressed, or if the individual comes to believe that selfhood lies in jettisoning one's entire life structure. In such situations, people are apt to make drastic decisions under the influence of poorly understood emotions. Such choices, especially those involving affairs, divorces, and major work transformations, often result in serious unraveling of the person's life, and these dramatic shifts may take years to repair.

THE SINGLE PARENT AT MIDLIFE

Divorce has increased the number of people living single at midlife. Depending on one's beliefs about what constitutes a worthwhile life, living single can be either a source of great pleasure (Anderson & Stewart, 1994) or a source of tremendous pain and anomie. Permanent singles have usually established a functional support network by midlife, but the newly divorced or widowed often have to develop a new support system. This is often difficult in midlife, when everyone else seems busy with their own families and networks. In such situations, depression is an ever-present possibility, especially among older single men.

The single custodial parent of adolescents, particularly if they have more than one child at home, is often under great stress. Even when one has financial and emotional support, teens are far more difficult to parent in the uncertain context of many single parents. Because most custodial parents are women (who are paid less at work and often receive little child support), trying to parent, work, and find time for a social life can be extremely complicated. If the parent is still depressed and bitter from the divorce, the situation often worsens. Noncustodial parents, most often fathers, may find it difficult to maintain a relationship with their children, and many disappear into new lives and families. As a man begins a life review, this sense of failure as a father may deeply impact his sense of himself. For men who are paying child support, finances may be stretched to the limit at a time they thought they would be free and clear.

GENDER AND CULTURE IN THE MIDLIFE FAMILY

GENDER

Gender deeply affects midlife issues and choices, including identity, work, and self-image. In most families, women provide most of the hands-on child care and emotional management, even when husbands or paid help participate. Even when women are in the labor force, their attention and time are divided in a way men's are not, and they are more apt to move in and out of work as family needs require. Women now in their late fifties often began new careers in midlife after the children left. Women now in their forties are likely to be already deeply involved in a career path in addition to child rearing. They may be extraordinarily busy, especially if they also want friends and a community life. In very high commitment careers, such as law or business, women often downsize their careers radically at around 35 in order to have children. The end of child rearing is usually experienced as a major shift in identity for women, and can mean liberation or a sense of worthlessness. Men, on the other hand, tend to see themselves as supporting the family by working. They are not likely to alter a career path for children, or to have a sense of changing identity when their children leave home. Launching may come as a shock, however, as they grieve the years they were disconnected from family life.

AGEISM

Ageism is also a serious issue, especially for women. Midlife and older women in this country are devalued in a society obsessed with youth, whereas midlife men are still seen as powerful and sexual beings. Divorced midlife men will most likely remarry, often to women 5 to 10 years younger. Divorced midlife women are apt to remain single, not necessarily by choice. Women's self-esteem often rises, however, as they learn to respond less to cultural norms and more to their own needs.

CULTURAL ISSUES

Although cultures differ in their assignment of roles for children and the elderly, all cultures assume that midlife persons will hold positions of respect and authority in the workplace or family. Class, however, strongly affects possible outcomes and choices at midlife. One's position at midlife is highly determined by the education and opportunities available in young adulthood. It is clearly more difficult for poor and working-class people to change their lives and to find new options at midlife. When they do, these changes are more likely to be in non–work-related areas, such as in their families or avocations. Because jobs for the poorly educated are often repetitious or physically demanding, workers get burned out physically or emotionally. Macroeconomic trends also determine issues and choices in midlife. Periods of economic growth and peace allow for more choices; in periods of economic retrenchment, midlife people may lose jobs they cannot replace.

THERAPY WITH MIDLIFE FAMILIES

Therapy goals for individuals and couples include the following:

1. Take midlife itself seriously as part of the therapy. Evaluate as much of the complex matrix of variables affecting the family as possible.
2. Work on acknowledgment and integration of undeveloped or hidden parts of the client's self.
3. Focus on helping each partner accept the other as a uniquely different and idiosyncratic human being.
4. Help the couple move to the place where they can see each other's often quite different needs.
5. Help the couple negotiate thoroughly any changes they plan to make in their lives.
6. Explore different stories of midlife that the partners bring to the marriage and to their lives. Help them choose optimistic and hopeful outcomes.

Three therapeutic problems stand out in the midlife family—how to treat couples whose dysfunctional patterns have been in operation for 20 years or more; how to help discouraged midlife people find meaning in their lives; and how to help complex step-family systems with multiple family members from previous marriages.

Dealing with long-married couples is a difficult art. Because the midlife transition has already made them question everything, some partners come to therapy ready to change. Some spouses are forced to come by the partner. Unless there is a compelling reason to do so, it is difficult to get people to change set patterns. Common pressures for change include desire for personal growth, the possibility of divorce, or an adult child who threatens to cut off a relationship unless a parent changes. The therapist must question the narrative of the couple and work toward one that permits possibilities for growth. This usually requires a careful search through the past for alternative stories.

Discouraged midlife individuals, coupled or not, need to understand the reasons for their sense of meaninglessness. Usually these involve multiple personal losses, a sense of personal failure, or a physiologically based depression. Depending on the situation, grief work, locating new support networks, antidepressants, and work on self-forgiveness are frequently helpful. In the face of the client's despair, the therapist's own optimism about life is perhaps the most central component of therapy.

Complex step-family systems require willingness to make careful family maps and to see multiple members of the family. Sessions in which everyone is included are difficult but helpful (Sager et al., 1983). When a child in the divorced family is experiencing difficulty, often we are contacted by only one parent or household. In many instances, the father is out of touch with his children, and it is extremely important to involve him (or the noncustodial parent) in the therapy. (For a discussion of these issues, see Isaacs et al., 1987; also see Kaslow, Chapter 18.)

The problem for the therapist of the midlife family is simple to state but difficult to resolve: It is very challenging for any one therapist to be versatile and wise enough to treat the wide range of life experiences in these complex systems. Therapists' feelings about midlife clients stem from their own midlife narratives and life experience. In general, it is easier to work with midlife couples when one is over 35 and has some sense of what aging issues are like. However, midlife therapists in the middle of their own transitions, or feeling burned out, may find it difficult to be reassuring or optimistic. Therapists over 60 must be sharply aware of the cultural changes that have shaped today's 40-year-olds. The male therapist in his late fifties or early sixties, for example, may find it difficult to understand the commitment to gender balance in the age-forty couple, and he may fail to support the wife's efforts to maintain her career while also being intimately involved with her children. The younger therapist may have an even more difficult time. How does the therapist with kindergarten age children understand and help the family with acting-out adolescents? Although intellectual grasp of the issues is vital, deeper levels of understanding and empathy may be lacking if the therapist has not passed through, and to some extent mastered, the stage of life he or she is attempting to help the client family through.

The therapist can ask the family to teach him or her about life events that are unfamiliar. But when the therapist's life experience limits him or her in working with a particular family constellation, bringing in a cotherapist or consultant may be the most effective bridge to the family's situation. A male-female cotherapy team is often a helpful solution to dealing with complex multigenerational family issues. In many instances the individual therapist's deficits are partly compensated for by mutual sharing and teaming, an arrangement that presents many modeling opportunities for the client family.

Therapists must also grasp, and help the family grasp, the three-generational context of their dilemmas. One of the most exciting aspects of working with the midlife couple is the opportunity—if not the necessity—of working intergenerationally. In many families, it is difficult to find a satisfying resolution that does not involve parents, children, and grandparents. For example, if a mother is being critical of her daughter and is fearful of her daughter's sexuality, and if the mother became pregnant with this daughter during her own rebellious and unsupervised adolescence, the deepest resolution of this problem may be to bring in the mother's parents to work on family-of-origin issues of hurt and abandonment (Vaillant, 1997). While the mother in this instance can improve her relationship with her daughter, working on her own adolescence with her parents allows her to bring a deeper level of hopefulness to her daughter.

The midlife family is a complex and difficult system to treat. Buffeted by time and circumstance, it can be stubbornly resistant to change, and at other times confusingly fluid and turbulent. This family encompasses such a wide range of human experiences that we can never be fully adequate in meeting its challenges, but in trying to help, we inevitably learn, and then learn some more.

REFERENCES

Anderson, C., & Stewart, S. (1994). *Flying solo: Single women in midlife.* New York: Norton.

Apter, T. (1990). *Altered loves: Mothers and daughters during adolescence.* New York: St. Martin's Press.

Apter, T. (1995). *Secret paths: Women in the new midlife.* New York: Norton.

Aquilino, W. S. (1991). Predicting parents' experience with coresident adult children. *Journal of Family Issues, 12,* 323–342.

Berquist, W., Greenberg E., & Klaum, G. (1993). *In our fifties: Voices of men and women reinventing their lives.* New York: Jossey-Bass.

Bersheid, E., & Reis, H. T. (1999). Attraction and close relationships. In D. T. Gilbert, S. T. Fiske, & G. Lindzey (Eds.), *The handbook of social psychology* (4th ed.) (pp. 193–281). New York: McGraw-Hill.

Blacker, L. (1999). The launching phase of the life cycle. In B. Carter & M. McGoldrick (Eds.), *The expanded family life cycle* (3rd ed.) (pp. 287–306). Boston: Allyn & Bacon.

Blankenhorn, D. (1995). *Fatherless America.* New York: Basic Books.

Blumstein, P., & Schwartz, P. (1983). *American couples: Money, work, and sex.* New York: Morrow.

Boszormenyi-Nagy, I., & Spark, G. M. (1973). *Invisible loyalties.* New York: Harper and Row.

Braverman, L., & Berman, E. (1995). *The middle of the journey.* Paper presented at the 18th Annual Family Therapy Networker Symposium, March 25, Washington D.C.

Braverman, L., & Berman, E. (1997). *Marriage at mid-life.* Paper presented at the 19th Annual Family Therapy Networker Symposium, March 27, Washington D.C.

Brumberg, J. (1997). *The body project. An intimate history of American girls.* New York: Random House

Carlson, J., & Sperry, L. (Eds.) (1998). *The disordered couple.* Philadelphia: Brunner/Mazel.

Carnegie Council on Adolescent Development. (1995). *Great transitions: Preparing adolescents for a new century.* New York: Carnegie Corporation.

Chodorow, N. (1978). *The reproduction of mothering.* Berkeley, CA: University of California Press.

Daniluk, J. (1998). *Women's sexuality across the life span* (pp. 241–270). New York: Guilford Press.

Erikson, E. (1963). *Childhood and society.* New York: Norton.

Everett, C. (1999). *Understanding and treating ADHD within the family.* New York: Guilford Press.

Gilbert, S. (1997, September 10). *Youth study elevates family's role.* New York Times.

Gilligan, C. (1982). *In a different voice.* Cambridge, MA: Harvard University Press.

Glenn, N. D. (1990). Quantitative research on marital quality in the 1980s: A critical review. *Journal of Marriage and the Family, 54,* 818–831.

Glick, P. (1990). American families: As they are, and were. *Sociology and Social Research, 74,* 139–145.

Goode, E. (1999, February 16). Middle age is prime of life. *New York Times.*

Gray-Little, B., & Burks, N. (1983). Power and satisfaction in marriage. *Psychological Bulletin, 933,* 513–538.

Hill, J. P. (1987). Research on adolescents and their families past and present. *New Directions for Child Development, 37,* 13–32.

Hines, P. (1998). Climbing up the rough side of the mountain. In M. McGoldrick (Ed.), *Revisioning family therapy: Race, culture and gender in clinical practice* (pp. 327–345). New York: Guilford Press.

Hunter, S., & Sondel, M. (Eds.). (1989). *Midlife myths: Issues, findings and practice implications.* Newbury Park, CA: Sage Publications.

Isaacs, M. B., Montalvo, B., & Abelson, D. (1986). *The difficult divorce.* New York: Basic Books.

Jacobs, J., & Gerson, K. (1998). Who are the overworked Americans? *Review of Social Economy,* Vol. LVI, No.4, Winter.

Jones, R. (Ed.). (1989). *Black adult development and aging.* Berkeley, CA: Cobb & Henry.

Jung, C. G. (1933). *Modern man in search of a soul.* New York: Harcourt, Brace.

Lachman, M. E., & James, J. (Eds.). (1997). *Multiple paths of midlife development.* Chicago: University of Chicago Press.

Napier, A., & Whitaker C. (1978). *The family crucible.* New York: Harper/Collins.

Napier, A. (1988). *The fragile bond.* New York: Harper/Collins.

Napier, A. (1999). Experiential approaches to creating the intimate marriage. In J. Carlson & L. Sperry (Eds.), *The intimate couple* (pp. 298–327). Philadelphia: Brunner/Mazel.

Pipher, M. (1994). *Reviving Ophelia.* New York: Ballantine Books.

Pittman, F. (1993). *Man enough: Fathers, sons, and the search for masculinity.* New York: G. P. Putman's Sons.

Rossi, A. (Ed.). (1994). *Sexuality across the life course.* Chicago: University of Chicago Press.

Ryff, C., & Seltzer, M. (Eds.). (1996). *The parental experience in midlife.* Chicago: University of Chicago Press.

Sager, C. J., Brown, H. S., Crohn, H., Engel, T., Rodstein, E., & Walker, L. (1983). *Treating the remarried family.* New York: Brunner/Mazel.

Sandmaier, M. (1996, May/June). More than love. *The Family Networker,* 21–33.

Shapiro, P. G. (1996). *My turn: Women's search for self after children leave.* Princeton, NJ: Peterson's.

Schnarch, D. (1997). *Passionate marriage.* New York: Norton.

Sheehy, G. (1974). *Passages.* New York: Dutton.

Sheehy, G. (1991). *The silent passage: Menopause.* New York: Random House.

Sheehy, G. (1995). *New passages.* New York: Ballantine.

Shweder, R. (Ed.). (1998). *Welcome to middle age (and other cultural fictions).* Chicago: University of Chicago Press.

Silverstein, O. (1994). *The courage to raise good men.* New York: Viking Press.

Steinberg, L. (1987). Recent research on the family at adolescence: The extent and nature of sex differences. *Journal of Youth and Adolescence, 16,* 191–198.

Stierlin, H. (1981). *Separating parents and adolescents.* New York: Jason Aronson.

U.S. Bureau of the Census (1999, January 7). *Estimated median age at first marriage, by sex: 1890 to the present.* Internet release.

Vaillant, G. (1977). *Adaptation to life.* Boston: Little Brown.

Vaillant, C. O., & Valliant, G. E. (1993). Is the U curve of marital satisfaction an illusion? A 40 year study of marriage. *Journal of Marriage and the Family, 55,* 230–239.

VonGennep, A. (1909/1960). *The rites of passage.* Chicago: University Chicago Press.

CHAPTER 12

Aging and the Family: Dynamics and Therapeutic Interventions

Adam Davey, Megan J. Murphy, and Sharon J. Price

I N THIS CHAPTER, our intention is to introduce current issues and controversies around aging and the family, as well as some of their primary implications for clinical practice. Whereas previous chapters on this topic have tended to emphasize either gerontological issues having clinical implications (e.g., Qualls, 1995) or clinical issues relevant to older adults and their families (e.g., Erlanger, 1997), the present work is directed toward integrating what is known across both disciplines to the fullest extent possible. We open with a section addressing the demographic aspects of aging. This section focuses on the trends that are most likely to affect marital and intergenerational issues, as well as changes in the composition of who is currently growing old in America. Adequate preparation to help the older client of today and tomorrow is thus a growing concern for clinicians. We next consider major research issues of aging and the family, concentrating on what is known about the principal transitions and circumstances that may bring elders or their relatives into a therapeutic context. In this section, we also examine how, from a multigenerational perspective, these issues affect the families or couples who confront them. Similarly, when we consider prevailing positions on each of these topics we strive to examine the intersections between clinical therapeutic approaches and social gerontological theories. Having set the context for therapeutic interventions around aging and the family, we next move to presentations of some integrated examples of how selected issues including caregiver stress, relationship loss in Alzheimer's disease, and the decision to institutionalize a relative may be manifested in the therapeutic context, along with some potentially useful interventions and roles that the therapist may consider in working with aging clients and their families.

DEMOGRAPHICS AND ASSUMPTIONS

DEFINING LATE-LIFE FAMILIES

In writing a chapter like this one, it is important to begin with a clear definition of the scope of "aging and the family." For example, should we confine consideration only to nuclear family units that include at least one older family member or only older couples, or should our emphasis lie with the effects of individual aging within a family context? Clearly, the scope of such a chapter could easily fill a book. For our purposes, we consider the effects of individual and family development on individuals, intergenerational, and intragenerational relationships. In other words, studying the intersection between aging and the family necessitates a dynamic and intergenerational approach. The circumstances and decisions (e.g., depression, functional limitations, divorce, or remarriage) made by members of one generation within the family necessarily have implications for the development of members within the same generation and for members of other generations.

As we shall see, there have been tremendous changes both in the experience of individual aging and in family form and function, which all warrant careful consideration. As well, it is important to appreciate the balance between the population level trends of interest to social science researchers, representing the "typical" intersections of aging and the family, and the situations that may lead individuals to the therapeutic context. Often, the portraits of aging and the family painted from each perspective differ in ways that have important implications for how presenting problems might best be addressed and resolved.

Aging and the Family: Trends to Watch

During this century, the Western industrialized world has seen a profound increase in the proportion of the population aged 65 and older. In fact, one recent estimate (Rowe & Kahn, 1998) suggests that roughly half of all individuals who have ever lived to be 65 years of age or older are alive today. In the United States, we have seen life expectancy at birth increase from 47 years to 76 years between 1900 and today. Similarly, whereas only 4 percent of the population was aged 65 and older in 1900, the U.S. population today is composed of 13 percent older adults. This dramatic increase in the older population has resulted from the combination of several demographic changes. Medical breakthroughs have greatly reduced premature deaths due to infectious diseases, poor nutrition, and death during childbirth. Decreases in fertility rates this century (except for the baby boom cohorts born between 1946 and 1964) are responsible for much of the increase in the population aged 65 and over. At the same time, rates of disability and mortality have also decreased among older age groups, extending life expectancy in old age. It appears, as well, that the phenomenon of population aging is likely to continue until well into the next century as the baby boom cohorts approach old age. By the year 2025, our best estimates suggest that more than 59 million individuals (or 20 percent of the population) will be at least 65 years old (Myers, 1990).

The aging population has often been described as the most heterogeneous segment of the population. That is, with increasing age, the utility of "age" as a marker for development becomes less and less useful. Thus, knowing only that an individual is 75 years old tells us little more than the year that he or she was born. We can only speculate about other characteristics such as cognitive abilities, health status, marital status, employment status, or a host of other variables that might be important. For this reason, it is important to consider each individual's situation very carefully, rather than bring preconceptions about older adults to the therapeutic context.

Demographic changes also reveal considerable changes in the older population itself. There are long-standing and widening differences between the life expectancies of men and women. Life expectancy for women currently stands at 79 years, whereas for men it is only 72 years (Kinsella, 1995). The added years at the end of the life span have resulted in a dramatic increase in the number and percentage of the oldest old, those aged 85 and over, who currently comprise 12 percent of the older population and are projected to account for nearly one-quarter of all older adults by the year 2050 (Hobbs & Damon, 1996). These individuals are also those who are most likely to experience functional limitations, cognitive impairment, and are most likely to reside in nursing homes. In fact, it has been estimated that 49.5 percent of those aged 85 have one or more physical limitations (Hobbs & Damon, 1996). Our best estimates of the prevalence of cognitive impairment in this age group is between 23.8 percent and 28.5 percent (Ebly, Parhad, Hogan, & Fung, 1994; Gatz, Kasl-Godley, & Karel, 1996), and 24.5 percent reside in an institutional setting (Pynoos & Golant, 1996). Comparable figures for those aged 65 to 74 are only 13 percent and 1.4 percent, respectively. However, despite the dramatic increase in the prevalence of dementia with age, it should still not be considered a part of normal aging.

There are also important differences in the experiences of various ethnocultural groups. Until approximately age 85, life expectancy of non-Hispanic whites exceeds that of African Americans. Beyond this age, however, mortality rates for African Americans are actually lower than for whites. Although immigration patterns complicate estimates of life expectancy, Asian Americans appear to have slightly greater life expectancies than whites; those for Hispanics are mixed, but generally comparable to those for whites. Native Americans, however, have the lowest life expectancies of any ethnocultural group, although there is encouraging evidence that differences in mortality rates have decreased very substantially in recent years. One important implication of ethnocultural differences in longevity, however, is that there are more older members of minority groups today than at any point in the past, a trend that is certain to continue into the foreseeable future. This aspect of the changing composition of the elderly population is only now beginning to receive the full treatment it deserves, with researchers focusing on differences in family structure, intergenerational assistance, and access to formal services, to name but a few issues.

Finally, we note that increases in the older population are no longer limited to Western industrialized nations. Although fertility rates remain high in most developing nations, the numbers of older adults are also growing rapidly. While population aging is truly a transnational phenomenon, the experience of aging in developing nations is a topic that has only recently begun to receive attention (e.g., Kinsella, 1995; Kinsella & Taeuber, 1993).

Changes in the population structure of the American population have clearly been considerable over the course of this century. Equally profound, however, are the changes in American family structure, particularly subsequent to World War II. We have seen changes in patterns of living arrangements, divorce and remarriage, decreases in fertility, and increases in women's labor force participation. Each of these has the potential to affect the experience of aging in a family context.

On the one hand, a longer time spent pursuing education has resulted in delay of both marriage and childbearing for many individuals. Additionally, increases in rates of cohabitation have largely accounted for the observed decrease in marriage rates. Starting a family later, coupled with decreased fertility, means that families are smaller today than at any point in the past, with the typical pattern being fewer children spaced more closely together in age than in previous generations. This pattern has resulted in what Bengtson, Rosenthal, and Burton (1990) refer to as the "beanpole family," in which each generation is smaller, but there are more generations alive at any one time with more years between each generation. Offsetting this trend to some extent is the rise in rates of teen pregnancy and out-of-wedlock births, which Bengtson and associates (1990) refer to as "age-compressed families." It is unclear how the nature of intergenerational ties may be affected by these changing family structures, and whether fewer and more enduring ties might lead to increased closeness between generations or serve instead to accentuate any conflict between generations (Bengtson, Rosenthal, & Burton, 1996).

The changing structure of intergenerational relationships is further complicated by the large increase in rates of divorce and remarriage. Divorce rates roughly doubled between the 1970s and 1990s and have since remained consistently high, now hovering at around 51 percent for first-time marriages (e.g., Cherlin, 1992; Martin & Bumpass, 1989). It is well known that most individuals who divorce will eventually remarry, and that divorce rates among subsequent marriages are even higher than those of first-time marriages. Marital dissolution and reconstitution affect intergenerational ties in ways that are only now beginning to be appreciated fully. For example, as we consider the cumulative effects of families being formed, dissolved, and reconstituted, an older adult may find himself or herself embedded in a complex web of ties with biological and step-children, as well as children-in-law. Given that a majority of baby boomers can expect to find themselves in one of these complex family forms, it will be important to learn more about precisely how these marital transitions affect the availability of support for future generations of older adults. One final trend in families that we wish to note here is the great increase in women's labor force participation. In order to make ends meet, the woman now works outside of the home in the vast majority of households. This labor force participation has implications for the individual's or couple's wealth upon retirement, timing of retirement, parent-child relationships, and also has implications for the availability of family caregivers for frail older adults (e.g., Zarit & Eggebeen, 1995). Additionally, cross-national work on the relationship between formal and informal systems of care reveals families will likely continue to provide high levels of assistance to older adults through adaptations of family functioning within changing family structures (Davey & Patsios, 1999; Davey & Patsios, 1998).

THEORETICAL PERSPECTIVES AND MAJOR RESEARCH ISSUES

ROLE TRANSITIONS

Aging is a time of transitions, many of which will involve losses, including loss of social role, loss of income, and loss of relatives and friends (Kane, Ouslander, & Abrass, 1994). Change and transition are often difficult for older persons, as they are with other people. Fears involved with transitions include financial insecurity, dependency, and losing family relationships (Kane et al., 1994). However, therapists might be confident that their older clients will be able to meet the challenges that are brought about by transitions because older clients are survivors—they are likely to have developed coping strategies to help them handle adversity in the past.

Many of the presenting problems therapists will face upon the initial meeting with an older client or couple derive from role transitions. Older persons usually deal with many role transitions, including retirement, death of a spouse, or physical illness. Unresolved intergenerational issues may emerge in the context of such role transitions as older clients attempt to renegotiate relationships with each other and their families. Not only are older clients likely to face multiple role transitions, but it is possible that younger members in the family are also experiencing such transitions (Erlanger, 1997). For example, an older client faces new challenges when her daughter gives birth to her first granddaughter. The older client probably works to separate her "mother" role from her "grandmother" role, both of which have different tasks and expectations. What might be expected in the "grand-mother" role may differ depending on whether the older client has retired from the work-force yet, or whether she still has children living at home. While the older client is learning what her new role entails, her daughter is also learning what is involved in the "mother" role, and she has her own expectations about what her mother's "grandmother" role should be. This example illustrates the complexity involved in role transitions for many family members as the result of a life event.

Although some role transitions are times for celebration and new challenges, others are times of loss for older clients (Erlanger, 1997). For example, a client may be excited at the prospect of being a grandparent because he can experience the joy of having a grandchild (perhaps) without the same responsibilities as rearing a child. He may also feel a sense of loss concerning a great geographical distance between himself and his grandchild. A more obvious example of a role transition associated with loss is widowhood. Not only do wid-ows lose a spouse and a companion, they also may face a decline in finances and loss of part of their social network (Hargrave & Hanna, 1997).

Role transitions do not necessarily involve major life events, such as birth, retirement, or widowhood. The loss of a driver's license may be devastating for an older client, because it signifies a loss of mobility, autonomy, and self-esteem (Duffy, 1984). The potential loss of a driver's license may be a burden or give a sense of relief to an older client's family. The older client may be reluctant to turn in her driver's license out of fear of being a bur-den to her family members, or she may not look forward to her sense of increasing depen-dency on others for mobility.

Today, the transition to new roles is fraught with complications because of the changing structure of the family and changing social and economic conditions. The younger gener-ation may be dependent on their parents for a longer period of time, due to a prolonged educational career, birth of a child at a young age, divorce, and the difficulty of reaching financial independence (Duffy, 1984). What were once thought of as clear role transitions become unclear as family relationships become multifaceted (Hanna & Hargrave, 1997) and family structures change. For example, couples who look forward to retirement as a chance to devote time to their marital relationship may be faced with the fact that their son needs to move back into the house because of financial difficulties. Concerns over care-giving is another example of murky role transitions that may have been clearer in the past. It may have been expected, for example, that adult children were responsible for taking an ailing parent into the home for caregiving. Discussions and decisions about caregiving responsibilities today may become more complicated if the older person has children from different marriages, all of whom have the potential to be caregivers. Who is responsible now in the constellation of offspring—the biological children, adopted children, or step- and half-siblings?

Retirement may be one of the first transitions experienced by older persons and couples. Older persons may have mixed responses to retirement, as it offers a freedom from work responsibilities and time constraints, as well as the opportunity to develop new relation-ships and work on old relationships (Erlanger, 1997). Couples in retirement can take time to nurture their relationship, which may not have been possible in the past because of responsibilities with children and work. If an older person in retirement has grandchildren, then he or she may look forward to and enjoy spending more time with grandchildren. On the other hand, a retiree may experience a loss of identity, status, income, and purpose in life (Duffy, 1984; Erlanger, 1997). At best, retirement involves a renegotiation of relationships, boundaries, and meanings for life (Hargrave & Hanna, 1997). These tasks can be difficult for those older persons who have previously had difficulty with transitions. Paid work no longer serves as a diversion from difficulties in family relationships. Members of a couple who had been used to spending time apart must work through a new increase in overlap in their lives. Furthermore, an older person may be involved in a "new" job of caretaking, particularly if the spouse is ill.

Many of the role transitions experienced by older persons involve a loss of power. Losing income and status may result in a real or perceived loss of power by an older person. A rescinded driver's license or the changed nature of the "parent" role may result in a loss of respect by the younger generation for the older person. Each of the role transitions may be occurring for an older person who seeks therapy, although clients may not present a problem using such language. In the first session, therapists should be aware of and investigate possible role transitions that are occurring in the family, including transitions experienced by family members not present for therapy. For example, an older client may come to therapy for depression. Although there are many causes for depression, the client may be upset at her son's pending divorce, and she may also be fearful of "losing" a grandchild. If the older client is feeling powerless, she may attempt to regain power by diminishing others' power in the family (Duffy, 1984). Thus, this client may un-invite her daughter-in-law to holiday gatherings. The therapist can help this client appropriately express her concern and fears, and also gather support from other family members to help her and her son move through this transition.

CAREGIVING AND THE STRESS PROCESS

Perhaps no issue within the literature on aging and the family has received as much attention as family caregiving. This topic is complex from both a research and a clinical standpoint. Most attention has been devoted to investigation of the stress and burden often associated with providing care to a frail older relative, particularly in the context of Alzheimer's disease or other dementias. One of the most striking features of this topic is that, faced with objectively identical circumstances, two caregivers can have dramatically different responses. Understanding the sources of these individual differences is thus one important task for researchers and clinicians alike.

One theoretical perspective that has proven to be extremely useful in understanding the process of family caregiving is the stress process model (e.g., Aneshensel, Pearlin, Mullan, Zarit, & Whitlach, 1995; Gaugler, Davey, Pearlin, & Zarit, 1999; Pearlin, Mullan, Semple, & Skaff, 1990). According to this model, primary stressors originate from the process of providing care itself, and include both objective (e.g., level of cognitive impairment, number of functional limitations, problematic behaviors) and subjective (e.g., sense of role overload, role captivity, loss of intimate exchanges) components. Aneshensel and colleagues (1995), in a longitudinal study of 555 caregivers to a relative with dementia, reported that all forms of primary objective stressors appeared to contribute to loss of intimate exchanges, but problematic behaviors were most important in determining feelings of role overload and role captivity.

Primary stressors, which stem directly from the caregiving context, may infiltrate into other roles occupied by the caregiver, and may lead to conflict in other family relationships, to work conflict, or to financial strain. These stressors are secondary to the care situation, although they are no less important in terms of their effects on caregivers. The role strains and intrapsychic strains caregivers experience as a result of stress in the caregiving context can be very detrimental to their well-being. For example, common outcomes of the prolonged stress of providing care to an older relative include depression, poor physical health, and impaired immune function (for a review, see Zarit, Davey, Edwards, Femia, & Jarrott, 1998).

Fortunately, these detrimental outcomes are not a necessary part of the caregiving process. The stress process emphasizes the role of family relationships (including history, quality, type, support, and conflict) and of caregiver resources (including coping strategies and assistance) in moderating stress proliferation and negative outcomes of providing care. We discuss the importance of each of these factors below.

FAMILY CONTEXT OF CAREGIVING

Research on family caregiving has identified a great number of structural variables associated with the person who is most likely to become a caregiver. By any estimation, gender is the single strongest predictor of who will become a caregiver, with women comprising approximately 70 percent of all caregivers (Aneshensel et al., 1995; Stone, Cafferata, & Sangl, 1987). Most research has suggested that caregivers assume their role hierarchically within the family structure. Married individuals will turn first to a spouse for assistance in times of need. In the absence of a spouse, adult children are the next choice, followed by siblings, more distant relatives, and finally neighbors and friends (e.g., Penning, 1990).

Demographic and social trends make wives, daughters, and daughters-in-law the most common female caregivers, and husbands the most common male caregivers, followed distantly by sons (Aneshensel et al., 1995), who are only likely to assume the caregiving role in the absence of a female sibling (Horowitz, 1985).

Chappell (1990) and Tennstedt and associates (1993) investigated whether living arrangement was more important than relationship to the care recipient. With regard to receipt of instrumental activities of daily living (IADL) assistance (e.g., help with shopping, housework, transportation) it matters more that the care recipient lives with at least one other person than does their marital or parental status. Because so few spouse caregivers are not coresident with the care recipient, it is difficult to design a formal test of this hypothesis, however. Nevertheless, the findings do underscore the importance of living arrangements in caregiving.

Marital status of parents and their children have emerged as important predictors of caregiving and exchange. Specifically, parental divorce has been shown to affect the quality of relationships and frequency of contact with fathers, and the frequency of contact with mothers (Webster & Herzog, 1995). In general, these authors found that the effects were much greater for fathers than for mothers, which is confirmed in research adopting the older parents' reports (e.g., Cooney & Uhlenberg, 1990; White, 1992).

Disruption in adult children's marital status has also been found to relate to lower levels of help given to elderly parents, perceptions that parents need less assistance, and a lower sense of filial obligation to provide assistance (Cicirelli, 1983). A study by Brody and others (1994) elaborates on these findings, suggesting that daughters' marital status can have considerable effects on the amount of care they provide to an older parent. In particular, never-married and widowed daughters were found to provide the greatest proportion of care needed by a frail older parent. Never-married daughters, in particular, were most likely to be sole caregivers for their elderly parents. Conversely, married daughters were more likely to receive assistance with care tasks from informal sources, and divorced daughters were more likely to report using formal services.

CAREGIVER-CARE RECIPIENT RELATIONSHIPS

Providing care to an elderly relative with dementia presents stressors that differ in fundamentally important ways from situations in which cognition is spared or recovery is possible. In a comparison of caregivers of relatives with dementia and of relatives with cancer, Clipp and George (1993) found that dementia caregivers reported poorer self-rated physical health, greater substance use, poorer emotional health, reduced social functioning, and poorer financial status, even when the effects of employment status, age, and duration of illness were controlled. These findings offer support to the idea that there is something uniquely debilitating about dealing with dementia in a spouse as compared to another terminal illness in which cognitive functioning is typically spared. Surprisingly, however, we are only now beginning to gain insights into the ways in which caregiving alters the relationship between caregivers and care recipients.

Wright (1993) compared a small, nonrepresentative sample of Alzheimer's disease caregiving couples with well couples across a variety of dimensions. While the generalizability of her findings are likely quite limited, the study is unique in that she considered the perspective of both members of the couples in each group, having each report on specific aspects of their marriage. Briefly, she found that Alzheimer's caregivers reported decreased companionship and difficulty dealing with changes in sexual intimacy. She also found that ratings of past marital happiness were associated with current valuing of the afflicted spouse as a unique individual, but not with future commitment, which was lowest among caregiving spouses.

Majerovitz (1995) examined the moderating relationship between family adaptability, as measured retrospectively using the Family Adaptability and Cohesion Scale (Olson, 1991). In her study of 54 caregivers to a spouse with dementia, she found that, for spouses reporting low levels of family adaptability, the memory problems spouses experienced and the hours of care provided were both related to higher levels of depression, whereas there was no such relationship for spouses reporting high levels of family adaptability. More interestingly, her follow-up analyses of low-adaptability spouses indicated that these individuals were more likely to cling to an unrealistic role for their dementing spouse, expecting their partner to continue to meet former expectations. While these data are cross-sectional, they do suggest that caregivers with more realistic expectations of their dementing spouse are likely to experience fewer negative consequences as a result of the care they provide.

With married couples, relationship quality between the caregiver and care recipient may also play a role in the decision to institutionalize. Pruchno and colleagues (1990) found that spouses reporting a better quality of relationship with the care recipient reported less desire to institutionalize, but this finding did not extend to actual decisions regarding institutionalization. By the same token, desire to institutionalize was a strong predictor of actual institutionalization, suggesting that an indirect link may exist.

There are also important consequences of dementia caregiving for adult children's relationships with their parents. Feelings of attachment and obligation have both been found to predict the amount of help daughters provide to their older parents (Cicirelli, 1993). Those who reported stronger attachment experienced lower levels of burden, whereas those who reported higher levels of obligation experienced higher levels of burden. Thus, children providing care out of a sense of obligation rather than affection may experience greater negative consequences.

There are other important implications of prior relationship quality for the caregiving experience. Caregivers with a poor relationship with the care recipient are less likely to assume the caregiving role and, if they do, to experience more stress within it (Whitlach & Noelker, 1996). In a study by Uchino, Kiecolt-Glaser, and Cacciopo (1994), higher ratings of preillness affection for the care recipient were associated with lower heart rate reactivity, a physiological indicator of stress, measured two years later.

Walker, Martin, and Jones (1992) examined the role of intimacy in predicting adult daughters' and mothers' perceived costs and benefits of caregiving. Adult daughters' feelings of intimacy were associated with fewer feelings of having insufficient time for extra-caregiving activities, less frustration with caregiving, and less anxiety about providing care. For mothers receiving care, intimacy was related only to less anger and resentment about the care they received. Other research has found conflict in the caregiver-care recipient relationship to be associated with greater caregiver strain and negative affect (Sheehan & Nuttall, 1988).

Townsend and Franks (1995) found that adult children's perceptions of relationship quality with their parent was an important mediator between the parent's cognitive impairment and the adult child's well-being. In their study of 90 adult-child caregivers, perceived closeness was associated with lower levels of reported caregiver burden and a greater sense of caregiving efficacy. Their study also underscores the importance of conflict in the relationship, which was associated with higher levels of stress, lower self-efficacy, and greater depression.

Even after institutionalization, families retain a high level of involvement in their relative's care (Aneshensel et al., 1995). Pruchno and colleagues (1994) found that children's perceptions of their parent's affective state are predictive of feelings of attachment toward their institutionalized parent.

One extreme outcome of a poor relationship between caregiver and care recipient is violence directed toward the elderly care recipient. In a study of 236 caregivers to a relative with dementia, Pillemer and Suitor (1992) examined predictors of violence and violent feelings toward the care recipient. With regard to care recipient characteristics, they found that both violent behaviors and disruptive behaviors were associated with caregivers' greater fear of becoming violent with their relative. Violent behaviors by the care recipient were also associated with a greater likelihood of actual violence on the part of the caregiver. Caregivers who lived with their relative were more likely to report being afraid of acting violently toward their relative, and spouse caregivers were more likely to have acted violently toward their relative than were adult children. Thus, there is evidence to suggest that aspects of the past and present relationship quality between caregivers and care recipients play an important role in the caregiving experience, and that these characteristics have an effect, for both spouses and adult children, on the burden experienced as a result of caring.

Because dementia has such profound effects on all aspects of an older adult's functioning, it can be expected to alter the nature of interaction dramatically. For this reason, new patterns of interaction can be a source of stress for caregivers. Pruchno and Resch (1989) examined the effects of care recipient behaviors on the mental health of caregivers. They found that asocial and disoriented behaviors on the part of the care recipient are associated with greater burden, decreased social participation, and less satisfaction with caregiving. For forgetful behaviors, the consequences for caregiver mental health increase at first, and again diminish as the severity of behavior problems increases, suggesting a curvilinear relationship between the two. Disruptive behaviors and social functioning resulting from cognitive impairment have also been shown to predict poorer relationships between caregivers and care recipients, more restricted caregiver social activities, and poorer caregiver health (Deimling & Bass, 1986; Poulshock & Diemling, 1984).

In a study of depression in dementia caregivers, Redinbaugh and colleagues (1995) found that caregivers who experienced chronic depression over a 3-year period reported experiencing their relative's behavior as more problematic, and experiencing higher levels of upsetting social support than nondepressed caregivers, or caregivers who had experienced a transient depressive episode during the course of the study.

Vitaliano and associates (1993) were interested in examining the possibility that caregiver behaviors, specifically in the form of expressed emotion, were predictive of subsequent care recipient behaviors one and a half years later. Controlling for initial levels of negative care recipient behaviors, those individuals cared for by an individual with high levels of expressed emotion displayed significantly more negative behaviors at follow-up. These findings are significant because caregiver expressed emotion is correlated with higher levels of depression, suppressed anger, and lower life satisfaction (Bledin, MacCarthy, Kuipers, & Woods, 1990; Vitaliano et al., 1993).

INTERVENTIONS FOR FAMILY CAREGIVERS

One goal of clinical interventions can be to help bolster caregivers' skills to provide care in an effective manner and may involve addressing issues such as family conflict, managing difficult behaviors, or dealing with relationship loss (Zarit, Orr, & Zarit, 1985). An additional and often overlooked goal of clinical interventions with family caregivers is to bring additional resources to the caregiving context. These might include such things as increasing the involvement of other family members in the process of providing care, linking caregivers with available community resources such as respite services (e.g., in-home respite or adult day care), support group participation, or even assistance in the process of institutionalizing a relative (Zarit et al., 1998).

While it need not be so, giving and receiving care can be quite problematic for many members of a family, depending on the context in which support is given and received (Davey & Eggebeen, 1998; Davey & Norris, 1998). Older persons usually prefer to care for themselves and remain independent as long as possible (Gelfand, Olsen, & Block, 1978). Furthermore, outside of physical illness or other needs, older adults may not be as dependent as children and society tend to think they are (Erlanger, 1997). Yet if the time comes for moving in with a child out of necessity, previous difficulties in family relationships can be magnified, particularly since relationship history, past patterns of support, expectations for support, and feelings of obligation may all be superseded by social norms for children to provide assistance to older parents in times of need (Davey, 1999; Eggebeen & Davey, 1998). Children and older persons both struggle with expectations regarding the new roles of caregiver and caretaker (Shaw, 1987). Issues of dependence and independence can cause conflict, particularly if these issues have not been resolved in the past. All family members shift expectations when adult children suddenly become responsible for the care of their parents, which is a role-switch for both generations. Older persons being cared for still need to be valued by children for their experience and expertise on life. Therapists can encourage caregivers to seek the advice of their parents—encouraging children to value their parents' thoughts and feelings.

As alluded to above, taking care of aging parents is not the same as taking care of children. Caregivers have experienced the stages that young children move through, and thus can empathize with children's feelings. Caregivers, if they are taking care of a parent, have not yet passed through the same stages as their parents, and may not have the same ability to empathize with their parents as they can with their children (Sterns, Weis, & Perkins, 1984). Furthermore, the ultimate goal of parenting is seen as the independence of children, whereas caregiving for parents can be seen as increasing in dependency. Therapists can challenge caregivers to encourage independence in their parents, which offers some hope for caregivers and ill parents alike.

Being cared for by children can be difficult for older persons as well as for caregivers. All family members may be embarrassed by the physical aspects of caregiving. The older person may experience a loss of privacy in having to be bathed and dressed. Losing eyesight or hearing can be challenging for the older person and for family members. Communication in a caregiving arrangement is crucial, yet may be extremely difficult if the older person has trouble communicating as a result of physical illness (Green, 1991). Difficulty communicating can be devastating for an older person because he or she may not be able to discuss needs with family members. If the relationship between caregiver and the older person has been strained in the past, then it is possible that the caregiver may question the validity of the older person's physical or psychological illnesses, perhaps seeing dependency as a way to get attention (Shaw, 1987). A therapist can help older family members identify their needs. Older persons may wish for more autonomy and independence from their children, whereas adult children may want to discuss maintaining appropriate boundaries between grandparents and parents in the household (Qualls, 1993).

The issue of caregiving is often linked with elder abuse. Abuse can be physical, psychological, financial, or take place in the form of neglect (Hanna, Hargrave, & Miller, 1997). Little is known about the phenomenon of elder abuse. Therapists are often reluctant to address these issues for fear of alienating the client (Hanna et al., 1997). Elder abuse usually does not take place in a vacuum—there tend to be patterns of abusive relationships in families who do report elder abuse, particularly between parent and child (Qualls, 1995). Therapists who suspect that an older client is being abused can collect information on past abuse in the family, which could indicate current problems in this area (Qualls, 1995). Older persons experiencing elder abuse in caregiving situations can feel powerless to escape the situation because they may be financially dependent on caregivers for physical care. In such situations, therapists can work collaboratively with the potential abuser and attempt to address and understand his or her concerns (Hanna et al., 1997).

The decision to place an older family member in a nursing home is usually fraught with stress and tension. Adult children tend to feel guilty if they decide to place their parent in a nursing home, and placement for an older person can symbolize the loss of independence. Older persons placed in nursing homes may fear being cut off from their families altogether. The decision to place an elder person is not a singular event but rather is a process (Caron, 1997). Therapists can capitalize on this process, as it allows time for the family to discuss their fears and concerns with each other prior to placement. Some families pull together in the process of deciding, whereas other families break down (Caron, 1997). Examining family history of experiencing crisis can be useful for therapists in helping the family anticipate and cope with the decision to place an older family member in a nursing home.

DEPRESSION AND SUICIDE

Depression is perhaps the most likely problem older clients will bring to therapy (Kane et al., 1994). While the prevalence of major depressive episodes is actually lower among older adults than younger adults (e.g., Fiske, Kasl-Godley, & Gatz, 1998; Gatz et al., 1996), between 1.5 percent and 5 percent of older adults meet diagnostic criteria for clinical depression, whereas another 10 percent to 20 percent express sadness or other depressive symptoms (Fiske et al., 1998; Gatz et al., 1996; Kane et al., 1994). Similar to younger populations, the suicide rate of males is higher than for females (Kane et al., 1994). Older persons may experience depression, often related to role transitions such as bereavement (e.g., Fiske et al., 1998). However, depression is not a part of the normal aging process (McQuellon & Reifler, 1989).

When any client presents with depression, it is important to consider the possible causes, which may include physical problems, past or current losses, damaged relationships with family, fears of aging, and role transitions. Suicide attempts may be a way for older persons to elicit help from family members (Duffy, 1984). Treatment for the depressed, including older persons, includes evaluations to determine whether medication is needed, support groups, and family therapy. Therapists can mobilize the family system to help depressed and suicidal family members (Osgood, 1989), particularly if strained family relationships are determined to be contributing to an older adult's depression.

CLINICAL APPROACHES AND CONSIDERATIONS

Intergenerational family therapy can be helpful for older clients and their families who are struggling with role transitions and other problems. Focusing on intergenerational relationships can add another dimension to the therapist's understanding of the client's presenting problem. As indicated earlier, therapists can inquire about an older client's relationship with his or her children, grandchildren, siblings, nieces, and nephews. Intergenerational family therapy can still be valuable if close or extended family members live too far away to regularly attend therapy sessions. Letter writing is helpful in this case (Duffy, 1984). Working to repair and improve relationships between family members is an excellent way to reconnect older clients to family members.

Solution-focused therapy can also be beneficial for older clients. Using this approach, therapists can emphasize clients' strengths and abilities so that clients can find their own solutions for their problems (Bonjean, 1997). Older clients have rich life histories that are likely filled with successes and challenges faced. This approach emphasizes older clients as the experts on their own lives, underscoring the fact that they have the power to make it through any difficult time in their lives. By focusing on strengths and positive outcomes, the solution-focused approach challenges the way the world tends to see older people and thus challenges the way older people see themselves and their capabilities.

Group therapy is also indicated for older clients. By serving many purposes and clients at once, group therapy is a particularly efficient means of helping older persons. Group therapy can help older persons with feelings of depression, loneliness, and rejection by family members (Grotjahn, 1978). Open communication can be facilitated by the group leader, often a therapist, on topics such as death and dying, nursing home placement issues, physical illness, and family relationships. Group participants can provide social and emotional support for one another by simply talking with one another about shared concerns (Berland & Poggi, 1979; Sterns et al., 1984). Finally, group therapy can be beneficial to older clients by normalizing the struggles each member is experiencing.

Techniques from many schools of family therapy can be helpful for the older client. Simply eliciting an oral history from an older client or couple can afford an opportunity to think through significant events in their lives (Baum, 1980). Older clients are likely to get satisfaction from the narration of their life stories. Therapists can encourage their clients to make a written record of their histories to share with younger generations. The goal of an oral history is not therapeutic in the sense that problematic events and relationships are examined. Rather, the therapeutic value lies in the simple telling of a story in which the client is the central character.

Similar to the oral history, exploring an older client's genogram can be a highly positive experience. This technique can be helpful for clients who feel uncomfortable in the therapy session, as the client is given the opportunity to be the "expert" on his or her family (Erlanger, 1990). A genogram can be used in a variety of ways, including highlighting clients' and families' strengths, pointing out successful negotiation of previous role transitions, and pointing out accomplishments. Genograms can be used to help older clients and their families explore detrimental relationship patterns and foster understanding of current behaviors and attitudes.

OTHER SUGGESTIONS FOR WORKING WITH OLDER CLIENTS

Although family therapists generally are not experts in physical health, they do need to attend to physical problems in older clients that may or may not be known to the client. Some health problems can inhibit communication in the therapeutic process. For example, a client with hearing difficulties may not wish to share this possibly embarrassing problem with family members or a therapist (Kane et al., 1994). Therapists should also evaluate the older client's socioeconomic functioning and psychological state. Collaboration with other professionals, including physicians, psychiatrists, social workers, nursing home aides, and lawyers may be necessary in assessing and helping older clients with many aspects of their lives.

Therapists should be aware of potential challenges in working with older clients. Like other clients, older clients may underreport complaints, have vague or nonspecific problems, or have multiple complaints (Kane et al., 1994). Older clients may have difficulty with growing dependency on family members and other age-related problems. Often, older clients have difficulty accepting help from family members as well as therapists and other members of the helping profession. The fear of losing connection and/or involvement with the family by entering into therapy may also be present (Gelfand et al., 1978).

Despite these challenges, therapists can take an active role in reassuring older clients regarding such concerns. Involving other family members in therapy can alleviate older clients' fears of becoming less involved in the family. The therapist can instill a sense of optimism in the client through maintaining hope and a positive stance throughout the course of therapy (Knight, 1996). Finally, older clients may be interested to hear about their therapists' previous work with older clients in similar situations (Knight, 1996). This both normalizes clients' concerns and communicates the therapist's experiences and successes with other older clients. As with clients of any age, a therapist's sensitivity to the older client's concerns can help foster a warm and helpful therapeutic relationship.

Looking beyond older clients to their social support network is also a key factor in their overall mental health (Wykle & Musil, 1993). The presence of and connection to friends can be helpful in preventing an overreliance on family for support and identity. Therapists can encourage older clients to remain active in their social environments and community

(Harris & Bodden, 1978). Social activity can result in a higher level of psychological functioning, increase independence and activity level, and potentially decrease depressed feelings (Harris & Bodden, 1978). A connection to the community through social interaction is a healthy way for older persons to experience themselves as a valued and integral part of society.

When working with older clients, therapists need to check and continually reassess their values and beliefs about the older community. Many therapists are reluctant to work with older people out of fear that they need some special skills. Other therapists may believe that older clients are fragile and not open to direct confrontation (Duffy, 1984). Still other therapists may have unresolved issues with their own older parents or grandparents. Even if therapy proceeds with older clients and a (presumably) younger therapist beyond these initial concerns, therapy can trigger therapists' own positive and negative memories of parents and grandparents (Erlanger, 1997). Fears of death and dying may also be elicited for a therapist working with an older client. Consultation with a supervisor, seasoned consultant, or other helping professional can help the therapist work through these issues and fears.

Therapists should examine any assumptions they have about older persons. Messages from society about older persons and their functioning can be detrimental to the therapeutic relationship. For example, a therapist should not assume that a sexually active older client is married (Garrison, 1989). Similarly, the therapist should not assume that older clients are no longer sexual beings. Therapists need to be aware of the effect that their assumptions have on their older clients and the therapeutic relationship. Older persons can be productive, happy, healthy members of society, with concerns that are just as valid and real as those of younger clients.

CONCLUSION

In considering the intersections and implications of families and aging for the clinical context several features stand out. First, whereas there has always been considerable heterogeneity within the older population, it is clear that the extent of diversity among older adults is greater today than at any point in the past. Additionally, it is projected that these changes will continue in the foreseeable future. To meet the needs of an older population, clinicians need to understand and be prepared to address this diversity within their practice.

Second, the profound changes experienced by families in the United States, such as higher rates of divorce, remarriage, cohabitation, delayed and reduced fertility, and increased labor force participation, can be expected to fundamentally alter the circumstances, experiences, and transitions that older clients will bring to the therapeutic context. These changes need to be considered from both a developmental and a multigenerational perspective. Clinicians should be aware of, and prepared to address, the wide range of potential family supports available, as well as the increased potential for conflict that may accompany this greater number of transitions.

Finally, we have presented several conceptual frameworks and therapeutic strategies that may be particularly useful when working with older clients or issues that derive from changes in aging and the family. Those strategies that emphasize the importance of changing roles, and that draw on the rich tapestry of experiences older adults bring to the therapeutic context, may prove particularly useful.

REFERENCES

Aneshensel, C. S., Pearlin, L. I., Mullan, J. T., Zarit, S. H., & Whitlach, C. J. (1995). *Profiles in caregiving: The unexpected career.* New York: Academic Press.

Baum, W. (1980). Therapeutic value of oral history. *International Journal of Aging & Human Development, 12,* 49–53.

Bengtson, V., Rosenthal, C. J., & Burton, L. (1990). Families and aging: Diversity and heterogeneity. In R. H. Binstock & L. K. George (Eds.), *Handbook of aging and the social sciences* (3rd ed., pp. 263–287). New York: Academic Press.

Bengtson, V., Rosenthal, C. J., & Burton, L. (1996). Paradoxes of families and aging. In R. H. Binstock & L. K. George (Eds.), *Handbook of aging and the social sciences* (4th ed., pp. 254–282). New York: Academic Press.

Berland, D. I., & Poggi, R. (1979). Expressive group psychotherapy with the aging. *International Journal of Group Psychotherapy, 29,* 87–108.

Bledin, K. D., MacCarthy, B., Kuipers, L., & Woods, R. T. (1990). Daughters of people with dementia: Expressed emotion, strain, and coping. *British Journal of Psychiatry, 157,* 221–227.

Bonjean, M. J. (1997). Solution-focused brief therapy with aging families. In T. D. Hargrave & S. M. Hanna (Eds.), *The aging family: New visions in theory, practice, and reality* (pp. 81–100). New York: Brunner/Mazel.

Brody, E. M., Litvin, S. J., Albert, S. M., & Hoffman, C. J. (1994). Marital status of daughters and patterns of parent care. *Journals of Gerontology, 49,* S95–S103.

Caron, W. A. (1997). Family systems and nursing home systems: An ecosystemic perspective for the systems practitioner. In T. D. Hargrave & S. M. Hanna (Eds.), *The aging family: New visions in theory, practice, and reality* (pp. 235–258). New York: Brunner/Mazel.

Chappell, N. L. (1990). Living arrangements and sources of caregiving. *Journals of Gerontology, 46,* S1–S8.

Cherlin, A. J. (1992). *Marriage, divorce, and remarriage.* Cambridge, MA: Harvard University Press.

Cicirelli, V. G. (1983). A comparison of helping behavior to elderly parents of adult children with intact and disrupted marriages. *The Gerontologist, 23,* 619–625.

Cicirelli, V. G. (1993). Attachment and obligation as daughters' motives for caregiving behavior and subsequent effect on subjective burden. *Psychology and Aging, 8,* 144–155.

Clipp, E. C., & George, L. K. (1993). Dementia and cancer: A comparison of spouse caregivers. *The Gerontologist, 33,* 534–541.

Cooney, T. M., & Uhlenberg, P. (1990). The role of divorce in men's relations with their adult children after mid-life. *Journal of Marriage and the Family, 52,* 677–688.

Davey, A. (1999). *Longitudinal predictors of emotional and instrumental support between older parents and their adult children.* Manuscript submitted for publication.

Davey, A., & Eggebeen, D. J. (1998). Patterns of intergenerational exchange and mental health. *Journals of Gerontology: Psychological Sciences, 53,* P86–P95.

Davey, A., Femia E. E., Shea, D. G., Zarit, S. H., Sundstrom, G., Berg, S., & Smyer, M. A. (1999). How much do families help? A cross-national comparison. *Journal of Aging and Health, 11,* 199–221.

Davey, A., & Norris, J. E. (1998). Social networks and exchange norms across the adult life-span. *Canadian Journal on Aging, 17,* 212–233.

Davey, A., & Patsios, D. (1999). Formal and informal care to older citizens: Comparative analysis of the United States and Great Britain. *Journal of Family and Economic Issues, 20,* 210–239.

Deimling, G. T., & Bass, D. M. (1986). Symptoms of mental impairment among elderly adults and their effects on family caregivers. *Journal of Gerontology, 41,* 778–784.

Duffy, M. (1984). Aging and the family: Intergenerational psychodynamics. *Psychotherapy, 21,* 342–346.

Ebly, E. M., Parhad, I. M., Hogan, D. B., & Fung, T. S. (1994). Prevalence and types of dementia in the very old: Results from the Canadian study of health and aging. *Neurology, 44,* 1593–1600.

Eggebeen, D. J., & Davey, A. (1998). Do safety nets work? The role of anticipated support in times of need. *Journal of Marriage and the Family, 60,* 939–950.

Erlanger, M. A. (1990). Using the genogram with the older client. *Journal of Mental Health Counseling, 12,* 321–331.

Erlanger, M. A. (1997). Changing roles and life-cycle transitions. In T. D. Hargrave & S. M. Hanna (Eds.), *The aging family: New visions in theory, practice, and reality* (pp. 163–177). New York: Brunner/Mazel.

Fiske, A., Kasl-Godley, J. E., & Gatz, M. (1998). Mood disorders in late life. In A. S. Bellack & M. Hersen (Series Eds.) & B. A. Edelstein (Vol. Ed.), *Comprehensive clinical psychology: Vol. 7. Clinical geropsychology* (pp. 193–229). Oxford, UK: Elsevier Science.

Garrison, J. E., Jr. (1989). Sexual dysfunction in the elderly: Causes and effects. In G. A. Hughston, V. A. Christopherson, & M. J. Bonjean (Eds.), *Aging and family therapy: Practitioner perspectives on Golden Pond* (pp. 149–162). New York: Haworth Press.

Gatz, M., Kasl-Godley, J. E., & Karel, M. J. (1996). Aging and mental disorders. In J. E. Birren & K. W. Schaie (Eds.), *Handbook of the psychology of aging* (4th ed., pp. 365–382). New York: Academic Press.

Gaugler, J. E., Davey, A., Pearlin, L. I., & Zarit, S. H. (1999). *Interrelationship of objective and subjective primary stressors over time: A growth curve modeling approach.* Manuscript submitted for publication.

Gelfand, D. E., Olsen, J. K., & Block, M. R. (1978). Two generations of elderly in the changing American family: Implications for family services. *The Family Coordinator, 27,* 395–403.

Green, C. P. (1991). Clinical considerations: Mid-life daughters and their aging parents. *Journal of Gerontological Nursing, 17*(11), 6–12.

Grotjahn, M. (1978). Group communication and group therapy with the aged: A promising project. In L. F. Jarvik (Ed.), *Aging into the 21st century: Middle-agers today* (pp. 113–121). New York: Gardner.

Hanna, S. M., & Hargrave, T. D. (1997). Integrating the process of aging and family therapy. In T. D. Hargrave & S. M. Hanna (Eds.), *The aging family: New visions in theory, practice, and reality* (pp. 19–38). New York: Brunner/Mazel.

Hanna, S. M., Hargrave, T. D., & Miller, R. B. (1997). Future directions for family therapy with aging families. In T. D. Hargrave & S. M. Hanna (Eds.), *The aging family: New visions in theory, practice, and reality* (pp. 295–307). New York: Brunner/Mazel.

Hargrave, T. D., & Hanna, S. M. (1997). Aging: A primer for family therapists. In T. D. Hargrave & S. M. Hanna (Eds.), *The aging family: New visions in theory, practice, and reality* (pp. 39–58). New York: Brunner/Mazel.

Harris, J. E., & Bodden, J. L. (1978). An activity group experience for disengaged elderly persons. *Journal of Counseling Psychology, 25,* 325–330.

Hobbs, F. B., & Damon, B. L. (1996). *65+ in the United States* (U.S. Bureau of the Census International Population Report No. P23–190). Washington, DC: U.S. Government Printing Office.

Horowitz, A. (1985). Sons and daughters as caregivers to older parents: Differences in role performance and consequences. *The Gerontologist, 25,* 612–617.

Kane, R. L., Ouslander, J. G., & Abrass, I. B. (1994). *Essentials of clinical geriatrics.* New York: McGraw-Hill.

Kinsella, K. (1995). Aging and the family: Present and future demographic issues. In R. Blieszner & V. H. Bedford (Eds.), *Aging and the family: Theory and research* (pp. 32–56). Westport, CT: Praeger.

Kinsella, K., & Taeuber, C. (1993). *An aging world II* (U.S. Bureau of the Census International Population Report No. P95/92–3). Washington, DC: U.S. Government Printing Office.

Knight, B. G. (1996). *Psychotherapy with older adults* (2nd ed.). Thousand Oaks, CA: Sage.

Majerovitz, S. D. (1995). Role of family adaptability in the psychological adjustment of spouse caregivers to patients with dementia. *Psychology and Aging, 10,* 447–457.

Martin, T. C., & Bumpass, L. L. (1989). Recent trends in marital disruption. *Demography, 26,* 37–51.

McQuellon, R. P., & Reifler, B. V. (1989). Caring for the depressed elderly and their families. In G. A. Hughston, V. A. Christopherson, & M. J. Bonjean (Eds.), *Aging and family therapy: Practitioner perspectives on Golden Pond* (pp. 97–116). New York: Haworth Press.

Myers, G. C. (1990). Demography of aging. In R. H. Binstock & L. K. George (Eds.), *Handbook of aging and the social sciences* (3rd ed., pp. 19–44). New York: Academic Press.

Olson, D. H. (1991). Commentary: Three-dimensional (3-D) Circumplex Model and revised scoring of the FACES-III. *Family Process, 30,* 74–79.

Osgood, N. J. (1989). A systems approach to suicide prevention. In G. A. Hughston, V. A. Christopherson, & M. J. Bonjean (Eds.), *Aging and family therapy: Practitioner perspectives on Golden Pond* (pp. 117–131). New York: Haworth Press.

Pearlin, L. I., Mullan, J. T., Semple, S. J., & Skaff, M. S. (1990). Caregiving and the stress process: An overview of concepts and their measures. *The Gerontologist, 30,* 583–594.

Penning, M. J. (1990). Receipt of assistance by elderly people: Hierarchical selection and task specificity. *The Gerontologist, 30,* 220–227.

Pillemer, K., & Suitor, J. J. (1992). Violence and violent feelings: What causes them among family caregivers? *Journals of Gerontology, 47,* S165–S172.

Poulshock, S. W., & Diemling, G. T. (1984). Families caring for elders in residence: Issues in the measurement of burden. *Journal of Gerontology, 39,* 230–239.

Pruchno, R. A., Michaels, J. E., & Potashnik, S. L. (1990). Predictors of institutionalization among Alzheimer disease victims with caregiving spouses. *Journals of Gerontology, 45,* S259–S266.

Pruchno, R. A., Peters, N. D., Kleban, M. H., & Burant, C. J. (1994). Attachment among adult children and their institutionalized parents. *Journals of Gerontology, 49,* S209–S218.

Pruchno, R. A., & Resch, N. L. (1989). Aberrant behaviors and Alzheimer's disease: Mental health effects on spouse caregivers. *Journals of Gerontology, 44,* S177–S182.

Pynoos, J., & Golant, S. (1996). Housing and living arrangements for the elderly. In R. H. Binstock & L. K. George (Eds.), *Handbook of aging and the social sciences* (4th ed., pp. 303–325). New York: Academic Press.

Qualls, S. H. (1993). Family therapy with older adults. *Generations, 17*(1), 73–74.

Qualls, S. H. (1995). Clinical interventions with later-life families. In R. Blieszner & V. H. Bedford (Eds.), *Aging and the family: Theory and research* (pp. 474–488). Westport, CT: Praeger.

Redinbaugh, E. M., MacCallum, R. C., & Kiecolt-Glaser, J. K. (1995). Recurrent syndromal depression in caregivers. *Psychology and Aging, 10,* 358–368.

Rowe, J. W., & Kahn, R. L. (1998). *Successful aging.* New York: Pantheon.

Shaw, S. B. (1987). Parental aging: Clinical issues in adult psychotherapy. *Social Casework: The Journal of Contemporary Social Work, 68,* 406–412.

Sheehan, N. W., & Nuttall, P. (1988). Conflict, emotion, and personal strain among family caregivers. *Family Relations, 37,* 92–98.

Sterns, H. L., Weis, D. M., & Perkins, S. E. (1984). A conceptual approach to counseling older adults and their families. *The Counseling Psychologist, 12*(2), 55–61.

Stone, R., Cafferata, G. L., & Sangl, J. (1987). Caregivers of the frail elderly: A national profile. *The Gerontologist, 27,* 616–626.

Tennstedt, S. L., Crawford, S., & McKinlay, J. B. (1993). Determining the pattern of community care: Is coresidence more important than caregiver relationship? *Journals of Gerontology, 48,* S74–S83.

Townsend, A. L., & Franks, M. M. (1995). Binding ties: Closeness and conflict in adult children's caregiving relationship. *Psychology and Aging, 10,* 343–351.

Uchino, B. N., Kiecolt-Glaser, J. K., & Cacciopo, J. T. (1994). Construals of preillness relationship quality predict cardiovascular response in family caregivers of Alzheimer's disease victims. *Psychology and Aging, 9,* 113–120.

Vitaliano, P. P., Young, H. M., Russo, J., Romano, J., & Magana-Amato, A. (1993). Does expressed emotion in spouses predict subsequent problems among care recipients with Alzheimer's disease? *Journals of Gerontology, 48,* P202–P209.

Walker, A. J., Martin, S. S. K., & Jones, L. L. (1992). The benefits and costs of caregiving and care receiving for daughters and mothers. *Journals of Gerontology, 47,* S130–S139.

Webster, P. S., & Herzog, A. R. (1995). Effects of parental divorce and memories of family problems on relationships between adult children and their parents. *Journals of Gerontology, 50B,* S24–S34.

White, L. (1992). The effect of parental divorce and remarriage on parental support for adult children. *Journal of Family Issues, 13,* 234–250.

Whitlach, C. J., & Noelker, L. S. (1996). Caregiving and caring. In J. E. Birren (Ed.), *Encyclopedia of gerontology* (pp. 258–264). New York: Academic Press.

Wright, L. K. (1993). *Alzheimer's disease and marriage: An intimate account.* Newbury Park, CA: Sage.

Wykle, M. L., & Musil, C. M. (1993). Mental health of older persons: Social and cultural factors. In M. A. Smyer (Ed.), *Mental health and aging: Progress and prospects* (pp. 3–17). New York: Springer.

Zarit, S. H., Davey, A., Edwards, A. B., Femia, E. E., & Jarrott, S. E. (1998). Family caregiving: Research findings and clinical implications. In A. S. Bellack & M. Hersen (Series Eds.) & B. A. Edelstein (Vol. Ed.), *Comprehensive clinical psychology: Vol. 7. Clinical geropsychology* (pp. 499–523). Oxford, UK: Elsevier Science.

Zarit, S. H., & Eggebeen, D. J. (1995). Parent child relationships in adulthood and old age. In M. H. Bornstein (Ed.), *Handbook of parenting: Volume 1, Children and parenting* (pp. 119–140). Mahwah, NJ: Lawrence Erlbaum.

Zarit, S. H., Orr, N. K., & Zarit, J. M. (1985). *The hidden victims of Alzheimer's disease: Families under stress.* New York: New York University Press.

PART IV

VARIATIONS IN FAMILY STRUCTURE

CHAPTER 13

Families by Choice:
Adoptive and Foster Families

Lita Linzer Schwartz

S OME FAMILIES are created by conscious personal choice rather than by more traditional applications of biology (or even modern reproductive technology). This does not make them better or worse than those created in more basic ways; it does make them different under some circumstances (Schwartz, 1996). Two types of such families by choice will be discussed here: adoptive families and foster families. These have some similarities and, again, some differences, even from each other.

Adoptive families are those in which a couple, and sometimes today a single person, chooses an infant or child to rear as their own child. What adoption means in terms of family is that the parents and child acquire, by judicial action, the same legal relationship as parents and the children born to them. The biological parents have had to sign documents in which they terminated their parental status, and usually have no further contact with the child. (The lack of contact is not the case in "open" adoptions, a controversial practice that will be discussed later.)

Today an adoptive family may be transracial or intentional in composition as well as what was almost universally true years ago—then the child bore some physical resemblance to one or both parents as a result of a "matching" search by the adoption agency. It may even mean, today, that the child has two parents of the same gender, as when homosexuals succeed in adopting a child, as cohabiting but unmarried parents (In re Jacob, 1995), or may have only one adoptive parent. Each of these relatively new practices brings its own potential complications to the family. One other practice, surrogate motherhood with its inherent partial adoption, can also raise problems within the family in general as well as for the child in particular (Schwartz, 1991, in press-b).

It is also important to be aware of the differences between the adoption of a newborn and that of an older child, and between a healthy child and one with special needs. Each of these situations places different demands on the adoptive parents and may be contrary to their expectations. Transracial and international adoptions add the complications of dealing with federal, and sometimes international, law, as well as affecting relationships with the extended family and larger community.

Foster families, on the other hand, are perceived as temporary families, although a given child may remain in the same family for several years. The task here is to care for the infant or child until the biological parent is once again able to care for the child, although in some cases the foster parents are the caretakers prior to an adoption. Foster families are usually supervised by community agencies, but the quality of supervision is often questioned. There are also other situations, however, in which the foster parent arrangement is less formal, as in the case of grandparents raising grandchildren, and these may function without supervision.

Foster care requires that the foster parents not only be willing to share their lives and their homes with children who have been removed from their biological parents, but also that they be capable of letting go of that child when outsiders—usually in the social welfare system—decide that the child should return to the original home or be moved on to an adoptive home. This can raise some questions about how close a bond foster parents should or actually do develop with the foster child. Agency-sponsored foster care also involves payment to the caretakers for services rendered, unlike adoption where the prospective parents typically bear all the expenses (although they may be eligible for a federal adoption tax credit or the child may be eligible for a government subsidy). Unlike neonates or infants adopted within the first few months of birth, foster children removed from their original home have often experienced abuse. As a result, they may well bring with them emotional "baggage" that makes adjustment to the foster family more difficult. Are the foster parents mature enough and emotionally stable enough to handle these problems constructively?

In both types of families, there may be incidents, questions, or problems that bring one or more family members to the family therapist. These may range from lack of bonding between the parents and child(ren) to laws that affect the viability of the family. Members of a family may already be in therapy for other reasons (e.g., marital therapy or "acting-out" behavior of a child) when issues relating to the family structure arise. Therapists need to be alert to the fact that it is not always the family arrangement that is at the root of the child's problem, or that of the parent's, but that, as in biological families, the interaction of varied personalities and perhaps particular situations can exacerbate latent difficulties.

MAJOR ISSUES

There are a number of issues in both adoption and foster placement that can bring people to therapists. These begin with why the adults involved chose this route to familyhood, and can concern the age, special needs, or origin of the child, and continue on to legal problems arising from the adoption or foster placement. Each of these will be briefly discussed to provide background for sources of potential psychological problems. The focus here is on the adoptive or foster family rather than on the surrendering parent(s), but therapists should also have an awareness of their emotional needs and choices (see, e.g., Sobol & Daly, 1992).

ADOPTION

Why, How, and Who to Adopt
Perhaps the most common reason for deciding to adopt one or more children is that the would-be parent(s) cannot conceive, carry, or deliver a biological child. There are other

people, however, who simply want to help one or more children to have a better chance in life than the one they had been dealt at birth. In some cases, they have biological children and decide to adopt more (or they choose to adopt and at a later date are able to have their own biological child).

There are many aspects of adoption about which they should be aware in order to minimize later complications (Horwich, 1997). Domestic adoptions can be arranged through social service agencies, typically with a wait of several years for a healthy infant, perhaps less time for a "hard-to-place" child, or through private sources that may have a shorter wait. Fees vary with the agency and, in the case of private adoptions, with any costs of pregnancy paid to the mother (the nature and amount of which may vary by state). Interstate adoptions can add problems of jurisdictional disputes if a biological parent withdraws consent to the adoption (Crawford, 1994). International adoptions, usually of older infants, toddlers, or preschoolers, can also be handled by agencies, but are often accomplished in less than 2 years, even with the complications of foreign laws (Gallagher, 1998).

Decisions to be made before deciding which route to take include whether the adoptee must be an infant or whether the prospective parents will welcome an older child. Is the child to be of the same racial or religious background as theirs or is that not critical? Will they only take a healthy child, or do they feel a "call" to adopt a child with special needs? It should be noted that the older child, or the one with special needs, may have had prior negative experiences, and so come to the new parents with the same kinds of emotional baggage as a child who has been in several foster homes. In the case of unmarried couples, whether heterosexual or homosexual, there may be additional questions about whether their state of residence will recognize their relationship and permit the adoption by one partner (where the other is the biological mother) or both partners (where the child is unrelated) (Goodheart, 1998).

The "why's" and "how's" of adoption have rarely been in the forefront of the news, unless an adoption ended tragically or was arranged illegally. In October 1998, however, *The New York Times* ran a series of three articles on adoption, each more than two full-size newspaper pages in length and each beginning on the front page, that touched on a few of the key issues to be discussed here (Fein, 1998; Lewin, 1998; Mansnerus, 1998). Giving adoption such a large role in the public's consciousness suggests that this is becoming a more important way of building a family than may have been true heretofore. The series, "In Search of a Child," alerted readers to the many questions all members of the adoption triad—biological parents, adoptive parents, and adoptees—ask themselves at some point. It also made the public aware of the significant legal differences among the states on such critical questions as permissible payments by the adoptive parents, when the birth mother may sign her consent to the adoption, and whether she has time afterwards to withdraw that consent (Mansnerus, 1998).

Transracial Adoption
When people of one race seek to adopt a child of a different racial background, they need to examine not only their own motives, as in any other prospective adoption, but also the community in which they live. An urban neighborhood with residents of varying backgrounds may be more receptive and supportive than one where families of only one or two backgrounds live, or than a small town. Although transracial adoption is far more common today than it was before, unfortunately bias and discrimination still exist and their possible effects on the child should be at least considered before making a commitment.

Transracial adoptions became a bit more common than they had been previously when veterans and their spouses adopted children orphaned in World War II, the Korean War, and Vietnam. At the same time (from the late 1940s into the 1970s and 1980s) there was a gradual movement in parts of the Caucasian community from the total disgrace of out-of-wedlock motherhood to an acceptance of that state. (For an overview of the changes in the world of adoption in the last quarter of that period, see Howe, 1983.) This reduced the availability of white infants for adoption. This was not as true in the African American community. However, a variety of studies cited by McRoy (1997) indicate that there are not enough African American homes available to welcome the tens of thousands of same-race children into foster care or adoption. Rather than have them remain in abusive or otherwise hazardous homes, many child welfare agencies have become more open to transracial placements.

On the opposing side, complications may arise from pressure groups within the second racial group that oppose transracial adoption, such as the National Association of Black Social Workers or supporters of the Indian Child Welfare Act of 1978 (Hollingsworth, 1998; Schwartz, in press-a). Minority placement agencies were organized in some locations to encourage and implement in-race adoptions (McRoy, 1997). The Multiethnic Placement Act of 1994 originally attempted to ban any consideration of race, color, or national origin of child or foster or adoptive parent by agencies or entities receiving federal aid, but this was modified in 1996 (Hollingsworth, 1998), and has varying effect depending on a number of factors.

Prospective parents should seek counseling to help prepare themselves for conflicts arising from one of these sources, or for guidance in explaining the differences in appearance to the children as they mature. Harris (1997) has noted a number of interesting and potentially embarrassing interpersonal-type problems that may arise, particularly for the daughter whose race differs from that of her adoptive or foster parents. In addition, foster parents involved in a transracial placement who seek to adopt the child may find themselves in a controversial situation that has each side claiming to be focused on the child's "best interests," and may need a highly knowledgeable attorney to help them wade through state legislation that appears to ban transracial adoptions. As in many other contested adoptions, there is "right" on both sides: On the one hand, should the child be separated from the family that loves and cares for him or her; on the other, should the child be separated from those who are physically and culturally like him or her?

International Adoption

Although Pearl Buck, a popular author a few decades ago, promoted the adoption of Chinese babies, overseas adoptions were a relative rarity in the past, except, perhaps, for those unwed and pregnant women sent out of their home countries to have their babies in the United States (Hunt, 1998), or for those abandoned in war-torn countries. The practice has increased markedly in recent years as the number of babies available for adoption decreased in the United States. Some countries that were formerly part of the Soviet Union have permitted foreign adoptions, as have China, Vietnam, Peru, Guatemala, and many others. Sometimes this becomes part of a political battle, so that the status of adoptions can change even while the prospective parents are meeting their potential child at the orphanage. In addition, laws may change as conditions in the home country are perceived differently at various times or by different pressure groups, again having unforeseeable impact on overseas adoptions (Farley, 1998).

There are legitimate concerns about the adequacy of preadoptive care in some of the overseas adoptions. Were children in an orphanage given enough food, affectionate handling, and exercise? Is the information on the birth parents complete in terms of health problems, substance abuse, prenatal care, and nutrition? How long has the child been in institutional or foster care? Are the medical records informative, accurate, and complete? Albers and her associates (1997) found that birth dates were often missing, itemized diagnoses and medications were unfamiliar to American physicians, children had apparently not been appropriately immunized against a variety of diseases ranging from polio to rubella, and there was often developmental delay in the adoptees unaccounted for in the available documents. They suggested, as have other researchers (e.g., Mainemer, Gilman, & Ames, 1998), that parental stress among the adopting parents might be reduced if it were recognized that children coming from the orphanages in what had been the Soviet Union should initially, at least, be regarded as children with special needs. Many of them certainly have memories of parents as well as the orphanage since these children may not be infants, and they may have been traumatized by the loss of parents in wartime. Another problem, more of legal concern, is whether the child was, perhaps, taken from the mother without her agreement (Ellison, 1998). To be emotionally secure, it behooves the adopting parents to acquire as much accurate information as possible about the child they hope to rear.

It should be remembered that many international adoptions involve the transracial element as well. Accordingly, "what children think of themselves as they grow up is crucial and their race is one of the basic ingredients of their self-concepts" (Rickard Liow, 1994, p. 378). They may also need help in coping with any trauma they might have experienced in wars (like Kosovo), floods (as in Nicaragua after Hurricane Mitch), or similar calamities.

Special Needs Adoptions

Special needs adoptees include older children, sibling groups, and children with a variety of physical, cognitive, and/or emotional disabilities. They may need special services, equipment, or care, and certainly prospective adoptive parents should be aware of their particular problems and needs prior to assuming their care. In some cases, the child is eligible for financial aid from Medicaid that eases the family's burden in providing needed medical care, although such a subsidy is rarely the stimulus for adopting special needs children. Most families who have adopted special needs children report great satisfaction with their decision (Lightburn & Pine, 1996), but many also cite the need for more sensitive professional workers and for some arrangement for respite care (Groze, 1996).

Older children may have been removed from their biological families as infants and been reared in one or more foster homes, or the removal may occur later because of a severe change in circumstances in the home such as physical or emotional abuse, parental imprisonment, substance addiction, or death of parent(s) with no extended family available to adopt. In any case, the children have had experiences that may lead them to have nightmares, anxieties, or inappropriate behaviors. If this is the case, the adoptive families need guidance from the placement agency, an appropriate support group, or a mental health therapist to help them help the children.

Sibling groups provide a different challenge. It is almost always highly desirable to keep siblings together as they move into a strange situation such as adoption. They tend to be their own support group and do not experience the loss of everyone familiar to them. However, finding prospective parents who are willing and able to assume the responsibility for two or more children at the same time may be a challenge for agencies. If there are biological children in the adoptive family as well, the adoption of more than one child at one time can lead to an "us versus them" conflict that needs defusing at times, and therapists can help the parents develop the skills to handle such situations.

Children with severe or chronic medical, cognitive, or emotional problems need more time and attention than healthy children and the adoptive parents not only need the temperament to deal with them, but they also need all of the relevant information about the nature and, where possible, the origin of the problems. The placement agency should certainly advise the new parents about any ongoing therapy the children are receiving and from what sources. It should be noted that although there is a legitimate concern about the number of babies born to substance-abusive mothers and who have drugs in their systems at birth, at least one study suggests that 4 years postadoption, such children "appear to function very much like other children as do their adoptive parents" (Barth & Needell, 1996, p. 49). Not every child responds so well to tender loving care, however, and some children may have developmental problems stemming from their mothers' addiction during pregnancy that are not remediable.

Step-Parent Adoption

Step-parent adoptions can take place either as a result of death or divorce preceding the other parent's remarriage. In the case of a still living and actively involved nonresidential parent, the step-parent is less likely to take such a step than if there is no contact with the noncaretaker. Adoption is a strong statement of commitment on the part of the step-parent to both the biological parent and the child(ren) involved, and may represent, at least in part, an attempt to establish a legal as well as an emotional bond to the child(ren) in the family unit. The move to adopt may vary with the age of the children involved, as midadolescents and older children may not feel the need or have the desire for such a tie, and they are often consulted by judges when adoption petitions are presented. Psychological parenting does not require judicial permission, however (Buser, 1991).

As Ganong and his associates (1998) have pointed out, this is a case where the step-parent is the newcomer in the family unit, not the child, as is true in more typical adoptions. They caution that there are many factors to be considered in step-parent adoption, including financial responsibility, as presumably child support from the child's other parent (in the case of divorce) would cease upon adoption. They discuss the possibility of adapting a British legal concept of "parental responsibility" in which the step-parent would have certain legal rights vis-à-vis the stepchild (e.g., school permissions, health care) but would not change the nonparent's status or responsibility.

Step-parent adoption can cause difficulty, however, with the grandparents and other extended family members of the displaced/deceased parent, and the courts vary in how they resolve questions about the resulting visitation rights of these biological relatives. As Hintz (1994) has indicated, some states have amended their adoption laws to permit continued postadoption visits if the biological relatives have previously had an ongoing relationship with the child. There is, however, a need to avoid perception of the child(ren) as "property" in any such legal conflict.

"Upset" Adoptions

There is typically a waiting period between the time the child comes home to the prospective adoptive parents and the time when the adoption is finalized in court. This may vary from 90 days to a year or slightly more, depending on the jurisdiction. One source of anxiety for the would-be parents is the possibility that one or both of the biological parents will withdraw consent for the adoption. The "Baby Jessica" and "Baby Richard" cases in the early 1990s were highly publicized examples of such problems (Schwartz, 1983, 1986, 1993a, 1993b, 1996). If the adoption has crossed state lines, the legal picture grows even murkier, despite the existence of a Uniform Adoption Act approved by the American Bar Association in 1995 and referred to state legislatures for their approval (Czerwinski, 1996, n. 15; Rodier, 1997). The courts vary in whether they emphasize the importance of biology or the child's "best interests," with the result that adoptive parents caught in such a suit cannot be certain that the child they have reared, possibly for years, will remain with them. Therapeutic support may well be warranted to help the family weather this stressful period.

Adoption in Surrogate Motherhood Cases

The most common form of surrogate motherhood involves paying a woman to carry her own ovum, fertilized by the sperm of the husband of the prospective parent couple, to delivery, after which the woman releases the new baby for adoption by the wife of the couple. Even if the surrogate is the wife's sister or other close relative, a legal adoption must occur (Schwartz, 1991, in press-b). Normally, this goes smoothly; occasionally, as in the "Baby M" case, the surrogate mother decides that she will not consent to the adoption because she either will not surrender the child at all (despite a possible legal suit by the child's father/sperm donor) or wants at least a partial caretaking arrangement—akin to a very open adoption. As with an "upset" adoption, the latter situation may provoke enough anxiety, stress, and hostility among the people involved, including the child, that therapeutic intervention is warranted.

Occasionally, the surrogate mother is really a surrogate in the sense that she is carrying the wife's fertilized ovum to term because the wife cannot carry it and so the surrogate has no genetic tie to the child although she certainly has a physiological one. (Technically, she is a "gestational carrier," not a surrogate mother.) Whether an adoption needs to occur legally in this latter case is highly questionable, but can (and has) run into the same legal battle as when a biological parent withdraws consent for an adoption (Schwartz, in press-b).

A third situation that involves surrogacy has arisen in recent years—carrying a baby for gay men (Bruni, 1998). Typically, the arrangement is made through a surrogacy agency, with the woman being artificially inseminated by one of the male partners involved. Since homosexuality is itself a controversial topic, and outside the purview of this chapter, all that will be said here is that the parents involved must prepare themselves to deal with intrusive and intolerant people who will criticize them for their way of life as well as for their way of becoming parents, and who may be offensive to their child. In the case of lesbian couples, usually one of the women is the biological mother, with her partner assuming a psychological parent role that may or may not be supported by the courts if the couple separates some years later.

FOSTER FAMILIES

Foster families are caretaking families that provide a temporary, sometimes a long-term, home for children from just after birth in some cases to adulthood in other cases. If the placement is under the auspices of a social welfare agency, there may be payment involved for the care, but there is no legal change of custody or termination of parental rights as there is in adoption. One of the long-standing problems in foster care has been that children either remained in foster homes for indeterminate periods or were moved from one foster home to another, but permanency of relationships or a return to the original home seemed not to happen. This is part of what the Adoptions and Safe Families Act of 1997 was designed to remedy. Two standards have been suggested as guidelines for agencies:

> (1) No child who enters nonkinship foster care as an infant should remain in foster care on their second birthday unless they are in a pre-adoptive home and (2) every child placed into nonkinship foster care as an infant who does not go home should have a legalized adoption by their third birthday. (Barth & Needell, 1996, pp. 53–54)

Although this seems highly appropriate in most cases, what effect would these standards have on the following case?

Consider a case that involves a formerly drug-addicted mother (African American) who completed an 18-month drug recovery program, has continued outpatient therapy, and holds two jobs, all part of an agreement with welfare authorities as the route to reunion with her child. Her two older children are being raised by their grandmother. She had given birth to a boy, who was, at the time of writing, age 2 1/2 years, and who was born with cocaine in his system. The infant was placed in the foster care of a politically connected, mature white couple, who had four grown children of their own plus another foster child. (The husband is an alderman in Chicago and the wife is an appellate judge in Illinois.) The foster placement agency had intended to return the boy to his mother through July 1997, when apparently the couple decided that they wanted to adopt the boy. "The agency said it changed the goal because [the mother] . . . had yelled at social workers in an alarming way when she thought she might lose her son" (Associated Press, 1998). The child's mother wanted him returned to her, in keeping with the earlier agreement. Meanwhile, the boy has known only one home for his entire life and presumably has established emotional bonds with his foster parents. Should he be returned or should he be adopted? (It is not known whether or how much contact he had with his mother or other family members over this period.) Should the transracial factor be considered here? Should the mother be denied her child after she has successfully met the goals set for her? Should the foster parents be denied their wish to adopt? Truly a dilemma calling for the wisdom of a King Solomon!

The Illinois Supreme Court appointed a Juvenile Court judge from another county to hear the case on the mother's fitness. Her decision was that the mother was fit to care for her son, and the petition to adopt was denied (Associated Press, 1998).

The Social Welfare System

Social service departments of municipalities and states have an inherent obligation to see that the children for whom they are responsible are placed in homes where they will receive the nurturance, both physical and emotional, that they need. What we have seen in recent years is the overburdening of agency staff with too many placements to supervise. When this happens, the workers may become apathetic or superficial in their monitoring and the children may experience abuse, neglect, or worse (Colapinto, 1997; Hansen, 1998; Kestin, 1998; Swarns, 1998). Foster parents, the very ones entrusted with providing safety for defenseless children, have, on occasion, become the abusers and even murderers of these youngsters because they did not have sufficient support from the system that "hired" them.

Reasons for Foster Placement

Children are usually placed in foster care because their parent(s) cannot care for them appropriately or at all. Sometimes, especially in a single-parent family, that parent has taken ill or been injured and cannot care for the children for a limited period until he or she recovers from the health problem. In other cases, of which we are perhaps more aware, the parents have been emotionally or physically abusive to the children, or are themselves substance abusers, so the youngsters are removed from a dangerous environment to a presumably more nurturing and safer one. In still other instances, the single parent, usually the mother, has been incarcerated and the children must be cared for, perhaps informally, by grandparents or another extended family member, or more formally by a foster family. Figures on the number of children whose parents are in custody are incomplete, but the estimate is 1.5 million or more (Seymour, 1998). The potential effects of this enforced separation on the children vary with several factors, but certainly may include anger, loss, guilt, loss of self-esteem, and shame, among other negative feelings no matter what the child's socioeconomic environment. Their therapeutic needs are increased by the parent's imprisonment and consequent traumatic separation as well as the social stigma associated with the punishment, and some effort may have to be made by the foster parents, case worker, and therapist to minimize negative behavior by others toward the child(ren).

Grandparents Rearing Grandchildren

Grandparents have helped to rear their grandchildren for many centuries; this is not new. However, taking on total responsibility for the children's care and welfare as if they were the parents occurs somewhat less frequently, although it is quite common in some communities. Burnette (1997) has asserted that a disproportionate number of affected families are in the poorer sections of cities and involve women and children of color (i.e., African American and Latino) who have HIV/AIDS, are substance abusers, or where the mothers are in prison. Many of the caretakers in these families need assistance in finding legal, medical, and social services.

Several other questions arise with respect to grandparents rearing their grandchildren (Schwartz, 1994): Is the health of the grandparent(s) good enough to allow them to be primary caretaker for young children? Is their income, whether current or from retirement, sufficient to meet the needs of the children in terms of clothing, medical care, cost of day care if needed, or school expenses? In what ways does re-assuming the role of parent affect the grandparent's lifestyle and relationships with others? Does the grandparent have greater difficulty interacting with the child and the child's teachers because of generational differences? Support from other family members, in terms of respite care for the child(ren) or shared decision making, can make the difference between the grandparents being overburdened or handling the resumption of child-rearing responsibilities with comparative ease.

Child Safety versus Family Reunification

The basis for foster care is the idea that such placements are temporary, that the child(ren) will return to the biological family within a relatively short period. Indeed, the stated goal of foster care is family reunification. Too often, as one can read in almost any newspaper or journal today, the children remain with the foster family for several years and the likelihood of their ever being reunited with their birth family is remote because that family does not become fit to rear the children. The welfare system has not been known for recommending an alternative to this ongoing foster care; rather, it has typically removed the child from a foster family that wanted to adopt the youngster and moved him or her else-where—but not back to the birth family either. An alternative has been to reunify the family on the grounds that familial unity is the best thing for the child(ren) even when the safety of the child(ren) is in doubt. Unfortunately, this sometimes ends in tragedy, with the children beaten, starved, burned, or suffocated.

The Adoption and Safe Families Act of 1997 (P. L. 105-89), mentioned earlier, includes provisions that seek to improve the foster care system as well as to see that foster children are either reunited with their families or placed in permanent homes more quickly. For example, "permanency" hearings are now required to begin within 12 months of the date the child is considered to have entered foster care (Title III). Also, by January 1, 1999, the states were required to certify that they were developing and implementing standards to ensure that children in foster care placements would receive quality services that protected their health and safety (Title III).

POTENTIAL PSYCHOLOGICAL PROBLEMS

"Closed" versus "Open" Adoptions

"Closed" adoptions include most of those that took place until about the 1970s to 1980s. The biological and adoptive parents were kept completely apart, with minimal knowledge about the biological mother given out by the agency or intermediary and all records as to her identity kept in a sealed record once the adoption was court-approved and final. The children were given birth certificates amended to show only the adoptive parents' names. Adopted children had no way to find out anything about their heritage, including medical history that might be important later in their lives, and had no opportunity to meet any of their biological relatives. So-called "open" adoptions, on the other hand, involve direct contact between the biological and adoptive parents, varying from a restricted exchange of information and photos for a limited period of time to a direct contact relationship that continues as the child grows up (Berry, 1991).

There are both benefits and risks to some or all of the parties in any of these arrangements, and good summaries of these may be found in Berry (1991), Siegel (1993), and Lee and Twaite (1997). The agency or intermediary involved in an infant's placement should help both sides evaluate what is feasible and comfortable for them, and help them to recognize that the decision is for the long term. Lifton (1988), herself an adoptee, is a strong advocate of open adoption, but all parties concerned might consider, as she did not in many of her presentations, what might be the effects on the children if there are two, three, or four adopted children in one family, each with different biological parents who are interacting with them and the adoptive parents.

If the adoptee is a preschooler or older, the situation is different. The child has already lived with parents or other caretakers for a few years and formed bonds with the caretakers. There are memories of relationships and events, obviously more numerous as the child grows older. There are also ties to extended family members, like cousins and grandparents. Here, open adoption would seem to be warranted unless there is a good reason against it, such as removal of the child because of child abuse.

Yet another situation arises when the adoptee decides, as an adolescent or adult, to look for biological family connections. If the individual was adopted with the past in a sealed record (the traditional closed adoption), it might be well for a neutral counselor or therapist to suggest some "food for thought." Whatever the reason the older adoptee may have for seeking the biological parent, and it may be primarily for medical history reasons rather than for seeking "roots" and biological connections, has that adoptee thought through the consequences of finding that parent? To begin with, the biological parent may not want to be found, especially if the placement took place 25 or more years ago when out-of-wedlock births were regarded more negatively than they are today. He or she may never have told a current spouse or other family members about the birth of this child and the subsequent release for adoption. This could create difficulties within that individual's family. (It is possible in some jurisdictions for birth mothers to indicate their willingness to be contacted by the children they placed for adoption should those children decide to seek information.)

Given today's litigious society, it is even possible that, once found, the surrendering parent may demand some kind of financial support or compensation from the child or the adoptive family. Indeed, as this chapter was being written, the story of such a case was printed, and is, according to one source cited, the only case of which the source was aware "in which a birth mother's discovery had escalated into litigation" (Testa, 1998). Found more than 35 years after she had given up her daughter for adoption, the mother has filed suit "against the private investigator hired by her daughter, alleging invasion of privacy and intentional infliction of emotional distress" (Testa, 1998). Part of the suit is focused on the investigator's use of information that was allegedly obtained illegally, but the case also raises the question of which "right" is more important, the right to privacy or the right to ancestry. As in other cases mentioned in this chapter, where is King Solomon when he is needed?

On the other hand, what happens within the adoptee's family of nurture or marriage? In one distressing case, the adoptee's 6-year-old child met members of the mother's family of origin and soon thereafter blurted out to her grandmother (adoptive mother of the child's mother), "You're not my real grandmother! ____ is!" This not only distressed the grandmother, but also created an area of conflict between the child's parents and grandmother, for the child had obviously gotten this view from one or both of her parents (Author's files).

Delays and Disappointments in Transracial and International Adoptions

Bartholet (1993) has authored one of the most knowledgeable books on the subject of international adoption and its possible complications, especially the political "games" that can cause governments to change their stance with respect to out-of-country adoptions while the process is in progress. Despite the promises of "quick" overseas adoptions by some agencies, the prospective parents need to be prepared for delays and disappointments. Similarly, if an agent for either Native Americans or another ethnic group seeks to upset a transracial adoption, claiming possible harm to the child by removing her from her ancestry, either the adoption process can become very convoluted and delayed, or the child may be removed from the would-be adoptive parents on a temporary or permanent basis (Schwartz, 1996).

Children Adopted When Older

Children who are adopted after they pass infancy, and particularly once they are of school age, come to the family with emotional bonds and a variety of experiences that younger adoptees do not have. If the adoptee has been in one or more foster families and is now being adopted by one of them, that is one kind of situation; if the adoptive parents represent yet another change of family, that is a different situation. If the child is being adopted by relatives subsequent to the death of his or her parents, again that is different from being adopted by nonrelatives after the same kind of trauma. Does the child come with a background of abuse or of affection? Were the adopting parents made aware of the child's history prior to placement? Clearly, these variables and others contribute to the overall adjustment of the child to the adoptive family and that of parents (and siblings) to the adopted child. Usually, the more negative the child's previous experiences, the wiser it would be to seek therapeutic support to help all family members make a healthy transition. (One mother's story [Hurlburt, 1998] amplifies some of these problems and makes the reader aware of the dangers of poor professional "help.") Glib statements about all that the child needs is love are not truly helpful.

Children with Special Needs

Youngsters with problems beyond the usual range of developmental challenges, whether adopted, biological, or foster in their relationships, can experience even more self-doubts or have weaker self-esteem because they perceive how others perceive them. For example, many learning disabled youngsters are well aware that their reading level lags behind that of their classmates' or a child with physical coordination problems is aware that he is not riding a two-wheeler when his friends are or that she cannot throw a ball as well as her friends do. In any of these cases, the other children may tease the less able child so much that emotional problems erupt; therapy may provide the needed skills or coping techniques.

Searching for the Biological Parents or Interaction with Them

It is quite common for children aged 6 years or so to ask where they came from, and for a reappearance of that question as they approach adolescence. The younger ones tend to be seeking a biological explanation ("No, you were not hatched!"), while the older ones, who have a better understanding of what adoption means, are asking about specific people. If they have not been part of an open adoption it would be appropriate to provide as much information as a preteen or young adolescent can comprehend, although not necessarily names and street addresses at this point. This is going to vary by state in terms of confidentiality and needed permissions to search for the biological family if this has been a traditional adoption. Potential psychological problems calling for therapy may arise if the youngster becomes obsessed with the idea of a search or is angered by an inability to acquire needed information.

On the other hand, if there is an open adoption in place and the youngster does interact with biological parents or siblings, does conflict arise as to which is the "better" family? Do feelings of guilt arise, perhaps, in an adoptee because he or she is part of an adopted family that is socioeconomically more affluent than the biological one? Is there a temptation, or a desire, to play off one family against the other?

Families with Biological and Adopted or Foster Children

Navigating the waters of the parent-child relationship when there are both biological and adopted or foster children within the same family unit can be a very challenging task. Some of the factors that may determine whether the family sails effectively or sinks under conflicts include (1) which came first, the biological or the nonbiological child(ren); (2) favoritism shown by one or both parents; (3) extrafamilial influences, such as extended family roles vis-à-vis the children or religious strictures that place genetic ties above nongenetic ones (Rosenberg, 1998); and (4) the tendency of children to tease each other on points where they are vulnerable. If the biological children came first, do they resent the entrance of adopted or foster children into the family, perhaps because of the extra caretaking the newcomers need? If the adopted children came first, do the parents feel a kind of loyalty or gratitude to them as "enablers" of the subsequent sibling births, or do they allow the newcomers to displace the adopted children in their affections? If teasing occurs that goes beyond the usual sibling inter-action, do the parents try to explain to the children why it is inappropriate or do they allow it to continue? How do the children swim in this changing waterway? Might therapeutic inter-vention, probably short term, provide an effective lifeboat?

Ames Reed (1994), a British researcher, did one of the relatively few studies on rela-tionship between biological and foster children, the latter with learning disabilities. An interesting item in her paper mentions a video about fostering made by a birth children's support group in Yorkshire. This reflects the sometimes ambivalent feelings that the birth children may have as a result of the impact of having foster siblings on their lives. The ambivalence among Ames Reed's 23 subjects is perhaps most clearly stated as "These young people were concerned to safeguard the welfare of the young person living with them and worried and upset about the effects of caring on their parents and on themselves" (p. 171). For therapists intervening in a situation with such a combined family, it would be appropriate to ascertain whether the adults give their own children enough time and energy, whether the biological children have been asked to assume too many responsibilities with respect to the foster child(ren), whether they could discuss their feelings with their parents, and whether there is enough physical room for everyone in the family home. As Ames Reed points out, these may seem like "commonsensical" factors, but they may be over-looked too often. Twigg's study (1995), with a smaller sample in central Canada, found that the biological children tended to experience a narcissistic loss when the foster children came into the family and, as a result, tried to distance themselves from the foster siblings. In some cases this may have been partly because the foster children were juvenile delin-quents on probation. The two samples are not equivalent, so caution must be used when comparing their findings.

Child Abuse
There is no question that child abuse in any form is dangerous to children's mental health as well as their physical being. If children have never known any other pattern in the care-taker-child relationship, they may learn over time both avoidance and adaptive techniques that keep them from being beaten too badly, while denying to others that any such abuse ever occurs. Of course, if they are too young to acquire survival mechanisms when abuse occurs, they may be permanently harmed or indeed may not survive. It is upsetting enough to outsiders that child abuse occurs, but when a child has been removed from a threaten-ing parent as a protective measure, and then is returned from foster care to that parent who has not received therapy for abusive behaviors and who subsequently kills or severely injures the child, great public and professional condemnation is justifiably heaped on the welfare agency responsible.

PREVAILING POSITIONS

CONFLICTS OVER TRANSRACIAL ADOPTIONS: WHICH IS MORE IMPORTANT: THE CHILD OR THE RACE?

Transracial adoption itself is not found to be negative. Indeed, Rickard Liow (1994) has found that studies indicate that disruption rates of transracial adoptions do not differ from those of intraracial adoptions, and success rates are comparable. The adopting parents are certainly aware that they are bringing home a child who is of a different race, and the child will only need to look in a mirror to be aware of the difference. Whether this becomes a problem outside the home may be more a political matter than a psychological one (i.e., if the child is subject to teasing or emotional abuse by others, or if a racial group seeks to upset the adoption on the grounds of intraethnic placement as a primary goal).

THE BIOLOGICAL PARENTS AND ADOPTEES: IS IT VITAL FOR ALL ADOPTEES TO SEEK THEIR BIOLOGICAL PARENTS?

The answer to this question depends very much on who is asked to respond. Many case workers and some mental health professionals would say that it is vital for all adoptees; others would reply that it might be important if there is suspicion of a genetically based illness, but that otherwise it is not essential and might even be traumatic. Some adoptees have to work out their own questions of why they were given up for adoption, no matter what the adoptive parents have told them. For whatever reason, they may feel betrayed, abandoned, rejected, worthless, or all of these (Jones, 1997). The roots of such feelings may be very subtle, but are very real and very painful. Searching for the biological parents may only reinforce these feelings, or it may reduce them; no therapist can know which is the case for certain. Therapists, if asked, should not dictate the adoptee's behavior, but rather should ask the adoptee why it is important, what he or she expects to find, and what the impact of any discovery might be on existing relationships.

CHILD SAFETY VERSUS FAMILY REUNIFICATION: CAN PROBLEMS IN FOSTER CHILD PLACEMENTS BE AVOIDED?

There are several responses to this question. One is that family reunification has priority over all other considerations. That has been the policy of many welfare agencies, sometimes resulting in tragedy for the children. Another response is that the child's safety is paramount, and that if this means remaining in foster care rather than returning to the biological family, so be it. A third reply focuses on the need for more proactive interaction with the biological parent(s) in an effort to rehabilitate the parent(s) and ensure the child's safety and well-being. What is clearly not desirable is to have the child moving back and forth between family home and foster home(s) several times over the course of childhood.

IMPACT ON THE FAMILIES

CONFLICTS BETWEEN PARENTS OVER WHY, HOW, AND WHO TO ADOPT

If either parent has reservations about adoption or foster care, the couple should postpone any such action until they can go forward in agreement and with a positive attitude, even if they have some natural anxieties about how the placement will work out. If, on the other hand, they are in agreement about wanting to go ahead but disagree on the agent to use or whom to adopt, they might be well advised to consult experienced professionals in the field. For example, if the question is a domestic versus an international adoption, they might not only explore the practical and legal questions, but also make lists of advantages and disadvantages of each approach. If the question has to do with the age or race of the child, again they might want to seek professional advice, and perhaps from more than one source. What is not needed in an adoptive family is reluctance on the part of one parent that will inevitably affect that parent's relationship with the child and probably with the spouse as well. That state of affairs could lead to divorce and further trauma for the child as well as for the adults.

INTERACTION WITH BIOLOGICAL PARENTS CAN BE STRESSFUL FOR ALL INVOLVED

As has already been suggested, interaction with the adoptee's biological parents and other family members can be more or less stressful for all parties depending on the time when the adoption took place and the precipitating circumstances. In a period when out-of-wedlock pregnancy was perceived as highly disgraceful and so was hidden, the woman may never have told anyone that she had had a baby and placed it for adoption, as in the case mentioned earlier. The appearance of that child 20, 30, or 40 years later could be tragically traumatic for her and her current family—or might be welcome. For the adoptive parents, the search for the biological family may seem to be a repudiation of all the care and affection they have given the child, and as such could create negative feelings in what had been a warm relationship. Birth mothers who placed their babies in more recent years, on the other hand, might welcome a certain amount of communication with their children (Cushman, Kalmuss, & Namerow, 1997). As already mentioned, in some jurisdictions it is possible for birth mothers to register their willingness to be contacted by the children they bore.

The adoptee in either situation is likely to have ambivalent feelings—curiosity about the biological family mixed with anxiety about their nature and circumstances. "What if they are substance abusers?" "What if they're illiterate?" "What if my mother was a prostitute?" "What if they carry some terrible disease?" These questions may not stop the desire to search, but they will certainly provoke stress.

INCOMPATIBILITY OF CHILD AND ADOPTIVE/FOSTER PARENTS

A number of longitudinal studies (e.g., Fergusson, Lynskey, & Horwood, 1995) point to reasons for adjustment and behavior problems among adoptees and foster children as well as difficulties that their caretaking parents may have. In the case of adoptive parents, there may be a reluctance to accept their infertility that reduces their ability to respond to the adoptee with warmth to the child's arrival, or they may simply be unrealistic in their expectations of what the child will be like (Berry, 1992). On the child's side, especially if older when adopted or placed in foster care, there may have been multiple placements or abusive experiences in the past that subtly encourage the child to test the limits of what the new parents will accept. In addition, as noted elsewhere, incomplete background data may not prepare the parents for a child who has special problems due to lack of prenatal care or maternal substance abuse. These and other factors can lead to poor adjustment of the child and disruptive behavior that interferes with a successful adoption (Schwartz, 1996). If the latter occurs, the would-be adoptive parents may feel that the deficiency was theirs, that they did not know how to be effective parents. Although erroneous, such a self-perception can be very damaging to them.

FAMILIES AND THERAPY

As Janus (1997) has indicated, adoption has been primarily the province of social workers, but for any professional working with families in which adoption has played a role, the knowledge and sensitivity needed to help them can be acquired. Mental health specialists can certainly learn, through a variety of modes, about the preadoption needs of birth parents and prospective parents, about the doubts that any of the parents may have concerning the adoption or how they are handling the child, about the conflicts an adoptee may feel about searching for a biological parent, and about the effects that being an adoptee may have on that individual's self-esteem or behavior.

Some professionals, notably social workers, tend to perceive adoptive parents who see themselves as parents in a garden-variety nuclear family as being "in denial" of their status as a "different" kind of family. Other professionals, more often psychologists and psychiatrists, see adoptive parents who emphasize their different status as being the ones with a problem. There is a need on the part of the therapist to consider the context in time and social or ethnic group as well as clients' personas in determining whether their views on the infertility that stimulated adoption, or their feelings about creating a family without a biological connection, are healthy or not. Which is healthier: to lament one's infertility 15 or 20 years after opting to adopt children that one cannot have otherwise, to continue to wonder many years later (and to verbalize it) about what biological children of the couple would have looked like, or to be thankful for the opportunity to rear children who regard you as their parent and call you "Mom" or "Dad"?

Certainly there are many other issues to which the therapist must attend, from "special needs" children to those adopted by people of a different racial, religious, or national background. The therapist can learn not only the basic information needed to begin working with families where one or more of these factors may be involved, but also has to know where to find more information, whether of a psychological, educational, or legal nature. Much information can be found on the World Wide Web today, although care needs to be taken about which websites are visited. Whether it is urgent that genograms showing adoptive and biological families be developed in the therapy setting is debatable, despite their utility in many situations and the pressure by some therapists for their use (Groze & McMillen, 1994; Rosenberg & Groze, 1997).

It behooves all of these professionals—mental health, educational, or judicial—to be aware that some of their views make things more difficult or stressful for adoptive families rather than less so. Nickman and Lewis (1994) have indicated four principal areas in which professionals may do more damage than good:

1. Failure to be aware of the different kinds of placement and the distinctions among them, such as adoption versus foster care; dealing with an infant versus an adolescent; closed or open adoption.
2. Failure to recognize and support family bonds that exist even during stress, with the result that the troubled or troubling adoptee may be separated from the adoptive parents rather than trying to work out the problem within the adoptive family unit.
3. Inappropriate intrusions into family life, such as asking when and how the child was adopted when that is not at issue.
4. Failure to provide appropriate psychotherapy (i.e., ignoring or overvaluing the child's past history, depending on age at adoption).

Too often, professionals operate from stereotypes or their own biases, such as attributing a quasi-"malignant" denial to parents who prefer to have or sustain a closed adoption, much to the detriment of the family with a presenting problem. Therapists in particular need to guard against such behavior because (1) they will be less helpful ultimately to their clients, and (2) they need to be alert to any such behavior in others that may hurt their clients. They might consider, to begin with, under what circumstances the adoption took place and whether there had been support groups or mentors who might have guided parents and children alike in developing healthy attitudes and relationships vis-à-vis their family status.

A particularly tragic case that involved two sets of professionals making a situation worse, with damage to at least three families, was the slaying and sexual assault of a little girl in a Las Vegas women's restroom by a bright high school senior, Jeremy S. (Walters, 1998). The first professional misdeed was that Jeremy's biological parents had extensive histories of psychiatric hospitalizations and substance abuse and this was not revealed to his adoptive parents by the placement agency when they adopted him as a "hard-to-place" toddler. Whether or not this predisposed him to alcoholism and drug abuse when he was 17 and 18 was not offered as a defense by Jeremy or anyone else, but his adoptive parents believe that the information might have guided their behavior to be more proactive. The second professional error occurred when "at least four" counselors and therapists to whom they took Jeremy in the year before the killing each shrugged off his changed behavior as in typical adolescent rebellion and negative .peer influence, despite the fact that this behavior represented a 180-degree turn from his status as a college- and Air Force-bound honor student. Whether they regarded Jeremy as a stereotypical adolescent or as a stereotypical adoptee is unimportant, other than as relevant to their failure to provide appropriate psychotherapy.

Adoption per se does not create mental health problems, but adoptive parents tend to be willing to seek professional assistance for their children (as was true in this case), which appears to inflate the figures when comparing adopted and biological children in treatment (Schwartz, 1996). It might be noted that when someone commits a crime and is found to have been adopted, at any age, that fact is sometimes overstressed in the media. This is inappropriate and can create false images of adoption outcomes in the minds of some people.

EMERGENCE OF CONFLICTS OR DIFFICULTIES DURING INDIVIDUAL/MARITAL/FAMILY THERAPY: WHAT THE THERAPIST NEEDS TO KNOW IN TERMS OF RESOURCES AND STATE LAWS

Adolescence can be a troubling time for youths and their parents. In the case of some adoptees, it may be a time of becoming more curious about their biological forebears and why they were placed for adoption, but therapists should neither take this for granted as the root of misbehavior nor dismiss it as irrelevant. Similarly, there may be unresolved feelings regarding infertility held by one or both adoptive parents, but again, this should neither be assumed nor dismissed, contrary to the position taken by McDaniel and Jennings (1997). McDaniel and Jennings quite correctly urge, however, that therapists in training be made aware of the role of adoption in families where this is part of the history. What is important is that therapists be sensitive to these possibilities as relevant to adoptive families, but not be blinded to other factors as possibly more critical to the problem that brought the family in.

If, indeed, an adolescent wants to locate and perhaps visit the original biological family and was adopted as a newborn or infant, the therapist needs to know where to find out what such a search requires and whether it is permitted in the state of residence. The therapist also needs to be able to point out the possible outcomes of such a search, if allowed, and have the young adoptee think about the ramifications for everyone involved before acting.

If the adoptee was placed as a toddler or later, there may be memories that are troubling or are treasured and warm. In this case, the therapist should be made aware of why the child was placed when he was, and whether the adoptive parents are from the extended biological family. There is a vast difference between being placed because one's parents died with no one in the family to assume their roles and being removed from abusive parents.

Dealing with Disappointments: Rescinded Adoptions, Adoptions That Fail or Do Not Happen

There are a variety of disappointments that can occur en route to adoption. For instance, no agency or legitimate intermediary may find a particular couple to be suitable as potential parents—for whatever reason. The rejection is a blow to the couple's self-esteem as well as a mortal defeat to their hopes. Would-be parents may travel thousands of miles to adopt a child only to have the laws of a country change as they wait for the paperwork to be completed, as we have seen. Either biological parent may decide not to place the newborn even before the child leaves the hospital. Any of these situations can cause great distress for the would-be parents.

The most difficult disappointment to deal with, however, would be the one where the child has already been welcomed into the adoptive home and then a biological parent rescinds the agreement to terminate parental rights, before the final adoption papers have been signed in court, or, as has occurred in several cases, the welfare agency removes the child(ren) with or without warning from a transracial placement (Samuels, 1998). The pain to the prospective adoptive parents may equal that of losing a child to death. If there are other adopted children in the home, the parents may simply say that the baby "left," and never discuss the matter again (Schwartz, 1996). If old enough, the other adopted children may wonder why their parents never came for them. The repressed feelings of either parent and the repressed curiosity of any of the older children aware of this loss may be appropriate to deal with years later in therapy, but the need to do so should not be taken for granted. As with any other client's situation, each one is unique.

The Difficult Child: Roots of the Problems

The perception of a child as "difficult" may be more in the eye of the beholder than in the reality of the child. To a rigid parent, the child who does not obey instantly is difficult. To the teacher who is threatened by a curious or nonconformist child, that child is difficult. The child whose preferences in friends or goals differs from those of siblings or parents may be perceived as difficult. Children labeled "difficult" typically may be brought for therapy at the instigation of a frustrated parent or teacher. If the adult involved cannot be persuaded to be more flexible, the strategy for the therapist may be to teach the child how to cope with difficult adults.

Other children who are difficult indeed have emotional problems that interfere with appropriate behavior at home, on the street, or at school. They may have conditions that can be classified as one of those in the *Diagnostic and Statistical Manual of Mental Disorders, 4th ed.,* of the American Psychiatric Association (1994), or the roots of the child's difficulties may lie in a physical condition, diagnosed or not. Beyond these possibilities, which are equally true for adopted, foster, and biological children, the roots of foster and adopted children's difficulties may be found in maternal substance addiction during pregnancy, or neglect or abuse in the family home before the child is removed. The point here is that it is the child and his or her presenting problem that need to be addressed, as we can rarely go back to undo what has happened in the past, although we may be able to modify the adverse effects.

EFFECTIVE THERAPIST INTERVENTION

BE ABLE TO HELP PARTIES EXPLORE PROS AND CONS OF THE PROJECTED NEW ROLE AND BE ABLE TO GUIDE THEM TO APPROPRIATE RESOURCES/AGENCIES

The Decision to Adopt

What facts of life lead to adoption? Inability to become pregnant or to carry a pregnancy to successful termination is probably still the major reason why a couple decides to adopt a child born of someone else. Modern reproductive technologies do not resolve that problem for everyone, in addition to which these treatments are expensive, not always covered by medical insurance, and therefore may not be obtainable by all those seeking to become pregnant. In still other cases, a couple with or without children may want to provide the opportunity for a better life to a child from a third-world country or from a distressed situation in this country. Or, within families, the adoptee may be an orphaned niece or nephew for whom the aunt and uncle choose to be legally responsible.

If the couple, or one of the partners, is in therapy it is necessary to explore why they want to adopt a child and how they plan to do so. Another question for the therapist to ask may be whether the partners are equally desirous of going the adoption route. If they are not, the therapist can work with both of them to try to reconcile their different viewpoints to one they can both live with rather than having one undermine an adoption with negative feelings.

FOCUS ON AND ENABLE DISCUSSION OF INVOLVEMENT WITH BIOLOGICAL PARENTS: CONSIDER BIOLOGICAL MOTHER'S FEELINGS ABOUT RELINQUISHMENT

If the therapist is working with the biological mother (and possibly the father as well), it may be appropriate to have her try to verbalize her feelings about giving up her baby. There may have been perfectly sensible reasons for doing so, such as being little more than a child herself, or feeling unable or unwilling to be a parent, but that does not mean that the mother has not had second thoughts about surrendering the child to someone else.

An interesting study by Cushman and colleagues (1997) provides at least some insight into the biological mother's feelings. From their original base of 272 unmarried African American and white mothers under age 21 who were planning to place their babies for adoption, 4 years later they were able to interview 171 who had placed their babies, 60 percent of whom had helped to choose the couple who eventually adopted their child. "Without exception, those who had a role in choosing the couple report lower levels of grief, regret, worry, and sadness, and higher levels of relief and peace, than do their counterparts who did not have this opportunity" (p. 14). Most of the birth mothers apparently would have welcomed some information, a "moderately open" arrangement, even if not direct contact with the adopting parents. Overall, however, the birth mothers reported low levels of the negative feelings, "and high levels of relief and feelings of peace regarding the placement decision, at four years post-relinquishment" (p. 17).

Assist Parties in Determining What Is Best for the Child (If Already Part of the Family)

Most parents, particularly first-time parents, may be unsure of how to be "good" parents unless they themselves have had the good fortune to have nurturing and supportive parents. Very often, they need to be oriented to the realities of child development, which include such things as some children trying to manipulate parents to get what they want, or behaving in ways of which the parents do not approve. For example, if the parents are having difficulty making a decision about a particular move for an adopted child, perhaps in being fearful that sending the child away to overnight camp will be perceived by the child as rejection, the therapist can be helpful in resolving the question by providing information and suggestions as well as seeking the child's actual views. In other situations, the therapist may also need to supply content rather than therapy per se, but that, too, may be therapeutic.

If Adoption Fails, for Whatever Reason, Provide Support for Grief and Help for Facing the Situation and Other People

As suggested earlier, the failure of an adoption has many parallels to the death of a child. In most such cases, the parents suffer great grief. They may also be berating themselves for events they could not control, and be totally unable to tell others that the failure has occurred, let alone why. Grief therapy is appropriate and should include any other children in the family, as well as, perhaps, grieving grandparents.

Interaction with Social Worker in Foster Care Cases If Appropriate

There are times, especially when a toddler-age or older child is moving into foster care or an adoptive home, when it may be appropriate for therapists to do an assessment of the child's needs, abilities, and potential mental health problems. It would be helpful if the social worker or welfare agency asked specific questions or expressed the concerns that the therapist should address in such an evaluation. Since that may not always be the case, it is important for the therapist to seek from the referring source all the needed pertinent information so that time and funds available for testing are used in an optimal manner (Kirby & Hardesty, 1998). The therapist may also make recommendations concerning the most advantageous placement for an older child, based on the evaluation, and for continuing therapy if that is needed.

It is also necessary for professionals to recognize that their work overlaps at different points in the placement process and that they can be more helpful to the clients they serve if they cooperate than if they remain remote from each other. Confidentiality is important, but a child's well-being, if endangered in a specific setting, should have a higher priority. If the therapist feels that honest answers are not forthcoming from the foster parents, consultation with the case worker may reveal where the truth lies and whether intervention is needed in the foster care situation. On the other hand, the therapist needs to be informed if the case worker sees progress or problems for the child.

RECOMMENDATIONS

The principal goal of adoption and of foster care is to give a child a nurturing, healthy, and safe environment in which to mature. That the adults' need and desire to be parents is also satisfied—and they usually are—is secondary.

Adopted children should be told how much they have enriched the family by becoming part of it, although whether adoptions should be open will vary with each situation. Open adoption should not be mandated by legislators or welfare agencies, although there probably should be a requirement for fuller medical information from the biological parents than is now supplied. Honesty on the part of placement intermediaries, public or private, is also essential to successful placement.

Foster children, who are possibly more vulnerable and emotionally fragile than their adopted peers, may need more therapeutic support because of the multiple separations they experience. Closer supervision of foster homes with therapeutic support for the foster parents also seems to be needed, for they, too, often have more challenges to meet than they may be prepared for.

Finally, mental health, social welfare, and legal/judicial professionals need to be aware of their prejudices and try diligently to reduce them when working with adoptive and foster families. Although these families may not be exactly the same as those created biologically, the difference does not mean that they are problem-laden or that every problem they have derives from the nonbiological relationship. They should try to look at statistics regarding the youngsters involved from a more positive point of view (i.e., if as many as 25 percent of them are in therapy, that means that 75 percent are not in therapy). They should then find out what has contributed to the apparently happier life of this 75 percent and teach it to the adoptive and foster families with whom they are involved.

Perhaps a key thought ought to be held and conveyed by those working with adoptive and foster families: Bonds of affection are not a matter of biology; they are an effect of caring. If some doubt that, let them think of married couples. Most married couples have no biological relationship; the marriage (or "significant other" relationship) thrives on their caring for each other. Most adoptions and foster care relationships similarly work out well because they are based on mutual bonds of affection derived from caring. A former judge of the District of Columbia Juvenile Court has stated the case for adoptive and foster families well:

> Those who make the laws and those who administer and enforce them must acknowledge that the consistent, day-to-day loving and guiding parental relationship that a child needs to mature and grow into a wholesome and law-abiding citizen can be provided by psychological or adoptive parents just as effectively as by biological parents (Ketcham, 1998).

REFERENCES

Adoption and Safe Families Act of 1997, Public Law 105–89.
Albers, L. H., Johnson, D. E., Hostetter, M. K., Iverson, S., & Miller, L. C. (1997, September 17). Health of children adopted from the former Soviet Union and Eastern Europe: Comparison with preadoptive records. *Journal of the American Medical Association, 278,* 922–924.
American Psychiatric Association. (1994). *Diagnostic and statistical manual of mental disorders* (4th ed.). Washington, DC: Author.
Ames Reed, J. A. (1994). We live here too: Birth children's perspectives on fostering someone with learning disabilities. *Childhood & Society, 8,* 164–173.
Associated Press (1998, November 5). Ex-addict prevails over powerful foster couple in adoption. *The New York Times,* p. A27.

Barth, R. P., & Needell, B. (1996). Outcomes for drug-exposed children four years post-adoption. *Children and Youth Services Review, 18*(1/2), 37–56.

Bartholet, E. (1993). *Family bonds: Adoption and the politics of parenting.* New York: Houghton Mifflin.

Berry, M. (1991). The effects of open adoption on biological and adoptive parents and the children: The arguments and the evidence. *Child Welfare, 70,* 637–651.

Berry, M. (1992). Contributors to adjustment problems of adoptees: A review of the longitudinal research. *Child and Adolescent Social Work Journal, 9,* 525–540.

Bruni, F. (1998, June 25). A small but-growing sorority is giving birth to children for gay men. *The New York Times,* p. A 12.

Burnette, D. (1997). Grandparents raising grandchildren in the inner city. *Families in Society, 78,* 489–499.

Buser, P. J. (1991). Introduction: The first generation of stepchildren. *Family Law Quarterly, 25,* 1–18.

Colapinto, J. (1997, November/December). The patterns that disconnect: The foster care system is a classic catch-22. *Family Therapy Networker, 21*(6), 43–44.

Crawford, M. (1994). In the best interests of the child? The misapplication of the UCCJA and the PKPA to interstate adoption custody disputes. *Vermont Law Review, 19,* 99–136.

Cushman, L. F., Kalmuss, D., & Namerow, P. B. (1997). Openness in adoption: Experiences and social psychological outcomes among birth mothers. *Marriage & Family Review, 25,* 7–18.

Czerwinski, E. C. (1996). Comment: Adoption law: Congratulations! For now—Current law, the Revised Uniform Adoption Act, and final adoptions. *Oklahoma Law Review, 49,* 323–330.

Ellison, K. (1998, August 24). In Brazil, judge comes under fire for role in global adoptions. *The Philadelphia Inquirer,* p. A3.

Farley, M. (1998, November 15). China passes a law that will change its policy for adopting orphans. *The Philadelphia Inquirer,* p. A5.

Fein, E. B. (1998, October 25). Secrecy and stigma no longer clouding adoptions. *The New York Times,* pp. 1, 30–31.

Fergusson, D. M., Lynskey, M., & Horwood, L. J. (1995). The adolescent outcomes of adoption: A 16-year longitudinal study. *Journal of Child Psychology and Psychiatry, 36,* 597–615.

Gallagher, S. (1998, April). The many roads to adoption. *Kiplinger's Personal Finance Magazine,* pp. 50–52.

Ganong, L., Coleman, M., Fine, M., & McDaniel, A. K. (1998). Issues considered in contemplating stepchild adoption. *Family Relations, 47*(1), 63–71.

Goodheart, A. (1998, July 22). Families broken for gender's sake. *USA Today,* p. 11A.

Groze, V. (1996). A 1 and 2 year follow-up study of adoptive families and special needs children. *Children and Youth Services Review, 18*(1/2), 57–82.

Groze, V., & McMillen, J. C. (1994). Using placement genograms in child welfare practice. *Child Welfare, 73,* 307–318.

Hansen, J. O. (1998, November 1). Series prompts agency to examine practices. *The Atlantic Journal/The Atlantic Constitution,* p. D9.

Harris, S. R. (1997). Race, search, and my baby-self: Reflections of a transracial adoptee. *Yale Journal of Law and Feminism, 9,* pp. 5–16.

Hintz, P. A. (1994). Comments: Grandparents' visitation rights following adoption: Expanding traditional boundaries in Wisconsin. *Wisconsin Law Review,* 483–510.

Hollingsworth, L. D. (1998). Promoting same-race adoption for children of color. *Social Work, 43*(2), 104–116.

Horwich, T. F. (1997). Legal issues: What every couple considering adoption should know. *Insights into Infertility, 12*(2), 9–10.

Howe, R-A. W. (1983). Adoption practice, issues, and laws 1958–1983. *Family Law Quarterly, 17*(2), 173–197.

Hunt, K. (1998, March 15). Veil of secrecy lifts on Irish children brought to America. *The Los Angeles Times,* p. 1.

Hurlburt, A. (1998). *The limits of hope: An adoptive mother's story.* Charlottesville: University Press of Virginia.

In re Jacob, 86 N.Y.2d 651 (November 2, 1995).

Janus, N. G. (1997). Adoption counseling as a professional specialty area for counselors. *Journal of Counseling & Development, 75,* 266–274.

Jones, A. (1997). Issues relevant to therapy with adoptees. *Psychotherapy, 34*(1), 64–68.

Kestin, S. (1998, October 29). System pulls kids from bad to worse; Abuse, neglect, apathy—The failures of foster care series. *Sun Sentinel,* Broward County, FL.

Ketcham, O. W. (1998, November 6). Parental laws must put children first. *The Sacramento Bee,* p. B9.

Kirby, K. M., & Hardesty, P. H. (1998). Evaluating older pre-adoptive foster children. *Professional Psychology, 29,* 428–436.

Lee, J. S., & Twaite, J. A. (1997). Open adoption and adoptive mothers: Attitudes toward birthmothers, adopted children, and parenting. *American Journal of Orthopsychiatry, 67,* 576–584.

Lewin, T. (1998, October 27). New families redraw racial boundaries. *The New York Times,* pp. A1, A12–A13.

Lifton, B. J. (1988). *Lost and found: The adoption experience.* New York: Harper & Row.

Lightburn, A., & Pine, B. A. (1996). Supporting and enhancing the adoption of children with developmental disabilities. *Children and Youth Services Review, 18*(1/2), 139–162.

Mainemer, H., Gilman, L. C., & Ames, E. W. (1998). Parenting stress in families adopting children from Romanian orphanages. *Journal of Family Issues, 19,* 164–180.

Mansnerus, L. (1998, October 26). Market puts price tag on the priceless. *The New York Times,* pp. A 1, A16–A17.

McDaniel, K., & Jennings, G. (1997). Therapists' choice of treatment for adoptive families. *Journal of Family Psychotherapy, 8*(4), 47–68.

McRoy, R. G. (1997). Achieving same-race adoptive placements for African American children: Culturally sensitive practice approaches. *Child Welfare, 76*(1), 85–104.

Nickman, S. L., & Lewis, R. G. (1994). Adoptive families and professionals: When the experts make things worse. *Journal of the American Academy of Child and Adolescent Psychiatry, 33,* 753–755.

Rickard Liow, S. J. (1994). Transracial adoption: questions on heritage for parents, children and counsellors. *Counseling Psychology Quarterly, 7,* 375–384.

Rodier, D. N. (1997, November 3). Out-of-state ruling bars action in PA. Adoption case; Decision was final. *Pennsylvania Law Weekly* (State Court Rulings; Family Law), p. 1.

Rosenberg, K. F., & Groze, V. (1997). The impact of secrecy and denial in adoption: Practice and treatment issues. *Families in Society: The Journal of Contemporary Human Services, 78,* 522–530.

Rosenberg, S. K. (1998). *Adoption and the Jewish family: Contemporary perspectives.* Philadelphia: The Jewish Publication Society.

Samuels, T. (1998, April 27). Race called issue in N. J. adoptions. *The Philadelphia Inquirer,* p. R3.

Schwartz, L. L. (1983). Contested adoption cases: Grounds for conflict between psychology and the law. *Professional Psychology, 14,* 444–456.

Schwartz, L. L. (1986). Unwed fathers and adoption custody disputes. *American Journal of Family Therapy, 14,* 347–355.

Schwartz, L. L. (1991). *Alternatives to infertility: Is surrogacy the answer?* New York: Brunner/Mazel.

Schwartz, L. L. (1993a). The interaction of field theory, family systems theory, and children's rights. *American Journal of Family Therapy, 21,* 267–273.

Schwartz, L. L. (1993b). What is a family? A contemporary view. *Contemporary Family Therapy, 15,* 429–442.

Schwartz, L. L. (1994). The challenge of raising one's nonbiological children. *American Journal of Family Therapy, 22,* 195–207.

Schwartz, L. L. (1996) Adoptive families: Are they non-normative? In M. Harway (Ed.), *Treating the changing family* (pp. 97–114). New York: John Wiley & Sons, Inc.

Schwartz, L. L. (in press-a). Adoption: Parents who choose their children and their options. In F. W. Kaslow (Ed.), *Handbook of couples and family forensics.* New York: John Wiley & Sons, Inc.

Schwartz, L. L. (in press-b). Surrogacy: Third leg of the reproductive triangle. In F. W. Kaslow (Ed.), *Handbook of couples and families forensics.* New York: John Wiley & Sons, Inc.

Seymour, C. (1998). Children with parents in prison: Child welfare policy, program, and practice issues. *Child Welfare, 77,* 469–493.

Siegel, D. H. (1993). Open adoption of infants: Adoptive parents' perceptions of advantages and disadvantages. *Social Work, 38,* 15–23.

Sobol, M. P., & Daly, K. J. (1992). The adoption alternative for pregnant adolescents: Decision making, consequences, and policy implications. *Journal of Social Issues, 48,* 143–161.

Swarns, R. L. (1998, April 3). City houses foster children with runaways in Brooklyn. *The New York Times,* p. B2.

Testa, K. (1998, November 8). A birth mother sues person who found her. *The Philadelphia Inquirer,* p. A12.

Twigg, R. C. (1995). Coping with loss: How foster parents' children cope with foster care. *Community Alternatives: International Journal of Family Care, 7*(1), 1–12.

Walters, B. (1998, October 30). *20–20.* ABC-TV Network.

CHAPTER 14

Gay and Lesbian Families

Jerry J. Bigner

THERE IS A widespread belief that gays and lesbians do not participate in family life and that the very nature of their lifestyle is antifamily and singles-oriented. Nothing could be further from the truth. This belief and others that are like it reflect deep-seated cultural attitudes known as homophobia (an irrational fear or hatred of homosexuals and/or homosexuality) and heterosexism (the prejudicial belief that heterosexuality is superior and preferable to homosexuality due to the high value placed on procreativity) (Blumenfeld, 1992). These attitudes are insidious within our culture and serve as oppressive devices to marginalize sexual minorities in our society. These attitudes also serve to lock people into rigid sex-role definitions and functions; lead others to mistreat, harm, and even kill gays and lesbians; legitimize discrimination and denial of basic human and civil rights guaranteed by the U.S. Constitution; inhibit the ability of gays and lesbians to participate in legitimized intimate relationships; minimize the value of diversity in society; and generally stigmatize a segment of the population. No one is unaffected by these attitudes, which are acquired, communicated, and reinforced throughout society over the entire life span of individuals.

In reality, gay and lesbian people participate in family forms that are not easily recognizable among others found in society. A common denominator of homosexual culture is the lack of constraints that force rigid adherence to culturally defined norms, roles, and behaviors. Gays and lesbians have been busily focusing on reinventing notions of what it means to have a family, how this family functions, and who participates in it (Benkov, 1994; Weston, 1997). These families are referred to as *families of choice,* meaning that gays and lesbians make conscious choices about who constitutes their family, how this family is defined, and what it means to be a participant. By not having to conform to standards that control how other families are formed and maintained, gays and lesbians have approached a basic problem of human beings in ways that are highly creative: how to provide a social network of like-minded people with whom one is compatible and who can provide acceptance, love, support, recreation, intimacy, emotional warmth, as well as a sense of community. Looking to one's family of origin to meet these needs is not a realistic choice for many gays and lesbians because of the problem of estrangement. Likewise, the committed relationships of gays and lesbians are denied recognition, socially as well as legally, by the larger culture. By creating families of choice, gays and lesbians are able to meet their needs in ways that require a different set of criteria than is usual for most other types of families in the United States (Becker, 1991).

There are threads of commonality that are shared among many families of choice but there are distinctions as well that are germane only to a particular family of choice. Families of choice may base membership on certain culturally defined traits found in homosexual lifestyles. Gay and lesbian parents may come together as families of choice since they share parenthood in common with others. Elderly lesbians may participate in families of choice basing membership on the age criteria exclusively. Religiously oriented gays and lesbians may form a composite family of choice based on spirituality as a common denominator.

Gays and lesbians also form nuclear-type families, especially when children are involved. Distinct differences can be found, however, in this regard when considering gay fathers and lesbian mothers. Children exist in gay and lesbian families as a product of past heterosexual involvement (i.e., from marriage), but also from adoption or from artificial insemination. Children are more prominently found in lesbian mother families since women typically are more likely to hold physical custody of children following divorce. Even more interestingly, there appears to be greater numbers of lesbian mothers in recent years, prompting one researcher to term this a lesbian baby boom (Patterson, 1994b). Gay fathers, usually being no different from divorced nongay fathers, often are involved with children, but on a limited basis as defined by visitation agreements.

Many gay fathers and lesbian mothers form committed partnerships with another man or woman and function in a type of nuclear family experience. However, it is not unusual to find that parenthood may be pursued using different arrangements not usually found in heterosexual families. For example, two gay men and a lesbian woman may decide to pursue parenthood using donor insemination provided by the two men, although little is known about such arrangements.

This chapter explores the variations found in gay and lesbian families that distinguish them from others. Formation of gay and lesbian families of choice will be described along with an examination of the issues faced in gay and lesbian families that include children. A final section focuses on therapeutic issues involved in working with gay and lesbian families.

PREVALENCE OF GAY AND LESBIAN FAMILIES

One of the earliest and most well-known estimates of the prevalence of homosexual men and women in the United States was made by Kinsey and his associates (1948, 1953). Basing the estimate on the continuum of sexual orientation, Kinsey believed that 2 percent of men and 2 percent of women were exclusively homosexual in orientation. Other researchers have also provided estimates of the prevalence of homosexual men and women (Ellis & Ames, 1987; Gagnon, 1977; Harry, 1990; Hunt, 1974; Knox & Wilson, 1991), which are similar to and vary slightly from the initial estimate made by Kinsey. Many people remain closeted or keep their sexual orientation private for various reasons due to the stigma associated with having this information made public.

Currently, it is believed that there are about 10.4 million men and about 5.2 million women who are exclusively gay or lesbian in sexual orientation in the U.S. population of about 260 million. The figures are even less clear when trying to estimate the percentage of gay and lesbian individuals who are also parents. Researchers estimate that about 20 percent to 25 percent of self-identified gay men are also fathers (Bell & Weinberg, 1978; Bozett & Sussman, 1989; Maddox, 1982; Miller, 1979; Weinberg & Williams, 1974). A substantial number of gay men and lesbian women have become parents while in a heterosexual marriage, having disclosed or realized their homosexual orientation often following divorce. It is likely, however, that there are greater percentages of lesbian women who are mothers since many lesbians choose to become a parent by adoption or use of artificial insemination by donor. These groups of gay fathers and lesbian mothers clearly constitute a minority within a minority in our culture.

The demographics of gay and lesbians in the United States appear to mirror those of the heterosexual population when considering age, sex, gender, and ethnicity (Briggs, 1994). A sample of gays and lesbians in the study by Briggs were reported to have significantly higher levels of education than the heterosexual sample but this did not equate with having higher incomes than heterosexuals in the study. The gay and lesbian sample had slightly lower incomes than the heterosexual sample, which was attributed to the gay men having lower incomes than heterosexual men.

Gay men and lesbian women typically congregate in large numbers in metropolitan areas of the United States in all geographic areas. The tendency is also to group in ghettolike areas of cities in keeping with the practice of many ethnic groups as a means of maintaining the culture and lifestyle associated with homosexuality. For gays and lesbians, however, the grouping together assists in forming a sense of community that is necessary for survival and safety as well as for providing an arena for participating in the culture. Designated areas provide places of recreation and socializing and have distinctive institutions associated with homosexual culture. For example, there may be parks for play and socializing as well as bars that specialize in serving particular segments of the gay population such as leather-oriented individuals or those who enjoy drag (cross-dressing or female impersonation). These areas also include church and synagogue groups that serve homosexual congregations, social service and health care agencies, and community outreach agencies that meet legal, political, and social needs of gays and lesbians.

Gays and lesbians are found in all ethnic groups represented in the United States (Peterson, 1992) and these individuals may align themselves in certain places of the designated gay ghetto area of a city. Unfortunately, there is little known from the research literature about these ethnic representatives in the gay and lesbian communities.

GAY AND LESBIAN FAMILY FORMATION

There are similarities as well as distinctions between gay and lesbian families and those found among heterosexuals. Hunt (1987) and Blumenfeld (1992) suggest that stereotypes and misconceptions are responsible for creating an imperfect, limited, and misleading impression of what homosexuality is like and how it is experienced by large numbers of gays and lesbians in the United States. Many believe that there is a single gay/lesbian lifestyle and a typical gay/lesbian personality, although there is as much diversity in these among gays and lesbians as is found among heterosexuals (Allen, 1997; Demo & Allen, 1996; Hildebrand, Phenice, Gray, & Hines, 1996; Reigot & Spina, 1996).

DIVERSITY IN GAY/LESBIAN LIFESTYLES

A comprehensive study by Bell and Weinberg (1978) of approximately 1,000 gay men and lesbian women illustrates the range of lifestyles that are associated with these individuals. The researchers developed a typology of five central lifestyles into which about 70 percent of their sample could be placed. The remaining 30 percent were too diverse in nature to be placed into any one of these categories. These include: (1) *Close-coupled.* In this lifestyle, people are involved in a one-to-one relationship that is monogamous and closely resembles the heterosexual ideal marriage. It is characterized also by close, emotional warmth in interpersonal interactions. Couples in this category reported having fewer sexual problems and the highest levels of happiness and fulfillment. The majority reported happiness and satisfaction with their sexual orientation. The group contained 10 percent of the gay men and 28 percent of the lesbian women of the sample. (2) *Open-coupled.* Individuals in this category were coupled but permitted sexual involvement with others outside the relationship. This group reported more sexual problems than the first and were more likely to regret having their sexual orientation. This group contained 17 percent of the lesbians and 18 percent of the gays. (3) *Functional.* Individuals in this category were not participating in a relationship. They reported having a higher number of sexual partners than in any other group and reported having the fewest sexual problems. In addition, they were the least likely to regret their sexual orientation. Approximately 15 percent of the men and 10 percent of the women in the sample fell into this group. (4) *Dysfunctional.* Individuals who reported having a high number of sexual partners as well as sexual problems fell into this group. They were considered by the researchers to have overall poor psychological and social adjustment. About 5 percent of the lesbians and 12 percent of the gays were identified in this category. (5) *Asexual.* People classified into this category had a low interest in sexual activity and little involvement, socially or sexually, with others. They had the greatest number of sexual problems and experienced difficulty finding sexual partners. They were the most secretive about their sexual orientation as well. Eleven percent of lesbians and 16 percent of gay men were in this group.

This classification scheme of gay and lesbian lifestyles is helpful in emphasizing the range of diversity found in gay and lesbian communities and that certain groupings lend themselves to producing greater happiness and satisfactory adjustments than others.

FAMILIES OF CHOICE: GAY AND LESBIAN KINSHIP

While to some the term gay and lesbian family is at best an oxymoron, gays and lesbians have been revolutionary in their approaches to creating a family form that will meet a variety of needs and functions. They have known, many for a great length of time, that they will have to make choices in formulating and determining kinship following disclosure of their sexual orientation to members of their family of origin. A substantial number of gays and lesbians are not accepted, welcomed, or tolerated as members of their families of origin following disclosure of their sexual orientation. For many, this is the first introduction to the notion that family membership and kinship may be more of an effort that requires choice and careful decision making than a birthright as is assumed by so many heterosexuals (Weston, 1997). Many gays and lesbians have had first-hand experience in learning that blood is much thinner than water and that kinship is more successfully formed when based on friendship and/or a variety of other ties such as nonbiological parenthood and committed relationships where support and emotional sustenance can be found.

Kinship for many gays and lesbians is based on forming a family of choice where informal and formal, explicit and implicit configurations tie one to another. These families typically are loosely organized in keeping with a homosexual subculture that is supported and maintained with fewer rules or boundaries. For example, kinship may be more inclusive than is found among genealogically based families. Family members may include friends as well as lovers or partners, past lovers or partners, co-parents, children from past heterosexual marriages, and adopted children as well as those conceived through artificial insemination. These ways of defining kinship contribute to the misunderstandings about gays and lesbians by many heterosexuals since families of choice are devoid of definition of family ties based on procreation and do not easily fit into the more conventional notions of kinship based on blood and institutionalized marriage. For gay and lesbian families of choice, personal discretion is the key to defining kinship.

The beginning point for the eventual family of choice *formation* is the initiation of the coming-out process where individuals acknowledge their homosexual orientation and begin sharing this information and its meanings to those who are important in their lives. This is considered a lifelong process that dynamically unfolds and influences someone throughout his or her life span, as a realization and acceptance of a vital and critical aspect of one's basic personal identity. Sharing this information, especially with members of one's family of origin, is pivotal for most gays and lesbians (Patterson, 1994a). It is a multifaceted transformational process that Cass (1979) describes as occurring in six stages. These are not discretely separate from one another but may be sequential. In addition, they are not age- or time-specific. Although many gays and lesbians initiate this process during adolescence, for many others it occurs later in early adulthood.

These stages include: (1) *Identity confusion stage.* This is characterized by the realization that one is somehow different from others. There may be an initial meek acknowledgment of homosexual feelings but a heterosexual self-image is maintained. Many increasingly acknowledge inconsistencies about sexuality issues. For some, denial of these feelings and activities may be implemented. (2) *Identity comparison stage.* Individuals enter this stage when they begin to acknowledge that they might be gay or lesbian. There is a heightened feeling of alienation, a willing relinquishment of a heterosexual self-image, and increasing feelings of alienation from one's family of origin, acquaintances, and society as a whole. This is dealt with by (a) emphasizing the positive aspects of being different and de-emphasizing the place of heterosexuals in one's life; or (b) accepting the homosexual identity based on one's behavior rather than on the nature of ones' internal self; or (c) accepting one's behavior and self as being homosexual but fearing others' negative reactions should this become known. (3) *Identity tolerance stage.* This occurs when an individual recognizes that there are sexual, emotional, and social needs that go with being gay or lesbian. There may be more acknowledgment of one's homosexual orientation and seeking out of other gays and lesbians as a means of inhibiting feelings of alienation. (4) *Identity acceptance stage.* When other gays and lesbians are contacted, new friendships are formed that encourage the person's acceptance of his or her true sexual orientation. Acceptance rather than tolerance for one's sexual orientation occurs. There is initial disclosure made to family members and friends who appear to be trustworthy. (5) *Identity pride stage.* A definite "we versus them" attitude is noticeable. There are intensive efforts to make identifiable acts that label oneself as gay or lesbian. A pride begins to develop about one's homosexual orientation, often in angered reaction to homophobic and hetero-sexist attitudes manifested by those assumed or known to be heterosexual. (6) *Identity synthesis stage.* At this point, the homosexual aspect becomes interwoven with all other aspects of one's personal identity. This assists in a feeling of completion of self and marks the end of the identity formation process. Anger subsides about heterosexuals with the recognition that there are heterosexual allies who can be counted on for support.

Many gays and lesbians disclose first to friends and only later to family of origin members, if at all. The pattern of disclosure to family members occurs in accordance with the degree of emotional closeness felt toward a particular family member. For example, disclosure is more likely to occur first with the mother, followed by siblings, and lastly to the father (Bigner, 1998). A child's disclosure of homosexual orientation acts as a stressor event for a heterosexual family system, producing a crisis reaction and disturbing family equilibrium. The child's revelation challenges the family's perceptions of him or her, and a conflict often develops as members attempt to reconcile negative stereotypes and beliefs about homosexuality with what they know about the child as a person (Strommen, 1989a, 1989b). Reactions to the disclosure affect everyone in the system but in different ways. Parents typically react with shock, anger, and feelings of guilt for what is happening to the child, but denial and feeling ashamed are also possible. Siblings may react with anger and confusion rather than guilt and develop feelings of alienation toward the gay or lesbian sibling. The family system as a whole struggles with this situation as they try to understand what this means to have a homosexual child. It is particularly disturbing for family members who thought they truly knew the homosexual child only to discover that an important aspect of that child's personality was hidden and not obvious until disclosure occurred.

Reconciling the disclosure is also a process for families of origin. When the family of origin deals with this crisis in healthy ways, they seek out information about homosexuality, refuse to create the disclosure as a family secret, participate in support groups, and create a new family role for the child as "our gay/lesbian child" (Bigner, 1998). Family systems that fail to react to this situation in healthy ways invariably promote the continued dysfunctionality of the system that can lead to serious impairments. When these systems react negatively to a child's disclosure, the likelihood of the child's formation of a family of choice is heightened. For example, these systems may shun or reject a gay or lesbian child; limit participation in or refuse to include the child in family events; refuse to discuss anything relating to the child's homosexuality, relationships, or lifestyle; or shame the child or act in ways that communicate intolerance such as disinheriting or banishing the child from the family system.

GAY AND LESBIAN RELATIONSHIPS

Just as a coupled relationship is the foundation of family life among heterosexuals, gays and lesbians also participate in a similar type of committed relationship that can lead to the formation of a different kind of family life (Scrivner & Eldridge, 1995). Considering the denial of legitimacy and lack of support for these relationships by society, however, it is surprising that gays and lesbians are able to form and participate in a coupled relationship that is sustained over a long period of time. Gays and lesbians recently witnessed first-hand the hostile homophobic attitudes of society emerge in the federal legislation known as the Defense of Marriage Act of 1998, which defined the only legally recognized marriage as one involving opposite-sex adults.

Nevertheless, gays and lesbians, contrary to misleading stereotyping (Testa, Kinder, & Ironson, 1987), participate in intimate relationships, many of which endure over a long period of time and are similar in some ways to those found among heterosexual or straight individuals (Peplau & Cochran, 1981). These relationships, when successful, are marked by trust, willingness to share intimacy, caring actions and words, mutual understanding, and love. Like heterosexuals, gays and lesbians desire steady, predictable relationships (Kurdek, 1995; Peplau, 1981, 1991; Peplau & Cochran, 1981; Peplau & Gordon, 1983), although this appears to be more desired by women than men; and seek affection, companionship, personal development, honesty, affection, and emotional closeness from the partner. Research findings refute a popular stereotype that regards sex as the basis for any relationship between homosexuals. As noted, many of the same variables that are valued among heterosexual couples are just as important to same-sex couples (Kurdek, 1995; Peplau, 1991). Relationship duration has been found to be a good predictor of relationship satisfaction regardless of the type of couple studied (lesbian, gay, heterosexual married, heterosexual unmarried but cohabiting).

Distinct differences, however, distinguish gay and lesbian intimate relationships from those of heterosexuals. If there is a generic template for the intimate, committed relationships formed by gays and lesbians, it might best be described as egalitarian in function and nature, because they are not forced to adopt or incorporate traditional sex role models into their committed relationships. A study by Tuller (1988) reports that there is often one personality that is prominent in gay couples but that this is not an indicator that this personality is the more masculine one and the other assumes a more feminine position. A conscientious emphasis placed on equality of the partners that is accentuated by the de-emphasis on power and control of one person over the other has been found to produce greater degrees of satisfaction with a relationship than those based on gender-based role typing (Maracek, Finn, & Cardell, 1988).

Many gays and lesbians are less likely to value sexual exclusivity as an ideal for their relationship (Peplau & Cochran, 1981), allowing a more open boundary on this aspect of relationship. What actually may be different from heterosexual couples is the degree of permissiveness and agreement among open-coupled gays and lesbians that such involvement does not threaten the stability or functioning of the relationship (Markowitz, 1993).

Another difference often encountered among gay and lesbian couples relates to labels that designate relationship. Heterosexual couples have the benefit of using culturally accepted labels such as spouse, husband, and wife to designate the relationship to another. Gay and lesbian couples, lacking similar legitimatization by society, flounder with the problem of what to call one another to designate relationship. Some rely on using the term lover and others often use partner or significant other. It is not unusual, however, to hear gay male couples refer to one another as husband and lesbian couples to refer to one another as wife. Not having such words readily for use in referring to one another in a meaningful relationship is a statement itself on the nebulous status of gay and lesbian couples in our society.

The issue of domestic partnership involves legal as well as economic implications. The relationships established by same-sex couples test a variety of legal, social, and economic policy issues (Hartman, 1996). Only a handful of states allow the category of domestic relationship or partnership to be applied to same-sex couples (Wisenkale & Heckart, 1993). In dealing with the legal ambiguity of same-sex relationships, many same-sex couples find it necessary to execute wills, living wills, medical living wills, and durable or general power-of-attorney documents to ensure that the partners can receive benefits that are similarly accorded heterosexual couples via the legal institution of marriage. The dire importance of having such legal instruments on hand was clearly discovered during the early years of the AIDS crisis. Family-of-origin relatives of lovers have denied access to their partner during hospitalizations and even when death occurred. In the absence of a will, property that may have been jointly purchased was confiscated by blood relatives of a deceased partner. It has not been unusual for the surviving partner to be excluded from making plans for burial and participating in funeral services.

The use of common-law marriage statutes also has been considered as a means of achieving legal recognition of same-sex relationships. Court cases are emerging that are helping to establish this as a likely route that may accomplish this recognition (Wisenkale & Heckart, 1993). These cases closely resemble those that established palimony as a plausible claim among heterosexual cohabiting couples who experienced property disputes and other financial claims following dissolution of their relationship. Same-sex palimony cases are currently being tried in some states such as Colorado (Tolleson, 1998). One case in particular is an example of how these cases may assist in establishing precedence toward legal recognition of sex-same relationships (*Braschi v. Stahl Association Company*, 1989). A same-sex male couple jointly owned a home and designated each other as beneficiary in their wills. One of the partners died and the surviving partner's legal right to the property was upheld by the judge. In awarding the judgment, the court used four standards for the definition of a family: (1) exclusivity and longevity of a relationship; (2) level of emotional and financial commitment of the partners; (3) the way the couple conducted their everyday lives in society; and (4) the couple's reliance on one another for daily services. Such standards reflect a definite change in the meaning of legal family recognition (Hildebrand et al., 1996).

DEVELOPMENTAL MODELS

Gay and lesbian couples experience relationship transitions and developmental changes over time just as do heterosexual couples. The development of these couples, however, remains largely speculative. Two models have appeared that describe such developmental changes.

Gay Couple Development

McWhirter and Mattison (1984, 1988, 1996) provide a comprehensive description of gay couple development based on observations of 156 male couples ranging in age from 20 to 69 years. The mean duration of their relationship was 8.7 years. Six stages emerge from these observations: (1) *Blending* (First Year), marked by intense romantic involvement where similarities are emphasized and differences minimized, exploration of ways to express equality, and intense sexual activity and feelings; (2) *Nesting* (Years 1–3), characterized by focusing of the couple on building and shaping a home environment, acknowledgment of flaws in each other, concern over declines in romanticism, and searching for evidence of deeper compatibility; (3) *Maintaining* (Years 3–5), emphasizing establishment of balance between autonomy and independence, togetherness and individuation, autonomy and dependence, conflict and its resolution, and confusion and understanding leading to deeper levels of togetherness, self-insight, and self-disclosure; (4) *Building* (Years 5–10), featuring cooperative and collaborative efforts, promotion of greater independence with complementarity between partners; (5) *Releasing* (Years 10–20), marked by increased trust, positive mutual regard, and sense of togetherness; and (6) *Renewing* (Years 20+), based on a sense of self-discovery and revitalization of the relationship, reliving of the past, enjoying financial security, and overall sense of renewal.

Lesbian Relationship Development

A developmental model of lesbian relationships described by Clunis and Green (1988) also includes developmental changes occurring in six stages and is based in part on ideas generated by Campbell (1980) regarding male-female relationships and those of McWhirter and Mattison (1984, 1988) describing gay male relationships outlined above: (1) *Prerelationship* (may be only days or a few weeks in duration), features a number of choices to be made by both individuals—whether to invest time and energy getting to know the other person better, whether or when to commence sexual involvement, and resolving confusion about how to act around the other person; (2) *Romance* (indefinite duration), has the primary goal of melding two separate identities into a central one and is experienced by mutual sharing of feelings tempered by realistic appraisal of each partner that is not clouded by false images presented by both partners; (3) *Conflict* (indefinite duration), commences with recognition of each partner's character flaws requiring use of conflict-resolution skills, learning to negotiate differences and attaining win-win solutions, and establishing basic ground rules and boundaries for the relationship; (4) *Acceptance* (indefinite duration), is recognized when both partners express mutual acceptance of each other as is, and introspection to discover how one contributes to disharmony when it occurs; (5) *Commitment* (indefinite duration), commences with dedication to the relationship's existence, working to maintain stability within the relationship, letting go of the desire to have a perfect partner, and developing a deepening trust for the partner; (6) *Collaboration* (indefinite duration), occurs when the partners acknowledge that conflicts can occur without threatening the strength of the relationship, working together on something that is an extension of the relationship (such as building a home), and looking forward to sharing the future together.

WORKING WITH GAY AND LESBIAN COUPLES AND FAMILIES

Therapists are likely to encounter gay and lesbian couples and families as part of their client load. Although most presenting problems may not appear to be significantly different from those of heterosexual couples and families, treatment of gay and lesbian couples and families inevitably requires awareness of the uniqueness of these individuals and the issues that are germane to homosexual clients in particular.

There is a mounting literature of studies describing treatment of homosexual clients for a variety of problems (Beane, 1981; Gonsioreck, 1985; Kominars & Kominars, 1996), but a paucity of those describing research on therapeutic methods, techniques, and issues affecting gay and lesbian couples and families (Anderson, 1996; Bigner, 1996; Cabaj, 1996; Kerewsky & Miller, 1996; Laird, 1996; Ussher, 1991). Despite this lack of resources, therapists may expect to encounter certain problems germane to gay male couples and gay father families that are shared as well as others that are distinct from those of lesbian couples and lesbian mother families. Issues that are likely to be shared by both gay and lesbian couples include (1) therapist-client issues; (2) boundary issues; (3) gender issues; (4) high-risk issues; and (5) coping with HIV status and AIDS-related issues. Gay father and lesbian mother families also have particular issues that may be observed by therapists including (1) resolving same-sex parent–step-family issues; (2) resolving gay father and lesbian mother identity issues; and (3) disclosure issues with children.

THERAPIST-CLIENT ISSUES

Gay and lesbian clients are a wary group when it comes to participating in therapy. They may have significant issues regarding how much to trust a therapist based on past experiences with others in society. Some may feel shame and embarrassment (also known as internalized homophobia) about discussing sexual issues with the therapist, especially if this person is known or assumed to be heterosexual in orientation. Because gays and lesbians grow up in the same society as everyone else, they learn and incorporate the same negative messages and meanings that society in general assigns to homosexuality. This same shame and guilt can play a prominent role in the course of therapy if the clients have not sufficiently processed these feelings and attitudes and have difficulty in achieving self-acceptance and self-love. This situation is compounded when the therapist, by way of words and/or body language, communicates a personal level of discomfort in discussing sexual issues or in observing gestures of love and nurturance by a same-sex couple. Gays and lesbians have years of experience in developing a heightened sensitivity to any sign or indication of unacceptance, discomfort, or intolerance from others. When there is any sign of this from a therapist, the clients are likely to discontinue treatment and may or may not decide to pursue work with another therapist. It is imperative that the therapeutic climate be one in which gay and lesbian clients can feel safe and not exposed to the hurtful presence of homophobic and heterosexist attitudes from the therapist.

It is uncertain if there is any importance to the client and therapist being similar in sexual orientation. However, some work suggests that openly gay or lesbian therapists facilitate successful therapy with gay and lesbian clients (Gonsiorek, 1985; Riddle & Sang, 1978; Rochlin, 1982). The findings of these studies and others suggest that it is therapeutically significant for a gay or lesbian therapist to disclose this information to gay or lesbian clients. This should set an example of disclosure for clients as well as being helpful in promoting levels of trust and comfort (Eichberg, 1990). The therapist should have worked through his or her own same-sex attraction feelings and conquered the tendency to impose heterosexist and homophobic stereotypes on gay and lesbian clients. If a therapist has not done his or her own personal work in this area, it will be demonstrated in some manner inevitably to gay and lesbian clients. When it becomes apparent that working with gay or lesbian clients is not comfortable for whatever reasons relative to sexual orientation issues, heterosexual therapists can seek gay-oriented or gay-affirmative supervision and training (Clark, 1987). Heterosexual therapists working with gay and lesbian clients can improve the likelihood of providing appropriate treatment by gaining such supervision and from participating in the culture of the gay, lesbian, bisexual, and transgendered (GLBT) communities (Markowitz, 1993). For example, gay fiction can be read as a means of forming an image of GLBT lifestyles rather than relying on misleading stereotypes and myths. By working with a competent supervisor, heterosexual therapists can safely examine their own homoerotic feelings by creating a genogram based on every homosexual they have known, the relationship to them, and feelings about them. If such supervision is not available or appropriate, the clients should be referred to a new therapist who specializes in working with gay and lesbian clientele.

BOUNDARY ISSUES

Boundaries have long been a part of systemic family therapy (Minuchin, 1974). These are traditionally understood to be "the rules defining who participates and how" (p. 53) in relationships. Minuchin (1974) believes that boundaries function to provide protection of a system's unique identity and viability and serve as an indicator of its functional effectiveness. Both lesbian and gay couples typically have complex processes for creating and maintaining boundaries. This is due to the lack of legitimacy afforded to gay and lesbian couples by society. Lacking viable role models, gays and lesbians devise the avenues for living and existing as couples by their own methodologies that are often experimental in nature. However, gay men and lesbian women, while sharing this commonality of using invention to solve boundary issues, also differ in some ways regarding these issues.

Gay male couples experience certain boundary issues that heterosexual therapists may find confusing and that appear to work against the integrity of the relationship. Some couples operate their relationship within the confines of monogamy while others permit sexual activity with others not typically included in their relationship. This may conjure up stereotypes of the typical gay man as being highly promiscuous and being incapable of sustaining a long-term committed monogamous relationship. Such behavior is seen as acceptable by segments of the gay community and the couple. Sex for gay men can be recreational, emotional, signifying a bond, and so on. Some gay men may be dependent on the excitement generated by having a new sex partner to sustain interest in their long-term partner. Like all others, gay men may seek sex with others outside of their relationship as a means of distracting themselves and for avoiding feelings. Heterosexual therapists will need to examine how their own value systems serve as filters for coloring their perceptions of gay men who are in relationships. Using therapeutic rituals (i.e., holding a commitment ceremony), using a Bowen-based approach of systems coaching, examining male gender role constructions, and validating the relationship by executing appropriate legal documents may be helpful in providing boundary support for gay male couples (Johnson & Keren, 1996).

Lesbian couples experience other kinds of boundary issues, often having high degrees of difficulty involving enmeshment. The tendency for these individuals to devote considerable time and attention to maintaining their highly valued relationship per se is often at the core of boundary issues (Krestan & Bepko, 1980). Likewise, lesbian couples experience similar negative stereotyping that is misleading. For example, while both gay and lesbian couples are depicted as assuming gender roles in relationships similar to those found in heterosexual ones, the butch (more masculine woman)–femme (more feminine woman) image of lesbian couples persists today. Because of changes experienced in the women's movement in general over the years, lesbian couples today are more likely to place greater emphasis on sexual activity, but are more likely to confine this within the relationship.

A common problem found by many therapists who treat lesbian couples is that the relationship suffers from long-term familiarity because of boundary creation and maintenance resulting in abated sexual activity (Markowitz, 1993). While this is essentially no different from other long-term couples regardless of sexual orientation, it is especially critical among lesbian couples because of the meanings assigned to sexual activity. For many lesbians, sex equates to the affirmation that a couple is a great deal more than just good friends. For some unknown reason, the frequency of sexual activity often declines after its newness wears off, giving rise to fears, self-doubts, self-questioning, and the risk of too much closeness. Therapists can assist couples having such problems by using a Bowen-based system coaching, therapeutic use of rituals (i.e., also having commitment ceremonies), and defining sex as much more than actions that are genitally based resulting in orgasm.

GENDER ISSUES

Gay and lesbian couples are freed from social convention that places everyone into a gender envelope of one type or the other when participating in relationships. They have the opportunity to explore how to define their roles in relationships based on something other than gender, which lacks significance because of the same-sex configuration. Homosexual individuals, because they have an outlaw position in society, perhaps have greater license to pursue role ideations, behaviors, and configurations as gender nonconformists. This often leads to being labeled as androgyns or as individuals who incorporate both masculine and feminine aspects into their roles and behaviors (Bigner, 1996; Morales, 1996). In gay and lesbian families, reliance on traditional gender roles to determine who does what and how in child rearing is largely absent. However, performing such androgynousness may be difficult for some same-sex families. Although both adults, for example, may be highly committed to co-parenting responsibilities, one person may have to assume primary parenting responsibilities. Among gay father families, this may be problematic because of the way males are socialized in our culture. If one of the partners of a gay family finds it necessary to quit his work role to provide care for children, this may be seen as suicidal to career goals (Bigner, 1996).

HIGH-RISK ISSUES

Gay and lesbian couples and families, like all others, are subject to behaviors and situations that place them at high risk for injury, threaten effective functioning, and endanger personal health. At the forefront of these are couples and families that experience violence, dependencies and addictions to various substances and experiences, and coping with the devastation associated with AIDS.

Dependencies and Addictions

There is a general belief that gays and lesbians are especially vulnerable to developing a variety of dependencies and addictions to various substances, experiences, and even people (Kominars & Kominars, 1996). This vulnerability is thought to be due to the significant role of internalized and externalized homophobia and heterosexism as well as daily exposure to a society that is hostile to their very existence (Glaus, 1989). The widespread prevalence of these conditions is believed to affect approximately one in three gay men or lesbian women in the general population (National Institute on Alcohol Abuse and Alcoholism, 1995). The deep feelings of shame that can be generated by exposure to these attitudes are thought to drive the development and operation of dependencies and addictions. This can make it difficult for gays and lesbians to seek out the help they need to begin the recovery process. Unless clients have begun to process and resolve their own issues relating to internalized homophobia, progress in recovery will be less certain and more problematic (Kominars & Kominars, 1996).

Gays and lesbians recovering from addictions and dependencies can make use of the numerous types of Twelve Step Programs as an important aspect of their recovery process. Ordinarily, Twelve Step Programs such as Alcoholics Anonymous (AA) or Narcotics Anonymous (NA) can provide gays and lesbians with considerable help in recovery, but there are AA groups, for example, that are made up solely of same-sex orientation individuals. Such groups may better serve the needs of particular gays and lesbians who may feel more safe and welcome in these types of recovery groups.

THE ROLE OF HIV/AIDS STATUS

Therapists should be aware of the deep significance that HIV infection has had on the GLBT communities. This disease will make its presence known in the therapy room as clients share their experiences that reflect the anxiety, fear, and deep losses that have accompanied it as it has ravaged the GLBT communities during the past 15-plus years. The gay male community has been hardest hit by this disease in the United States. For example, many gay men have had their entire social network wiped out by deaths of their important partners and friends from AIDS-related diseases. Before the advent in 1996 of the triple drug cocktail used commonly today to treat those with full-blown AIDS diagnosis, many gay men typically could expect to attend anywhere between two and four memorial services each month for friends who had died of this disease. The negative stigmas such as the shame associated with this disease can have devastating effects not only on an individual's sense of well-being but can play out negatively in the relationships with others. This is further complicated by the physical symptoms of the disease that make everyday functioning difficult and problematic.

The AIDS epidemic also takes it toll on the gay men and other individuals who serve as primary caregivers of partners who have been disabled by the infection. Caregiver burnout has been high as the stressors associated with providing care have severe cumulative effects. The chronic nature of the disease is a large contributor to caregiver burnout as are the drastic changes that occur in conducting day-to-day activities. In addition, the economic aspects associated with providing health care can be devastating, especially for individuals who are not adequately covered by medical insurance.

But being HIV-positive or having AIDS are not the only casualties of this epidemic. There is a significant segment of the gay male population that is HIV-negative who manifest feelings and reactions described as survivor guilt (Johnston, 1995). Along with having seen partners and friends die horrible deaths from this disease, the stress of having the constant presence of a fatal disease as a part of daily life that is associated with life-affirming sexual activity has been devastating. Combining this situation with the losses of lovers, friends, and companions, one wonders how gay men and those who love and care for them cope successfully and in healthy ways with such high levels of stress and anxiety.

There are a number of gay couples who find that they have a mixed-HIV-status relationship in that one partner is HIV-positive or has AIDS and the other is HIV-negative (Johnston, 1995). People often become infected with the disease agent prior to entering a relationship. Many men have not allowed themselves to be tested for HIV antibodies (that indicates infection) because of the high levels of stress associated with knowing that a positive result is highly indicative of future diagnosis of full-blown AIDS. This also poses problems in the long run that can affect potential social relationships in dating as well as in forming a committed relationship. The additional stress in mixed-status couples can add further burdens that relate to survivor guilt (from not being infected) to being fearful of leaving an unhealthy relationship because of the HIV-positive or AIDS diagnosed partner who needs the assistance from his healthy partner.

HIV infection also affects gay and lesbian parents and their family members (Shuster, 1996). There are not only the presence of problems shared by individuals who have been infected but others that impose additional difficulties. For example, infected parents need to disclose the diagnostic information to children and former family members. Everyone will usually need assistance in responding to the disclosure, as well as a support network in the period when the disease manifests itself in full-blown AIDS symptomatology and subsequent fatal consequences. A more detailed discussion of the more complicated family reactions and treatment approaches is provided by Shuster (1996).

There are support groups in most communities that focus on assisting those who are HIV-positive or have been diagnosed with full-blown AIDS and their partners, those who are HIV-negative, and those couples who are mixed HIV-status. Referral to such groups can facilitate therapy as well as provide assistance to clients who are involved in grieving the death of significant friends or life partners.

Therapists are obligated to examine their feelings and attitudes about HIV/AIDS in the same light as homophobic and heterosexist attitudes. In addition, they should examine their issues relating to death and dying. Therapists also will need to be thoroughly informed about safer sex practices, approaches, and problems so that they can communicate with clients about such matters and the role that this plays in a variety of types of relationship issues.

GAY AND LESBIAN PARENT ISSUES

Research consistently indicates that gay fathers and lesbian mothers are effective in providing care for their children and that children are not harmed by being raised in such households (Barret & Robinson, 1990; Bigner, 1998; Golombok & Tasker, 1994; Patterson, 1992). In general, both gay father and lesbian mother clients share similar problem situations that relate to coming-out issues, disclosure to children issues, and managing step-family issues.

Coming-Out/Identity Issues

Because most gay fathers and lesbian mothers come out following divorce or separation from a heterosexual relationship, a central task in therapy is working through disclosure issues, which include coming out to the self and learning to accept positively a homosexual orientation. This also involves eventually coming out to a spouse or ex-spouse, children, and to family-of-origin members.

Most gay and lesbian parents have spent years prior to entertaining the notion that they are homosexual in orientation either in denial or even being completely unaware, at least at a conscious level, of their true sexual orientation. Internalized homophobia and heterosexism, again, are at fault here in not allowing most of these individuals to acknowledge who and what they are and leading them into a charade of heterosexuality in order to avoid the negative stigmatization associated with homosexuality in our society. For many people in this situation, self-recognition of homosexual orientation is the longest and most difficult phase of coming out (Eichberg, 1990). Once this is accomplished, the process is set in motion to construct a positive self-image of a person who is a gay man or lesbian woman and who is also a parent.

This knowledge often is shared first with someone who can be trusted, and this may be a therapist who has demonstrated that he or she can provide this safety. However, it is important to note that initially there are ambivalent feelings among many clients about whether this self-recognition is "okay" or not (Bigner, 1996). Many individuals typically self-identify at first as being bisexual in orientation rather than homosexual, since homosexuality is viewed more negatively. Clients at this time gain in self-aware-ness as therapists lay the groundwork for more intensive self-examination via biblio-therapy that helps to reframe many of the negative stereotypes and images of homosexuals and homosexuality. Participation in support groups that focus on the com-ing-out process also are beneficial.

It is at this point that many clients request assistance in coming out to spouses or ex-spouses and the focus of therapy may shift to this issue. Clients may need assistance in examining options available as they deal with the insight that maintaining a conventional marriage may be inappropriate to one's newly acknowledged sexual orientation. Assistance may be needed in helping clients end their marriages constructively.

The next major developmental task of gay and lesbian parents is constructing a positive identity as a gay father or lesbian mother. This is thought to occur primarily through a process known as *integrative sanctioning* (Bozett, 1981a, 1981b). This is accomplished by the client's disclosing to heterosexuals who validate the homosexual aspect of the person's self-identity and with gay men and lesbian women who validate the parental aspect of the client's self-identity while distancing themselves from those of both orientations who can-not do so.

A positive identity as a gay or lesbian parent is promoted by socialization experiences that teach the individual about homosexual culture. In-depth experiences in the GLBT communities assist in destroying misleading stereotypes about homosexual lifestyles. This is especially the case for many gay fathers who have acquired a genitally based conception of what it means to be a gay man. Both gay fathers and lesbian mothers will have to develop new social skills that facilitate learning how to date and interact socially with someone of their own sex who is homosexual in orientation. In addition, participating in homosexual cultural events such as Pride Week parades and festivities, gay and lesbian choral concerts, and other affairs assists in a client's socialization process.

Disclosure to Children Issues

Disclosure to children is probably the most feared but desired task facing gay and lesbian parents. At the heart of this fear is that of losing the love and respect of one's children upon learning of the parent's sexual orientation. Gay and lesbian parents can be expected to request assistance from therapists as well as support group members in developing strate-gies and scripting for disclosure to children. Clinical experience suggests that this is best accomplished prior to children experiencing puberty since sexual identity issues often sur-face among adolescents following disclosure, especially among same-sex children (Bigner & Bozett, 1989). However, there is no research available that presents findings about the effects on children upon disclosure or on factors that influence this event. However, guide-lines have been published that describe ways to help gay and lesbian parents to discuss their sexual orientation with children (Bigner & Bozett, 1989).

Gay and Lesbian Step-Family Issues

Therapists are likely to encounter gay and lesbian step-families who seek assistance with resolving a variety of problems and issues that threaten effective, healthy functioning of the group. For all practical purposes, gay and lesbian step-families resemble heterosexual step-families in most respects (Baptiste, 1882, 1987, Barret & Robinson, 1990; Mitchell, 1996; Patterson, 1995). Problems and issues commonly shared include, for example, the experience of divorce, custody issues involving children, problems in the affectional relationships of step-parents and step-children, difficulty in accepting the new adult, and disciplinary issues between step-parents and step-children.

Unique challenges are experienced, however, by gay and lesbian step-families. As mentioned previously, there is a general lack of acceptance and ensuing lack of legitimization of these families in their communities-at-large. This results in a variety of situations that do not directly affect heterosexual families. For instance, the lack of legal and community support makes incorporation of the new adult partner into the new step-family problematic. Gay and lesbian families lack the use of recognized rituals (such as a legal marriage ceremony) that confirm and establish kinship. Next, gay and lesbian step-family functioning may be strained by fears of public exposure of the sexual orientation of the adults. This may be more of an issue for gay male step-families than lesbian step-families since society holds more harsh and hostile views about male than female homosexuality.

Relationships with ex-spouses are also strained among some gay and lesbian step-families. Some parents may not disclose to former spouses for fear of having custody agreements modified to reduce their involvement in child rearing. Acrimony usually is often intense between a gay or lesbian parent and their ex-spouses following disclosure, making resolution following divorce even more problematic.

When therapists begin working with gay and lesbian step-families, it is appropriate to approach the process of therapy as one would with a heterosexual step-family. The beginning point often focuses on the relationship of the two adults (Martin & Martin, 1992). When this relationship can be strengthened, the entire step-family is strengthened. Gay and lesbian step-family problems frequently focus on problems between the step-parent and step-children. Like their heterosexual counterparts, gay and lesbian step-families may benefit from assistance in forming new family rules, boundaries, and rituals that enhance emotional bonding of the family members. Conflicts between the step-parent and step-children can be reduced by restricting the exercise of discipline only to the biological parent. This frees the step-parent and step-child to work on a relationship that is facilitated in an atmosphere of friendship and attachment. The step-parent's use of authority is gradually introduced when bonding between step-children appears to be intact.

Therapists need to become aware that demonstrations of affection between adults in gay and lesbian step-families also are described as problem areas. When adults remain closeted, this is a strong point of strain in their relationship. The strain comes from acting in ways that are viewed as unnatural and confining since the adults must constantly be on guard about actions and must edit carefully what is said around children. Even when adults have disclosed to children, expressions of affection between adults can be a source of stress in the step-family. Children are known to exert boundary control over adults' behavior especially as this relates to public behavior (Bozett, 1987). Step-families may benefit from working through these issues therapeutically.

Some gay and lesbian step-families benefit when therapists help members to define the nature and scope of family relationships. Children can be encouraged to discuss their perceptions of how the various roles in the gay step-family are similar and different from those observed in their heterosexual family or step-family. When all family members can discuss the changes they observe, it is helpful to step-family members to see that family roles often are not parallel in each type of family (Martin & Martin, 1992; Ross, 1988). Therapists also can assist gay and lesbian families in dismantling the tendency to promote secrecy and isolation from others. They can be helped to connect with support systems and to network with others.

CONCLUSION

Gay and lesbian families share many aspects with other families but also have unique distinctions. This places them on the cutting edge of efforts to reinvent notions of family definitions and functioning. They assist in expanding the very idea of family that transcends traditional limitations. They help in broadening our thinking about homosexuality, parenting roles, and the sociocultural contexts in which the meaning of family is explored and expressed. They also eloquently articulate the effects of homophobic and heterosexist attitudes in influencing personal as well as social development of individuals and families and how these effects can be dealt with in healthy ways.

REFERENCES

Allen, K. R. (1997). Lesbian and gay families. In T. Arendell (Ed.), *Contemporary parenting: Challenges and issues* (pp. 196–218). Thousand Oaks, CA: Sage Publications.

Anderson, S. C. (1996). Addressing heterosexist bias in the treatment of lesbian couples with chemical dependency. In R.-J. Green & J. Laird (Eds.), *Lesbian and gay couple and family relationships: Therapeutic perspectives* (pp. 370–403). San Francisco: Jossey-Bass.

Baptiste, D. A., Jr. (1982). Issues and guidelines in the treatment of gay stepfamilies. In A. Gurman (Ed.), *Questions and answers in the practice of family therapy* (Vol. 2,) pp. 225–229). New York: Brunner/Mazel.

Baptiste, D. A., Jr. (1987). The gay and lesbian stepfamily. In F. W. Bozett (Ed.), *Gay and lesbian parents*. New York: Praeger.

Barret, R. L., & Robinson, B. E. (1990). *Gay fathers*. Lexington, MA: D. C. Heath.

Beane, J. (1981). "I'd rather be dead than gay": Counseling gay men who are coming out. *Personnel and Guidance Journal, 60,* 222–226.

Becker, C. S. (1991). A phenomenology of friendship families. *Humanistic Psychologist, 19,* 170–184.

Benkov, L. (1994). *Reinventing the family*. New York: Crown Publishers, Inc.

Bell, A. P., & Weinberg, M. S. (1978). *Homosexualities: A study of diversity among men and women*. New York: Simon & Schuster.

Bigner, J. J. (1996). Working with gay fathers: Developmental, post-divorce, and therapeutic issues. In R-J. Green & J. Laird (Eds.), *Lesbian and gay couple and family relationships: Therapeutic perspectives* (pp. 370–403). San Francisco: Jossey-Bass.

Bigner, J. J. (1998). *Parent-child relations: An introduction to parenting* (5th ed.). Upper Saddle River, NJ: Prentice Hall.

Bigner, J. J., & Bozett, F. W. (1989). Parenting by gay fathers. *Marriage and Family Review, 14,* 155–176.

Blumenfeld, W. J. (1992). *Homophobia: How we all pay the price*. Boston: Beacon Press.

Bozett, F. W. (1981a). Gay father: Evolution of the gay father identity. *American Journal of Orthopsychiatry, 51,* 552–559.

Bozett, F. W. (1981b). Gay fathers: Identity conflict resolution through integrative sanctioning. *Alternative Lifestyles, 4,* 90–107.

Bozett, F. W. (1987). Gay fathers. In F. W. Bozett (Ed.), *Gay and lesbian parents*. New York: Praeger.

Bozett, F. W., & Sussman, M. B. (1989). Homosexuality and family relations: Views and research issues. In F. W. Bozett & M. B. Sussman (Eds.), *Homosexuality and family relations* (pp. 4–10). New York: Harrington Park Press.

Braschi v. Stahl Association Co. (1989). New York Court of Appeals, WL 73109.

Briggs, J. R. (1994). *A Yankelovich monitor perspective on gays/lesbians*. Norwalk, CT: Yankelovich Partners, Inc.

Cabaj, R. P. (1996). Psychotherapeutic interventions with lesbian and gay couples. In R. P. Cabaj & T. S. Stein (Eds.), *Textbook of homosexuality and mental health* (pp. 485–501). Washington, DC: American Psychiatric Press.

Campbell, S. M. (1980). *The couple's journey: Intimacy as a path to wholeness.* San Luis Obispo, CA: Impact Publishers.

Cass, V. C. (1979). Homosexual identity formation: A theoretical model. *Journal of Homosexuality, 4,* 32–39.

Clark, D. (1987). *Loving someone gay* (rev. ed.). Berkeley, CA: Celestial Arts.

Clunis, D. M., & Green, G. D. (1988). *Lesbian couples.* Seattle, WA: Seal Press.

Demo, D. H., & Allen, K. R. (1996). Diversity within lesbian and gay families: Challenges and implications for family theory and research. *Journal of Social and Personal Relationships, 13,* 415–434.

Eichberg, R. (1990). *Coming out: An act of love.* New York: Viking Penguin.

Ellis, L., & Ames, M. A. (1987). Neurohormonal functioning and sexual orientation: A theory of homosexuality-heterosexuality. *Psychological Bulletin, 101,* 233–258.

Gagnon, J. (1977). *Human sexualities.* Glenview, IL: Scott, Foresman.

Glaus, K. O. (1989). Alcoholism, chemical dependency, and the lesbian client. *Women and Therapy, 8,* 131–144.

Golombok, S., & Tasker, F. (1994). Children in lesbian and gay families: Theories and evidence. *Annual Review of Sex Research, 5,* 73–100.

Gonsiorek, J. C. (Ed.). (1985). *A guide to psychotherapy with gay and lesbian clients.* Binghamton, NY: Harrington Park Press.

Harry, J. (1990). A probability sample of gay males. *Journal of Homosexuality, 19,* 89–104.

Hartman, A. (1996). Social policy as a context for lesbian and gay families: The political is personal. In J. Laird & R.-J. Green (Eds.), *Lesbians and gays in couples and families: A handbook for therapists* (pp. 69–85). San Francisco, CA: Jossey-Bass.

Hildebrand, V., Phenice, L. A., Gray, M. M., & Hines, R. P. (1996). *Knowing and serving diverse families.* Upper Saddle River, NJ: Prentice Hall.

Hunt, M. (1974). *Sexual behavior in the 1970s.* Chicago: Playboy Press.

Hunt, M. (1987). *Gay.* New York: Michael di Capua Books.

Johnson, T. W., & Keren, M. S. (1996). Creating and maintaining boundaries in male couples. In R.-J. Green & J. Laird (Eds.), *Lesbian and gay couple and family relationships: Therapeutic perspectives* (pp. 231–250). San Francisco: Jossey-Bass.

Johnston, W. I. (1995). *HIV-negative: How the uninfected are affected by AIDS.* New York: Plenum Press.

Kerewsky, S. D., & Miller, D. (1996). Lesbian couples and childhood trauma: Guidelines for therapists. In R.-J. Green & J. Laird (Eds.), *Lesbian and gay couple and family relationships: Therapeutic perspectives* (pp. 370–403). San Francisco, CA: Jossey-Bass.

Kinsey, A. C., Pomeroy, W. B., & Martin, C. E. (1948). *Sexual behavior in the human male.* Philadelphia: Saunders.

Kinsey, A. C., Pomeroy, W. B., & Martin, C. E. (1953). *Sexual behavior in the human female.* Philadelphia: Saunders.

Knox, D., & Wilson, K. (1981). Dating behaviors of university students. *Family Relations, 4,* 255–258.

Kominars, S. B., & Kominars, K. D. (1996). *Accepting ourselves & others: A journey into recovery from addictive and compulsive behaviors for gays, lesbians, and bisexuals.* Center City, MN: Hazelden.

Krestan, J. A., & Bepko, C. S. (1980). The problem of fusion in the lesbian relationship. *Family Process, 19,* 277–289.

Kurdek, L. (1995). Lesbian and gay couples. In A. R. D'Augelli & C. J. Patterson (Eds.), *Lesbian, gay, and bisexual identities over the life span.* New York: Oxford University Press.

Laird, J. (1996). Family-centered practice with lesbian and gay families. *Families in Society, 77,* 559–572.

Maddox, B. (1982). Homosexual parents. *Psychology Today, 56,* 62–69.

Maracek, J., Finn, S. E., & Cardell, M. (1988). Gender roles in the relationships of lesbians and gay men. In J. P. DeCecco (Ed.), *Gay relationships* (pp. 156–188). New York: Harrington Park Press.

Markowitz, L. M. (1993). Understanding the differences: Demystifying gay and lesbian sex. *Family Therapy Networker, 17*(2), 50–59.

Martin, D., & Martin, M. (1992). *Stepfamilies in therapy: Understanding systems, assessment, and intervention.* San Francisco: Jossey-Bass.

McWhirter, D. P., & Mattison, A. M. (1984). Psychotherapy for gay male couples. In J. C. Gonsiorek (Ed.), *A guide to therapy with gay and lesbian clients* (pp. 79–95). New York: Harrington Park Press.

McWhirter, D. P., & Mattison, A. M. (1988). Stages in the development of gay relationships. In J. P. DeCecco (Ed.), *Gay relationships* (pp. 65–90). New York: Harrington Park Press.

McWhirter, D. P., & Mattison, A. M. (1996). *Male couples.* Washington, DC: American Psychiatric Press.

Miller B. (1979). Unpromised paternity: The lifestyles of gay fathers. In M.P. Levine (Ed.), *Gay men,* New York: Harper & Row.

Minuchin, S. (1974). *Families and family therapy.* Cambridge, MA: Harvard University Press.

Mitchell, V. (1996). Two moms: Contribution of the planned lesbian family to the deconstruction of gendered parenting. In R.-J. Green & J. Laird (Eds.), *Lesbian and gay couple and family relationships: Therapeutic perspectives* (pp. 343–357). San Francisco, CA: Jossey-Bass.

Morales, E. (1996). Gender roles among Latino gay and bisexual men. In R.-J. Green & J. Laird (Eds.), *Lesbian and gay couple and family relationships: Therapeutic perspectives* (pp. 272–315). San Francisco, CA: Jossey-Bass.

National Institute on Alcohol Abuse and Alcoholism. (1995). *Assessing alcohol problems: A guide for clinicians and researchers.* Publication No. 95-3745. Washington, DC: National Institutes of Health.

Patterson, C. J. (1992). Children of lesbian and gay parents. *Child Development, 63,* 1025–1042.

Patterson, C. J. (1994a). Lesbian and gay families. *Contemporary Directions in Psychological Science, 4,* 62–64.

Patterson, C. J. (1994b). Children of the lesbian baby boom: Behavioral adjustment, self-concepts, and sex-role identity. In B. Greene & G. M. Herek (Eds.), *Psychological perspectives on lesbian and gay issues* (Vol. 1, pp. 156–175). Thousand Oaks, CA: Sage Publications.

Patterson, C. J. (1995). Sexual orientation and human development: An overview. *Developmental Psychology, 31,* 3–1.

Peplau, L. A. (1981, March). What homosexuals want. *Psychology Today,* pp. 19–27.

Peplau, L. A. (1991). Lesbian and gay relationships. In J. C. Gonsiorek & J. D. Weinrich (Eds.). *Homosexuality: Research implications for public policy* (pp. 146–179). Beverly Hills, CA: Sage Publications.

Peplau, L. A., & Cochran, S. D. (1981). Value orientations in the intimate relationships of gay men. *Journal of Homosexuality, 6,* 1–19.

Peplau, L. A., & Gordon, S. L. (1983). The intimate relationships of lesbians and gay men. In E. R. Allgeier & N. B. McCormick (Eds.), *Changing boundaries: Gender roles and sexual behavior* (pp. 226–244). Palo Alto, CA: Mayfield.

Peterson, J. L. (1992). *Black men and their same-sex desires and behavior.* Boston: Beacon Press.

Reigot, B. P., & Spina, R. K. (1996). *Beyond the traditional family: Voices of diversity.* New York: Springer.

Riddle, D. I., & Sang, B. (1978). Psychotherapy with lesbians. *Journal of Social Issues, 34,* 84–100.

Rochlin, M. (1982). Sexual orientation of the therapist and therapeutic effectiveness with gay clients. *Journal of Homosexuality, 7,* 21–30.

Ross, J. L. (1988). Challenging boundaries: An adolescent in a homosexual family. *Journal of Family Psychology, 2,* 227–240.

Scrivner, R., & Eldridge, N. S. (1995). Lesbian and gay family psychology. In R. H. Mikesell, D.-D. Lusterman, & S. H. McDaniel (Eds.), *Integrating family therapy: Handbook of family psychology and systems theory* (pp. 327–345). Washington, DC: American Psychological Association.

Shuster, S. (1996). Families coping with HIV disease in gay fathers. In R.-J. Green & J. Laird (Eds.), *Lesbian and gay couple and family relationships: Therapeutic perspectives* (pp. 404–419). San Francisco, CA: Jossey-Bass.

Strommen, E. F. (1989a). Hidden branches and growing pains: Homosexuality and the family tree. *Marriage and Family Review, 14,* 9–34.

Strommen, E. F. (1989b). "You're a what?": Family member reactions to the disclosure of homosexuality. *Journal of Homosexuality, 18,* 37–58.

Tasker, F. L., & Golombok, S. (1997). *Growing up in a lesbian family: Effects on child development.* New York: Guilford Press.

Testa, R. J., Kinder, B. N., & Ironson, G. (1987). Heterosexual bias in the perception of loving relationships of gay males and lesbians. *Journal of Sex Research, 23,* 163–172.

Tolleson, J. (1998). Same-sex palimony case under trial in Colorado: Colorado Legal Initiatives Project. Personal communication.

Tuller, N. R. (1988). Couples: The hidden segment of the gay world. In J. P. DeCecco (Ed.), *Gay relationships* (pp. 36–45). New York: Harrington Park Press.

Ussher, J. M. (1991). Family and couples therapy with gay and lesbian clients: Acknowledging the forgotten minority. *Journal of Family Therapy, 13,* 131–148.

Weinberg, M. S., & Williams, C. J. (1974). *Male homosexuals: Their problems and adaptations.* New York: Oxford University Press.

Weston, K. (1997). *Families we choose: Lesbians, gays, kinship.* New York: Columbia University Press.

Wisenkale, S. K., & Heckart, K. E. (1993). Domestic partnerships. *Family Relations, 42,* 199–204.

CHAPTER 15

Diversity of New American Families: Guidelines for Therapists

Raksha Dave Gates, Sylvia Arce de Esnaola, Georgi Kroupin,
Ciloue Cheng Stewart, Manfred van Dulmen, Blong Xiong,
and Pauline G. Boss

THIS CHAPTER is about New American families. For many, uprooting has meant loss, for others hope; for most, an ambivalent mixture of both. As participants in the immigrant experience ourselves, we were reminded repeatedly of the primacy of diversity in contemporary family therapy as we wrote this chapter. Differences occurred within and across our ethnicity, cultures, races, genders, and ages; we became aware of differences in our socialization and life experiences. Yet, we found commonalities among us—the value of families to care for the young and old; concern for preserving the institution of marriage; concern about family violence and abuse; and genuine respect for the incredible strengths we see in so many who have come here to overcome traumatic uprooting from discrimination and war.

How these commonalities are manifested varies, however, and this is where misunderstandings abound. Our professional experience has taught us to set aside strategies and stereotypes and begin by simply listening to each family's unique story. This sets the stage for collaboration, a necessity with New American families. A family's history cannot be erased no matter how terrible it is, but, together, we can help its members live more comfortably with the inherent tension and ambiguity in their dual reality—life as it was in the old country and now, as it is in the new.

Our aim in this chapter is to provide a stimulus for therapists to become more curious and knowledgeable about the wonderful diversity of families who are settling in North America. We also raise questions. Although we speak in a unified voice about the strengths of diversity and the need for even veteran clinicians to listen more, each of the first six authors writes separately based on his or her country of origin.

Appreciation is expressed to the University of Minnesota Experiment Station for their partial support of Dr. Boss for this project.

NEW AMERICANS FROM INDIA
RAKSHA DAVE GATES

Nina and her husband, Prem, were 27-year-old Hindus who had immigrated to Canada from India at an early age. They experienced a second miscarriage 1 year before going to therapy. Their cultural stigma about talking with anyone outside the family about problems was sufficient to prevent either of them from seeking family therapy earlier to deal with their grief and loss. They said that if they could overcome the stigma, the therapy would need to help them understand what the miscarriages meant beyond the medical perspective. For Nina and Prem, exploring these meanings would be critical because they appeared to be acculturated to the Canadian host culture with respect to their dress, food, and identification with values of personal control and autonomy. Yet, to their surprise, Nina reported, "Western concepts didn't work for me; they increased turmoil, confusion, and anxiety. I returned to my culture." "My culture" meant that she perceived the miscarriages had occurred due to karma or past life experiences, of their souls, the connections of their souls to the souls of the lost babies, or to the possibility that someone may have cast an "evil eye" or *nazar* upon them. Furthermore, according to their *kundli* (i.e., palmistry and astrological readings), they believed that their next 7 years were destined to be a struggle and could be counterbalanced by fasting.

For them the mind and body were interlinked. Their quest for "why" led them to culturally specific coping strategies: fasting, astrology and palmistry, herbal foods, rituals to remove the nazar, and strength in the belief that "every situation has a lesson to teach" as a preparation for future lives. They did not discount medical possibilities but their explanations of "why" also disclosed that Nina's mother was a significant cultural resource for them; not only did she coach them in traditional rituals, but she contacted a priest in India regularly to conduct prayers on behalf of the family. Issues concerning who was inside the family emerged for the couple (Boss, 1988).

It is essential to engage couples about their beliefs, attributions, and values, as well as their location on the continuum of acculturation to the host culture. In this case, the therapist took the role of learner and listener so the couple was empowered to teach her what would be most helpful for them.

DEMOGRAPHICS ON ASIAN INDIANS IN THE UNITED STATES

The country of origin, diverse cultural backgrounds, and the time and reason for immigration contribute to the complexity of Asian Indian immigrants—a group often referred to as South Asian, East Indian, or by other identifiers reflecting the geographic, linguistic, and religious diversity of India. A lack of a unified identifier for Asian Indians creates confusion and contributes to their invisibility in the discourse on culture. "Asian Indian" is used here to identify the ethnic group that originates in India. Estimates of demographics are difficult because many Asian Indians come to the United States from countries other than their country of birth or ancestry.

Migration of Asian Indians to the United States occurred in two waves. The first wave was prior to 1946 and was composed largely of men from Punjab (Leonard, 1993) who worked on farms and in construction (Leonhard-Spark & Saran, 1980). They settled in California, concentrating in rural areas (Leonard, 1993). The second wave came after the 1965 Immigration Act was passed. This revised policy created new criteria for visas based on family, finance, and occupation, and drew highly educated and professionally skilled Asian Indian immigrants who settled according to locations of their jobs rather than as a concentrated community. This trend for Asian Indian immigrants, skilled in the fields of engineering, mathematics, and computer science, was especially apparent between 1988 and 1990 and continues today. Increasingly, a higher unmarried proportion of Asian Indians are in the United States as migrant professional workers (Kanjanapan, 1995). They use immigration to raise their family income for a better economic standard when they return to India or other parts of South Asia. Experiences in other countries prior to arriving in the United States, exposure to Western beliefs and values as a result of the British colonialization of India, and their urban background familiarize Asian Indians with Western culture and the English language (Leonhard-Spark & Saran, 1980; Pais, 1997).

Although some Asian Indians fit the "model minority" stereotype of high education, income, and professional status, Asian Indians who come to the United States due to the Family Reunification Act are not highly educated or trained (Borjas, 1990). Hence, family therapists in the United States may meet Asian Indian families who, because of less education, face greater language, economic, and cultural barriers.

WHAT DOES A FAMILY THERAPIST NEED TO KNOW TO WORK EFFECTIVELY WITH ASIAN INDIANS?

Despite within-group diversity, similarities arise from a common social structure and spiritual world view. First, intergenerational and gender difficulties are likely to occur for Asian Indian New Americans, often arising due to a clash of values between the younger, more acculturated generation, and their more traditional parents. Open expression of individualism and acculturation by the younger generation is often perceived as a threat to parental status and right to control their children (Kar, Campbell, Jimenez, & Gupta, 1996). These clashes are often a greater source of conflict between daughters and their parents as compared to sons, especially in situations of dating and marriage (Kar et al., 1996).

This intergenerational difference is reflected in the dual identities for daughters and their subsequent ambivalence as their mothers often want them to have greater freedom in education and careers, yet also want them to stay close to home so their social activities can be monitored. For Asian Indian women, new roles bring a new sense of independence that often clashes with the expectations of older generations as well as with males within their own generation (Kar et al., 1996).

Elder Asian Indian women, even in the United States, are often dependent on their husband's or son's status, and if widowed, are unlikely to remarry (Keskar, 1990). Although the cultural norm is for elders to live with their sons, the current trend suggests that the social stigma associated with elder parents living with married daughters (Keskar, 1990) is diminishing. Five out of six widowed persons are women, and when they choose to live with relatives, they are more likely to live with a daughter than a son (Keskar, 1990). Increasingly, the elderly are confronting issues of living independently. One elder woman said:

> Once my daughter thought that independent housing will be good for me; we applied at senior housing and I got an apartment, but I did not go there because I was not courageous enough to live alone. Three other Indian families were living there, but I thought I would feel very lonely in the evenings. At least the children around me make me self-assured.

Another said:

> This the first time for living alone. I didn't live alone my whole life like here. Aging in India, we don't live by ourselves as I am living here. We live together

with our older son. We live together you know. So we don't feel that we are lonely, not wanted.

Hikey (1996) notes that elder Asian Indian women express a longing for the extended family they grew up in, perceiving the nuclear family as cold, sterile, and lacking a sense of nurturing. Their immigrant daughters, on the other hand, feel less attached to the extended family structure and are more comfortable in a nuclear family.

Second, family therapists must be aware of commonalities and differences among Asian Indians about spirituality and world view. Asian Indians are diverse in their religions: Hinduism, Islam, Sikhism, Jainism, Buddhism, Christianity, Zoroastrianism, and so on (Almeida, 1996). The Hindu tradition, representing 83 percent of India's population, proposes a continuity between past and future lives where *moksa,* or liberation of the soul, is attained in the final stage of life as a transition to future lives (Joseph, 1991). Other key values include *karma,* the cycle of birth and rebirth; *dharma,* the rules for appropriate conduct in life, responsibility, and duty; *kama,* the physical satisfaction of sexual desire, or personal well-being; and *artha,* material well-being and wealth (Ram-Prasad, 1995). Hindus believe in an *asrama* theory of normative life stages composed of (1) *Brahmacarya* or student; (2) *Grhstha* or householder; (3) *Vanaprastha* or forest-dweller; and (4) *Sannyasa* or renouncer (Ram-Prasad, 1995). A key aspect of the Hindu ideal of life is to maintain an outward involvement with life and expected roles while internally renouncing physical and material attachments. This ability to manage the dialectical nature and boundary ambiguities of life enables Asian Indians to balance their entry into American life in the context of economics and education while maintaining a traditional Indian pattern of behavior at home (Saran, 1985).

Asian Indians are metaphysical in their world views because of their ancient religious and philosophical traditions. Hindus reject the self or "I" as an empirical or physical entity but rather, believe in a "pure consciousness" most closely represented by *atman* or an undefinable spiritual self. Hence, the world view of Asian Indians is more closely tied to unconscious, nonrational, and cosmic processes that reflect an acceptance and fatalism regarding occurrences in the world rather than a need to master or control. This often affects the attitude of Asian Indians who report, "I will cross that bridge when I come to it," "why worry now," or "what will happen will happen." These attitudes may be changing, however, because Asian Indians adjust to the social context of the United States with more planful and mastery-oriented attitudes. Hence, a consequence of immigration for many may be their greater discomfort with ambiguity, contradictions, and dialectical logic in order to meet the need for consistent, clear, and linear logic in the host culture.

Whether educated professionals fluent in English or less fluent family members who come to join extended families, New American Asian Indians face adjustments related to gender and generation. If explored, their world view and spiritual perspective can serve as significant sources of strength and coping as they balance continuity and change.

NEW AMERICAN FAMILIES FROM HISPANIC COUNTRIES

SYLVIA ARCE DE ESNAOLA

Hispanic-Latinos are increasing almost four times as fast as the rest of the U.S. population. By the year 2050, one in every four Americans will be Hispanic/Latino, not one homogeneous ethnic group, but a mixture of differing races, languages, and traditions from 22 Latin American countries (Robinson, 1998). Within each are white Europeans, Africans, Afrocaribbeans, Mestizos, as well as indigenous groups (Vargas-Willis & Cervantes, 1987). The following case illustrates therapeutic resistance resulting from language and cultural confusions.

An indigenous family from South America requested help because the teacher said their daughter showed ADHD behaviors at school. The parents could not communicate fluently in English, nor could they speak Spanish. They were disappointed and distressed because their daughter showed a 3-year developmental delay in language and speech. The family was labeled "neglectful." Mother felt blamed for her daughter's diagnosis and was upset because of what she considered an intrusion into her privacy and a disqualification of her as a mother. Father, on the other hand, was highly suspicious of the medication prescribed, saying that in his homeland he knew that they used indigenous people to test medications. At the time that this family requested help, they already had six different providers involved in their lives. Most spoke little or no Spanish. The use of an interpreter from yet another culture complicated things further.

The family was overwhelmed with the many weekly appointments and did not know how to balance the demands of their daughter's treatment with their own work schedules. Father ended up unemployed due to his many absences to attend the mandated treatments; mother had to work fulltime to support the family, leaving little time to breastfeed her newborn baby. Mother's distress and anger were interpreted by the psychotherapist as refusal to comply with treatment; her quietness was interpreted as depression and a rejection of her daughter.

The lack of cultural sensitivity and awareness by some of the treating professionals harmed this family. Instead of empowering the family and particularly the parental dyad, the parents were in constant fear of being reported to child protection, raising their levels of mistrust and impeding therapeutic progress. Mother's sadness and silence had a different meaning for her than for the translator and the therapist. Mother reported, "I am so angry with the disqualification that they make of me as a mother that I prefer to remain silent." The language barrier, the lack of sensitivity in the use of an unskilled interpreter, and the counselor's premature and erroneous interpretation of the mother's nonverbal actions throughout the session left the mother feeling frustrated and that the interventions were not at all helpful.

WHAT DOES A FAMILY THERAPIST NEED TO KNOW TO WORK WITH THIS GROUP?

Family and Health Definition

A culturally based definition of health for Hispanic families implies wellness of the total person, including spiritual health (Vargas, 1980). Among very poor and working-class families, children are commonly seen as parental property, so family wealth means having as many children as possible. A large family is considered valuable not only as a way to obtain cheap labor and ensure security in the parents' old age, but also as a form of human capital since the family is the economic unit. What is not possible to acquire without economic resources can be easily obtained through having more children. Latin American society justifies and promotes this behavior directly and indirectly. A commonly heard phrase among low-income Hispanic/Latinos is, "Our children are the treasures of the poor; we may have nothing, but if God gives us children then we are rich." What makes a family then is children.

It is also a collective belief that the extended family should socialize the young. To offer support and informal education there are parents, grandparents, uncles, and aunts, all with a common language that becomes a valuable resource because the children always find a familiar face to take care of them while their parents work. But the extended family is becoming scarce due to the mobility of the modern world. While Latin America has not escaped this transformation, this effect is most noticeable in New American families.

Political and religious officials in the majority of Latin American countries continue to stress the importance of families as the building blocks of the society (Valle & Vega, 1980), but this emphasis places Latina women in a precarious position. While their first role continues to be the production of future citizens, and they are expected to fulfill their traditional roles as housewife and educator-mother in almost full measure, they are now also expected to contribute to their national economies through active participation in the work force.

Another problem Hispanic/Latino immigrants face is the lack of economic resources, reflected in feelings of insecurity, instability, and emotional imbalance. If the pervasive fear related to undocumentation is added to this list, therapists can assume that Hispanic/Latinos certainly are at risk. In the case of documented immigrants, Hispanic/Latinos also have to face the reality of the regulations that each state has regarding the professional practice of a career. Even when immigrants hold degrees from a foreign university they are forced to take underpaid positions, thus jeopardizing the whole family as they now face low income and often poverty. Such situations increase stress and the possibility of violence in the family (De Juan Gomez, 1990).

Indeed, predisposing factors may cause high levels of stress in immigrant Hispanic families—no clear boundaries between family members, social legitimization of use of violence, rigid roles, and indirect and abusive communication patterns (Flores-Ortiz & Bernal, 1989; Flores-Ortiz, Esteban, & Carillo, 1994). After immigration, stress escalates from the ascribed minority status of Hispanics in general, rapid changes in the family, loss of support systems, contradictory expectations related to gender roles, low income, high fertility, single parenting, and different levels of acculturation among family members (Arroyo, 1997a, 1997b).

The crucial first step in building a therapeutic relationship with Hispanic/Latinos is the establishment of *confianza* (trust, bonding) in order to develop an acceptance of the therapeutic relationship. As a cultural group, Hispanic/Latinos of various origins are people oriented. It is extremely important, therefore, to develop rapport with clients and demonstrate a genuine interest in them, their family, and their problems, and to work collaboratively to seek solutions to their problems. *Respeto* is important for Hispanic/Latinos, who like to be treated in an atmosphere of mutual respect. First impressions will determine if they come back or withdraw. Reasons for resistance to the intake and assessment process, and later to interventions, may stem from past negative experiences such as racism and discrimination by whites in positions of authority. Being discriminated against for one's color is a new and extremely painful experience for Hispanics since discrimination in Latino countries is more frequently limited to socioeconomic status.

Legal status also plays an important role in building a therapeutic relationship. Being undocumented adds an additional threat of *la migra,* and the constant fear of deportation or being reported to officials is a barrier to establishing a therapeutic relationship as well as to developing personal self-worth. After many months in therapy, a father told me, "I am not myself—I am of no value." In order to survive in the United States, he had taken the identity of another person; thus he did not exist in this country, which brought an inner conflict intertwined with the reality of his legal status.

When treating Hispanic/Latino families or individuals, it is important to explore the circumstances involved in their decision to leave as well as to return for visits (Rogler, Cortes, & Malgady, 1991). For example, the fact that Puerto Ricans are U.S. citizens gives them immediate freedom to move back and forth between homeland and the continental United States. They do not have to deal with long periods of mourning over permanent losses, harsh immigration policies, and discriminatory treatment due to legal status. In addition, being U.S. citizens allows them to look for jobs without having to obtain or renew work permits, an obligation that legal aliens have to face every year.

For some South American, Central American, and Caribbean groups—Argentineans, Uruguayans, Chileans, Nicaraguans, Salvadorians, Guatemalans, Hondurans, Haitians, and Cubans—the situation is different. Their immigration was often forced by political issues, war, oppression, exploitation, political torture (Vargas-Willis & Cervantes, 1987) and forced exile (Olea-Guldemont, 1992). Many may fear people in positions of authority such as the police, the military, and representatives of the court or "the system" due to past negative experiences with officials either in their country of origin or in the United States. Refugees and immigrants often fear deportation or other forms of government reprisal. Therapists must empathize when they view seeking outside help from an agency or organization as unsafe and risky.

When exploring the sources of strength for Hispanic/Latinos, invariably we see the spiritual realm. The majority of Hispanic/Latinos are Christians, ranging from traditional observant Catholics to "magico-religious" practices of historical-cultural heritage. Many religious celebrations weave the primitive with the modern. In Minnesota, for example, there is "Dia de muertos" (November 1st, the Day of the Dead) in which tribute is paid to loved ones who have passed away. Another highly valued religious celebration is "La Purisima" for Nicaraguans (December 8th). Even during wartime, they stopped to celebrate the protection of the Virgin Mary who intercedes for their children before God.

The therapeutic relationship with Hispanic/Latinos must start with a mutual agreement in which the shared responsibility for solving the problem is clearly stipulated. Client and therapist work together to specify goals, objectives, areas of improvement, and evaluation. Feedback is given on unique strengths and competencies, which are valued and built upon. Passive, reticent, timid, overly polite, and stereotypic behavior is respectfully challenged. Women are encouraged to be more active and validate their expressive behavior. While also encouraging expression of feelings in male clients, as well as instrumental behaviors, it may be appropriate to challenge sexist language and behaviors (Herrera & Esnaola, 1990).

NEW AMERICANS FROM RUSSIA

GEORGI KROUPIN

Immigration from Russia to the United States has a relatively long history with the first major wave from Czarist Russia arriving in America in the first two decades of the twentieth century (Thomas & Znaniecki, 1984). The second wave, which came from the Soviet Union after World War II, was ethnically mixed and consisted mostly of those who were scattered across Europe as a result of war. From the 1960s to the 1980s, ethnic problems caused the third wave of immigration from the former Soviet Union as a number of ethnic groups—Germans, Chechens, Crimean Tatars, Estonians, Meshketin Turks, Lithuanians, Latvians—were uprooted under Soviet rule. Starting from the late 1960s, in an effort to resolve existing ethnic problems, the Soviet Union permitted controlled, limited immigration, assuming that it would exhaust itself soon (Salitan, 1992). Radical positive changes in immigration policy came after 1986, when Gorbachev came to power, and *perestroika* began. With Germans and Armenians immigrating mostly to Western Europe, Soviet Jews came to the United States.

The Relationship between Jewish and Russian Cultures

Jews played an important role in the Bolshevik Revolution of 1917, and by the end of Lenin's life a majority of the members of the Politburo were of Jewish origin (Andreski, 1979; Gitelman, 1991; Ryvkina, 1996). During these early years the decision was made, with the agreement of Jewish Communists, to abolish traditional, "high" Jewish culture, and campaigns were launched against the Judaic religion and Hebrew, Zionist, and Jewish political movements (Gitelman, 1991).

By the late 1920s an attempt was made to reconstruct a Jewish culture, based on a secular and socialist foundation. Yiddish, the language of ethnic Jews, was chosen to replace the "high culture" Hebrew language, with its historical and religious associations. "Many Jews eagerly abandoned the Yiddish culture, which they associated with a way of life they had been taught to regard as backward, and embraced the Russian language and culture" (Gitelman, 1992).

The situation started changing rapidly in the 1930s, when Stalin (who was not an ethnic Russian himself and spoke Russian with a very heavy accent) began more actively enforcing Russian nationalism as a means of consolidating and manipulating a gigantic, culturally diverse country. "High" culture of Bolshevist international socialism became the center of this new Soviet nationalism, which sought to displace the "local cultures" of the different states and ethnic groups. One of the major results of this policy "was the virtual destruction of Jewish culture" (Brym, 1994).

Russian/Soviet Immigrants Have More Ambiguity about Leaving

Soviet Jewish immigrants come from a geographic and cultural background that ranges from Central Asia to the Baltic, so generalizations about this group are of limited validity. In the United States, Soviet Jews often call themselves Russian, partly for simplicity, but also for reasons of cultural self-definition and to acknowledge their being part of the Soviet population.

Although the pre-1974 Jewish immigration from the Soviet Union was primarily Zionist in nature and consisted of less-educated rural Jews from territories that were annexed after World War II, the second period of mass immigration (1974–1979) was characterized by the diminishing importance of Zionism, and the flow consisted mostly of urban professionals, who immigrated for cultural and political reasons (Feigin, 1996). Usually highly educated (Freedman, 1989; Gitelman, 1992; Miller, 1984; Ryvkina, 1996), they actively participated in social and intellectual movements for change and identified themselves with the Russian intelligentsia.

With the end of the Cold War fewer Russian immigrants are granted the status of refugees. Recent immigration is seen as mostly pragmatic (Brym, 1994; Ryvkina, 1996), with major reasons, along with fleeing from anti-Semitism and reunification with the family, being the welfare of children, political stability, and increased standards of life. The fact that motivation for immigration became relative, but not absolute (Portes & Rumbaut, 1996), helps to explain why recent immigrant families struggle with much more ambiguity and ambivalence about immigration and its consequences.

Family Dynamics of Russian Immigrant Families

A high educational level characterizes Russians coming to the United States, the majority having high school diplomas and a significant percentage having college degrees. Upon arrival, however, most Russian immigrants occupy lower niches in the labor market that offer few chances for upward mobility (Portes & Rumbaut, 1996). This has several consequences, including first the fact that many Russian immigrants with a relatively high educational level either fail to find a professional job in the United States or find one at a much lower level of professional competency than they had in the country of origin. The result is a severe loss of social status, particularly for older immigrants (aged 50 to 65), who experience difficulties with employment in spite of having left high-status jobs in the country of origin.

Second, motivation for education and achievement in both the first and the second generation of immigrants from Russian is very high, but it is mostly the second generation that achieves in this area. This creates distance between the two generations, who formerly were close, which is thus perceived as a deterioration of family relationships. With children separating both physically and emotionally, aging parents who immigrated "for the sake of children" have to "reinvent" the meaning of their immigration, or face a severe identity crisis.

Third, former Soviet society was characterized by a double standard in gender expectations. Women were in most cases working as hard as men and doing most of the housework at the same time, but the prevalent Russian convention still equated femininity with weakness and therefore demanded that women act helpless and vulnerable (du Plessix Gray, 1990, cited in Althausen, 1996). Paradoxically, this expectation of feminine domesticity is often beneficial for Russian immigrant women, who because they can keep doing housework in the United States did not experience as much guilt and loss as did men who remained unemployed. Losing the only source of their social value, men often experience a profound crisis of identity.

Fourth, in Russian culture, friends are highly valued and often are like family members, providing moral, financial, and sometimes physical support. Being a good friend to others is also an important and a valuable part of one's self-image. Loss of friends who stayed behind has a strong negative effect on the adjustment of Russian immigrants.

Definition of the Family and Family Development

Due to many socioeconomic and cultural factors, the life cycle of a typical Russian family is different from the one described in developmental theory (Duvall & Miller, 1985). Many Russian families do not go through the phases of "independent young adult," or "nuclear family." Most children live with parents until they marry, and many live with them after they get married and have children. Grandparents are often involved in rearing grandchildren while both parents work. This arrangement provides help for the second generation and creates additional meaning in the life of the elders. Later, it is assumed that children will take care of their parents as they grow old, a pattern of mutual care that remains a part of the mentality of many Russian immigrants when they come to the United States (Althausen, 1996).

Meanwhile, the realities of immigration create other dynamics. Different living arrangements, social status, and life objectives cause many adult children to separate from their family of origin both physically and emotionally, creating an "existential vacuum" for their parents. Accustomed to caring for children and grandchildren, their only experience of caring that centered on themselves was when they fought for survival, or when they were sick.

Younger Russian immigrants have challenges of their own. Those who come to the United States during the young adult phase have the greatest potential for adapting in terms of career and culture. However, they also may be most vulnerable to cutting off their heritage, which may be associated with poorer mental health outcomes (Vega & Rumbaut, 1991).

A Russian immigrant family with adolescent children in the United States is at high risk of intergenerational conflicts. Cultural differences between the United States and the former Soviet Union in attitudes toward adolescence are dramatic. I was once asked by an American mother of a 14-year-old, "What was adolescent culture like in Russia in your time?" My answer was, "There was no such thing, there were only 'children' and 'adults'." Many Russian/Soviet immigrants see "adolescent culture" as a foreign concept, largely created by consumerism. Russian families who are not ready to embrace this concept are either being overprotective, trying to keep their children out of this culture, or think that their children are out of control. The former behavior often results in more peer adjustment difficulties, the second, in open family conflict often amplified by the exposure of the younger generation to the adolescent culture of the urban underclass in the United States, due to the concentration of immigrant households in poorer urban areas (Portes & Rumbaut, 1996).

CLINICAL ISSUES

The diagnosis of depression, or dysthymia, is one of the most common mental health problems in immigrant populations (Rumbaut, 1994). For Russians,

> suffering is not only a natural part of life, but it also has a certain redemptive value. Toska means melancholy, depression, yearning, anguish, pangs of love, ennui, weariness, tedium, boredom, and nostalgia all rolled into one. Any thinking individual was expected to have this malaise to some degree. (Althausen, 1996)

When two Russian friends meet and one of them asks a trivial "How are you?," the other is expected to share his problems to some degree. The answer "Fine" might be perceived as distancing and unwillingness to communicate. My colleagues are sometimes puzzled when after they ask a Russian-speaking patient, "How do you feel," the answer is, "Pretty bad, but that's okay; I don't think anybody can help me."

A common complaint of Russian immigrants about the health care system in the United States, and most of all about primary care, is that "They don't care." The type of "care" that a Russian immigrant typically expects from a physician can be best described as palliative care, where besides scientifically accurate information and relevant medications, the patient receives advice that enhances a subjective feeling of competency in dealing with a health problem. For example, a common flu lasts about a week, whether one treats it or not, but one still feels better when told to drink hot milk with honey, put some mustard in his or her socks at night, and breathe over a pot of fresh boiled potatoes.

Other issues that therapists must note center on disabilities, addiction, and sexual identity. Due to the lack of facilities and accommodations, as well as to stigmatization, disabled people in Russia did not have access to many areas of life and were virtually confined to isolation and lower social strata. Working with attitudes toward disability will be an important factor in helping families with chronic illness. Issues of sexual identity and sexual orientation also present a significant challenge for Russian immigrant families because same sex intimate relationships were prosecuted by law in the former Soviet Union until late 1980. Older Russian immigrants were therefore socialized to view homosexuality as a perversion or pathology.

Finally, alcoholism or casual drinking is viewed more normatively in Russian culture, with much more tolerance and often compassion. A culturally sensitive, but thorough exploration of indicators of alcoholism can be an important part of initial family assessment because what was tolerated in the old country may now be labeled as addiction and need for treatment in the United States.

An essential part of successful therapy with New Americans from Russia is identifying and utilizing the ethnic values and former beliefs clients wish to retain. Among them are a value of high educational and professional levels, mutual support and strong family ties, and the ability to tolerate adversity and to accept life as it comes.

NEW AMERICANS FROM TAIWAN—
THE INTERGENERATIONAL PERSPECTIVE

CILOUE CHENG STEWART

Contemporary Chinese families who have immigrated to the United States from Taiwan since the 1950s and who are predominantly professionals, merchants, or restaurateurs, have not until recently been specifically addressed in the family studies field (McAdoo, 1993). Although people from Taiwan are generally considered to be ethnic Chinese, their socio/economic/political/historical background is distinctively different from that of any other Chinese.

BRIEF ETHNIC AND HISTORICAL BACKGROUNDS

Two groups most likely to be represented in contemporary Chinese immigrant families from Taiwan are Taiwanese and Mainlanders (those who escaped Communist Mainland China in 1949 and their offspring). They share similarities in culture and customs and yet differ significantly in historical experience and dialects. Both immigrant populations are generally financially sound prior to emigration to the United States, which is mostly voluntary in nature. However, contrary to the common categorization that polarizes voluntary and forced emigration, the meaning of emigration is much more complex when factors of time and generation are taken into account. Many of the older members of the Mainlander households that had enjoyed a sociopolitically privileged, upper-middle-class lifestyle in Taiwan also had catastrophic experiences and suffered great personal loss as they fled from mainland China about 1949. For them, a refugee/survival mentality became a central familial dynamic, with an intensified emphasis on education, family solidarity, geographic mobility, and ultimate safety for future generations—values that may seem contradictory. For example, the adult child's emigration to a politically safe and prosperous country may at once symbolize a psychological safety link for the family in times of potential political crisis (an act of filiation), and yet, a sacrifice of immediate familial solidarity (Stewart, 1996, 2000).

IMMIGRATION FACTORS

The emigration process in the Chinese immigrant population follows a sequential pattern (Lin & Liu, 1993). Often the parents, upon retirement, emigrate to join an adult child years after the child obtains resident/citizen status. Drawing a family's boundary can be an elusive task when we look at families whose elders maintain more than one residence both before and after they officially acquire immigrant status. Many immigrant parents rotate regularly between a home in Taiwan and those of their children in the United States and, in some cases, the homes of children who live in other countries. Family boundaries are fluid.

Being uprooted from one's homeland can be especially difficult for elderly parents. Although immigration may have globalized families with a home becoming wherever the adult offspring reside, at the same time, it can create a fragmented sense of home and belonging. The uprooting effects are that family members may become out of touch with both their original and immediate communities. They no longer know where "home" is.

In the case where families have fluid boundaries as their members move "to and fro" between households and continents, individuals may experience an incoherent sense of identity, loyalty, and future vision of the family. This prolonged sense of transition is captured by the concept of boundary ambiguity (Boss, 1999). In such a perpetually ambiguous state, family members are less able to anchor life experiences—births, marriage, career, aging—that are the result of natural development.

As a family's external/internal boundaries continue to fluctuate with ambiguity, the family's need for cohesion may increase; consequently, family members often become each other's sole support, unable or unwilling to tap into the available community resources. As a cyclical result, the family becomes externally more isolated, internally more dependent, and members are overburdened on both physical and emotional levels. Dialogue within, between, and among members becomes rigid; rules and strategies of the past and family narratives may freeze in time and space without room for negotiation or reintegration within their new contexts.

DICHOTOMOUS FAMILY NARRATIVES

According to the Chinese wellness paradigm, the physical, interpersonal, and collective well-being in a family comprise integrated parts of the whole. A disturbance in the intergenerational familial relationship often shows itself in an individual's physical or emotional symptoms. Similarly, the strain on a couples' relationship may reflect a loyalty conflict with elderly parents. To work with Chinese families from Taiwan and collaboratively arrive at a culturally sound therapeutic approach, we must examine the validity of commonly mentioned culprits permeating many families' narratives as well as those in the popular and academic culture. The attributions may contribute to the confusion family members experience.

Effects of Immigration

A sequential pattern of immigration may lead to differing degrees of acculturation and adjustment between generations. In times of family distress, "immigration" becomes a natural and automatic explanation for any intergenerational difficulty. The common complaint is that the young are overly westernized and estranged from their cultural traditions, while the old anxiously hold onto the eastern ways of life, unwilling to let go of unrealistic expectations. Although this narrative provides a perspective to look at existing "frictions," it does not help clinicians move toward the necessary "repair" efforts. Rather, this reasoning serves to widen the gap between the old and the young, the distance between the East and the West, between homeland and the host society.

The overall changes confronting Chinese American families are not an exclusive effect of "immigration." Balancing the new and the traditional is a fundamental element of human experience. In fact, due to globalization, the weaving of both western and eastern cultures takes place even in Chinese families who remain in Taiwan or live in countries other than the United States.

Filial Piety

Chinese familism is derived from the interwoven influence of moral/religious/cultural ideologies, such as Confucianism, Taoism, and Buddhism. Adhering to this paradigm, the Chinese stress mutual obligation and encourage solidarity among family members. Filial piety (Hsiao Shuen) refers to the belief and conduct of one's respect for one's parents. Hsiao means being filial, and Shuen refers to the children's sense of deference to parents' wishes.

Although "filial piety" has been scapegoated as the culprit of many modern Chinese family dilemmas, it is important to note that filial piety has been an evolving concept. There may be modern-day solutions available in a living ideology. However, in a problem saturated narrative, what is presented about one's ideology can be fragmented and out of context. Clinicians must explore and cocreate with family members contextually sound solutions using filial ideology. The following delineation is offered for clinical consideration.

Filial Piety Reexamined

One of the most frequently offered scenarios of intergenerational filial failure in Chinese families is the dilemma in which parents rigidly grasp onto old filial expectations, while adult children fail to adhere to the filial mandates. The undesirable choices lie, presumably, between what the parents want and what the children want. In fact, conflicts of interest have been attributed by many as in the nature of intergenerational relationships and, thus, the cause of their difficulties (e.g., Bray & Williamson, 1987; Brody, 1979; Pyke & Bengtson, 1996; Quinn & Keller, 1983). Filial dilemma is likened to issues of power and control.

An alternative interpretation (Stewart, 2000), however, may be suggested. First, the same filial ideology that prescribes deference of self to parents also speaks of a good family relationship in which the parents act *Tse* (kindly/mercifully/lovingly), while the child is Hsiao (being filial). In other words, to adhere to filial ideology is to be mutually loving across generations. One does not uphold the other at one's own expense. Thus, conflicting interests do not create relational difficulties; rather, the lack of or failed attempt at the negotiation of these varying needs of the old and the young is the true culprit of filial breakdown.

Second, family members, as social beings, not only have individual needs for autonomy, but also have needs of togetherness and cohesion. Below the surface, what the old and the young want may be more similar than different. This delicate balance of the two has been illuminated by the systems concept of dialectics. Under the seeming struggle of control in intergenerational families, other fundamental dynamics may be at play—a sense of belonging and inclusion. This is particularly relevant in Chinese immigrant families, where some elderly parents' experiences of war deprived them of home, childhood, or even their own filial connection. Three elderly parents residing in three separate cities in Taiwan volunteered the same "hearsay" tale to me:

Upon arriving in the USA to visit her adult son and daughter-in-law, an elderly widow was picked up by her son, only to be dropped off at the doorstep of an elderly Chinese gentleman. It turned out a marriage had been arranged for her by her son. It was said that the old woman cried for an entire week before the old man came to his senses and eventually sent her back to her home in Taiwan (Stewart, 2000).

Whether this is a true story and how unrealistic its premise are not important. What is important is that the circulation of this tale epitomizes the deepest fear of filial rejection and abandonment and the subsequent tentativeness experienced by some elderly parents as they reunite with their adult children overseas.

CLINICAL IMPLICATIONS

Overall, the primary dynamics and potential issues concerning these intergenerational families include the compounding issues of emigration and isolation, the entrapment of a dichotomous view, and tension around filial piety, with issues of trust and abandonment underlying them all. In order to revitalize a family's sense of harmony, the therapeutic goal should be to enhance an ethically sound sense of inclusion of all members; to anchor sense of self in fragmented contexts; and to encourage integrative and constructive story telling, individually and jointly. For many Chinese people, "home dirt should not be revealed." Although the general stigma has begun to break down in Taiwan, seeking mental health services may still be perceived by many as bringing shame and "loss of face" to the individuals and the entire family. Descriptions, other than the common "worried, troubled, confused, hurt," of deep emotions are often not voluntarily uttered. What often is presented to a therapist is only a partial representation. Even in cases in which the entire family is physically present, one's view of the family may still be blinded by the interactional patterns prevalent in the therapy process. It becomes imperative to enter into the family's meaning-world by encouraging family members to share their stories. In order to create a meaningful therapeutic experience and useful results with Chinese immigrant families from Taiwan, the following questions may serve as a guide as therapeutic solutions are co-constructed:

Who/what/where is your family?

What does it mean to you to be an immigrant in the United States?

How has your experience of intergenerational living or maintaining intergenerational relationships been in the United States, Taiwan (and other countries)?

Knowing filial piety is an important concept in your culture, what do you consider to be the prevalent filial/relational issues for your family?

What are the most relevant cultural beliefs concerning intergenerational relationships that have influenced you and your family?

The nature and dynamics of people's relationships often evolve due to time, place, age, social roles, stages of career/family life, social contexts, and so on; filial relationship may be no exception. How does each of your family members deal with such changing filial dynamics?

Since ideologies about intergenerational relationships often speak of how to sustain love and a sense of loyalty in hardship and about giving and receiving mutually between generations, what has your cultural teaching offered you in loving reciprocally?

NEW AMERICAN FAMILIES FROM NORTHWESTERN EUROPE

Manfred Van Dulmen

Although there has been a shift in origin of immigrants coming to the United States, and although Northwestern Europeans currently make up a smaller proportion than people of color, it would be unrealistic to think that immigration from Northwestern Europe has ceased. Close to one million people from Great Britain and Germany have immigrated to the United States since 1960 (Rumbaut, 1997).

Definition of Northwestern Europe and History

Northwestern Europe refers here to England, Scotland, Wales, Norway, Denmark, Sweden, Northern Ireland, Ireland, Finland, the Netherlands, Belgium, Luxembourg, Switzerland, Austria, France, and Germany. There is wide variety among these countries. In some, for example England, Scotland, Wales, Northern Ireland, and Ireland, English is the main language spoken, whereas in others, English is secondary or nonexistent. Yet families often emigrate from all these countries for similar reasons—job opportunities in companies that are located both in Europe and the United States. Overall, the reason is better career opportunities. Except for language differences, people from Northwestern Europe have experienced a similar social-political atmosphere, since most are part of the European Union. Such intercontinental collaboration tends to decrease differences among people in Northwestern Europe and enhance their acculturation when they come to the United States.

From Involuntary to Voluntary Emigration

Emigration from Northwestern Europe to the United States has a long history and started in the "peasant heart of Europe" (Handlin, p. 1979, p. 6). Beginning in the nineteenth century, immigration to the United States was often a reaction to economic circumstances. In the first half of the twentieth century, World Wars I and II played a major role and, until about 1960, immigration was often motivated by economic reasons because the United States was the only really stable economic power in the Western world (Chirot, 1986).

Since the 1960s, with more stable economic and political situations in Western Europe, emigration from Western Europe to the United States has been characterized as much by those who want to enhance their careers as those who uproot because of poverty or political or religious persecutions. Emigration today is more voluntary than it has ever been before, which is one of the most important changes in the meaning of immigration for families from Northwestern Europe in the United States. The decision to move to the United States is often in the hands of the family itself. They choose to come; uprooting is volitional, although there may be differing perceptions among family members.

Working Clinically with Families and Individuals from Northwestern Europe

World View: From Social Support to Survival of the Fittest

Most Northwestern European countries are characterized by a political system that provides a fair amount of support for those in need of financial and medical help; housing and education are subsidized. In the Netherlands, for example, most benefits are based on an insurance scheme (Van der Horst, 1996). In the United States, these benefits are more the responsibility of self than government; this can be challenging. Personal conflicts about social justice and what is fair often arise, especially when there are financial problems or when differences in the old and new country conflict. For example, if one becomes disabled or sick, benefits in the United States are very different from those received in any one of the Northwestern European countries. Whereas unemployment and disabilities often lead to family stress, in the case of immigrants from Northwestern Europe, they can lead to additional stress as a result of the different experience from that in one's country of origin.

Attitudes about Work: From Long Lunches and Holidays to a 24-Hour Economy

The place of work in people's lives and their work ethic varies and thus must be explored by family therapists. In most Northwestern European countries Sunday is a "protected day," which means that most stores are closed. Many stores also close early on Saturday in preparation for the Sabbath. Although many Northwestern European countries are now moving toward a 24-hour economy, people who have come to the United States did not grow up with this view. In addition, Northwestern Europeans are accustomed to several weeks of holiday each summer. A common saying has thus emerged: In Northwestern Europe someone questions whether or not you work too hard, whereas in the United States someone questions whether or not you work hard enough.

For a therapist, this means that the work ethic of these families may be less intensive than in the United States. Individual stress can therefore result from additional work pressures, which can lead to family difficulties. Also, the place of the family in the lives of individuals changes. Whereas in most Northwestern European countries a family vacation of several weeks during the summer is more the rule than the exception, in the United States such vacations often are not possible. Family time has to be constructed in new ways.

Work, Gender, and Gender Roles: Who Does the Job?

Dual income families are not as common in Northwestern Europe as in the United States, and there are a great number of part-time workers (20 hours a week) and full-time jobs that are only 32 to 36 hours a week. These work patterns were encouraged in order to create jobs in the context of a relatively high unemployment rate in many Northwestern European countries. That, plus the fact that part-time jobs are more common in Northwestern Europe, could affect the gender roles of Northwestern European families in the United States. Haas (1993) showed from a 1986 survey that only 6 percent of Swedish women would like full-time work.

Both partners arrive in the United States with perceptions of what their work-family life was like or would have been like in Northwestern Europe; thus gender roles need to be renegotiated in light of new work responsibilities for each person. This can be especially stressful for women since they tend to do the majority of housework even if they work the same number of hours as their husbands outside the home. While they face the same problems other American wives and mothers face, the Northwestern European women have to deal with the fact that in their country of origin a better family-work balance would have been more culturally supported.

Boundary Ambiguity and Ambiguous Loss

Whereas emigrant families from Northwestern Europe often have financial resources to regularly return to their home country, the visits can also result in more ambiguity about one's own identity and culture. The husband of a couple who emigrated to the United States, and who returns yearly to the Netherlands to visit family, said, "I don't really know to which culture I belong nor where I really live now. When I am here (in the Netherlands), I don't feel like I belong here, and when I am in the U.S., I also feel not at home." This reflects Boss's idea that boundary ambiguity is inherent in most immigrant families (Boss, 1990).

Working preventively and clinically with families who emigrated recently from Northwestern Europe is challenging. At first, differences might not be as apparent because the historical roots of many American families originated in Western Europe. However, taking a closer look at their world view, attitudes about work, issues around work and gender roles, and boundary ambiguity is critical.

Therapists may assume that the frame of reference for new immigrants is the same as other families in the United States, but it could just as well be like that of other families in their country of origin. Therefore, the changes that are going on in the United States today, and also the changes that are going on in the country of origin, become contextual material for therapy. How well are they doing? How good do they feel about their choice to come to the United States? The answers to these questions will depend on how well other families fare in their country of origin as well as how their neighbors in the United States function.

HMONG NEW AMERICAN FAMILIES

BLONG XIONG

The first wave of Hmong to set foot on the lands of Southeast Asia, including Burma, Thailand, Laos, and Vietnam, were believed to have arrived from China during the period from 1810 to 1850 (Bliatout, Downing, Lewis, & Yang, 1988). These Hmong ancestors came seeking freedom and independence from external Chinese controls and forced assimilation (Hamilton-Merritt, 1993). The independence and peace they sought in Southeast Asia, particularly in Laos, lasted only for a short period of time prior to entry into another war that claimed a third of the Hmong population in Laos (Rumbaut, 1995), and drove half of the remaining population to Western countries, such as Canada, Australia, France, French Guyana, and the United States (Hamilton-Merritt, 1993). Currently, there are approximately 125,000 to 150,000 Hmong residents in the United States. Approximately 85 percent live in California, Minnesota, and Wisconsin (Yang & North, 1988).

Traditional Hmong culture includes a mixture of animism and ancestor worship in its religious practices. Animism refers to a belief that all natural objects have spirits and that humans and spirits live interdependently with each other. Ancestor worship refers to the linkages between the living and the spirits of the deceased family members for health, wealth, and prosperity. However, a sizable number of Hmong in the United States have converted to Christianity. Therefore, when speaking of Hmong culture and values, diversity exists within our group. But despite changes from acculturation, Hmong people still speak the same language, celebrate the Hmong New Year, attend the same festivities, and listen to Hmong music, and they share many values of ethnic identity, including filial piety and harmony.

The values of filial piety and harmony are critical for therapists to know about because they often contribute to family conflicts and threaten family cohesion. Filial piety refers to children's obligation to pay deference to their parents and elders; this value organizes family rules regarding who should carry over the family name and learn the familial spiritual rites.

The value of harmony underscores interpersonal relationships and interactions. Hmong try to avoid conflicts or potential conflictual situations in order to maintain harmony and to save face. Families who come to therapy may be more likely to passively accept what the therapist tells them to do rather than take an active role. Asking questions and sharing opinions with a person in authority is a violation of this principal value. For Hmong, the purpose of therapy is to find a way to minimize conflicts and maximize harmonious relationships.

The values of filial piety and harmony have significant implications for therapy because much Western therapy is based on an individual orientation. Hmong, on the other hand, believe that if there is a misunderstanding between individuals, they have to find ways to control the misunderstanding in order to maintain harmony. Understanding this value and the focus on family rather than the individual will help therapists to understand the cultural world view of Hmong family life. It is necessary to work from the perspective of the Hmong, to develop rapport, and to support change without isolating the family from its community or isolating individuals from their own family.

INTERGENERATIONAL CONTINUITY AND CHANGE IN HMONG FAMILIES

Because Hmong culture emphasizes human relationships and harmony, generation is a critical value that determines rules of family interaction and roles of respect for individuals. For instance, when meeting a Hmong stranger, a child is instructed to find out about that stranger's clan and spiritual family and subsequently his or her generation in order to properly address him or her. By answering these questions, the stranger will soon become an acquaintance, relative, or cousin because everybody belongs to the web of the Hmong community. Through this relational quest, people develop respect for one another, thereby forming a close-knit community.

Parents wish to transmit this value of intergenerational continuity to their children despite living in a contemporary urban culture. However, not all adolescents are interested in knowing about the Hmong culture and values. When this occurs, conflicts in the family intensify. For example, when Kao, a 15-year-old boy, calls a relative by his first name without accompanying his generation identifier (such as uncle), Kao has violated one of the most fundamental rules of respect in interpersonal relationships. He has shamed his parents for not knowing the proper way to address others. Because of the critical role that cultural and generational continuity play in Hmong interpersonal relationships, every child is socialized about the rules. However, despite this socialization, many Hmong adolescents try to liberate themselves from the old cultural practices as they become more "Americanized." The pressure to continue the Hmong cultural practices taught in the family collides with the pressure from peers to behave like a "cool" American teenager.

Therapists usually work with families during fragile times, so it is critical to understand the significance of balancing intergenerational continuity with change in the bicultural environment of most Hmong families. We assist them in developing meanings and in constructing adaptive strategies to solve their problems during tough times. When parents bring their adolescent to therapy, the first step is to attempt to understand the parents' and the adolescent's ideas about what is expected of the "good" adolescent or "good parent" and their expectations for each other, for the family, and for others. Without such understanding, we may make suggestions that are either insensitive or invasive to the family.

GENDER ISSUES IN HMONG FAMILIES

Hmong families are based on a patrilineal system and on an ancestral worship where women are socialized to take on roles of daughter-in-law, wife, mother, and caretaker of the family. According to the Hmong proverb, "A girl is a guest daughter." This means that when the girl reaches adulthood she will marry and move out to dwell with her husband's family. Hence, it is assumed that the investment of educating and training a girl will not pay off in the long run for the family because she will use these skills to enhance the survival of her husband's family and/or clan, instead of her family of origin. Hmong therefore invests in boys for the survival and betterment of the family. This has perpetuated unfair treatment toward female children. In the United States, many adolescent Hmong girls are often restricted and denied the same freedom and autonomy their brothers enjoy—the ability to socialize with friends and be free from overwhelming household responsibilities (Detzner, Xiong, & Eliason, 1999).

In the realm of education, however, parental attitudes toward girls have changed in a positive manner. In the past, girls were to be mother's helpers and family caretakers, while boys traveled miles away from home to attend school. Now, both boys and girls are encouraged to stay in school and excel. However, in family responsibilities and dating girls are still treated unfairly. Women, particularly educated women, feel isolated in their extended families because they belong neither to the men's table nor in the kitchen with other older women. Their only place of special recognition is in the workplace.

To effectively help Hmong women and thereby New American Hmong families, we need to assure our clients that not every culture views gender in the same manner. We can collaborate with our clients to develop a new understanding of their roles as males and females and strategize ways to cease violence and abuse in their relationships while at the same time respecting their culture. Only through this basic understanding and collaborative effort can we begin to develop culturally appropriate plans to help clients resolve their problems. The following case illustrates this point:

> Mr. and Mrs. Lee, a Hmong couple, were referred for consultation regarding their constant marital conflicts. Mr. Lee is a high school graduate while Mrs. Lee is a graduate student. Mr. Lee believed that his wife should stay home and care for the children and the house, while he went out to serve relatives and friends every weekend. Mrs. Lee believed that weekends should be reserved for their family life since both of them work during the weekdays while putting their two young children in a child care center.

This is a typical case for a married couple living in a dual cultural context. In traditional Hmong mediation with the elders, a strategy would be to reaffirm to Mrs. Lee that her husband is making contributions to the community and to her family and that she needs to be patient and broaden her narrow heart. To effectively help Mr. and Mrs. Lee solve their problem without blame and shame the therapist needed to understand that married men have many responsibilities to the community in contemporary urban Hmong culture while Hmong women want to be more than just housewives, mothers, or silent bystanders. By understanding the dual cultures in the couple's marriage, therapists are better able to work with the couple to prioritize and sacrifice each other's needs for the betterment of their marriage, family, and community.

IMPACT OF WAR ON HMONG FAMILIES

The aftermath of war in Laos has had a profound effect on the adjustment of Hmong families. The war transformed the Hmong social and familial structure from its original form. For instance, prior to the Indochinese war, elders and spiritual leaders were the "few" to gain recognizable social status in the Hmong communities. However, during and after the war, a sizable number of soldiers gained significant recognition and social status within the Hmong clan structure and family system. During the Indochinese war in Laos, hundreds of men attained military rank that gave them social status within the Hmong community and which continues today. Not only were typical Hmong farmers transformed into high military officials but also their ranks brought pride and respect. As refugees in an urban environment, these respected people are the ones who feel the sharpest decline of respect and authority, both in their own families and in the community. Usually, they refuse to accept help and decline to be involved in therapy.

The second negative effect of the aftermath of war is posttraumatic stress disorder (PTSD). The majority of Hmong refugees in the United States have endured tremendous suffering and have survived multiple traumatic experiences prior to coming here (Nicassio, 1985; Williams & Westermeyer, 1983). As they resettled in America, many experienced more losses, particularly loss of country, important kin relationships, culture, and identity (Lin, 1986; Lin & Masuda, 1981); new stressors continued—learning a new language, finding work, loss of authority for men, and parents loss of control over the children (Bennett & Detzner, 1997; Detzner et al., 1999; Xiong, 1997). Such problems, when added on top of PTSD, result in family dysfunction, helplessness, hopelessness, and suicides. To cope, some adults formed Hmong political groups to reclaim Laos from the Communists. Others isolated themselves from anything that had to do with Laos. Some became disabled and/or died. There were many cases of the sudden unexpected nocturnal death syndrome (SUNDS) (Bliatout, 1982).

Therapists need to be aware of the converging of multiple and severe stressors that produce a high level of distress which in turn exerts negative influences on individuals and families. These issues need attention, both in doing therapy and in connecting clients to the right resources in the community to meet their basic needs. Failing to incorporate both strategies can lead to the Hmong feeling of being used by therapists, which leads to a mistrust of Western services. Therapists need to merge Eastern and Western cultural strengths to acquire adaptive ways to respectfully intervene with the problems families endure.

CONCLUSION

In this chapter we emphasize collaboration and the raising of questions more than one specific strategy. Yet some common guidelines emerged for performing therapy with most immigrant families regardless of origin:

- How elderly parents interact with the middle and younger generations varies from country to country and region to region. What appears to be common is that there is some caring and sharing across generations, and caregiving from birth to death.
- Worldwide, patriarchy still predominates; therapists who enjoy egalitarianism must recognize that it was not always a choice for women and men, especially those who live under totalitarian regimes. We must empathize and understand the context from

which they came and help clients create new ways of being that are more consistent with their new culture.

- Concepts of independence may clash if the older generations value collective family life and youth value self-sufficiency and autonomy. At the same time, what looks like enmeshment to U.S. therapists may be normal caring in immigrant families.

- Spirituality may be viewed differently from our own, so we must ask family members to tell us about their beliefs and values and how they see the world.

- The effects of war, torture, and life-threatening upheaval may leave a legacy in individuals and families that requires special treatment. Stories of traumatic experiences may emerge through music, narratives, embroideries, and paintings. All are valid expressions and have clinical value. Many family therapists have never experienced the trauma of war, torture, or rape, so it is imperative that we listen to the stories of those who have. Creating a safe environment and then listening may be our main therapeutic task.

- Cultural ideologies such as communism, capitalism, or socialism influence individual identity development because external contexts enhance or impede processes of growth and change. What appears to a therapist as passivity or indecisiveness may simply be a product of an ideology that discouraged self-determinism.

- People's reasons for leaving their country of origin and their reasons for coming to the United States are important considerations. Was their uprooting volitional or was it forced? What are the specifics in either case? Did all family members have the same experience?

- With a rapidly aging worldwide population and increasing employment of women, the value of filial piety may lead to more marital and family stress. As the pressures on family caregivers (primarily women) increase, the value of intergenerational support needs to be shared across more members of the family.

- The cultural value of harmony may suppress disagreements in family discussions. Asking a family member to express his or her anger at another family member may be resisted. Asking a child to express anger at a parent will clash with the value of filial piety. Asking the head of the family or clan to become a cotherapist in such discussions would enhance a collaboration that could lead to eliciting feelings within the family's tolerance.

- By collaborating with people from inside the family or group, new ways of being for husbands, wives, children, grandparents, and kinfolk may be more easily developed.

- Realities of immigrant life (legal and illegal) are part of the clinical picture. Past experiences with authority figures will influence development of trust for a therapist.

- Traditional ethics for refusing gifts from clients may be viewed as disrespectful by low-income immigrant families.

- The economic status of New Americans may vary greatly from their previous status. The drop in status, economically and professionally, of New Americans is missed when therapists look for symptoms and do not listen to contextual stories.

What becomes clear is that the traditional family therapy models may not always fit the needs of immigrant families. We may not agree on what normal families are or what good family therapy is, but there is agreement on the need for child and elder care and for preserving the marital bond whenever possible. There is also disdain for violence and abuse. As family therapists, we can play a central role in setting the stage for collaborating with

New American families as they meld assumptions, perceptions, and behaviors from one culture to another.

REFERENCES

Almeida, R. (1996). Hindu, Christian, and Muslim families. In M. McGoldrick, J. Giordano, & J. K. Pearce (Eds.), *Ethnicity and family therapy* (2nd ed., pp. 395–423). New York: Guilford Press.

Althausen, L. (1996). Russian families. In M. McGoldrick, J. Giordano, & J. K. Pearce (Eds.), *Ethnicity and family therapy* (2nd ed., pp. 612–618). New York: Guilford Press.

Andreski, S. (1979). Communism and the Jews in Eastern Europe. *International Journal of Comparative Sociology, XX*(1–2), 151–161.

Arroyo, W. (1997a). Central American children. In G. Johnson-Powell & J. Yamamoto (Eds.), *Transcultural child development: Psychological assessment and treatment* (pp. 80–91). New York: John Wiley & Sons, Inc.

Arroyo, W. (1997b). Children and families of Mexican descent. In G. Johnson-Powell & J. Yamamoto (Eds.), *Transcultural child development: Psychological assessment and treatment* (pp. 290–304). New York: John Wiley & Sons, Inc.

Bennett, J., & Detzner, F. D. (1997). Loneliness in cultural context: A look at the narratives of older Southeast Asian refugee women. *The Narrative Study of Lives, 5,* 113–146.

Bliatout, T. B. (1982). *Hmong unexpected nocturnal death syndrome: A cultural study.* Oregon: Sparkle Publishing Enterprises.

Bliatout, T. B., Downing, T. B., Lewis, J., & Yang, D. (1988). *Handbook for teaching Hmong-speaking students.* Folsom, CA: Folsom Cordova Unified School District, Southeast Asia Community Resource Center.

Borjas, G. (1990). *Friends or strangers.* New York: Basic Books.

Boss, P. (1988). *Family stress management.* Newbury Park, CA: Sage Publications.

Boss, P. (1990). Ambiguous loss. In M. Goldrick & F. Walsh (Eds.), *Living beyond loss: Death and the family* (pp. 164–175). New York: W.W. Norton.

Boss, P. (1999). *Ambiguous loss.* Cambridge, MA: Harvard University Press.

Bray, J. H., & Williamson, D. S. (1987). Assessment of intergenerational family relationships. In A. F. Hovestadt & M. Fine (Eds.), *The family therapy collection* (pp. 31–43). Rockville, MD: Aspen Publication.

Brody, E. (1979). The etiquette of filial behavior. *Aging and Human Development, 2,* 87–104.

Brym, R. J. (1994). *The Jews of Moscow, Kiev and Minsk: Identity, antisemitism, emigration.* New York: New York University Press.

Chirot, D. (1986). *Social change in the modern era.* San Diego, CA: Harcourt, Brace, Jovanovich Publishers.

De Juan-Gomez, A. (1990). *An assessment of the awareness of Hispanic/Latino students of career development and placement services at The Pennsylvania State University.* Master's thesis, The Pennsylvania State University, State College, PA.

Detzner, D. F., Xiong, B., & Eliason, P. (1999). *Helping youth succeed: Bicultural parenting for Southeast Asian families.* St. Paul, MN: University of Minnesota Extension Service.

Duvall, E. M., & Miller, B. (1985). *Marriage and family development.* New York: Harper & Row.

Feigin, I. (1996). Soviet Jewish families. In M. McGoldrick, J. Giordano, & J. K. Pearce (Eds.), *Ethnicity and family therapy* (2nd ed., pp. 631–645). New York: Guilford Press.

Flores-Ortiz, I., & Bernal, G. (1989). Contextual family therapy of addiction with Latinos. In G. W. Saba, B. M. Karrer, & K. V. Hardy (Eds.), *Minorities and family therapy* (pp. 123–142). New York: Haworth Press.

Flores-Ortiz, I., Esteban, M., & Carillo, R. (1994). Violence in the family: A contextual, intergenerational, & therapeutic model. *Interamerican Journal of Psychology, 28*(2), 235–250.

Freedman, R. (Ed). (1989). *Soviet Jewry in the 1980s: The politics of anti-Semitism and emigration and the dynamics of resettlement.* Durham, NC: Duke University Press.

Gitelman, Z. (1991). The evolution of Jewish culture in the Soviet Union. In R. O'I & A. Becker (Eds.), *Jewish culture and identity in the Soviet Union* (pp. 3–24). New York: New York University Press.

Haas, L. (1993). Nurturing fathers and working mothers: Changing gender roles in Sweden. In J. C. Hood (Ed.), *Men, work and family* (pp. 238–261). Newbury Park, CA: Sage Publications.

Hamilton-Merritt, J. (1993). *Tragic mountains: The Hmong, the Americans, and the secret wars for Laos.* Indianapolis, IN: Indiana University Press.

Handlin, O. (1979). *The uprooted: The epic story of the great migrations that made the American people* (2nd ed.). Boston, MA: Little, Brown & Company.

Herrera, D., & Esnaola, S. (1990). *Hospital de Dia una experiencia psicoterapeutica. ["Hospital de Dia" a day care program a psychotherapeutic experience.]* Unpublished paper presented later at the XXIV Interamerican Congress of Psychology, Santiago, Chile, July 1993.

Hikey, M. G. (1996). "Go to college, get a job, and don't leave the house without your brother": Oral histories with immigrant women and their daughters. *Oral History Review, 23*(2), 63–92.

Joseph, J. (1991). *Aged in India: Problems and personality.* Allahabad, India: Chugh Publications.

Kanjanapan, W. (1995). The immigration of Asian professionals to the United States: 1988–1990. *Internation Migration Review, 29*(1), 7–32.

Kar, S. B., Campbell, K. C., Jimenez, A., & Gupta, S. R. (1996). Invisible Americans: An exploration of Indo-American quality of life. *Amerasia Journal, 21*(3), 25–52.

Keskar, A. (1990). *Adjustment to the changing status and role of old age: A study of aged persons in Pune city.* Gultekdi, Pune: Tilak Maharastra Vidyapeeth.

Leonard, K. (1993). Historical constructions of ethnicity: Research on Punjabi immigrants in California. *Journal of American Ethnic History,* (Summer), 3–26.

Leonhard-Spark, P. J., & Saran, P. (1980). The Indian immigrant in America: A demographic profile. In E. Eames & P. Saran (Eds.), *The new ethnics: Asian Indians in the United States* (pp. 136–162). New York: Praeger.

Lin, C., & Liu, W. (1993). Intergenerational relationships among Chinese immigrant families from Taiwan. In H. P. McAdoo (Ed.), *Family ethnicity: Strength in diversity* (pp. 271–286). Newbury Park, CA: Sage Publications.

Lin, K. M. (1986). Psychopathology and social disruption in refugees. In C. L. Williams & J. Westermeyer (Eds.), *Refugee mental health in resettlement countries* (pp. 61–71). Washington, DC: Hemisphere.

Lin, K. M., & Masuda, M. (1981). *Impact of the refugee experience: Cultures-social work with Southeast Asian refugees* (pp. 32–53). Los Angeles: Asian American Community Mental Health Training Center.

McAdoo, H. P. (Ed.). (1993). *Family ethnicity: Strength in diversity.* Newbury Park, CA: Sage Publications.

Miller, J. (Ed.). (1984). *Jews in Soviet culture.* New Brunswick, NJ: Transaction Books.

Nicassio, P. (1985). The psychosocial adjustment of the Southeast Asian refugee: An overview of empirical findings and theoretical models. *Journal of Cross-Cultural Psychology, 16*(2), 153–173.

Olea-Guldemont, M. (1992). Recuerdos de un exilio en Suiza. (Memories of an exilee in Switzerland). Santiago, Chile: Arygo Ltd a.

Pais, S. (1997). Asian Indian families in America. In M. K. DeGenova (Ed.), *Families in cultural context: Strengths and challenges in diversity* (pp. 173–190). Mountain View, CA: Mayfield.

Portes, A., & Rumbaut, R. G. (1996). *Immigrant America: A portrait* (2nd ed.). Berkeley, CA: University of California Press.

Pyke, K. D., & Bengtson, V. L. (1996). Caring more or less: Individualistic and collectivist systems of family eldercare. *Journal of Marriage and the Family, 58,* 379–392.

Quinn, W. H., & Keller, J. F. (1983). Older generations of the family: Relational dimensions and quality. *The American Journal of Family Therapy, 11*(3), 23–33.

Ram-Prasad, C. (1995). Classical Indian philosophical perspectives on aging and the meaning of life. *Aging and Society, 15,* 1–36.

Robinson, L. (1998, May 11). Hispanics don't exist. *U.S. News & World Report,* pp. 27–32.

Rogler, L. H., Cortes, D. E., & Malgady, R. G. (1991). Acculturation and mental health status among Hispanics. *American Psychologist, 46*(6), 585–597.

Rumbaut, R. G. (1994). The crucible within: Ethnic identity, self-esteem, and segmented assimilation among children of immigrants. *International Migration Review, 28,* 784–794.

Rumbaut, R. (1995). Vietnamese, Laotian, and Cambodian Americans. In P. G. Min (Ed.), *Asian Americans: Contemporary trends and issues* (pp. 232–270). Thousand Oaks, CA: Sage Publications.

Rumbaut, R. G. (1997). Ties that bind: Immigration and immigrant families in the United States. In A. Booth, A. C. Crouter, & N. Landale (Eds.), *Immigration and the family: Research and policy on U.S. immigrants* (pp. 3–46). Mahwah, NJ: Lawrence Erlbaum.

Ryvkina, R. (1996). *Jews in post-soviet Russia—Who are they?* Moscow: URSS Publishing House.

Salitan, L. (1992). *Politics and nationality in contemporary Soviet-Jewish emigration, 1968–89.* New York: St. Martin's Press.

Saran, P. (1985). *The Asian Indian experience in the United States.* Cambridge, MA: Schenkman Publishing Company.

Stewart, C. C. (1996). *Elderly parents at the crossroads of emigration.* Proceedings from the 18th International Federation for Home Economics Pre-Congress Workshop on Social Services for Families in Society, Thailand, July 18–20.

Stewart, C. C. (2000). *Chinese American families from Taiwan:* A transnational study of filial connections. University of Minnesota dissertation.

Thomas, W. I., & Znaniecki, F. (1984). *The Polish peasant in Europe and America: 1918-1920* (Ed. and abr. Eli Zaretsky). Reprint. Chicago, IL: University of Illinois Press.

Valle, R., & Vega, W. (1980). *Hispanic natural support systems. Mental health promotion perspectives.* Sacramento, CA: Department of Mental Health.

Van der Horst, H. (1996). *The low sky: Understanding the Dutch.* Schiedam/The Hague (The Netherlands): Scriptum Books/NUFFIC.

Vargas, R. (1980). *Raza health promotion project.* Sacramento, CA: Department of Mental Health.

Vargas-Willis, G., & Cervantes, R. C. (1987). Consideration of psychosocial stress in the treatment of the Latina immigrant. Hispanic. *Journal of Behavioral Sciences, 19*(3), 315–329.

Vega, W. A., & Rumbaut, R. G. (1991). Ethnic minorities and mental health. *Annual Review of Sociology, 17,* 351–383.

Williams, C. L., & Westermeyer, J. (1983). Psychiatric problems among adolescent Southeast Asian refugees: A descriptive study. *Journal of Nervous and Mental Disease, 171,* 79–85.

Xiong, B. (1997). *Southeast Asian parenting: Meaning and conflicts.* Unpublished master's thesis. St. Paul, Minnesota: University of Minnesota.

Yang, D., & North, D. (1998). *Profiles of the Highland Lao communities in the United States: Final report.* Prepared for the U.S. Department of Health and Human Services, Family Support Administration, and Office of Refugee Resettlement.

CHAPTER 16

Single-Parent Families: Dynamics and Treatment Issues

Craig A. Everett and Sandra Volgy Everett

DEFINING SINGLE PARENTHOOD

Single parenthood, as a concept, has been analyzed in a variety of contexts including custodial and access patterns, postdivorce family adjustment, parental absence, economic resources, and the roles of postdivorce fathers and mothers. The historical view represented single-parent families as dysfunctional anomalies in comparison to the more accepted and stable intact nuclear families (Anthony, 1974, 1982; Guttmann, 1993; Levitan, 1979; Morrison, 1995; Walsh, 1991). Because early custodial award patterns of children favored mothers, the concept became synonymous with single mother-headed families (Guttmann, 1993).

Several authors suggest that the concept, itself, is a "misnomer" (Ahrons & Rodgers, 1987; Ahrons & Perlmutter, 1982; Guttmann, 1993; Kaslow & Schwartz, 1987). Ahrons and Perlmutter argue that a postdivorce family is more accurately described as "a one-parent household" when both parents continue to be involved, and as a single-parent family when one of the parents is not active in parenting. The prevalence of joint custody over the past decade further challenges the usefulness of the single-parent concept since both parents retain a legal identity as parents and share, to varying degrees, in the physical parenting of the children.

The single-parent family concept can be seen as further limited, from a broader family systems perspective, when its use fails to recognize the ongoing supportive roles of family-of-origin members, particularly grandparents (Hilton & Macari, 1997), as well as other community resources (Niepel & Nestmann, 1997). Morrison (1995) and Walsh (1991) offer a caution regarding the common practice in the literature of overlooking the significance of this broader support network: "We need to be careful that the term 'single parent' does not blind us to the important influences and potential resources in other significant relationships in and outside of the primary residence" (Walsh, 1991, p. 527). The importance of these support systems for low-income, minority, single-parent families has been identified by Lindblad-Goldberg (1989).

Several alternative definitions of single parenthood have been offered. Sager and associates (Crohn et al., 1981) introduced, perhaps more accurately, the concept of the "double single-parent family to describe the continuing role of both parents in postdivorce families. Ahrons (1979, 1980, 1994; Ahrons & Perlmutter, 1982) introduced the concept of the "binuclear family," which has been widely used to describe the evolution of dual, postdivorce family systems, each headed by one of the former parents. These systems encompass two households and may include the roles of step-parents and step-siblings. The residential patterns of the children and the relative involvement of each parent may vary widely. Pam and Pearson (1998) suggest, however, that even the use of the binuclear and blended concepts, despite their wide recognition, is 'misleading' because these families remain "disconnected and conflictual."

Most single-parent families are the product of a divorce. The exceptions would include widowhood and intentional single parenthood. The focus of this chapter will be on single parenthood that is the product of divorce. Glick (1994) estimated that one-half of present marriages represent a second, third, or more marriage for the spouses and that 60 percent of these will also end in divorce. Despite the high divorce rate of second and third marriages, the rate of remarriages also continues to be high with estimates that one in seven minor children live in a step-family (Glick, 1994). Glick (1994) and Visher and Visher (1993) suggest that the true rate, after statistics are redefined for second divorces and unmarried former spouses, may be closer to one in three minor children living in step-families.

Single parenthood, based on the demographic patterns, may be defined more accurately as a transitional period for postdivorce parents who are seeking and/or waiting for an opportunity to remarry. Further demographic data, summarized by Bianchi (1995), indicate that the dramatic increase in single-parent families during the 1960s and 1970s was based on divorce, while the continued increase, particularly of single mother-headed families, during the 1980s was based more on delayed marriage and unmarried childbearing. The proportion of male-headed single families, in the population of single families, nearly tripled between 1970 and 1990 (Greif, 1995), and rose to one in five by 1990 (Bianchi, 1995). Laosa (1988) used 1980 census data to contrast the proportion of Caucasian children living with single parents (14.4 percent) to that of African American children, 45.8 percent (see also Fine, McKenry, & Chung, 1992), Hispanic children, 23.5 percent, and American Indian children, 28.6 percent.

There are, of course, subpopulations of single parents who do not plan to remarry. These are reflected by widows and widowers, as well as those who choose to remain single for reasons of gender orientation. A number of studies investigate the parenting roles (single or with a partner) of homosexual parents and children who are raised in these single-parent families (Belcastro, Gramlich, Nicholson, Price, & Wilson, 1993; Causey & Duran-Aydintug, 1997; Duran-Aydintug & Causey, 1996; Patterson, 1992; Tasker & Golombok, 1997). Unmarried adults who become parents through adoption or artificial insemination represent another subpopulation of single parents.

We view single-parent families, for the purposes of this chapter, to mean postdivorce parents who have established a new family system centered on their role as a continuing parent. This family system may be dual and parallel to the one similarly established and headed by the former spouse. However, the definition of legal custody may vary widely for these families and the actual physical involvement by a parent with the children may include such patterns as split (50 percent/50 percent) residential time, 90 percent to 10 percent for an out-of-state parent, or no time. The goal of remarriage and the formation of a step-family may also vary among these single parents. These single-parent households may also include either permanent or occasional live-in romantic partners or family-of-origin members. This broader view of single-parent families is reflected in the concept of the "permeable family" (Elkin, 1994), which describes the relative ease with which nonblood individuals and paid child-care workers are included in family life.

AN OVERVIEW OF CHARACTERISTICS OF SINGLE-PARENT FAMILIES

Single-parent families, in comparison with intact families, experience more disadvantages that affect their everyday life experiences in a variety of areas: economic resources and stability, physical and emotional health, and housing conditions. Single mothers suffer greater postdivorce financial stress, which is well documented in the literature, than single fathers (Ali & Avison, 1997; Cohen, 1995, 1996; Dixon & Rettig, 1994; Draughn, LeBoeuf, Wozniak, Lawrence, & Welch, 1994; Lino, 1995; Mahler, 1994; Stroup & Pollock, 1994; Wijnberg & Weinger, 1998). This factor is based on the observation that single mothers have fewer marketable skills and resources to aid their roles in work and career settings (Kissman & Allen, 1993; Schwartz & Kaslow, 1997). Never-married, single mother-headed families and their children are the most economically disadvantaged group (Bianchi, 1995; Foster, Jones, & Hoffman, 1998). These factors of financial disadvantage are significant contributors to the overall subjective well-being and postdivorce adjustment in all populations (Cohen, 1995; Thiriot & Buckner, 1991).

The emotional well-being and developmental experiences of children living in predominantly female-headed or male-headed single-parent families have been debated in the literature. Early theories (see Goldstein, Freud, & Solnit, 1973) suggested that the continuing role of a mother in a postdivorce child's life should be paramount to that of a father's. However, the efficacy and contribution of a father's parenting resources, as well as the relative lack of differences observed in children living predominantly with male-headed or female-headed single families, has been supported more recently in the literature (Demaris & Greif, 1997; Greif, 1985; Risman & Park, 1988). Schnayer and Orr (1989), for example, found no differences between children living with single mothers and single fathers in areas of self-perceptions and behaviors, and Watts and Watts (1991) found few differences in adolescents' academic achievement levels. Downey (1994), using a large national and longitudinal sample of 8th graders, reported no significant difference in school performances between children in female-headed or male-headed single-parent families. However, both of these groups performed below the levels of children from intact families. Entwisle and Alexander (1996) reported similar academic findings for single-parent family children and suggested that economic factors were greater predictors of school performance than male- or female-headed households. Cohen (1994) used the well-known FACES-III in a comparative study of dynamics and roles in single male-headed and female-headed families with no significant differences reported.

Children living in single-parent families were found to display few differences on a personal attribute checklist (Johnson & Hutchinson, 1989) when compared with children living in step-families and intact families. Similarly, the interactional patterns of preschool siblings, when compared with that of siblings in intact families, were found to be similar (Summers, Summers, & Ascione, 1993), while few differences were noted in mother-child interactional stress in single-parent families as compared to intact families (Sander &

Ermert, 1997). However, a more clinical study (Huntley, Phelps, & Rehm, 1987) reported that boys living with single mothers displayed greater levels of depression than did a comparative sample of girls.

An important broad issue was noted for researchers and practitioners when Hutchinson and Spangler-Hirsch (1989) suggested the need to "reframe" the work with children of single-parent families so that more positive resources from their experiences are identified and explored. They make the point that children from single-parent families have been found to display many positive traits, such as greater maturity and enhanced decision making, than is otherwise assumed.

There are, of course, a variety of patterns and issues observed in single parents. Many of these reflect the continuation of parenting roles and resources from the formerly intact family of origin. There are several interesting patterns that have been noted. For example, single mothers are less firm and use less discipline with sons than with daughters (Heath & MacKinnon, 1988), and mothers who use more active behavioral and cognitive parenting strategies feel greater authority and control with their children (Holloway & Machida, 1991). Single fathers, who are rearing only preadolescent girls, report fewer problems than those raising both preadolescent and adolescent girls, children of both sexes, or boys only (DeMaris & Greif, 1992). The observation that fathers have fewer "private talks" (a more common behavior of mothers) with their children but engage in more play time and focus on more "masculine" household tasks, as well as other gender-specific traits between female and male single parents, have been reported by Hall and associates (1995).

CLINICAL PATTERNS AND FAMILY DYNAMICS

FAMILY STRUCTURAL ISSUES

The nuclear family system, following a separation or divorce, divides into two households, each headed by one of the parents (former spouses). Each respective parent's prior roles in areas such as family management, affective availability, and interaction with the children are mirrored, subsequently, in her or his new role as a single parent. However, while a child's adjustment to the new postdivorce dual households is stressful and disruptive, experiences with her or his respective parents are often still familiar and predictable. Each of these new "mini" systems must evolve and maintain a new balance (homeostasis) that will shape its ongoing and future survival. Of course, an effective balance may have been lacking for many years in the predivorce nuclear system due to the prior marital and/or family conflict. The initial balance that develops early in this new single-parent family is fragile and can be easily disrupted by four common postdivorce dynamics:

1. Ongoing animosity and adversarial issues stemming from the prior or continuing divorce litigation
2. Individual parental adjustment conflicts and stress
3. A child's difficulty with personal adjustment, sibling and/or step-sibling conflicts, and/or school and peer problems
4. The former spouse's intrusions into the new single-parent system

A new single parent, for example, fearing loneliness and financial ruin, may feel devastated by the divorce and withdraw her or his emotional availability from a child. The child's loss of this support, which she or he relied on for emotional survival during the divorce, may cause serious adjustment issues in areas such as affective disorders, anger, and/or acting-out behaviors. When high levels of conflict and animosity have been present and continue between the former spouses, such as in an adversarial divorce that lasts a year or longer, a child's normal development is interrupted and she or he may feel pulled into several potentially disruptive roles—taking sides with one of the parents, attempting to bring the parents back to their former marriage, trying to mediate the parents' conflicts, and/or emotionally withdrawing from interactions with one or both parents.

However, we have worked with many postdivorce families where a less involved parent, typically the father, became an attentive, caring, and involved single parent (often to the surprise of the other parent as well as the children). We have often observed this phenomenon in families where the uninvolved parent may have been pushed aside or overwhelmed by an overfunctioning and over-enmeshing partner. (In the context of our clinical roles as custody evaluators, we will often recommend equal time for this formerly underinvolved parent, even when she or he may have been less involved for many years, in order to provide her or him the opportunity to develop a more effective parental relationship with the children.) The enhancement of a formerly uninvolved parent's role can dramatically affect a healthier postdivorce balance for the children with each parent and provide an accommodation for the periodic emotional unavailability experienced by the children with either parent during the divorce adjustment period. On the other hand, the emergence of this newly functioning parent can create unexpected jealousy and resentment by the other parent in at least two areas:

1. She or he may resent that this parent is now performing an effective role with the children when she or he failed to do so throughout their marriage; this parent may have assumed that, following the divorce, she or he would have remained the primary caretaker and that the other parent would have played a less intrusive role in her or his life and that of the children.
2. This parent may fear, and later resent, that the formerly uninvolved parent is now gaining favor with the children and worry that she or he may lose the children's time, affection, and attachment.

We have conceptualized the development of this postdivorce, single-parenting, and dual household phenomena in three systemic terms (Everett & Volgy-Everett, 1991, 1994). Developed from the concept of *structural coupling,* discussed originally by Maturana and Varela (1980), the separation and/or divorce process for a nuclear family begins with and includes the stage of *structural decoupling.* Here the adults alter their roles and withdraw their former emotional loyalties to one another and to the family system. Children tend to maintain their identities, at this early stage, with the former predivorce parental and marital roles of their parents as well as toward their image of their formerly intact family system. The relative success of this decoupling process for each parent defines the basis for their postdivorce adjustment. A spouse who clings, often for years, to the hope of reconciling and reuniting with a former partner, despite clear indications that this is unrealistic, delays her or his own adjustment, and perhaps that of one's children. The delay of this process seriously inhibits a parent's effectiveness to parent as well as to pursue new social and/or career goals.

As the decoupling process proceeds, parents and children begin the second stage, which we have termed *network coupling.* This stage often involves the renewal of kinship ties with family of origin and extended family members for both emotional and financial support. This can be positive in aspects of supporting temporary adjustment for the parent, but it can also reinforce new or continuing dysfunctional patterns of excessive intrusion by family-of-origin members. The other healthy aspect of this process is that it gradually broadens to include the development of new social relationships. These new networks (family and social) substitute, in part, for the parents' and the children's loss of the former nuclear system. It is this process that increases the involvement of many grandparents, as well as aunts and uncles, in the ongoing lives of a single-parent family. The need to renew these family ties often prompts a single parent to relocate geographically to be near her or his family of origin. However, this move often can be made precipitously (and prematurely), prompted by the single parent's panic and/or the enmeshing pull of one's family of origin.

The relocation can be a double-edged sword because it provides needed emotional and financial support for the single-parent family, but it can also create a variety of potentially dysfunctional situations:

1. Disruption of relocating children from the security of the relationship with the other parent, as well as from their school and peer attachments
2. Severe limitation of the other parent's caretaking role, bonding to the children, and legal parental rights
3. Uncomfortable and potentially problematic dependency of the relocating parent on her or his family of origin
4. Greater emotional and physical intrusions from family-of-origin members experienced by both relocating parents and children
5. Job and career, as well as social support disruptions for the relocating parent
6. Potential renewal of adversary litigation between the parents to determine the one parent's right to move away with the children and the other parent's right to continue her or his parenting role (legal criteria governing these "move away" situations will vary according to jurisdictions)

Clinicians working with these potential "move away" single parents need to familiarize themselves with their local court-defined rules and criteria. Most states have requirements that the parent considering a relocation must notify the other parent within a certain time frame before leaving and this parent may also need to have formal approval from the court to remove the children from its jurisdiction. Postdivorce parents struggling with these issues can benefit from working with a therapist or mediator to attempt to work out a plan that is mutually acceptable and one that benefits the developmental needs of the children.

However, clinicians need to be careful not to get caught in the middle or take one side over the other in these struggles. One of the authors (CAE) was involved in a "move away" case in which the mother's therapist had supported the mother's relocation across the country. The rationale was that she would be somewhat closer to her family of origin and she would be able to obtain a higher paying job. No consideration was given to the 11-year-old child's needs. The father filed suit to keep the child in the community but by the time it was heard the mother had relocated, found a new job, and bought a new home. The author met with the child, who was clear that she did not want to leave her father, school, or extended family. He recommended to the court that the child should remain in the community and that the relocation had been unnecessarily disruptive. The court ruled in the father's favor and returned the child to the community.

These initial two stages may occur over several months or require several years to complete satisfactorily. When delays or disruptions in the completion of these tasks occur, they can produce serious imbalances and difficulties for the single parent and the children. A single mother's career, for example, may require her to live thousands of miles from her family of origin and, even though her parents wish to be supportive after the divorce, she is unable to take advantage of their offers of support because of the great distance and limited financial resources. If she considers giving up her career to relocate, the financial and emotional consequences must be taken into account. In another example, a single father's family of origin may live nearby. However, his father is an alcoholic and both of his parents were abusive toward him and his siblings when they lived at home. He would like to believe that the parents have changed but he cannot trust them with his young children. He has distanced himself from his siblings who, because of the abuse, refuse to have contact with their parents. In both cases these single parents, and their children, experience little direct support from their families of origin and struggle to replace that family support by developing new social networks. However, the search for an effective social network is often limited by the financial struggles experienced by many single parents, forcing some to take on two or more jobs, which limits their time and energy for parenting and social pursuits. Many issues can delay the process of these two stages.

Structural recoupling is the final stage of the postdivorce process. It involves redefining and realigning the former parent-child subsystem (from the predivorce nuclear family) such that the single-parent-headed systems, representing the dual households, are able to function independently, but in a parallel and interactive manner in which both parents are involved in caretaking and residential responsibilities with the children. The parenting roles (typically co-parenting roles) become the nucleus of the new single-parent family. This new system is also defined by its access to extended family members (e.g., grandparents) and to a new social network. This single-parent system has an evolving life of its own even though the everyday interactive patterns may be further defined by custody and access patterns, the geographical location of the other parent, and the relative involvement of the other parent. The successful completion of this stage of structural recoupling involves the redefinition of co-parenting roles (which may take a variety of shapes) and the establishing of the continuing structural link that is maintained between the predivorce parental roles. This new single-parent system, typically, will eventually face the challenge of integrating new spouses (remarriage) and additional siblings (step-family) into its functioning and balance.

CLINICAL ISSUES FOR PARENTS AND CHILDREN

A variety of parent-child clinical issues are present in single-parent families. Kaslow and Schwartz (1987) summarized a variety of pitfalls for single parents, including responding to a child as a reminder of the former spouse, the parent's overdependence on a child (and/or her or his family of origin), perception of the child as a burden, and focusing on one's personal survival rather than parenting and losing sight of the developmental needs of a child.

Many single parents report feeling overwhelmed by the dual roles of parenting and career responsibilities, yet others seem to thrive on these experiences. However, most parents report problems in child management, often erring in the direction of being too lenient with discipline and rules for the children. They may fear hurting the child emotionally or making the child's adjustment to the divorce more painful. A single parent who is continuing to struggle with her or his own decoupling from the marriage and personal adjustment may rely on a child, often the eldest, to take on a pseudo-adult and parentified role in their single-parent system. Many children are comfortable assuming such a role because it is a reflection of their underlying sympathy and protective feelings toward the parent. Such a role also provides a child with greater adult status within the family.

These parentified children may become the confidants to their often sad and unhappy single parents; others may become their protectors and defenders. If the expectations of these roles are excessive, the child may give up normal developmental experiences to better perform the expected responsibilities with the parent or in the family. Some of these children report that they stop attending after-school activities, such as clubs or athletic teams, because they "feel needed" by their single parent at home. Sometimes they feel responsible to care for younger siblings or to manage household responsibilities. A 12-year-old reported, "I miss playing soccer with my friends, but my mom needs me to get home early to take care of my sister and fix dinner before she gets home from work." Another stated: "I miss seeing my friends after school but my dad says he will lose his job if I can't be there to take care of my brother and sister."

Although single parents report that they recognize the problems of placing their child in these parentified roles, they often state, "I couldn't make ends meet if I had to hire a babysitter," or "I can't make it on my own without my daughter helping with the chores." We often work with clinical families where children as young as 5 and 6 years of age have assumed these pseudoparental responsibilities. A 14-year-old parentified son, acting as his single mother's protector, physically attacked her new boyfriend in front of the house, warning him, "Don't get involved with my mother!" A 16-year-old son stated to his mother, "I hate your boyfriend, if you let him live here I will move in with Dad (an alcoholic in another city) or I will run away."

In addition to the postdivorce adjustment drama of their parents, children living with single parents face their own adjustment issues. The variety of tasks and struggles for these children include:

- Adapting to two households, often miles apart
- Struggling with the emotional and geographical transitions between households
- Balancing time with peers and activities with the need to spend time with their other parent
- Managing differing parenting values, styles, and expectations
- Adjusting to each parent's new partners and step- and/or half-siblings in their lives
- Remaining neutral when parents are often trying to get them to align against the other parent
- Learning how to become more self-reliant and self-directed when their dependency needs are being denied

A single parent is also vulnerable to the parallel activities and behaviors of her or his former spouse when she or he becomes intrusive and quizzes the children about their father's or mother's new friends, the cost of new acquisitions, or what kind of food is in the refrigerator. The involvement of the former spouse with a new romantic partner is one of the more dramatic disruptive dynamics that we see clinically with postdivorce families. The presence of a new partner often represents a serious threat for some parents in terms of having to give up one's fantasy or wish for a potential reconciliation. For other single parents the situation triggers a fear that the children will either be in physical and/or emotional jeopardy from this new partner or that they will identify with this new individual as a replacement parent for them. This situation can be the stimulus for the single parent to return to court, often with vengeful allegations of abuse and/or drug use, directed at either the former spouse or her or his new partner.

As the first of the former spouses approaches remarriage the other partner is challenged with more abrupt decoupling, particularly if she or he has maintained the wish for a reconciliation. One of the more vulnerable roles for a single parent occurs when the former spouse has remarried and she or he has not. The single parent often sees herself or himself as less adequate or less attractive, and can become jealous that her or his former partner has now gone on with life. This jealousy may be framed in the context of the other spouse having created a "whole family" again, for themselves and the children—they eat meals, travel, and celebrate holidays together—while the unmarried single parent remains single, lonely, and now even outnumbered.

The remarriage of the former partner pushes some single parents into premature and unsatisfactory relationships, just to show the former spouse and children that she or he, too, can create a family of one's own. For other parents it triggers revenge and anger—often latent aspects of the former marital conflict and now of unsatisfactory decoupling. Accusations, old marital secrets, and demeaning statements are shared with the children in an effort to discredit the other parent or a new partner, and to maintain a degree of self-esteem for oneself. Such a single parent, in an extreme reaction, may begin a vindictive process of attempting to withhold and/or alienate the children from the remarried parent. This is evidenced in the growing number of cases that involve parental alienation (see Cartwright, 1993; Dunne & Hedrick, 1994; Gardner, 1992, 1994, 1998).

FAMILY THERAPY STRATEGIES

Therapists often seem perplexed about how to offer or develop family therapy strategies for single parents and their children. Their concerns are often expressed as, "But there is only one parent available," or "They are divorced and don't want to see each other, particularly in therapy," or "The children just want to talk about the parent they are not living with." These comments reflect a therapist's focus solely on individual issues rather than having conceptualized the single-parent family's clinical needs in a broader systemic orientation. Family therapy approaches to working with general divorce and postdivorce families are described elsewhere in the literature (Ahrons & Rodgers, 1987; Ahrons & Perlmutter, 1982; Brown, 1985; Crohn et al., 1982; Crosbie-Burnett & Ahrons, 1985; Everett & Volgy, 1991; Fulmer, 1983; Goldner, 1982; Issacs, 1983; Kaslow, 1981; Kaslow & Schwartz, 1987; Nichols, 1985; Schwartz & Kaslow, 1997; Visher & Visher, 1996; Walsh, 1991). We have also described, elsewhere, 14 clinically predictable stages in the divorce process that can aid the clinician with assessment and treatment interventions (Everett & Volgy-Everett, 1991, 1994). These stages included such dynamics as predivorce ambivalence, spousal distancing, separation and pseudo-reconciliation, postdivorce co-parenting, remarriage, and dual-family functioning.

The postdivorce nuclear system does not cease to exist but it is restructured around two single-parent "mini" systems. A nonresidential single-parent family system evolves and continues to exist, a fact often ignored by many therapists, even when this system is located many miles away from the child's primary residence. A nonresidential parent's role continues, even though visitation may occur only during holidays and summers, through telephone and mail contacts during the school year, as well as in a child's images, fantasies, and attachment to that parent.

The therapist working with single-parent families also needs to recognize the bigger picture of the intergenerational and social networks that are present as both resources and influences (positively or negatively) for the postdivorce family. Treatment strategies for single-parent families need to involve more than focusing solely on the single parent's or a child's postdivorce adjustment through individual or group therapy. We believe that family therapy with postdivorce families is most effective when it includes in the treatment process as many of the system's relevant members as possible. The therapist may wish to invite a broad range of extended family and nonfamily members, such as

- A former spouse
- A step-parent
- Step-siblings
- Grandparents (from nearby or distant locations)
- Other family-of-origin members
- Live-in partners (heterosexual or homosexual)
- Individual therapists who are working with a parent or a child

A single father may spend months in individual therapy lamenting his former wife's new boyfriend, this boyfriend's influence on the children, what the children are telling him about the mother's boyfriend's drinking behavior, how long the children spend with this person, and whether he should talk to an attorney about modifying custody. A therapist can become frustrated with these reflections because they lack definitive corroboration and action. However, when the family therapist offers to schedule a joint meeting between the father, the former wife and boyfriend, and perhaps the children, the father will focus very quickly on the issues he is willing to deal with and the relative seriousness of his concerns. The therapist's rationale for a joint session includes several goals:

1. To improve the former spouses' communication and block mixed messages regarding the children
2. To clarify, define, and expand, if necessary, their co-parenting roles
3. To clarify the roles of new partners in their lives and that of their children
4. To remove the children as messengers and/or mediators between the two households
5. To block the children's potential manipulations between each household

The father's concerns may subside quickly when he recognizes that he was feeling sorry for himself because the "children seem to have so much fun at their mother's house with her new boyfriend," and that he "wishes he were not so lonely." When the proposed joint therapy session is conducted, the underlying clinical goals include further completion of the decoupling process for the parents and the children, and a focus on the structural recoupling stage to enhance their co-parenting.

A single mother may focus, in individual therapy, on her wishes to improve and spend more time with her parents, who live a thousand miles away and who, since the divorce, send her money to pay for her apartment and attorney's fees. However, she remembers unhappy issues from her adolescent years that may cause her to remain emotionally distant and unresponsive to their requests to visit. During her early years at home she was somewhat rebellious and her experimentation with drugs and sexual behaviors angered and disappointed her parents. She left home precipitously at 17 years of age, after getting pregnant, to marry the man whom she recently divorced. Her parents warned her that he was not right for her and that she was not ready for marriage or parenthood. She worries that her parents will still be angry and that they will compare her to her older brother who finished college and is now happily married.

When the therapist treats these family-of-origin issues solely in individual therapy they remain primarily a cognitive and speculative exercise. They do not become "live" clinical issues until the mother can deal with them in a face-to-face meeting with her parents. We believe that family-of-origin consultation sessions (Framo, 1992) are an effective and underutilized resource for single-parent families. We often invite family-of-origin members to attend clinical sessions, whenever possible, even if they reside in distant communities. When these members are not physically accessible we schedule telephone consultations and/or conference calls. We have found that well-planned family-of-origin sessions can accomplish many more clinical goals in just 2 to 4 hours of interaction than can often be accomplished in several months of individual psychotherapy for a single parent.

The clinical goal in the case above was to repair the mother's premature separation from her family of origin and to address her unresolved concerns regarding her parents' unhappiness about her former adolescent behaviors and early marriage. These clinical issues can usually be processed and improved in a couple of hours in a family-of-origin meeting. Here the door can be opened clinically for the mother to receive support and feel connected once again to her family of origin (network coupling), and her parents can feel that they have open access to their daughter and grandchildren. Such an intervention can be a dramatic resource for a single parent in her or his process of balancing and stabilizing one's new postdivorce family system.

We shape our family therapy interventions with single-parent families around their relative progress through the three postdivorce tasks of decoupling, network coupling, and recoupling. There is certainly overlap in these stages and the therapist must use her or his clinical judgment as to which areas to prioritize. We find, however, that there is a clear developmental process in these stages—a single parent needs to make progress in decoupling from her or his former marriage before one can successfully recouple as co-parents. It is unrealistic for the therapist to encourage a single parent to be more objective in communication regarding parenting with a former spouse when, in fact, she or he is still hoping for reconciliation (despite the fact that the spouse has moved on with life or even remarried).

Clinical interventions in the decoupling stage initially involve a combination of individual sessions to help the single parent focus on the struggle and ambivalence of letting go emotionally, resolving issues of the one who is leaving versus the one who is left (Everett & Volgy-Everett, 1994), and beginning the process of network coupling with family-of-origin members and social relationships. This process often leads to an invitation for the former spouse to attend several joint sessions. In these joint sessions the former marital and divorce issues can be resolved more quickly when both spouses are present. This therapeutically prescribed interaction enhances more effective decoupling, clearer co-parenting roles, and improved communication.

If a former spouse is reluctant to attend a joint session because she or he is working with another therapist, we offer to schedule joint meetings so the other therapist might attend— although many individual therapists decline and defer to our working with the relationship issues. (Some former spouses may wish to attend joint sessions with their attorneys, which we typically decline. If the couple is continuing to struggle with postdivorce disputes, we refer them to a mediator.) When former spouses live too far away to attend a joint session we may conduct a telephone consultation with the distant parent to encourage increased correspondence or telephone contact with the other parent in the interim before they visit the community. We simply wait to schedule these joint sessions when the parent visits the community to pick up the children. On occasions when a former spouse simply refuses to participate in a joint session, we work on relevant issues individually through simulations and role playing.

Children's experiences during the decoupling process, which vary according to age, involve ambivalence about their altered family structure and dual households as well as fantasies of their parents' potential reconciliation. Unhappy and insecure children can be quite direct in creating crises or employing manipulations to keep their parents in touch with one another, albeit in a negative manner. Family interventions with these children often proceed initially with sibling sessions, to which their step- and/or half-siblings may also be invited, which can help in a variety of ways:

1. Children can share the struggles and/or disappointments with one or both parent's attitudes, behaviors, and availability
2. Children can discuss the differences they experience in parenting values and styles that are now more evident due to their parents living in single-parent households
3. Children may deal with the transitional problems and the actual access schedules of changing residences
4. Children may express wishes for additional time with one of the parents
5. Children may comment on one or both parent's involvement with new partners
6. Children may work on getting to know and relate to new step- and/or half-siblings

These sibling sessions may also focus on helping the children express, and eventually accept, their fears or anger that their parents will never reunite. A 5-year-old boy, in one of these sibling sessions, scheduled 18 months after his parents had divorced, said to one of the authors, "I will give you all of the pennies in my piggy bank if you can get Daddy to come back home."

The children's issues, particularly those raised in the sibling session, can be processed in several family sessions, ideally involving both parents. When this is not possible, we meet first with the children and one parent and then take the issues from that session to a similar session with the children and the other parent. Although this is a less desirable format, it makes it possible to address the children's concerns in a therapeutic context. It is a critical mistake, from a family therapy perspective, for the therapist not to make every effort possible to involve the former spouse. This would also include invitations to step-parents and step-siblings if one, or both, of the parents have remarried, and a half-sibling with a new child is present. When the other spouse is not willing to participate, we turn to other resources in the family system for the children, namely the further involvement of the grandparents and/or aunts, uncles, or cousins. The clinical goal is to assist the children with the decoupling process by rebalancing their lives with whatever resources are available in the family (this may include individual and/or play therapy sessions for more overwhelmed or depressive children, and/or referrals to children's postdivorce support groups offered by schools, churches, or courts).

Network coupling is an ongoing process, paralleling the decoupling and recoupling stages, and continuing throughout the postdivorce and remarriage periods. However, a single parent experiencing rage for having been "left" by the former spouse, or who has an unrealistic fantasy of reconciliation, may experience seriously inhibited and delayed success in establishing support from either one's family of origin or one's social networks. The therapeutic interventions discussed above for the decoupling process are often helpful here and can be interspersed with ongoing individual sessions as well as referral to community support groups.

A 45-year-old man, for example, who had been divorced 2 years, was referred by his physician because of serious depression and malnutrition. He continued to function in his career and saw his one child a couple of days a month. However, he had developed a pattern of rushing home from work most nights with a fast-food dinner to sit quietly in his apartment. His fantasy was that he was waiting for his former wife to "knock on the door and tell me she wants me to take her back." She had remarried a couple of years ago to a former friend of his. He fantasized that she would "dump her new husband, realizing her error, and ask me to accept her back." He did not date or socialize. His wife refused the therapist's invitation for a joint meeting, but since she was fearful that he could potentially begin stalking her, she agreed to meet with the therapist individually. She expressed clearly that she disliked her former husband, that she was well decoupled, and that she planned to remain married to her present husband. The therapist reported these observations to the former husband who struggled through several sessions to accept the reality of the divorce and to process his own need to decouple. Within 6 weeks he was able to request spending more time with his son, and 3 months later he became interested in dating.

Therapy during the stage of structural recoupling involves the primary task of redefining co-parenting roles and healthy patterns for the children in each household. Single parents who reside in the same community, particularly those who may have alternating-week access plans, must deal with considerable transitional logistics and co-parent management issues, in addition to the ongoing emotional processes. These issues are complicated by three common problem areas:

1. Poorly defined access plans and financial responsibilities that require too many negotiations between the parents
2. Difficult or complicated transitional access patterns (too frequent or too few) that create difficulties for children and parents (both of these situations draw parents, and the children, into chronic patterns of conflict)
3. Unresolved marital and divorce (decoupling) issues observed as hurt feelings, jealousy, and/or rage that overshadow even well-defined access plans

Joint sessions with both single parents are the treatment of choice. These clinical sessions focus on resolving and/or redefining the above problem areas. When the single parents are unable to meet jointly, due to refusal or geographical factors, the therapist may deal with this problem in several ways: alternating individual parent sessions, joint sessions that involve a parent's individual therapist (or two), or telephone conference calls with an out-of-town parent. A reluctant parent may be persuaded to attend a joint or individual session when the goals are clearly defined as helping the children adjust to the divorce. Sometimes they are cautious because they expect the goals to be working on the marriage, getting back together, or resolving old marital conflicts. Occasionally we receive calls from an attorney, representing a parent, who wants to clarify our goals (and intentions) for these joint clinical meetings. When we explain our goals most attorneys support the therapeutic orientation of these sessions, even when litigation is still in progress.

We have found that it is more effective, clinically, to involve children in joint family sessions after the parents have made some progress themselves in defining their co-parenting roles (recoupling) and, if necessary, defusing underlying emotional and/or former marital issues. These family therapy sessions are, again, the treatment of choice. The overall goal is to provide a structured setting for the single parents to present, mutually, to the children their plan for co-parenting, communication, and access. This experience can be a powerful statement to the children regarding their parents' concerns for reducing stress, making their lives more predictable and manageable, and reinforcing unified co-parenting roles. The latter goal, for example, will be productive in eliminating a child's engaging in go-between or manipulative behaviors.

Step-parents, if any, are not invited to the initial family session. (The exception would be a step-parent who has been involved with the children for some years.) It is important to respect the members of the original nuclear system and provide them a private time to complete this recoupling process (typically one initial session is satisfactory). However, the presence of a step-parent is mandatory, even when her or his involvement in the therapy sessions is postponed until the second or third family session.

Co-parenting issues cannot be defined realistically or resolved clinically without the input and response from the step-parent(s). The therapist who does not invite such participation early will soon discover that this absent step-parent can easily sabotage clinical changes in co-parenting and improvements in the family's interaction. However, the therapist's proposal for involving a step-parent in the family sessions may trigger latent decoupling issues for the single parent. If this occurs, the invitation should be delayed until the single parent has had an opportunity to work through her or his concerns and fears. Even when a parent and step-parent reside out of town, these sessions can be conducted effectively for several hours over a weekend or (somewhat less effectively) by telephone prior to extended visitations.

The physical absence and/or continuing animosity on the part of the other parent makes clinical interventions with the recoupling process much more difficult. When this occurs, the therapist needs to creatively involve additional resources from the single parent's family-of-origin system. For example, a single parent who feels overwhelmed by primary residential responsibilities for the children can benefit from emotional, child care, and financial help provided by grandparents. Other extended family members (aunts, uncles, and cousins) who live nearby can also help on a daily or weekly basis when the other parent is absent. The availability of these extended family members can also be instrumental in providing support for a child when her or his other parent is absent or unavailable. Friends in the community, who may have known both parents before the divorce, can also provide supportive services for both a parent and the children. Distant family-of-origin members can help, in more limited ways, by providing regular telephone calls, letters, and cards to the children. They may also consider planning more frequent trips to the residential city. If a child is old enough to travel, these family members can invite her or him for visits at their residence for portions of holidays and summers, thus providing the single parent with free time from parenting.

The postdivorce single-parent family may take many forms and be characterized by a variety of child custodial patterns. Due to this family form's prevalence in the culture, it is no longer viewed as the dysfunctional anomaly of the prior decades. Efforts to describe its overall functioning and dynamics have ranged from that of the "double single-parent family" (Crohn, 1983) to the "permeable family" (Elkin, 1994) to the "binuclear family" (Ahrons, 1979, 1980, 1994).

Effective clinical interventions with single-parent families involve broad systemic family assessment therapy. Family therapy assessment and interventions may follow the post-divorce family's progression through the three stages identified in this chapter: structural decoupling, network coupling, and structure recoupling. The therapist working with single-parent families will benefit from a recognition of the research and theoretical variables that shape these families, an appreciation of the broader interactive and family system patterns that define these families' experiences, a willingness and ability to involve former spouses and extended family members in the therapy process, and creativity to resolve conflicts and provide supportive resources.

REFERENCES

Ahrons, C. R. (1979). The binuclear family: Two household, one family. *Alternative Lifestyles, 2,* 499–515.

Ahrons, C. R. (1980). Redefining the divorced family: A conceptual framework for postdivorce family systems reorganization. *Social Work, 25,* 437–441.

Ahrons, C. R. (1994). *The good divorce.* New York: HarperCollins.

Ahrons, C. R., & Perlmutter, M. S. (1982). The relationship between former spouses: A fundamental subsystem in the remarriage family. In Messinger, L. (Ed.), *Therapy with remarriage families* (pp. 31–46). Rockville, MD: Aspen.

Ahrons, C. R., & Rodgers, R. H. (1987). *Divorced families: A multidisciplinary developmental view.* New York: Norton.

Ali, J., & Avison, W. R. (1997). Employment transitions and psychological distress: The contrasting experiences of single and married mothers. *Journal of Health and Social Behavior, 38,* 345–362.

Anthony, E. J. (1974). Children at risk from divorce: A review. In E. J. Anthony & C. Koupernik (Eds.), *The child and his family* (pp. 115–138). NY: John Wiley & Sons, Inc.

Belcastro, P. A., Gramlich, T., Nicholson, T., Price, J., & Wilson, R. (1993). A review of data based on studies addressing the affects of homosexual parenting on children's sexual and social functioning. *Journal of Divorce and Remarriage, 20,* 105–135.

Bianchi, S. M. (1995). The changing demographic and socioeconomic characteristics of single parent families. *Marriage and Family Review, 20,* 71–97.

Brown, M. D. (1985). Creating new realities for the newly divorced: A structural-strategic approach for divorce therapy with an individual. *Journal of Psychotherapy and the Family, 1,* 101–120.

Cartwright, G. F. (1993). Expanding the parameters of Parental Alienation Syndrome. *American Journal of Family Therapy, 21,* 205–215.

Causey, K. A., & Duran-Aydintug, C. (1997). Tendency to stigmatize lesbian mothers in custody cases. *Journal of Divorce and Remarriage, 28,* 171–182.

Cohen, O. (1994). Family functioning: Cohesion and adaptability of divorced fathers and mothers raising their children. *Family Therapy, 21,* 35–45.

Cohen, O. (1995). Divorced fathers raise their children by themselves. *Journal of Divorce and Remarriage, 23,* 55–73.

Cohen, O. (1996). The personal well-being of single-parent family heads rearing their children by themselves: A comparative study. *Contemporary Family Therapy, 18,* 129–146.

Crohn, H., Sager, C. J., Brown, H., Rodstein, E., & Walker, L. (1982). A basis for understanding and treating the remarried family. In L. Messinger (Ed.), *Therapy with remarriage families* (pp. 159–186). Rockville, MD: Aspen.

Crohn, H., Sager, C. J., Rodstein, E., Brown, H. S., Walker, L, & Beir, J. (1981). Understanding and treating the child in the remarried family. In I. R. Stuart & L. E. Abt (Eds.), *Children of Separation and Divorce.* NY: Van Nostrand Reinhold.

Crosbie-Burnett, M., & Ahrons, C. R. (1985). From divorce to remarriage: implications for therapy with families in transition. *Journal of Psychotherapy and the Family, 1,* 121–137.

DeMaris, A., & Greif, G. L. (1992). The relationship between family structure and parent-child relationship problems in single father households. *Journal of Divorce and Remarriage, 18,* 55–77.

DeMaris, A., & Greif, G. L. (1997). Single custodial fathers and their children: When things go well. In A. J. Hawkins & D. C. Dollahite (Eds.), *Generative fathering: Beyond deficit perspectives. Current issues in the family series, 3* (pp. 134–146). Thousand Oaks, CA: Sage Publications.

Dixon, C. S., & Rettig, K. D. (1994). An examination of income adequacy for single women two years after divorce. *Journal of Divorce and Remarriage, 22,* 57–72.

Downey, D. B. (1994). The school performance of children from single-mother and single-father families: Economic or interpersonal deprivation? *Journal of Family Issues, 15,* 129–147.

Draughn, P. S., LeBoeuf, R. C., Wozniak, P. J., Lawrence, F. C., & Welch, L. R. (1994). Divorcees' economic well-being and financial adequacy as related to interfamily grants. *Journal of Divorce and Remarriage, 22,* 23–36.

Dunne, J., & Hedrick, M. (1994). The parental alienation syndrome: An analysis of sixteen selected cases. *Journal of Divorce and Remarriage, 21,* 21–38.

Duran-Aydintug, C., & Causey, K. A. (1996). Child custody determination: Implications for lesbian mothers. *Journal of Divorce and Remarriage, 25,* 55–74.

Elkin, D. (1994). *Ties that bind. The new family imbalance.* Cambridge, MA: Harvard University Press.

Entwisle, D. R., & Alexander, K. L. (1996). Family type and children's growth in reading and math over the primary grades. *Journal of Marriage and the Family, 58,* 341–355.

Everett, C. A., & Volgy-Everett, S. S. (1994). *Healthy divorce.* San Francisco, CA: Jossey-Bass.

Everett, C. A., & Volgy, S. S. (1991). Treating divorce in family-therapy practice. In A. Gurman & D. Kniskern (Eds.), *Handbook of family therapy* (Vol. 2, pp. 508–524). New York: Brunner/Mazel.

Fine, M. A., McKenry, P. C., & Chung, H. (1992). Post-divorce adjustment of black and white single parents. *Journal of Divorce and Remarriage, 17,* 121–134.

Foster, E. M., Jones, D., & Hoffman, S. D. (1998). The economic impact of nonmarital childbearing: How are older, single mothers faring? *Journal of Marriage and the Family, 60,* 163–174.

Framo, J. L. (1992). *Family-of-origin therapy: An intergenerational approach.* New York: Brunner/Mazel.

Fulmer, R. H. (1983). A structural approach to unresolved mourning in single parent family systems. *Journal of Marital and Family Therapy, 9,* 259–269.

Gardner, R. (1992). *The parental alienation syndrome: A guide for mental health and legal professionals.* Cresskill, NJ: Creative Therapeutics, Inc.

Gardner, R. (1994). Differentiating between true and false sex-abuse accusations in child-custody cases. *Journal of Divorce and Remarriage, 21,* 1–20.

Gardner, R. (1998). Recommendations for dealing with parents who induce a parental alienation syndrome in their children. *Journal of Divorce and Remarriage, 28,* 1–23.

Glick, P. C. (1994). American families: As they are and were. In A. S. Skolnick & J. H. Skolnick (Eds.), *Family in transition* (8th ed., pp. 91–104). New York: HarperCollins.

Goldner, V. (1982). Remarriage family: Structure, system, future. In L. Messinger (Ed.), *Therapy with remarriage families* (pp. 187–206). Rockville, MD: Aspen.

Goldstein, J., Freud, A., & Solnit, A. J. (1973). *Beyond the best interests of the child.* New York: The Free Press.

Greif, G. L. (1985). Single fathers rearing children. *Journal of Marriage and the Family, 47,* 185–191.

Greif, G. L. (1995). Single fathers with custody following separation and divorce. *Marriage and Family Review, 20,* 213–231.

Guttmann, J. (1993). *Divorce in psychosocial perspective: Theory and research.* Hillsdale, NJ: Lawrence Erlbaum.

Hall, L. D., Walker, A. J., & Acock, A. C. (1995). Gender and family work in one-parent households. *Journal of Marriage and the Family, 57,* 685–692.

Heath, P. A., & MacKinnon, C. (1988). Factors related to the social competence of children in single-parent families. *Journal of Divorce and Remarriage, 11,* 49–66.

Hilton, J. M., & Macari, D. P. (1997). Grandparent involvement following divorce: A comparison of single-mother and single-father families. *Journal of Divorce and Remarriage, 28,* 203–224.

Holloway, S. D., & Machida, S. (1991). Child-rearing effectiveness of divorced mothers: Relationship to coping strategies and social support. *Journal of Divorce and Remarriage, 14,* 179–201.

Huntley, D. K., Phelps, R. E., & Rehm, L. P. (1987). Depression in children from single-parent families. *Journal of Divorce and Remarriage, 10,* 153–161.

Hutchinson, R. L., & Spangler-Hirsch, S. L. (1989). Children of divorce and single-parent lifestyles: Facilitating well-being. *Journal of Divorce and Remarriage, 12,* 5–24.

Issacs, M. B. (1982). Facilitating family restructuring and relinkage. In L. Messinger (Ed.), *Therapy with remarriage families* (pp. 121–143). Rockville, MD: Aspen.

Johnson, M. K., & Hutchinson, R. L. (1989). Effects of family structure on children's self-concepts. *Journal of Divorce and Remarriage, 12,* 129–138.

Kaslow, F. W. (1981). Divorce and divorce therapy. In A. Gurman & D. Kniskern (Eds.), *Handbook of family therapy* (pp. 662–696). New York: Brunner/Mazel.

Kaslow, F. W., & Schwartz, L. L. (1987). *The dynamics of divorce. A life cycle perspective.* New York: Brunner/Mazel.

Kissman, K., & Allen, J. A. (1993). *Single-parent families.* Newbury Park, CA: Sage Publications.

Laosa, L. (1988). Ethnicity and single parenting in the United States. In E. M. Hetherington & J. D. Arasteh (Eds.), *Impact of divorce, single parenting, and stepparenting on children* (pp. 23–49). Hillsdale, NJ: Lawrence Erlbaum.

Levitan, T. E. (1979). Children of divorce: An introduction. *Journal of Social Issues 35*(4), 1–25.

Lindblad-Goldberg, M. (1989). Successful minority single-parent families. In L. Combrinck-Graham (Ed.), *Children in family contexts* (pp. 244–268). NY: Guilford.

Lino, M. (1995). The economics of single parenthood: Past research and future directions. *Marriage and Family Review, 20,* 99–114.

Mahler, S. R. (1994). A comparison of single and married working parents' agency and desire for money. *Journal of Divorce and Remarriage, 22,* 73–86.

Maturana, H., & Varela, R. (1980). *Autopoiesis and cognition: The realization of the living.* Dordrecht, the Netherlands: Reidel.

Morrison, N. C. (1995). Successful single-parent families. *Journal of Divorce and Remarriage, 22,* 205–219.

Nichols, W. C. (1985). Family therapy with children of divorce. *Journal of Psychotherapy and the Family, 1,* 55–68.

Niepel, G., & Nestmann, F. (1996). The social networks of single mothers [German]. *Grupendynamik, 27,* 85–108.

Pam, A., & Pearson, J. (1998). *Splitting up: Enmeshment and estrangement in the process of divorce.* New York: Guilford Press.

Patterson, C. J. (1992). Children of lesbian and gay parents. *Child Development, 63,* 1025–1042.

Risman, B. J., & Park, K. (1988). Just the two of us: Parent-child relationships in single-parent homes. *Journal of Marriage and the Family, 50,* 1049–1062.

Sander, E., & Ermert, C. (1997). Interaction behavior of preschool children from single and two parent families. *Journal of Divorce and Remarriage, 26,* 57–63.

Schnayer, R., & Orr, R. R. (1989). A comparison of children living in single-mother and single father families. *Journal of Divorce and Remarriage, 12,* 171–184.

Schwartz, L. L., & Kaslow, F. W. (1997). *Painful partings: Divorce and its aftermath.* New York: John Wiley & Sons, Inc.

Stroup, A. L., & Pollock, G. E. (1994). Economic consequences of marital dissolution. *Journal of Divorce and Remarriage, 22,* 37–54.

Summers, M., Summers, C. R., & Ascione, F. R. (1993). A comparison of sibling interaction in intact and single-parent families. *Journal of Divorce and Remarriage, 20,* 215–227.

Tasker, F., & Golombok, S. (1997). Young people's attitudes toward living in a lesbian family: A longitudinal study of children raised by post-divorce lesbian mothers. *Journal of Divorce and Remarriage, 28,* 183–202.

Thiriot, T. L., & Buckner, E. T. (1991). Multiple predictors of satisfactory post-divorce adjustment of single custodial parents. *Journal of Divorce and Remarriage, 17,* 27–48.

Visher, E. B., & Visher, J. S. (1993). Remarriage families and stepparenting. In F. Walsh (Ed.), *Normal family processes* (2nd ed., pp. 331–353). New York: Guilford Press.

Visher, E. B., & Visher, J. S. (1996). *Therapy with stepfamilies.* New York: Brunner/Mazel.

Walsh, F. (1991). Promoting healthy functioning in divorced and remarried families. In A. Gurman, & D. Kniskern, D. (Eds.), *Handbook of family therapy* (Vol. 2, pp. 525–545). New York: Brunner/Mazel.

Watts, D. S., & Watts, K. M. (1991). The impact of female-headed single parent families on academic achievement. *Journal of Divorce and Remarriage, 17,* 97–114.

Wienberg, M. H., & Weinger, S. (1998). When dreams wither and resources fail: The social support systems of poor single mothers. *Families in Society, 79,* 212–219.

CHAPTER 17

Families Experiencing Divorce

Florence W. Kaslow

THE PROCESS OF DIVORCE: A TIME OF PAIN AND GRIEF

Divorce can and does occur any time during the family life cycle. The impact, which is almost always very potent and lingering, will differ depending on numerous variables, including but not limited to the age of the family members, the length of the existence of the marriage, the family's socioeconomic status, religion, race, ethnic/cultural background, and educational level. No matter when in one's life or why the divorce occurs, it almost always involves a heart-wrenching series of events; it is one of the most painful processes a family can undergo (Schwartz & Kaslow, 1997) at any stage in its life together. For many months, and sometimes years, before, during, and after the actual legal divorce occurs, there is either high conflict between the partners or retreat into semisilence. Many individuals describe the divorce process as akin to a roller coaster ride—the climbs upward are slow and tedious, the down periods come rapidly with a crash.

Over time the vicissitudes decrease in frequency and intensity; however, predictably, the leveling out and re-equilibration process takes 2 to 5 years from the time the inevitability of divorce becomes obvious. Thus for the partner who decided he or she was determined to end the marriage, this time frame commences around the date the decision becomes irreversible. For the partner who was told "the marriage is over and there is nothing you can do to salvage it," the recuperation process is more complex and usually begins later—at the time their spouse announces the declaration of intended exodus from the partnership. It is complicated by the sense of rejection, of failure to fulfill the spouse's needs and expectations, and anger over multiple losses. The above portrays the most frequently encountered scenario of divorcing spouses.

It is important to highlight several divergent scripts. In some marriages, particularly those characterized by violence and physical abuse, and often by severe and long-standing alcohol or drug abuse, the decision to separate en route to divorce may bring a wave of relief. The beckoning prospect of freedom from the abuse and the chronic fear of violence can be very appealing. At the same time, it is frequently tinged with remorse over (1) having originally selected a partner whose faults were not recognized, or if seen, were minimized; (2) having been unable to rescue or fix the person, if he or she is is perceived as having a disease or psychological problem; (3) having prolonged making the choice to end the marriage despite years of turbulence and unhappiness; (4) the children having witnessed and/or heard arguments, obscene language, physical fights; and/or (5) the children also were victims of abuse while the other parent felt helpless to protect them adequately (Courtois, 1988: Walker, 1990). In addition, the delicious taste of potential freedom is all too often laced with fear of being tracked down and further victimized by the former spouse, if he or she was a perpetrator of violence (Guyer, 1999; Walker, 1994). When they finally seek to break out of the marital prison that has entrapped them, they need a solid plan for leaving that includes providing for safety for themselves and their children.

To set the framework for this chapter, an analogy will be used to illuminate how many individuals traversing the divorce pathway perceive the experience. A synopsis, based on the descriptions of numerous patients, is:

> It is like entering a dark tunnel. The entryway is narrow and you cannot fathom what lies ahead; you just grope around in the strange darkness, feeling befuddled and panicky. Slowly some crevices emerge and some light filters in, as if there are now little windows in the tunnel. It begins to widen, and bit by bit you can breathe a little better and know you are moving forward and will not trip and be unable to recover. You begin to feel occasional spurts of energy to tackle the myriad chores and attend to the problems and issues that need to be solved. As you continue going further into the tunnel, the windows get larger and some sunshine beams in. Your pace quickens and a little optimism bubbles up to replace the confusion and despair. Then, one day you realize there is light at the end of the dungeon of divorce and there will be a new life beyond. You can help design that life for yourself; it will take into account what has gone before but does not need to be dictated and circumscribed totally by this experience.

Often therapists have the privilege of coaching (Bowen, 1988) people through the journey, and knowing what it is apt to resemble enables them to be a much more empathic and knowledgeable guide. (Many of the statements made about divorcing couples also apply to and describe unmarried couples who have lived together for a long period of time in a committed relationship [especially if they have children]. This includes gay and lesbian couples [Kuehlwein, 1999] as well as heterosexual couples.)

SEVEN ASPECTS OF DIVORCE

Seven facets or phases of divorce have been identified and articulated in the past 30 years. Initially Bohannan (1970) described six stations of divorce. In the ensuing years, I have expanded the model to include a seventh facet, the religious/spiritual divorce (Kaslow, 1994; 1995; Kaslow & Schwartz, 1987), and have refined and elaborated what transpires during the process, adding new elements like divorce mediation in the legal phase (Kaslow, 1990, 1995, 1999; Schwartz & Kaslow, 1997). The stages do not occur in an invariant sequence nor are they discrete; rather they overlap. To clarify what is entailed, it is preferable to analyze and describe them separately. The process is depicted in Table 17.1 and discussed in detail below.

TABLE 17.1 "Diaclectic" Model of Stages in the Divorce Process

Phase	Stage and Aspects	Feelings	Behaviors and Tasks	Therapeutic Approaches	Mediation Issues
Predivorce: A time of Deliberation	I. Emotional divorce	Disillusionment Dissatisfaction Alienation Anxiety Disbelief Denial Despair Dread Anguish Ambivalence Shock Emptiness Anger Chaos Inadequacy Low self-esteem Loss Depression Detachment	Avoiding the issue Sulking and/or crying Confronting partner Quarreling Withdrawing (physical and emotional) Pretending all is fine Attempting to win back affection Asking friends, family, clergy for advice Changing residence for one or both partners	Marital therapy (one couple) Couples group therapy Individual therapy Marital therapy (one couple) Divorce therapy Couples group therapy	Contemplation of mediated vs. litigated divorce Deciding which is best option
During divorce: A time of legal involvement	(II. Legal divorce	Self-pity Helplessness Fear of loneliness Apprehension about future	Consulting an attorney or mediator Accepting that divorce is probably inevitable Filing for legal divorce Bargaining Screaming Threatening Attempting suicide	Family therapy Individual adult therapy Child therapy	Set the stage for mediation orientation session Ascertain parties' understanding of the process and its appropriateness for them

(continued)

343

TABLE 17.1 Continued

Phase	Stage and Aspects	Feelings	Behaviors and Tasks	Therapeutic Approaches	Mediation Issues
(	(III. Economic/ financial divorce	Confusion	Separating physically	Children of divorce group	Define the rules of mediation
(		Fury	Considering financial settlement	Child therapy	
(		Sadness, loneliness	Determining amount of child support and/or alimony	Adult therapy	Identify the issues and separate therapeutic issues from mediation
(		Relief			
(		Vindictiveness			Focus on parental strengths, children's needs, and formulating best possible co-parenting and residential arrangement
(		Greed	Deciding on custody/visitation schedule		
	IV. Co-parental divorce/issues of residence and contact	Concern for children	Grieving and mourning	Same as above, plus family therapy	Negotiate and process the issues and choices
		Ambivalence	Telling relatives and friends		Reach agreement
		Numbness	Re-entering work world (unemployed woman)		Analyze and formalize agreement
		Uncertainty	Feeling empowered to make choices		Take to attorneys for finalizing and filing
		Fear of loss	Possible relocation		
			Arranging child care		
	V. Social/community/ extended family issues	Indecisiveness	Dealing with others' reactions	Adults and adolescents	
		Optimism		Individual therapy	
		Resignation	Interpreting changes to extended family	Singles group therapy	
		Excitement	Finalizing divorce		
		Curiosity	Reaching out to new friends	Children	
		Regret		Child play therapy	
		Sadness	Undertaking new activities	Children's group therapy	
				Sibling system therapy	
			Stabilizing new life style and daily routine for children		
			Exploring new interest and possibly taking new job		

TABLE 17.1 Continued

Phase	Stage and Aspects	Feelings	Behaviors and Tasks	Therapeutic Approaches	Mediation Issues
	VI. Spiritual/religious divorce	Self-doubt Desire for church approval Fear of God's displeasure or wrath	Gaining church acceptance Having a religious divorce ceremony Making peace with one's spiritual self	Divorce ceremony for total family Adult therapy Pastoral counseling Children—same as above	Return to mediation when changed circumstances warrant a renegotiation of the agreement
Postdivorce: A time of exploration and re-equilibration	VII. Psychic divorce	Acceptance Self-confidence Energetic Improved self-image Wholeness Exhilaration Independence Autonomy	Resynthesis of identity Completing psychic divorce Seeking new love object and making a commitment to some permanency Becoming comfortable with new lifestyle and friends Helping children accept finality of parents' divorce and their continuing relationship with both parents	Parent-child therapy Family therapy Group therapies Children's activity group therapy Individual therapy	

Source: For earlier versions see Kaslow, 1984, 1988, 1995, 1997 (in Schwartz & Kaslow). Table periodically revised and expanded. (Updated for this chapter, 1999). © 1984, F. Kaslow.

I. THE EMOTIONAL DIVORCE—THE MARRIAGE DISINTEGRATES

Stage One

This commences when one or both partners realize they have become disenchanted with and/or dissatisfied in the relationship. The feeling of disillusionment is not just episodic but has become chronic. It can happen any time, from the first year of marriage to 40-plus years later.

Severe disappointment experienced during the first year or two of marriage usually emanates from one of several sources. The person may have entered into living together and/or marriage with a fantasy vision imprinted from early childhood when fairy tales promising "some day my prince (or princess) will come and we will ride off into the sunset to live happily ever after" were heard. When the person learns all too soon that his or her partner is not a prince or princess but an imperfect human being with strengths and weaknesses, admirable traits and flaws, he or she may become quite angry at being short-changed. Unless the fantasy is tempered with reality, the ire of not having one's dream fulfilled can become pervasive and stir up much resentment about what one does not have rather than savoring and building upon what one does have. Fortunately, many people recognize the unreality of their childhood and adolescent fantasies and accept their partner lovingly as a person who has the entire gamut of emotions, a large repertoire of behaviors and interests, and a separate self that will become close but not symbiotically enmeshed. The prognosis for this latter group of achieving a long-term satisfying marriage is much higher (Kaslow & Hammerschmidt, 1992; Sharlin, 1996).

Others enter marriage feeling empty and desperately hope their partner will quickly and repeatedly fill in the void. They often come from homes in which their affective, physical, spiritual, or intellectual needs were not met. Their home may have been characterized by physical, emotional or sexual abuse; parental absenteeism and/or neglect; substance abuse; poverty and/or homelessness; or great wealth being substituted for love and nurturance. They come into marriage very needy and expect their partner to be all giving; to play the multiple roles of spouse, lover, parent, best friend, caretaker and protector, playmate, and confidante, and to know exactly when to switch into the role they need to comfort and fulfill them. This is, of course, virtually impossible. Frequently, the person they gravitated toward and who was attracted to them shares similarities in key areas. Whether this is conceptualized in Bowenian terms (1988) that people tend to pick a partner at the same level of individuation from their family of origin, or Whitaker's enigmatic idea that in marriage all things are equal (Whitaker & Bumberry, 1988), it becomes apparent that at any moment in time that we select a partner, we choose a person who embodies exactly what we need, consciously or unconsciously, at that point in time. Often potential mates understand the needs very well, because they have a similar family background and similar or interlocking needs. The opposite may also be true; that is, they select someone who seems to come from a totally different background into which they can escape. If both feel deprived, neither may have enough to give to the other for them to feel nurtured and satisfied. Sometimes, the opposite occurs and one is a rescuer and overfunctioner and the other has been a victim who wants to be taken care of. This frequently gets presented in therapy as follows:

One partner's litany is, "I never get enough"—be it attention, understanding, money, assistance with chores/work/children. The other spouse states, with equally great frustration, "No matter how much I give, it's never enough." Or "Nothing I do is appreciated; all I get is criticism."

Eventually, if the giver wants the "I give, you take" equation to become more reciprocal (i.e., to shift to we both give and we both receive), the more needy partner may feel even more depleted at the thought of having to give from his or her very limited emotional reservoir. The wrath incurred when one is unable to acquire what he or she so desperately needs can be overwhelming to the partner and, at times, to the therapist, especially if the patient has a borderline personality (Lachkar, 1992; Solomon, 1996). These are among the most difficult couples to treat in marital therapy; one or both may decide they have no choice but to end the marriage, and therapy may get converted into divorce therapy.

Others become disaffected when they realize the person they are living with is quite different from (their image of) the person with whom they fell in love. The person may have been secretive about an addiction, about prior involvement in a criminal lifestyle, about an out-of-wedlock child or an abortion, or about a history of serious mental illness in the family. The partner may feel that he or she has been duped and that the secrecy about salient factors in the other's background does not bode well for building and having a trusting relationship based on integrity and open communication. He or she may not be able to forgive this "sin of omission" and may decide that divorce is a preferable option to living with someone who has been deliberately deceitful.

Then there are the more usual reasons given for partners dissolving their union—including sexual incompatibility, in-law problems, disagreements over money, childrearing and/or values and lifestyle differences, and religious differences. Often the specific issues identified mask the deeper level conflicts, which are about power and control: Who will get their way? Who will establish dominance, and how? Is the passive control more insidious and hard to deal with than are the active, aggressive mechanisms (Kaslow, 1983; Parsons & Wicks, 1983)? In therapy, one should get beneath the superficial battlegrounds on which the power machinations get played out, and determine what is really causing the repetitive discord. One goal may be to see if the couple can find a way to share or rotate the power, as appropriate, and move toward a win-win modus operandi rather than a win-lose imbalance of power. For this to occur, it is essential that both partners be interested in a more egalitarian relationship, or if they want a complementary relationship contingent on a power differential, that this is acceptable to both and can be renegotiated if it ceases to be so.

One's involvement in an affair is a precipitant of many marital crises and is another precursor to divorce. The converse is also true; this behavior can signify the marriage is already headed for a breakup and one or both partners are seeking excitement, understanding, or ego gratification outside of the marriage. There have been several substantial books that categorize affairs (Brown, 1991; Pittman, 1989), and describe the dynamics and impact these extramarital dalliances have on all whose lives are touched by this behavior. The affair, often clandestine, can initially be enticing, fabulous, and fun (Kaslow, 1993a) for the infidel, and be experienced by the cuckolded partner (Lusterman, 1998) as a total violation of the covenant of marriage and as an unforgivable betrayal of love and trust. Some couples consider the affair and what it has meant to both of them and can work through the hurt, pain, and rage it has caused. The unfaithful partner needs to acknowledge and take responsibility for his or her desires and actions, and ultimately apologize for the hurt caused and damage wrought. The betrayed partner also needs to address any contribution he or she may have made to their spouse's discontent in the arena of not being available emotionally and/or sexually because of (over) absorption in vocational or avocational pursuits, children, school, or friends. Although they can argue this would not justify as extreme a measure as resorting to an affair, if the errant partner has tried to discuss his or her distress or indicated that the distance within their relationship is widening and they should do something about it, but these pleas have fallen on deaf ears, both members of the marital dyad have contributed to the triangulation and turning outward, albeit in very different ways.

Sometimes one or both partners do not wish to try to move beyond the affair and build a better and different marriage. Their love for each other, at least from the unfaithful partner to the (assumed) faithful one, may have diminished and cannot be rekindled. Or the spouse who feels rejected and humiliated may believe he or she can never forgive or trust again. If a child is born from the extramarital involvement, this adds an additional layer of complexity (Kaslow, 1993) that is often insurmountable. An affair that started as a casual diversion can become an important, serious relationship and provide the momentum for someone to depart from a marriage that is no longer satisfying. Or it can cause the couple to reassess their marriage and make a commitment to improving it so both will be much more satisfied, content, sensitive to each other, and trustworthy. When the former is the case, even the best therapy may not be able to help them repair the damage wrought, and divorce becomes the route taken. The rage over the betrayal runs too high and hot.

Children may be drawn into the fray and take a stance against the "wicked" affairee, whom they blame for tearing their family asunder. Often it is too difficult to believe that one's parent has cheated voluntarily, so the onus is projected onto the lover for having cast a spell over the parent (attribution to magic, not participatory choice).

Until several decades ago, most states officially decried adultery and considered it grounds for a "fault" divorce. Part of the legal punishment, which undergirded the moral ethos, was that the adulterer, if male, might have to pay more alimony than might otherwise be meted out, or if female, the amount of alimony might be less money or not granted at all. *The Scarlet Letter* (Hawthorne, 1850) was not laid to rest in Salem centuries ago.

Couples further sever their ties when one partner moves out and into his or her own living quarters (sometimes with one's own parents). This makes the impending divorce more public. The children become more fully aware of what is transpiring and have to cope with the reality of "heart surgery of the family," their reactions to this massive procedure, and questions from their friends. Concern over "what's going to happen to me" or "what will the implications be for my future" enter consciousness, no matter what the age of the child. Unquestionably, the divorce will cause major changes in their lives and these repercussions will be experienced for many years into the future.

When one really decides the emotional attachment is gone and the marriage is irretrievably broken and beyond repair, there is little the other can do to salvage it and make it a happy relationship. The other spouse may become symptomatic with a psychosomatic illness, withdraw, become depressed, and/or threaten suicide if left, and this may serve to keep the partner physically in the home a little longer. However, eventually, if the person who wants to leave is determined enough, he or she will leave what they have come to regard as imprisonment, once the coercive threat becomes less ominous.

The G Case*

The G's were referred by her psychiatrist for couple therapy. They had relocated from Chicago to South Florida several years prior to coming to see me. Mr. G was still involved in his business up north. He resided with his wife every third or fourth weekend in Florida and joined her to attend major functions with family and friends. She did not wish to return to Chicago and he had no desire to relocate totally. He was still vigorous and business oriented. He also was "tired of his critical, never satisfied, demanding wife" and believed he had "served out his term" (implied prison) waiting until the children were grown up and had moved out of their house before he made clear his intention to get divorced. He did this early in the session when queried as to why he wanted to begin therapy at this time. Mrs. G crossed her arms and stated icily, "There's no way I will let you divorce me." He retorted, "I've talked to lawyers in Illinois and Florida, and I can file and ultimately attain a divorce, even if you don't want one." She became infuriated and screamed, "Never! You can't do this to me. You can live a separate life, have a girlfriend in Chicago, even travel with her. But you will continue to support me and come here once a month and pretend we are still a happily married couple. I don't want to go from being 'Mrs. Somebody' to being 'Miss Nobody'. I won't let you do this to me." He tried to de-escalate by answering calmly but firmly, stating, "You can no longer badger and threaten me. You've always gotten your way. Now I want some pleasure and enjoyment in life and I don't have that with you." She stood up in a rage and screamed, "If you persist, I will commit suicide tomorrow. I already have enough pills. I will call each of the children tonight and tell them you are killing me and I will say good-bye to them and they will hate you. I cannot be divorced and live." There was something chilling in her threat and he cowered. Asked if he thought she might carry it out, he nodded, looking rejected and defeated. I asked if he felt he could cope with the suicide and he said, "No, she would make the burden of guilt impossible to bear." Instead he acquiesced and accepted her terms of living separate lives most of the time, maintaining the pretense of marriage, and being involved in an extramarital liaison if he so chose.

The next day I spoke to the referring psychiatrist. He concurred that she was desperate enough to commit suicide and that, despite his empathy for the husband, this was obviously not the time for him to seek his freedom. We both doubted she would ever let go. As this case illustrates, the only way he could depart would be with the risk of her suicide hanging over him. There are times we can neither do marital nor divorce therapy if the impasse is so entrenched that it defies being responsive to any interventions; that is, no therapeutic wizardry is potent enough when someone is determined to hang on at all costs.

The short-term and long-term impact and emotional and financial sequelae of divorce vary markedly depending on numerous variables. Basic demographic data on three drastically different families drawn from my clinical files are presented below. Although they share the unitary event of a divorce of the adult couple in 1999, the ages, ethnic/cultural and religious backgrounds, socioeconomic status, and family compositions differ. It is not hard to deduce that they perceive and are dealing with the experience differently, and that divergent outcomes are predictable (Table 17.2).

---

* All case material has been carefully camouflaged so that the original parties involved are unrecognizable.

TABLE 17.2 Family 1—Marriage of 2 years

Members	Age	Occupation	Income	Race	Religion	Ethnic/Cultural Background
Henry	27	Engineer	$60,000	C	Episcopal	Both born in U.S.
Sheila	24	Teacher	$32,000	C	Methodist	

Given the short duration of their marriage, the fact that each is already employed in the career of choice, that there are no children, and both have grown up in the community in which they are residing at the time of their divorce and their respective families live there also, they feel confident that all will go well postdivorce and they will quickly re-enter the singles scene. Both believe they made a mistake and that they are cutting their losses by dissolving their union quickly. They are sorry, but there is no deep grief or projection of blame onto the other. Henry and Sheila are high-functioning young adults who should do well. Couples therapy was brief and was followed by an individual wrap-up session with each that was devoted to considering "where to from here." They attended two mediation sessions and were able to come to agreement quickly on the division of assets (Table 17.3).

Mr. R has adapted well to South Florida and is glad he has relocated. His wife longs to return to Buenos Aires; she misses her family of origin and homeland. He has learned to speak English fluently; she still speaks mostly Spanish. She works in an import-export firm where many of the letters and other documents are written in Spanish, so this is not an obstacle in her job. She does not like the freedom accorded the children in the United States and abhors their sassy, assertive behavior. Mr. R continues to adhere to the prerogatives of his machismo background (Comas-Diaz, 1996) while espousing equality and pushing his shy wife to work longer hours and earn more money. He has a girlfriend and is quite indiscreet, believing he is entitled to this extramarital pleasure. Felicia cannot tolerate this betrayal and feels alone and abandoned. Despite their Catholic upbringing, Guillermo would welcome a divorce but insists his wife may not take the children and move back to Argentina as they need to be near their *padre*. At the inception of therapy Felicia was despondent and confused; she spoke softly—trying desperately to conceal her hurt, rage, and financial worries about her future. Therapy is protracted, given the numerous issues that abound in this tale of the conflict between two sets of values and the pull between two countries and two desired lifestyles. What is clear is Mr. G's stubbornness and his willingness to stay married but only on his terms with no complaints or criticisms from

TABLE 17.3 Family 2—Marriage of 14 years

Members	Age	Occupation	Income	Race	Religion	Ethnic/Cultural Background
Guillermo R	43	Construction Business	$50,000	C	Catholic	Hispanic from Argentina
Felicia R	38	Secretary (part-time)	$10,000	C	Catholic	Hispanic from Argentina
Jesus	12	School	—	C	Catholic	Emigrated to U.S. 5 years before divorce
Consuelo	10	School	—	C	Catholic	Emigrated to U.S. 5 years before divorce
Arturo	7	School	—	C	Catholic	Emigrated to U.S. 5 years before divorce

Felicia. She feels trapped in the image of a good wife and by the dictates of her antidivorce brand of Catholicism. The children are exposed to much tension and many arguments, and have grown fearful about what will happen to them. A visit here by a parent from Argentina has been recommended so they can provide support and be parties to the future planning so that Felicia knows what she can expect from her extended family (Table 17.4).

Jacob had been brought from Russia to the United States when he was 10 years old. A bright, inquisitive, and ambitious child, he learned quickly and excelled in school. His father had gradually progressed from selling small items from a pushcart in Manhattan to opening a retail store. Jacob joined him after finishing 2 years of college; they expanded until they had four stores in suburban New York towns. He retired at age 60 and relocated to Florida.

He had met, fallen in love with, and married Sophia when she was 19 years old and a college freshman. She graduated just before their first son was born and became a home-maker and devoted mother for the next 20 years, and she enabled her husband to grow his business. She enjoyed her life and when she decided that she wanted a fourth child, prefer-ably another daughter, and they could not conceive any more, she courageously decided to adopt a foreign orphan. The family had handled the issues of becoming and being a bicul-tural unit very well, although sometimes Jacob intimated he would have preferred a child of their own faith and color.

When Kim entered nursery school, Sophia decided to pursue another of her personal dreams and enrolled in law school. Jacob was surprised; he was also proud of his wife. Upon graduation she got a position with a well-respected law firm in New York and was made a partner within 3 years. When her husband was ready to relocate, it did not pose a problem for her since her firm had several branch offices in Florida.

However, once they settled in and her husband began spending his time playing golf, bridge, and poker, Sophia began to find her husband's life and conversation boring. Her career was in ascendance and she loved the professional terrain. She craved the challenges of being a litigator and could not understand how her husband could be content playing all day "with the boys" and no longer being part of the business world. The gulf between them widened and Sophia began talking about wanting a divorce. Jacob and all of the children, except Kim, found the idea unfathomable. Sophia had always put everyone else's needs before her own and they were astounded by her enormous ambition, which had not been expressed until her 40s. Jacob did not want to lose his beloved Sophia; neither did he want to return to the workaday world. Sophia was now earning more per year than Jacob had made, and liked earning her income and spending much of it as she desired. She saw her world as expanding and her husband's as shrinking. She dreaded being confined in even a

TABLE 17.4   Family 3—Married 38 years

Members	Age	Occupation	Income	Race	Religion	Ethnic/Cultural Background
Jacob	65	Retired retail store owner	$25,000	C	Jewish	Russian
Sophia	57	Attorney	$185,000	C	Jewish	United States
Ephraim	35	Attorney	$70,000	C	Jewish	United States
Rachel	32	Cantor	$30,000	C	Jewish	United States
Mendel (Manny)	29	Physician	$50,000	C	Jewish	United States
Kim	25	Writer	$15,000	Asian	Buddhism	Korean

very beautiful gated golf club community, and had come to realize she and Jacob were no longer compatible. Despite her gratitude for many good decades of marriage and family life, Sophia grew up during the heady days of the women's liberation movement and now she wants to strike out on her own.

It is likely that divorce will at first be devastating to Jacob, but he will soon be sought after by many divorced and widowed women in his community. The grown children will miss receiving what they expected to from the traditional grandmother they thought Sophia would become, but they all adore and respect her and will probably come to accept this other dynamic aspect of their mother, the lawyer.

Given the extent of variables in each of these three family constellations, it is not hard to fathom why the outcomes will vary so greatly.

II. THE LEGAL DIVORCE—A TIME OF TURBULENCE, CONSTERNATION, AND HEARTBREAK

In the United States for a marriage to be legitimized there must be a document granted by the civil authorities that legally recognizes and sanctions the union and serves as a contract of commitment. The actual marriage ceremony may be performed by a justice of the peace or other duly designated civil official, or a minister, priest, or rabbi. If an ordained religious leader officiates, the requisite civil documents must still be acquired, signed, and witnessed. If the couple opts to have a religious ceremony to solemnize their vows, then their covenant is also religiously sanctioned. But the religious ceremony is insufficient in the absence of the necessary civil documents; the reverse is not true, in keeping with the precept of separation of church and state.

Any and all of these contracts will shape the nature of the relationship the couple will evolve (Kaslow, 1999). Once they are wed, the state will not intrude upon the couple or their family if they pay their taxes and do not come to the court's attention because someone has filed charges against them or because they engage in an action, such as adoption or divorce, that brings them under the court's jurisdiction. A religious divorce (such as an annulment in the Catholic church or a *Get* in Orthodox Judaism [Schwartz & Kaslow, 1997]) may be required by their church or synagogue before they can remarry, but it is not deemed sufficient for one to be considered divorced by the state. As with marriage, one must also obtain a civil, legal decree.

Civil law, which encompasses family law, is partially derived from criminal law. As such, it has been predicated upon the assumption that there are both a guilty and an innocent party, or a perpetrator and a victim, and that the one adjudicated guilty should be punished and/or pay some kind of damages to the aggrieved victim. This belief system is congruent with Aristotelian logic, which is predicated on the supposition that causality is linear. When extrapolated and applied in divorce cases, traditionally this has meant that one partner has had to bear the blame for what went amiss in the marriage (i.e., to be held responsible for the demise of their union).

Adversarial Divorces—Litigated Win-Lose Battles

Once women ceased to be regarded as chattel of their husbands (19th Amendment to the Constitution, 1920) and were accorded recognition as separate entities under law entitled to rights of their own, a shift took place from the presumption that fathers should retain custody of children after divorce to a standard of maternal preference. This eventuated from a confluence of many factors after centuries of patriarchal supremacy and legal entitlement. These forces included (1) the expansion and strong impact of ideas based on psychoanalytic theory brought to the United States by analysts trained in Germany and Austria who promulgated the importance of the formative early childhood years and the centrality of the mother-child bond in fostering a child's healthy development (Brenner, 1955; Freud, 1933); (2) the translation of this developmental attachment theory concept into the legal doctrine of the tender years; that is, that a child belongs primarily with his or her mother until age 7 unless there are mitigating circumstances, like prostitution or insanity; and (3) the transformation of our society from a basically agricultural economy, where fathers worked on the family farm and extended families lived together in kinship arrangements so that a grandmother or an aunt was available to care for children if the mother were absent, to a predominantly industrial society composed of small nuclear family units living in cities. With the advent of industrialization, men worked long hours in plants and factories, spent a great deal of time commuting to and from work, and left their wives at home alone for long hours to care for the children. The father's role as a participant in his children's daily lives decreased markedly. The easy access to loving relatives also diminished as extended family members no longer lived together or nearby.

During the next five to six decades, almost invariably custody of children was granted to their mothers upon divorce, since mothers had become the main nurturing parent. Generally, since the man was the only or major income producer, attorneys for the wives sought to prove the husbands guilty of something serious in order to obtain the largest possible settlement for wives so they and the children would be well provided for and mothers could save face and retain their dignity if they were the rejected and abandoned parties (Kaslow, 1999). A man adjudicated guilty was mandated to pay child support and often lifelong spousal support or alimony also (terms will be used interchangeably). The objective of most women and their lawyers was to garner the biggest possible settlement. Knowing that this is what was likely to happen, the goal of the man's attorney was to retain as big a portion of the extant assets for him as was possible. The battle over the division of tangible and intangible assets often dragged on for many years in protracted, costly, and emotionally debilitating legal battles. Periodic demeaning interactions produced bitterness, pettiness, and retaliatory behaviors. The continuing warfare impeded each party's ability to arrive at closure to the relationship and to seek a more satisfying life beyond divorce.

Often children became the pawns on the divorce battlefield, being drawn in to take sides. Not infrequently, the custodial parent curtailed visitation if the noncustodial parent did not send the check(s) that were due. Sometimes the noncustodial parent disappeared or faded out of the child's life, for such reasons as (1) it was too painful to be so peripheral; (2) the custodial parent made contact and involvement so difficult; or (3) he or she did not want continuing financial or emotional responsibility to interfere with his or her new life. Such behaviors were detrimental to the well-being of children and exasperated those who viewed what was transpiring.

When a father desired and thought he warranted being the custodial parent, or wanted to punish his wife by taking the children away from her, almost invariably he was counseled by his lawyer not to expend time and money to wage a court battle since his chances of winning were negligible. (The movie *Kramer v. Kramer* demonstrated the centrality of the concept of the tender years and the principle of maternal preference that guided judges' verdicts during this time frame.)

From about 1920 to 1970, if both spouses agreed to getting a divorce, they could not file for a no-fault, uncontested divorce. During that era divorce was still construed to mean one partner was at fault, or guilty, and therefore had to be held accountable. "No fault" was not yet an accepted concept or doctrine; rather, mutual agreement to divorce was deemed an illegal collusion. Thus couples who wanted to terminate their marriage resorted to deciding jointly who would file for divorce, who would be designated the guilty party, and what the alleged grounds would be. Legally stipulated grounds included, depending on state variations, adultery, alcoholism, mental cruelty, mental illness, and prostitution. If someone wanted a divorce badly enough, he or she might confess to a behavior that had never taken place. This could mean a mandate for the male to pay life-long alimony as a way of atoning for ostensible transgressive behavior. Conversely, as a consequence, a female might forfeit alimony in order to obtain freedom from an abusive or otherwise intolerable spouse.

Judges, reflecting the mores of society, often held that a man had an obligation to pay permanent support to his ex-wife. This coincided with women's beliefs that they were entitled to this income because they had given birth to and raised their ex-husband's children, kept a home for him, and perhaps enabled him to build his career. When a man could not afford to shoulder this permanent indebtedness, he might resort to vanishing. Some men settled in other countries and camouflaged their identities. Their children were the main victims, losing all contact with their fathers and often being subjected to the fallout from their mother's dire downward spiraling financial plight.

A third significant shift in ideas and ideals about divorce, custody, child support, alimony, and property distribution occurred during the 1970s and early 1980s. The doctrine of the "best interest of the child" (Goldstein, Freud, & Solnit, 1973) had finally taken hold (Florida, 1982, 1992). This highlighted the importance of perceiving the child's needs as primary. Child advocates and many mental health professionals posited that if a child's needs and a parent's rights and desires conflicted, the child's needs were to be considered paramount. Ironically, because most children have no voice or representation in adversarial divorce proceedings (and often none is needed) unless there is a court-appointed child advocate or guardian ad litem, which is a rarity, what is in their best interest may not be what is prescribed in the prevailing guidelines, like visiting one parent every other weekend and one night per week. It can be too little if the parent is very involved positively, and too much if the parent is an addict, abusive, or emotionally detached. It is rarely clear who is to determine what the best interest is—the judge, one parent, a custody evaluator, a therapist, or the lawyers.

Mediation Erupts on the Scene

In light of the horrendous repercussions of hundreds of thousands of acrimonious divorces following World War II, many therapists and lawyers recognized the dire need for something different and kinder, a more equitable and benign pathway through divorce. O. James Coogler, an Atlanta, Georgia, based lawyer, who underwent his own disastrous marital breakup in the 1970s, also recognized that there had to be a more humane way to end a marriage legally. He pioneered the evolution of such a process and founded the contemporary divorce mediation movement. His seminal book, *Structural Mediation in Divorce Settlement* (Coogler, 1978), was greeted enthusiastically by those who were seeking an alternative dispute resolution process for marital dissolution. Some therapists, clergy, and attorneys who heard about his work went to him for training in what was originally an apprentice model. Soon Coogler and his followers, including John Haynes (1981, 1982), Steven Erickson (Erickson & McKnight, 1988), and Will Neville (1984) began doing formal training and writing about their work, thereby disseminating the substantive information and necessary how-to skills quite widely. In the past two decades the number of publications have proliferated (see for example, *Family Mediation Quarterly,* 1983 to present), and mediations occur quite frequently.

The majority of mediators hold degrees in law or one of the mental health professions. In addition, by the mid-1980s several graduate programs emerged that grant degrees in mediation. Mediation has become a viable and more peaceful pathway through and beyond divorce. The key principles of mediation, initially articulated by Coogler, have been elaborated subsequently by many leading practitioners in the field (Folberg & Milne, 1988; Gold, 1992; Kaslow, 1988, 1990, 1999; Marlow, 1992; Marlow & Sauber, 1990). These include:

- Negotiating in good faith
- Full disclosure of assets
- Empowering both parties to speak on their own behalf
- Belief in the clients' ability to know their own and their children's best interests and to make wise decisions on their own behalf
- Seeking a win-win collaborative and equitable agreement
- Sharing of the cost of the mediator's services
- Giving real attention to the best interests of the child
- That either party or the mediator can terminate the process if they do not believe it is progressing in a positive and fair direction

These precepts were and are compatible with the principles of no fault divorce that were then evolving throughout the United States and that were eclipsing the earlier doctrine of "fault" divorce. They are also congruent with the basic premises of family systems theory that rests on circular or curvilinear rather than linear logic, and thereby posits that both members of the pair contribute to its dynamics and functioning and, by extension, to its disintegration.

Ideally, negotiations within mediation take place between the separating partners and the mediator, who functions as a neutral, objective third party in the sessions, promoting understanding, encouraging compromise and tradeoffs, fostering good will, and fashioning mini-agreements on each issue. Mediators who still practice in accordance with the original philosophy and ideals dub their approach client-centered mediation (Erickson & McKnight, 1998, 2000). This is an empathic and focused conflict resolution process utilized to arrive at an agreement. The parties are encouraged to brainstorm solutions to each concern that is raised; the mediator may suggest other alternatives also. Cooperation, mutual consideration, and respect are fostered.

Another approach is transformative mediation (Bush & Folger, 1994). Adherents believe that this approach enables the parties to transform their relationship so that they can become better attuned to each other and build a positive relationship to carry them into the postdivorce era. Underlying assumptions are that clients are well informed about themselves and can be considerate toward one another. This style seeks to help clients strive for wholeness and emotional health; its goals and techniques are congruent with those of many psychotherapy approaches. It is a more free-flowing strategy than the client-centered approach (Erickson & McKnight, 2000), but also emphasizes empowering and encouraging clients to be proactive in making their own decisions rather than relying on lawyers or a judge to do this for them.

There is another very different school of mediation called "muscle mediation." Practitioners of this genre go beyond suggesting options to placing pressure on the disputants to make specific choices quickly. This jeopardizes the client's right to self determination and appears to be in contradiction to the very respectful value base of mediation.

In some states mediation has become increasingly legalistic during the last decade and the contribution of mediators drawn from the mental health disciplines has been denigrated. To illustrate, in Florida court-based mediators and those who receive referrals from court mediation offices must be certified and recertified by the Florida Supreme Court. Some jurisdictions urge that the disputants' respective attorneys participate in the mediation conferences, which often means the mediator negotiates between the attorneys and not between the divorcing couple. Like muscle mediation, this goes counter to the precept that mediation empowers the couple to speak and act on their own behalf in making decisions that will profoundly affect the rest of their lives. It also makes mediation much more costly.

When the lawyers are present and/or muscle mediation techniques are employed, mediations tend to become more adversarial in tone and content, and far less cooperative than client-centered or transformative mediations. The latter two types are geared to crafting an agreement that the two parties and their significant others, especially their children, will view as their own and as a positive road map for the future. In states where financial affidavits are expected to be attached to the mediated memorandum of understanding that goes to the attorneys for finalization into a marital settlement agreement, the mediation process is a less voluntary one and comes to resemble the discovery aspect of a litigated divorce rather than the agreed upon good faith and full disclosure procedures of client-centered mediation.

Some arbitrators also conduct divorce mediations. Although they may try to accomplish as much as possible by nonbinding arbitration, at times the contract has a clause giving the arbitrator the authority to make binding decisions on any issues on which the spouses cannot reach accord. People who do not wish to take total responsibility for what happens to them so they can blame someone else instead, like a judge or arbitrator, may prefer transferring final decision-making authority to another. For them, binding arbitration may be an acceptable, less anxiety-producing highway to divorce.

Given the many variations in mediation practice, it is incumbent upon mediators to tell consumers what their orientation is so they can decide if the mediator's approach is congruent with what they are seeking. Clients should feel free to ask about the practitioner's philosophy and style, as well as about fees and how these are to be paid. Generally, what occurs in mediation is held to be confidential. No records similar to therapy notes are made; one only records the mini-agreements evolved in each session. Since many mediators request financial statements and write up everything in triplicate, all involved have copies of what they need throughout the negotiations. The parties can provide these to their lawyers if they choose to, or can ask the mediator to send the mini-agreements arrived at in each session, as well as the final memorandum of understanding.

Whenever couples engage in acrimonious divorce actions, the embitterment and rage felt are likely to be emotionally debilitating to them and their children for years to come. These are the couples who frequently return to court seeking retribution. They cannot let go and move on; instead they wreak havoc within themselves, toward each other, their children, and in the courts. Whenever possible, such warfare should be avoided. Since therapists are often consulted by clients embarking on divorces, it behooves them to be aware of the different options their clients can select to deal with the legalities so they are equipped to help them sort through what is likely to be most ego syntonic and fruitful for them.

III. Economic and Financial Issues

The major categories of financial issues that must be dealt with and resolved are (1) property settlement and the division of all tangible and intangible assets; (2) child support; and (3) spousal support or alimony. The tax implications of any plans being devised must be calculated to ascertain which plan will permit maximum assets to be retained now and to accrue in the future to the couple. Since there are various ways to slice up the economic pie, the one chosen should be that which leaves the largest amount of money and property in the hands of the family. Since money also has emotional value and is perceived as being related to status and personal worth, this subject is often highly charged and explosive. Objective advice from a knowledgeable tax attorney or accountant should be sought whenever such issues come to the fore. Discussions should be anchored in financial realities like tax returns and ongoing fixed expenses, while taking account of emotional wish lists.

All assets and liabilities must be disclosed and calculated, including but not limited to real estate holdings, certificates of deposit, stocks and bonds, mutual funds, coin and other collections, jewelry, items such as boats or horses, individual retirement accounts, and profit sharing and pension plans. Liabilities encompass all debts, including credit card bills. Provisions need to be made regarding items to be sold and those that need to be transferred from joint names (tenants by the entirety) to single name.

Intertwined with concerns about parenting, residence, and visitation is the matter of child support. Our society posits that children should be maintained at the same socioeconomic level postdivorce as predivorce. Yet, except in very affluent families, this is not possible; when the family income has to be divided and shared by two single-parent households neither will have as much as the couple did preseparation. Questions about what child support is to cover, how often it is to be paid, and whether it is to be lowered during periods of time when the children are staying with the nonresidential payor parent for longer than a week, need to be addressed. This should be handled calmly, with the mediator or lawyers providing information, if requested, about how others have resolved these issues successfully. In jurisdictions where there are child support guidelines (Schwartz & Kaslow, 1997), couples should use these to keep their discussions tied to the legal expectations, with flexibility exercised if there are extenuating circumstances such as a chronically ill child or an incapacitated parent. Use of these external guidelines can neutralize controversies about what is a fair amount to be paid.

It is crucial to bear in mind that the end point of the legal and economic phases are not co-terminus. The legal divorce ends the day the final decree is issued by the judge. The economic divorce is not final until:

1. The period for payment of child support comes to its predetermined end. For example, if a couple divorces in 1999 and their youngest child is then 2 years old, whatever child support has been awarded, plus increases granted, would have to be paid by the wealthier ex-spouse to the less affluent parent, if he or she is decreed the primary parent, until 2015 in those states in which the age of legal majority is 18 years of age. If special circumstances exist, such as with a mentally retarded or severely physically handicapped child, the payment of child support may have been awarded for as long as the payor parent lives. Once mandated child support payments end, money can be

provided directly to the child by the former payor parent, or if he or she decided to cover post-secondary school expenses by sending tuition directly to the educational institution, such payments no longer fall within the category of child support.

2. The period stipulated for payment of spousal support runs out. As mentioned earlier, in the United States until the 1970s, alimony was usually permanent. It did not cease until either of the parties died or the recipient spouse remarried. Thus if a pair were divorced when the woman was 40 years of age and both lived into their 70s, the man had to continue supporting his ex-wife for more years than he had been married to her. Yet she offered him nothing in return once the children were out of the home. Scores of men believed this to be unfair; they could not fathom why the ongoing obligation was non-reciprocal. If the man remarried, often he was supporting two women; how odd to be mandated to commit economic bigamy when bigamy is illegal! (Kaslow, 1999)

In the past four decades women sought equality in all domains of life, and multitudes entered the paid work force as competent employees and independent professionals, earning their own incomes and making their own investments. In response, many men objected to having to pay spousal support ad infinitum. They believed that if divorce was no longer interpreted as the end result of a conflict between a guilty and an innocent party, and took place within a no fault context, then continuous spousal support could only be justified for women who were either incapacitated or who were elderly, lacked salable skills, and were (probably) unemployable. Many state legislatures passed laws adding short-term or rehabilitative alimony as an option to be considered. When temporary alimony is awarded, it usually runs from 3 to 10 years, long enough for the youngest child to be in school full-time so the mother does not need to be home. She can take training or go to college to augment her skills and earning potential, or return directly to work if further schooling is not essential in her field. Sadly, many women still do not have the ability to earn a sufficient income to cover the amount lost when alimony ceases.

According to Weitzman (1985), women's and children's financial status deteriorates after divorce; that is, they are likely to slide downward on the socioeconomic ladder. Men are apt to remain at the same level or to move upward. It is apparent that in our laws, we still have not developed a formula that leads to a resolution that is fair to both ex-husbands and ex-wives. Although many postdivorce battles allegedly are waged about the children, it is the seething tensions about money that bubble beneath the surface and keep the fight raging. The disagreement may be over who is entitled to what, whether child support and alimony can and should be renegotiated, or how to get a resistant, incommunicado ex-spouse to pay what he (or she) owes (Palmer & Tangel-Rodriguez, 1995) short of threatening incarceration. Even if this eventuates, one cuts off his or her potential source of income, so it boomerangs. This is a terrible web in which all too many people get entangled.

The division of assets has to be completed before the divorce decree is issued. The property settlement, once finalized, is not renegotiable. Thus it must be well thought out. When a couple are poor, each will remain at the poverty level after divorce (unless a major change occurs in either of their lives). Still, they have to reach agreement on how they will pay off their debts and afford the costs of daily living. Those who have accumulated assets need to agree on how to divide these and how remaining liabilities will be defrayed. This all must occur within the parameters of the laws of their state. The vast majority of states adhere to the equitable distribution of property standard. Equitable means fair, not equal, and this leaves room for negotiation over entitlement, the relative value of what each has contributed to the marriage, about future earning potential, and the other's claim to future income. Other states are governed by a community property standard (i.e., the assets are jointly co-owned and must be equally divided—regardless of special needs or contributions). Each asset does not need to be partitioned in half; rather the total of the two halves distributed must be identical. Much resentment is engendered as one has to give up items of sentimental and monetary value and/or one finds that no matter what his or her beliefs and values, the ultimate authority to decide how much one receives or retains rests with the court and not with the parties to the dispute.

These three components of the financial picture should be carefully considered so that the final division of assets produces a fair and balanced package for each, although each of the segments may need to be deliberated separately and then reassessed in light of the totality.

When assets are substantial and the woman has good financial know-how and/or an expert financial advisor, she may be wise to opt for a larger up-front settlement instead of permanent alimony. This way she will acquire a lump sum that she can invest in a business, in real estate, or in securities, and perhaps garner more money over time than she would receive from spousal support. She can avoid becoming permanently financially dependent on her ex-mate and his payment vicissitudes. Once the funds are hers, they cannot be taken back. Conversely, if she is counting on receiving spousal support for the ensuing 20 to 30 years and the ex-husband dies in 3 years, the support she has assumed will continue will vanish and she has no recourse to her ex-husband's estate. She may fare well, however, if she remained his beneficiary on a large life insurance policy.

For the man who can handle it, a lump sum up-front settlement can also have definite advantages. He can be finished with spousal support payments much sooner, ending the sense of bondage many men face when they have to continue paying for the remainder of their lives. He then has more energy and a better outlook to become involved in building a new life postdivorce. The couple may be able to reach a compromise in which in return for his offering a substantial up-front settlement, she relinquishes all claims to his pension and/or retirement plan. For many men, being assured this asset will be wholly his provides a modicum of security.

If the woman is the wealthier party by virtue of her earnings, dividends from investments, or an inheritance, and she is the one paying child support and/or alimony, the same principles, assumptions, and considerations apply. Thus all decisions should be gender neutral. Such cases are occurring slightly more often now as an increasing portion of the wealth in this country is owned by women.

IV. CO-PARENTAL AND VISITATION ISSUES

Children need to be told about their parents' impending divorce as soon as the decision is definite and one parent is moving into separate living quarters. They should be protected against name calling, hearing and witnessing physical and verbal abuse, drunkenness, and other demeaning, frightening behaviors. It is best if the parents tell the children jointly what is going on and answer their questions together. The children will need to be reassured, perhaps repeatedly, that (1) it is not their fault and they are not to blame in any way; (2) there is nothing they can do to change their parents' decision and they should not try or feel responsible for keeping the family together; (3) both parents will continue to love them and be involved in their lives emotionally, physically and financially; (4) they will not be expected to take sides and are free to love both parents (and all grandparents); and (5) their lives will be disrupted as little as possible.

The children have a right to ask questions and express their own thoughts, feelings, and reactions, and should not be punished for their anger, tears, or withdrawal. As is indicated in Table 17.1, they may need therapy and it should be the treatment of choice at any moment during and after the divorce process—family therapy, parent-child therapy, individual child therapy, sibling group therapy, or children of divorce group therapy (Kessler & Bostwick, 1977; Roizblatt et al., 1990). All explanations and interventions should be age appropriate and tailored to the specific child.

Children need to derive some sense of security from having a schedule that is fairly predictable, yet still allows for flexibility of parents' needs occasionally to trade off when a child will be in residence. This can be emphasized in therapy and/or in mediation when the parents are discussing which homes will be the primary and secondary residences (see, e.g., Florida 1982, 1992), how and when shifts from one parent to the other will take place, and how to make certain that the transitions from one household to the other will be neither too often nor too disruptive. The adults should be encouraged to respect each other's parenting skills and to reinforce the image that each is a loving, caring parent who will remain involved with the child and will refrain from being critical of the other parent. Whenever possible, parents should continue to share the same activities with their progeny as before and share the best of themselves in their skills and talents. They need to work out a schedule for holidays and special occasions, like children's birthdays, mother's day, and father's day. They should understand that initially divorce for children is extremely traumatic and personal.

If there are three children of vastly different ages, such as 5 months, 3 years, and 8 years of age, three different parenting plans would be ideal. A 5-month-old infant who is being nursed should not be away from its mother for any prolonged period of time, nor should it be weaned abruptly. The father might have regularly scheduled brief visits between feedings until the child stops nursing, so that his son or daughter is familiar with him. Such visits need to be carried out in a way that is mutually acceptable, nonintrusive on the mother, and peaceful. The 3-year-old may or may not be ready to live part-time in two residences because he or she needs the security of living in one home. Overnight sleepaways may need to wait until the child is 5 years old and less attached to the mother. Being with the father can occur on day outings and visits, and on weeknights for dinner and playtime instead. Conversely, the 8-year-old may be quite ready and eager to spend every other weekend with the nonresidential parent, plus one or two nights per week. Working out the different schedules is a complicated task and has to take into account not only the ages and needs of the children, but also the parents' work schedules, availability to drive, and the other demands on their time. Sometimes it is not feasible and children will need to rotate back and forth as a unit, even if this is not the optimal plan for each developmentally.

Clinicians and mediators should counsel separating parents, based on their expertise in child development, that it is important to minimize the number of disruptions and changes the children have to handle at any one time. For instance, if the person designated the primary residential parent can remain in the family home for several years postdivorce, the children will not be faced with adapting to a new school and new friends at the same time they are losing one live-in parent. The professional may convey to them that sometime in the future the child may wish to spend more time with the nonresidential parent in order to get to know him or her better, or to have a fuller chance to identify with the same-sex parent. Reassurance that this frequently happens around early adolescence may offset the dismay if and when it occurs, and set the stage for their reworking the agreement later without the child having to cause "a crisis by getting into trouble by using drugs, truanting, developing anorexia or bulimia, or attempting suicide in order to have his or her needs attended to" (Kaslow, 1999). It is wise for the couple to agree to hold annual major conferences to review what is transpiring in their child's life and to consider whatever changes appear warranted. If they find later that they cannot discuss concerns that arise alone together, they can (re)enter therapy or mediation to resolve the dilemmas rather than engage in a new legal battle.

When mediation is the route taken to work out the divorce agreement, the importance of assessing the children's needs and how these are likely to change over the course of a child's normal development will be stressed. For example, the professional might point out that a 7-year-old child who eagerly anticipates going to his or her father's home alternate Fridays after school may wish at around age 12 years to have that schedule altered when he or she enters high school and Friday night is when football games and special peer group activities occur that he or she does not want to miss. If the parents are sensitive to the child's normal and predictable requests, the minor modifications necessary to change the starting time of visitation from Friday night to Saturday morning and the return from Sunday night to Monday morning will be made congenially without needing to resort to legal action. If, however, the former spouses are still embroiled in postdivorce squabbling, the father may perceive such a request as an attempt to interfere with his wishes and rights, and the result of his ex-wife's chronic efforts at parental alienation (Gardner, 1989; Palmer, 1988).

Children of divorce tend to fare reasonably well if their parents do (Wallerstein & Kelly, 1980); some report later that they have grown stronger, more independent, and more resilient from learning how to cope and survive the exigencies wrought by their parents' divorce. Others remain distraught, feeling that the whole world was shattered, often identifying with a parent who reacts in this way. It is incumbent upon lawyers, therapists, relatives, close neighbors, teachers, and others involved in the children's lives to listen to them, provide rational guidance and affection, and be patient and available to help them through the turbulence and confusion if the parents are too enmeshed in their problems to be accessible to the children. If they are loved, respected, and encouraged, and not used as pawns, they usually perk up and get back onto a healthy developmental track.

V. EXTENDED FAMILY, FRIENDS, AND COLLEAGUES: THE COMMUNITY AND PSYCHOSOCIAL ASPECTS

It is ironic and disconcerting that important interpersonal decisions and legal machinations must occur at the same time that the divorcing individuals are highly emotional, experiencing feelings including extreme pain, rage, hurt, disappointment, grief, confusion, uncertainty, and resentment (see Table 17.1). Yet they are supposed to act rationally since some of the choices they make now are irrevocable and will shape not only their futures, but those of their children and other valued family members. Probably they will impact on future partners also. How they behave now toward each other will also influence their postdivorce relationship. It will affect whether they will continue to wallow in self-pity and a desire to retaliate for the narcissistic and other wounds inflicted or whether they will be able to eventually reach beyond anger and arrive at a point of some acceptance and even forgiveness of their ex-spouse, so that they can achieve the requisite psychic closure to move on to a fruitful life beyond divorce (Schwartz & Kaslow, 1997).

Whether they act in ways that enhance self-respect and respect of the other will also determine their future ability to be in the same place simultaneously when, for example, their children are in athletic events or school performances, graduate from high school and college, get married, have babies, and celebrate other significant life events, or in times of stress, like when a child has surgery (Kaslow, 1999). There will also be reverberations with friends who may feel constrained about inviting them both to the same function. If the rift is intensified by meanness or deceit during the divorce proceedings, such behavior will interfere with everyone's postdivorce recovery.

During the time the details of the divorce agreement are being negotiated, opinions from others, solicited and unsolicited, are likely to be proffered. The couple may be deluged by suggestions from parents, friends, or colleagues as to what they should or should not do or agree to. Such gratuitous ideas may be offered by loving, well-intentioned people; nonetheless they can be a negative force because they add to the confusion and may stir up more animosity. Instead, the parting pair should tune into their own inner thoughts, feelings, and wishes, and determine what suits them and their circumstances, as each divorce is idiosyncratic and unique.

Throughout the divorce process, various forms of therapy (Table 17.1) can be beneficial to the several members of the parting family—separately or in different subsystem combinations. Therapy offers a haven in which distressed individuals can express the entire gamut of emotions, rational and irrational; the oscillating and inundating depressed moods; the sense of failure and decline of self-esteem; the wish for retribution against one's departing spouse; and the desires and fantasies for the future. Ideally the therapist encourages patients to consider the alternatives available as they progress toward creating and later implementing a sound agreement. The therapeutic focus may center on making the process as constructive and growth oriented as possible within the current situation.

Many divorced individuals report the three most arduous days in the divorce process are (1) the day they tell or are told by their partner that the marriage is irreparable and a divorce is imminent; (2) the day one of them moves out of the marital home, adding proof to the idea that the marriage is irretrievably broken; and (3) the day of the final court hearing.

Ironically, on the happy wedding day friends and family congregate to celebrate with the new couple, signifying their support of the union, and to wish them well. Usually many more people want to attend the festivities than either the bride or groom would like to have present. Conversely, the very unhappy day of the issuance of the legal divorce decree, even if some relief is experienced as when divorce marks the end of an abusive, turbulent, or intolerable marriage, is usually an ultralonely one. The divorcing person goes alone to court, accompanied only by his or her attorney, to face not only an unknown and unpredictable judge but also the soon to be ex-spouse with whom one once shared so many hopes and dreams. This is a day when close friends and relatives would be sagacious to rally around and offer to go along to court to make these last rites for the marriage easier. Perhaps they might also take the newly divorced person out for lunch or dinner afterwards to mark what is an auspicious occasion and transition that should not be spent alone, as if no one cares. Children might be included, too, as this day is also a significant occasion in their lives (Kaslow, 1999) and will have a long-lasting effect on what comes to pass based on the provisos that have been made for them for the present and into the future.

Friends who wish to be helpful should listen when the person wants to talk and complain, cry and bemoan his or her fate, or scream about many frustrations. They should be willing to share some silences when the distressed person needs quiet and to tolerate mood swings. They can make themselves available to go places and do things when the person is ready to, pushing this gently but not too much. Offers of child care from friends and family may be most welcome, so that the residential parent gets some respite from the constant demands of single parenthood without feeling guilty.

When necessary, family members might also offer financial assistance to tide someone over a rough period. Sometimes temporary shelter is needed and if it can be offered, perhaps with some outside time limit specified so the arrangement does not drag on, it can provide a most welcome and needed oasis.

Friends and colleagues are well advised not to stigmatize the divorcing/divorced person; there are enough problems to cope with without further loss of self-esteem. Critical statements such as "You should have" or "Why didn't you" cut too deep. Children's playmates and their parents can offer solace and comfort, as can the adult's peers and colleagues, by not excluding or ostracizing them. The more accepting and supportive people in their extended network are, the better and quicker the recuperation process. It is critical that divorcing family members, including children and senior generation parents, feel valued and respected and not "shunned."

Different work situations can exacerbate or ameliorate the pressures of divorce. When a particular profession or vocation has a basically antidivorce attitude, it adds to the negativity of this life process. A prime example is that of the clergyperson, who after much sturm and drang decides he or she can no longer survive in an intolerable marriage. Sometimes congregants censure the quest to escape and build a more fulfilling life. Other times officials in the church hierarchy decry the behavior and may go so far as to remove the person from his or her ministry—multiplying the losses experienced and becoming the extra stressor that breaks the person's spirit. What an anathema in light of the fact that religion and the church ostensibly are there to provide comfort and a safe haven in times of crisis. In my clinical practice, clergy of a variety of faiths have been among the most troubled and most abandoned divorcing/divorced patients with whom I have worked.

VI. SPIRITUAL/RELIGIOUS ASPECTS

As alluded to earlier, the majority of people have some religious component to their wedding, symbolizing that the marriage is consecrated in the eyes of God. Even if they do not adhere to all of the teachings of their religion, they see themselves as belonging and being blessed within their faith. When they decide to part, they also want their divorce to be deemed acceptable by their church. Since emotional health entails feeling an internal sense of coherence (Antonovsky, 1982), those who are rejected or extruded by their church for divorcing will be further ostracized and estranged from their heritage when they desperately need the church's support and guidance. Some divorced people leave the religion they were reared in, disillusioned by its rigid abhorrence of divorce. Often they have postponed the divorce longer than is tenable to avoid these grave consequences.

In recent decades liberal churches have been much more accepting of the reality of divorce and have even run groups for the newly single and for children of divorce. Such activities lend substance to the verbal acknowledgment that divorce is a viable choice.

Many individuals who have been married by a minister, priest, or rabbi want the divorce to be acknowledged in a religious as well as in a civil, legal procedure. Unfortunately, in some religions divorce is the only major life cycle event, happy or sad, for which there is no ritual or ceremony. It stands to reason that if divorce is not accepted as valid, and that one is expected to stay in a marriage and "turn the other cheek" no matter how horrid it is, then there will be no ritual to mark and ease the transition.

In the mid-1970s when some of my divorcing patients first brought the desire for such a ceremony to my attention, I searched the literature for this material; all I could find was reference to the *Get* ceremony performed by orthodox rabbis (see Schwartz & Kaslow, 1997 for information on this document). But at least this gave credibility to the recognized need for such a ceremony by one of the world's great religions. I asked some liberal Protestant clergy friends if they could and would compose such a ritual, and Henry Close, ThD, obligingly did (Close, 1977). Others found the idea farfetched at that time, although subsequently several denominations have developed religious divorce ceremonies.

In the interim, to respond to the longing of various patients to have such a ceremony administered, I created a therapeutic ceremony that participants have found to be quite spiritual and to have strong healing properties. It should not be utilized prior to 2 years after the legal divorce since it pushes the divorced parties to go beyond anger and incorporate the early good memories with the later bitter ones. Few people are able to do this even at the 2 year point; it is often advisable to wait a few years longer until they are ready for psychic closure. Even several decades later it can and has proven invaluable to the now adult children of divorce as they share with their parents how they felt when the divorce occurred, what they worried about, and what they would like from their parents now.

This quasi-spiritual therapeutic ceremony has turned out to be a brief, strategic, and profound healing instrument. It has also become an intervention I use for training of professionals who do divorce therapy and/or mediation which, even in a simulation, rapidly gets them in touch with the pain, pathos, and long-lasting resentments and sorrows that emanate from divorce. (See Kaslow, 1993b, for a full description of this divorce ceremony.) Religious leaders who attend have been deeply touched and some indicated they have later adapted the ceremony for use with their parishioners.

Many individuals find they must arrive at some inner peace as well as greater outer harmony with their children, former in-laws, and former spouse before recuperation and closure can be obtained. Thus the religious/spiritual aspect must be attended to by those to whom this matters, and its importance should not be denigrated by others who may be more agnostic or atheistic in their beliefs.

VII. The Psychic Divorce: Resolution, Moving Forward, and Life beyond Divorce

It is important that therapist, mediator, and lawyer fees be paid in full to add another note of closure, that all documents and property that need to be transferred into one name are, and that any other legal details be wrapped up as soon as possible. This helps one conclude the items that should be relegated to the past.

For adults who are reasonably healthy and have good recuperative powers, it takes from 2 to 5 years to feel optimistic and confident again and to move from living in and obsessing about the past, or the there and then, to concentrating on the present, or here and now, and be thinking about the future. It takes this long for any necessary relocations and job changes to take place, for the parenting/visitation schedule to be functioning well for all, for the adults to be dating if they wish to do so, and for them to risk being willing to trust again after having been hurt, disillusioned, and possibly betrayed. During this phase, the emotional tasks to be accomplished include rebuilding one's self-image and self-confidence, looking and feeling better physically, feeling good about one's skill and ability as a single parent, reaching acceptance about what has transpired, and reactivating old or developing new hobbies, activities, and friendships (Kaslow, 1999). If one is no longer comfortable in the mainly couples world they traveled in while married, he or she will have to form new friendships among single peers: the never married, divorced, or widowed. The divorced person may have more in common with them in terms of concerns about single parenting, visitation snags, vacations, and hobbies. Some divorced people remain involved with many of their married friends and continue to be included by them in social activities while also developing a network of single friends. Each person has to ascertain what works for him or her, and where and with whom they feel most welcome, stimulated, and content.

Ahrons and Rodgers (1987, pp. 114–121) have developed an illuminating typology depicting five relationship styles of former spouses. These are:

1. *Perfect pals:* Those who get along quite amicably and have decided to remain friends but did not wish to remain married to each other.
2. *Cooperative colleagues:* Those who are able to cooperate well as parents, but who do not see themselves as good friends.
3. *Angry associates:* Those who remain embittered and resentful toward one another and find co-parenting difficult. Their children often get "caught in their parents' struggles and experience ongoing loyalty conflicts."
4. *Fiery foes:* Those who are still so infuriated with one another, even many years post-divorce, that they are unable to co-parent. They cling to memories of all that went wrong and can recall nothing good in their marriage. Repeated legal battles are waged.
5. *Dissolved duos:* Those who discontinue all contact with the former spouse; usually one relocates quite a distance from the other, often disappearing totally from the family orbit.

We concur with this classification schema and note that children whose parents fall in types 1 and 2 are likely to fare best, while the prognosis for healthy development of the children diminishes markedly in categories 3 to 5. The adults should be apprised of this by any professionals involved in their lives so they will be aware of the chaos and damage they can cause. The goal of parenting classes instituted by many courts for divorcing couples has been to diminish such noxious and harmful attitudes and behaviors on the part of parents, who often claim to love their children.

Rapidly remarrying after divorce is usually not a good idea. Prior to the 2-year mark there is rarely enough closure on the prior spousal relationship to allow for a full commitment to a new partner, and too much residual hurt and hostility may spill over onto the new loved one. Then, too, if the current love affair predated the divorce and was one of the factors that ignited the divorce, one needs to be reasonably sure that the lover will also be the right spouse for him or her now that the secretive, forbidden fruit mystique no longer is operative. In addition, one is more likely to have to cope with intense resentment from the children if the betrothed is viewed as someone who tore their family asunder.

Ultimately most divorced people do decide to try again and remarry within 5 years of the divorce. It is valuable for a person considering remarriage to show his or her intended the marital settlement agreement since there is a legal, ethical, and existential commitment and obligation to fulfill it in terms of an ongoing financial and emotional investment in the children of the previous marriage(s) (Kaslow, 1993c) that predates the new relationship. Everyone involved should recognize the fact that although one is legally divorced from an ex-spouse, one is never legally (or financially) divorced from one's children.

Despite the complexities of the remarriage family (Visher & Visher, 1991), many do find great satisfaction in this new life after divorce. So do those who choose to remain single because they like the freedom and independence it affords. There is definitely life beyond divorce, and it can be happy, if one is willing to let go of the past and is proactive in creating the present and future.

REFERENCES

Ahrons, C. R., & Rodgers, R. H. (1987). *Divorced families: A multidisciplinary developmental view.* New York: Norton.

Antonovsky, A. (1982). *Unraveling the mystery of health.* San Francisco, CA: Jossey-Bass.

Bohannan, P. (1970). The six stations of divorce. In P. Bohannan (Ed.), *Divorce and after: An analysis of the emotional and social problems of divorce* (pp. 29–55). New York: Doubleday.

Bowen, M. (1988). *Family therapy in clinical practice* (2nd ed.). Northvale, NJ: Jason Aronson.

Brenner, C. (1955). *An elementary textbook of psychoanalysis.* New York: International Universities Press.

Brown, E. M. (1991). *Patterns of infidelity and their treatment.* New York: Brunner/Mazel.

Bush, R. A. & Folger, J. P. (1994). *The promise of mediation.* San Francisco, CA: Jossey-Bass.

Close, H. (1977, Spring). Service of divorce. *Pilgrimage, 5*(1), 60–66.

Comas-Diaz, L. (1996). Cultural considerations in diagnosis and treatment. In F. W. Kaslow (Ed.), *Handbook of relational diagnosis and dysfunctional family patterns,* (pp. 152–168). New York: John Wiley & Sons, Inc.

Coogler, O. J. (1978). *Structural mediation in divorce settlement.* Lexington, MA: D. C. Heath.

Courtois, C. A. (1988). *Healing the incest wounds: Adult survivors in therapy.* New York: Norton.

Erickson, S., & McKnight, M. (1998, July 8). *Academy of Family Mediators Pre-Conference Workshop.* San Francisco, CA.

Erickson, S. & McKnight, M (2000). *A practitioner's guide to mediation.* New York: John Wiley & Sons, Inc. (in press).

Florida Dissolution of Marriage—Children Act, Chapter 82–96 (1982), Chapter 61 (1992 Revision).

Folberg, J., & Milne, A. (1988). *Divorce mediation.* New York: Guilford Press.

Freud, S. (1933). *New introductory lectures on psychoanalysis.* J. Strachey, Ed. and Trans.) (1964). New York: Norton.

Gardner, R. A. (1989). *Family evaluation in child custody mediation, arbitration and litigation.* Cressbill, NJ: Creatine Therapeutics.

Gold, L. (1992). *Between love and hate: A guide to civilized divorce.* New York: Plenum.

Galdstein J., Freud, A., & Solnit A. (1973). *Beyond the best interests of the child.* New York: Free Press.

Guyer, C. (1999). Spouse abuse. In F. W. Kaslow (Ed.), *Handbook of couple and family forensic issues* (pp. 206–234). New York: John Wiley & Sons, Inc.

Hawthorne, N. (1948). *The scarlet letter.* New York: Washington Square Press. (Original work published 1850.)

Haynes, J. M. (1981). *Divorce mediation.* New York: Springer.

Haynes, J. M. (1982). A conceptual model of the process of family mediation: Implications for training. *The American Journal of Family Therapy, 10*(4), 58–66.

Kaslow, F. W. (1983). Passive aggressiveness: An intrapsychic, interpersonal and transactional dynamic in the family system. In R. D. Parsons & R. J. Wicks (Eds.), *Passive aggressiveness: Theory and practice* (pp. 134–152). New York: Brunner/Mazel.

Kaslow, F. W. (1984). Divorce mediation and its emotional impact on the couple and their children. *American Journal of Family Therapy. 12*(3), 58–66.

Kaslow, F. W. (1988). The psychological dimension of divorce mediation. In J. Folberg & A. Milne (Eds.) *Divorce mediation: Theory and practice* (pp. 83–108). New York: Guilford.

Kaslow, F. W. (1990). Divorce therapy and mediation for better custody. *Japanese Journal of Family Psychology, 4,* 19–37 (In English).

Kaslow, F. W. (1993a). Attractions and affairs: Fabulous and fatal. *Journal of Family Psychotherapy, 4*(4), 1–34.

Kaslow, F. W. (1993b). The divorce ceremony: A healing strategy. In T. Nelson & T. Trepper (Eds.), *101 favorite family therapy interventions* (pp. 341–345). New York: Haworth Press.

Kaslow, F. W. (1994). Painful partings: Providing therapeutic guidance. In L. L. Schwartz (Ed.) *Midlife divorce counseling* (pp. 67–82). Alexandria, VA: American Counseling Association.

Kaslow, F. W. (1995). The dynamics of divorce therapy. In R. H. Mikesell, D. D. Lusterman, & S. H. McDaniel (Eds.), *Integrating family therapy: Handbook of family psychology and systems theory* (pp. 271–283). Washington, DC: American Psychological Association.

Kaslow, F. W. (1999). Divorce and its sequelae: A psychological perspective. In F. W. Kaslow (Ed.), *Handbook of couple and family forensic issues* (pp. 235–257). New York: John Wiley & Sons, Inc.

Kaslow, F. W. & Hammerschmidt, H. (1992). Long term good marriages: The seemingly essential ingredients. *Journal of Couples Therapy, 3*(2/3), 15–38, and in B. J. Brothers (Ed.), *Couples therapy: Multiple perspectives* (pp. 15–38). New York: Haworth Press.

Kaslow, F. W. & Schwartz, L. L. (1987). *Dynamics of divorce: A life cycle perspective.* New York: Brunner/Mazel.

Kessler, S., & Bostwick, S. (1977). Beyond divorce. Coping skills for children. *Journal of Clinical Child Psychology, 6,* 38–41.

Kuehlwein, K. T. (1999). Legal and psychological issues confronting lesbian, bisexual and gay couples. In F. W. Kaslow (Ed.), *Handbook of couples and family forensic issues* (pp. 164–187). New York: John Wiley & Sons, Inc.

Lachkar, J. (1992). *The narcissistic/borderline couple.* New York: Brunner/Mazel.

Lusterman, D. D. (1998). *Infidelity: A survival guide.* Oakland, CA: New Harbinger.

Marlow, L. (1992). *Divorce and the myth of lawyers.* Garden City, NY: Harlon Press.

Marlow, L., & Sauber S. R. (1990). *The handbook of divorce mediation.* New York: Plenum Press.

Mahler, M. S., Pine, F., & Bergman, A. (1975). *The psychological birth of the human infant.* New York: Basic Books.

Mediation Quarterly (1983 to present). Journal of the Academy of Family Mediators. San Francisco, CA: Jossey-Bass.

Neville, W. G. (1984). Divorce mediation for therapists and their spouses. In F. W. Kaslow (Ed.), *Psychotherapy with psychotherapists* (pp. 103–122). New York: Haworth Press.

Palmer N. (1988). Legal recognition of the parental alienation syndrome, *American Journal of Family Therapy, 16*(4), 361–363.

Parsons, R. D., & Wicks, R. J. (Eds.) (1983). *Passive aggressiveness; Theory and practice.* New York: Brunner/Mazel.

Pittman, F. (1989). *Private lies.* New York: Norton.

Roizblatt, A., Garcia, P., Maida, A. M., & Moya, G. (1990). Is Valentine still doubtful? A workshop model for children of divorce. *Contemporary Family Therapy, 12,* 299–310.

Schwartz, L. L., & Kaslow, F. W. (Eds.) (1997). *Painful partings: Divorce and its aftermath.* New York: Wiley.

Sharlin, S. (1996). Long term successful marriages in Israel. *Contemporary Family Therapy, 18,* 225–242.

Solomon, M. (1996). Understanding and treating couples with borderline disorders. In F. W. Kaslow (Ed.) *Handbook of relational diagnosis and dysfunctional family patterns* (pp. 251–269). New York: Wiley.

Visher, E. B., & Visher, J. S. (1991). *How to win as a stepfamily.* (2nd ed.) New York: Brunner/Mazel.

Walker, L. E. A. (1990). Violence in the family. In F. W. Kaslow (Ed.) *Voices in family psychology* (Vol. 2, pp. 139–158). Newbury Park, CA: Sage.

Walker, L. E. A. (1994). *Abused women and survivor therapy: A practical guide for the psychotherapist.* Washington, DC: American Psychological Association.

Wallerstein, J. S., & Kelly, J. B. (1980). *Surviving the breakup: How children and parents cope with divorce.* New York: Basic Books.

Weitzman, L. J. (1985). *The divorce revolution: The unexpected social and economic consequences for women and children in America.* New York: Free Press.

Whitaker, C. A., & Bumberry, W. M. (1988). *Dancing with the family: A symbolic experiential approach.* New York: Brunner/Mazel.

PART V

FAMILIES WITH SPECIAL NEEDS AND PROBLEMS

CHAPTER 18

Remarried Families of 2000: Definitions, Description, and Interventions

Roni Berger

W HEN MRS. CARTER called to schedule an appointment to see me because she and her husband were experiencing difficulties with 15-year-old Angela, I asked who else lives in the family. The response was, "Well, it depends what day we are talking about. . . . " She went on to explain that she and her husband have been divorced from previous spouses and consequently remarried, bringing into the new union two daughters each. Her daughters, 15 and 13, live with the remarried couple "full time." His 18-year-old daughter lives with them during weekdays because she attends a school nearby. On vacations and alternative weekends she goes to live with her mother, step-father, sister, two younger half-siblings, and a step-sister (a daughter of her mother's current husband from his first marriage). His 15-year-old lives with her remarried mother and comes to visit the Carters regularly without any prearranged schedule.

The Carters are not alone. The number of such complex "accordion" families that challenge the language and expertise of family therapists as well as traditional definitions of family boundaries, roles, and development is large and growing. Current estimates suggest that "eventually the majority of people will be married more than once during their lifetime" (Ihinger-Tallman & Pasley, 1997, p. 24), making remarried families a dominant family configuration in our society. Men remarry more frequently and more quickly than women, whites more than blacks. Age, education, and income have been shown to correlate with the tendency to remarry (Ihinger-Tallman & Pasley, 1997). The likelihood of a remarriage ending in a divorce is somewhat higher than that of a first marriage. The reason may be that remarried families face more difficulties and/or because divorce is a solution that has been tried and demystified and is therefore recognized as an option when the marriage does not work well.

When either or both spouses bring to the remarriage household children from a previous marriage, a step-family is created. More than one-fifth of married couples raising children include a step-parent and about one-fourth of all children born in the 1980s live in a step-family (Mason, 1998). Step-families are classified into simple and complex step-families. Simple step-families (a misleading concept because families, let alone step-families, are never simple) are created by the remarriage of a parent to a nonparent. Complex step-families are the result of a remarriage of two parents. Most step-families are step-father families, as women gain custody in the majority of divorces. A recently multiplying type of step-family is that of an unmarried mother who marries a man who is not the biological father of her child (Mason, 1998).

REMARRIED FAMILIES IN HISTORICAL CONTEXT

Remarriage is not a new phenomenon. It has been a part of the social scenery in all societies at all times as evidenced by ancient nuptial laws, proverbs, and folk tales. Frequency of remarriage in Western Europe and in the United States in the seventeenth and eighteenth centuries was similar to the current situation (Beer, 1992; Chandler, 1991; Noy, 1991). Abraham Lincoln, Thomas Jefferson, James Madison, Ronald Reagan, Bill Clinton, many of the Kennedys, Leonardo da Vinci, Constantin Brancusi, and most Hollywood stars were and are members of remarried families. Earlier remarriages tended to follow the death of a spouse. Since the 1960s most remarriages that occur follow a divorce. This is reflected in the concept *stoep,* an old English word meaning bereaved. The constant growth in the number of remarried families and the changes in their nature have been attributed to economic and social forces. Women's growing economic independence following the industrial revolution and the world wars, social mobility, liberalization of family norms, and the emphasis on personal happiness in the postmodern era have contributed to step-families fast becoming the most common family form (Beer, 1992; Pasley, Rhoden, Visher, & Visher, 1996).

In spite of the fact that remarried families have been around for a long time, with a few earlier exceptions, scholars neglected to study them systematically until the 1970s (Berger, 1998; Ihinger-Tallman & Pasley, 1997). Only in the past two decades have we witnessed a growing flux of studies (Everett, 1995; Visher & Visher, 1996). Most studies have been based on clinical populations and have examined the effects of remarriage from a problem-oriented viewpoint (Berger, 1998; Ganong & Coleman, 1994a). This yielded the deficit-comparison paradigm that implicitly assumes the relative inferiority of remarried families, portrays them as fragile and unstable, and blames them for diverse social, economical, and psychological ills (Berger, 1998; Carter & McGoldrick, 1990; Cherlin, 1978; Ganong & Coleman, 1994a; Kaslow, 1993; Mason, 1998). The negative perception of remarried families is reflected in the absence of "step" language that is free of negative connotations. Most available concepts are awkward, inadequate, and inaccurate and there is an absence of laws and norms (Nichols, 1996).

As most remarried families seek help in early phases of their life cycle, many studies have focused on newly formed families and the initial phases of the remarriage (Pasley et al., 1996). Recent years have brought some efforts to know more about long-lasting, normative aspects of remarried families. Recent studies offer knowledge about step-family relationships, the antecedent conditions under which step-families succeed, changes in step-families over time, diversity of step-families, and typical dynamics such as decision making, past orientation, and role allocation (Berger, 1993; Bray & Berger, 1993; Bray & Hetherington, 1993).

Three "generations" of knowledge can be noticed in the literature heretofore. The first generation, during the 1960s and early 1970s (Bohannan, 1975; Bowerman & Irish, 1962;

Hetherington, Cox, & Cox, 1981; Rosenberg, 1965) was characterized by comparing remarried families to first-time marriages. Remarried families have been described as lacking in cohesion and suffering from fragmentation and marital discord. Children who grow up in them were anticipated to experience more academic, emotional, psychological, and social difficulties (Berger. 1998; Pasley & Ihinger-Tallman, 1987). Most of this research was conducted from an individual perspective and had serious methodological limitations. This pathologizing viewpoint characterized earlier works and is still present in some recent books (e.g., Popenoe, 1996).

The second generation started with a paradigm shift pioneered by Visher and Visher (1979), who advocated acknowledging the differences of step-families from first marriage families and the need to understand them in their own context. The focus became understanding step-families as a different species rather than comparing them to first marriage families to their disadvantage. This generation of knowledge started to entertain systemic perspectives in addition to the traditional individualistic viewpoint. Studies focused on understanding normative processes, characteristics, issues, and the life cycle of remarried families (Papernow, 1993). Studies addressed patterns of communication, cohesion, intimacy, permeability of boundaries, split loyalties, complexity of the metafamily, ambiguity of roles, conflicting needs of diverse family members and subsystems, and additional intrafamilial relationships and family organization (Atkinson, 1986; Bernstein, 1997; Bray & Berger, 1993; Bumpass, Sweet & Martin, 1990; Crosbie-Burnett, 1984; Erera-Weatherky, 1996; Martin & Martin, 1992; Mason & Mauldon, 1996; Pasley & Ihinger-Tallman, 1987; Peek, Bell, Waldern & Sorell, 1988; Pill, 1990; Pink & Wampler, 1985; Wilson & Clarke, 1992). Other studies sought to identify factors that affect marital satisfaction, adjustment, and quality of the remarriage (Hobart, 1989).

Currently we are in the midst of the third generation of step-family studies. The focus has shifted from understanding remarried families vis-à-vis other family configurations to understanding differences within the population of step-families. Current studies move away from lumping all step-families together and muting the myriad variations to studying different kinds of step-families and the idiosyncratic characteristics that typify families in each category. They use more sophisticated research methods, examine nonclinical families, and conduct longitudinal studies to address complexities and refined subtleties in understanding processes and relationships. This leads to more clarity about and awareness of the diversity of remarried families (Ihinger-Tallman & Pasley, 1997; Kaslow, 1998).

NOT MADE IN ONE MOLD: DIVERSITY OF REMARRIED FAMILIES

The diversity of step-families was recognized first in relation to their structure, such as the difference between simple and complex step-families, step-father and step-mother families, and so forth. Several typologies of dynamic characteristics of step-families were suggested. Burgoyne and Clark (1984) distinguished five types of step-families based on their self-perceptions: "Not really a step-family" type are step-families that divorced and remarried while children were very young and perceive their step-family as an ordinary family. In "looking forward for the departure of children" type of step-family spouses remarry when children are adolescents or young adults, do not wish to have children in the remarriage, and wait for the children to leave so that they can focus on the marital relationship. Families of the "progressive" type emphasize the advantages of their current situation.

"Conscious pursuit of an ordinary family life together" families imitate non–step-families, with new children and step-parents accepting full parental roles. The "conscious pursuit of ordinary family life frustrated" step-families are those whose efforts to be like a non–step-family are undermined by continuing problems from the first marriage.

Gross (1986) identified four types of families based on the perceptions of adolescents who lived in them. "Augmentation" describes a family perception that includes both the divorced natural parents and the step-parent. "Reduction" is a family perception that includes only the remarried natural parent and excludes both the noncustodial natural parent and the step-parent. "Alternative" family perception includes the remarried natural parent and the step-parent but not the noncustodial natural parent. "Retention" maintains the original situation by including the natural parents and excluding the step-parent.

A study of Israeli step-families (Berger, 1993, 1998) yielded three types of families. "Integrated families" combine past and present, maintain parenting roles according to biological lines, perceive themselves as different from non–step-families, and view the marriage as the focal subsystem. In most of these families both spouses have been married and have children, who are currently adolescents (wife) or young adults (husband), on their way to leaving the family. "Invented families" are often created by a childless husband and a mother of young children, who bear at least one child together and focus on raising a family and sharing parenting responsibilities. These families are present-oriented, perceive the current family as "the real family" and minimize the meaning of previous marriages. "Imported families" lead their present life as if the new family is a continuation of the original marriage. Their orientation to the past is limited, the focal subsystem is marital, and step-parents take over roles vacated by noncustodial biological parents.

Recognition of step-families' diversity calls for substituting the singular model of "functional step-family" that dominates the field traditionally with acceptance of a broader variety of ways to be a successful step-family. Such a broad approach is supported by postmodernistic and feministic theoretical perspectives (Elliot, 1997).

CHARACTERISTICS OF REMARRIED FAMILIES

In spite of their diversity, all remarried families share structural and dynamic characteristics. First, remarried families have a complex structure because they are composed of two units that carry with them baggage from the families of origin of each spouse as well as ghosts from previous marriages and divorces. Children belong to two households and multiple parental figures and numerous subsystems and kin relationships from past and current marriage exist, including grandparents, in-laws, and other relatives. Siblings have different parents and are typically in different phases in their life cycle (Bohannan, 1975; Visher & Visher, 1996). The absence of concepts to describe these complex relationships makes social introductions and filling of medical, insurance, and other administrative forms uncomfortable and a source of embarrassment and confusion.

Structural complexity of remarried families is intensified by the need to merge the cultures of the original units to create the miniculture of the new family. The effort to integrate two separate units creates friction. This friction is amplified by the competing and sometimes incongruent needs of children from different marriages, and often of spouses, who are in different phases of their life cycle, as well as by a marriage that is younger than some of the children (Rosenberg & Hajal, 1985). For example, creating a step-family may include forming a new marital system, educating young children born in the remarriage while launching postadolescents from previous marriages, allowing adolescent children to gain autonomy within a young remarriage that seeks cohesion and bonding, and so forth.

Family structure affects the allocation of power. In remarried families, power and authority are divided among various adults (Nichols, 1996). The force of sole custodial parents who share with the children a lifelong history, intensive common memories, and having gone through critical phases of divorce and single parenthood overpowers the power of step-parents. This lack of symmetry in parental power within the remarriage may strengthen the position of the natural parent in the spousal relationship, in extreme cases to the degree of marginalizing the step-parent. Differences in economic strength color the spouses' power in the remarriage, typically gaining more strength for men because they tend to enter remarriage financially stronger than women do. Remarried parents may try to abuse their power and control the household of the noncustodial parent. Noncustodial parents have more power than their new spouses (step-parents married to noncustodial parents) do and, at least at the beginning, also more power than step-parents married to the custodial parents. They draw their power from the predivorce relationship and, depending on the circumstances of the divorce, the child's guilt for living with the other parent, especially if the noncustodial parent is not remarried or lives in poorer financial conditions than the remarried family. While step-parents who reside with the step-children have initially little power, they gradually gain power, especially if they fulfill parental roles for the step-child and if custodial parents allow them to gain it. Step-mothers often gain power earlier and more intensively than step-fathers because they get involved in homemaking, attending parent-teacher conferences, and so forth. When a mutual child is born in the remarriage, step-parents becomes more central and gain more parental power (Beer, 1992).

The power of children from a previous marriage is fueled by the existence of an additional parent outside the remarried family and by guilt feelings of the custodial parent. Typical expressions of such power include overdependency, overdemanding behavior, and efforts to create a cross-generational coalition with the natural parent against the step-parent. The position of outsiders held by visiting step- and half-siblings is a source both of power and the lack of it. They have the powerful status of desirable guests, yet may feel left out when other family members refer to events of which they are not part. The power children of the remarriage gain by having both parents present is limited by being the youngest, and unlike children from previous marriages, by lacking support from an external parent.

Coupled with the complexity of structure is the lack of clarity and permeability of external and internal boundaries. Ambiguity of boundaries results from differences between family members' perceptions of the family, parental subsystems that transcend the boundaries of the remarried family, and children who vacillate between households for visitation or because custody arrangements change (Gorell-Barnes, 1997; Keshet, 1987; Visher & Visher, 1988). Some parents include their spouses' visiting children and some do not; a child may see the noncustodial parent as part of the family, unlike the remarried parent and step-parent, and so forth. This creates uncertainty regarding affiliation, distance-proximity, and togetherness-separateness and may become a source of stress (Furstenberg & Spanier, 1984; Ganong & Coleman, 1994a; Visher & Visher, 1996). Lack of clear boundaries combined with the heightened sexual atmosphere around the remarital relationship and an absence of taboo on relationships between nonblood kin who did not grow up together may lead to loosening of sexual boundaries and create incestuous issues (Kaslow, 1993; Sager et al., 1983).

In addition to ambiguity of boundaries remarried families experience ambiguity of norms to guide them in fulfilling step roles as well as a lack of social opportunities to learn those roles (Nichols, 1996). Cherlin (1978) relates this role ambiguity to incomplete institutionalization of step-families. In the current decade, norms for the role of step-parent are emerging (Bray, Berger & Boethel, 1995; Ganong & Coleman, 1994b; Ihinger-Tallman & Pasley, 1997). While normative step-parents' roles are being developed, absence of cultural norms remains regarding many step roles. Step-mothers and step-parents in families where noncustodial natural parents are highly involved in the children's life and for families with young step-children in early phases of the step life cycle still lack normative consensus (Fine, 1996). This leads to competition, role strain, and issues of loyalty.

Split loyalties are a common issue in remarried families. Remarried parents feel torn between their loyalty to their children and to their new partners and in some cases between their current and previous spouses (especially, but not exclusively in remarriage following death). Step-parents experience conflicts between their loyalty to their step- and to natural children. Children are conflicted between their loyalty to step- and to natural parents and between their loyalties to each of the divorced natural parents. Preadolescent and adolescent children tend to have a hard time, especially if one parent is not remarried or is not in a new relationship. This is expressed in boycotting a remarried parent, refusing to visit and accept presents, and occasionally, refusal to communicate and invite the parent to weddings, birthday parties, and so on. These loyalty conflicts may cause guilt, anger, and emotional distance as a defense against the guilt.

In the absence of norms for remarried families, myths develop. Typical myths are that remarried families are less good than first marriage families and that step-mothers, specifically, are wicked and evil (the Cinderella myth). Step-fathers were subjected less to negative myths, probably because they often are perceived as saviors who rescued the single mother and her children from poverty and misery. Another myth is that remarried families can and should become as similar as possible to first marriage families or that the adjustment to remarriage is fast and easy, resulting in one big happy family (the Brady Bunch syndrome). An additional myth is that of "instant love" (Schulman, 1972). These stereotypes are fostered by the media and folklore fairy tales of all cultures and have penetrated into everyday language. For example, the term "being a step-child" describes being deprived, second-class, and neglected.

Myths regarding remarried families shape the attitude that members of such families are subject to as well as their own self-expectations, stimulating a cycle of negative attitudes and dysfunctional behaviors through the process of self-fulfilling prophecy. Teachers, social workers, lawyers, and other professionals are not innocent of adopting these myths, as evidenced by research (Coleman & Ganong, 1987) and by reports of members of remarried families about their encounters with educators, social agencies, and medical staff. Stereotyping is often used, or one may say abused, to "explain" problems.

Common challenges for remarried families grow out of the gap between their reality and their legal status. Although remarriage creates a legal commitment between adults and no commitment or a limited commitment exists between step-parents and step-children, the latter often become central figures in each other's life. The legal status of step relationship is changing gradually (Fine & Fine, 1992; Mahoney, 1994) to establish mutual rights and obligations among step-parents and step-children. However, remarried families still live with a considerable discrepancy between their de facto and de juro situation. Step-parents are not allowed to approve medical treatment or claim custody or visitation regarding step-children if a divorce occurs. Eligibility of step-children for child support and inheritance varies and is at best unclear even though the income of a step-parent is often crucial in preventing or ending the poverty of step-children and securing their welfare during and following the remarriage (Mason & Mauldon, 1996). Incongruent with this lack of clarity and consistency, step-parents rear, parent, support, and discipline step-children and make major decisions regarding their life. This discrepancy is a source of stress and hard feelings on the part of children, and natural parents and step-parents alike.

BECOMING A REMARRIED FAMILY: DEVELOPMENTAL ASPECTS

The road to becoming a remarried family is long and bumpy. It has been estimated to last 4 to 7 years (Papernow, 1993). The marital transitions from an intact to a divorced to one-parent to a remarried family involve disorganization, reorganization, and reassigning of roles. Relocation and reorganization of space and belongings cause loss of exclusivity of relationships, autonomy, privacy, social status, role fantasies, and assets that have been acquired during pre-remarriage. These losses reactivate previous losses, emphasize the finality of the termination of previous marriages, and challenge the fantasy of reunion common in children of divorced families. Transition passages in the life cycle of the remarried family tend to recurrently reignite experiences of loss associated with the previous marriage.

The process of becoming a remarried family requires family members to adjust quickly to a new situation, one that some of them do not choose, and simultaneously to develop their new reality as a unit while freeing themselves of previous perceptions (Jacobson, 1996; Visher & Visher, 1988). There is no opportunity for a gradual process and reality presses people into taking on multiple roles at once. This may cause confusion and bewilderment, especially to children who feel that they have no control over what is happening in their lives and who often tend to blame the step-parent for the situation, since they are afraid to risk blaming their parent.

Throughout this process, remarried families need to come to terms with the past and cope with financial obligations such as child support and alimony payments, unresolved issues with previous spouses and their extended family, patterns and rituals, friends and colleagues, feelings, perceptions, emotional wounds, and memories.

Seven phases in the process of becoming a remarried family have been described by Papernow (1993): (1) Fantasy—adults expect the new system to be established instantly; (2) immersion characterized by constant conflicts and tension; (3) awareness—of difficulties and splits along biological lines; (4) mobilization—clashes among diverse needs of individuals and subsystems; (5) action—solidifying of the couple and responding to needs of children; (6) contact—step-parent–step-child relationship develops and some stability has been achieved; (7) resolution—the family gains cooperation and stability. Understanding and addressing the issues of a given remarried family requires taking into consideration its location in the step–life cycle.

ISSUES OF REMARRIED FAMILIES

Remarried families encounter issues in different subsystems within the family as well as with extended family and society at large.

ISSUES WITHIN THE FAMILY

The Couple: Issues Related to the Remarriage

Marital issues in remarriage include "ghosts from the past," the presence of children, property, money, and inheritance issues (Nichols, 1996). Ghost from the past refers to the need to deal with residues from the former marriage. How to relate to the first marriage within the remarriage is a central issue. Does the couple unite against previous partners to cement the current spousal relationship? Do they ignore the previous partners as if they never existed? Do they maintain or repeat past patterns? Do they see the remarriage as an improved version in which families try to amend failures and correct mistakes of previous marriages? To what extent are expectations from the remarriage colored by experiences in previous marriages? In some families the first marriage is very much part of the remarriage: "there is no forgetting of the ex . . . there she is, forever a part of your past and often enough, your present. She has become a permanent fixture . . . a reference point for gleaning new insights from old patterns" (Garfinkel, 1990, p. 24). "My wife's first marriage is always in the air . . . it is part of our collective memory . . . it is not her first marriage but our first marriage . . . it serves as a reference point in our life. In a way I live as if I was married to him" (Berger, 1998, p. 52).

The existence of children may hinder the establishment of appropriate internal boundaries (Nichols, 1996). A major task in remarried families is to define a clear boundary around the new couple and avoid triangulation caused by parent-child relationships that predate the current marriage. Establishing clear boundaries around the couple and strengthening its bonding emerge in step-family literature as the single most important factor in building family stability (Kaslow, 1993; Visher & Visher, 1996). In the process of constructing a marital world and establishing a sense of togetherness, the newly married couple may exclude others. Children from previous marriages often experience this as rejection and attempt to split the new couple.

An additional task is defining a focal subsystem and the boundaries of the family and the subsystems. The focal subsystem describes which subsystem (marital vs. parental) is dominant, functions as the uniting means between adults, and has priority in situations of conflicting interests. The issue of focal subsystem exists in all families. In families with a marital focal subsystem, adults unite around spousal and intimate relationship concerns. In families with a parental focal subsystem, adults unite around building and raising a family and parenting children. In remarried families the issue of focal subsystem is amplified by the unbalanced investment of the spouses in the marital and parental roles and the competition between children from previous marriages and the new spouse. The former seek to maintain the exclusivity of their relationship with their natural parent and the latter struggles to prioritize the relationship with the partner (Berger, 1998). In extreme situations, this may reach a "he or me" ultimatum.

Traditionally, functional remarried families were believed to have a marital focal subsystem (Goetting, 1983) as reflected in the common recommendation to focus in therapy initially on validating and solidifying the couple before involving additional family members (e.g., Sager et al., 1983; Visher & Visher, 1996). However, in recent research no association was found between the type of focal subsystem and levels of functioning and satisfaction (Berger, 1998).

Financial and monetary issues regarding assets that each spouse brings from the pre-remarriage phases and especially lack of balance in financial situations place economic and emotional strain on many remarriages (Berger, 1998; Nichols, 1996).

Custodial, Noncustodial, and Step-parenting

Multiple parents exist in remarried families: custodial and noncustodial natural parents, a step-parent who resides with the child, and often a step-parent who is married to the non-custodial parent. This paves the way to disagreement about disciplinary issues and child-rearing practices. For example, a step-parent may think that a natural parent spoils the child and is being manipulated, a natural parent may view the step-parent as not caring enough or being too strict, and the parents in each household may have criticisms of parenting practices in the other household. Conflicts regarding parenting can easily ignite a marital problem and consistently have been found to be a major source of conflict in remarried couples (Elliot, 1997; Visher & Visher, 1996).

Custodial parents' parenting is often guided by guilt feelings for having caused the child to live through a divorce and to be in a step-family. Noncustodial parents are sometimes "Disney parents," providing presents and fun when the child visits. Competition between the natural parents is not uncommon, often leaving the custodial parent angry and frustrated: "He takes them to the movies and I have to take them to the dentist."

Custodial natural parents and their current spouses share parental responsibilities in varying degrees. In some families, the custodial natural parents remain the primary or exclusive disciplinary and nurturing figures for their children from previous marriages, sometimes becoming a buffer between the step-parent and the step-children. In other families, spouses share parenting responsibilities. Step-parents attend parent-teacher meetings, discipline the children, and function as a full parent. When a child is born in the remarriage, the step-parent's parental position often expands to include the step-children. Step-parents' parental responsibility depends on permission by natural parents and step-children, length of remarriage, age of step-children at the time of remarriage, degree of availability of noncustodial natural parents, nature of the step-parents' relationship with their own children, family type, and cultural norms (Berger, 1993; Ihinger-Tallman & Pasley, 1997). Traditionally, it has been recommended that in early stages of the step–life cycle natural parents maintain responsibility for managing children's behavior while the step-parent remains neutral and gradually assumes authority (Elliot, 1997). An additional approach is for the step-parent to enter an authority role through "the soft side" of authority with control over resources and the power to allocate them rather than the power to discipline (Berger, 1998). The involvement of noncustodial parents in the life of children varies from full parenting to involvement limited in intensity and domains to minimal or absence of parenting.

Full, Half-, and Step-Siblings

Family reorganization following remarriage impacts on children individually and as a family subsystem (Nichols, 1984, 1986). Remarriage potentially creates three major types of sibling relationships: full, half-, and step-siblings. Full siblings share both parents and are traditionally raised in the same household, sharing everyday life experiences. Half-siblings share one parent but not the other. They may or may not grow up in the same household and have relationships of diverse intensity and frequency. Step-siblings are children of remarried partners by previous marriages, and they have no common natural parent. The parent of one is the step-parent of the other.

Ruth and John Simon are remarried. Each has been married before. Richard, age 14, and Albert, age 12, Ruth's sons by her first husband, live with the Simons. Louise,

John's 17-year-old daughter from his previous marriage, lives with her mother in a nearby town and visits frequently. Ruth and John parent together 3-year-old Jessica. Richard and Albert are full siblings, Louise is their step-sibling, and Jessica is a half-sibling of all three adolescents.

Nichols (1984, 1986) discusses factors that determine the effects of family reorganization on the sibling subsystem. Children's personalities, attitudes and actions, and availability of parents shape the level of intensification of sibling subsystem and its effects. Step-siblings may develop a relationship that is similar in many ways to that of siblings in non–step-families. This is especially true for step-siblings who grow up together from an early age. They also face all the usual issues of siblings such as rivalry and jealousy. However, these issues gain unique flavor in remarried families because different sets of siblings may or may not be equally provided depending on financial differences between the households to which they belong (Berger, 1998; Elliot, 1997). Specific to remarried families are coalitions among siblings from different cohorts, creating the "your children and my children hit our children" situation. Sexual tension, sexual abuse, and a great deal of discomfort may grow out of lack of clear social norms and rules regarding step- and half-siblings, specifically, the absence of the incest taboos. At the same time, a major strength of the sibling subsystem is that it can offer children support and a sense of togetherness in times of uncertainty and family reorganization (Nichols, 1984, 1986). If children are young when their parents remarry and their half-siblings are born, their relationships are more similar to siblings in non–step-family. Opportunities for spending time together while growing up contributes to closeness, and sometimes to more stress and competition, among step-siblings. The number of children in each sibling cohort and the gender of the mutual parent/step-parent also determine the nature and quality of sibling relationships (Bernstein, 1997).

Remarried Families and the Extended Family

Remarriage has an impact on the relationship with the extended family. Parents and previous in-laws of a remarrying parent may feel displaced, as the new couple builds the boundary around the new unit. This is especially true for the parents of the noncustodial parent and more so if the new spouse has parents that embrace their new step-grandchildren. Grandparents are often concerned about whether the new step-parent will treat their grandchildren properly and whether the remarriage will take away from the attention given to the children by the remarried parent. Some may experience loyalty conflicts between their child's previous and new spouses. As the remarrying couple develops their relationships with the extended families of each other, connections with the extended family of the noncustodial parent typically loosen.

Jealousy and competition between previous and current spouses radiate to the relationships within the extended families. Resentment toward step-children who "took the place" of natural children is not uncommon and colors attitudes of uncles, aunts, cousins, and other relatives. Some extended families treat step-kin as equals while others discriminate against them openly or implicitly.

Many grandparents serve as support to their grandchildren during the phases of divorce and single-parent family, when the parents are often busy with their own difficulties and may be less available to the children. These relationships need to be reshaped to adjust to the new family configuration to enable continuous support by grandparents without it being perceived as intrusive or undermining the remarriage. In many cases such a relationship with a grandparent may be helpful for the children to find their place in the new family more easily.

REMARRIED FAMILIES IN THE BROAD SOCIAL CONTEXT

One major issue of remarried families is that schools, community centers, and educational, medical, and social agencies, as well as the general public lack awareness about the issues of remarried families and are not geared and prepared to address them properly. Greeting cards for step-parents are rare and rituals for remarried families, norms for including step-parents in graduations, formal documents, and transition ceremonies are nonexistent. Five-year-old Eve came home crying because the teacher corrected her when she included in her family drawing her half-brother from her father's first marriage who lives with his remarried mother, saying: "This is not a brother. This is a cousin." The girl insisted that this is her brother, but the teacher would not accept it because "brothers and sisters live in the same house." Such incidents indicating the failure of educators, social agencies, medical staff, and other professionals to understand issues of remarried families are not uncommon.

Remarried families report anti-remarriage biases and the use of biased language. Emma, a remarried divorcee, reported that when she discussed her son with his teacher and described the family configuration, the teacher responded: "I did not know David is from a broken family." This teacher failed to understand that what has been broken is the marriage, while the family is reorganized in a different configuration. She used a concept that carries negative connotations and caused Emma discomfort.

Remarried stereotyping is often abused to explain problems such as underachievement, behavior, and emotional difficulties ("No wonder she or he is academically weak/acting out and so forth . . . the parents are divorced and remarried"). Conveyed to children of remarried families and to their classmates, these stereotypes create negative expectations and may become a self-fulfilling prophecy. Such stereotyping exists in schools, the workplace, the media, and in the arena of public opinion.

Absence of clear policies is an additional issue remarried families face. The growing attention given in recent years to remarried families by scholars and clinicians has not been matched by a similar development in family policy. The legal status of these families is uneven in different states, unclear or lacking in most of them, and inconsistent in state and federal policy. Two competing models dominate laws, regulations, and policies regarding remarried families: the "dependency" model and the "stranger" model. The former treats step-parents as in loco parentis (in place of a parent) who are responsible for step-children. The latter treats step-parents as unrelated legally to step-children and as bearing no rights or obligations (Mason, 1998). Federal policies follow the first model, entitling step-children to Social Security and benefit programs in most cases while states tend to favor the second, denying step-children's rights (Mahoney, 1994; Mason, 1998). However, there is inconsistency across federal programs in defining step-relationships and step-children's eligibility. Federal and state programs that grant step-children rights to the support of step-parents and benefits limit them to the duration of the remarriage. Even step-children who depend on a step-parent have no rights to inheritance and cannot bring a negligence suit. Where they exist, rights and obligations of step-parents are limited. This can cause many problems following a divorce or the death of the natural custodial parent. For example, giving up child support from the natural parent as part of the divorce agreement is not uncommon; therefore, children's welfare may be endangered by a divorce of their custodial parent (typically mother) from their step-parent (typically step-father), on whose income they have depended during the remarriage. When a natural custodial parent dies, even a remote natural parent who had no contact with the child is preferred for custody over the step-parent who might have parented the child since infancy. Recent years have brought many proposals, from active discouragement of step-families to a consideration of step-parents as full parents with all rights and obligations during the remarriage and following its dissolution by divorce or death of the biological parent.

TREATING REMARRIED FAMILIES

Several guidelines can be offered for addressing the challenges that the aforementioned issues of remarried families present in family therapy. Interventions need to be multisystemic; that is, professionals should work with individual remarried families, with social institutions, and with the public.

IMPLICATIONS FOR DIRECT PRACTICE

An important recommendation for direct practice with individual remarried families is that therapists educate themselves as to what is normative and what is pathological for remarried families rather than approach them from a first marriage families perspective. In a recent study of step-family therapy (Pasley et al., 1996), knowledge and understanding on the part of therapist (or lack of it) of the dynamics and issues of remarried families was reported as the single most significant factor in the evaluation of therapy by remarried couples. For example, in working with remarried families one should expect permeable external boundaries, diversity in allocation of parental roles, a wide range of feelings and relationships among family members, a gradual process of building of relationships, and the need for much negotiation and decision making to bridge the absence of norms and rituals.

Assessing Remarried Families
Assessing remarried families should reflect awareness of their difference from non-remarried families. Special attention should be given to assessing permeability of external boundaries, parental effectiveness, family cohesion, flexibility and creativity, skills of communication and decision making, and developmental phase in the life cycle. These components are important for the functioning of remarried families and their normative levels are different from those of non-remarried families.

Given the diversity of remarried families, the assessment and intervention plan should also be type specific. To this end, prior to developing a therapeutic strategy it is of utmost importance to assess the type of remarried family. Berger (1998) suggests a schema for differentiating remarried families by their past orientation, acceptance/rejection of difference, and focal subsystem. This schema can be used to define the type of step-family as a basis for tailoring an intervention plan that addresses specific needs and takes into consideration typical strengths and issues of step-families.

Assessment can be done by means of interviews, genograms, or standardized instruments, or a combination of these methods. Interviews can be conducted with individuals, dyads, triads, and large family units. Examples are a remarried couple, a child or children with their natural parents, a step-parent with step-child, natural and step-siblings, the divorced natural parents and step-parent(s), a remarried couple with living-in and/or visiting children, and all the adults who parent the children full-time or part-time with the children.

Genograms with remarried families are extremely helpful in gaining an organized picture of their very complex matrix, and they enable family members to work on encapsulating parts of the past and relating to them in a safe setting (Kaslow, 1993). At the same time, they are complicated because of the large number of individuals involved, and the multiple marriages and parental relationships that cut across families. For some types of remarried families (Imported and Invented) the genogram serves as a mediator that facilitates dealing with past issues.

Standardized instruments that can be used to assess remarried families include those used for understanding all families as well as those specific to remarried families (e.g., Stepfamily Time Orientation Scale [STOS], Berger, 1993). Such instruments can provide systematic and comparable data. A combination of methods gives the therapist a comprehensive and rich picture that enables understanding of the remarried family in the context of other remarried families.

The Role of Family Therapy with Remarried Families
The uniqueness of the step-family should also guide the treatment. One task of the therapist is to help families find themselves within the variety. This includes accompanying, guiding, normalizing, and encouraging them in their struggle to negotiate rules, roles, and role allocation (e.g., the role of the step-parent). Also, clarifying and respecting everybody's definitions of "who is the family" and developing their subsystems and self-perception as a unit in a way that is comfortable to all family members is crucial. Theresa, whose mother remarried four times, reports that her mother put her men before her children. At 42, married and a mother of three, she still carries the pain of having to live in a family configuration that was not sensitive to the kind of family in which she wished to live.

Living in the shadow of myths, false expectations, and scrutinization by the noncustodial parent, extended family, friends, neighbors, teachers, and the community, members of remarried families need support and validation in their struggle to establish their norms and create their family history.

A major task of remarried families is to define subsystems and develop appropriate boundaries around them. This requires redefining subsystems that existed throughout the single-parent phase. Often this phase is characterized by close relationships between custodial parents and their children. Remarriage brings into the picture a new adult that is perceived as competition to the same-sex noncustodial parent and as an intruder in the custodian parent-child intimacy. Therapists need to help the newly re-wed couple to deliberately allocate time and space for their spousal relationship and not allow the multiple roles imposed on them by the remarriage to rob them of opportunities for privacy and intimacy. Guilt-stricken remarried parents should be encouraged to spend time together without their children around and without talking about children. Sometimes remarried couples need the permission of a professional to allow themselves to leave for a honeymoon (and later vacations) without their children. Time and space also need to be allocated for the natural parent and his or her children without the step-parent and for the step-parent with the step-children without the natural parent to allow them to bond.

Helping families develop clear boundaries within step- and half-sibling subsystems is also crucial. Elena and George, both 16, had been dating for 3 months when their divorced parents started dating each other and eventually remarried. The former high school sweethearts now became step-siblings, sharing a house on alternative weekends and during summer vacations. In light of this new situation, the family faces questions regarding acceptable rules about their relationship. Can they go on? What will happen if they break up? What about intimate relationships? While this may be an extreme, although not impossible situation, issues of sexual attraction between non–blood-related step-kin are common.

Adults in remarried families often feel incompetent and guilty about their attitude both toward their natural and their step-children. It is of utmost importance to validate them, let them know that their struggles are typical and normal, and offer them practical ways to address specific situations. In a recent meeting of the American Association of Stepfamilies, a remarried stepmother of an 11-year-old boy described her guilt for not loving him as affectionately as his late mother did. She was amazed at the question "Who said that you should?" and was then able to relate to specific aspects of her step-son's behavior that she likes and those she dislikes. Guiding and helping members of remarried families to develop this process of differentiation in their mutual relationships is a major task of the family therapist.

Useful Strategies and Techniques for Therapy with Remarried Families

Decisions regarding with whom to work, on what to work, and how to work depend on the type of the step-family and the phase in the step–life cycle. However, family therapy with all remarried families requires focusing on developing creativity, flexibility, negotiation skills, and strategies for decision making. The absence of clear normative expectations for the "right" way to do things in remarried families combined with limited knowledge about effective proven strategies and techniques in the young field of remarriage family therapy requires families and their therapists to invent strategies tailored for their specific situations. Therapists should teach remarried families techniques for generating unusual solutions and encourage them to originate their own norms without feeling guilty or anxious about judgment from their environment rather than trying to fit preconceived expectations.

Attention should be given to helping remarried families originate their own rituals. Mutual support groups are especially useful since they offer families opportunities to learn from others in similar family configurations and discover what works for them. Given the intensity of life in remarried families, teaching them techniques for stress control and anxiety reduction also is helpful.

Although all models of family therapy are applicable and useful when working with remarried families, it has been suggested that a multitheoretical approach is to be preferred (Elliot, 1997). The evolving collaborative conversational models, such as the reflecting team (Andersen, 1991) and Michael White's approach (White & Epston, 1990), are especially helpful because they provide families with tools to originate their own solutions effectively. These approaches value differences, underscore the role of the family as a generator of ideas, and address preconceived biases. Hypothetical future-oriented questions are used as a key technique in helping families to separate themselves from their old problem-saturated story and develop a new story that fits the current situation. These approaches are useful in providing a focus for change and generating new possibilities for complex systems, especially families that are caught in an endless maze of their past (Dickerson & Zimmerman, 1993; Lax, 1994). Consequently, they are valuable in helping remarried families cope with typical issues of complex structure, differences of views, absence of acceptable social norms, and life in the shadow of social myths and of their own past, including previous marriages and single-parent family (Berger, in press).

WORKING ON BEHALF OF REMARRIED FAMILIES

In addition to their work with remarried families to help them with their issues, professionals need to intervene more globally on behalf of remarried families. One important area is that of stimulating public discussion to develop appropriate remarried families language so that these families will have satisfactory terminology (Kaslow, 1998). Socialization channels for step roles should be developed and role models enhanced. Bringing to the public eye remarried celebrities who speak to issues related to remarriage in their life and share their way of coping can serve this purpose.

Family therapists might help lobby for the development of federal and state legislation to regulate obligations and the rights of step-kin. Mason (1998) suggests a model for regulating the legal status of remarried families based on the nature of their living and financial arrangements and the length of the remarriage without invalidating the natural noncustodial parent. Although this model may be criticized, it represents the beginning of a public dialogue on remarriage and step-family issues. There is a need for many more voices to lead to innovative legislative and policy-making action.

Family therapists might also become active in fostering a public campaign for debates on the topic of social norms regarding remarried families. In the absence of role models, members of remarried families do not have socialization channels. Family therapy could be an active force in developing ways to learn how to be a remarried family and in providing role models for identification. One such way is fostering nonstigmatized mutual help groups in which remarried families share experiences and dilemmas and learn from each other. Family therapy can also promote a nonstigmatized profile of remarriage on television, in magazines, and in the movies. Therapists should work to encourage social recognition of remarried families as a legitimate family configuration. Training teachers to include in class discussions remarried families as an acceptable alternative, creating invitations and report cards that include step-parents, fostering recognition of step-parents in Father's Day and Mother's Day, and including reference to roles in remarried families in formal forms can contribute to this end.

A CASE EXAMPLE

Rachel, 43, and Robert, 54, have been remarried for 8 years. Rachel, a high school teacher, had been divorced from 44-year-old Roger for 5 years and was the mother of 12-year-old Ruth and 5-year-old Michael when she met Robert. Robert came to a parent-teacher meeting for Milly, his only daughter from his first marriage. Rachel was her English teacher. Milly was 14 at the time and lived with her remarried mother, Rose, her step-father, and two half-sisters, and often visited with her father. Robert, a salesman, had been involved at the time with another woman and lived with her and her young son from a previous marriage. Soon after he met Rachel he broke up with his girlfriend and started dating Rachel exclusively. A few months later, at the end of the school year, he moved into her house and he and Rachel married a couple of months later. Figure 18.1 describes the family genogram.

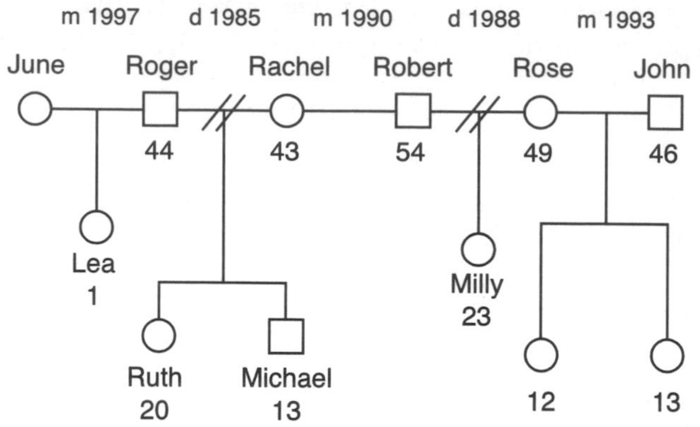

FIGURE 18.1   The Roth family.

Roger, Rachel's ex-husband, had not been involved in Ruth's or Michael's life and has paid no child support, claiming that he did not have the means to meet his financial obligations specified in the divorce agreement. Rachel and her children welcomed Robert as a paternal figure. He had a dominant role in raising Michael. Together with Rachel, he attended parent-teacher meetings, was active in the PTA, accompanied class trips, and was an active father. While in the beginning there was distance between each adult and their spouse's children, at the time of coming to therapy Rachel was closer to Robert's daughter than was Robert and Robert was closer to Michael than was Rachel.

The relationships between the step-siblings took longer to develop. Rachel and Robert took their three children with them on their honeymoon and "there hell broke loose." The new step-siblings could not tolerate each other and were instigating their natural parents against one another. Gradually, the relationships were worked out. Milly visited regularly with her father's new family and became especially close with Ruth, particularly as they were growing up and were both involved with the same theater group. The relationship with Michael was characterized by conflicts typical of adolescent siblings with age and gender differences.

The family requested help when Michael turned 13 and decided to change the living arrangement and move in with his biological father, with whom he had maintained minimal contact. Roger had recently remarried June, a much younger never-married woman, and he had with her a baby girl, Lea.

Robert, Rachel, and Michael showed up for the first appointment. Michael expressed his wish to live with his natural father, learn to know him better, and become closer with him. He felt that his step-father and his mother ganged up on him and did not understand him in this matter as in many other matters. Robert expressed feeling hurt and betrayed. His message was mixed: "I understand that he wants to reconnect with Roger, especially now that he has a new comfortable house, but where was Roger all these years? . . . Michael is like my own son." Rachel appeared to be torn between feeling rejected by her son's wish, empathizing with her husband's disappointment, and cognitively realizing that Michael's wish was legitimate and understandable:

> I know that it is good for him [for Michael to be closer with his father, R.B.], but I am concerned. It's like reopening all these old scars, going again through the divorce.

We decided about the arrangement a long time ago and he [Roger] did not live up to them when they were uncomfortable for him. Now he is suddenly there. It is a good thing that finally he is there for Michael but it breaks our family . . . Robert was more of a father to Michael than his own father.

The therapist validated the reactivated feelings of loss and explained to the parents that Michael's wish is not uncommon. Many adolescents request such changes in custody arrangement to have a chance to get closer with their noncustodial parent. Rachel and Roger were somewhat relieved to hear that Michael's wish was neither an indication of their mistake nor a reflection on their relationship with Michael. Michael was delighted to find somebody to support his wish without blaming him or making him feel guilty. Milly and Ruth were invited to join the next meeting. In the following meeting it became clear that the two young women were more sympathetic to Michael's wish but warned him that he could be back home soon because he would not be able to tolerate the hard disciplinary demands of his father's new wife. The third meeting included the four adults (Rachel and Robert, Roger and his current wife) and focused on understanding everybody's reaction to the intended move and negotiation of a timetable and arrangements comfortable to all. In the following meeting those arrangement were shared with Michael, Milly, and Ruth and their feedback helped shape the details of visitation procedures as well as decisions about how and when the change will occur. It was clear to all that Michael would move on a trial basis on a given date. Arrangements for communication and making decisions concerning the move were made and the family was scheduled for a follow-up meeting a month after the move.

CONCLUSION

Having existed throughout history, remarried families are becoming a dominant family configuration, generally formed following a divorce. Studies of remarried families shifted from focusing on problems and clinical populations to efforts to understand normative characteristics and issues of functional remarried families. The process of becoming a remarried family is long and complicated. Remarried families are diverse. In spite of their diversity, all of them share ambiguity of roles and boundaries, absence of norms, gaps between legal and reality status, and living in the shadow of stigma and myths. These characteristics create typical issues in the marital, parental, and sibling subsystems as well as with the extended family and society at large. The task of family therapy is to provide to remarried families type-specific direct services and to lobby in the public arena for social and legal changes to address their needs. A multitheoretical approach, conversational models, validation, depathologizing, psychoeducation, and fostering creativity are crucial in working with remarried families.

REFERENCES

Andersen, T. (1991). *The reflecting team: Dialogues and dialogues about dialogues.* New York: Norton.
Atkinson, C. (1986). *Stepparenting: Understanding the emotional problems and stresses.* Wellingorough: Thorns.
Beer, W. R. (1992). *American stepfamilies.* New Brunswick, NJ: Transaction Publishers.

Berger, R. (1993). *Past orientation, acceptance/rejection of difference and focal sub-system in non-clinical stepfamilies.* Jerusalem: The Hebrew University of Jerusalem.

Berger, R. (1998). *Stepfamilies: A multi-dimensional perspective.* New York: Haworth Press.

Berger, R. (in press). The goodness of fit between the reflective team approach and stepfamilies' problems and issues. *Journal of Systemic Therapies.*

Bernstein, A. C. (1997). Stepfamilies from siblings' perspectives. *Marriage and Family Review, 26*(1–2), 153–175.

Bohannan, P. (1975). *Stepfathers and the mental health of their children. Final Report.* La Jolla, CA: Western Behavioral Sciences Institute.

Bowerman, C. E., & Irish, D. P. (1962). Some relationships of stepchildren to their parents. *Marriage & Family Living, 24,* 113–121.

Bray, J. H., & Berger, S. H. (1993). Developmental issues in stepfamilies research project: Family relationships and parent-child interactions. Special section: Families in transition. *Journal of Family Psychology, 7*(1), 76–90.

Bray, J. H., Berger, S. H., & Boethel, C. L. (1995). Role integration and marital adjustment in stepfather families. In K. Pasley & M. Ihnger-Tallman (Eds.), *Stepparenting: Issues in theory, research, and practice* (pp. 69–86). Westport, CT: Greenwood.

Bray, J. H., & Hetherington, E. M. (1993). Families in transition: Introduction and overview. *Journal of Family Psychology, 7*(1), 3–8.

Bumpass, L., Sweet, J., & Martin, M. C. (1990). Changing patterns of remarriage. *Journal of Marriage and the Family, 52,* 747–756.

Burgoyne, J., & Clark, D. (1984). *Making a go of it: A study of stepfamilies in Sheffield.* Boston: Routledge & Kegan Paul.

Carter, B., & McGoldrick, M. (Eds.). (1990). *The changing family life cycle.* Boston: Allyn & Bacon.

Chandler, J. (1991). *Women without husbands: An exploration of the margins of marriage.* New York: St. Martin's Press.

Cherlin, A. (1978). Remarriage as an incomplete institution. *American Journal of Sociology, 84,* 634–650.

Coleman, M., & Ganong, L. (1987). The cultural stereotyping of stepfamilies. In K. Pasley & M. Ihnger-Tallman (Eds.), *Stepparenting: Issues in theory, research, and practice* (pp. 19–41). Westport, CT: Greenwood.

Crosbie-Burnett, M. (1984). The centrality of the step relationship: A challenge of family theory and practice. *Family Relations, 33,* 459–463.

Dickerson, V. C., & Zimmerman, J. L. (1993). A narrative approach to families with adolescents. In Friedman, S. (Ed.), *The new language of change* (pp. 226–250). New York: Guilford Press.

Elliot R. (1997). Therapy with remarried couples—a multi-theoretical perspective. *The Australian and New Zealand Journal of Family Therapy, 18*(4), 181–193.

Erera-Weatherley, P. I. (1996). On becoming a stepfamily: Factors associated with the adoption of alternative stepparenting styles. *Journal of Divorce and Remarriage, 25*(3–4), 155–174.

Everett, C. A. (Ed.). (1995). *Understanding stepfamilies: Their structure and dynamics.* New York: Haworth Press.

Fine, M. A. (1996). The clarity and content of the stepparent role: A review of the literature. In C. A. Everett (Ed.), *Understanding stepfamilies: Their structure and dynamics* (pp. 19–34). New York: Haworth Press.

Fine, M. A., & Fine, D. R. (1992). Recent changes in laws affecting stepfamilies: Suggestions for legal reform. *Family Relations, 41,* 334–340.

Furstenberg, F. F., & Spanier, G. (1984). *Recycling the family: Remarriage after divorce.* Beverly Hills, CA: Sage.

Ganong, L. H., & Coleman, M. (1994a). *Remarried family relationships.* Thousand Oaks, CA: Sage.

Ganong, L. H., & Coleman, M. (1994b). Adolescent stepchild stepparent relationship: Changes over time. In K. Pasley & M. Ihnger-Tallman (Eds.), *Stepparenting: Issues in theory, research, and practice* (pp. 87–104). Westport, CT: Greenwood.

Garfinkel, P. (1990, October 14). The best man. *New York Times,* pp. 24, 56.

Goetting, A. (1983). The relative strength of the husband-wife and parent-child dyads in remarriage: A test of the Hsu model. *Journal of Comparative Family Studies, 14*(1), 117–128.

Gorell-Barnes, G. (1997). *Growing up in stepfamilies.* Oxford: Clarendon Press.

Gross, P. E. (1986). Defining post-divorce remarriage families: A typology based on the subjective perceptions of children. *Journal of Divorce, 10,* 205–217.

Hetherington, M., Cox, M., & Cox, R. (1981). The aftermath of divorce. In E. M. Hetherington & R. D. Parke (Eds.), *Contemporary readings in child psychology* (pp. 99–109). New York: McGraw-Hill.

Hobart, C. (1989). Experiences of remarried families. *Journal of Divorce, 13,* 121–144.

Ihinger-Tallman, M., & Pasley, K. (1997). Stepfamilies in 1984 and today: A scholarly perspective. *Marriage and Family Review, 26*(1–2), 19–40.

Jacobson, D. (1996). Incomplete institution or culture shock: Institutional and processual models of stepfamily instability. In C. A. Everett (Ed.), *Understanding stepfamilies: Their structure and dynamics* (pp. 3–18). New York: Haworth Press.

Kaslow, F. W. (1993). *Understanding and treating the remarried family. Directions in marriage and family therapy.* New York: Hatherleigh Comp. Division of Clinical Psychology, 1(3), (November).

Kaslow, F. W. (1998). Foreword. In R. Berger, *Stepfamilies: A multi-dimensional perspective* (pp. xiii–xiv). New York: Haworth Press.

Keshet, J. K. (1987). *Love and power in the stepfamily.* New York: McGraw-Hill.

Lax, W. D. (1994). Offering reflections. In S. Friedman (Ed.), *The reflecting team in action* (pp. 145–166). New York: Guilford Press.

Mahoney, M. (1994). *Stepfamilies and the law.* Ann Arbor: University of Michigan Press.

Martin, D., & Martin, M. (1992). *Stepfamilies in therapy.* San Francisco, CA: Jossey-Bass.

Mason, M. A. (1998). The modern American stepfamily: Problems and possibilities. In M. A. Mason & A. Skolnick (Eds.), *All our families: New policies for a new century* (pp. 95–116). New York: Oxford University Press.

Mason, M. A., & Mauldon, J. (1996). The new stepfamily requires a new public policy. *Journal of Social Issues, 52*(3), 11–27.

Nichols, W. C. (1984). Therapeutic needs of children in family system reorganization. *Journal of Divorce, 7*(4), 23–44.

Nichols, W. C. (1986). Siblings sub-system therapy in family system reorganization. *Journal of Divorce, 9*(3), 13–31.

Nichols, W. C. (1996). *Treating people in families.* New York: Guilford Press.

Noy, D. (1991). Wicked stepmothers in Roman society and imagination. *Journal of Family History, 16,* 345–361.

Papernow, P. (1993). *Becoming a stepfamily: Patterns of development in remarried families.* San Francisco: Jossey-Bass.

Pasley, K., & Ihinger-Tallman, M. (Eds). (1987). *Remarriage and stepfamilies: Current research and theory.* New York: Guilford Press.

Pasley, K., Rhoden, L., Visher, E. B., & Visher, J. (1996). Stepfamilies in therapy: Insights from adult stepfamily members. *Journal of Marital and Family Therapy, 22,* 343–357.

Peek, C. W., Bell, N. J., Waldern, T., & Sorell, G. T. (1988). Patterns of functioning in families of remarried and first marriage couples. *Journal of Marriage and the Family, 50,* 699–708.

Pill, C. J. (1990). Stepfamilies: Redefining the family. *Family Relations, 39,* 186–193.

Pink, J. E., & Wampler, S. (1985). Problem areas in stepfamilies: Cohesion, adaptability and the step-father-adolescent relationship. *Family Relations, 34,* 327–335.

Popenoe, D. (1996). *Life without father.* New York: Martin Kessler Books.

Rosenberg, B., & Hajal, F. (1985). Stepsiblings relationships in remarried families. *Social Casework, 66,* 287–292.

Rosenberg, M. (1965). *Society and the adolescent self image.* Princeton, NJ: Princeton University Press.

Sager, C. J., Brown, H. S., Crohn, H. M., Engel, T., Rodstein, E., & Walker, L. (1983). *Treating the remarried family.* New York: Brunner/Mazel.

Schulman, G. (1972). Myths that intrude on the adaptation of the stepfamily. *Social Casework, 53*(3), 131–139.

Visher, E. B., & Visher, J. S. (1979). *Stepfamilies: A guide to working with stepparents and stepchildren.* New York: Brunner/Mazel.

Visher, E. B., & Visher, J. S. (1988). *Old loyalties, new ties.* New York: Brunner/Mazel.

Visher, E. B., & Visher, J. S. (1996). *Therapy with stepfamilies.* New York: Brunner/Mazel.

White, M., & Epston, D. (1990). *Narrative means to therapeutic ends.* New York: Norton.

Wilson, B. F., & Clarke, S. C. (1992). Remarriage: A demographic profile. *Journal of Family Issues, 13*(2), 123–141.

CHAPTER 19

Families Experiencing Violence

Michele Harway

OMESTIC VIOLENCE, a phenomenon that recently has received widespread attention, has been a factor in families for generations and has been written about extensively over the last 20 years. Social scientists (Davidson, 1977; Dobash & Dobash, 1979) and legal scholars (Hart, 1993) note that domestic violence is reported in religious and historical writings going back to the time of the Romans. Although much of this chapter is focused on violence between marital partners, and there is a specific focus on the treatment of women who have been battered and on the men who battered them, we will consider the general area of relationship violence as well as the impact on the children in the home of witnessing this violence. Child abuse, as a separate issue, will not be considered here. Elder abuse in the home will be discussed briefly.

PREVALENCE STUDIES

PARTNER VIOLENCE

The home, safe haven for many, remains the single most dangerous place for victims of domestic violence. Former U.S. Surgeon General Antonia Novello (1992) reported that "every 5 years, domestic violence claims as many [American] lives as were lost in the Vietnam War—about 58,000." Although the figures about how many Americans are affected by domestic violence vary, there is general agreement that it is a widespread problem affecting millions of families from a wide variety of backgrounds. A long-ignored problem, domestic violence is now being seriously addressed in almost every venue, from Congress (with the enactment of the Violence Against Women Act), to local law enforcement

---

Portions of this manuscript are modified from Harway and O'Neil (1999), Harway and Evans (1996), and Hansen and Harway (1993).

(with more frequent mandatory arrest statutes), to the mental health community (with more domestic violence training).

ADULT MARITAL AND COMMITTED PARTNERS

Gelles and Straus's (1989) widely cited prevalence studies derived from the 1975 First National Family Violence Survey and the 1985 Second National Family Violence Survey indicate that one out of six wives reported being hit by her husband at some point during the marriage; that one out of 22 women said she was the victim of physically abusive violence each year; and that the average battered wife was attacked three times during that year, with severe beatings occurring in six cases out of 1,000 and guns or knives being used in two cases out of 1,000. More recent studies, such as the National Crime Victimization Study (Bachman & Saltzman, 1996), support the high incidence of domestic violence, with 29 percent of violence committed against women by a lone offender being perpetrated by an intimate. Although exact prevalence figures vary depending on the study and the manner in which data were collected, it remains clear that relationship violence is a serious problem affecting millions of American families.

That marital violence can have serious consequences is supported by data from Okun's (1986) study of residents of battered women's shelters, who had experienced an average of 59 assaults each with more than 20 percent indicating that they had been assaulted two or more times per week. Of the women who had ever been pregnant during their abusive relationships, 62 percent had been assaulted during pregnancy. Six percent had experienced at least one assault in which they were extensively beaten up or worse. At intake, among the 300 women studied, there were 28 fractures (usually of the nose or jaw) and 22 other serious injuries (e.g., torn ligaments, dislocations, ruptured eardrums, broken teeth, stab wounds, bullet wounds). Sixty-nine percent of these women experienced at least one assault that involved police intervention and 17 percent had received multiple police visits.

Many incidents of marital and other forms of relationship violence have lethal consequences. In 1994, 62 percent of women homicide victims were killed by intimate others, relatives, or friends (Federal Bureau of Investigation, 1994). Campbell (1992) indicates that at least two-thirds of partner femicide victims had a history of having been battered prior to the killing.

DATING VIOLENCE

Dating violence includes physical injuries, verbal assaults, and threats of violence in the context of a dating relationship. Dating violence has been reported to affect 10 percent of high school students (Roscoe & Callahan, 1985) and 22 percent (Sorenson & Bowie, 1994) to 39 percent of college students (White & Koss, 1991). Jealousy and anger are given as the primary motives for dating violence and most incidents are reported to occur when the partners have been dating each other steadily (Burke, Stets, & Pirog-Good, 1989; Makepeace, 1986; Roscoe & Callahan, 1985). As with other forms of acquaintance violence, young women are more likely than young men to indicate that they were victims of severe physical violence in the context of dating (Gamache, 1991).

Few victims actually report dating violence and, if they seek help at all, generally it is from their friends. Roscoe and Kelsey's (1986) study of dating violence indicates that 25 percent to 35 percent of victims and perpetrators consider the violence a sign of love. The victim often reasons that her partner became violent because she denied him sex. Most violent young men say that they become violent with their date to exert power over her or to intimidate her (Makepeace, 1986; Sorenson & Bowie, 1994).

There are a number of antecedent factors implicated in dating violence. For example, there is some evidence that observing violence in the family is related to a fourfold increase in adolescent males' likelihood to assault their dates, a greater probability for adolescent males convicted of violent offenses (including rape) to repeat these crimes, and a one-third greater chance for adolescent females to be victims of date rape and other forms of assault by peers (Jaffe, Sudermann, & Reitzel, 1992). It is also clear that dating violence can have serious consequences: Young women are three times more likely to report severe emotional trauma as a result of a violent episode in the dating context (Makepeace, 1986).

GAY AND LESBIAN RELATIONSHIP VIOLENCE

Battering is not restricted to heterosexual couples (Island & Letellier, 1991; Renzetti, 1992). Renzetti's (1992) study of lesbian couples indicates that 54 percent had experienced 10 or more abusive incidents, 74 percent had experienced six or more incidents, 60 percent reported a pattern to the abuse, and 71 percent said it grew worse over time.

There are no parallel studies of gay men and domestic violence, which Island and Letellier (1991) attribute to the double taboo surrounding both the topics of domestic violence and that of gay men. This is compounded by the fact that in most cities, domestic violence is a problem that the gay community has been reluctant to address, although a changing political climate has encouraged its confrontation. Finally, the lack of community services available to gay battered men makes them unlikely to come to the attention of authorities or service providers. In the absence of empirical data, Island and Letellier (1991) estimate (from heterosexual prevalence figures and population statistics on sexual orientation) that as many as 500,000 gay men are victims of domestic violence.

ELDER ABUSE IN THE HOME

Abused elders are new participants in the prevalence statistics on domestic violence, not because this is necessarily a new phenomenon, but because until recently it has received little attention. Although some of the early research is inconsistent as to characteristics of victims and perpetrators, the prevalence figures suggest that it is not an insignificant problem. For example, 200,000 cases of elder abuse were reported by Tatara in 1990; this is estimated to represent only one out of 14 cases. Pillemer and Finkelhor's (1988) study of Boston residents aged 65 or older indicated that 2 percent of elders are victims of physical abuse in any given year. This percentage rises to 3.2 percent when psychological abuse and neglect are included in the figures. This study also indicated that 58 percent of respondents reported being abused by spouses, 24 percent by children, and 18 percent by others. Most other studies of elder abuse indicate that the perpetrator is most often a relative who lives with the elder and has cared for him or her over many years. A 1993 study of elder abuse in Los Angeles County found that two-thirds of suspected abusers of elders were family members, of whom 35 percent were offspring, 14 percent spouses, and 18 percent other relatives (Taler & Ansello, 1985). Elders living alone are less likely to be abused than those living with others (Pillemer & Finkelhor, 1988), but abused elders are also more likely to be isolated (from contact with family and friends) than nonabused elders (Wolf & Pillemer, 1994)

CHILDREN WHO WITNESS DOMESTIC VIOLENCE

The number of children said to have been exposed to violence between adults in their home ranges from 3.3 million to 10 million (Carlson, 1984; Straus, 1991). Witnessing violence includes both seeing violence and being aware of the existence of violence even though it may not have been directly seen. Many parents believe that their children are protected from the effects of witnessing the violence because they are sleeping and therefore unaware of the violence. However, Jaffe, Wolfe, and Wilson (1990) note that these same children are able to report in detail about incidents of domestic violence to which they were supposed to be oblivious. Children are known to be present in cases of domestic violence anywhere from 41 percent of the time (according to police records; Bard, 1970) to 71 percent (Jenkins, Smith, & Graham, 1989).

ETIOLOGY OF DOMESTIC VIOLENCE

Although much has been published about violence in the family, many of the available articles and books have provided conflicting information about the etiology and sequelae of familial violence. It is beyond the scope of this chapter to extensively review the many theories proposed to explain men's violence against women. The interested reader is referred to a partial listing of the many books and articles on theories about men's violence against women (American Psychological Association, 1996; Barnett, Miller-Perrin, & Perrin, 1997; Carden, 1994; Crowell & Burgess, 1996; Dutton, 1985, 1988; Gelles, 1979, 1985; Gelles & Straus, 1979; Hamberger & Renzetti, 1996; Kantor & Jasinski, 1997; Koss et al., 1994; Okun, 1986; McCall & Shields, 1986; Straus, Gelles, & Steinmetz, 1988; Thorne-Finch, 1992). In spite of a multiplicity of books and chapters on this topic, it is clear, as Gelles (1993) indicates, that theory development in this area is primitive and that specific theories on violence against women are in the very early stages of development.

The theoretical literature in this area is fragmented and confusing for a number of reasons. First, individual theories of violence have been developed in reaction to prevalent paradigms. The first decade of theorizing about causes of family violence was dominated by biological explanations. In reaction to single-factor biological explanations, sociocultural explanations that linked social structures to family violence were created. In reaction to these theories, feminist and sociopolitical theories emerged. Psychological theories about domestic violence are just beginning to be created. As a result of each of these shifts in theory development, much emotion has been generated and controversies have occurred about the causes of domestic violence.

Second, many of the theories are single-factor theories, limited to a single discipline, rather than more complex ones that hypothesize multiple factors explaining violence across disciplines. Furthermore, the different disciplines have used different terminology to explain family violence, thereby sometimes discouraging discussion across disciplines. However, the complexity of explaining the causes and risk factors of violence requires multidisciplinary explanations.

O'Neil and Harway (1997) and Harway and O'Neil (1999) have presented a multivariate model for understanding men's violence against women (in particular domestic violence). This model posits that six sets of factors explain men's risks for violence against women and that such violence results from the effects of men's psychological learning experiences, socialization experiences, psychosocial risk factors, biology, and relationships, all in the context of the larger macrosocietal dimension. All of these factors interact and contribute to the multiplicity of risks for men's violence against women. Vulnerability to violence is also affected by exposure to counterbalancing protective factors in the man's life. The absence or possession of the protective factors is directly related to men's resilience and vulnerability to violence against women.

UNDERSTANDING BATTERING—THE CYCLE OF VIOLENCE

That battering occurs in cycles was first documented by Walker (1979) in the Cycle of Violence, which effectively depicts typical behavior patterns of abusive relationships and helps us understand the predictable and cyclic nature of the violence. The Cycle of Violence consists of three phases: the tension rising phase, the explosion phase, and the honeymoon phase. The world external to the relationship tends to see the couple during the honeymoon period, when the man looks loving and rational. However, the woman has the symptoms of traumatic stress disorder, which make her look emotionally unstable, angry, vacillating, hysterical, and so on. Seen from the outside, most viewers expect the battered woman to take action against her batterer. Understood from the perspective of the Cycle of Violence it becomes clear why she fails to act: This is because her partner is someone upon whom she has depended in the past, who has just terrified her but is now acting like the loving man whom she originally chose as partner. The Cycle of Violence also helps us understand why both man and woman are motivated to minimize and deny the violence and the abuse in order to support the loving relationship the honeymoon period seems to prove they have.

Usually, the tension and violence continue if not interrupted. The tension and violence often get worse and more frequent. Because the violence recurs so often, eventually the honeymoon period may disappear because neither partner can pretend it will not happen again. The Cycle of Violence predicts that the cycle will keep going: The relief from tension that follows the explosive violence is sufficient to reinforce the cycle. The cycle also reflects a kind of predictability, a dynamic homeostasis, that can also keep the cycle self-regenerating.

An additional factor is what has been dubbed the "battered woman syndrome" (Walker, 1984), which predicts that a battered woman, like an abused child, will take on responsibility for the abuse and focus intensely on changing herself in order to stop the violence. This keeps the victim firmly locked into the cycle and reinforces the violence, because the batterer gets his way without significant negative consequences.

The main use of the Cycle of Violence model clinically has been to help battered women. Survivors can use the model to see past the honeymoon period and past their own excessive guilt and to understand that the abuse and violence will continue, no matter what they do within the relationship. They learn that they cannot ever change enough to affect the cycle.

The key to understanding battering is to know that the Cycle of Violence is controlled by the abuser's behavior. Until and unless the survivor steps outside the cycle, she will be enmeshed in this violence cycle. The batterer's pattern of behavior is independent of the behavior of his immediate partner, as Jacobson's (1993) research showed. Unlike many other family problems, violence controls the family system, not the other way around.

Walker's Cycle of Violence has been updated by the Duluth Minnesota Domestic Violence Project's "Power and Control Wheel" (Pence & Paymar, 1990). The wheel illustrates the idea that the core issue in an abusive relationship is not the cycle of violence, nor violence itself, but the pervasive issue of control. It has taken time to identify this as the most crucial issue because the drama of violence has been so compelling. However, it is crucial to effective intervention to understand that violence is the "enforcer" for the control the man tries to have in many contexts. Battered women find both the Cycle of Violence and the Power and Control Wheel models to make sense of their phenomenological experience.

THE PHENOMENOLOGICAL EXPERIENCE OF BATTERERS

However helpful battered women find these models to be, abusers do not find them to be as useful. They often do not believe that these models fit their phenomenological experience. Admittedly, this is partly because men are in denial of the effects and the reality of their behavior. In addition, men who batter often do not experience themselves as particularly powerful in the world or in their relationships. When these men are accused of being in control, they feel misunderstood. Some have insisted that at the very moment that they were the most abusive, they were terrified. They felt "out of control." The batterer's experience is captured by the Cycle of Feeling Avoidance developed by Evans (and described in Harway & Evans, 1996), which focuses on the man's phenomenological experience: his feelings, his behavior, and the consequences of his behavior, from his viewpoint.

THE CYCLE OF VIOLENCE FROM AN ABUSER'S VIEWPOINT—FEELING AVOIDANCE

The Cycle of Feeling Avoidance is related to the Cycle of Violence with a focus on how the abuser experiences it. Most abusers in relationship experience tension and other unacceptable emotions. This tension may or may not be about events within the relationship. It also may be a distant or unclear experience. Eventually the tension becomes too much for the abuser's usual coping style and there is a crisis. The crisis is initiated when feelings overwhelm the person. The feelings include such things as hurt, shame, helplessness, fear, guilt, inadequacy, loneliness, or other feelings dubbed bad or felt by weaklings. Because these feelings are unacceptable, he feels a need to use defenses. It is important to notice that the defenses are against the feelings. They are not a solution to the problems that led to the feelings. The defenses against feelings can include:

- Blame and denial, making the other an enemy that must be attacked (this is partner abuse)
- Control of everyone and everything around (also abuse)
- Alcohol or drugs to take away the pain temporarily (addiction)
- Negative excitement, such as one-night stands, to distract (acting-out)

All of these defenses can lead to relief in the short run. This reinforces the use of these defenses, despite the fact that they also lead to increased problems. Early in a relationship, the abuser at this point in the cycle may feel remorse or be apologetic; this leads to remorse and honeymoon behavior and other defenses against blame, guilt, and loss (such as placating, submitting, apologizing, manipulating, and so on).

This phase of remorse may drop out after awhile, when repeated abuse makes it impossible for either partner to believe the abuser's apologies. Relief still keeps the cycle going, however. The consequences of the defenses actually cause increased bad feelings and continued tension rising. This cycle of behavior regularly repeats, gets more frequent, more abusive, and more dangerous over time unless it is interrupted or controlled by external factors.

In this cycle, the partner's behavior is irrelevant: Whether she is passive or placating does not matter. This cycle is the individual abuser's cycle. Moreover, an abuser may only be violent in intimate relationships, but he is usually controlling and abusive in most of his relationships. Often we do not label his behavior as abusive, because it is within the ordinary range of what is expected of men. Noticed or not, it is the controlling behavior that men exhibit and the coercion abusers use to enforce the control that is the core of partner abuse as experienced by the survivor. It is the cycle of avoiding dealing with one's central issues by being abusive that is the core issue for batterers themselves. If this behavior pattern is not changed, abuse will continue.

This model is consistent with the work being done in the fields of alcohol and addiction treatment and sex offender treatment, especially in relapse-prevention work. This is no accident. Alcohol and drug abuse are related to domestic violence, as many correlational studies have shown (Dutton, 1988; Edleson & Tolman, 1992). But the relationship between the factors remains elusive unless one assumes that alcohol and drug abuse are related to domestic violence by being part of the cycle of defense against feelings. Although it is almost impossible for an abuser who is actively abusing substances to stop abusing his partner, a sober abuser will generally still be abusive toward his partner unless he gets specific treatment to stop abusive behavior.

CLINICIANS AND DOMESTIC VIOLENCE

Clinicians are increasingly required to be knowledgeable about treating clients affected by violence in the family. Most clinicians are not aware of the frequency with which they may be called upon to intervene in cases of domestic violence. Many erroneously believe that only professionals who plan to specialize in working with family members affected by domestic violence need special training in this area. The high percentages of clients seeking treatment for a variety of issues who are in fact affected by domestic violence require that all clinicians be knowledgeable about how to identify it.

Hansen, Harway, and Cervantes' (1991) and Harway and Hansen's (1993) research indicates that therapists have difficulty recognizing domestic violence and making appropriate interventions. Holtzworth-Munroe and colleagues (1992) contacted therapists to identify maritally distressed but supposedly nonviolent couples. In five different samples recruited through their therapists, 55 percent to 56 percent of the supposedly nonviolent men reported that they had been violent toward their partners in the previous year. Clearly those therapists were unaware of the domestic violence in their caseload.

Until recently, few graduate training programs provided training in the assessment and treatment of domestic violence. This is a particular problem because individuals and families affected by domestic violence do not often volunteer that violence is an issue. Unless therapists are properly trained in assessment of domestic violence, it is likely that they, like the therapists contacted by Holtzworth-Munroe and associates (1992), will miss the indicators for violence and be unable to intervene appropriately.

ASSESSMENT FOR DOMESTIC VIOLENCE

Unless they are specifically doing batterer intervention, where they know domestic violence is a problem, clinicians must routinely assess for violence in the family. It is rare that an individual who is abusive will present for therapy on his or her own volition. It is much more common that a couple involved in domestic violence or a survivor of such violence will present for psychotherapy. Occasionally, a symptomatic child will be the client.

Because clients seldom volunteer information about the battering, assessing for the existence of violence is critical. O'Leary, Vivian, and Malone (1992) indicate that fewer than 5 percent of couples seeking marital therapy spontaneously report violence as a problem during the intake, yet as many as two-thirds of these couples admit to some form of violence on self-report measures (this is also consistent with Cascardi, Langhinrichsen, & Vivian, 1992). Ehrensaft and Vivian (1996), in exploring why couples do not report violence at intake, note that these couples do not consider the violence itself the problem, because the violence is unstable and infrequent and thus it appears to be secondary to other problems. Moreover, the shame that both parties in domestic violence feel (whether they are perpetrator or victim) serves to keep them from volunteering the information at intake. Some survivors may already have experienced the misguided reactions of family members, friends, clergy, and medical personnel who have encouraged them to modify their behavior in order to effect a change in the relationship. Consequently, they think that they will not be believed or that no one is interested in their predicament. Indeed, Goodstein and Page (1981) report that battered women who presented at emergency rooms for treatment following a violent episode had often sought out psychotherapy, but had only had one session and had not returned because the therapist failed to ask them about the battering. Finally, survivors of domestic violence experience the very real fear of increased danger if they tell. All of the above make it clear that mental health professionals must ask about the existence of violence, even (especially) when clients do not mention it.

An example of my intake approach follows:

> Sheila called my office late one afternoon, indicating that she wanted to see me along with her husband Bob. In spite of a long marriage (14 years) and two children, they had been having communication difficulties and she felt that it was time they seek some marital counseling. Could they come see me? I explained that I would be happy to see them for an evaluation session, but that I wanted to be clear up front about how such a session would proceed. I told her that I would see them together for a few minutes at the beginning of the session, that I would next spend about 15 minutes with each partner alone, and that in the final minutes of the evaluation, we would come together briefly to discuss treatment options. I cautioned her not to expect that the issues that were being brought into marital counseling would be addressed or resolved in this first session.

In laying the groundwork in such a way for my intake session, I was ensuring that I would be able to ask the questions necessary to ascertain whether domestic violence was an issue with this couple. If domestic violence were an issue, I would be unlikely to get the information by doing the intake with both members of the couple present. The victim would be unwilling to tell me in her partner's presence, since doing so would endanger her and it would clearly be inadvisable for me to push her to tell me. By seeing them each alone for a few minutes, I can provide the safety needed to get the information that will then allow me to intervene appropriately.

> When Sheila and Bob arrive at my office, I spend a few minutes taking a history of their relationship. I remind them of the game plan for the session, and then by design I interview Sheila first and then Bob. During my interview with Sheila, I learn that

during their latest disagreement, Bob became violent and slapped Sheila. She also tells me that this is not a first-time occurrence. Once things got so out of hand that she ended up at the emergency room needing five stitches to her chin. After assuring her that Bob will not learn from me that I know about the violence and after encouraging her to steadfastly deny that she has told me anything about it, I bring Bob into my office.

I suspect that getting him to acknowledge the violence is likely to be far more difficult. However, armed with the information that Sheila has given me, I know to be infinitely persistent with my questioning. Eventually, Bob does indeed reveal the violent episode.

It is particularly important during the individual questioning that I speak first with the potential victim since she is most likely to acknowledge the violence. Batterers are typically in denial about the violence and even when they do acknowledge it, they minimize and underplay a great deal. In addition, many batterers are also extremely charming and it may be difficult to believe that such a charming individual can be violent with someone he loves. Batterers are also likely to try to control the therapist and the therapy session. Without direct evidence about violence, it is easy for a therapist to fail to be persistent enough to uncover violence. Questions about possible violent interactions need to be consistent and specific. Batterers will seldom acknowledge that they have been violent or abusive when asked directly. However, they may acknowledge that they have pushed her—a little— or slapped her—but only to get her attention.

My questions to Sheila eventually veer toward "All couples have disagreements. Tell me about your last disagreement (or your worst disagreement). What happened? What did you say? What did he say? What did you do? What did he do? And what did you do/say next? What did he do/say next? And then . . . "

The questions ask the woman to recount the disagreement step-by-step, one freeze-frame at a time. It is important to slow the questioning down to this speed because otherwise there is a tendency (on the part of both) to gloss over the violence, and it would be easy to overlook the push or the slap and get to the end of the discussion without ever recognizing that a violent interaction had taken place. I also look for any evidence of fear on her part. Once she has acknowledged the violence to me, I have two responsibilities to her—both related to keeping her safe. I must let her know that no matter what he says to me, I will not acknowledge that she has given me information about the violence. Letting him know that she has informed me about the violence would endanger her since he would surely beat her upon their return home. This means that I will steadfastly maintain my client's confidentiality in order to ensure her safety. My second responsibility to her is to give her information about how to stay safe during the next violent episode. This will usually involve a brief overview of the safety planning that is a standard part of early treatment with a domestic violence survivor.

When Bob comes into the room for his individual interview, I have a bigger challenge. Knowing about the violence, I must somehow create a context that will enable him to tell me about it. It is crucial that the information come from him. My questions to him are along the same line as they were with her, except that I am likely to prolong the questioning and ask for more details if he fails to reveal the violence the first time around. I am also looking to see if he describes the conflict as being resolved using win/lose strategies where a resolution requires one person to emotionally overpower or control the other. I look for patterns of control in their relationship. I assess whether I feel controlled by this client. I listen to see whether he blames everything on his partner and whether he seems willing to hurt her in order to win. I assess his ability to be empathic to his partner and also whether he speaks as if he knows *the* right way or answer.

Some of these patterns may already have been evident to me during the first part of the interview when they were together in my office. Usually through persistent questioning, especially where I have been forewarned that violence did in fact occur, he will acknowledge that there was some violence. It is almost always minimized in its intensity and duration. However, I do not need him to acknowledge a whole list of infractions. A single one will do. Should he ever directly say to me "Did my wife say I hit her? She did, didn't she?", I would deny any such information, but would also redirect it "She didn't, but why don't you tell me about your argument?" Now comes the tricky part.

> I bring Sheila and Bob back together in my office. I now have information that violence does seem to be a problem in this relationship and I know that I will not work with them as a couple. I now have to tell them about my suggested treatment plan. I begin by telling them that while they indeed have a number of issues as a couple that will need marital counseling it would be premature to work on these prior to resolving some of the individual issues that get in the way first. At that point, I would recommend that Bob attend a men's group with men who have similar relational issues and that Sheila work on her individual issues that may affect their relationship.

Note that I never use the word violence, abuse, anger, control, or any of those other trigger words in making my referral to Bob. I refer him to a group that will work not just on the anger and the violence, but on the underlying issues that the violence represents. I refer Sheila to an individual therapist, not because she has myriad individual issues that need resolving, but because she needs support in dealing with the battering. I cannot suggest a battered women's group at this point or I risk scaring them both away from treatment. I have to be realistic. I know that they both would much rather undergo couples therapy than deal with the issues related to violence. There is also a strong probability that they will not follow my suggested treatment plan, but will instead seek out another therapist whom they hope will see them as a couple. I do try to get them into what I consider the more appropriate treatment modality.

WHY NOT COUPLES THERAPY?

The use of couples therapy with couples who have experienced domestic violence is considered controversial. The controversy dates back to feminist critiques of family systems approaches to battering (Pressman, Cameron, & Rothery, 1989; Yllo & Bograd, 1988). Systemic approaches inherently blame the victim and attribute co-responsibility for the battering to her by virtue of approaching the problem from a systemic perspective. Even where the victim is not overtly blamed for the battering, the focus on identifying characteristics of the victim or her behavior supports a conceptualization of the violence as a response provoked by the victim (Hansen, 1993). Moreover, diagnosing victims on the basis of preexisting psychological characteristics leads to the development of interventions based on these diagnoses (Bograd, 1984; Hansen et al., 1991; Harway & Hansen, 1990; Weitzman & Dreen, 1982). Women who experience this process in therapy are likely to continue to regard themselves as responsible for the battering. Because this perception is at least in part responsible for the couple entering therapy, changes in the pattern of inter-action as a result of therapy is unlikely. No matter how well informed the therapist is about the dynamics of battering or how well-meaning she is about her approach to working con-jointly with a battered woman and her batterer, couples therapy implies that the problem is systemic when it is not. Secondly, couples therapy, by its nature, focuses on the problems of the relationship. Looking at these problems under a microscope increases the tension in the couple's relationship, which in turn may increase the risk of harm to the woman.

There are data that suggest that the battering behavior is unrelated to the recipient's behavior. Jacobson (1993) reported that in the course of an argument between a batterer and his partner, her behavior had no effect on the outcome or the process of the argument. Her attempts to placate, confront, or exhibit other forms of behavior were irrelevant to whether the batterer escalated and the argument got worse. If this is so, then systemic inter-ventions to stop abusive behaviors are at best doomed to fail. Focusing on the relational behaviors of the members of the couple and urging modifications of these behaviors will not be an effective way of ending the violence.

Thus, the data suggest that couples therapy is at best an ineffective way of intervening in cases of domestic violence, at worst an approach that puts the victim at increased dan-ger. Both proponents and opponents of couples therapy with clients affected by domestic violence generally agree that once the violence is under control, there remain many rela-tional issues that will benefit from couples interventions (Hansen & Goldenberg, 1993). Most of the proponents of couples therapy reserve this approach for couples experiencing only mild forms of violence (Geffner, Mantooth, Franks, & Rao, 1989).

OTHER ASPECTS OF ASSESSMENT

Once it has been ascertained that domestic violence is indeed a part of the presenting pic-ture, then other levels of assessment must be conducted. These include assessing the level of danger or risk because this has implications for the type of intervention that would be most effective. For example, Gelles (1998) asserts that assessing the severity of risk along with the stage of change (from Prochaska & DiClemente, 1982) can help determine whether incarceration or psychotherapy would be most effective. Others, such as Sonkin (1998) also indicate that knowing the comorbidity, if any, of the batterer will give impor-tant information about treatment options. Finally, assessing for the possibility of lethality is crucial to keeping the client safe. Key factors in determining whether a batterer has the potential to kill include threats of homicide or suicide, acute depression and hopelessness, possession of weapons, obsessive feelings about the partner and family accompanied by beliefs that he cannot live without them or that they are the center of his universe, rage, drug and alcohol consumption combined with despair, history of pet abuse, and easy access to the battered woman and/or family members (Harway & Hansen, 1994).

ASSESSMENT WHEN BATTERED WOMEN PRESENT FOR TREATMENT

Just as couples who have experienced violence will seldom volunteer information about the violence, a woman who has survived battering over a period of time is unlikely to vol-unteer the information. This may be due to her own shame over her mistaken notion that she is responsible for the violence, because she has minimized the violence she has expe-rienced, or because she is unaware that the symptoms that have brought her to therapy are the result of having been battered. Many women who have experienced battering have developed symptoms of posttraumatic stress disorder and these will be the presenting problems that they will bring into therapy. Thus, it is not unusual for a battered woman to enter therapy because she is suffering from depression, anxiety, a sleep or eating disorder, substance abuse, suicidality, intrusive thoughts, somatization, hypervigilance, or because she has victimized others. Determining that these symptoms are the result of a history of abuse is part of the intake. Because of her own feelings of responsibility for the violence, the questioning must follow a similar path to that followed when doing an intake with a couple. That is, the therapist must be persistent and must ask specific questions about specific behaviors. Once it is clear that domestic violence is at the root of the client's symptoms, then normalizing her symptoms is an important step in treatment. The therapist must let the client know that "Disorganized and unusual behaviors following horrible experiences are normal responses to traumatic events." (Root, 1992, p. 237). The client's goal for therapy may include getting some help in having the violence stop but almost never is she in therapy to get help in leaving the abusive relationship. Thus, it is critical that the therapist not revictimize the client by focusing on getting her out of the relationship. Moreover, the client may not return if she feels even subtle pressure by the therapist to end the relationship. At the same time, she may be in extreme danger because of her partner's violence. Consequently, as soon as the therapist is aware of the violence, she and the client must develop and practice a safety or danger-management plan.

Marilyn has been teary throughout much of our initial session. Her 5-year relationship with Peter has been punctuated by several violent episodes, followed by long periods of calm. Each violent episode has seemed to get progressively more dangerous. The last one ended in the hospital emergency room, where Marilyn's broken wrist was set. Accomplished at covering up her violent relationship, Marilyn convinced the medical staff that she broke her wrist during a game of tennis.

She came to see me the very next day and we have been tracing the progression of violence in her relationship. Marilyn has told me up front that she loves Peter and wishes nothing more than to have the violence cease. I know that I must find a way to protect her and keep her safe in the home she shares with Peter and twin 8-year-old boys.

In our first session, we sketch out how she might stay out of harm's way during the next violent outburst. But first, I have to educate Marilyn about the cycle of violence. She learns that for many couples who experience domestic violence there is a definite cycle that occurs. It consists of increasing tension in the home (due to external or internal factors), followed by a violent outburst (the battering) and then by a period that has been dubbed the honeymoon period. It is during this time that Peter has typically apologized profusely for his behavior, promised never to do it again, and has gone out of his way to be especially sweet and loving. Marilyn readily recognizes the cycle, although she had never been aware of it before. Knowing about the cycle organizes her experience, which until now had seemed random. She had often described Peter to her family as sometimes being Dr. Jekyll and other times Mr. Hyde. Of course, she always believed that Mr. Hyde was an aberration and that the man she fell in love with (the real Peter) was the sweet loving man who appeared during the honeymoon period. Now, she realizes that Peter is both men and that she must find a way to keep herself from getting hurt the next time the cycle becomes violent (and she is easily convinced that there will be a next time).

The safety plan involves packing a suitcase containing all the necessities (money, medications, change of clothing for herself and the children). It includes putting this suitcase in a convenient location so that she can quickly take it with her and leave the premises while he explodes. It also involves having a plan for where she will go and how she will get there. Every contingency must be considered: At whose house can she stay? Where will he not think to find her? If he is physically between her and the exit, how will she get out? The plan must be developed and rehearsed repeatedly until it becomes second nature. Variants of the plan must also be developed to consider all eventualities. Finally, because he is likely to become even more agitated if he thinks she has left him, the plan must include a process for letting him know that she is only temporarily removing herself from the premises and will return when he is once again safe.

If a battering outburst is conceptualized as toothpaste out of the tube, it is obvious that when the batterer reaches the point where he is about to explode, he will be unable to stop the explosion midstream (or return the toothpaste to the tube). Once he has had the explosion, he is likely to be ready once again to be loving to his partner. Thus safety planning comes with a recognition of the point of inevitability of the explosion as the time for the woman to exercise the safety plan.

ASSESSING THE EFFECTS ON CHILDREN EXPOSED TO DOMESTIC VIOLENCE

There is no doubt that children exposed to violence in the home suffer from its consequences. Some have described exposure as a kind of psychological maltreatment or emotional abuse (Brassard, Germain, & Hart, 1987). Exposure to marital violence is believed to be more detrimental than exposure to marital discord by itself (Forsstrom-Cohen & Rosenbaum, 1985; Jouriles, Murphy, & O'Leary, 1989). And the effects are likened to being exposed to parents' alcoholism or to seeing a homicide (Rutter, 1979). It is certain that exposed children exhibit far more behavioral problems than nonexposed children. Data suggest that exposed children suffer damage in four areas, including the immediate trauma of the violence, longer term adverse consequences on development, living under conditions of high levels of stress because of fear of injury to self and to the mother, and finally the by-now well-documented impact of exposure to violent role models, particularly on boys.

Wolfe (1997) cites numerous studies describing the effects of observing interparental violence on children. Effects include internalizing and emotional effects such as anxiety, low self-esteem, depression, suicidality, withdrawal, stress reactions, feelings of loss/anger/sadness/confusion, self-blame, and physical problems. Problems may also manifest in the areas of school and social competence and may include learning problems, social incompetence, low empathy, poor problem-solving and conflict-resolution skills, issues of acceptance/legitimization, and poor cognition. Finally, children so exposed may experience externalizing behavioral problems such as aggression and alcohol or drug abuse. Because of the overlap in symptoms between exposure to domestic violence and other clinical presentations, clinicians are strongly cautioned to rule out whether the cause is trauma (exposure to violence, or other forms of trauma), conduct disorder, or attention-deficit disorder. A family history is critical to rule out symptoms that are not due to exposure. Assessing a child's developmental level is also important because one effect of exposure to violence is a developmental lag. It is also important to rule out the coexistence of child abuse because 30 percent to 70 percent of batterers are said to also abuse their children (Hughes, 1992; Pagelow, 1989; Straus et al., 1980). Moreover 35 percent of abused children are abused by their battered parent and another 15 percent by both parents (Stark & Flitcraft, 1988).

ASSESSING ELDER ABUSE

Assessing elder abuse is particularly difficult because it is unlikely that the elder will be brought in for psychotherapy and thus, unless some other service provider becomes involved, elder abuse may continue unheeded. Even when an elder is seen by a mental health professional, the fear of retaliation may prevent an elder from talking about the abuse, especially when his or her continued survival is dependent on the abuser. Shame, guilt, or self-blame are also often factors preventing the elder from disclosing the abuse. Because of the complicated relationship with extended family, wanting to protect family members—either of the perpetrator or of others—may be another reason the elder does not disclose. The clinician must therefore be proactive and assess such things as family boundaries, deviance of the caregiver, and any history of perpetrating abuse against others or of abusing substances. Sexual victimization may also be present: "Therapists must be alert to the patient who sometimes makes a 'coded' disclosure, which is a hint rather than a direct statement of sexual victimization" (Ramsey-Klawsniyk, 1993, p. 90).

> Mathilda, an 85-year-old who lives with her grandson Jonathan, his wife Elizabeth, and their five children has been brought into therapy by Elizabeth. She has become concerned because Mathilda is refusing to eat at the dinner table and cries quietly for hours. Mathilda appears alert and well-groomed and seems eager to tell me about her life. After taking a general history for some minutes, I ask her about her move into Jonathan's home. It is obvious to me that this is a difficult subject but I don't know to what extent her loss of independence is implicated. After a few minutes, I ask her to describe a recent family crisis for me.

As in the earlier case of Sheila and Bob, my questions are very specific and require Mathilda to report the family crisis in a freeze-frame manner.

> I soon find out that Jonathan has been physically abusive with Mathilda a few times during recent months. These episodes almost always occurred when Elizabeth and the children were out of the home and Mathilda was needing Jonathan's assistance in getting from one room of the house to another. The violence has been mild, but nonetheless its occurrence has been extremely traumatic to this loving but aging grandmother. In my home state, I am a mandated reporter when abuse to an elder 65 or over is involved, so I must meet that responsibility first. I also must develop a strategy to ensure that Mathilda's future safety is ensured—especially as she intends to continue living in Jonathan and Elizabeth's home. I may need to serve as an advocate for Mathilda or find an agency who will take on that role.

The disposition of cases involving elder abuse is almost always difficult because, unlike abused children who are not capable of determining what is in their best interest, most abused elders have the cognitive capacity to make such decisions. They may not be physically well enough to remain on their own, however. Conversely, not all elders will be in a cognitive state that will allow disclosure of existing abuse and it may be necessary to involve medical personnel in making such assessments.

TREATMENT ISSUES FOR BATTERERS

Intervening with the perpetrator of family violence is the most important goal in working with domestic violence. Although this section focuses on treatment of men who batter, with small variations it could be applied to other perpetrators of abuse in the family. Also, the focus here is on the perpetrator, because although recipients or witnesses of violence will need to be treated, nothing will change in the family unless the violence is stopped. Domestic violence does not remit on its own; instead, battering usually escalates in severity and occurs more frequently. Although most battered women who leave an abusive relationship go on to form healthy relationships, the same is not true for a batterer who is not treated. Men who batter, unless they are treated for partner abuse, are likely to go on to additional battering relationships (U.S. Commission on Civil Rights, 1982). When a battered women refuses to put up with the abuse, the batterer simply cycles women: He finds another woman whom he can control at least for some time. This is because battering is not the result of a dysfunctional relationship, but rather the result of an individual man's dysfunctional relational style (Harway & Hansen, 1993). The dilemma is that unless a batterer is court-mandated to treatment he will rarely seek it out on his own. The sole exceptions are men who are "wife mandated" to treatment, that is, whose spouses give them a choice of seeking treatment or losing the relationship.

It is important in working with batterers to be clear about what the presenting problem is. Battering is an act of control by one intimate partner over another. It may involve physical violence (i.e., using one's physical strength or presence to control another), or it may involve verbal and emotional abuse (e.g., using one's words or voice to control another). Men who use verbal or emotional abuse often graduate to using physical violence to control their partner. Even when verbal abuse does not eventuate in physical abuse, the psychological mechanisms that stimulate and maintain these two forms of control are the same.

Battering may include a variety of behaviors that range from those appearing moderate (e.g., holding down, unplugging the phone) to those appearing more extreme (e.g., trying to run over with a car, using guns and knives). However, it is extremely important from a treatment perspective to recognize that batterers use a spectrum of violent behaviors. Consequently, battering is recognized not as a response to anger, but as a strategy to maintain power in the relationship, which is seen as the man's entitlement. It is this faulty belief system and the maintenance of the sense of entitlement through self-pity, denial, rationalization, manipulation, and general disregard for the partner that need to be challenged in treatment.

Although batterers have been described in the literature in a variety of ways, it is currently believed that no single profile of batterers exists, but that there are subtypes of batterers. Holtzworth-Munroe and Stuart (1994) indicate that there are three subtypes: family-only, dysphoric, and violent antisocial batterers. Sonkin (1998) describes batterers as organized along two different bipolar dimensions: undercontrol/overcontrol and instrumental/impulsive with three different types resulting from that classification: Overcontrolled, Borderline Personality Disordered/Cyclical, or Psychopathic. He also suggests that the first two types of batterers are more effectively treated using psychodynamic unstructured groups, whereas the third type would do better in a structured cognitive-behavioral group. Gelles (1998) suggests that the level of risk and stage of change of the batterer determine whether incarceration, individual, conjoint, or group treatments are most appropriate, with the highest risk individual at the precontemplative stage of change most suited for incarceration, and the lowest risk and at maintenance level of change suited for couples therapy.

EXISTING TREATMENT APPROACHES

A batterer uses a wide variety of abusive behaviors. At the same time, his primary goal is to maintain control over his partner while allowing him to deny responsibility for the violence. Both of these factors suggest that confronting the violence and the underlying psychological mechanisms will be difficult if not impossible to accomplish effectively in individual therapy. Group therapy is usually recommended for effective treatment. But as Gondolf (1993) points out not all interventions are of equal value.

The three major approaches to group treatment of batterers include programs that focus on anger management, those addressing skill building in a psychoeducational setting, and finally, those confronting men's tendency toward power and control with a view toward making men accountable for their behavior. Some treatment programs include several of the above components.

Anger management programs are based on the belief that battering is caused by a man's inability to control his temper. Intervention consists in teaching the batterer to avoid outbursts by identifying the cues that precede them and the behaviors of the partner that provoke them. As Gondolf (1993) suggests, however, anger control programs by themselves are ineffective in part because they give the batterer, whose problem is due to wanting to control his environment, yet one more thing to learn to control. Moreover, Gondolf also suggests that anger management programs do not properly identify men's sense of entitlement and privilege as causes of battering. Modifications in batterers' behaviors, consequently, seem to be relatively superficial rather than leading to long-lasting and deep change.

Similarly, skill-building programs do not lead to permanent change. Rather than attempting to modify underlying psychological processes, skill-building programs focus on communication skills, stress reduction, gender roles, conflict management, and the like. Some also include attention to cognitive restructuring. Skill-building programs by themselves often yield batterers who become more effective at controlling others through psychological abuse.

Other interventions confront men's tendency toward power and control and teach batterers to take responsibility for the abuse. However, this type of intervention tends to use shame and guilt, leading to large dropout rates among already defensive men. Nonetheless, when properly incorporated into a broader program of intervention, confrontation is a critical component of treatment.

EVALUATION OF BATTERER TREATMENT PROGRAMS

It is unclear how effective batterer treatment programs have proven. Gondolf (1993), citing Tolman and Bennett (1990) and Edleson and Syers (1990), notes that these programs are effective in curbing physical violence: Sixty percent of men who complete the programs are not physically violent 6 months after completion. However, these programs appear not to be as effective at removing the cycle of violence and abuse from these men's repertoire because 60 percent of these men continue to be verbally abusive. This may be because most batterer treatment programs fail to deal with the underlying dynamics of the abuse. Unless and until this aspect is included in treatment, we can expect continuation of the patterns of abuse in families.

Most experts on the treatment of batterers agree that group work should be the primary intervention modality. One rationale for group treatment is that men are socialized together into the culture of women-blaming and violence and can best be resocialized in groups of men. Another more practical reason is that the more experienced men can, more effectively than a therapist, confront the denial and abusive beliefs of the newer group members and reinforce their own changes at the same time.

The best reason for group work may be that it facilitates working with men in the area of their interpersonal functioning. Some men are so filled with shame that it takes hearing that other men have the same problems and have found a way to be different, to give them the courage to examine themselves. For example, clients who espouse feminist convictions, and a conscious commitment to nonviolence, may in fact be controlling and attacking in their interactions with others. This behavior in group provides the focus for change.

The intervention that is most effective with batterers combines therapy and education, a blend of cognitive-behavioral techniques, traumatology, feminist analysis, and psychodynamic approaches. Like therapy with other resistant clients, with batterers behavior change remains the most important goal and is the most common topic of group conversation.

Durable personality change depends on building an effective group process and involving each man in personal relationships that support frequently painful self-awareness and difficult self-confrontation. Shaming a client by forcefully confronting him without a supportive relationship rarely results in positive change, and often has the opposite effect. Moreover, men rarely listen to input that contradicts their own beliefs unless they feel heard and understood. In particular they need to have their pain and feelings of powerlessness validated before they are ready to deal with how they create their own problems through their abusive behavior.

Although many of the treatment approaches described earlier are limited in effectiveness when applied alone, they are each important and necessary components in the treatment of domestic violence. Batterers' treatment must be comprehensive. Focus on the behavior of violence and control is important, as is teaching anger control techniques. At the same time, anger control strategies must be recognized as only another tool to a man who still wants control. Therefore, although communication and other relationship skills have to be taught, attitude change, and more important, personality change, also have to be goals. Understanding how a batterer is repeating family-of-origin behaviors may also help plan appropriate interventions. Working with the individual circumstances of each person's life is critical too. Treatment is predicated on understanding battering and the phenomenological experience of the batterer. Treatment must also emphasize the effects and consequences of the abuser's behavior and it is necessary for there to be social consequences, such as arrest and jail, for batterers' treatment to succeed. It is also important to acknowledge that the abuser is not just his abuse. He is many other human things as well—a total person.

USING THE CYCLE OF FEELING AVOIDANCE IN GROUP TREATMENT

The Cycle of Feeling Avoidance is a core component of a group treatment program encompassing both psychodynamic and cognitive-behavioral approaches. The program has been successfully implemented in a probation-approved batterer's treatment program called Another Way, developed by Kendall Evans. Treatment consists of long-term (52 weeks are mandated) ongoing same-sex groups. In general, these clients blame others in every area of their lives. However, there are a few who come in taking full responsibility for their behavior, motivated by their own awareness that their lives are not working. The violence perpetrated by the court-referred men varies in seriousness, with injuries requiring hospital treatment being the minority. Men causing more serious injury apparently are more frequently sentenced to jail time. In the group, treatment generally focuses on emotional violence more often than physical because emotional abuse recurs frequently. Nevertheless, there is often the threat of serious injury in the situations described by the clients, and safety is the first priority issue. In addition, there does not seem to be a reliable way to discriminate in a few assessment sessions between low- and high-risk cases.

Using this model, group work with batterers seems to follow a loose pattern or progression, partially dictated by the treatment priorities inherent in the situation. For example, one way of clarifying seemingly competing priorities is to make safety the clear number one priority.

The clients who are not court-referred are usually wife-referred, meaning that they are trying to keep her or get her back by coming to therapy. These clients have a higher dropout rate, and frequently are actually less motivated than court-referred clients. A few enter therapy motivated to change.

The women referred by the court seem to have some of the same dynamics as the men, but are also significantly different. They seem to be more likely to be battered women fighting back, or to be more emotionally disturbed than male referrals. Also, being violent is not generally accepted behavior for women in the same way that it is for men. Some programs include women in coed groups and report good results (Richardson, 1990). However, the state of California requires that court referrals go to "same-gender" groups. The group sessions do not always focus solely on domestic violence. The clients talk about work, friendships, childhood, and many other topics. Talking about the Cycle of Feeling Avoidance in any area of their life will lead to personal change and to a reduction in violence and abuse. Abuse is a symptom of a human being living a dysfunctional pattern of behavior, as a result of dysfunctional life experiences, within a dysfunctional society.

After a year in the program, most men appear to have changed significantly, based on clinical assessment and interviews with their partners. Most have completely stopped being violent and are significantly less emotionally abusive. Some men actually stay beyond their 1-year commitment for 2 to 3 years, and they tend to be the men who change the most. After the first year, clients also often participate in individual and couples counseling with generally excellent results.

At the same time, there are also some clients, perhaps as many as 20 percent, who do not change significantly. They may maintain an awareness of legal consequences that will reduce their violence, but they are just as emotionally abusive as when they started. A small number of men drop out within the first four sessions when they realize that they will be confronted and pushed to participate. Voluntary clients also have a high probability of dropping out if their initial attendance immediately resulted in reunification with their partner.

Some batterers have invested major parts of their identity in their "maleness," as defined by being different from and dominant over women. Talking about feelings, cooperating, walking away from an aggressive challenge, and being considerate can all be seen as being "not male" and therefore threatening to such clients' sense of identity. Some clients were raised in emotionally abusive environments that left them filled with shame, so that questioning any aspect of their behavior becomes very painful. For them, the need to be right is experienced as a survival issue. For almost all clients, a confrontation that shames the client does not lead to significant or useful change. Shame is toxic, counterproductive, and easily stimulated.

For other men, the work revolves around the difficulty of giving up the power they feel when they use coercion successfully to control another person. Men who are generally doing well and use intellectual defenses are frequently too proud to let themselves learn anything different from another person. Many men feel relatively powerless in their lives and fear giving up any power they may have attained. Others feel powerful, enjoy the power, identify with power, and fear having nothing if they give up misusing power. Many clients feel unable to change, or appear unable to even conceive of changing. Surprisingly, high proportions of men in these batterers groups appear to be quite passive generally and resist change indirectly, by simply not acting.

The group process provides both the support for and examples of change. The newer or more resistant clients learn from the examples, the support, and the confrontations of the more experienced men. The more experienced men learn from seeing themselves in others' stories. Educational material, such as facts about the consequences of violence, is presented to clients as situations come up in their lives, so that they are more emotionally ready and desirous of learning new ideas and behaviors than they would be with a simple didactic approach.

The power of the group process is sometimes very surprising. Passive avoidant men often learn to become more assertive. Inconsiderate, aggressive men learn to soften and show nurturing. It is not possible to predict in an individual client's case how successful he will be in group. It is possible to maximize each person's chance of success by observing his group process and using the group to draw him out or confront controlling or aggressive behavior. Clients identify with and utilize the Cycle of Feeling Avoidance. It makes sense of their experience, offers them a way out of being trapped, and explains their behavior without blaming and shaming them.

Clients from ethnic minority groups sometimes have a hard time feeling comfortable enough to open up to the group experience. It is important to make sure each client has at least one other person with whom he can identify in the group. Learning to understand the lives of men different from oneself is part of the value of group for many batterers, who can be racist as well as sexist. Learning self-respect is also a powerful gain from effective group process.

TREATING BATTERED WOMEN

Although many women can benefit from the support they receive from others in a battered women's support group, individual therapy is the first type of clinical intervention to which many women will be exposed. There are three distinct treatment phases in individual therapy with battered women. During the crisis intervention phase, the most important aspects are to assess thoroughly for the existence of violence and the level of danger. Educating her about battering and validating her experience are also important components of this phase because others in her life may have ignored the violence or downplayed the danger. Developing and practicing a safety or danger-management plan, as described earlier, is a key component of this phase of treatment. During the next phase of treatment, the single most important goal is to work on empowerment issues. A woman who has been battered has seen her self-esteem systematically eroded away. She may well feel incompetent or too frightened to carry out the simplest task. Paradoxically, as she gains in strength, unless her partner is simultaneously being treated for battering, she is in even greater danger of being hurt by her partner, so safety issues must be constantly revisited.

Because many battered women have indeed been sheltered in their relationship, they may have failed to develop independent living skills and attitudes that may be necessary for survival if the relationship is to end. Finally, an important goal in the therapy at this stage is to grieve the loss of the idealized relationship because regardless of whether she chooses to leave her partner or stay, the relationship that she has is not the one she imagined it to be. Realizing the limitations of her partner and acknowledging the parameters of her actual relationship are important aspects of treatment.

Later in therapy, work is focused on healing the past. A battered woman who is empowered often gets in touch with a great deal of anger and must move through the anger and on to forgiveness in order to continue to improve. Because trust has been repeatedly violated, battered women also have much work to do to develop trust, first in their relationship with the therapist and then with others in their life. Women who have experienced prior boundary violations (such as women with histories of child abuse) will have even more intense work to do on this issue. Finally, exposure to battering over a period of time may have resulted in the development of psychological problems. Conceptualizing these as normal reactions to an abnormal situation (using a trauma recovery model; Root, 1992) and helping the battered woman find meaning in her experience so that she might reorganize her perception of the world and her sense of self are important aspects of the later phases of treatment.

Simultaneously with her individual therapy, battered women can do much healing in battered women's support groups. These groups help her get through her denial, understand her experience, and normalize her reactions to her abusive relationship. Bonding with group members can also help ease the isolation in which many battered women find themselves as a result of the batterer's control.

TREATING OTHERS AFFECTED BY FAMILY VIOLENCE

> Tommy, age 9, was brought to therapy because of suddenly plummeting school grades and aggressive behavior on the playground. During the course of our work together, I learned that in the previous 2 months Tommy had witnessed several episodes of mild violence between his parents. Reenactment through play therapy and the parents' willingness to seek their own therapy were effective with this family.

Because the symptoms developed by children exposed to domestic violence comprise the gamut of symptoms with which children present for therapy, it is difficult to describe here all the appropriate interventions. Of course, interventions should always be age appropriate. With young children, play therapy and other symbolic interventions are often quite effective. Depending on symptomatology, older children may be referred to group treatment.

For elders experiencing violence, pragmatic interventions, including advocacy, are of highest priority.

> Mathilda, the abused grandmother described earlier, experiences great shame because of her victimization. Her guilt vis-à-vis her grandson who is now experiencing legal difficulties because of the abuse is enormous. Much of our time in therapy is spent exploring alternative living options for Mathilda and discussing other pragmatic issues related to her situation. At the same time, we must carefully work through the feelings that the abuse and the ensuing legal problems have elicited for Mathilda.

Much of the therapeutic work with abused elders is focused more on advocacy than on traditional therapeutic interventions. The inevitable feelings surrounding the abuse must also be processed. In addition, following a proper assessment to ascertain whether the elder is also suffering trauma symptoms, working from a trauma recovery model may be appropriate as well.

SOME CONCLUDING REFLECTIONS ON THE FUTURE OF FAMILY VIOLENCE

Family violence is a problem that will not go away soon. The prevalence figures cited earlier argue for the importance of proper training for mental health professionals and the necessity for clinicians to be proactive in their work with those affected by violence in the family. In particular, the availability of intervention programs for violent individuals and the societal pressure to ensure that individuals mandated for treatment comply are essential. Most juridisdictions still permit battering interventions that have not been effective or are of too short duration. Ensuring consistency across jurisdictions is important. And, most important, as Senator Joseph Biden has indicated "this type of violence has been allowed to continue because the problem has been protected by a wall of silence, denial and neglect. . . . We must end the silence." (Biden, 1999).

REFERENCES

American Psychological Association (1996). *Violence and the family: Report of the American Psychological Association Task Force on Violence and the Family.* Washington, DC: Author.

Bachman, R., & Saltzman, L. E. (1996). *Violence against women: Estimates from the redesigned survey* (Bureau of Justice Statistics special report). Rockville, MD: U.S. Department of Justice (NCJ No. 154348).

Bard, M. (1970). Role of law enforcement in the helping system. In J. Monahan (Ed.), *Community mental health and the criminal justice system* (pp. 99–109). Elmsford, NY: Pergamon.

Barnett, O. W., Miller-Perrin, C. L., & Perrin, R. D. (1997). *Family violence across the lifespan.* Thousand Oaks, CA.: Sage Publications.

Biden, J. R. (1999). Foreword. In M. Harway & J. M. O'Neil (Eds.), *What causes men's violence against women.* (pp. ix–xi). Newbury Park, CA.: Sage Publications.

Bograd, M. (1984). Family systems approaches to wife battering: A feminist critique. *American Journal of Orthopsychiatry, 54,* 558–568.

Brassard, M. R., Germain, R., & Hart, S. N. (1987). *Psychological maltreatment of children and youth.* New York: Pergamon.

Burke, P. J., Stets, J. E., & Pirog-Good, M. A. (1989). Gender identity, self-esteem and physical and sexual abuse in dating relationships. In M. A. Pirog-Good & J. E. Stets (Eds.), *Violence in dating relationships: Emerging social issues* (pp. 72–93). New York: Praeger.

Campbell, J. C. (1992). "If I can't have you, no one can": Power and control in homicide of female partners. In J. Radford & D. E. H. Russell (Eds.), *Femicide: The politics of woman killing* (pp. 99–113). New York: Twayne.

Carden, A. D. (1994). Wife abuse and the wife abuser: Review and recommendations. *The Counseling Psychologist, 22*(4), 539–582.

Carlson, B. E. (1984). Children's observations of interparental violence. In A. R. Roberts (Ed.), *Battered women and their families* (pp. 147–167). New York: Springer.

Cascardi, M., Langhinrichsen, J., & Vivian, D. (1992). Marital aggression, impact, injury, and health correlates for husbands and wives. *Archives of Internal Medicine, 152,* 1178–1184.

Crowell, N. A., & Burgess, A. W. (1996). *Understanding violence against women.* Washington, DC: National Academy Press.

Davidson, T. (1977). Wife beating: A recurring phenomenon throughout history. In M. Roy (Ed.), *Battered women: A psychosocial study of domestic violence* (pp. 1–23). New York: Nostrand Reinhold.

Dobash, R. E., & Dobash, R. P. (1979). *Violence against wives: A case against the patriarchy.* New York: Free Press.

Dutton, D. G. (1985). An ecological nested theory of male violence toward intimates. *International Journal of Women's Studies, 8*(14), 404–413.

Dutton, D. (1988). *The domestic assault of women.* Boston: Allyn & Bacon.

Edleson, J., & Syers, M. (1990). The relative effectiveness of group treatments for men who batter. *Social Work Research and Abstracts, 26,* 10–17.

Edleson, J. L., & Tolman, R. M. (1992). *Intervention for men who batter.* Newbury Park, CA: Sage.

Ehrensaft, M. K., & Vivian, D. (1996). Spouses' reasons for not reporting existing marital aggression as a marital problem. *Journal of Family Psychology, 10*(4), 443–453.

Federal Bureau of Investigation. (1994). *Uniform crime reports, Supplemental homicide report.* Washington, DC: Author.

Forsstrom-Cohen, B., & Rosenbaum, A. (1985). The effects of parental marital violence on young adults: An exploratory investigation. *Journal of Marriage and the Family, 47,* 467–472.

Gamache, D. (1991). Domination and control: The social context of dating violence. In B. Levy (Ed.), *Dating violence: Young women in danger* (pp. 69–83). Seattle, WA: Seal Press.

Geffner, R., Mantooth, C., Franks, D., & Rao, L. (1989). A psychoeducational conjoint therapy approach to resolving family violence. In P. L. Caesar & L. K. Hamberger (Eds.), *Psychotherapeutic interventions with batterers: Theory and practice* (pp. 103–133), New York: Springer.

Gelles, R. J. (1979). *Family violence.* Beverly Hills, CA: Sage Publications.

Gelles, R. J. (1985). *Intimate violence in families.* Beverly Hills, CA: Sage Publications.

Gelles, R. J. (1993). Family violence. In R. L. Hampton, T. P. Gullotta, G. R. Adams, E. H. Potter, & R. P. Weissberg (Eds.), *Family violence: Prevention and treatment* (pp. 1–24). Newbury Park, CA.: Sage Publications.

Gelles, R. J. (1998, October 21–24). Presentation at the 4th International Conference on Children Exposed to Domestic Violence. San Diego, CA.

Gelles, R. J. & Straus, M. R. (1979). Determinants of violence in the family: Toward a theoretical integration. In W. R. Burr, R. Hill, F. I. Nye, & I. L. Reiss (Eds.), *Contemporary theories about the family. Vol. 1* (pp. 549–581). New York: The Free Press.

Gelles, R. J., & Straus, M. R. (1989). *Intimate violence: The causes and consequences of abuse in the American family.* New York: Simon & Schuster.

Goodstein, R. K., & Page, A. W. (1981). Battered wife syndrome: Overview of dynamics and treatment. *American Journal of Psychiatry, 138,* 1036–1044.

Gondolf, E. W. (1993). Treating the batterer. In M. Hansen & M. Harway (Eds.), *Battering and family therapy: A feminist perspective* (pp. 105–118). Newbury Park, CA: Sage Publications.

Hamberger, L. K., & Renzetti, C. (1996). *Domestic partner abuse.* New York: Springer.

Hansen, M. (1993). Feminism and family therapy: A review of feminist critiques of approaches to family violence. In M. Hansen & M. Harway (Eds.), *Battering and family therapy: A feminist perspective* (pp. 69–81). Newbury Park, CA: Sage Publications.

Hansen, M., & Goldenberg, I. (1993). Conjoint therapy with violent couples: Some valid considerations. In M. Hansen & M. Harway (Eds.), *Battering and family therapy: A feminist perspective* (pp. 82–92). Newbury Park, CA: Sage Publications.

Hansen, M., & Harway, M. (1993). *Battering and family therapy: A feminist perspective.* Newbury Park, CA: Sage Publications.

Hansen, M., Harway, M., & Cervantes, N. N. (1991). Therapists' perceptions of severity in cases of family violence. *Violence and Victims, 4,* 275–286.

Hart, B. J. (1993). The legal road to freedom. In M. Hansen & M. Harway (Eds.), *Battering and family therapy: A feminist perspective* (pp. 13–29). Newbury Park, CA: Sage Publications.

Harway, M., & Evans, K. (1996). Working in groups with men who batter. In M. Andronico (Ed.), *Men in groups* (pp. 357–375). Washington, DC: APA Books.

Harway, M. & Hansen, M. (1990). Therapists' recognition of wife battering: Some empirical evidence. *Family Violence Bulletin, 6*(3), 16–18.

Harway, M., & Hansen, M. (1993). Therapist perceptions of family violence. In M. Hansen & M. Harway (Eds.), *Battering and family therapy: A feminist perspective* (pp. 42–53). Newbury Park, CA: Sage Publications.

Harway, M., & Hansen, M. (1994). *Spouse abuse: Treating battered women, batterers and their children.* Sarasota, FL: Professional Resource Press.

Harway, M., & O'Neil, J. M. (1999). *What causes men's violence against women?* Newbury Park, CA: Sage Publications.

Holtzworth-Munroe, A., & Stuart, G. L. (1994). Typologies of male batterers: Three subtypes and the differences among them. *Psychological Bulletin, 116,* 476–497.

Holtzworth-Munroe, A., Waltz, J., Jacobson, N. S., Monaco, V., Fehrenbach, P. A., & Gottman, J. M. (1992). Recruiting nonviolent men as control subjects for research on marital violence: How easily can it be done? *Violence and Victims, 7,* 79–88.

Hughes, H. M. (1992). Impact of spouse abuse on children of battered women: Implications for practice. *Violence Update, 2*(17), 1, 9–11.

Island, D., & Letellier, P. (1991). *Men who beat the men who love them: Battered gay men and domestic violence.* New York: Harrington Park Press.

Jacobson, N. (1993, October). *Domestic violence: What the couples look like.* Paper presented at the annual convention of the American Association for Marriage and Family Therapy. Anaheim, CA.

Jaffe, P. G., Sudermann, M., & Reitzel, D. (1992). Working with children and adolescents to end the cycle of violence: A social learning approach to intervention and prevention programs. In R. DeV. Peters, R. J. McMahon, & V. L. Quinsey (Eds.). *Aggression and violence through the life span* (pp. 83–99). Newbury Park, CA: Sage Publications.

Jaffe, P. G., Wolfe, D. A., & Wilson, S. K. (1990). *Children of battered women.* Newbury Park, CA: Sage Publications.

Jenkins, J. M., Smith, M. A., & Graham, P. J. (1989). Coping with parental quarrels. *Journal of the American Academy of Child and Adolescent Psychologists, 28,* 182–189.

Jouriles, E. N., Murphy, C. M., & O'Leary, K. D. (1989). Interpersonal aggression, marital discord, and child problems. *Journal of Consulting and Clinical Psychology, 57,* 453–455.

Kantor, G. K., & Jasinski, J. L. (1997). *Out of the darkness: Contemporary perspectives in family violence.* Thousand Oaks, CA: Sage Publications.

Koss, M. P., Goodman, L. A., Browne, A., Fitzgerald, L. F., Keita, G. P., & Russo, N. F. (1994). *Male violence against women at home, at work and in the community.* Washington, DC: APA Books.

Makepeace, J. M. (1986). Gender differences in courtship violence victimization. *Family Relations, 32,* 101–109.

McCall, G. J., & Shields, N. M. (1986). Social and structural factors in family violence. In M. Lystad (Ed.), *Violence in the home: Interdisciplinary perspectives* (pp. 98–123). New York: Brunner/Mazel.

Novello, A. C. (1992). From the Surgeon General, U. S. Public Health Service; A medical response to domestic violence. *Journal of the American Medical Association, 267* (23), 3132.

Okun, L. (1986). *Women abuse: Facts replacing myth.* Albany, NY: State University of New York Press Albany.

O'Leary, K. D., Vivian, D., & Malone, J. (1992). Assessment of physical aggression against women in marriage: The need for multimodal assessment. *Behavioral Assessment, 14*(1), 5–14.

O'Neil, J. M., & Harway, M. (1997). A multivariate model explaining men's violence toward women: Predisposing and triggering hypotheses. *Violence Against Women, 3*(2), 182–203.

Pagelow, M. D. (1989). *The forgotten victims: Children of domestic violence.* Paper presented at the Domestic Violence Seminar of the Los Angeles County Domestic Violence Council.

Pence, E., & Paymar, M. (1990). *Power and control, tactics of men who batter: An educational curriculum.* Duluth, MN: Minnesota Program Development, Inc.

Pillemer, K. A., & Finkelhor, D. (1988). The prevalence of elder abuse: A random sample survey. *The Gerontologist, 28*(1), 51–57.

Pressman, B., Cameron, G., & Rothery, M. (Eds.). (1989). *Intervening with assaulted women: Current theory, research, and practice.* Hillsdale, NJ: Lawrence Erlbaum.

Prochaska, J. O., & DiClemente, C. C. (1982). Transtheoretical therapy: Toward a more integrative model of change. *Psychotherapy: Theory, Research and Practice, 19*(3), 276–288.

Ramsey-Klawsnik, H. (1993). Interviewing elders for suspected sexual abuse: Guidelines and techniques. *Journal of Elder Abuse and Neglect, 5*(1), 73–90.

Renzetti, C. M. (1992). *Violent betrayal: Partner abuse in lesbian relationships.* Newbury Park, CA: Sage Publications.

Richardson, A. (1990). *The effects of the presence of female batterers on male batterers.* Unpublished master's paper. Encino, CA: California Family Study Center.

Roscoe, B., & Callahan, J. E. (1985). Adolescents' self report of violence in families and dating relations. *Adolescence, 20,* 545–553.

Roscoe, B., & Kelsey, T. (1986). Dating violence among high school students. *Psychology, 23,* 53–59.

Root, M. P. P. (1992). Reconstructing the impact of trauma on personality. In L. S. Brown & M. S. Ballou (Eds.), *Personality and psychopathology: Feminist reappraisals* (pp. 229–265). New York: Guilford Press.

Rutter, M. (1979). Protective factors in children's responses to stress and disadvantage. In M. W. Kent & J. E. Rolf (Eds.), *Primary prevention in psychopathology: Vol. 3. Promoting social competence and coping in children* (pp. 49–74). Hanover, NH: University of New England.

Sonkin, D. (1998, October 21–24). Presentation at the 4th International Conference on *Children Exposed to Domestic Violence,* San Diego, CA.

Sorensen, S., & Bowie, P. (1994) Vulnerable populations: Girls and young women. In L. Eron, J., Gentry (Eds.), *Reason to hope: A psychosocial perspective. Schlegel, P. on violence and youth.* (pp. 167–176). Washington, DC: American Psychological Association.

Stark, E., & Flitcraft, A. H. (1988). Women and children at risk: A feminist perspective on child abuse. *International Journal of Health Services, 18,* 97–118.

Straus, M. A. (1991, September). *Children as witness to marital violence: A risk factor for life-long problems among a nationally representative sample of American men and women.* Paper presented at the Ross Roundtable titled "Children and violence," Washington, DC.

Straus, M. A., Gelles, R. J., & Steinmetz, S. K. (1980). *Behind closed doors: Violence in the American family.* Garden City, NY: Doubleday.

Taler, G., & Angello, E. F. (1985). Elder abuse. *Association of Family Physicians, 32,* 107–114.

Tatara, T. (1990). *Elder abuse in the United States: An issue paper.* Washington, DC: National Aging Resource Center on Elder Abuse.

Thorne-Finch, R. (1992). *Ending the silence: The origins and treatment of male violence against women.* Toronto: University of Toronto Press.

Tolman, R. M., & Bennett, L. W. (1990). A review of quantitative research on men who batter. *Journal of Interpersonal Violence, 5,* 87–118.

U.S. Commission on Civil Rights (1982). *Under the rule of thumb: Battered women and the administration of justice.* Washington, DC: U.S. Government Printing Office.

Walker, L. E. A. (1979). *The battered woman.* New York: Harper & Row.

Walker, L. E. (1984). *The battered woman syndrome.* New York, Springer.

Weitzman, J., & Dreen, K. (1982). Wife beating: A view of the marital dyad. *Social Casework, 63,* 259–265.

White, J. W., & Koss, M. P. (1991). Courtship violence: Incidence in a national sample of higher education students. *Violence and Victims, 6,* 247–256.

Wolf, R. S., & Pillemer, K. A. (1994). What's new in elder abuse programming? Four bright ideas. *The Gerontologist, 1*(34), 126–129.

Wolfe, D. (1997). Children exposed to marital violence. In O. W. Barnett, C. L. Miller-Perrin, & R. D. Perrin (Eds.), *Family violence across the lifespan: An introduction* (pp. 133–157). Newbury Park, CA: Sage Publications.

Yllo, K., & Bograd, M. (Eds.). (1988). *Feminist perspectives on wife abuse.* Newbury Park, CA: Sage Publications.

CHAPTER 20

Families with Learning Disabilities, Physical Disabilities, and Other Childhood Challenges

Sandra A. Rigazio-DiGilio and Darci Cramer-Benjamin

IT IS ESTIMATED that 4.5 million children in America experience a disabling condition (Cedarbaum & Mashaw, 1995). Concomitantly, they, their families, and their communities are dealing with the associated challenges (Breslau, 1988; Seligman, 1985). Some disabilities are primarily psychosocially based, being identified by those who determine that the child's developmental path and psychological functioning are not in synchrony with her or his normative group or with family and societal expectations. Learning disabilities, attention deficit disorder/hyperactivity disorder (ADD/HD), and some speech and language difficulties typify the types of disabilities that are defined through social exchanges with parents, teachers, caregivers, and peers. Other childhood challenges are primarily physically based, with specific biological anomalies, including impairment of movement, speech, vision, hearing, and growth.

Individual and family reactions to childhood disabilities are likened to the experience of grieving and loss (Bevan, 1988; Cohen, 1995; Fortier & Wanlass, 1984; Shontz, 1965). Although variations exist, this process includes phases of shock, refusal, guilt, bitterness, envy, rejection, and finally adjustment—in relation to the child's disability and the response of the wider community. Seligman (1985) notes that multiple influences on family life and family coping render these stages flexible and not necessarily linear (p. 64).

The mediating role of families in the management of childhood disabilities is well documented (Ferrari & Sussman, 1987; Rolland, 1994). However, although early research suggests that most families experience adverse reactions, current research indicates that the variability and intensity of family reactions are greater than originally expected (Norton & Drew, 1994). Some families do not experience increased levels of adversity (Dyson, 1991) or relational issues (Carr, 1988). They meet needs for security and change, and create environments to integrate disabilities in ways that access unity and resources (Cobb, 1987). However, some families do struggle with associated stressors, experiencing disruptive parent-child relations (Yando & Zigler, 1984), damaged sibling relations (Powell & Gallagher, 1993), contentious marital relations (Lambie & Daniels-Mohring, 1993), or strained family-community relations (Goode, 1984).

It has long been argued that the family is the most appropriate unit of analysis for understanding the manifestation and meaning of childhood disabilities as co-constructed between individuals and families (Drotar, Crawford, & Bush, 1984; Shapiro, 1983). More recent dialogues broaden the social exchange arena to include the wider community (Rigazio-DiGilio in press; Wynne, Shields, & Sirkin, 1992). The extant literature, however, continues to examine primarily the pathogenic effects of the disability on the child and its impact on the family. This research is largely based on a cognitive-behavioral framework (Quittner & DiGirolamo, 1998) and focuses on variables consistent with operating within this paradigm. Seldom do researchers begin with an examination of the family in context and then investigate the specific systemic dynamics that facilitate or impede effective development and functioning within and between individuals, families, and communities. Instead, most focus on the impact of specific disabilities on the family and on the coping strategies generated by the family (Kazak, 1986).

The findings of this research suggest that family stress is related to the child's age and the uncertainty of the diagnosis. That is, when a child is diagnosed early and with less ambiguity (e.g., Down's syndrome), family stress is limited, whereas increased stress and coping difficulties are present when a child is diagnosed at a later age and when the illness life course is uncertain (e.g., Rett's disorder). These findings, while important, are of limited value in understanding the unique family dynamics and family-community interface variables that influence effective coping, management, and development (Mowder, 1991).

This chapter reviews this literature base and offers a perspective on family adaptation to childhood disability based on co-constructive, developmental, and biopsychosocial principles. The integrative analysis is used to suggest treatment, research, and training implications.

RELATIONAL STRESSORS AND CHILDHOOD DISABILITIES: A MULTICULTURAL, METAPERSPECTIVE

Culberston and Silovsky (1996) delineate diagnostic criteria to assess the relational stressors that emerge and influence childhood disabilities. Based on their analysis of research targeting learning disabilities and ADD/HD, they suggest a set of relational problems that could exist, to varying degrees, between individuals, families, and communities faced with identifying and managing these disabilities. These criteria include relationships typified by inappropriate parental expectations for achievement and/or behavior; impaired levels of family control; devaluing interactions that lower the child's status within the family by virtue of the problems associated with the disability; high levels of parent-child conflict related to day-to-day living; and an interactional pattern characterized by overprotection, rejection, or criticism associated with low self-esteem in the child and/or difficulty in interpersonal problem solving. These criteria are pertinent in four interactional domains: parent-child, sibling, teacher-school, and peer relations.

Because individuals and families are embedded within broad systems, relational interactions within and among individuals, families, and communities are influenced by cultural determinants (Pare, 1996). Therefore, while Culberston and Silovsky (1996) provide a broad framework for understanding relational stressors associated with and influencing childhood disabilities, a multicultural metaperspective provides appreciation for the unique relational arrangements occurring within and across cultures and how persons sharing particular customs and interpretations collectively develop (Anderson & Sabatelli, 1999).

Cross-cultural research indicates that a child's disability has different meanings for each family (Barnwell & Day, 1996; Lynch & Hanson, 1992; Rogers-Dulan & Blacher, 1995). Therapists working with these families should understand the predominant beliefs, customs, and practices of their own and the family's particular ethnic groups and communities, while being aware of the tendency to overgeneralize. Any appreciation of ethnicity must include both an understanding of the central tendencies of each group and various other factors that contribute to family diversity (e.g., immigration patterns, religious ties, intercultural partnering, socioeconomic factors, acculturation processes). General themes about childhood disabilities found within ethnically diverse families can be used to appreciate how different families understand and react to disability. Therapists could use these themes to hypothesize about collective meaning making, and then refine these themes as they learn more about other factors affecting family diversity.

In Anglo-European culture, the etiology of childhood disability is generally perceived as based in science, primarily genetics and psychology (Lynch & Hanson, 1992). Native American tradition usually places the causality of illness on supernatural (i.e., spirit loss or intrusion) and natural (i.e., disturbances of balance brought on by breaching cultural taboos) causes. In Native American tradition, genetic explanations may explain how disabilities occurred, but only cultural factors explain why these occurred (Barnwell & Day, 1996). For African Americans, disabilities may be interpreted in one of two ways: as bad luck or misfortune or as the result of "sins of the fathers." However, practical realities usually supersede any causative mythology, and families do what they must to survive (Boyd-Franklin, 1989). Latino American families tend to have an underlying belief that illness occurs due to the presence of evil in one's environment. These ideas are related to beliefs in a punishing God, folk beliefs about the power of evil, or beliefs that life is laden with tragedy, where one accepts good and bad as they occur (Steinberg, Davila, Collazo, Loew, & Fischgrund, 1997). Asian American traditions may use naturalistic and metaphysical explanations focused on a mother's presumed failure to follow health care practices during pregnancy or postpartum. Asian Americans also may see disability as a divine punishment for sins committed by parents or ancestors (Campion, 1982). Parental responsibility is often seen as the cause of the birth of a child with a disability by families of Middle Eastern cultures. Guilt is felt by the mother, who is usually held responsible for the child's well-being and shame is felt by the father, who often views his child's disability as a personal defeat and a scar on the family's pride (Barnwell & Day, 1996).

FRAMEWORKS FOR UNDERSTANDING CHILDHOOD DISABILITIES

Traditional services provided for families dealing with childhood disabilities rely heavily on educational and medical frameworks. Services tend to be unidirectional and focus on the child's needs separate from family and community (Beckman, 1996; McDaniel, Hepworth, & Doherty, 1992). Biopsychosocial models and family stress models provide a more interactive understanding of the family's mediative role in assisting its child and other members to adapt to associated challenges. Co-constructive models view disability identification and management as a transactional phenomenon that includes how the community influences and is impacted by the disability. Thus, frameworks for understanding childhood disabilities range from narrow, individualistic, deficit-based perspectives to holistic, transactional, and competency-based perspectives that include extended territories for assessment, intervention, and evaluation.

EDUCATIONAL PERSPECTIVES

Educational services seldom deal with family dynamics that support or hinder the growth and development of a disabled child (Christiansen, Olson, & Gentry, 1997). Children are assessed to determine special education eligibility (Public Law 94-142, 1975). Although parent participation is required in planning, the plans seldom encourage parent involvement or parent-teacher collaboration. In 1990, the role of public schools and agencies was extended to provide services for preschool children with disabilities (Public Law 101-476, 1990). Services are meant to help families stimulate the development of their children. Plans are based on family strengths and needs, and services are aimed at assisting families to interact with and be involved in their child's development. In reality, however, services are often provided directly to the child, and the family is not party to the strategies created by involved professionals working on behalf of the child.

MEDICAL PERSPECTIVES

The medical model primarily attributes pathology to biological processes and does not account for social, psychological, or interactional variables that promote or hinder childhood development (McDaniel et al., 1992). Not only are child and family separated, but the totality of the child also is undermined—treating disabilities apart from humaneness. This fragmentation of patient care has been challenged for more than two decades. Engel (1980) proposed a biopsychosocial model that considered biological, social, and psychological variables as part of a comprehensive medical assessment. He cautioned professionals to account for these variables in assessments of disease or disorder. Others have extended Engel's work to include the concepts of development (Hobbs, Perrin, & Ireys, 1985) assessment, treatment, and collaboration (McDaniel et al, 1992), and bidirectionality (i.e., how illness affects families and how families affect illness) (Wood, 1993).

THE BIOBEHAVIORAL PERSPECTIVE

Wood (1995) proposes a biobehavioral disease continuum to conceptualize childhood disabilities. She constructed a framework to account for the relative proportions of psychological and physical factors inherent in any disability. At one end of the continuum are disabilities with strong psychosocial influences (e.g., learning disabilities), and at the other are disabilities with strong physical influences (e.g., cerebral palsy). The middle ground represents disabilities such as ADD/HD.

Although each disability has unique characteristics, there are universal developmental and biopsychosocial features (Serrano, 1993). Issues concerning the impact of disabilities on the child, the family, and the management of the disability hold true for severe cognitive and emotional, as well as physical illnesses (Wood, 1995). The commonalities in the adaptative styles of individuals and families are the basis for a comprehensive, developmental intervention model.

Wood places her continuum within a wider biopsychosocial and developmental framework and suggests that the well-being of children with disabilities depends on a dynamic balance among individual physical functioning, individual psychological functioning, and family-social functioning. She offers a three-domain assessment process to determine levels of balance in the family: the member (questions focus on well-being, developmental milestones, and identity); the family level (factors such as proximity and intimacy, generational hierarchy, responsivity, and subsystem relational quality are examined); and the social level (issues of proximity, hierarchy, responsivity, and triangulation for the child and the family as they interact with external agencies and institutions are considered).

FAMILY STRESS PERSPECTIVES

Hill (1949) introduced the family stress model to investigate the psychosocial impact of normative and nonnormative stressors on families. Models frequently used to examine families dealing with childhood disabilities build on the basic elements of this model (e.g., McCubbin & Patterson, 1982; Thompson, Gustafson, Hamlett, & Spock, 1992). While each is somewhat different, all rely on similar constructs and assumptions regarding how families respond to stress (e.g., constructs such as stress, stressor events, coping strategies and resources, and adaptive or ineffective coping responses). Further, most models assume that (1) ongoing demands for change continually place families under some degree of stress, (2) at times, families need to alter task management strategies to respond to stress, (3) a family's ability to adapt to stress influences its capacity to function effectively over time, and (4) adaptive families construct strategies that reduce individual and collective stress while concomitantly supporting the growth of all members (Anderson & Sabatelli, 1999).

Research stemming from these models suggests that although the diagnoses and management of childhood disabilities place children and family members at risk for particular relational and psychological disorders (e.g., depression, anxiety, marital discord), these effects are variable, with a majority of families making a successful adaptation (Drotar, 1992). In their meta-analysis of such studies, however, Quittner and DiGirolamo (1998) found that although broad indices of behavioral and emotional functioning suggest general adjustment, well-controlled epidemiological studies indicate a higher incident rate of psychological disorders for children with chronic illnesses and their parents when compared to families without disabled children. Although one has to question if these pathogenic labels are a socially constructed phenomena that do not take into account natural and logical consequences of dealing with a disability (Rigazio-DiGilio, Ivey, & Locke, 1997), their findings do point out that studies based on family stress models are not specific enough to predict when developmentally and contextually specific stressors may surface in response to a childhood disability.

CO-CONSTRUCTIVE PERSPECTIVES

Co-constructive conceptualizations regarding relational and psychological distress (e.g., Wynne et al., 1992) help us understand the interactive processes that occur across individuals, families, and wider systems (i.e., the interactive triad) to identify and manage childhood challenges. For example, Wynne and colleagues (1992) provide a conceptual framework that looks at the definition and management of physical and emotional disability as a transactional process wherein experiences among individuals, families, and health professionals serve to construct meaning-making systems that label and respond to disability. In terms of childhood challenges, both the ontology of disability (i.e., culturally defined impaired functioning, observable and attributable to a particular challenge) and the phenomenology of disability (i.e., the transactional interpretation of a child's functioning that attributes his or her behavior to a challenge) are inextricably linked, quickly becoming part of a discourse among members of the interactive triad. The collective meaning that emerges from this discourse comes to govern how members of the triad will identify and manage particular childhood challenges. This framework helps us conceptualize how families and wider communities come to construe childhood challenges in ways that either promote or inhibit healthy adaptation.

World Views

Rigazio-DiGilio (in press) articulates a co-constructive perspective that identifies several variables affecting the transactional process described by Wynne and colleagues (1992). That is, families construct their experience, perception, and reaction to childhood disabilities within three main parameters: (1) those inherent in the family's collective world view, (2) those inherent in the individual world views of family members and significant others directly and indirectly participating in naming and managing the disability, and (3) the wider sociocultural constructions governing conceptualizations of health and dysfunction. The degree to which families respond to and influence their members and wider contexts depends on these parameters and on the degree of instrumental power and influence potentially exercised by each component of the interactive triad.

Power Differentials

Power differentials across components of the triad change the interaction. For example, social and economic oppression negatively influence the development of personal and collective competencies in relation to defining and managing disabilities. This also occurs when families experience pronounced dissonance from external narratives that are outside their physical, psychological, cultural, moral, or spiritual sense of self or self-in-context, or when the environment labels a family's familiar ways of perceiving and acting as substandard or deviant (Miller, 1976).

Embeddedness

This concept is used to represent the degree of power and influence any member of the individual-family-community system exerts during transactions that define childhood disabilities. Influence is generated by the extent to which components of the interactive triad are interrelated when defining and managing a disability. For example, if an individual's primary source of consensual validation and identity is based within the family's world view, then that individual will be strongly influenced by how the family defines and manages the childhood disability and will help perpetuate the shared world view. This is often the case for younger children with disabilities who depend on family validation to construct a basic sense of self and self-in-context. On the other hand, if an individual's sense of self and others is based in a multitude of environments (e.g., school, community, peers), the individual will be less affected by the family's world view of the disability and may question or rebel against the family's version and management of the disability, as is often the case with adolescents.

FRAMEWORKS FOR UNDERSTANDING INDIVIDUAL AND FAMILY DEVELOPMENT AND CHILDHOOD DISABILITIES

Research on how individuals and families adapt to childhood disabilities focuses on how the disabilities affect childhood psychosocial development and family adaptation, and on how family responses affect the child's ability to cope. Such foci are derived from general theories of individual and family development and adaptation (Quittner & DiGirolamo, 1998).

STAGE-SPECIFIC DEVELOPMENTAL FRAMEWORKS

Over the last five decades, theorists have devised frameworks to explain family life stages (e.g., Carter & McGoldrick, 1988). Some of these models emphasize concepts of reciprocity (e.g., Nichols & Everett, 1986), family transitions (e.g., Bruenlin, 1988), multigenerational influences (e.g., Combrinck-Graham, 1983), alternative stages (e.g., Carter & McGoldrick, 1988), and cultural context (e.g., Falicov, 1988). Although most models look through filters of culturally defined normative tasks and demands, the core assumptions can be used to understand families dealing with nonnormative demands for change.

These stage-specific models use childbearing and rearing as focal points and describe varying ways changes occur in family composition, structure, roles, tasks, demands, and strategies over the life course. Models highlighting reciprocity issues remind clinicians that individuals are on their own life path within a broader collective life phase, each influencing the other. Transitional theories connect developmental transitions with models of stress and coping and offer ways to examine family transitions that relate to managing childhood disabilities.

Multigenerational models help clinicians look at the impact that generational stressors and strategies have on the life course of each generation. Alternative theories assist clinicians to view forced life situations, such as childhood disability, as a disruption in a traditional developmental journey, as a new developmental challenge that needs to be superimposed on traditional models, or as requiring a family life cycle model in its own right. Finally, theories that highlight contextual issues focus clinicians on how the predominant culture influences ways individuals and families experience and respond to nonnormative stressor events.

Clinicians can use the dimensions inherent in these theories to guide comprehensive assessment. For example, the birth of a disabled child requiring extensive medical intervention will affect the family's ability to bond together. Another example would be how the parents' tendency to overprotect a child will affect their own and the child's psychosocial development. At the time of diagnosis, any family is faced with the necessity of changing rules and strategies to meet the needs of the child. The elder generation may be asked to temporarily forgo their developmental trajectory to assist in caretaking. While morphostasis will occur, it will be interrupted when changing individual or family needs are not in synchrony with the biopsychosocial demands of the disability. This could occur as siblings surpass the developmental milestones attained by an older disabled child. Finally, if the disability is not embraced by institutions involved in its definition and management, the family members will need to rely on their own sense of normative development in order to challenge deficit-based perspectives.

CO-CONSTRUCTIVE DEVELOPMENTAL FRAMEWORKS

Unlike the linear, normative assumptions underlying most stage models, co-constructive frameworks focus on human and systemic meaning making (e.g., Rigazio-DiGilio, in press). Such models represent holistic perspectives on how individuals and families come to understand and act upon life events. Four assumptions undergird these models: (1) Individuals and systems co-construct unique world views, (2) world views develop in a person-environment dialectic transaction, (3) change occurs in nonhierarchical, recursive ways, influenced by a need to balance constancy and change, and (4) developmental impasses reflect incongruities between world views and change demands. Impasses occur when families cannot balance management of a stressor and concomitant needs to help members and subsystems grow and adapt (Rigazio-DiGilio, 1999).

The child with a disability is embedded in multiple systems that overtly and covertly interact to influence the illness experience and its management. Families are central mediators in this exchange process and understanding how they interpret and respond to this world is essential. They make choices that directly influence the coping strategies that will have an impact on their well-being and the well-being of the child with a disability.

Adaptive families utilize resources to meet their needs in relation to the experience and management of the disability. Belief systems, based on past successes, enable them to exercise influence on members and the wider context to minimize stress and ensure successful development of members and subsystems. Nonadaptive families are constrained by a limited use of options, have difficulty balancing change and constancy, and may exaggerate their responses in either direction. On the one hand, if a constrained family rigidly adheres to patterns of blame and anger in response to change demands, and a child is diagnosed with a disability, the family may enter into a cycle of blaming one another and outside helpers. On the other hand, if a nonadaptive family's coping style is diffuse and not anchored in behavioral, cognitive, or emotional patterns, the family haphazardly attempts any new idea or belief in an effort to respond to the stress associated with a childhood disability. In both circumstances, the family's ability to manage both the disability and its own development is hindered.

A SYSTEMIC CO-CONSTRUCTIVE–DEVELOPMENTAL PERSPECTIVE OF CHILDHOOD DISABILITIES

Systemic cognitive-developmental theory (SCDT) (Rigazio-DiGilio, in press, 1994) is a co-constructive perspective regarding human and systemic adaptation. It offers a framework for understanding how families come to experience, understand, and operate in their worlds and in relation to normative and nonnormative life tasks such as childhood disabilities.

SCDT does not situate pathology within the child or family, but posits a dialogic process that encompasses the disability, the mediating role of the family, and the interactions that occur across the interactive triad. SCDT suggests that adaptive or nonadaptive responses to disabilities evolve from the interactions that occur across individual and family biological and social history, cultural contexts that influenced them over time, and contexts currently involved in assessing and managing the disability.

Families are often called upon to be primary mediators in the interactive triad when a child is considered to be disabled. In this role, families function in ways that either promote or inhibit the child's development and the continued growth of all its members and subsystems. How well they manage these two tasks is influenced by their particular phase of systemic development.

PHASES OF SYSTEMIC DEVELOPMENT AND CHILDHOOD DISABILITIES

A systemic, co-constructive–developmental framework focuses on meaning-making processes, or ways families cognitively, affectively, and behaviorally integrate normative and nonnormative life tasks. This approach directly links developmental constructs to practice and research (Borders, 1994). Accordingly, families and their members are understood to recycle through four meaning-making phases as they interact together and within significant contexts. These phases represent varying (1) internal family arrangements, (2) individual and collective meaning-making processes, and (3) levels of permeability among members, subsystems, and the environment.

Family adaptation is facilitated or constrained by the family's unique structure, collective identity, and interactive style as these change over time and in response to specific circumstances. Clinicians and researchers can look at the demands of childhood illnesses (e.g., Rolland, 1984) and associated management tasks, and determine if these are developmentally matched or mismatched to the family's competencies at any particular point in its collective development.

System Exploration Phase

In this phase, forming or established systems begin to negotiate an initial or alternative sense of collective identity. It takes a period of time for individuals to establish boundaries that will protect the integrity of their relationship so that they can co-construct shared meanings and a sense of collective identity. During this time, partnerships primarily rely on (1) each individual's history and world view, and (2) significant contextual influences that govern mores and norms and define health and dysfunction. The relationship might be described as a diffuse interpersonal environment, grappling with system precursors from these individual and community domains and linking some of these together to form common themes that influence continued interaction and meaning making (Gray, 1981). This is a vulnerable time, as partners have yet to build a coherent identity, and are susceptible to variations within individual and wider contextual domains. This susceptibility threatens effective partnering with one another, or with outside contexts in response to nonnormative events like childhood disabilities. Secondary issues may arise that manifest the lack of coherent identity and structure and a perceived need to depend on the expertise and strength of others.

When established families initially encounter the prospect of a childhood disability, they recycle through this exploratory phase as they attempt to redefine a collective sense of themselves and rearrange their functioning to adapt to or challenge this circumstance. Families that have established a coherent yet flexible collective meaning-making process will be best able to handle these ontological and phenomenological challenges to identity and functioning. Those who have yet to construct a coherent family identity or those who have constructed a reified sense of family may have difficulty developing partnerships within the family and with significant others to effectively handle internal and external demands for change, and may tend toward interpretations, emotions, and behaviors that exacerbate individual and relational stressors.

System Consolidation Phase

During this phase system precursors connect to form organizing themes, and a relational structure is established that supports and reflects these themes. Families establish strong boundaries to consolidate and protect the integrity of their internally supported themes as they establish a firm foundation that ensures the continuity of the system. They reinforce shared, more predictable ways of experiencing, interpreting, and acting in the world and in response to certain circumstances. During this phase, their tendency is to reject alternative intrafamilial or extrafamilial opinions or attitudes. Families that remain embedded in this phase have difficulty effectively evaluating alternative perspectives and may demonstrate complications in collaborating with family members and outside systems.

When integrating the needs of a disabled member, families tend toward two options: incorporating the disability within their existing image of themselves and accommodating to the needs of the child and affected members in ways already familiar to them; or solidifying around a deficit-based image of blame, shame, and scapegoating because their consolidated image is threatened by the prospect of a disability. At this phase, the dynamics to coerce member or contextual compliance can lead to secondary presenting problems that reflect the family's inability to alter its image and strategies to effectively manage life tasks.

System Enhancement Phase

During this phase, families are more likely to operate with clear boundaries concerning their collective sense of themselves as a family-in-context. Information from family members and significant others is more readily accepted to extend and enhance their image. Although the impetus to alter strategies comes from multiple sources, families weigh the relevance of these alternatives and use those that reinforce a sense of competence. They expand the influence and centrality of mutual goals, values, and views by elaborating their ideas and beliefs to cover a range of issues. At this phase, variations are more easily accepted in terms of types of internal and external change demands, such as a childhood disability. This is often a phase where the entrance of a nonnormative stressor does not easily threaten the integrity of the family, as the collective unit can more readily integrate the needs of all family members and the challenges of the wider context. A stumbling block can occur, however, if the type of disability, the range of management, or the demands of the wider context require the unit to transform its identity as opposed to altering family life strategies. Secondary issues can arise for those members who are prone to hold outdated images of self and system that are not in synchrony with the life course changes required to integrate the childhood disability.

System Transformation Phase

During this phase, families go through a process of significantly changing images of themselves, their members, and wider contexts, questioning the foundations of their identity. They question the viability of their preexisting identity in light of demands for change that challenge the parameters within which they experience, understand, and operate in the world. The external process of making boundaries moves toward increasing levels of permeability. Families deconstruct less useful assumptions and options and reconstruct alternative ones that provide continuity while also encouraging the evolution of an alternative identity that is more in synchrony with their circumstances. This process may return families to systems exploration. Stumbling blocks occur if families are faced with multiple challenges to their preexisting identity, so much so that synthesizing each challenge could dismantle their system (e.g., the diagnosis of a childhood disability concurrent with the diagnosis of a life-threatening illness in a partner).

How families move through these phases depends on the degree to which variations can be effectively incorporated into their preexisting identity. As Constantine (1986) suggests, when confronting unfamiliar stressors, families tend to respond in ways that are consistent with their preexisting world view. This often leads to an exaggeration of their established repertoire (Kantor & Lehr, 1975). Therefore, families with coherent yet flexible identities are better able to traverse through these phases when faced with a childhood disability. Such families might represent those that do not experience debilitating stress in relation to a disability. For example, the literature indicates that a strong marital relationship is a primary factor that can mediate parental distress associated with childhood disabilities (cf. Bristol, 1984). Guralnick (1989) asserts that optimal child development corresponds with the extent that parents become competent and confident in their roles. On the other hand, families with weak or reified identities—indicative of systems that are arrested at a particular phase or that drift toward the system exploration phase, where wide latitude is given to try less coherently based interpretations and options—are not able to successfully negotiate changes in family strategies or collective identity required to successfully understand and manage a childhood disability over the life course.

THE FAMILY-ILLNESS INTERFACE

To balance continuity and change, families must manage a multitude of coexisting individual, family, and contextual variables. This balance can be skewed, depending on the phase of collective development dominating a system at a given point. We highlight the interdependent relationship between developmental phases and the introduction and life course management of a childhood disability. Although these two variables also have many dimensions (e.g., illness onset and course, family themes and strategies), the primary dimensions we focus on are the evolution of collective meaning making and boundary creating processes between individuals, families, and communities as these relate to systemic development and to illness identification and management.

Adaptive families effectively manage childhood disability while concomitantly supporting the growth of members, subsystems, and the collective unit. Adaptation is less assured for families that attend to one of these life tasks at the sacrifice of another; families that manage illness in a way that hinders individual, subsystem, or family development; or families that promote the development without embracing the ill member. The interface of these two dimensions is explicated in Table 20.1. For each developmental phase four options are available to handle the family needs and the disability. In option one, the family demonstrates an ability to effectively manage both aspects of development. Option two represents a skewed response, privileging illness management over individual and family development. Option three represents the opposite response, favoring individual and family development over illness integration. The final option represents families that are unable to manage either aspect of development.

The table offers a framework that clinicians and researchers can use to understand how families traverse developmental phases as collective units while integrating the disability and its life course management. The table suggests cognitive and behavioral indicators that may assist clinicians and researchers to target the particular point of interface experienced by a family. This may assist clinicians to tailor treatment to the developmental needs of the family and illness, and may guide researchers to construct developmentally versus pathologically oriented investigations.

TABLE 20.1   The Family–Illness Interface

	System Exploration Phase	System Consolidation Phase	System Enhancement Phase	System Transformation Phase
Pathway One: Families are able to manage both individual, subsystem, and family development, and illness onset and course.	Themes related to individual and system development and illness meaning and management move toward integration as family searches for a coherent, collective identity.	Themes related to individual and system development and illness meaning and management become integrated into a coherent collective identity.	Family can contemplate multiple perspectives and options for alternative identities, structures, and strategies to manage the illness and continue as a collective unit.	Family deconstructs portions of individual and collective identities that marginalize illness meaning and management and reconstruct identities that synthesize development and illness course.
Pathway Two: Families manage illness onset and course, but have difficulty managing individual, subsystem, and/or family development.	Family moves toward a collective identity that is predominantly based on the meaning and management of the illness, deemphasizing other individual, subsystem, and collective roles, positions, and tasks.	The collective identity remains intact so long as illness meaning and management can be incorporated into this image. However, individual and relational life tasks could be sacrificed if major change is necessary.	Family may divert energy from individual and relational development and instead emphasize finding creative solutions to understand and manage the illness.	Family may deconstruct and reconstruct only those parts of individual and relational identity that are focused on illness meaning and management, arresting other components of these identities.
Pathway Three: Families manage individual, subsystem, and family development, but have difficulty managing illness onset and course.	Family moves toward individual and relational images apart from the disability and its management. May result in ineffective care or in a primary reliance on external support systems.	Family members may slightly alter strategies or bring in outside support so individual and relational tasks are not hindered.	Solutions to adapt may favor alternative strategies for individual and relational development while sacrificing the growth of those members involved in managing the disability.	Individual and collective transformative issues continue that do not adequately address the needs of the child with a disability or those involved in management over time.
Pathway Four: Families are not able to manage individual, subsystem, and family development, or illness onset and course.	Individual and relationship stressors, along with illness integration and management, may be seen as insurmountable.	Outdated individual and collective identities are reified, marginalizing the disability and promoting linear patterns of blame, denial, and anger.	Many surface level perspectives and strategies are generated but magical thinking about the "perfect cure" or the "perfect family" may come to dominate.	The added variation of an illness may promote a rapid deconstruction and affect a dismantling of the system.

CLASSIFICATION OF CHILDHOOD CHALLENGES: RESEARCH FINDINGS AND ANALYSIS

Using Wood's (1995) biobehavioral continuum of disabilities, we classify various childhood challenges within two groups: (1) those primarily psychosocial (learning, speech and language, ADD/HD), and (2) those primarily physical (general, congenital or acquired, mental retardation, neurological, developmental, autism, impairments of vision, hearing, growth).

INCIDENCE REPORTS AND DEFINITIONS

Definitions and incident levels for each examined disability are provided in Table 20.2. Translating incidence levels to family demographics, it is estimated that one in four American families have a child experiencing a disability, with a disproportionate number of children and families dealing with socially defined psychosocial disabilities.

In a "best" construction of social reality, we might imagine that this is related to our increasing ability to identify psychological and educational childhood challenges that have heretofore been unrecognized or misdiagnosed. A "worst case scenario" also can be entertained. That is, one can imagine that the dominant culture increasingly pathologizes children and families who are not in synchrony with mainstream institutions and policies and that this trend may absolve wider contexts from the responsibility to make contextual changes more tailored to increasing diversities inherent in our pluralistic society (Rigazio-DiGilio, 1999; in press):

> To illustrate, consider two sets of parents attending parent-teacher conferences to discuss indicators being used to determine whether or not their sons require evaluative testing for . . . ADHD. The parents embedded within the social, political, and economic realities dominating the local educational community and carrying their own sense of real or perceived power, might define themselves as a family that will stand up for the rights of their child. These parents may use the dialogue to address the deficiencies of an overpopulated, understaffed school system. They may note that the use of Ritalin™ in the local school system has increased over 20% in the last decade and that teachers have received inadequate training. . . . However, the parents more peripheral to social, political, and economic trends, or carrying less of their own sense of real or perceived power, might define themselves and their child as somehow dysfunctional or inadequate. These parents may listen to the steps that school personnel envision they need to take to ensure that their child accommodates to the classroom environment. They may not recognize that the classroom environment may have an inadequate structure or inadequately trained teachers to tailor to the needs of their child.
>
> In the latter case, the wider systems of influence could, intentionally or not, neglect the interactional forces at work between the child and his environment, and move toward the ADHD diagnosis. However, in the first case, the systems of influence may in fact be required to reflect upon how social, political, and economic trends have affected the classroom environment, and how these changes are now affecting the child's perception of himself and his educational and behavioral competence. (p. 25)

AN ANALYSIS OF THE EMPIRICAL STUDIES

A literature review is presented for both physically and psychosocially based disabilities, organized around two main issues: (1) how these diagnoses affect child and family iden-

TABLE 20.2   Incidence Reports and Definitions for Primary Childhood
Problems/Challenges

Psychosocially Based Problems/Challenges

Learning disabilities: [5% of school-aged children] Deficiencies in one or more psychological
processes involved in spoken/written language, resulting in an imperfect ability to listen, think,
speak, read, write, spell, or do mathematical calculations (NICHCY, 1998a).

Speech and language impairments: [approximately 1,000,000 students during 1995–96]
Problems in communication and related areas (e.g., oral motor function) and range from sound
substitutions to the inability to understand or use language or the oral-motor mechanism for
functional speech and feeding (NICHCY, 1998b).

ADHD: [3–5% of school-aged children] A neurobiological disorder manifest in developmentally
inappropriate behaviors like poor attention skills, impulsivity, and hyperactivity. ADHD typically
arises before age 7, is chronic, and lasts at least 6 months (NICHCY, 1998c).

Physically Based Problems/Challenges

Spina bifida: [1 out of 1,000 births] Spina bifida is identified by an incomplete closure in the
spinal column. Symptoms include muscle weakness or paralysis below the area of the spine
where the incomplete closure (or cleft) occurs, loss of sensation below the cleft, and loss of
bowel and bladder control (NICHCY, 1998d).

Cerebral palsy: [500,000–700,000 Americans] A condition caused by damage to the brain,
affecting musculature. Symptoms can include tight limb muscles, purposeless movements, rigidity, and lack of balance. Cerebral palsy is often accompanied by seizures, drooling, incoordina-
tion, abnormal speech, hearing/visual impairment, and/or mental retardation (NICHCY, 1998e;
United CP Association of Washington, 12/2/98).
http://weber.u.washington.edu/~wscchap/NoMoreLabels/palsy.html

Autism: [5 to 15 per 10,000 births]: A neurological disorder that affects a child's ability to
communicate, understand language, play, and relate to others. Evidenced by a moderate to
severe range of communication, socialization, and behavior problems, and often accompanied by
mental retardation (NICHCY, 1998f).

Visual impairments: [12 per 1,000 children] Types include *partially sighted* problems requiring
special education; *low vision* or being unable to read newsprint at a normal viewing distance,
even with eyeglasses or contacts; *legally blind* persons with less than 20/200 vision in their best
eye or with a limited field of vision (20 degrees at its widest point); and *totally blind* students
who learn via braille or other nonvisual media (NICHCY, 1998g).

Hearing impairments: [68,070 students, age 6–21, in 1995–96] Impairments include permanent
or fluctuating difficulties that adversely affect educational performance. Deafness is an impairment in processing linguistic information through hearing, with or without amplification
(NICHCY, 1998h).

Mental retardation: [585,308 students, age 6–21 in 1995–96] Subaverage general intellectual
functioning existing concurrently with deficits in adaptive behavior that adversely affect a
child's educational performance (NICHCY, 1998i).

Growth impairments: [1 in 140 children experience muscle and skeletal disabilities] Disorders
include human growth hormone deficiency, Cushing's syndrome, hypothyroidism, nutritional
short stature, intrauterine growth retardation, Russell Silver syndrome, disproportionate short
stature, and achondroplasia. Although each of these disorders manifest with different symptoms,
in general symptoms can include growth retardation, muscle or bone tissue atrophy, and asym-
metrical or disproportionately sized extremities (Human Growth Foundation, 12/2/98).

tity, and (2) bidirectional accounts of the impact of family dynamics on child psychosocial
functioning and vice versa. This analysis reveals three significant findings concerning (1)
the paradigmatic approach of investigators, (2) the nature of the recursive interaction
between family and disability, and (3) the role of family therapy in treatment.

Paradigmatically, two significant findings emerge. First, most research examines the
impact of the disability from a deficit-based perspective. That is, the predominant research
examines coping styles and impediments to healthy development for the child, the family

subsystems, and the family as a whole. The presumption undergirding most studies is that the disability will significantly interrupt individual and relational development. For example, some studies report the comorbidity of psychiatric symptoms associated with childhood disabilities (e.g., Biederman, Faraone, Milberger, & Guite, 1996). Only recently have we come to recognize that many of these families also have positive resources to draw upon and are able to continue on their developmental journey while still embracing the disability (e.g., Singh et al., 1997; Stein et al., 1997).

Secondly, while there is a predominant use of developmental conceptualizations to explore growth over time, the traditional chronological application of development is most commonly offered (Piaget, 1954), and seldom are developmental constructs used to frame the exploration of the investigation (e.g., Hanline, 1991). The co-constructive views provided above might help investigators use competency-based models to explore the impact of childhood disabilities from a developmentally based rather than a deficit-based paradigm.

Most studies do not adequately address recursive transactions across illness, individuals, families, and wider systems. This finding is consistent with results from reviews conducted by Black, Danseco, and Krishnakumar (1998) and Bauman, Drotar, Leventhal, Perrin, and Pless (1997). Most studies look at the unidirectional impact of the disability on the child and the family (e.g., Holder-Brown, Bradley, Whiteside, Brisby, & Perette, 1993; Norton & Drew, 1994).

Studies that attempt to examine issues of bidirectionality employ global measures of family dynamics such as FACES III (Olson, 1987), The Family Environment Scales (Moos & Moos, 1981), and behavioral checklists and aggregate the data around issues of cohesion and hierarchy (e.g., Varni, Rubenfeld, Talbot, & Setoguchi, 1991). The fact that few studies (e.g., Bennett, 1988; Hanline & Daley, 1992) provide a culturally sensitive analysis of the interaction between family dynamics and disabilities speaks to the fact that there is little emphasis on issues of bidirectionality as these occur across individuals, families, and communities. One explanation might be that work conducted thus far has primarily been carried out by researchers trained in a specific disability or in individualistic psychology who do not bring a systemic perspective to their work.

Recent efforts (e.g., Kaslow, 1996; McDaniel et al., 1992) have offered theoretically based relational lenses to examine these issues. However, a comprehensive agenda of research based on such lenses has yet to be advanced. If it is presumed that family dynamics and societal norms play a significant role in the evolution and manifestation of problems associated with childhood disabilities, and that, concomitantly and interdependently, the challenges and stressors associated with disabilities have a significant influence on individuals, relationships, families, and societal institutions and policies, then it follows that more empirical work needs to be accomplished in this area to inform theory and practice.

Five treatment approaches are available in the mainstream identification and management of childhood disabilities: psychoeducation and preventive models, grieving and coping skills models, medical and psychopharmacological models, consultation and mediation models, and family therapy models. The first two dominate the literature. The behavioral, deficit-oriented model that pervades existing literature is reflected in the treatment options of choice. For example, medical, technical, and drug interventions have proven successful in orthopedic (e.g., Holder-Brown, et al., 1993) and ADD/HD (e.g., Barkley, Guevremont, Anastopoulos, & Flecher, 1992). Some interventions rely on the work of therapists as advocates for the child and/or family with school, medical, and social service agencies (e.g., Correa, Silberman, & Trusty, 1986). A few studies report the effect of family therapy on these disabilities (e.g., Barkley, et al., 1992). Those studies that directly mention the type of family therapy used in the intervention process most often highlight structural (Minuchin, 1974) and behavioral family therapy (Patterson, 1982) models. Unfortunately, what is proposed as a family approach usually is reduced to employing the assistance of the family through psychoeducational or family support group treatment approaches (e.g., Dunst & Trivette, 1988; McPhail, 1996).

In sum, the research literature presents information on a wide diversity of childhood disabilities. However, it does not concentrate on the recursive nature of the individual, relational, systemic, and developmental transactions that occur across all domains of the interactive triad dealing with the ontological and phenomenological aspects of particular childhood disabilities. Although research demonstrates how particular treatment interventions can aid in the management of stress and the amelioration of some psychosocial factors (e.g., school problems, generational stressors, peer relations), the research does not adequately address how individuals, families, and wider systems do, or can be assisted to, interact and realign around revised identities that embrace the disability over time.

TREATMENT IMPLICATIONS

The literature is replete with suggestions for clinical interventions.

Psychoeducational Needs

Some focus on psychoeducational needs, such as helping families develop social support networks and learn new language to communicate information about their child's disability to members of the interactive triad (e.g., Holder-Brown et al., 1993). A current emphasis in this area focuses on family empowerment in which clinicians assist families to develop capacities for accessing knowledge, skills, and resources that help them gain positive control of their lives and effectively partner with service providers (e.g., Singh et al., 1997; Stein et al., 1997). Other areas of focus include methods for attending to crisis management; securing and refining appropriate services; training in educational, medical, and tailored child rearing; and locating economic and social support networks (e.g., Harbin, 1993).

Family Dynamics

Other reports focus on family dynamics (e.g., Anastopoulous, Barkley, & Shelton, 1996; Powers, 1991; Serrano, 1993), indicating that clinical work with this population needs to emphasize (1) the integration of the disability in the family, (2) the creation of a positive and coherent family and individual identity, (3) the realignment of family structure and organization, and (4) the development of facilitative interactions with outside services. Powers (1991) specifies the need to assess cross-generational coalitions, hierarchical conflict, and executive and sibling subsystem discord. Steinberg and associates (1997) extend the assessment terrain to include family meaning making and individual and collective self-image.

Tailoring Treatment

Some authors recognize a need to tailor treatment to the unique needs of this population. For example, Heflinger and Nixon (1996) offer three guidelines to assist therapists in this effort. First, a range of therapeutic options should be available, including format (e.g., individual, relational, family, group), orientations (e.g., psychodynamic, cognitive-behavioral, developmental, structural, transgenerational), duration, and frequency. Second, therapists need to be aware of the risk of negative treatment effects based on their own assumptions of family pathogenesis or dysfunction, or when treatment is mandated (or strongly suggested) by an outside agency. Third, the quality of the therapeutic alliance cannot be overestimated. Effective interventions will be grounded within a therapeutic relationship built on respect and empathy, and an understanding of the ontological and phenomenological reality of these families and the illnesses they face.

Expanding Assessment and Treatment

Relational (Culbertson & Silovsky, 1996) and co-constructive perspectives (Rigazio-DiGilio, in press) offer new opportunities to expand our domains of assessment and treatment. Working with the internal dynamics of a family system will be enhanced when external relationships (e.g., peers, teachers) and community influences (e.g., cultural mores, sociopolitical forces) are accounted for, not only diagnostically, but also in terms of treatment. Therapy with these populations cannot simply occur inside the walls of the therapy office. Often, clinicians will be involved in treatment regimens that actively include members of the interactive triad. For example, treatment must address the degree of congruency across various world views inherent in the interactive triad, and the trends of these views toward salutogenic or pathogenic perspectives of the illness and its management. Additionally, clinicians need to determine the phases of systemic development a family is grappling with, including both the collective family unit and its understanding and management of the disability.

CASE EXAMPLE

Lisa (44) and Mike (47) Slater, an intact, dual-career couple with two children (Angela, 10, and Matthew, 6) came to therapy after a series of incidents involving Matthew's behavior at school. The last incident resulted in Matthew's suspension after he verbally threatened his teacher, and the couple deciding to seek therapy. The couple's explanation of the incident revealed a narrow and reified meaning and interactional structure that revolved around various ways of conceptualizing Matthew's learning disability (LD) and its management. The critical nature of Matthew's behavior required his immediate removal from school, and administrators called Lisa at her workplace, when Mike, the usual contact person, was not reached. While she was able to make arrangements to pick up Matthew, both the request and the situation activated Lisa's usually unexpressed feelings of anxiety about her son and anger toward her husband for not being consistently available to rectify such situations. The couple's management of such emotions usually escalated unresolved conflict and a family split along gender lines.

Always a part of their interaction, the unresolved conflict and distancing behaviors had increased over the years, revolving mainly around parenting issues. During their transition to parenting, Mike assumed most household management and child-care duties, while Lisa concentrated on career advancement and social position. Lisa was an involved, yet peripheral parent during periods of lesser stress. During escalated periods of stress, she entered more as a critical and anxious evaluator of Mike's child-care competencies. This pattern became narrower and more reified after Matthew's LD diagnoses and continued to meet the needs of the couple for external social status and internal emotional distance.

Matthew's language processing difficulties were evident early on and prompted a physical way of interacting with his environment. Within the home, his behaviors were labeled "cute and typical of little boys." Both parents focused on his more childlike behaviors, Mike enjoying a relationship revolving around physical activities and Lisa mainly interacting in affectionate and cuddling behaviors. As Matthew entered wider environments, however, the image held by his parents was not congruent with emergent labels.

By contrast, Angela had an unremarkable developmental history and was seen as a well-mannered, intelligent child—much unlike her brother. Parent-child interactions with Angela were more achievement-based and focused on her school and community involvement. Parental and community images about Angela's success were congruent. Angela's discontent with Matthew was not questioned, given that he was so disruptive, and thus she was not discouraged from using verbal power tactics to disrupt Matthew's intrusive and demanding behaviors.

Family dynamics regarding distancing and conflict resolution were fueled as Lisa became increasingly anxious about the emerging image of their son as an aggressive, out-of-control young boy. She avoided conferences related to her son and Mike easily took on the role of family representative and mediator of Matthew's outside activities, to the point that the couple did not discuss scheduling or the results of such conferences, and Lisa took on responsibilities for Angela. The argument that preceded treatment resulted from the coming together of Lisa's anxiety about having to be in the company of school officials, hearing about Matthew's escalating negative behavior, and having to pretend that Mike had been fully honest with her about all the previous reports. Mike had been a teacher and felt comfortable in the school environment. Lisa had negative memories about school and school officials and felt more comfortable in social and nonschool achievement-oriented activities.

ANALYSIS AND TREATMENT

This family reflects the types of internal and external arrangements consistent with pathway three under the system enhancement phase of development depicted in Table 20.1. Mike and Lisa had split the children. Lisa was comfortable establishing normative growth paths for Angela but helped to maintain an arrested picture of Matthew as a cute little boy, thus avoiding having to deal with the mounting academic and emotional problems related to his learning disability. These functions, along with Mike's business with household responsibilities and filtering information to Lisa about Matthew, allowed Mike to control the environment in an autocratic fashion, which also pushed Lisa out with Angela.

Therapy helped the couple to shift the internal image of the children and the relationship between Lisa and Mike. Mike was helped to understand that his go-between role was keeping Lisa out and maintaining a false image of Matthew. He came to see that he alone did not have sufficient resources to protect or develop Matthew. Lisa was encouraged to work with Matthew's teacher to help her see him as having difficulty in school because of his learning difficulties, which led to his action-oriented way of managing his environment. The therapist provided information about special education laws, and both parents attended a local support group for parents of children with learning disabilities and rehearsed being a unified team as they prepared for upcoming parent-teacher conferences.

Assisting the parents to have equal access to knowledge about both Matthew's disability and their own management style permitted them to reconsider how they would be involved in his care. As Lisa's knowledge increased, she was able to be more active in cogenerating competency-based, solution-oriented alternatives for their son as well as in predicting and managing her own anxieties in domains of discomfort. Using strategies coached in treatment, the parents were able to hold school officials accountable for planning a school program for Matthew's success and discontinuing the casting of Matthew as a troubled, out-of-control child. This shift helped the family move to pathway one in the system consolidation phase described in Table 20.1. A strong, positive image of Matthew's learning disability was being integrated into the collective identity in a manner that allowed all individuals to continue to grow and develop in normative ways.

The new joint parenting behavior was transferred to the relationship between the children, with the parents assisting Angela to be a support for Matthew and not an antagonist and helping Matthew to negotiate with Angela. Angela was helped to see that relationships are based on mutual negotiations and not on the previous typical unilateral decision-making patterns. Moving past their original division of labor, the parents were able to reconnect on emotional levels as well as parenting levels and to find satisfaction in helping their children to grow together.

CONCLUSION

Adding a co-constructive/developmental/biopsychosocial lens enhances our perspectives of family development and childhood disabilities. However, establishing a strong theoretical, clinical, and empirical base is difficult, as the hegemony of the individualistic paradigm still imbues dominant institutions, tending toward singular and unidirectional attributions of blame and responsibility concerning disabilities (Wynne et al. 1992). To show plainly the persistence of this perspective, Denton (1996) notes that in the *Diagnostic and Statistical Manual (Fourth Edition)* (DSM-IV), "each of the mental disorders is conceptualized as a clinically significant behavioral or psychological syndrome or pattern that occurs in an individual" (APA, 1994, p. xxi). Even when the locus of explanation shifted to families (e.g., Bateson, Jackson, Haley, & Weakland, 1956; Wynne, Ryckoff, Day, & Hirsch, 1958), a positivistic influence still prevailed. The subject moved from the individual to the family as a unit of analysis, but the emphasis remained primarily on the "subject" (i.e., the family). The subject as conceived within a dialectic subject-environment is not proposed or investigated, on a broad level, to supplant the traditional individualistic paradigm (Rigazio-DiGilio, Gonçalves, & Ivey, 1996).

Although many believe "the family [undergoes] changes that parallel society's" (Minuchin, 1974, p. 46), this recursive process has been omitted from theory construction and empirical inquiry related to disorder and disability (Denton, 1996). As a result, theories maintain status quo perspectives regarding hierarchical and static pathways of individual and family development, and reflect predominant, sociopolitical expectations (McWilliams, 1993). Alternative concepts such as idiosyncratic developmental paths, relational influences on distress, power differentials within the interactive triad, and cultural and social forces that facilitate and guide conceptualizations of health and disorder remain marginalized. To the degree that these concepts are peripheralized from DSM-IV nosology (Kaslow, 1996), relational stressors and family dynamics will assume a secondary role behind individualistic, medical, and psychopharmacological interventions.

Individualistic perspectives are important to include in our repertoire of interventions, but these should not be the sole option available to clinicians working with families dealing with childhood disabilities. The biopsychosocial model as employed in medical family therapy (McDaniel et al., 1992) offers alternative options for treatment. Developmental and co-constructive frameworks (e.g., Nichols, 1996; Rigazio-DiGilio, in press) also provide operationalized constructs that can be used in research and practice. The advantage of such frameworks is that a wide variety of factors directly impacting on the well-being of children and families can be identified, modified, and enhanced to provide a context for optimum development. The disadvantages are that the complexities of these models often discourage research endeavors and that the theories and integrative practice are often too complex for anyone but seasoned therapists.

The integration of these alternative perspectives affords the field an opportunity to examine the intrafamilial dynamics surrounding a disability and challenges the field to account for salutogenic principles and wider social influences. For example, we might come to question whether what we now consider to be the evolution of secondary symptoms considered pathological are, in actuality, natural and logical consequences of dealing with disabilities-in-context. Further, we might better incorporate the fact that cultural and community dynamics exercise significant influence over the course of development and the evolving identities of the child and her or his family (Lynch & Hansen, 1992). As our field of vision expands to include the totality of life forces shaping a family's and child's experience, we will begin to design alternative interventions that can be tailored to the unique needs of each individual, family, illness type, and context. This contextual frame will help us move from an individualistic-positivistic paradigm to an ecosystemic-developmental paradigm and provide guidelines for future research, theory building, and practice.

REFERENCES

American Psychiatric Association (1994). *Diagnostic and statistical manual of mental disorders* (Fourth Edition). Washington DC.

Anastopoulos, A. D., Barkley, R. A., & Shelton, T. L. (1996). Family based treatment: Psychosocial intervention for children and adolescents with attention deficit hyperactivity disorder. In E. D. Hibbs & P. S. Jensen (Eds.), *Psychosocial treatments for child and adolescent disorders: Empirically based strategies for clinical practice* (pp. 267–284). Washington, DC: American Psychological Association.

Anderson, S., & Sabatelli, R. (1999). *Family interaction: A multigenerational developmental perspective.* Boston, MA: Allyn & Bacon.

Barkley, R. A., Guevremont, D. C., Anastopoulos, A. D., & Fletcher, K. E. (1992). A comparison of three family therapy programs for treating family conflicts in adolescents with attention-deficit hyperactivity disorder. *Journal of Consulting and Clinical Psychology, 60*(3), 450–462.

Barnwell, D. A., & Day, M (1996). Providing support to diverse families. In P. J. Beckman (Ed.), *Strategies for working with families of young children with disabilities* (pp. 47–68). Baltimore: Paul H. Brookes.

Bateson, G., Jackson, D., Haley, J., & Weakland, J. (1956). Toward a theory of schizophrenia. *Behavioral Science, 1,* 251–264.

Bauman, L. J., Drotar, D., Leventhal, J. M., Perrin, E. C., & Pless, I. B. (1997). A review of psychological interventions for children with chronic health conditions. *Pediatrics, 100,* 244–251.

Beckman, P. J. (1996). Theoretical, philosophical and empirical bases of effective work with families. In P. J. Beckman (Ed.), *Strategies for working with families of young children with disabilities* (pp. 1–16). Baltimore: Paul H. Brookes.

Bennett, A. T. (1988). Gateways to powerlessness: Incorporating Hispanic deaf children and families into formal schooling. *Disability, Handicap and Society, 3*(2), 119–151.

Bevan, R. C. (1988). *Hearing-impaired children: A guide for concerned parents and professionals.* Springfield, IL: Charles C Thomas.

Biederman, J., Faraone, S., Milberger, S., & Guite, J. (1996). A prospective 4-year follow-up study of attention-deficit hyperactivity and related disorders. *Archives of General Psychiatry, 53*(5), 437–446.

Black, M., Danseco, E., & Krishnakumar, A. (1998). Understanding pediatric health concerns in a social-ecological context: A review of the intervention research. *Children's Services: Social Policy, Research, and Practice, 1*(2), 111–126.

Borders, D. L. (1994). Potential of DCT/SCDT in addressing two elusive themes of mental health counseling. *Journal of Mental Health Counseling, 16*(1), 75–78.

Boyd-Franklin, N. (1989). *Black families in therapy.* New York: Guilford Press.

Breslau, N. (1988). Childhood disabilities: Economic and psychological effects. In W. A. Gordon, J. A. Herd, & A. Baum (Eds.), *Perspectives on behavioral medicine, Vol. 3: Prevention and rehabilitation* (pp. 143–168). San Diego: Academic Press.

Breunlin, D. C. (1988). Oscillation theory and family development. In C. J. Falicov (Ed.), *Family transitions: Continuity and change over the life cycle* (pp. 133–155). New York: Guilford Press.

Bristol, M. M. (1984). Family resources and successful adaptation to autistic children. In E. Schopler & G. B. Mesibov (Eds.), *The effect of autism on the family* (pp. 289–310). New York: Plenum Press.

Campion, J. (1982). Young Asian children with learning and behaviour problems: A family therapy approach. *Journal of Family Therapy, 4*(2), 153–163.

Carr, F. (1988). Six weeks to twenty-one years old: A longitudinal study of children with Down's syndrome and their families. *Journal of Child Psychology and Psychiatry, 29*(4), 407–431.

Carter, B., & McGoldrick, M. (1988). *The changing family life cycle: A framework for family therapy.* New York: Gardner Press.

Cedarbaum, J., & Mashaw, J. (1995). *Policies for children with disabilities: Connecticut, Virginia and some national trends* (draft working paper). Washington, DC: National Academy of Social Insurance, Disability Policy Project.

Christiansen, J., Olson, J., & Gentry, D. (1997). Students with disabilities and their families. In T. N. Fairchild (Ed.), *Crisis intervention strategies for school-based helpers* (2nd ed.), (pp. 101–130). Springfield, IL: Charles C Thomas.

Cobb, P. S. (1987). Creating respite-care programs. *Exceptional Parent, 15*(5), 31–33.

Cohen, R. A. (1995). Working with visually impaired infants and their families: Implications for other physically challenged patients. In J. A. Incorvaia (Ed.), *The handbook of infant, child, and adolescent psychotherapy: A guide to diagnosis and treatment. Reiss-Davis Child Study Center, Vol. 1* (pp. 199–210). Northvale, NJ: Jason Aronson, Inc.

Combrinck-Graham, L. (1983). The family life cycle and families with young children. In H. A. Liddle (Ed.), *Clinical implications of the family life cycle* (pp. 35–53). Rockville, MD: Aspen.

Constantine, L. L. (Ed.). (1986). *Family paradigms: The practice of theory in family therapy.* New York: Guilford Press.

Correa, V. L., Silberman, R. K., & Trusty, S. (1986). Siblings of disabled children: A literature review. *Education of the Visually Handicapped, 18*(1), 5–13.

Culbertson, J. L., & Silovsky, J. F. (1996). Learning disabilities and attention deficit-hyperactivity disorders: Their impact on children's significant others. In F. W. Kaslow (Ed.), *Handbook of relational diagnosis and dysfunctional family patterns* (pp. 186–209). New York: John Wiley & Sons, Inc.

Denton, W. H. (1996). Problems encountered in reconciling individual and relational diagnosis. In F. W. Kaslow (Ed.), *Handbook of relational diagnosis and dysfunctional family patterns* (pp. 35–45). New York: John Wiley & Sons, Inc.

Drotar, D. (1992). Integrating theory and practice in psychological intervention with families of children with chronic illness. In J. T. Akamatsu & M. A. Stephens (Eds.), *Family health psychology* (pp. 175–192). Washington DC: Hemisphere Publishing Corp.

Drotar, D., Crawford, P., & Bush, M. (1984). The family context of childhood chronic illness: Implications for psychosocial intervention. In M. G. Eisenberg, L. C. Sutkin, & M. A. Jansen (Eds.), *Chronic illness and disability through the life span: Effects on self and family.* New York: Springer.

Dunst, C. J., & Trivette, C. M. (1988). A family systems model of early intervention with handicapped and developmentally at-risk children. In D. R. Powell (Ed.), *Parent education as early childhood intervention: Emerging directions in theory, research and practice. Annual advances in applied developmental psychology, Vol. 3* (pp. 131–179). Norwood, NJ: Ablex.

Dyson, L. (1991). Families of young children with handicaps: Parental stress and family functioning. *American Journal on Mental Retardation, 95,* 623–629.

Education for All Handicapped Children Act of 1975, PL 94-142. (August 23, 1975). Title 20, U.S.C. 1401 et seq: *U.S. Statutes at Large, 89,* 773–796.

Engel, G. (1980). The clinical application of the biopsychosocial model. *American Journal of Psychiatry, 137,* 535–544.

Falicov, C. J. (Ed.). (1988). *Family transitions: Continuity and change over the life cycle.* New York: Guildford Press.

Ferrari, M., & Sussman, M. B. (1987). *Childhood disability and family systems.* New York: Haworth Press.

Fortier, L. M., & Wanlass, R. L. (1984). Family crisis following the diagnosis of a handicapped child. *Family Relations, 33*(1), 13–24.

Goode, D. A. (1984). Presentation practices of a family with a deaf-blind, retarded daughter. *Family Relations, 33,* 173–185.

Gray, W. (1981). The evolution of emotional-cognitive and system precursor theory. In J. E. Durkin (Ed.), *Living groups: Group psychotherapy and general system theory* (pp. 199–215). New York: Brunner-Mazel.

Guralnick, M. J. (1989). Recent developments in early intervention efficacy research: Implications for family involvement in PL 99-457. *Topics in Early Childhood Special Education, 9,* 1–17.

Hanline, M. F. (1991). Transitions and critical events in the family life cycle: Implications for providing support to families of children with disabilities. *Psychology in the Schools, 28*(1), 53–59.

Hanline, M. F., & Daley, S. E. (1992). Family coping strategies and strengths in Hispanic, African-American, and Caucasian families of young children. *Topics in Early Childhood Special Education, 2*(3), 351–366.

Harbin, G. L. (1993). Family issues of children with disabilities: How research and theory have modified practices in intervention. In N. J. Anastasiow & S. Harel (Eds.), *At-risk infants: Interventions, families, and research* (pp. 101–112). Baltimore: Paul H. Brookes.

Heflinger, C. A., & Nixon, C. T. (1996). *Families and the mental health system for children and adolescents: Policy, services and research.* Thousand Oaks, CA: Sage.

Hill, R. (1949). *Families under stress.* New York: Harper.

Hobbs, N., Perrin, J., & Ireys, H. (1985). *Chronically ill children and their families.* San Francisco: Jossey-Bass.

Holder-Brown, L., Bradley, R. H., Whiteside, L., Brisby, J. A., & Parette (1993). Using the HOME Inventory with families of children with orthopedic disabilities. *Journal of Developmental and Physical Disabilities, 5*(3), 181–201.

Human Growth Foundation. (1998). What are growth disorders? [On-line]. Available: http://www.genetic.org/hgf/disordersframe.html.

Individuals with Disabilities Education Act of 1990 (IDEA), PL 101-476. (October 30, 1990). Title 20, U. S. C. 1400 et seq: *U.S. Statutes at Large, 104,* 1103–1151.

Kantor, D., & Lehr, W. (1975). *Inside the family. Toward a theory of family process.* San Francisco, CA: Jossey-Bass.

Kaslow, F. W. (Ed.). (1996). *Handbook of relational diagnosis and dysfunctional family patterns.* New York: John Wiley & Sons, Inc.

Kazak, A. E. (1986). Families with physically handicapped children: Social ecology and family systems. *Family Process, 25,* 265–281.

Lambie, R., & Daniels-Mohring, D. (1993). *Family systems within educational contexts.* Denver, CO: Love.

Leyser, Y., Heinze, A., & Kapperman, G. (1996). Stress and adaptation in families of children with visual disabilities. *Families in Society, 77*(4), 240–249.

Lynch, E. W., & Hanson, M. J. (Eds.). (1992). *Developing cross-cultural competence: A guide for working with young children and their families.* Baltimore: Paul H. Brookes.

McCubbin, H. I., & Patterson, J. M. (1982). The family stress process: The Double ABCX Model of adjustment and adaptation. In H. I. McCubbin, M. B. Sussman, & J. M. Patterson (Eds.), *Social stress and the family: Advances and developments in family stress theory and research* (pp. 7–38). New York: Haworth Press.

McDaniel, S. H., Hepworth, J., & Doherty, W. J. (1992). *Medical family therapy: A biopsychosocial approach to families with health problems.* New York: Basic Books.

McPhail, E. R. (1996). A parent's perspective: Quality of life in families with a member with disabilities. In R. Renwick & I. Brown (Eds.), *Quality of life in health promotion and rehabilitation: Conceptual approaches, issues, and applications* (pp. 279–289). Thousand Oaks, CA: Sage.

McWilliams, S. (1993). Construct no idols. *International Journal of Personal Construct Psychology, 6*(3), 269–280.

Miller, E. (1976). The social work component in community-based action on behalf of victims of Huntington's disease. *Social Work in Health Care, 2*(1), 25–32.

Minuchin, S. (1974). *Families and family therapy.* Cambridge, MA: Harvard University Press.

Moos, R. J., & Moos, B. S. (1981). *Family environment scale.* Palo Alto, CA: Consulting Psychologists Press.

Mowder, B. A. (1991). *Working with parents: Challenges and opportunities.* Keynote presentation to the New York City Board of Education's District IV Staff Development Conference, Brooklyn, NY.

National Information Center for Children and Youth with Disabilities (1998a–i). General information about specific childhood challenges. *Disability Fact Sheets and Briefing Papers* [On-line]. Available: http://www.nichcy.org/pubs/factshe/fs7txt.htm.

Nichols, W. C. (1996). *Treating people in families: An integrative framework.* New York: Guilford Press.

Nichols, W. C., & Everett, C. A. (1986). *Systemic family therapy: An integrative approach.* New York: Guilford Press.

Norton, P., & Drew, C. (1994). Autism and potential family stressors. *American Journal of Family Therapy, 22*(1), 67–76.

Olson, D. H. (1986). Circumplex Model VII: Validation studies and Faces III. *Family Process, 25*(3), 337–351.

Pare, D. (1996). Culture and meaning: Expanding the metaphorical repertoire of family therapy. *Family Process, 35,* 21–42.

Patterson, G. R. (1982). *A social learning approach to family intervention. Vol. 3, Coercive family process.* Eugene, OR: Castalia.

Piaget, J. C. (1954). *The construction of reality in the child.* New York: Basic Books.

Powell, T. H., & Gallagher, P. A. (1993). *Brothers and sisters—A special part of exceptional families.* Baltimore: Paul H. Brookes.

Powers, M. D. (1991). Intervening with families of young children with severe handicaps: Contributions of a family systems approach. *School Psychology Quarterly, 6*(2), 131–146.

Quittner, A. L., & DiGirolamo, A. M. (1998). Family adaptation to childhood disability and illness. In R. T. Ammerman & J. V. Campo (Eds.), *Handbook of pediatric psychology and psychiatry, Vol. 2: Disease, injury, and illness* (pp. 70–102). Boston: Allyn & Bacon.

Rigazio-DiGilio, S. (1994). A coconstructive developmental approach to ecosystemic treatment. *Journal of Mental Health Counseling, 16,* 43–74.

Rigazio-DiGilio, S. (in press). Reconstructing psychological distress and disorder from a relational perspective: A systemic co-constructive developmental framework. In R. Neimeyer & J. Raskin (Eds.), *Constructions of disorder.* Washington, DC: American Psychological Association.

Rigazio-DiGilio, S. A. (1999). Ethics and family therapy: Working within a coconstructive, ecosystemic paradigm. *Guidance and Counseling, 14*(2), 22–28.

Rigazio-DiGilio, S. A., Gonçalves, O. F., & Ivey, A. E. (1996). From cultural to existential diversity: The impossibility of an integrative psychotherapy within a traditional framework. *Applied and Preventive Psychology: Current Scientific Perspectives, 5,* 235–248.

Rigazio-DiGilio, S., Ivey, A., & Locke, D. (1997). Continuing the post-modern dialogue: Enhancing and contextualizing multiple voices. *Journal of Mental Health Counseling, 19,* 233–255.

Rogers-Dulan, J., & Blacher, J. (1995). African American families, religion, and disability: A conceptual framework. *Mental Retardation, 33*(4), 226–238.

Rolland, J. (1984). Toward a psychosocial typology of chronic and life-threatening illness. *Family Systems Medicine, 2,* 203–221.

Rolland, J. S. (1994). *Families, illness and disability.* New York: Basic Books.

Seligman, M. (1985). Handicapped children and their families. *Journal of Counseling and Development, 64*(4), 274–277.

Serrano, J. A. (1993). Working with chronically disabled children's families: A biopsychosocial approach. *Child and Adolescent Mental Health Care, 3*(3), 157–168.

Shapiro, J. (1983). Family reactions and coping strategies in response to the physically ill or handicapped child: A review. *Social Science and Medicine, 17*(14), 913–931.

Shontz, F. (1965). Reactions to crisis. *Volta Review, 67,* 364–370.

Singh, N. N., Curtis, W. J., Ellis, C. R., Wechsler, H. A., Best, A. M., & Cohen, R. (1997). Empowerment status of families whose children have serious emotional disturbance and attention-deficit/hyperactivity disorder. *Journal of Emotional and Behavioral Disorders, 5*(4), 223–229.

Stein, M. T., Coleman, W. L., & Epstein, R. M. (1997). "We've tried everything and nothing works": Family-centered pediatrics and clinical problem-solving. *Journal of Developmental and Behavioral Pediatrics, 18*(2), 114–119.

Steinberg, A. G., Davila, J. R., Collazo, J., Loew, R. C., & Fischgrund, J. E. (1997). "A little sign and a lot of love . . . ": Attitudes, perceptions, and beliefs of Hispanic families with deaf children. *Qualitative Health Research, 7*(2), 202–222.

Thompson, R., Gustafson, K., Hamlett, K., & Spock, A. (1992). Psychological adjustment of children with cystic fibrosis: The role of child cognitive processes and maternal adjustment. *Journal of Pediatric Psychology, 17*(6), 741–755.

Varni, J. W., Rubenfeld, L. A., Talbot, D., & Setoguchi, Y. (1991). Family functioning, temperament, and psychologic adaptation in children with congenital or acquired limb deficiencies. In S. Chess & E. Hertzig (Eds.), *Annual progress in child psychiatry and child development* (pp. 279–291). New York: Brunner/Mazel.

Wood, B. L. (1993). Beyond the "psychosomatic family": A biobehavioral family model of pediatric illness. *Family Process, 32,* 261–278.

Wood, B. L. (1995). A developmental biopsychosocial approach to the treatment of chronic illness in children and adolescents. In R. H. Mikesell, D. Lusterman, & S. H. McDaniel (Eds.), *Integrating family therapy: Handbook of family psychology and systems theory* (pp. 437–455). Washington, DC: American Psychological Association.

Wynne, L., Shields, C., & Sirkin, M. I. (1992). Illness, family theory, and family therapy: I. Conceptual issues. *Family Process, 31,* 3–18.

Wynne, L., Ryckoff, I., Day, J., & Hirsch, S. (1958). Pseudo-mutuality in the family relationships of schizophrenics. *Psychiatry, 21,* 205–220.

Yando, R., & Zigler, E. (1984). Severely handicapped children and their families: A synthesis. In J. Blacher (Ed.), *Severely handicapped young children and their families: Research in review* (pp. 401–416). Orlando, FL: Academic Press.

CHAPTER 21

Families with Chronic Physical Illness

Joan C. Barth

F AMILIES WITH CHRONIC PHYSICAL ILLNESS deal with it in their own way. There is no typical cancer family or a typical diabetes family. Families can have illness as their theme or family life as their theme. Each family is unique.

DEFINITION

Before we consider the effects on families with chronic physical illness, we must define chronic physical illness. Many professional articles and books tell us how to deal with chronic physical illness without actually defining it (Berkman, 1996; Dorfman, 1996; Proctor, 1996; Turner, 1996; Baker, 1997; and Hochstenbach, 1997). In her book *Chronic Physical Illness: Impact and Intervention,* Eileen Morof Lubkin (1986) cites eight definitions of chronic physical illness, each of them a bit different from the other. Basically, they are either medically oriented or behaviorally oriented.

Disagreement on the definition of chronic illness shows us why there is no consensus on the handling of such illnesses. The Centers for Disease Control and Prevention in Atlanta uses the definition of chronic physical illness taken from the book *Chronic Disease: Epidemiology and Control* (Brownson, R., 1993):

> Chronic diseases can be defined as those that have a prolonged course that do not resolve spontaneously and for which there a complete cure is rarely achieved (p. 9).

The definition of chronic physical illness used throughout this chapter is:

> Chronic Physical Illness is a less than normal physical condition that continues beyond 3 months and for which there is no known cure.

That definition allows victims of amyotrophic lateral sclerosis (ALS), commonly called Lou Gehrig's disease, for example, who cannot do anything to lessen the progress of their disease, to be included as having chronic physical illness. The symptoms may worsen or go into remission but the illness lasts over time. Some illnesses, such as AIDS (acquired immunodeficiency syndrome), have been redefined as chronic.

As treatments change, so do the definitions of illnesses. What was once terminal, may no longer be (Goodheart & Lansing, 1997).

LOCALE OF SUSCEPTIBILITY

Neither are certain area beds of illness. However, there are pockets of chronically ill people scattered throughout the country. Although studies do not prove that certain areas such as the Love Canal in New York State or Toms River in New Jersey produce specific illnesses, certain areas do have higher incidences of chronic physical illnesses than others. There seems to be more liver disease in New Jersey, more brain tumors in Chicago, more breast cancer in Washington, D.C., and more thyroid problems in Pennsylvania (Anderson, Kochanek, & Murphy, 1997). AIDS is more prevalent in major cities such as San Francisco, New York, and Los Angeles (Beaudin & Chambré, 1996). People at risk for certain ailments might investigate what illnesses seem prevalent in the area where they choose to live.

Throughout the United States the three major causes of death—heart disease, cancer, and stroke, can all be chronic. Although a person can have an acute heart attack or stroke and die instantly or in a few days, both heart disease and stroke can be long-term illnesses and they are considered here as chronic. Further, this chapter will provide the words of families just as a therapist would hear them in his or her office. In their role of "fixers of the problem," therapists often do not listen long enough. In listening, it is important to recall that there is no typical diabetic family, asthmatic family, or any other typical chronic illness family. There is also no typical way of handling chronic physical illness for a therapist. Each family handles chronic physical illness in its own way. No two families are alike (Tolstoy, 1961).

STAGES OF DEVELOPMENT

Family members are also in different stages of development. A boy whose younger brother was in a bicycle accident and sustained a spinal injury as a result may be entering puberty. His sister had recently married. His father was starting a new job while his mother was completing her Master's degree. Each of them was at a significant stage in his or her own development. So, too, was the person having the illness. The therapist must consider at what stage of development each family member faces.

Certain chronic physical illnesses are prevalent at birth while others develop later in life. Families that have to deal with congenital heart defects in a child at birth cope differently than families that must deal with heart failure later in life.

Technological advances may help families deal with chronic illness. For example, a mother felt uncomfortable leaving her cancer-ridden adult daughter on her own. I recommended that she purchase a beeper to use whenever she was out and her daughter needed her. A person in her thirties with diabetes was willing to have a pump inserted in her abdomen so she could provide insulin into her system when necessary. A 91-year-old woman with progressive hearing loss began to use a hearing aid that used a remote to focus sound when she was on the phone or in a crowd. Making use of technology is often more acceptable for the person having the disease than the nondisabled family members think it would be (Pope & Tarlov, 1997).

RESPONSIBILITY

In interviewing families for this chapter, it was demonstrated that those patients who were living with their illness successfully were those who took responsibility for themselves. No one had to ask them if they had taken their medication or whether they had made an appointment for a check-up. It is important for family members to refuse to provide those services. They must practice a love that holds the sick member responsible for doing as much as he or she is capable of doing, a kind of "tough love" (York & York, 1982).

> Olivia spoke of how her husband, Karl, who had end-stage renal disease, was feeling sorry for himself and not taking care of himself. She let him know about his irresponsibility. After that he did more for her and thought more about her feelings, despite the fact that he was unable to do any more for himself physically. Karl has learned that the caregiver needs support too.

NEEDS OF CAREGIVERS

Indeed, although caretakers need support, frequently they do not get it. "As long as my dad was taking care of my mother, no one else stepped in. When he had a stroke, others helped," a daughter told me.

A person who can give financial or emotional support may be unable to cut toenails. A family needs to respect what each caregiver can give (Goodheart & Lansing, 1997).

Because many people will have to deal with chronic physical illness, especially as the "Baby Boom" generation ages, it is helpful for professionals to know how to be useful to them. Although professionals are usually called upon when there is little hope, it is necessary that they have resources that are hopeful, not full of doom. At the end of this chapter an Appendix listing is provided taken from the National Genetic Voluntary Organizations. These organizations are available to discuss current treatment and to make referrals to self-help groups. Many other genetic associations available that may be contacted. Looking in the Yellow Pages or perusing the guide listed in the Appendix will be helpful (National Center for Education in Maternal and Child Health, 1989). All professionals working with a family with an illness should know as much as possible about resources the family can call upon.

LISTENING

Therapists need to respect the work the family has already done and listen to what impediments there are to their living a fulfilling life. The following are two examples of parental reactions to chronic illness in a child:

"I was totally unprepared for my son's having his eye poked out at 12," said a mother who felt that her son, a natural ballplayer, could no longer casually walk down to the school playing field and bat some balls.

"We knew from the start that our daughter had Maple Sugar Urine Disease," said a father about his little girl. This family had a genetic defect and was expecting that it might show up. When it did, they were nonplussed by its diagnosis but nearly overwhelmed with its day-to-day requirements.

ACCEPTANCE

Even when an adult who lives far away from his or her family develops an illness, the entire family can be affected. When one person develops breast cancer, Parkinson's disease, adult-onset diabetes, or kidney failure, the lifestyle of the entire family may change. Whether it results in the need for family members to do more shopping, cleaning, errand-running, or having the sick person move in with them or visiting more often there will be changes.

One family had to deal with their daughter and wife's multiple sclerosis (MS) (Noble Topf, 1995). It was not until the couple had been married for 10 years that they finally had a definitive diagnosis. The diagnosis explained what had been affecting Annie for many years. Ultimately, she was confined to a wheelchair and the couple had to alter their lifestyle so Annie could maneuver her wheelchair easily thoughout the house. When I interviewed her husband he told me:

> I think everybody grows up with a picture and an expectation about how life is supposed to be. I believe that all children, through adolescence and teenage into young adulthood, grow up with a picture of what a relationship is supposed to be like. You grow up and you look for the One, the ideal man or woman to live a relatively normal life with. The man and/or woman goes out to work, maybe has a family, kids, love. You earn a living, live your life, do things normal people do. You just live your life.
>
> Shortly after we got married, my wife started getting symptoms of numbness. After having it checked out, she was diagnosed with "probable MS." It was a very frightening thing because we didn't know what to expect.

NEED FOR ILLNESS

Some family members focus on the disability to the degree that nothing else exists in their lives. "I can't imagine life without hydrocephalus," a woman said. She had given birth to a daughter whose umbilical cord was wrapped around her neck. The daughter required frequent surgeries to replace the shunt that kept fluid from building up in her brain. The daughter, now a mature woman, knows when her shunt is not working properly, and telephones her physician for an appointment to repair it. Yet her mother reacts as she did at the child's birth, nearly 40 years ago. The mother continues to worry about her daughter's health, while her daughter struggles to gain autonomy.

My interview with the mother revealed that her subsequent divorce was the result of the child's illness and the focus the mother placed on her. She said: "Having a brain-damaged child led to my divorce, directly and indirectly. We had a problem dealing with words like retarded or brain-damaged child. I also had this incredible desire to be near or close to the neurosurgeon." It is not uncommon for marriages that include a sick child to end in divorce. Professionals can warn couples of this possibility and work to help prevent it.

Some disabilities seem larger than life, but the therapist needs to listen to the family because all disabilities are different, and so is the family's attitude toward them. This attitude is a product of the family's ethnic background, their culture and religion, as well as other influences (Barth, 1993). In most Puerto Rican families it is expected that the family will sell everything for treatment despite the inevitability of death. In most Irish families, it is common not to discuss the burden that dealing with a chronic physical illness presents. In most African American families it is expected that everyone, including neighbors, helps out. Heinrich Boll, the Pulitzer Prize–winning writer, notes that in his native Germany losing an arm was a calamity, while in Ireland, that same accident brought sighs of "Lucky it wasn't his writing hand" (Boll, 1967).

In the following example, the father is Pennsylvania Dutch, a culture that often keeps personal health matters private. The mother has dealt with the deafness of her 4-year-old son: "The audiologist told us how severe the loss was and gave us some information on who to contact and told us what some of the options would be — sign language and different programs that he could get into." Through tears, the mother told me what the nurse said to her when her son underwent some hearing tests:

No matter what the outcome of those tests, you will love him just the same. Initially, I was fine with it until I met some deaf adults. That was the first time I really saw deafness as long-term. This wasn't going away. I don't think my son sees his deafness as a problem. I think he sees it as an advantage to get away with things with adults who don't know sign language.

I asked the mother if the family had gotten together to discuss the deafness. She told me: "When we initially found out that he was hearing-impaired the teacher and the audiologist met with the whole family for several evenings. By the whole family, I mean the grandparents, aunts, uncles, cousins with children."

Her ex-husband, the boy's father, stopped learning sign language after the marriage broke up, which Annabelle, the mother, thought was exacerbated by their son's "not being perfect." Their 6-year-old daughter chose not to learn while her father was uninterested, but since he no longer is in the picture, she has resumed learning sign language. The mother told me: "In the last three-and-a-half months they have not seen their father, and her signing skills have greatly improved. I think the fact that her father wasn't signing with her brother probably has had some effect."

We notice with Annabelle that there is a sense of denial about the significance of that malady relative to her son. She thinks he is fine and that he uses his deafness as a means to manipulate others. She doesn't see what effect it has on his relationships with other children, including his nondeaf sister. The only way she is aware of its affecting them as a family is that she insists on a sign-language–proficient babysitter. However, in a Pennsylvania Dutch family his disability also causes relationship distance with paternal relatives. The grandparents were unable to become intimate with the boy because of his disability. They felt guilty about having a grandson who could not hear.

Unlike Annabelle's son, the onset of most chronic physical illness occurs later in life rather than at birth. Multiple sclerosis, cancer, stroke, and Parkinson's disease usually appear in adulthood. Those families have become accustomed to a member of the family being healthy until he or she develops an illness. Their tendency is to ignore the potential seriousness of that illness.

"Funny that I had to get very sick to get healthy," said a man who had been overweight, smoked, and drank before being diagnosed with adult-onset diabetes. When I interviewed him and his wife, they were further examples of what I had already discovered — that it is usually the spouse who notices that the sick person has a problem. Further, the sick person often did not seek help until an acute event happened — an accident, sudden blindness, a heart attack.

When the acute event does happen, most people expect a quick cure. They fail to realize they need help to get well. Some of that help has to come from themselves. They need to take responsibility for themselves, including changing their lifestyles. They must be involved in their treatment. It is not helpful to keep them out of their own healing. Professionals must seek ways to help them to be interactive with their treatment.

In my interview with the man with diabetes and his wife, his wife said: "I noticed that he was grouchier than usual. And he was also drinking all the time." Her husband spoke of frequent urination, thirst, and diminishing eyesight. Finally he was forced to see the physician at his workplace and was hospitalized that day. He told me: "The doctor said I should be in a coma — my blood sugar was so high. He figured I would need two shots of insulin every day for the rest of my life. I said, 'No way.' Then I lost weight and started exercising. Three months later, I was off insulin."

When I asked about lifestyle changes, the husband answered: "I cut out drinking and eating so much. And like I said, 'it's too bad you have to get sick to become healthy.' Now, I'm healthy." In response to my question about lifestyle, the wife told me:

> He never ate breakfast before in his life and then he started. He cut out all the sweets he's been eating. He hadn't exercised and he started that. Now he walks six miles a day and golfs as often as possible. When he first was on insulin shots, he had to eat within 15 minutes of taking his shot, so that meant a really strict regimen as far as time was concerned. I had to plan supper so that he could sit down to it immediately after his shot.

This man told me there were other diabetics at his factory who had not changed their unhealthy lifestyles. He said of them: "They think that if they pop a pill, that's going to cure it all. It does not."

AIDS

There are illnesses that families feel are punishment for sin. One woman told her daughter-in-law, who developed cancer at 43, "You wouldn't have gotten this if you were more religious." AIDS certainly provides another case in point. In the 1980s, AIDS was considered an acute illness and one that only homosexuals had. In 1992, it was redefined as a chronic illness that many heterosexuals and children had. In the early years most people were afraid to be in contact with a person having the illness because it was not known how it was contracted or what the prognosis was. Many people, including some ministers and physicians, avoided those who had AIDS. Some religions believed that AIDS was punishment for violating God's rules. Families were often the only caregivers available when physicians, friends, or hospitals were unsympathetic. When individuals with the disease recovered, they often continued to stay with their families (Beaudin & Chambre, 1996).

Some families are able to focus on the sick member's life, rather than on their illness. Indeed, people who have chronic physical illnesses often do not factor in their illness symptoms when you ask them how they are (Kawaga-Singer, 1993). They say something like, "I'm fine, except for the day after I have my chemotherapy." It is as if they accept their illness as something outside of themselves. They do not see it as a major part of their bodies (Kane, 1996). For some this may be an effective coping strategy; for others, it may prove problematic.

TRANSPLANTS

There is a common belief that technology can cure anything. Technology has made treatment for some chronic physical illnesses more effective than was previously the case. Organ transplants are fairly recent innovations. However, even with those improvements, it is a long time before most people, especially men, admit there is something unusual happening in their bodies. Part of my interview with a woman whose husband died after receiving a lung transplant follows:

> The doctor would not believe he had given up drinking so he didn't want to give him a transplant. I had to assure him that he gave up drinking as soon as he was diagnosed. He kept asking me. My husband kept trying to protect me. We were both in denial. We had traveled a lot and when he got sick, he apologized for not being able to take me places. I told him I had traveled enough even if I never traveled again. The time he lived was a gift. I didn't resent any of it. I had to bathe him and take him to the bathroom. Now, I don't think I would have the strength to do it. After it was over, I grieved for a few years. During that time, I saw a counselor. I could tell you exactly when I returned to my former self. The cloud lifted. And it was after that, that I finally could get myself going.

HELPLESSNESS

Unlike mental illness, where the sick person is often encouraged to "get on with it," those with physical illness may be treated like invalids. People want to do things for them that they can do for themselves. It takes a lot of discipline to do things for yourself that others want to do for you when you are ill. And it also takes discipline to refrain from doing for a sick person what he or she is capable of doing for himself or herself.

It can be frustrating for professionals to deal with those who are chronically ill. They may become impatient with the habituality of family problems. There is no dramatic resolution as there may be after an acute incident. A woman with MS related that her physician told her "It was a fluke" when she recounted to him an event of being able to walk again after receiving a highly experimental treatment. He did not want to get his (or her) hopes up that there might be a cure for MS. A therapist cannot come up with a way to eliminate the illness. However, he or she may be able to foster a realistic sense of optimism.

HOPEFULNESS

Because of a lack of support from their physicians, 96 percent of the population seek help outside the medical profession, according to a report at a Harvard Medical School seminar (1997). Also reported was the fact that people did not tell their physicians they were using alternatives such as Chinese herbs, acupuncture, massage, Tai Chi, or yoga. If they do improve or are cured using these techniques, they are often told, "your tests must have been faulty," "it was a placebo effect," or "your healer is a quack." Because of the medical practitioner's lack of curiosity or hope, sick people and their families seek out professionals who possess those traits. Unfortunately, this also makes them vulnerable to false claims. At the same time, changes are occurring. Progressive hospitals and medical personnel open to learning those methods are inviting experienced practitioners of alternative methods to their sites (Doylestown Hospital, 1998).

Often people who want to use alternative methods of treatment do not for reasons other than skepticism. One person with Stage 4 cancer wanted to take herbs and go to Mexico for treatment. She continued with chemotherapy because if she did not, her illness would no longer be covered by her medical insurance.

A woman whose husband died of ALS told me:

My brother-in-law who was in medical school told me he thought my husband had Lou Gehrig's disease. The doctor didn't want to give him a diagnosis. He sent us for another opinion. No one wants to give a young man a death sentence. His mother said the physicians were wrong. My parents' way of dealing with it was to set up a fund-raising group for the illness.

Our daughter was 16 months old when he was diagnosed. She was 3 when he died. As she was learning to walk, he was losing his ability to do the same. It was very hard. He was getting worse but wouldn't get into counseling. And eventually he couldn't talk. My whole life changed. I was basically a single mother even though there was another parent in the house. I went from being a wife to being a nurse but I didn't have the skill. It was very hard.

WOMEN

As the average age of death increases (75.8 years), there is more chronic illness (see Chapter 13). Women are especially prone to developing an illness that lasts a long time (Mother's Day Report, 1987). Because they live longer than men, illnesses surface in women's lives as they age — stroke, cancer, Alzheimer's disease, and osteoporosis (Centers for Disease Control & Prevention, National Bureau of Statistics, 1997). Women are in a special category for chronic illness. Their family usually is accustomed to them being caretakers and the family is not prepared for playing the role that the mother traditionally played. One woman said:

> When my sister developed emphysema after being the family caregiver all her life, my father and brother never went to visit her or even called her. She told her neighbor that when she died her brother would be there immediately but would not visit her when she was sick.

Women are more accustomed to sharing their feelings with others. When sick, they feel comfortable discussing their illnesses.

ANGER

When married, usually it was the spouses who noticed that the sick person had a problem. Regardless of spousal warning, however, the sick person did not seek help until an acute event occurred. The resulting anger in the nonsick spouse remained unexpressed because the culture supports empathy toward the sick, not anger. A woman whose husband suffered a heart attack told me, "When I told my sister how angry I was with my husband after his heart attack, she was horrified. She couldn't believe I could be angry at a sick person." Professionals need to ferret out the anger that lies dormant. Family members need to speak about their underlying feelings in order to keep communication channels open.

Families may use some of the following techniques when a member is ill:

1. *Make specific suggestions:* "I am available to drive you on Tuesday and Fridays."
2. *Call frequently:* Be upbeat. Don't ask about the illness.
3. *Be a family member, not a physician:* Asking questions about the illness is not your domain. Be supportive, not inquisitive.
4. *Take the sick person out:* It is not healthy to only go out to the doctor's office or the hospital. Even if you need another person to help you with the sick person, go out for coffee or to see the leaves changing color.
5. *Listen:* The sick person may need to talk.

PROFESSIONALS

Professionals are required to attack the chronic physical illness from a more objective viewpoint than family members. It is important to recognize the theme of the family. Is it the illness or life? Some families focus on the illness as if it were the most important factor in their life. The professional must allow the family to see that they are more than the illness. They can help the caregiving family speak of their needs for support, nurturance, and free time. It is important that the family, spouse, or parent giving the majority of support speak of the sources available for their own personal sustenance. Perhaps a session has to be held apart from the person having the chronic physical illness for the caregiver to discuss his or her feelings. One woman told me:

I told my husband that when he had a heart attack I visualized bludgeoning him to death with a huge hammer. Despite the fact that I waited to say this until six months after his coronary, he never forgave me for having such feelings. It would have been better to have told a professional and not him.

Like family members, professionals have to listen to the story of how they remember what happened. They must realize that they are sought out for their humanity. If the questions asked are pertinent to the illness, the professional needs to listen until the speaker reveals his or her feelings about the occurrence itself. The following techniques are helpful for professionals:

1. *Listen:* The family may need to talk about how to deal with feeling drained or retell the particulars of the illness.
2. *Avoid scare tactics:* Be sure to use supportive statements. Don't paint the worst picture.
3. Be certain to say "I don't have any cure for this," not "There is no cure for this." Don't speak as if you are God. Be humble.
4. *Be respectful:* The family has done a lot of things before seeing you. Acknowledge that.

REFERENCES

Anderson, R., Kochanek, K., & Murphy, S., *Monthly Vital Statistics Report National Center for Health Statistics and Centers for Disease Control and Prevention, 45*(11) supplement, June 12, 1997.

Baker, L. M. (1997). Preference for physicians as information providers by women with multiple sclerosis a potential cause for communication problems? *Journal of Documentation 53*(3), 251–262.

Barth, J. (1993). *It runs in my family,* New York: Brunner/Mazel.

Beaudin, C., Chambre, S. (1996). HIV/AIDS as a chronic disease. *American Behavioral Scientist, 39*(6).

Berkman, B. (1996) The emerging health care world: Implications for social work practice and education. *Social Work, 41*(5), 541–551.

Böll, H. (1967). *Irish journal.* New York: McGraw Hill.

Brownson, R., Remington, P. L. (1993). *Chronic disease: Epidemiology and control.* Washington, DC: American Public Health Association.

Centers For Disease Control & Prevention (1997). National Bureau of Statistics.

Dorfman, L. T., Holmes, C. A. & Berlin, K. L. (1996). Wife caregivers of frail elderly veterens: Correlates of caregiver satisfaction and caregiver strain. *Family Relations 45*(1), 46–55.

Doylestown Hospital, May 1998.

Goodheart, C., & Lansing, M. (1997). *Treating people with chronic disease: A psychological guide.* Washington, DC: American Psychological Association.

Harvard Medical School Seminar, June 1997.

Hochstenbach, J., Donders, R., Mulder, T., Van Limbeck, J., & Schoonderwalot, H. (1996). Long-term outcome after stroke: A disability-orientated approach. *International Journal of Rehabilitation Research, 19*(30), 189–201.

Kane, R. L. (1996). Health Perceptions, *American Behavioral Scientist. 39*(6), 707–716.

Libow, J. (1989). Chronic Illness and Family Coping. In L. Combrinck-Graham (Ed.) *Children in family contexts* (pp. 214–229). New York: Guilford Press.

Lubkin, E. M. (1986). *Chronic physical illness: Impact and intervention.* Austin/Monterey: Jones and Bartlett Publishers.

Mother's Day Report (1987). *The picture of health for midlife and older women in America.* Washington, DC: National Center for Education in Maternal and Child Health.

Noble Topf, L. (1995). *You are not your illness: A fireside book.* New York: Simon & Schuster.

Pope, A. M., & Tarlov, A. R., (Eds.). (1997) *Disability in America: Toward a national agenda for prevention.* Washington, D.C.: Institute of Medicine.

Proctor, E. K., et al. (1996) Implementation of discharge plans for chronically ill elders dicharged home. *Health and Social Work, 21*(1), 30–40.

Statistical Abstract of the United States (1998). Washington, DC: U.S. Government Printing Office.

Tolstoy, L. (1961). *Anna Karenina.* New York: Penguin Books.

Turner, D. C. (1996) The role of culture in chronic illness. *The American Behavioral Scientist 39*(6), 717–728.

York, D., & York, P. (1982). *Tough love.* Garden City, NY: Doubleday.

APPENDIX: SOURCES OF INFORMATION AND SUPPORT

March of Dimes Birth Defects Foundation, 1275 Mamaroneck Avenue, White Plains, New York 10605, (914) 428–7100.

National Easter Seal Society, 2023 West Ogden Avenue, Chicago, Illinois 60612, (312) 243–8400.

National Foundation for Jewish Genetic Disease, Inc., 250 Park Avenue, Suite 1000, New York, New York 10177, (212) 682–5550.

National Organization for Rare Disorder, Inc. (NORD), P.O. Box 8923, New Fairfield, Connecticut 06812, (800) 447–6673, (203) 746–6518.

Sibling Information Network, University Affiliated Program on Developmental Disabilities, University of Connecticut, 249 Glenbrook Road, Box U-64, Storrs, Connecticut 06268, (203) 486–3783.

TAPSH: The Association for Persons with Severe Handicaps, 7010 Roosevelt Way, NE, Seattle Washington, 98115, (206) 523–8446.

* * *

Alexander Graham Bell Association for the Deaf (AGBAD), 3417 Volta Place, N. W., Washington, DC, 20007, (202) 337–5220 (Voice and TTY).

* * *

American Cancer Society, Inc., 3340 Peachtree Road, N.E., Atlanta, Georgia, 30026, (404) 320–3333.

Intestinal Multiple Polyposis and Colorectal Cancer (IMPACC) 1006-1001, Brinker Dr. Hagerston Md. 21740, (301) 791–7526.

Leukemia Society of America, Inc., 733 Third Avenue. New York, New York 10017, (212) 573–8484.

National Cancer Care Foundation (NCCF), 1180 Avenue of the Americas, New York, New York, 10036, (212) 221–3300.

* * *

Association for Children with Down Syndrome, Inc. (ACDS), 2616 Martin Avenue, Bellmore, Long Island, New York 11710, (516) 221–4700.

Fragile X Foundation, P.O. Box 300233, Denver, Colorado, 80203, (800) 835–2246 Ext. 58.

Fragile X Support, Inc., 1380 Huntington Drive, Mundelein, Illinois 60060, (312) 680–3317.

National Association for Down Syndrome (NADS), P.O. Box 4542 Oak Brook, lllinois 60521, (312) 325–9112.

Prader-Willi Syndrome Association (PWSA), 6490 Excelsior Boulevard, E-102, St. Louis Park, Minnesota, (612) 926–1947.

Turner's Syndrome Society, York University Administrative Studies, Building #006, 4700 Keele Street, Downsview, Ontario M3J IP3, Canada, (416) 736–5023.

* * *

National Marfan Foundation (NMF), 382 Main Street, Port Washington, New York 11050.

* * *

American Cleft Palate Association (ACPA), The Cleft Palate Foundation, 1218 Grandview Avenue, University of Pittsburgh, Pittsburgh, Pennsylvania 15211, (800) 24-Cleft, (412) 481–1376.

Association for Children and Adults with Learning Disabilities, Inc. (ACLD), 4156 Library Road, Pittsburgh, Pennsylvania, 15234, (412) 341–1515.

Autism Society of American (ASA), 1234 Massachusetts Avenue, N.W., Suite 1017, Washington, DC 20005–4599, (202) 783–0125.

Center for Hyperactive Child Information, Inc. (CHCI), P.O. Box 66272, Washington, DC, 20035–6272, (703) 920–7495.

Orton Dyslexia Society (ODS), 724 York Road, Baltimore, Maryland 21204, (301) 296–0232.

United Cerebral Palsy Associations, Inc. (UCPA)/UCP Research and Educational Foundation, 66 East 34th Street, New York, New York 10016, (800) USA–1UCP, (212) 481–6300.

* * *

American Celiac Society, 45 Gifford Avenue, Jersey City, New Jersey, 07304, (201) 432–1207.

American Liver Foundation (ALF), 998 Pompton Avenue, Cedar Grove, New Jersey 07009, (201) 857–2626.

Gluten Intolerance Group of North America (GIG), P.O. Box 23055, Seattle Washington, 98102–0353, (206) 325–6980.

National Foundation for Ileitis and Colitis, Inc., (NFIC), 44 Park Avenue, New York, New York 10016–7374, (212) 685–3440.

* * *

Cooley's Anemia Foundation, Inc., 105 East 22nd Street, Suite 911, New York, New York, 10010, (212) 598–0911.

Council on Cardiovascular Disease in the Young, American Heart Association National Center, 7320 Greenville Avenue, Dallas, Texas, 75231, (214) 373–6300.

Iron Overload Diseases Association, Inc. (IOD), 224 Datura Street, Suite 311, West Palm Beach, Florida 33401, (305) 659–5616, 5677.

National Association for Sickle Cell Disease, Inc. (NASCD), 4221 Wilshire Boulevard, Suite 360, Los Angeles, California 90010–3503, (800) 421–8453, (213) 936–7205.

National Hemophilia Foundation (NHF), The Soho Building, 110 Greene Street, Room 406, New York, New York 10012, (212) 219–8180.

* * *

American Lupus Society, 23751 Madison Street, Torrance, California 90505, (213) 373–1335.

Immune Deficiency Foundation (IDF), P.O. Box 586, Columbia, Maryland 21045, (301) 461–3127.

Sjogren's Syndrome Foundation, Inc. (SSF), 29 Gateway Drive, Great Neck, New York 11021, (516) 487–2243.

National Kidney Foundation Inc., Two Park Avenue, New York, New York 10016, (212) 889–2210.

* * *

American Diabetes Association, Inc., 1660 Duke Street, Alexandria, Virginia 22314, (703) 549–1500.

American Porphyria Foundation, P.O. Box 11163, Montgomery, Alabama 36111, (205) 265–2200.

Association for Glycogen Storage Disease, Box 896, Durant, Iowa 52747, (319) 785–6038.

Association of Neuro-Metabolic Disorders, 5223 Brookfield Lane, Sylvania, Ohio 43560, (419) 885–1497.

Cystic Fibrosis (CF) Foundation, 6931 Arlington Road, Bethesda, Maryland 20814, (800) FIGHT CF, (301) 951–4422.

Dysautonomia Foundation, Inc., 370 Lexington Avenue, New York, New York, 10017, (212) 889–5222.

Foundation for the Study of Wilson's Disease Inc., 5447 Palisade Avenue, Bronx, New York 104719, (212) 430–2091.

Lowe's Syndrome Association, Inc., 222 Lincoln Street, West Lafayette, Indiana 47906, (317) 743–3634.

Malignant Hyperthermia Association of the United States (MHAUS), P.O. Box 3231, Darien, Connecticut 06320, (203) 655–3007.

Maple Syrup Urine Disease (MSUD) Family Support Group, RR #2, Box 24-A, Flemingsburg, Kentucky 41041, (606) 849–4679.

ML (Mucolipidosis) IV Foundation, 6 Concord Drive, Monsey, New York 10952, (919) 425–0639.

National Gaucher Foundation, Inc. (NGF), 1424 K Street, NW, Fourth Floor, Washington, DC 20005, (202) 393–2777.

National Mucopolysaccharidoses (MPS) Society, Inc., 17 Kraemer Street, Hicksville, New York 11801, (516) 931–6338.

National Organization for Albinism and Hypopigmentation (NOAH), 1800 Locust Street, Suite 1811, Philadelphia, Pennsylvania 19102–4316, (215) 471–2278, (215) 471–2265.

National Tay-Sachs and Allied Diseases Association, Inc. (NTSA), 385 Elliot Street, Newton, Massachusetts 02164, (617) 964–5508.

Organic-Acidemia Association, Inc., 1532 South 87th Street, Kansas City, Kansas 66111, (913) 422–7080.

United Leukodystrophy Foundation, Inc. (ULF), 2304 Highland Drive, Sycamore, Illinois 60178, (815) 895–3211.

Williams Syndrome Association (WSA), P.O. Box 178373, San Diego, California 92117–0910, (713) 376–7072.

Wilson's Disease Association, P.O. Box 75324, Washington, DC, 20013, (703) 636–3003, 3014.

Zain Hansen MPS (Mucopolysaccharidoses) Foundation, P.O. Box 4768, 1200 Fernwood Drive, Arcata, California 95521, (707) 822–5421.

* * *

Arthritis Foundation/American Juvenile Arthritis Organization (AJAO), 1314 Spring Street, NW, Atlanta, Georgia 30309, (404) 872–7100.

Freeman-Sheldon Parent Support Group, 1459 East Maple Hills Drive, Bountiful, Utah 84010, (801) 298–3149.

National Scoliosis Foundation, Inc., 93 Concord Avenue, P.O. Box 547, Belmont Massachusetts 02178, (617) 489–0888, 0880.

Osteogenesis Imperfecta Foundation, Inc. (OIF), P.O. Box 14807, Tampa, Florida 34629–4807, (813) 855–7077.

Scoliosis Association, Inc., P.O. Box 51353, Raleigh, North Carolina, 27609, (919) 846–2639.

* * *

Alzheimer's Disease and Related Disorders Association, Inc. (ADRDA), 70 East Lake Street, Chicago, Illinois 60601, (800) 631–0379, (312) 853–3060.

American Narcolepsy Association (ANA), P.O. Box 1187, San Carlos, California 94070, (415) 591–7979.

CHAPTER 22

Families Experiencing Death, Dying, and Bereavement

Dorothy S. Becvar

The dark background that death supplies brings out the tender colors that life supplies in all their purity.

Santayana

WITHOUT DEATH, the concept of life would be meaningless. Nevertheless, we in Western society spend enormous amounts of time, money, and energy denying our inevitable finiteness and/or attempting to prolong life. The paradox is that in the process of avoiding acceptance and a related serious consideration of death we may miss the opportunity for enhancing the ability to live more fully that may be derived from such a focus. Further, when confronted with death, whether our own or that of someone about whom we care deeply, we are inadequately prepared and the event becomes a tragedy, often of seemingly insurmountable proportions. Therefore, in an effort both to expand our perceptions and enhance our therapeutic skills, this chapter provides an overview of the issues and attitudes that may be anticipated when death, dying, and/or bereavement become the dominant reality in the life of a family. Also considered will be appropriate preparation and response on the part of therapists working with individuals or families engaged in any stage of the process of dealing with death. The goal will be to help professionals to be able to facilitate a good death for those who are dying and to be a source of meaningful aid and support for those for whom the death of another designates them as the survivors, those experiencing bereavement. To begin, we will consider various definitions and perceptions that are essential aspects of this topic.

DEFINITIONS AND PERCEPTIONS

DEATH

In our society, the most prevalent perception of death has been that it is a phenomenon to be denied (Becker, 1973) or feared (Foos-Graber, 1989), or both. It may even be considered a social disease, something from which we attempt, often successfully, to remain aloof and to avoid incorporating in otherwise socially acceptable conversations (Shneidman, 1980a). Indeed, it has been noted that while sexual activity has become more and more "mentionable," death, as a natural process, has become increasingly more "unmentionable" (Gorer, 1980). Even when it is mentioned, death tends to be "discussed in hushed, solemn tones" (Hainer, 1997, p. 1D). Further, when death occurs, we are reluctant to acknowledge the reality. Even the embalming process, which is virtually unknown in Europe, may be understood as a refusal to accept death (Aries, 1980).

Dictionary definitions indicate that death refers to the loss of life, or anything so dreadful as to seem like death. Further, it is noted that death is often symbolized by a skeleton with a scythe. Indeed, we fear death as indicating the end of life as we know it. At the same time, however, it also represents perhaps the greatest mystery known to the human race:

> From the very beginning we sense the oxymoronic quality of death. Death is destroyer and redeemer; the ultimate cruelty and the essence of release; universally feared but sometimes actively sought; undeniably ubiquitous, yet incomprehensibly unique; of all phenomena, the most obvious and the least reportable, feared yet fascinating. (Shneidman, 1980a, p. 10)

In recent years, there has been a gradual transformation of our cultural stories about and professional responses to death. At the forefront of this transformation has been Elisabeth Kubler-Ross, who was lauded for her initial delineation of the stages of death and dying (1969) and subsequently vilified when she began to write about near-death experiences (Foos-Graber, 1989) and death as a final stage of growth (Kubler-Ross, 1975), revealing her belief in such phenomena as karma and reincarnation. Today, the fields of thanatology and traumatology (Figley, Bride, & Mazza, 1997) are recognized and accepted areas of specialty within the mental health professions.

Although the growing respect for and attention to this topic on the part of professionals are indicative of a shift in societal attitudes, we nevertheless must be sensitive both to the unique ways in which individuals in a given cultural context experience the phenomenon of death and to the various influences on the creation of meaning. Included in this regard are past experiences with death (Callanan & Kelley, 1992), family patterns related to loss and bereavement (Byng-Hall, 1991), stage in the family life cycle (McGoldrick & Walsh, 1991), and ethnic background (McGoldrick Almeida, Hines, Garcia Proto, Rosen, & Lee, 1991). In addition, the presence or absence of a religious or spiritual belief system may be extremely significant. Relative to this latter dimension, Kastenbaum (1986) summarizes various common interpretations of death as follows:

> (1) a more enfeebled form of life, (2) the continuation of personal existence more or less as usual, (3) perpetual spiritual development, (4) a triphasic progression from waiting to judgment and on to a final eternal culmination (the most traditional form of Christian belief), (5) cycling and recycling of the self through life-death-rebirth passages, and (6) nothing. (p. 34)

Regardless of our personal perceptions about death, however, and while its definition may at first glance appear to be clear-cut, with the advances in medical technology in recent years, the issue of what constitutes death has become somewhat ambiguous (Becvar, in press). Given the increased ability to prolong life by maintaining persons on life-support systems, the medical and legal communities have struggled, for example, with the distinction between a vegetative state and brain death (Iglesias, 1995). In 1968, a group of physicians at the Harvard Medical School created what have come to be known as the "Harvard Criteria" for determining that the brain has reached a state in which it is deemed to be irreversibly nonfunctional:

1. *Unreceptive and unresponsive.* No awareness is shown for external stimuli or inner need. The unresponsiveness is complete even under the application of stimuli that ordinarily would be extremely painful.
2. *No movements and no breathing.* There is a complete absence of spontaneous respiration and all other spontaneous muscular movement.
3. *No reflexes.* The usual reflexes that can be elicited in a neurophysiological examination are absent (e.g., when a light is shined in the eye, the pupil does not constrict).
4. *A flat EEG.* Electrodes attached to the scalp elicit a printout of electrical activity from the living brain. These are popularly known as brain waves. The respirator brain does not provide the usual pattern of peaks and valleys. Instead the moving automatic stylus records essentially a flat line. This is taken to demonstrate the lack of electrophysiological activity.
5. *No circulation to or within the brain.* Without the oxygen and nutrition provided to the brain by its blood supply, functioning will soon terminate. (Precisely how long the brain can retain its viability, the ability to survive, without circulation is a matter of much current investigation and varies somewhat with conditions.) (Kastenbaum, 1986, p. 9)

Although the Harvard Criteria have become the basis on which difficult decisions often are made, the new field of bioethics, or biomedical ethics (Beauchamp & Childress, 1994) has evolved more recently in order to respond to the need to be able to make prudent life and death decisions at an institutional level.

DYING

Indeed, the need for an institutional response such as the field of bioethics represents in part an outgrowth over the controversy regarding how we are to die and who is to have control over the process (Carter, 1996). Are the decisions regarding how we are to make the transition from life to death in the hands of the dying person or are such decisions to be made by our families and communities? On the one hand, there are those who have been instrumental in the development and support of the hospice movement in this country (Byock, 1997; Callanan & Kelley, 1992), one whose mission is the provision of supportive, palliative, rather than curative, care until physical death has been medically determined. On the other hand, many believe that a person who has determined that a reasonable quality of life has ceased should have the option to hasten the dying process through some form of euthanasia (Battin, 1994; Dying Well Network, 1996). Ironically, in both instances there is a shared goal of facilitating a good death (Becvar, in press), although the means to that end differ drastically.

According to Kubler-Ross's formulation (1969), the process of dying evolves through a series of five stages including (1) denial, or the inability to accept the truth that death is near; (2) rage and anger, or the resentment that is felt about the fact that one's life is indeed coming to an end; (3) bargaining, or the attempt to gain more time in exchange for the promise of altered behavior; (4) depression, or the grief and sadness that one's life will soon be over; and (5) acceptance, or a feeling of resignation that the end is near. Although such a model certainly is not invariant for every person, nor are the stages necessarily followed in the above sequence, this framework may be useful in understanding the behavior of an individual at a given point in the dying process. At the same time, it is important to be aware that, as Byock (1997, p. xiv) writes, "the actual range of human experience of dying is broad."

For some, the dying process may be understood and engaged in as a transformative experience (Callanan & Kelley, 1992). That is, "when we accept death, transform our attitude toward life, and discover the fundamental connection between life and death, a dramatic possibility for healing can occur" (Sogyal, 1992, p. 31). Similarly, based on Eastern philosophy, Foos-Graber (1989, p. 200) describes "deathing," which is comparable to birthing, as "a means of making an informed, safe, responsible, and joyous transition from the physically focused 'I' consciousness to the various subtle stages of life-after-death's expanded states, including humanity's birthright—full enlightenment, or liberation." Using a variety of breathing techniques and meditative practices, dying thus becomes part of a larger spiritual discipline, or art form, that facilitates transformation to a higher state of consciousness. Rather than seeing death as just another biological process that simply happens to us, we thereby are encouraged to embrace it and utilize it in a growthful manner.

BEREAVEMENT

Whether death is feared or embraced, and regardless of the manner of dying, those who survive experience the fact of the loss, which according to Kastenbaum (1986) denotes bereavement. Grief is one response to the experience of bereavement and mourning may be understood as "the culturally patterned expression of the bereaved person's thoughts and feelings" (p. 139). Typical responses in our society include feelings of confusion and despair, forgetfulness, sleep disturbances, extended periods of crying, and a variety of physical symptoms. However, the degree of intensity and the length of time in which such reactions are considered appropriate have been the subject of much debate.

Classical models of the grieving process were described by Freud (1917–1957) and Lindemann (1944), and until quite recently most professional explanations were derived from their work and included three basic assumptions. Accordingly, it was believed that the grieving process is time-limited (Peretz, 1970), with the standard being 2 weeks of shock and intense grief, 2 months of strong grieving, and 2 years during which the grief decreased, the bereaved individual recovered, and she or he returned to full, normal functioning. By the end of this 2-year period the grieving process was to have concluded. Throughout the grieving process, the basic goal was that of detaching from emotional ties to the deceased in order to be able to form new relationships with those who are still living (Bowlby, 1980). Should the grief not be resolved within the designated appropriate amount of time, then mourning was to be considered maladaptive (Raphael, 1983).

The above model was subscribed to for many years following its creation. However, during the 1980s a variety of studies challenged all three of its fundamental assumptions (Demi & Miles, 1987; Fish, 1986; Fulton, 1987; Knapp, 1987; McClowry, Davies, May, Kulenkamp, & Martinson, 1987; Osterweis, Solomon, & Green, 1984; Palmer, 1987; Zisook & Shuchter, 1986). Based on the findings reported in these studies, it became possible to conclude that the grieving process may have no fixed end point, and indeed, that it may last a lifetime. Although the bereaved person may return to normal functioning, she or he may never "get over" the loss, but rather learns to live with it. Secondly, complete detachment from the deceased came to be understood as neither desirable nor possible. Rather, there is recognition that the bereaved person is able to maintain a simultaneous attachment to both the living and to the one who has died and function perfectly well. Finally, there emerged an awareness that bereavement may take many forms and that the degree to which it is adaptive or maladaptive must be determined on an individual basis.

More recently, Silverman and Klass (1997, p. 16) have proposed what they call a new paradigm according to which it is understood that "interdependence is sustained even in the absence of one of the parties . . . the bereaved remain involved and connected to the deceased, and . . . actively construct an inner representation of the deceased that is part of the normal grieving process." What is more, according to Rando (1997, p. xvii) acute grief responses share similarities with those of posttraumatic stress disorder and include the necessity for the following:

> The working through of related affects, integration of conscious and dissociated aspects, mourning of relevant secondary physical and psychosocial losses, acquisition of new ways of being to move adaptively into the new world, development of a comprehensive perspective on the event and one's level of control therein, emotional relocation of what was lost, acceptance of fitting responsibility and relinquishment of inappropriate guilt, revisions of the assumptive world demanded by the event and its repercussions, creation of meaning out of the experience, integration of the event into the totality of one's life, formation of a new identity reflecting survival of the event, and appropriate reinvestment in life.

Given such a shift in perspectives, one is well advised to avoid pathologizing the grief process before understanding each person's reactions in the context of his or her world view and unique situation. That is, rather than overcoming and recovering from a major loss, the goal is to facilitate adaptation (Bernstein, 1997). In this process, values, attitudes, beliefs, perceptions, and relationships are affected and altered and people are forever changed. In order to be able to put the experience in context, it is essential to consider such variables as the impact of time, the role and life stage of the deceased, and the manner in which the death occurred. In each of these areas it is also important to be aware of gender differences that may emerge in the grieving process. In the following sections we consider each of these variables more fully.

THE IMPACT OF TIME

Time is significant in many ways, to both the dying and to those who survive. In the case of an anticipated death, the dying person has an opportunity to put his or her affairs in order, to participate in funeral arrangements and burial decisions, as well as to achieve closure in significant relationships. There is also an opportunity to assimilate what is happening and to realign beliefs and meaning systems. At the same time, having this knowledge also tends to initiate a period of anticipatory mourning in which everyone involved is faced with the inevitability of the loss and the grieving process begins even though the death has not yet occurred (Rolland, 1991). Further, in the case of an extended dying process, significant stress may be placed on caretakers and a sense of remorse about being a burden may emerge on the part of the one who is dying. Also, when the sick person dies, feelings of relief may be accompanied by feelings of guilt for what is a perfectly normal, if mixed, reaction.

The other side of the coin is illustrated in situations in which a death is sudden and unexpected, with no time to prepare for the experience. In this case, the person who has died may have made no arrangements or had an opportunity to express his or her wishes regarding issues such as organ donation, funeral arrangements, and burial preferences. What may be more significant, however, is the lack of closure experienced by survivors. There has been no time for farewells and guilt in this case may emerge regarding unresolved conflicts. Acute feelings of unreality, disbelief, and shock are common and a sense of there being many loose ends also is to be expected. Dissonance in terms of beliefs and meaning systems is highly likely, particularly if the death occurred under tragic circumstances or involved the loss of a child. In the later instance, the feeling of a death out of time is extremely significant (Gilbert, 1997).

THE IMPACT OF ROLE AND LIFE STAGE

DEATH OF A CHILD

The death of a child is considered to be one of the most traumatic experiences possible in this life (Gilbert, 1997), one that pushes parents almost "beyond endurance" (Knapp, 1986). It has been described most poignantly by a bereaved mother who is also a psychologist as follows:

> The sun rises in the east. Winter inevitably yields to spring. The tides ebb and flow with comforting predictability. Seeds take root, push their greenery toward the sun, bloom, produce new seed, wither, and die, all in orderly progression according to nature's plan. When an aged parent dies, though we may grieve deeply for the personal loss, the world is not turned upside down. Nature's plan, the predictability of the universe, remains intact. When a child dies, the very ground on which we depend for stability heaves and quakes and the rightness and orderliness of our existence are destroyed. Nothing in life prepares us; no coping skills were learned. Parents who lose children are thrown into chaos. The loss of a child is shattering, unique among losses. (Bernstein, 1997, p. 3).

According to Klass (1988), the uniqueness of parental grief grows out of the unique bond between parent and child. One's sense of identity as a parent, the intertwining of the relationship between parent and child and those with many other people, the parent's feeling of obligation and commitment to care for and safeguard the child are all assaulted by such a loss, while perceptions regarding the unjustness of the experience add to the grief experience.

Because the relationship with the child who dies is different at different ages and stages, the mourning experience will vary greatly. However, there is no evidence to suggest that the loss of a child is any more or less devastating as a function of the time of life at which his or her death occurs (Rando, 1988). Further, although often ignored or denied, this assessment also often applies to the loss of a child during pregnancy (Speckhard, 1997). Although all parents experience the destruction of their hopes, dreams, and expectations for the child when she or he dies, the cultural disenfranchisment of the loss of a pregnancy means less support than is generally available for parents who have lost a child following birth.

One of the most important things of which to be aware when working with parents who have lost a child is their need to talk about the experience (Bernstein, 1997; Knapp, 1986). As one bereaved parent writes, "The most essential ingredient, in fact, in surviving well— besides facing reality—is to speak of the dead child unashamedly" (Schiff, 1977, p. 101). When the opportunity to speak and to express emotions is denied, the parents may experience resentment and eventually choose to separate from those whom they perceive as uncaring and insensitive (Knapp, 1986).

The relationship between the parents also is at risk as each member of the couple may experience different ways of grieving and neither feels supported by the other (Bernstein, 1997; Lindbergh, 1998). Those working with bereaved parents might therefore wish to consider the following "caveats for couples" (Bernstein, 1997):

- Different paces and styles of mourning are to be expected. There is no right way to do this grief-work. Your way is not better than your spouse's. You each have to design your own route through the maze.
- Recognize that a marriage is not an all-purpose relationship that can meet all of your needs all of the time. Much of the time you may be out of synch with each other and be unable to provide support. Finding support among other family and friends takes the heat off the marriage.
- Read nonverbal communication. If your spouse is silent, that is not a failure to communicate. That is a loud and clear communication. Respect it.
- Resist the temptation to become a mind-reader and assume what your spouse is thinking or feeling. Ask!
- Touch!
- Readiness for reentry into sex, social activities, or any pleasurable pursuit varies widely.
- Make a concerted effort to be kind thoughtful, respectful, and forgiving. (p. 129)

DEATH OF A SIBLING

The siblings of a child who dies often experience a double loss. Not only has their brother or sister died, but at a time when parental support may be most needed, their mothers and fathers may be so immersed in their own grief that they are unable to respond fully to the needs of other children (Baker, 1997). The siblings' sense of security therefore may be threatened as their parents behave differently, are inconsistent, appear vulnerable, refuse to reminisce about the dead brother or sister, or are unable to support the grieving processes of their surviving children. Ultimately the relationships of siblings to their parents is likely to be forever changed, either for the better or the worse.

In addition, well-meaning others often deny what siblings may be experiencing when they inquire of them how their parents are doing without first or ever asking how they are doing. It is likely that these surviving children are struggling with a variety of reactions, among which may be "guilt (for survival, health, past actions, or jealousy), sadness, hurt feelings, loneliness, anger, confusion, fear, difficulty sharing feelings, disbelief, apathy, and numbness" (Nader, 1997a, p. 19). However, the degree to which the sibling experiences such emotions and is able to resolve the loss is affected by the relationship between the child who dies and his or her brother or sister as well as the manner in which the loss is handled by the family as a whole.

A major focus for those attempting to help facilitate the resolution of sibling loss is thus family communication (Baker, 1997). In addition to allowing each family member to tell his or her story, other important topics of conversation include the differences in coping and grieving styles among family members as well as the impact of past bereavement experiences on each; the need for a shift in roles that is necessitated by the death of the child; developmental tasks that may be in need of attention in terms of both individuals and the family; and ways in which the grieving process may be supported for each individual. Also important may be a consideration of how the family wishes to be or to create itself in the future.

DEATH OF A PARENT

Children who lose a parent are affected not only by the death but also by the circumstances surrounding it. Such circumstances include prior relationship patterns and issues, the manner of the death, as well as the availability of support. As with the loss of a sibling, the life of the family is forever changed in addition to the fact that the surviving parent is also experiencing his or her bereavement. Although parental loss continues to be extremely significant regardless of the ages of those involved, it is important to note that children in different developmental stages will experience the death of a parent differently and will have different ways of displaying grief (Steinberg, 1997).

According to Raphael (1983), very young children may experience a sense of grief, may continually request that the lost parent return, and may reject anyone who attempts to act as a substitute. Children between the ages of 2 and 5 may be assisted to understand the meaning of death and while they can be dealt with in an honest and direct manner may also revert to behaviors of an earlier age such as bedwetting. Between the ages of 5 and 8, children may experience a sense of guilt about their parent's death or may deny that the death is permanent. The reactions of children between the age of 8 and 12 tend to mimic those of adults and include increased fears about both their own mortality and that of their surviving parent. Further, the following observations have been made regarding young daughters who have lost mothers:

> Unlike the adult, who experiences parent loss with a relatively intact personality, a girl who loses her mother during childhood or adolescence co-opts the loss into her emerging personality, where it then becomes a defining characteristic of her identity. From learning at an early age that close relationships can be impermanent, security ephemeral, and family capable of being redefined, the motherless daughter develops an adult insight while still a child but has only juvenile resources to help her cope. (Edelman, 1994, p. xxv)

Enabling children to come to terms with parental loss may be facilitated by helping them to create inner constructions or representations of the deceased parent in order to maintain a sense of connection with him or her (Nickman, Silverman, & Normand, 1998). Surviving parents may become a crucial part of this process by encouraging the expression of memories and feelings, by supporting a realistic assessment of both the negative and the positive qualities of the parent who died, and by allowing the children to describe their feelings about what they have lost or miss most. Further questions that may be useful in support of a viable construction of the deceased person, for both the surviving parent as well as the child, include the following:

"Do you ever talk to him?" "Does she answer you?" "Do you dream of him?" "Where do you think she is now, or do you not think of her as being in a particular place?" "Do you sense him near you? Is that a good feeling, or not so good?" "Are there things you'd like to be able to tell her?" (p. 133)

DEATH OF A SPOUSE

The experience of losing a spouse varies considerably as a function of the suddenness of the death, the gender and age of the bereaved, and the family life cycle stage. Both widows and widowers who have the most severe reactions to the death of a spouse are those who have had little or no warning. However, women who lose a husband tend to feel abandoned while husbands are more likely to describe a feeling of dismemberment at the loss of their wives (Kastenbaum, 1986). Women often are freer in their ability to cry over their loss than are men, who are likely to attempt to behave in a manner consistent with societal prohibitions against the expression of emotions. Women may describe a sense of injustice as compared to men, who are more likely to experience guilt, although both groups share and express feelings of anger.

The reaction to widowhood is also significantly influenced by age and the point in the family life cycle at which the death occurs. For families with young children, loss of a spouse "is complicated by financial and caretaking obligations for the children, which can interfere with the tasks of mourning" (McGoldrick & Walsh, 1991, p. 36). A further complicating factor is that fathers who have lost wives are likely to be more supported in the domestic arena by friends and extended family members than are mothers who have lost husbands.

Individuals who experience widowhood in middle age lose a partner just at the point in their life cycle when greater freedom and financial ability might have enabled them to anticipate spending more time together and perhaps attaining some of the goals that previously had to be postponed because of responsibilities associated with child-rearing and career requirements. Indeed, once the children leave home, it is the marriage that becomes the primary focus (McCullough & Rutenberg, 1988), and loneliness and extreme disorientation are common grief reactions. Men, in particular, find the loss of their spouse to be more disruptive during the initial period of bereavement and are far more likely than women to resort to suicide (Walsh, 1988). However, over the long term, it is women who experience greater hardship given the likelihood of reduced financial resources and the decreased probability that they will remarry.

When an elderly wife or husband loses a spouse, the death may seem more appropriate, or more in the natural order of things. However, the pain associated with this loss should not be underestimated. In addition, there may be concerns on the part of both the bereaved person and other family members about the ability of the surviving spouse to care for himself or herself (Brown, 1988). Also important to note is that such deaths may mean the loss of long-term relationships, which "involve strong primary attachments that serve as a base for mutual security and protectiveness" (Moss & Moss, 1996, p. 163). What is more, the rate of remarriage for widowed persons decreases with age. As women are far more likely than men to outlive their husbands, they are also more likely to spend their remaining days alone.

DEATH OF AN EXTENDED FAMILY MEMBER, COLLEAGUE, OR FRIEND

Despite an inevitable experience of loss, the impact of the death of an extended family member, colleague, or friend will vary as a function of the degree of closeness experienced by surviving family members with the one who has died. Important factors include the role played by the person who died in the life of the family as well as whether there was emotional dependence on the individual (Brown, 1988). The more important the deceased and the more family members looked to him or her for support, the stronger the reactions on the part of the family as a whole are likely to be.

The same considerations may apply in the case of colleagues and friends. Also to be noted, however, is the fact that:

> the death of a co-worker no matter what the cause or circumstances, is always premature; it reminds those in good health that life is not forever and that mortality is fleeting and forces them to consider the impending reality of their own deaths. (Williams & Nurmi, 1997, p. 43)

The aftershocks of such deaths, therefore, may continue to reverberate through various systems even as they affect the ability of the bereaved to function normally.

Finally, in an era when violence is increasing, it is important to be cognizant of the fact that more and more children are being exposed to the death of schoolmates at an early age (Nader, 1997b). Not only does it appear to be essential to have support within the systems such as schools where the deaths occurred, but it also may be important for family members to be sensitive to needs a child may be experiencing to express and resolve his or her grief. Depending on the nature of the death, specialized methods of trauma treatment also may be required. Indeed, in all of the types of relationship loss described to this point, the manner in which the death occurs is a factor that must be taken into consideration.

THE IMPACT OF CIRCUMSTANCES

DEATH FOLLOWING AN EXTENDED ILLNESS

Although, as previously noted, an extended illness may be extremely stressful for those who are caring for the dying person, it does offer an opportunity to come to terms with death on many levels. Knowing that someone is about to die provides precious time that if used well, may be helpful to everyone involved. The first issue to be considered in this regard is whether to discuss the awareness of impending death with the person who is dying.

According to Kubler-Ross (1995, p. 7), "There is no one dying, whether he is five or ninety-five, who does not know that he is dying. And the question is not: do I tell him that he is dying? The question is: Can I hear him?" Others would agree that people have an awareness not only of the fact that they are dying but also when it is going to happen (Callanan & Kelley, 1992), a phenomenon described as "nearing death awareness." Assuming this awareness to be the case, what next becomes important is a sensitivity to the desires of the dying person to speak, or not, about his or her own death. If the dying person wishes to speak, then it is crucial to hear his or her sometimes subtle cues, to offer to listen and to be willing to engage in the conversation at the level that is appropriate for him or her. The dying person may thus be given an opportunity to express a variety of emotions as well as to deal with relationship issues. In addition she or he may be assisted in making appropriate financial and legal arrangements, all of which may enhance a sense of completion for the person whose life is coming to an end.

For the relatives of the dying person, the period of the illness allows time to make amends for past hurts, to come to terms with the inevitable, and to bid farewell in a meaningful way. Much healing can occur that facilitates greater acceptance of death when it finally arrives. Indeed, Byock (1997) views dying as a developmental process similar to the one that is initiated at birth; one that the family supports and is influenced by as each stage of growth is moved through and the achievement of goals is accompanied by a sense of mastery and accomplishment. He writes:

> People who are dying often feel a sense of constant pressure to adapt to unwanted change. As a person's functioning declines, the physical environment becomes threatening. A trip to the bathroom may become an hour's chore and then, a few weeks later, a major event. On learning of the grave prognosis, family and friends may begin acting differently, becoming serious or even solemn in one's presence. People may avoid one out of their own emotional pain, leaving one feeling awkward and isolated, an innocent pariah. New strategies are urgently needed to forestall a sense of personal annihilation. Mastering the taskwork may involve personal struggle, and even suffering, yet it can lead to growth and dying well. The tasks are not easy. But as a dying person reaches developmental landmarks such as experienced love of self and others, the completion of relationships, the acceptance of the finality of one's life, and the achievement of a new sense of self despite one's impending demise, one's life and the lives of others are enriched. (Byock, 1997, p. 33)

Although many dying persons are able to speak directly of their needs and desires, others are able to articulate their wishes only in indirect and often symbolic ways (Callanan & Kelley, 1992). Therefore, it is essential to be alert to very subtle requests, whether for assistance, for others to be contacted, or for there to be recognition that the person is about to die. Dying persons may be extremely sensitive to the emotional pain of those they are leaving behind and may even need permission to die or space in which to do it. For example,

> it's common for dying children to send their parents away so they can die in peace. It's as though they sense their parents could hold them back from dying peacefully, or they wish to spare them the anguish of witnessing their moment of death. (p. 207)

Also important is the awareness that as people approach death, they may speak of seeing or being in the presence of friends and relatives who are no longer living (Callanan & Kelley, 1992). Although this may be mistaken as mental confusion, particularly in the elderly, it is a fairly common experience that benefits from validation by those in the caretaking role. It is appropriate to respond with gentle inquiries about what is happening or about messages received; to pose open-ended questions; and to avoid arguing or challenging the perceptions of the dying person. The fact that the dying person does not experience himself or herself as being alone can provide a measure of reassurance and comfort, thus enhancing the coping ability for all.

SUDDEN OR ACCIDENTAL DEATH

The challenge to the coping ability of the bereaved is the distinguishing feature in the case of sudden or accidental death (Rando, 1988). Shock, disbelief, and extreme disruption are added to the pain of the loss as mourners struggle to make sense of an apparently meaningless event. Thus, the grieving process may take longer or be more complicated, with survivors experiencing a lack of control whose manifestations run the gamut from emotional numbness to heartrending reactions and outbursts (Nurmi & Williams, 1997). Kastenbaum (1986) notes that there is also a greater tendency for the unexpectedly bereaved to manifest physical symptoms such as high blood pressure, colds and other infections, arthritis, chest pains, and allergies. However, the long-term adaptation of those whose loved one died suddenly and/or in an accident tends to be similar to that of those experiencing a death that was anticipated (Bernstein, 1997).

Understanding the onslaught to the belief systems of survivors and their need to be able to create a meaningful story or context within which to make sense of the death is the key to helping in the case of sudden or accidental death. Indeed, for some, anger at God and a loss of religious or spiritual supports on which they previously relied may leave survivors feeling even more bereft. As one's old world view is shattered, a new one must be created or found in order to be able to recommit to life. Books such as *When Bad Things Happen to Good People* (Kushner, 1981) represent such an attempt to come to terms with loss through the embracing of a different perspective and thus may be helpful to some. Ultimately, however, what is needed is support through the process of making sense of the experience in a way that is useful to the persons involved. Throughout there needs to be understanding that this may require great periods of time and much searching in a variety of directions before a sense of peace is regained.

VIOLENT OR WRONGFUL DEATH

Yet another dimension is added to the grieving process following sudden death when a person is murdered or dies as the result of some other form of violence. In this instance, survivors may become obsessed with concerns that the victim suffered in the process of dying (Knapp, 1986). They also are likely to experience rage about the injustice of the situation (Bernstein, 1997). If the legal system becomes involved, insult may be added to injury by the requirement for an autopsy, by delays in the handling of the case, and by an ultimate lack of resolution.

At the same time, involvement with the legal system may provide an opportunity, particularly for parents, that enables them to feel like they are doing something to right a wrong. According to Klass (1988, p. 38), "In cases of wrongful deaths, parents often work tirelessly to ensure that the police and court systems bring justice to the death." The challenge for such parents is to avoid assuming a vengeful stance and to overcome a sense of helplessness even as they continue to do everything in their power to assure an appropriate outcome. When such efforts fail, they may turn to political activism or the creation of victims' rights organizations such as Mothers Against Drunk Driving (MADD), which provide useful and creative ways to channel their grief.

SUICIDE

In contrast to the experience of violent or wrongful death, feelings of guilt and an inability to speak about the death because of social stigma may complicate the grieving of those whose loved ones have died as a result of a completed suicide (Bernstein,

1997). Indeed, the many cultural stories about suicide include beliefs that it is a sinful act, that it represents criminal behavior, and/or that it indicates weakness or madness (Kastenbaum, 1986). Those left behind may feel anger and a sense of rejection as a result of the lack of warning when someone they cared about succeeds in ending his or her own life (Nurmi & Williams, 1997). For parents, resentment may emerge as a result of "having been electively and publicly abandoned by a son or daughter who, in the minds of the parents, catastrophically showed that their love was not enough" (Schiff, 1977, p. 42).

In addition to providing support to those who are bereaved as a function of suicide, it is extremely important to help with the process of putting self-blame in perspective (Martin & Romanowski, 1994). In fact, there is no clear evidence regarding the causes of suicide and even when notes are left, they may be ambiguous or incomplete. The act may be carefully planned or spontaneous and may be a response to either a single event or many. Each suicide must be understood as a unique, personal event and may be as much or more a statement about the person as it is about those left behind. However, survivors of suicide may be in great need of psychological support as they tend to be at higher risk for morbidity and mortality than others in the first year of bereavement (Shneidman, 1980b).

AMBIGUOUS DEATH AND LOSS

Lack of public validation and prescribed rituals that aid the bereaved characterizes the experience of death and loss that are ambiguous (Boss, 1991). In cases where family members are absent or lost for extended periods of time as, for example, with soldiers missing in action, or kidnapping or desertion, closure is prevented and those left behind must linger in limbo regarding the fate of their love one. In other cases, psychological absence as a result of disease processes, drug overdose, or accident-induced comas may create a void that produces confusion and conflict among family members.

Assisting such family members in their efforts to deal with ambiguous death and loss involves several steps (Boss, 1991). These include providing empathy for and understanding of the fact that it is a very stressful situation; allowing family members to express and hear each other's perceptions of the experience; offering and clarifying as much information about the ordeal as possible; putting family members in touch with support groups and others who have had similar experiences; and facilitating a process of resolution through the search for and creation of meaning. The overriding goal seems to be that of helping family members to be resilient in the face of stressful circumstances and to re-create their lives in ways that work for them in spite of the ambiguity of a situation in which who is in and who is out of the family remains unclear.

Just as with ambiguous death and loss the importance of social support cannot be underestimated; this seems to be a common thread that runs throughout the discussion of the various ways in which death, dying, and bereavement may occur and grief may be experienced. However, it appears that it is the perception of support relative to its availability and degree of experienced satisfaction that is critical to its ability to ameliorate reactions to death (Reif, Patton, & Gold, 1995; Sarason, Sarason, Shearin, & Pierce, 1987). Thus, while we may make efforts to help family members and clients, what we do must be perceived as meaningful if it is to be helpful. In the following section, therefore, we discuss some specific approaches that may be particularly useful in our efforts to tailor our work to meet clients where they are and thus to be a source of meaningful support.

ADDITIONAL THERAPEUTIC INTERVENTIONS

As noted particularly in the discussion of the death of a child, it is important for bereaved family members to be able to tell their story. As described by Sedney, Baker, and Gross (1994), encouraging clients to share the stories of their loss facilitates emotional relief, encourages the search for meaning, and helps to bring family members together. When used as an assessment tool, stories provide information about the way their narrators construct their reality and areas where assistance might be useful, for example, around such unresolved issues as guilt, blame, and a sense of responsibility for the death. The process of telling a story also may be understood as a therapeutic intervention in that it may provide new information, encourage feelings of competency and control, and provide an opportunity for clients and therapist to feel more connected. As therapy proceeds, changes in the clients may be reflected in changes in stories as new information is incorporated, shifts in emphasis occur, and new meanings emerge. With the use of this approach, "the death comes to be viewed as an experience that the family can talk about, cope with, and incorporate into their ongoing family story. The focus is on respect for each individual's unique experience within a family context" (p. 294).

The serendipitous benefits of having several of the participants write and then read to one another their reflections on the process of therapy are described by Levac, McLean, Wright, and Bell (1998). Therapeutic conversations were the mechanism chosen to understand and challenge, when appropriate, the beliefs of a couple who had recently lost their son in a sudden, accidental death. Specific interventions included the use of interventive questions to elicit core beliefs and provide information; reflecting teams to increase feedback and foster a collaborative relationship between clients and clinicians; letters sent to clients between sessions to highlight and confirm the therapeutic process; and externalizing the problem so that it might be experienced as a phenomenon separate from the client. After several sessions, the clients were invited to participate with two other members of the team in writing an article that would be submitted for publication. At a subsequent session, each of the four authors read what she or he had written. In the final session the manuscript was reviewed by all and the clients participated in clarifying their perceptions and correcting what they felt were misperceptions on the part of the therapists. The couple also expressed their belief that the writing of the article was part of the therapeutic process. However, the clinical team concluded that it was the use of a "reader's theater," or "the shared reading of each other's contributions to our article that provided the most profound opportunity for healing for this couple" (p. 92).

Other strategies include transitional family therapy (Horwitz, 1997), in which the focus is on mapping patterns over several generations in order to "locate epicenters of trauma and loss" (p. 215) and understand previous attempts by family members to resolve their grief. Armed with this information, the therapist then draws on a variety of systemic approaches to help alleviate the pain that is being experienced. Solomon and Shapiro (1997) suggest the use of eye movement desensitization and reprocessing (EMDR) in order to facilitate recovery from unresolved grief. EMDR is an eight-phase treatment method that involves taking a history, preparing the client, assessing the target of the intervention, desensitizing negative affect, enhancing positive cognitions, scanning the body for residual tension, closing the session, and re-evaluation. It is emphasized that before undertaking the use of EMDR, however, appropriate training is required. By contrast, no special training is required to implement thought field therapy (Callahan & Callahan, 1997) in order to help clients successfully move through the process of bereavement. In this case, clients are taught to tap on specific body points as they focus on upsetting emotions while also engaging in activities such as moving their eyes, humming, or counting. The procedure is individualized for each client and "the emphasis of therapy is on the effort to help the bereaved become as strong as possible in the face of the tragedy and to facilitate the wholesome survival of the family" (p. 255). Each of these latter approaches would seem to more suitable for use in cases of long-term unresolved grief than in the initial phase of the bereavement period, when the narrative approaches described first might be more appropriate. To reiterate, sensitivity to what is happening with the client, and what she or he feels is needed, is crucial to the ability of the therapist to be effective.

CONCLUSION

As noted elsewhere (Becvar, 1997), therapy represents the bestowing of a sacred trust when clients come to mental health professionals seeking help with their problems. Nowhere does this seem to be more the case than when presented with the opportunity and the challenge of hearing about and assisting with the resolution of the pain associated with the loss of a loved one. Rather than being an onerous burden, those who have worked in the field of death, dying, and bereavement often experience it as a great gift. As Callanan and Kelley (1992) write:

> The truth is that our work brings tremendous satisfaction, fulfillment, and even joy. How is this possible? Part of the answer is that we have come to recognize the parallels between being born and dying—between entering this world and leaving it—and this understanding helps us to define our function and rewards. (p. 21)

Moving beyond, and perhaps changing, the negative cultural stories and perceptions about death requires that we enter fully into this realm and that we become familiar with the needs of both the dying and the bereaved. Becoming effective therapists also requires recognition that this is a complex area with many subtle nuances. Therefore, we equip ourselves both personally and professionally as we become knowledgeable about the many ways in which this final stage in the life cycle of both individuals and families may be negotiated.

REFERENCES

Aries, P. (1980). Forbidden death. In E. S. Shneidman (Ed.), *Death: Current perspectives* (2nd ed., pp. 52–55). Palo Alto, CA: Mayfield Publishing Co.

Baker, J. E. (1997). Minimizing the impact of parental grief on children: Parent and family interventions. In C. R. Figley, B. E. Bride, & N. Mazza (Eds.), *Death and trauma: The traumatology of grieving* (pp. 139–157). Washington, DC: Taylor & Francis.

Battin, M. (1994). *The least worse death.* New York: Oxford University Press.

Beauchamp T., & Childress J. (1994). *Principles of biomedical ethics* (4th ed.). Oxford: Oxford University Press.

Becker, E. (1973). *The denial of death.* New York: The Free Press.

Becvar, D. (1997). *Soul healing: A spiritual orientation in counseling and therapy.* New York: Basic Books.

Becvar, D. (in press). Euthanasia decisions. In F. W. Kaslow (Ed.), *Handbook of couple and family forensics.* New York: John Wiley & Sons, Inc.

Bernstein, J. (1997). *When the bough breaks: Forever after the death of a son or daughter.* Kansas City, MO: Andrews & McKeel.

Boss, P. (1991). Ambiguous loss. In F. Walsh & M. McGoldrick (Eds.), *Living beyond loss: Death in the family* (pp. 164–175). New York: W. W. Norton.

Bowlby, J. (1980). *Loss, sadness and depression.* New York: Basic Books.

Brown, F. H. (1988). The impact of death on the family life cycle. In B. Carter & M. McGoldrick (Eds.), *The changing family life cycle: A framework for family therapy* (2nd ed., pp. 457–482). New York: Gardner Press.

Byng-Hall, J. (1991). Family scripts and loss. In F. Walsh & M. McGoldrick (Eds.), *Living beyond loss: Death in the family* (pp. 130–143). New York: W. W. Norton.

Byoctr, I. (1991). *Dying well.* New York: Riverhead Books.

Callahan, R. J., & Callahan, J. (1997). Thought field therapy: Aiding the bereavement process. In C. R. Figley, B. E. Bride, & N. Mazza (Eds.), *Death and trauma: The traumatology of grieving* (pp. 249–268). Washington, DC: Taylor & Francis.

Callanan, M., & Kelley, P. (1992). *Final gifts: Understanding the special awareness, needs, and communications of the dying.* New York: Bantam Books.

Carter, S. L. (1996, July 21). Rush to a lethal judgment. *The New York Times Magazine,* pp. 28–29.

Demi, A., & Miles, M. (1987). Parameters of normal grief: A delphi study. *Death Studies, 11,* 397–412.

Dying Well Network. (1996). *Helping people die well.* Spokane, WA: Dying Well Network.

Edelman, H. (1994). *Motherless daughters.* New York: Dell Publishing.

Figley, C. R., Bride, B. E., & Mazza, N. (Eds.). (1997). *Death and trauma: The traumatology of grieving.* Washington, DC: Taylor & Francis.

Fish, W. (1986). Differences of grief intensity in bereaved parents. In T. Rando (Ed.), *Parental loss of a child* (pp. 415–428). Champaign, IL: Research Press.

Foos-Graber, A. (1989). *Deathing: An intelligent alternative for the final moments of life.* York Beach, ME: Nicolas-Hays.

Freud, S. (1957). Mourning and melancholia. In J. Strachey (Ed.), *The standard edition of complete psychological works of Sigmund Freud, Vol. 14,* pp. 237–258. London: Hogarth Press and the Institute for Psychoanalysis. (Original work published 1917)

Fulton, R. (1987). The many faces of grief. *Death Studies, 11,* 243–256.

Gilbert, K. R. (1997). Couple coping with the death of a child. In C. R. Figley, B. E. Bride, & N. Mazza (Eds.), *Death and trauma: The traumatology of grieving* (pp. 101–121). Washington, DC: Taylor & Francis.

Gorer, G. (1980). The pornography of death. In E. S. Shneidman, (Ed.), *Death: Current perspectives* (2nd ed., pp. 47–51). Palo Alto, CA: Mayfield Publishing Co.

Hainer, C. (1997, August 11). At peace with death. *USA Today,* pp. 1–2D.

Horwitz, S. H. (1997). Treating families with traumatic loss: Transitional family therapy. In C. R. Figley, B. E. Bride, & N. Mazza (Eds.), *Death and trauma: The traumatology of grieving* (pp. 211–230). Washington, DC: Taylor & Francis.

Iglesias, T. (1995). Ethics, brain-death, and the medical concept of the human being. *Medical Legal Journal of Ireland,* pp. 51–57.

Kastenbaum, R. J. (1986). *Death, society, and human experience* (3rd ed.). Columbus, OH: Charles E. Merrill.

Klass, D. (1988). *Parental grief: Solace and resolution.* New York: Springer.

Knapp, R. (1986). *Beyond endurance: When a child dies.* New York: Shocken.

Knapp, R. (1987, July). When a child dies. *Psychology Today,* pp. 60, 62–63, 66–67.

Kubler-Ross, E. (1969). *On death and dying.* New York: Macmillan.

Kubler-Ross, E. (1975). *Death: The final stage of growth.* New York: Touchstone.

Kubler-Ross, E. (1995). *Death is of vital importance.* New York: Station Hill Press.

Kushner, H. S. (1981). *When bad things happen to good people.* New York: Avon Books.

Levac, A. M. C., McLean, S., Wright, L. M., & Bell, J. M. (1998). A "reader's theater" intervention to managing grief: Posttherapy reflections by a family and clinical team. *Journal of Marital and Family Therapy, 24*(1), 81–93.

Lindemann, E. (1944). Symptomatology and management of acute grief. *American Journal of Psychiatry, 101,* 141–148.

Lindbergh, A. M. (1998). *Dearly beloved.* New York: Buccaneer Books.

Martin, J., & Romanowski, P. (1994). *Our children forever: Messages from children on the other side.* New York: Berkley Books.

McClowry, S., Davies, E. B., May, K. A., Kulenkamp, E. J, & Martinson, I. M. (1987). The empty space phenomenon: The process of grief in the bereaved family. *Death Studies, 11,* 361–374.

McCullough, P., & Rutenberg, S. (1988). Launching children and moving on. In B. Carter & M. McGoldrick (Eds.), *The changing family life cycle: A framework for family therapy* (2nd ed., pp. 287–310). New York: Gardner Press.

McGoldrick, M., Almeida, R., Hines, P. M., Garcia-Preto, N., Rosen, E., & Lee, E. (1991). Mourning in different cultures. In F. Walsh & M. McGoldrick (Eds.), *Living beyond loss: Death in the family* (pp. 176–206). New York: W. W. Norton.

McGoldrick, M., & Walsh, F. (1991). A time to mourn: Death and the family life cycle. In F. Walsh & M. McGoldrick (Eds.), *Living beyond loss: Death in the family* (pp. 30–49). New York: W. W. Norton.

Moss, M. S., & Moss, S. Z. (1997). Remarriage of widowed persons: A triadic relationship. In D. Klass, P. R. Silverman, & S. L. Nickman (Eds.), *Continuing bonds: New understandings of grief* (pp. 163–178). Washington, DC: Taylor & Francis.

Nader, K. O. (1997a). Childhood traumatic loss: The interaction of trauma and grief. In C. R. Figley, B. E. Bride, & N. Mazza (Eds.), *Death and trauma: The traumatology of grieving* (pp. 17–41). Washington, DC: Taylor & Francis.

Nader, K. O. (1997b). Treating traumatic grief in systems. In C. R. Figley, B. E. Bride, & N. Mazza (Eds.), *Death and trauma: The traumatology of grieving* (pp. 159–192). Washington, DC: Taylor & Francis.

Nickman, S. L., Silverman, P. R., & Normand, C. (1998). Children's construction of a deceased parent: The surviving parent's contribution. *American Journal of Orthopsychiatry, 68*(1), 126–134.

Osterweis, M., Solomon, F., & Green, M. (Eds.). (1984). *Bereavement: Reactions, consequences, and care.* Washington, DC: National Academy Press.

Palmer, L. (1987). *Shrapnel in the heart: Letters and remembrances from the Vietnam Veterans Memorial.* New York: Random House.

Peretz, D. (1970). Reaction to loss. In B. Schoenberg (Ed.), *Loss and grief* (pp. 20–35). New York: Columbia University Press.

Rando, T. (1988). *Grieving: How to go on living when someone you love dies.* Lexington, MA: Lexington Books.

Rando, T. (1997). Foreword. In C. R. Figley, B. E. Bride, & N. Mazza, (Eds.), *Death and trauma: The traumatology of grieving* (pp. xiv–xix). Washington, DC: Taylor & Francis.

Raphael, B. (1983). *The anatomy of bereavement.* New York: Basic Books.

Reif, L. V., Patton, M. J., & Gold, P. B. (1995). Bereavement, stress, and social support in members of a self-help group. *Journal of Community Psychology, 23,* 292–306.

Rolland, J. (1991). Helping families with anticipatory loss. In F. Walsh & M. McGoldrick (Eds.), *Living beyond loss: Death in the family* (pp. 144–163). New York: W. W. Norton.

Sarason, I. G., Sarason, B. G., Shearin, E. N., & Pierce, G. R. (1987). A brief measure of social support: Practical and theoretical implications. *Journal of Social and Personal Relationships, 4,* 497–510.

Schiff, H. S. (1977). *The bereaved parent.* New York: Penguin Books.

Sedney, M. A., Baker, J. E., & Gross, E. (1994). "The story" of a death: Therapeutic considerations with bereaved families. *Journal of Marital and Family Therapy, 20*(3), 287–296.

Shneidman, E. S. (Ed.). (1980a). *Death: Current perspectives* (2nd ed.). Palo Alto, CA: Mayfield Publishing Co.

Shneidman, E. S. (1980b). Suicide. In E. S. Shneidman (Ed.), *Death: Current perspectives* (2nd ed., pp. 416–434). Palo Alto, CA: Mayfield Publishing Co.

Silverman, P. R., & Klass, D. (1997). Introduction: What's the problem? In D. Klass, P. R. Silverman, & S. Nickman (Eds.), *Continuing bonds: New understandings of grief* (pp. 3–30). Washington, DC: Taylor & Francis.

Sogyal, R. (1992). *The Tibetan book of living and dying.* New York: HarperCollins.

Solomon, R. M., & Shapiro, F. (1997). Eye movement desensitization and reprocessing: A therapeutic tool for trauma and grief. In C. R. Figley, B. E. Bride, & N. Mazza (Eds.), *Death and trauma: The traumatology of grieving* (pp. 231–248). Washington, DC: Taylor & Francis.

Speckhard, A. (1997). Traumatic death in pregnancy: The significance of meaning and attachment. In C. R. Figley, B. E. Bride, & N. Mazza (Eds.), *Death and trauma: The traumatology of grieving* (pp. 101–121). Washington, DC: Taylor & Francis.

Steinberg, A. (1997). Death as a trauma for children: A relational treatment approach. In C. R. Figley, B. E. Bride, & N. Mazza (Eds.), *Death and trauma: The traumatology of grieving* (pp. 123–137). Washington, DC: Taylor & Francis.

Walsh, F. (1988). The family in later life. In B. Carter & M. McGoldrick (Eds.), *The changing family life cycle: A framework for family therapy* (2nd ed., pp. 311–332). New York: Gardner Press.

Williams, M. B., & Nurmi, L. A. (1997). Death of a co-worker: Facilitating the healing. In C. R. Figley, B. E. Bride, & N. Mazza (Eds.), *Death and trauma: The traumatology of grieving* (pp. 193–207). Washington, DC: Taylor & Francis.

Zisook, S., & Shuchter, S. (1986). The first four years of widowhood. *Psychiatric Annals, 16*(5), 288–294.

Index

process of, 88–92
and psychotherapy, 99, 100–103
socioeconomic status and, 132–133
theory of, 87
Gene-environment correlations, 52–53, 59
Generative marriage, 224
Genetics
of alcoholism, 57–58
of anxiety, 54–55
of attachment, 50
backlash against, 42–43
of bipolar disorder, 57
and Darwin's theory, 26
of divorce, 50
eugenics, 42
heritability ratios, 53–54
Human Genome Project, 45, 58
of introversion/extroversion, 56–57
molecular, 54–55
of mood, 55–56
pervasiveness of conditions due to, 45
renewed interest in, 41
of schizophrenia, 57
of temperament, 54, 58–59
twin studies, 46–47
of violence, 50–52
vs. family influence, 47–49
Genogram(s)
of remarried families, 383
use in family therapy, 247
GIFT (gamete intrafallopian transfer), 180
Glick, Paul, 7
Glickman, Dan, 135
Goodwin, Frederick, 42–43
Gottman, John, 161–162
Gould, Stephen J., 59
Grandparent(s)
as foster parents, 263
and midlife family, 226–227
and remarried families, 380–381
Grieving process, 456–457
after sudden death, 464
after suicide, 464–465
therapeutic interventions in, 466–467
Group therapy
for batterers, 406, 407–409
for older clients, 246
Gunderson, John, 58

Haley, Jay, 15
Hamer, Dean, 56
Hamilton, W. D., inclusive fitness theory of, 34–35
Happiness, genetic basis of, 55
Harmony, value of, in immigrant families, 316, 319
Harris, Judith, 48
Harvard Criteria, 455
Havinghurst, Robert, 8
Haynes, John, 354
Health
in midlife, 228–229
socioeconomic status and, 134–136
Hearing impairments, 443
Heredity. *See* Genetics
Heritability ratios, 53–54
Heterosexism, 279
Hill, Reuben, 5, 6
Hindu tradition, 302

Hispanics
dilemma of rage for, 119–122
immigrant families, 302–305
life expectancy for, 237
perception of childhood disabilities by, 417
single-parent families, 324
therapy with, 303, 304–305
History
accumulated, of midlife family, 223–224
perspective on gender differences, 86
HIV/AIDS. *See* Acquired immune deficiency
syndrome
Hmong families, 315–318
Holman, T. B., 169
Holmes, Oliver Wendell, 42
Homophobia, 279
internalized, 292
Homosexuality. *See* Gay and lesbian families; Gays
and lesbians
Hospice movement, 455
Howells, J. G., 16
Human Genome Project, 45, 58
Human nature, evolutionary psychological
perspective on, 29–30

Illness
childhood (*See* Childhood disabilities)
chronic physical (*See* Chronic physical illness)
of close relative, effect on children, 197
death following, 462–463
family-illness interface, 425
Immigrant families, 299–320
commonalities in, 299
gender issues in, 301–302, 304, 307, 314, 317
Hispanic, 302–305
Hmong, 315–318
Indian, 300–302
intergenerational relationships in, 301, 308,
310–312, 316
from Northwestern Europe, 313–315
reasons for immigration, 305, 306–307, 313,
319
from Russia, 305–309
from Taiwan, 309–312
therapy with, 300, 303, 304–305, 308, 312, 315,
316, 317, 318–320
visits to home country, 314–315
In vitro fertilization (IVF), 180
Incestuous issues, in remarried families, 375
Inclusive fitness theory, 34–35
Income. *See* Socioeconomic status
India, immigrant families from, 300–302
Indians. *See* Asian Indians; Native Americans
Individual differences, evolutionary psychological
perspective on, 30–31
Individual life span development, and family
development, 10, 13–14
Individual therapy, with battered women, 409–410
Infancy, 190
Infant-parent psychotherapy, 202–203
Infertility, 177–181
couples' responses to, 173–174
definition of, 177
and life satisfaction, 175, 178
psychological effects of, 175, 177–178
psychotherapy for, 181–184
social attitudes toward, 177–178